The Death of Treaty Supremacy

The Death of Treaty Supremacy

An Invisible Constitutional Change

DAVID L. SLOSS

OXFORD
UNIVERSITY PRESS

OXFORD
UNIVERSITY PRESS

Library of Congress Cataloging-in-Publication Data
Names: Sloss, David, author.
Title: The death of treaty supremacy : an invisible constitutional change /
    David L. Sloss.
Description: New York : Oxford University Press, 2016. | Includes bibliographical
    references and index.
Identifiers: LCCN 2016009586 | ISBN 9780199364022 ((hardback) : alk. paper) |
    ISBN 9780197651797 (paperback)
Subjects: LCSH: United States—Foreign relations—Law and legislation. |
    Treaty-making power—United States—States. | International relations—United States—States. |
    Federal government—United States. | Constitutional law—United States—States. | States' rights
    (American politics)—History. | Separation of powers—United States.
Classification: LCC KF4651 .S73 2016 | DDC 342.73/0412—dc23 LC record available at
http://lccn.loc.gov/2016009586

9 8 7 6 5 4 3 2 1

Paperback printed by Marquis, Canada

Note to Readers

This publication is designed to provide accurate and authoritative information in regard to the subject matter covered. It is based upon sources believed to be accurate and reliable and is intended to be current as of the time it was written. It is sold with the understanding that the publisher is not engaged in rendering legal, accounting, or other professional services. If legal advice or other expert assistance is required, the services of a competent professional person should be sought. Also, to confirm that the information has not been affected or changed by recent developments, traditional legal research techniques should be used, including checking primary sources where appropriate.

(Based on the Declaration of Principles jointly adopted by a Committee of the American Bar Association and a Committee of Publishers and Associations.)

> **You may order this or any other Oxford University Press publication
> by visiting the Oxford University Press website at www.oup.com.**

*I dedicate this book to future generations
in the hope that all nations
will achieve the practical realization of the ideals
embodied in the U.N. Charter
and the Universal Declaration of Human Rights.*

CONTENTS

LIST OF TABLES

PREFACE TO THE PAPERBACK EDITION (OCT. 30, 2021)

The first edition of *The Death of Treaty Supremacy* demonstrated that—from the Founding until World War II—U.S. courts, commentators, and government officials conceived of treaty supremacy doctrine and self-execution doctrine as two independent, non-overlapping doctrines. Treaty supremacy doctrine governed the relationship between treaties and state law. Self-execution doctrine was a federal separation of powers doctrine that governed the division of power over treaty implementation among the three branches of the federal government. The treaty supremacy rule, rooted in the Constitution's Supremacy Clause,[1] meant that treaties supersede conflicting state laws, and that judges have a constitutional duty to apply treaties when there is a conflict between a treaty and state law. There was no exception to the treaty supremacy rule for non-self-executing (NSE) treaties because the concept of non-self-execution, as understood before World War II, was simply not relevant to cases involving alleged conflicts between treaties and state law.

However, the dominant understanding of the relationship between treaty supremacy doctrine and self-execution doctrine changed dramatically after World War II in response to the advent of modern international human rights law. In the late 1940s, litigants began invoking the human rights provisions of the UN Charter in conjunction with the traditional treaty supremacy rule in an effort to invalidate racially discriminatory state laws, at a time when the Equal Protection Clause still permitted southern states to maintain Jim Crow. In *Fujii v. California*,[2] a California state court applied the UN Charter together with the treaty supremacy rule to invalidate a state law that discriminated against Japanese nationals. That result was shocking. If *Fujii* was correct, it meant that the United States had effectively invalidated Jim Crow laws throughout the South by ratifying the UN Charter. That conclusion was politically unacceptable, even though the court's legal reasoning in *Fujii* was entirely consistent with the traditional understanding of the treaty supremacy rule.

In response to *Fujii*, a group of clever lawyers invented a novel legal rule, which I call the NSE exception to the treaty supremacy rule. Under the NSE exception, judges are free to disregard non-self-executing treaties that conflict with state laws, despite the clear command of the Supremacy Clause that "judges in every state shall be bound by" ratified treaties.[3] The lawyers who created the NSE exception claimed that the traditional treaty supremacy rule included an exception for non-self-executing treaties, at least since the Supreme Court's 1829 decision in *Foster v. Neilson*.[4] That claim was historically inaccurate, but it was politically convenient because it provided a plausible legal rationale for courts to refuse to apply human rights treaties to invalidate racially discriminatory state laws. Thus, the myth that the treaty supremacy rule had always included an exception for non-self-executing treaties soon became accepted as conventional wisdom. The NSE exception to the treaty supremacy rule was codified as black letter law in the Restatement (Second) of Foreign Relations Law, published in 1965.[5]

In the context of preparing the paperback edition of *The Death of Treaty Supremacy*, I reviewed state court decisions in treaty supremacy cases that have been published in the last several years. The most surprising finding from the current research is that there is a discrepancy between black letter law and state court judicial practice. Black letter law, per the U.S. Supreme Court decision in *Medellín v. Texas*, holds that "a non-self-executing treaty does not by itself give rise to domestically enforceable federal law."[6] Thus, according to the self-execution doctrine articulated by the Court in *Medellín*, U.S. courts may not apply a non-self-executing treaty as a rule of decision to decide the merits of a case.[7] Therefore, logically, courts must first decide whether a treaty is self-executing or non-self-executing before applying the treaty as a rule of decision. But that is not how state courts actually behave. In practice, in treaty supremacy cases involving human rights treaties, state courts apply the NSE exception to the treaty supremacy rule. However, in most treaty supremacy cases that do not involve human rights treaties, courts apply the treaty to decide the merits of the treaty supremacy argument without regard to whether the treaty at issue is self-executing or non-self-executing.

To assess the current status of the relationship between the treaty supremacy rule and self-execution doctrine, I did an electronic search to identify state court decisions published between January 1, 2016 and October 31, 2021 in which one party raised a treaty supremacy argument. (A treaty supremacy argument is an argument that a court should apply a treaty as a rule of decision to preempt state law or to reverse a judicial decision based on state law.) The search identified eighteen such state court decisions. Identifying treaty supremacy cases is not an exact science, but I am confident that those eighteen decisions constitute all, or a substantial majority, of the published state court decisions during the specified time frame in which a party raised a treaty supremacy argument.

Those eighteen treaty supremacy cases can be divided broadly into two groups: cases involving human rights claims based on the International Covenant on Civil and Political Rights (ICCPR) and everything else. The data set includes four cases in which a party raised a treaty supremacy argument based on the ICCPR.[8] In all four cases, the court said that the ICCPR is not self-executing. In all four cases, the court's rationale for rejecting the treaty supremacy argument relied at least partly on the modern NSE exception to the treaty supremacy rule.[9] (In three of the four cases, the courts also rejected the treaty supremacy argument on the merits.[10])

In contrast, none of the other fourteen decisions applied the NSE exception to the treaty supremacy rule.[11] Indeed, only one of those fourteen cases even used the term "self-executing." In that case, a California appellate court assumed, for the sake of argument, that the Hague Public Documents Convention is self-executing, but rejected the treaty supremacy argument on the merits.[12] In the other thirteen cases, courts decided the merits of the treaty supremacy arguments without explicitly considering whether the treaty at issue was self-executing or non-self-executing. Those cases include six where the party raising a treaty supremacy argument won on the merits[13] and seven where the party raising a treaty supremacy argument lost on the merits.[14]

In sum, apart from cases involving the ICCPR, state courts today typically apply treaty supremacy doctrine in much the same way that they did before World War II; they address the merits of treaty supremacy arguments without bothering to consider whether the treaty at issue is self-executing or non-self-executing. This pattern of judicial decision-making presents a puzzle that requires some explanation.

The apparent discrepancy between black letter law and state court judicial practice might be explained as follows. The data set of eighteen state court decisions includes thirteen cases where courts decided the merits of treaty supremacy arguments without any reference to self-execution doctrine. Nine of those thirteen cases involve The Convention on the Service Abroad of Judicial and Extrajudicial Documents in Civil or Commercial Matters, commonly known as the Hague Service Convention.[15] The Supreme Court has never explicitly decided whether the Hague Service Convention is self-executing.[16] However, a few lower federal courts have stated that the Convention is self-executing.[17] More importantly, in *Volkswagenwerk Aktiengesellschaft v. Schlunk*, the Supreme Court held: "By virtue of the Supremacy Clause . . . the [Hague Service] Convention pre-empts inconsistent methods of service prescribed by state law in all cases to which it applies."[18] In light of these authorities, one could argue that state courts presented with treaty supremacy arguments based on the Hague Service Convention routinely assume, *sub silentio*, that the treaty is self-executing, and decide cases on the basis of that unstated assumption.

However, the analysis in *The Death of Treaty Supremacy* suggests a different possible explanation. Perhaps judicial doctrine related to self-execution and treaty supremacy really is schizophrenic.[19] I have argued elsewhere that the distinction between public law and private law litigation helps explain judicial behavior in cases where litigants invoke treaty-based arguments before U.S. courts.[20] (In private law cases, the parties are all private parties. In contrast, public law cases involve litigation where a private party is adverse to a government actor.) Bearing in mind the public-private distinction, the following explanation seems plausible.

In public law cases, including cases implicating human rights treaties, courts apply modern treaty supremacy doctrine, which includes an exception to the treaty supremacy rule for non-self-executing treaties. However, in private law cases, courts apply traditional treaty supremacy doctrine, as it existed before World War II. Under that doctrine, the distinction between self-executing and non-self-executing treaties is simply not relevant to treaty supremacy cases. Hence, when presented with treaty supremacy arguments in private law cases, courts apply the treaty supremacy rule to decide the merits of treaty supremacy arguments, without regard to whether the treaty at issue is self-executing or non-self-executing. There are undoubtedly a few outlier cases where courts apply modern treaty supremacy doctrine in private law cases.[21] However, the vast majority of judicial decisions in the past few decades are consistent with a bifurcated approach in which courts apply modern treaty supremacy doctrine in public law cases and traditional treaty supremacy doctrine in private law cases.

In an important law review article published in 2012, Professor Oona Hathaway and her co-authors agreed that judicial practice from World War II until the Supreme Court's 2008 decision in *Medellín* generally followed a bifurcated approach between public law and private law.[22] However, they maintained, the Supreme Court decision in *Medellín* induced lower courts to restrict judicial enforcement even of private law treaties after 2008.[23] Without disputing that claim, it bears emphasis that neither of the two leading examples they cite— *McKesson Corp. v. Islamic Republic of Iran*[24] and *Gross v. German Foundation Industrial Initiative*[25]—is a treaty supremacy case. In neither case did a party urge the court to apply a treaty to preempt state law or to reverse a judicial decision based on state law. Thus, with respect to treaty supremacy cases, the pattern identified above seems to persist even after *Medellín*: courts apply modern treaty supremacy doctrine, including the NSE exception, in public law cases, but they apply traditional treaty supremacy doctrine without any exception for NSE treaties in private law cases.

Perhaps this conclusion is not as surprising as it initially appears, because the Supremacy Clause is addressed specifically to "the judges in every state." The evidence suggests that state court judges in private law cases choose to follow the clear text of the Supremacy Clause, rather than the black letter law expressed in *Medellín v. Texas* and the ALI's Restatement of Foreign Relations Law. Thus, notwithstanding the title of *The Death of Treaty Supremacy*, the traditional treaty supremacy rule may not be entirely dead. The traditional rule still survives in state court decisions in private law cases.

ACKNOWLEDGMENTS

I began work on this book in 2011. Over the past five years, many people have contributed to the project in various ways. It is a pleasure to take this opportunity to thank them for their contributions.

Several gifted Santa Clara law students provided invaluable research assistance over the past few years. In particular, I owe thanks to Lara Bahr, Michael Branson, Krysha Chatman, Cheri Kramer, Alexandra Logue, Timmoney Ng, Susan Shapiro, Ariel Siner, and Melissa Wheeler. Each of them made important contributions to the overall project. Two different faculty assistants—Channing McCabe and Abigail King—also provided valuable assistance over the years.

As a scholar, I greatly appreciate the support provided by research librarians. Two librarians, in particular, deserve special mention. Leslie O'Neill helped me get access to materials from the archives of the American Law Institute, which are housed at the University of Pennsylvania. I could not have completed this project without her assistance. Mary Sexton, at Santa Clara University, invariably tracks down every source I ask her to find, even when my requests are wildly unreasonable. I am forever in her debt.

I thank the Center for Comparative Constitutional Studies at the University of Melbourne for providing an exceptionally congenial environment where I was able to work on this book during my sabbatical in 2014. Special thanks go to Adrienne Stone, the Center Director, and Cheryl Saunders, the former director. Thanks also to Jeanette Goh for providing exceptional administrative assistance during my time in Melbourne.

Two different deans at Santa Clara University School of Law School provided funding over the course of this project. I thank Dean Donald Polden and Dean Lisa Kloppenberg for their generous support. Thanks also to the Center for Global Law and Policy at Santa Clara, directed by Professor Anna Han, for funding a conference where I received valuable feedback from several scholars on an early draft of the book.

I benefited greatly from the opportunity to present draft chapters at workshops and conferences at numerous universities over several years. In particular, I received valuable feedback when I presented draft chapters at the following fora: the ASIL research forum in Los Angeles (2011); a meeting of the European-American consortium on legal education at the University of Ghent (2012);

a faculty workshop at Santa Clara University (2012); faculty workshops at Temple University and George Mason University (2013); an AALS workshop in Washington, D.C. (2014); the ASIL research forum in Chicago (2014); presentations at Melbourne Law School, Australian National University, and University of Sydney (2014); faculty workshops at New York Law School and University of Wisconsin (2014); a faculty workshop at the University of North Carolina (2015); and a conference at Brigham Young University (2015). I thank the many scholars who commented on drafts of various portions of the manuscript during these workshops and conferences.

Duncan Hollis, David Moore, John Parry, Edward Purcell, and Carlos Vázquez reviewed portions of the manuscript and provided valuable feedback. I thank all of them for their insightful comments.

I hosted a conference at Santa Clara University in December 2014 for the purpose of receiving critical feedback on the manuscript. I want to thank John Coyle, William Dodge, Martin Flaherty, Jean Galbraith, Bradley Joondeph, Chimène Keitner, Thomas Lee, Michael Ramsey, Paul Stephan, Edward Swaine, and Michael Van Alstine for taking the time to read the entire manuscript, as it existed at that time. They all provided extremely helpful commentary and made significant contributions to the quality of the final product. Of course, I alone am responsible for any remaining errors or omissions.

I owe thanks, also, to my editors at Oxford University Press: John Louth, Blake Ratcliff, and Alden Domizio.

Finally, I am especially grateful to my wife, Heidi, my two children, Dakin and Kamala, and my daughter-in-law, Gabrielle Gatta. They have all provided tremendous support and encouragement over the years. Scholarly research can be a very solitary occupation. Time with my family provides a welcome opportunity to move from the realm of abstract ideas to the realm of concrete relationships.

Introduction

Not around the inventors of new noise, but around the inventors of new values does the world revolve; inaudibly it revolves.
— Friedrich Nietzsche, *Thus Spoke Zarathustra*

When the Framers of the U.S. Constitution met in Philadelphia in 1787, they drafted a Constitution designed to ensure that states would not violate the nation's treaty commitments. Before adoption of the Constitution, Alexander Hamilton noted, "the treaties of the United States ... [were] liable to the infractions of thirteen different legislatures ... The faith, the reputation, the peace of the whole Union, are thus continually at the mercy of the prejudices, the passions, and the interests of every member of which it is composed."[1] The Framers sought to rectify the problem of state treaty violations by vesting power over treaty compliance in the federal government. The draft Constitution sparked vigorous debates in the period from 1787 to 1789. No issue was more hotly contested than the balance of power between the states and the federal government. However, there was virtual unanimity on one point: the Constitution prohibited state government officers from violating national treaty obligations. The power to violate treaties belonged to the federal government, not the states.

On August 5, 2008, the State of Texas executed José Ernesto Medellín. His execution violated the nation's legal obligations under the U.N. Charter, the treaty that created the United Nations. President George W. Bush—a former Texas governor who supports the death penalty and believes strongly in states' rights—tried to block Medellín's execution, precisely because it violated U.S. treaty obligations. However, the Supreme Court ruled in a case called *Medellín v. Texas* that President Bush could not prevent Texas from putting Medellín to death, even though the execution violated international law.[2] The Supreme Court based its decision on an understanding of the Constitution that differed sharply from the Framers' understanding. How did we arrive at a shared understanding that the Constitution permits states to violate some treaties, even though the Framers purposefully adopted a Constitution that barred states from violating any treaties? That is the central question addressed in this book.

In taking up this question, I draw on a growing body of scholarship that explains constitutional change outside the courts, and outside the formal amendment process codified in Article V of the Constitution. Much of that literature celebrates constitutional change outside the courts as a democratic expression of popular sovereignty.[3] To cite just one example, the women's movement failed in its effort to promote adoption of the Equal Rights Amendment (ERA) through the formal Article V process, but succeeded in changing popular attitudes about gender discrimination. Those changed attitudes, in turn, gave rise to new federal legislation and key Supreme Court decisions that accomplished many of the goals of the women's movement. That process has come to be known as the "de facto ERA."[4]

The central story line in this book is similar to the ERA story in one respect, but quite different in other respects. The "treaty supremacy rule" is codified in Article VI of the Constitution, known as the Supremacy Clause. The rule, as traditionally understood, provided that treaties automatically supersede conflicting state laws. The traditional treaty supremacy rule served an important purpose: it helped ensure that state governments would not violate U.S. treaty obligations unless the federal political branches authorized them to do so. The United States ratified the U.N. Charter in 1945. Articles 55 and 56 of the Charter obligate the United States to promote "human rights . . . for all *without distinction as to race*."[5] In the late 1940s and early 1950s, human rights activists in the United States invoked the Charter's human rights provisions, together with the Constitution's treaty supremacy rule, to challenge the validity of state laws that discriminated on the basis of race or nationality. In 1950, in a case called *Fujii v. California*, a California court ruled in favor of human rights claimants, striking down a California law that discriminated against Japanese nationals because it conflicted with the Charter's human rights provisions.[6] The potential implications of that decision were shocking. If the court was right, the United States had effectively abrogated Jim Crow laws throughout the South by ratifying the U.N. Charter. That result was unacceptable to many Americans at the time. Responding to *Fujii*, conservatives mobilized support for a constitutional amendment, known as the Bricker Amendment, whose aim was to abolish the treaty supremacy rule. Like the feminists who failed to obtain passage of the ERA, but achieved some of their goals in other ways, proponents of the Bricker Amendment realized some of their goals without a formal constitutional amendment. I refer to that constitutional transformation as the "de facto Bricker Amendment."

In contrast to the de facto ERA, the history of the de facto Bricker Amendment is not a story about the triumph of democracy and popular sovereignty. Rather, it is a story about invisible constitutional transformation. The results of the de facto ERA were codified in federal statutes and Supreme Court opinions— sources that were readily accessible to all interested American citizens. One did not need a law degree to understand the significant expansion of women's rights that occurred in the 1970s. In contrast, most lawyers in the United States today are unaware that the Constitution's treaty supremacy rule was dramatically transformed in the 1950s. The substance of that transformation was initially expressed in American Bar Association (ABA) reports and Senate testimony by Eisenhower administration officials in the early 1950s.[7] Later, the de facto Bricker Amendment was "codified" in the Restatement (Second) of Foreign Relations Law, a document published by the American Law Institute (ALI) in 1965.[8] None of those sources were readily accessible to the American public. Moreover, neither the ABA nor the ALI exercises formal governmental authority.

The de facto Bricker Amendment remained largely invisible because the results were expressed in technical legal jargon that obscured the magnitude of the constitutional change. Before 1950, the treaty supremacy rule was simple: all treaties prevail over conflicting state laws because the Supremacy Clause says so. By 1965, though, a new constitutional understanding had emerged—"self-executing" treaties prevail over conflicting state laws, but states are free to violate "non-self-executing" treaties. The distinction between self-executing (SE) and non-self-executing (NSE) treaties has been a feature of U.S. constitutional law since the 1790s. According to the oldest version of self-execution doctrine, federal executive officials have the authority to implement SE treaties, but congressional legislation is needed to authorize the president to implement NSE treaties. For example, if treaty implementation requires an expenditure of money, legislation is needed to authorize federal officials to withdraw funds from the U.S. treasury. Hence, the treaty is "non-self-executing" in that respect. Before 1950, treaty supremacy doctrine and self-execution doctrine were independent, non-overlapping doctrines. Treaty supremacy governed the relationship between treaties and state law. Self-execution governed the division of power over treaty implementation between Congress and the president. (Actually, self-execution doctrine was somewhat more complicated, but I will address those complications later.) The de facto Bricker Amendment expanded the scope of self-execution doctrine to encompass the relationship between treaties and state law. In the process, lawyers created the "NSE exception to the treaty supremacy rule." The NSE exception allows state government officers to violate U.S. treaty obligations without authorization from the federal political branches.

In this respect, the NSE exception is starkly at odds with one of the primary goals of the Constitution's Framers. In the Federalist Papers, James Madison invited readers to consider the hypothetical example of a federal constitution that provided for the supremacy of state law over federal law. In that case, he said,

> [T]he world would have seen, for the first time, a system of government founded on an inversion of the fundamental principles of all government; it would have seen the authority of the whole society everywhere subordinate to the authority of the parts; it would have seen a monster, in which the head was under the direction of the members.[9]

In certain situations, the NSE exception to the treaty supremacy rule places the head under the direction of the members. In *Medellín v. Texas,* the Supreme Court held that Article 94 of the U.N. Charter is not self-executing.[10] The Court's decision was based on the NSE exception to the treaty supremacy rule that arose from the de facto Bricker Amendment (although the Court claimed, incorrectly, that it was applying nineteenth-century self-execution doctrine). As a practical matter, the Court's decision meant that Texas was allowed to violate U.S. treaty obligations. Moreover, Texas's actions meant that the federal political branches were forced to deal with the foreign policy consequences of a treaty violation that they did not authorize and that the president tried to prevent. This was precisely the type of situation that the Framers sought to avoid by codifying the treaty supremacy rule in Article VI of the Constitution.

The de facto Bricker Amendment gained acceptance because the NSE exception to the treaty supremacy rule was responsive to widely shared sentiments about American constitutional identity. Americans have long believed that we have the best constitution in the world. I refer to this view as American exceptionalism. The *Fujii* decision (referenced above) threatened the popular faith in American exceptionalism. In *Fujii*, not only did the court hold that California law violated the U.N. Charter's human rights provisions; it also held that the law *did not* violate the Fourteenth Amendment Equal Protection Clause. The juxtaposition of those two holdings was impossible to reconcile with the widely shared faith in American exceptionalism. Most Americans in the early 1950s were not prepared to accept the notion that international human rights law provided more robust protection against racial discrimination than did our own Fourteenth Amendment. Thus, at a time when the Fourteenth Amendment was generally understood to permit racial segregation, the NSE exception to the treaty supremacy rule served a useful purpose. Like other doctrines that are well known to lawyers, but that are generally unfamiliar to non-lawyers, the new NSE exception gave judges a convenient rationale for refusing to decide questions that they preferred to dodge. Specifically, it provided courts a rationale for refusing to answer the question of whether the U.N. Charter prohibited forms of racial discrimination that the Fourteenth Amendment permitted.[11] Thus, the NSE exception to the treaty supremacy rule helped preserve the public faith in American exceptionalism by enabling courts to dodge the uncomfortable question of whether the U.N. Charter prohibited racially discriminatory laws and practices that were still pervasive in the United States in the 1950s.

The legacy of the de facto Bricker Amendment continues today. The NSE exception to the treaty supremacy rule is still an entrenched feature of modern legal doctrine, although the precise contours of that exception are contested.[12] Perhaps more important, the Bricker debate generated an atmosphere in which human rights treaties are seen as political poison. Consequently, the United States refuses to ratify most human rights treaties, and the treaties we do ratify include unilateral reservations and declarations designed to ensure that ratification does not affect human rights protection in the United States.[13] The net result is that we cling to our faith in the superiority of the U.S. constitutional system, but domestic protection for human rights falls short of international standards.[14] International human rights law provides a mirror that tells us who is "the fairest of them all." Like the queen in Snow White, we do not like the answer, so we refuse to look in the mirror. NSE doctrine helps us avert our gaze from the unflattering answer that the mirror provides.

I. THE SUBSTANCE OF TRANSFORMATION

The substance of the constitutional transformation that occurred between 1945 and 1965 can be summarized briefly in two sentences. Before 1945, the treaty supremacy rule was a mandatory rule. After 1965, though, the treaty supremacy rule was generally understood to be an optional rule.

Article II of the Constitution grants the president the power to make treaties "by and with the advice and consent of the Senate."[15] I use the term "treaty makers" to refer collectively to the president and the Senate when they act together under Article II to make treaties. Article VI, Clause 2, of the Constitution, known as the Supremacy Clause, states in full:

> This Constitution, and the Laws of the United States which shall be made in Pursuance thereof; and all Treaties made, or which shall be made, under the Authority of the United States, shall be the supreme Law of the Land; and the *Judges in every State shall be bound thereby,* any Thing in the Constitution or Laws of any State to the Contrary notwithstanding.[16]

The treaty supremacy rule, as traditionally understood, consisted of two elements. First, all treaties supersede conflicting state laws. Second, state and federal courts have a constitutional duty to apply treaties whenever there is a conflict between a treaty and state law, because the Supremacy Clause specifies that judges are "bound thereby." Thus, the Supreme Court said in 1909: "We do not deem it necessary to consider the constitutional limits of the treaty-making power. A treaty, within those limits, by the express words of the Constitution, is the supreme law of the land, binding alike national and state courts, and is capable of enforcement, and must be enforced by them in the litigation of private rights."[17] Similarly, more than a century earlier, U.S. Supreme Court Justice Samuel Chase wrote: "That it is the declared duty of the State Judges to determine any Constitution, or laws of any State, contrary to that treaty (or any other) made under the authority of the United States, null and void. National or Federal Judges are bound by duty and oath to the same conduct."[18] Before 1945, no significant judicial, governmental, or scholarly authority claimed that Article II granted the treaty makers the discretion to opt out of the treaty supremacy rule. The treaty supremacy rule was understood as a mandatory rule, not an optional one.

In 1959, though, a preliminary draft of the ALI's Restatement on Foreign Relations Law expressed a very different view. It said:

> The provisions of Art. VI, § 2 of the Constitution [the Supremacy Clause] under which treaties may be self-executing are in effect, permissive rather than mandatory. Therefore, not all treaties concluded on behalf of the United

States are self-executing..... [A non-self-executing] treaty does not operate as a rule for the executive branch . . . *or the States* nor does an individual acquire rights under it until Congress has taken appropriate action to implement it.[19]

Before 1945, self-execution doctrine established that some treaties are non-self-executing, meaning that legislation is needed to authorize federal executive officers to implement the treaty. Moreover, the doctrine established that Article II grants the treaty makers discretion to decide which treaties are self-executing and which ones are non-self-executing.

The de facto Bricker Amendment expanded the concept of self-execution to address the relationship between treaties and state law. Before 1945, treaty supremacy doctrine and self-execution doctrine were two independent doctrines. Treaty supremacy governed the relationship between treaties and state law. Self-execution governed the division of power over treaty implementation between Congress and the president. Thus, Quincy Wright (the leading scholar of constitutional foreign affairs law at the time) wrote in 1951: "the distinction between self-executing and non-self-executing treaties has been used in American constitutional law only with reference to the agency of the Federal Government competent to execute the treaty and has had no reference to the relations between the Federal Government and the States."[20] By expanding the concept of non-self-execution to encompass the relationship between treaties and state law, the de facto Bricker Amendment effectively subsumed treaty supremacy doctrine within self-execution doctrine. In the process, the treaty supremacy rule was converted from a mandatory rule to an optional one, because it was generally agreed that Article II of the Constitution granted the treaty makers discretion to decide whether a particular treaty would be self-executing or non-self-executing. The idea that the treaty supremacy rule is optional developed organically in the 1950s in the context of debates over the Bricker Amendment and U.S. participation in the then-emerging system of international human rights treaties. The ALI's Restatement of Foreign Relations Law consolidated the transformation by expressing the NSE exception to the treaty supremacy rule in a manner that was accepted as authoritative by lawyers and judges.

II. THE RHETORIC OF TRANSFORMATION

Sometimes, lawyers and judges want to change the law without admitting that they are changing the law. They often use two different tools to achieve their goals. First, they cite judicial precedents as authority for legal claims, but reinterpret older precedents to support novel claims. Second, they employ familiar legal terms to express their ideas, but use those terms in new ways so that a legal term-of-art acquires a new meaning.[21] The lawyers who created the NSE exception to the treaty supremacy rule employed both strategies.

In modern parlance, lawyers and judges use the terms "self-executing" and "non-self-executing" to express three very different concepts. I refer to these as the "congressional-executive" concept, the "political-judicial" concept, and the "federal-state" concept. All three share one common feature: federal legislation is necessary to implement an NSE treaty, but not to implement an SE treaty. The three concepts express different understandings as to why legislation is needed.

Under the congressional-executive concept, an NSE treaty does not operate as a rule of conduct for federal executive officers unless Congress enacts implementing legislation. In contrast, federal executive officers apply SE treaties as law, and need not await legislative authorization to do so. Justice Brandeis expressed this concept when he said: "For in a strict sense the Treaty was self-executing, in that no legislation was necessary to authorize executive action pursuant to its provisions."[22] As discussed previously, treaties that require an expenditure of money are NSE in this sense of the term. Congressional-executive variants of NSE doctrine serve two purposes: they limit the president's power to implement treaties that conflict with prior federal statutes, and they preserve a role for the House of Representatives in creating federal laws to implement treaties. (Recall that the president makes treaties with the advice and consent of the Senate, but without House participation.) The congressional-executive concept dates back to the 1790s. It was the dominant concept of self-execution before World War II.

A different concept of self-execution arose in the nineteenth century. Under the political-judicial concept, SE treaty provisions are judicially enforceable, but courts may not apply NSE provisions unless Congress enacts implementing legislation. The Supreme Court applied the political-judicial concept in 1884 in *The Head Money Cases*.[23] There, the Court said that "the judicial courts have nothing to do [with NSE treaties] and can give no redress." However, SE treaties "are capable of enforcement as between private parties in the courts of the country."[24] Political-judicial variants of NSE doctrine prevent courts from deciding treaty-related issues in situations that require the exercise of political judgment in choosing how best to carry out U.S. treaty obligations. Under the political-judicial concept, unlike the congressional-executive concept, federal executive officers have the authority to implement NSE treaty provisions and need not await legislative authorization to do so. For example, federal executive officers do not need legislative authorization to implement an arms control treaty requiring the destruction of certain types of weapons. However, courts would be reluctant to enforce such a treaty if an individual sued the president to remedy an alleged treaty violation.

The federal-state concept of self-execution arose in the early 1950s in the context of disputes about U.S. participation in human rights treaties and judicial application of the U.N. Charter's human rights provisions. Under the federal-state concept, an SE treaty supersedes conflicting state laws, but an NSE treaty does not supersede state laws unless Congress enacts legislation to implement the treaty. A California Supreme Court decision in 1952 was the first published judicial decision to apply the federal-state concept of self-execution. (This case was the appeal from the *Fujii* decision discussed previously.) In an opinion rejecting a claim based on the Charter's human rights provisions, the court said: "A treaty ... does not automatically supersede local laws which are inconsistent with it unless the treaty provisions are self-executing."[25] As mentioned before, the federal-state variant of NSE doctrine served a useful purpose by providing a justification for courts to dodge the uncomfortable question whether the Charter's human rights provisions offered stronger protection against racial discrimination than did the Fourteenth Amendment.

Before World War II, lawyers and judges used the terms "self-executing" and "non-self-executing" to express both the congressional-executive concept and the political-judicial concept, without distinguishing clearly between them. The fact that these terms had already acquired two very different meanings before 1945 may have made it easier for lawyers and judges after 1945 to stretch self-execution rhetoric to encompass the federal-state concept. However, they still needed a judicial precedent they could cite as authority to legitimize the extension of self-execution doctrine into the previously distinct realm of treaty supremacy.

In the field of U.S. constitutional law, if a lawyer wants a precedent to support her position, she can find no better authority than an opinion by the great Chief Justice John Marshall. A legal claim gains instant legitimacy if the proponent cites a Marshall opinion as authority. In 1829, in a case called *Foster v. Neilson*, Marshall wrote that an NSE treaty "addresses itself to the political, not the judicial department; and the legislature must execute the contract before it can become a rule for the Court."[26] *Foster* involved a dispute over ownership of land in what is now Louisiana. The plaintiffs relied partly on a treaty to support their claim. The defendant's claim was based on a land grant from the federal government. *Foster* said nothing about the relationship between treaties and state law because both parties relied exclusively on federal law to support their claims.[27] Even so, in litigation involving the U.N. Charter's human rights provisions in the early 1950s, lawyers began citing *Foster* to support the idea that an NSE treaty does not supersede conflicting state laws. By the late twentieth century, the underlying facts had been shrouded in the mists of time, so the judges who cited *Foster* as authority did not realize that *Foster* said nothing about the relationship between treaties and state law. Thus, in *Medellín v. Texas*—where the Supreme Court effectively authorized Texas to violate U.S. treaty obligations—Chief Justice Roberts relied heavily on *Foster* to support the Court's decision.[28]

In sum, lawyers and judges in the early 1950s used the rhetoric of self-execution and the authority of Marshall's opinion in *Foster* to create a novel NSE exception to the Constitution's treaty supremacy rule. Virtually nobody other than Quincy Wright noticed that the newly minted NSE exception constituted a dramatic change from the mandatory treaty supremacy rule that prevailed from the Founding until about 1950. Thus, the de facto Bricker Amendment converted the treaty supremacy rule from a mandatory to an optional rule by means of a process of invisible constitutional change.

III. THE POLITICS OF TRANSFORMATION

The transformation of the treaty supremacy rule was closely linked to the emergence of a new constitutional rule barring racial segregation. Both were revolutionary constitutional changes. Both were responses to the emergence of a new body of international human rights law.

The U.N. Charter took effect in 1945; it codified a new international norm prohibiting racial discrimination. As a party, the United States is obligated to promote "human rights ... for all *without distinction as to race*."[29] The United Nations adopted the Universal Declaration of Human Rights in 1948, which states: "Everyone is entitled to all the rights and freedoms set forth in this Declaration, without distinction of any kind, such as race, colour, sex, language, religion, political or other opinion, national or social origin, property, birth or other status."[30] Adoption of the Universal Declaration reinforced the importance of the norm against racial discrimination in the emerging postwar international order. As of 1948, the United States was one of the few countries in the world with a system of legally sanctioned racial segregation. Jim Crow laws in the South were the most notorious example, but various western states had discriminatory laws restricting land ownership,[31] and states throughout the country used their judicial systems to enforce private agreements that maintained racially segregated housing.[32] In light of the glaring discrepancy between U.S. laws and practices and the international norm against race discrimination, the United States came under intense pressure from the international community to abolish race-based discrimination.[33] If the United States wanted to win the Cold War ideological battle with the Soviet Union, it would have to put an end to the uniquely American form of apartheid.

Shortly after the Charter took effect, lawyers in the United States began invoking the Charter's human rights provisions in domestic litigation. Between 1946 and 1954, U.S. courts decided dozens of cases in which civil rights plaintiffs relied on the Charter's human rights provisions to challenge discriminatory state laws.[34] The combination of international pressure and domestic civil rights litigation sparked a process of "acculturation" in the United States. Professors Goodman and Jinks define acculturation as "the general process by which actors adopt the beliefs and behavioral patterns of the surrounding culture." The touchstone of acculturation, they say, "is that varying degrees of identification with a reference group generate varying degrees of cognitive and social pressures to conform." Goodman and Jinks emphasize the "civilizing force of hypocrisy" as a crucial element in explaining how the process of acculturation can yield deep, meaningful human rights reform. They claim that "acculturation narrows the gap between public acts and private preferences through internal cognitive processes: Under certain conditions people change their beliefs to avoid the unpleasant state of cognitive dissonance between what they profess in public and what they believe in private."[35] Cognitive dissonance and the civilizing force of hypocrisy were key factors driving constitutional transformation in the United States between 1946 and 1954. Indeed, the Supreme Court's landmark 1954 decision in *Brown v. Board of Education*, holding that racial segregation in public schools is unconstitutional, was a product of acculturation. *Brown* can be explained as a decision to incorporate into the Fourteenth Amendment Equal Protection Clause the strong anti-discrimination norm codified in the U.N. Charter and the Universal Declaration of Human Rights.

The parties litigated *Brown* in tandem with its companion case, *Bolling v. Sharpe*. *Bolling* involved racial segregation in public schools in the District of Columbia. Petitioners in *Bolling* presented a detailed argument to the effect that racial segregation in public schools violated the U.N. Charter's anti-discrimination provisions.[36] The United States filed a key amicus brief in *Brown* and *Bolling*, arguing that continued racial discrimination in the United States hindered accomplishment of the nation's foreign policy goals. The government's brief emphasized that continued racial segregation at home undermined the nation's effort to win the Cold War ideological battle with the Soviet Union.[37] In light of the arguments presented, the Court had three basic options in *Brown* and *Bolling*. First, it could have adhered to established precedent under the "separate but equal" doctrine and held that state and local laws permitting racial segregation in public schools were valid. Second, it could have invalidated state and local laws by applying the U.N. Charter in conjunction with the Supremacy Clause. Both of these options were unsatisfactory because, as one contemporary commentator noted, it would be "a reproach to our constitutional system to confess that the values it establishes fall below any requirement of the Charter."[38] Not wanting to reproach our constitutional system, the Court selected the third option: it repudiated the doctrine of "separate but equal" and held that racial segregation in public schools violates the Fourteenth Amendment Equal Protection Clause (*Brown*) and the Fifth Amendment Due Process Clause (*Bolling*).[39] The third option was the only one that allowed the justices "to avoid the unpleasant state of cognitive dissonance between what they profess in public and what they believe in private."[40] The justices believed privately in American exceptionalism: the view that the United States has the best constitution in the world. In light of the newly emerging international norm prohibiting race-based discrimination, the justices could not reconcile their faith in American exceptionalism with the reality of racial segregation. So, they reinterpreted the Constitution to incorporate the U.N. Charter's strong anti-discrimination norm into the Equal Protection Clause.[41]

As other scholars have explained, *Brown* is properly viewed as a midpoint, not the endpoint, of the civil rights revolution in the United States.[42] Just as the U.S. Supreme Court's 1954 decision in *Brown* was a critical turning point in the transformation of the Equal Protection Clause, the California Supreme Court's decision in *Fujii v. State* was a crucial landmark in the transformation of the treaty supremacy rule.[43] The plaintiff in *Fujii* was a Japanese national who bought land in California. California's Alien Land Law barred Japanese nationals from owning land in California. Sei Fujii filed suit to challenge the validity of the California statute. In a landmark ruling in April 1950, a lower court held that the Alien Land Law was invalid because it conflicted with the U.N. Charter's human rights provisions and that the Charter trumped California law under the Supremacy Clause.[44]

The lower court's decision in *Fujii* was legally sound, but politically explosive.[45] Even before the *Fujii* decision, leaders of the ABA had been lobbying vigorously against U.S. participation in international human rights treaties. By the time the California court issued its decision, the ABA was officially on record opposing both U.S. ratification of the Genocide Convention and U.S. participation in the International Covenant on Human Rights, which was then in draft form. *Fujii* persuaded the ABA leadership that more drastic action was necessary. In September 1950, the ABA authorized a study of possible constitutional amendments to avert the perceived threat posed by international human rights treaties. *Fujii* also provoked a strong response from the U.S. Senate. In September 1951, Senator John Bricker introduced the first of several versions of a proposed constitutional amendment that came to be known as the Bricker Amendment. Like the ABA proposal, the Bricker Amendment was designed to address the perceived threat posed by international human rights treaties.[46]

In an effort to counter the political momentum supporting the Bricker Amendment, lawyers who favored U.S. ratification of human rights treaties began to invoke NSE doctrine. In particular, they argued that the draft Covenant on Human Rights could be rendered non-self-executing by including appropriate language in the treaty itself or in unilateral reservations attached to the treaty. Lawyers presented this argument in internal debates within the ABA. Senior officials in the Eisenhower administration made similar arguments during Senate testimony in hearings on the proposed Bricker Amendment. By invoking NSE doctrine in this way, they hoped to demonstrate that international human rights law was not as threatening as Senator Bricker and the ABA leadership claimed. However, by applying NSE doctrine in this manner, they obscured the critical distinction between treaty supremacy doctrine (which had previously governed the relationship between treaties and state law) and self-execution doctrine (which had previously governed the distribution of power over treaty implementation among the branches of the federal government). In the process, they created a novel NSE exception to the Constitution's treaty supremacy rule.[47]

Fujii illustrates this point. On appeal to the California Supreme Court, the California attorney general argued that the U.N. Charter did not "supersede" the Alien Land Law because the Charter is not self-executing.[48] The California Supreme Court accepted this argument. It said: "A treaty . . . does not automatically supersede local laws which are inconsistent with it unless the treaty provisions are self-executing."[49] The court then analyzed the U.N. Charter's human rights provisions, concluding that they are not self-executing.[50] The holding that the Charter is not self-executing enabled the court to dodge the uncomfortable question of whether the Alien Land Law violated the Charter's human rights provisions.[51] It bears emphasis that the California Supreme Court was not concerned about the division of power over treaty implementation among the branches of the federal government, which was the traditional focus of self-execution doctrine. Instead, the court applied NSE doctrine to protect California's autonomy, as a sovereign state, from the "foreign" influence of the Charter's human rights provisions. This was a very different concept of non-self-execution than any court had ever utilized before. *Fujii* was the first published decision by any state or federal court in U.S. history that applied NSE doctrine to support a decision that a treaty did not supersede conflicting state laws.

The ALI published the Restatement (Second) of Foreign Relations Law in 1965. As noted previously, the Restatement effectively codified the NSE exception to the treaty supremacy rule that the California Supreme Court articulated in *Fujii* (in 1952), and that the Eisenhower administration endorsed in Senate testimony on the proposed Bricker Amendment (in 1953). After 1965, judges and scholars accepted the NSE exception to the treaty supremacy rule on the strength of the ALI's authority.

Why did American lawyers accept the NSE exception to the treaty supremacy rule? Four factors help answer this question. First, reliance on the authority of *Foster v. Neilson*, combined with confusion about the proper definition of the term "non-self-executing," concealed the expansion of self-execution doctrine to encompass the previously distinct doctrine of treaty supremacy. Consequently, most of the lawyers responsible for the de facto Bricker Amendment probably did not realize that the NSE exception to the treaty supremacy rule was a dramatic departure from prior law. Second, President Eisenhower was firmly opposed to the proposed Bricker Amendment. Creation of an NSE exception to the treaty supremacy rule helped the Eisenhower administration defeat the Bricker Amendment in the Senate, because the NSE exception supported the administration's argument that human rights treaties were not as threatening as Senator Bricker feared. Third, the United States was engaged in a Cold War ideological battle with the Soviet Union, and the Soviets were exploiting every available opportunity to criticize racist policies and practices in the United States. In cases such as *Bolling* and *Fujii*, a judicial holding that state law did not comply with the Charter's human rights provisions would have caused a major diplomatic embarrassment for the nation. NSE doctrine conveniently allowed the courts to avoid that embarrassment by ducking the question of whether state law conflicted with the Charter.

Finally, cases such as *Bolling* and *Fujii* created severe cognitive dissonance for American lawyers and judges. If courts applied the U.N. Charter and traditional treaty supremacy doctrine to invalidate discriminatory state and local laws, they would have been tacitly admitting that the Charter provided stronger protection against racial discrimination than did the Fourteenth Amendment. Such an admission would have been contrary to their faith in American exceptionalism. To address that cognitive dissonance, the California Supreme Court in *Fujii* and the U.S. Supreme Court in *Brown* and *Bolling* reinterpreted the Fourteenth Amendment to incorporate the U.N. Charter's strong anti-discrimination norm into the Equal Protection Clause. Meanwhile, the *Fujii* court endorsed an NSE exception to the treaty supremacy rule. The NSE exception helped judges preserve their faith in American exceptionalism by enabling them to duck the uncomfortable question of whether international human rights law provides stronger protection for human rights than does the U.S. Constitution. In cases where it appears that the answer is yes, courts preferred to reinterpret the Fourteenth Amendment to satisfy international human rights standards, rather than apply the treaty supremacy rule.

IV. ORGANIZATION OF THE BOOK

The remainder of the book is divided into four parts. Part One addresses treaty supremacy in the Founding era. The analysis is fairly abbreviated. Part One touches briefly on the Articles of Confederation, the Federal Convention, the state ratification debates, and the first decade after adoption of the Constitution. The reason for brevity is *not* that the Founding era is unimportant. Rather, the reason is that there is no significant scholarly disagreement regarding the book's central claim about the Founding era. At that time, all key participants understood that treaty supremacy addressed the relationship between treaties and state law, whereas non-self-execution was a federal separation of powers doctrine. Therefore, no influential member of the Founding generation advocated an NSE exception to the treaty supremacy rule.[52]

Part Two covers the period from 1800 to 1945. In contrast to Part One, this part attempts to be fairly comprehensive. Comprehensiveness is necessary to debunk the myth that there was an NSE exception to the treaty supremacy rule before 1945. The lawyers, judges, and scholars who carried out a successful constitutional revolution after World War II did a remarkably good job of perpetrating that myth. Because falsehoods are buried deeply in contemporary understandings of the relevant legal history, quite a bit of excavation is needed to uncover the truth. The final chapter of Part Two discusses social, political, and intellectual developments between 1900 and 1945 that laid the groundwork for the ensuing constitutional transformation.

Part Three analyzes the period from 1945 to 1965. Whereas Part Two focuses heavily on courts, Part Three is primarily concerned with developments outside the courts. The ABA, the ALI, civil rights organizations, and the U.S. Senate feature prominently in this part of the story. In brief, the birth of modern international human rights law unleashed a torrent of human rights activism in both domestic and international fora. That human rights activism, in turn, sparked a strong political backlash in the United States. The backlash generated substantial political momentum in both the ABA and the U.S. Senate in favor of the proposed Bricker Amendment. Members of Washington's foreign policy establishment joined forces with leading international lawyers to defeat the proposed amendment. That coalition produced a new version of NSE doctrine that helped reverse the momentum supporting the Bricker Amendment. A similar coalition of foreign policy professionals and international lawyers joined forces under the umbrella of the ALI to produce the Restatement (Second) of Foreign Relations Law. The Restatement codified the new NSE exception to the treaty supremacy rule as black letter law, thereby consolidating the process of constitutional transformation.

Part Four addresses two questions. Chapter 14 discusses contemporary doctrinal controversies related to self-execution and treaty supremacy. The history examined in Parts One to Three provides an alternative perspective to help illuminate certain doctrinal issues that are still hotly contested today. Chapter 15 discusses the implications of the de facto Bricker Amendment for contemporary constitutional theory. I suggest that the phenomenon of invisible constitutional change is a subject that merits further study. Additionally, the story of the de facto Bricker Amendment injects a cautionary note into contemporary scholarship on "popular constitutionalism." Whereas much of that scholarship celebrates constitutional change outside the courts as a triumph of democracy and popular sovereignty, the history of the de facto Bricker Amendment suggests that constitutional change outside the courts is not always consistent with principles of democratic legitimacy.

PART ONE

Treaty Supremacy at the Founding

When the Constitution's Framers met in Philadelphia in 1787, one of their primary objectives was to persuade European powers that the United States could be trusted to fulfill its international obligations.[1] In the late eighteenth century, international obligations came in two varieties. Written international law was codified in treaties. Unwritten international law was known as "the law of nations."[2] In the decade since adoption of the Declaration of Independence, the United States had repeatedly violated obligations it owed to European states under treaties and the law of nations.[3] The failure to fulfill its international obligations created serious problems for the young nation.

Repeated infractions of international law were directly attributable to the structure of government under the Articles of Confederation. (The Articles of Confederation was effectively the Constitution of the United States from 1781 until the new Constitution took effect in 1789.) The Articles created a weak national government that was powerless to control the individual States. The Framers sought to rectify the problem of State treaty violations by vesting power over treaty compliance in the federal government. Thus, the Constitution was purposefully designed to grant the national government the power to restrain state governments from violating the nation's international obligations. National leaders envisioned "a new government that would have the capacity to fulfill the nation's international obligations and, by so doing, earn acceptance within the surrounding community of nation-states."[4]

The treaty supremacy rule, codified in the Supremacy Clause, was a central element of the Framers' plan for a Constitution that would ensure the nation's ability to fulfill its international commitments. Part One discusses the origins of the treaty supremacy rule during the Founding era. Part One consists of three chapters. Chapter One addresses the period from the Declaration of Independence in 1776 to the signing of the Constitution in September 1787. Chapter Two focuses on state ratification debates in 1787 and 1788. Chapter Three addresses two key foreign relations controversies during the Constitution's first decade: the Supreme Court decision in *Ware v. Hylton* in 1796 and debates about the Jay Treaty in 1795–1796. The analysis demonstrates that a broad and deep consensus supported the treaty supremacy rule in the Founding era. Several issues related to treaties generated substantial controversy during state ratification debates and during the 1790s. However, the Constitution's treaty supremacy rule was not controversial.

1

The Origins of Treaty Supremacy: 1776–1787

The United States declared its independence in 1776, creating a loose confederation among thirteen sovereign states. The United States concluded three treaties with France in 1778, including a Treaty of Alliance and a Treaty of Amity and Commerce.[1] The new nation did not adopt a formal document to codify the powers of the national government until 1781. The Articles of Confederation, in force from 1781 to 1789, stipulated: "Each state retains its sovereignty, freedom, and independence, and every power, jurisdiction, and right, which is not by this Confederation expressly delegated to the United States."[2] Thus, under the Articles, power was concentrated mostly in state governments. The national government consisted primarily of a single body, the Congress of the United States. Congress had "the sole and exclusive right and power of . . . entering into treaties and alliances."[3] Congress exercised this power to conclude treaties with the Netherlands, Sweden, France, Prussia, Morocco, and the United Kingdom between 1782 and 1786.[4]

I. TREATY VIOLATIONS UNDER THE ARTICLES OF CONFEDERATION

Although the Continental Congress had the power to make treaties, it lacked substantial legislative power. Hence, Congress depended on the states to implement treaties. The problems inherent in such a decentralized governmental structure became apparent soon after the United States concluded a peace treaty with the United Kingdom. Under Article 7 of the 1783 peace treaty, "his Brittanic Majesty" promised to "withdraw all his armies, garrisons, and fleets from the said United States, and from every post, place, and harbor within the same."[5] When Britain failed to implement this promise, John Adams, the minister plenipotentiary from the United States to Britain, delivered a diplomatic message to the British secretary of state, Lord Carmarthen, protesting Britain's failure to remove its troops.[6] Carmarthen responded by summarizing British complaints about U.S. violations of the peace treaty. Carmarthen's message described in detail "the grievances complained of by Merchants and other British Subjects having estates, property and debts due to them in the several States of America."[7] John Jay, the U.S. secretary for foreign affairs, concluded that the British had many legitimate grievances about U.S. treaty violations, which were generally attributable to the actions of state governments.[8] Jay and other national leaders wanted the states to comply with the peace treaty. Under the Articles of Confederation, though, Congress was unable to compel state compliance.

Lord Carmarthen concluded his note to Adams as follows: "I can assure you, Sir, that whenever America shall manifest a real determination to fulfil her part of the treaty, Great Britain will not hesitate to prove her sincerity to cooperate."[9] In short, treaty violations attributable to state governments provided a justification for Britain to postpone removal of its troops from U.S. territory, and Britain's willingness to remove its troops depended on a demonstration of U.S. resolve to halt such treaty violations. Thus, Congress's inability to compel state compliance with treaties posed a serious national security problem. "The continued occupation of the garrisons by the British Army jeopardized the security of the northern frontier and blocked vital trade routes."[10]

Meanwhile, the United States' economy suffered from a serious depression through much of the 1780s.[11] Thomas Paine quipped that the American states were "in want of two of the most essential matters which governments could be destitute of—money and credit."[12] Several factors contributed to the economic depression, but Britain's imposition of retaliatory trade measures was a significant one. "America was now subject to Britain's restrictive trade measures, excluded from the lucrative British West Indian trade . . . and liable to all the discriminatory duties levied against foreign bottoms in its direct trade with other countries."[13] To make matters worse, "restrictive trade measures were also being imposed by America's ally, France, and in turn by Louis XVI's ally, Spain."[14] A key goal of U.S. diplomacy during the 1780s was to negotiate commercial agreements with Britain and other European countries to help promote economic development at home. However, European nations were reluctant to enter into trade treaties with the United States because they knew that the national government could not guarantee treaty compliance by the states. "Continued treaty violations on the part of the American [states] served to dampen such sentiment as existed in England for a reciprocal trade treaty."[15] Thus, Congress's inability to compel state compliance with treaties created serious economic difficulties for the young nation.

Aside from national security and economic concerns, treaty compliance was a matter of national honor. John Jay wrote:

> Contracts between Nations, like contracts between Individuals, should be faithfully executed . . . honest nations like honest Men require no constraint to do Justice; and tho impunity and the necessity of Affairs may sometimes afford temptations to pare down contracts to the Measure of convenience, yet it is never done but at the expence of that esteem, and confidence, and credit which are of infinitely more worth than all the momentary advantages which such expedients can extort.[16]

Similarly, Alexander Hamilton was ashamed by the country's inability to fulfill its international obligations. He said:

> We may indeed with propriety be said to have reached almost the last stage of national humiliation. There is scarcely any thing that can wound the pride or degrade the character of an independent nation which we do not experience. Are there engagements to the performance of which we are held by every tie respectable among men? These are the subjects of constant and unblushing violation.[17]

In sum, the national government's inability to compel states to comply with treaties created both economic and national security problems. It was also a source of national shame and dishonor. Even under the Articles of Confederation, though, national leaders began to sow the seeds for a doctrine of treaty supremacy, which would come to fruition with adoption of the Constitution. The next two sections discuss those seeds in *Rutgers v. Waddington* and in John Jay's report to Congress.

II. *RUTGERS V. WADDINGTON*

The Mayor's Court of the City of New York decided the case of *Rutgers v. Waddington* in August 1786.[18] Mayor James Duane sat as chief judge and authored the court's opinion. During the Revolutionary War, Elizabeth Rutgers fled New York City when the British military occupied the city, leaving behind an abandoned brewhouse. Joshua Waddington, a British merchant, acting under the authority of the British military, occupied the brewhouse from September 1778 until June 1783.[19] After the war, the New York legislature passed a statute authorizing New York citizens whose property had been occupied to file trespass actions against British subjects. The statute provided specifically that no defendant "shall be admitted to plead in justification any military order or command whatever of the enemy for such occupancy."[20] Rutgers sued Waddington under the New York trespass law, seeking eight thousand pounds in compensatory damages for the occupation of her brewhouse. Thus, *Rutgers* presented an apparent conflict between the law of nations, which provided a "military orders" justification for Waddington, and the New York statute, which appeared to bar such a defense.

Alexander Hamilton represented Waddington in the case. Hamilton advanced several distinct arguments, but two are important for present purposes. First, under the law of nations, "[t]he enemy having a right to the use of the Plaintiffs property & having exercised their right through the Defendant . . . he cannot be made answerable to another without injustice and a violation of the law of Universal society."[21] Thus, in Hamilton's view, the law of nations barred a judgment requiring Waddington to pay damages to Rutgers. Second, "to make the Defendant answerable would be a breach of the Treaty of Peace,"[22] because under the law of nations every treaty of peace includes an implied amnesty for wartime actions that cause damage to property.

The court's opinion divided defendant's occupation of plaintiff's property into two phases. Before April 30, 1780, the occupation was not justified under the law of nations because defendant acted under the authority of the commissary general, a civilian officer who exercised no lawful authority under the laws of war. However, after April 30, 1780, the occupation was justified under the law of nations because defendant acted under the authority of the British commander in chief.[23] Hence, with respect to the period after April 30, 1780, the court said: "We are therefore of opinion, that restitution of the fruit, or in other words, the rents and issues of houses and lands, which have been *bona fide*, collected by or under the authority of the British Commander, while he held possession of the city, cannot, according to the law of nations, be required."[24]

The court also agreed partially with Hamilton's argument that the peace treaty with Britain included an implied "amnesty and oblivion of damages and injuries in the war."[25] However, the court said, the amnesty applies only to acts done in relation to the war, and the occupation before April 30, 1780, "had no relation to the war."[26] Moreover, as the peace treaty did not include an express amnesty provision, defendant's argument hinged on an implied amnesty under the law of nations. Thus, the "amnesty" argument and the "lawful occupation" argument both led to the same result: defendant had a valid argument under the law of nations for the period after April 30, 1780.

This conclusion, in turn, raised another question. The court had to decide "whether the courts of justice ought to be governed by the [New York] statute, where it clearly militated against the law of nations."[27] During the 1780s, courts in most states applied their own state laws, even where those laws conflicted with the peace treaty and/or the law of nations.[28] In contrast, Hamilton argued that "[t]he judges of each state must of necessity be judges of the United States. And they must take notice of the law of Congress as a part of the law of the land." Specifically, "in respect to foreigners they must judge according to that law which alone the constitution knows as regulating their concerns," that is, the law of nations.[29]

Several passages in the court's opinion addressed the relationship between international law and New York state law, but the court's pronouncements on this question were inconsistent. In one passage, for example, the court defended the principle of legislative supremacy. "The supremacy of the [New York] Legislature need not be called into question; if they think fit positively to enact a law, there is no power which can control them. When the main object of such a law is clearly expressed, and the intention manifest, the Judges are not at liberty, although it appears to them to be unreasonable, to reject it: for this were to set the judicial above the legislative, which would be subversive of all government."[30] This passage strongly suggests that, in the event of a conflict between the law of nations and a New York statute, state courts are bound by the statute.

However, other passages contradict this view. Hamilton argued in his brief that "[t]he power of Congress in making Treaties is of a Legislative kind. Their proclamation enjoining the observance of [the peace treaty] is a law. And a law

Paramount to that of any particular state."[31] In one passage, the court seemingly agreed with this argument: "The federal compact hath vested Congress with full and exclusive powers to make peace and war. This treaty they have made and ratified, and rendered its obligation perpetual. And we are clearly of opinion, that no State in this union can alter or abridge, in a single point, the federal articles or the treaty."[32] Thus, the court endorsed the principle of treaty supremacy, rather than (state) legislative supremacy.

In addition to defending treaty supremacy, Hamilton made a similar argument for the supremacy of the law of nations over New York law. "Congress have the exclusive direction of our foreign affairs & of all matters relating to the Laws of Nations. No single state has any legal jurisdiction to alter them. . . . While the Confederation exists a law of a particular state derogating from its constitutional authority is no law."[33] In one passage, the court appeared to endorse this argument as well. It said that the several states of the United States "must be governed by one common law of nations; for on any other principles how can they act with regard to foreign powers; and how shall foreign powers act towards them?" Moreover, the court continued, "to abrogate or alter any one of the known laws or usages of nations, by the authority of a single state, must be contrary to the very nature of the confederacy . . . as well as dangerous to the union itself."[34]

Ultimately, the *Rutgers* court dodged questions about the supremacy of international law over state law by construing the New York trespass statute in harmony with the law of nations. It said: "The repeal of the law of nations, or any interference with it, could not have been in contemplation, in our opinion, when the Legislature passed this statute; and we think ourselves bound to exempt that law from its operation."[35] The court concluded that whoever "is clearly exempted from the operation of this statute by the law of nations, this Court must take it for granted, could never have been intended to be comprehended within it by the Legislature."[36] Thus, despite what appeared to be a stark conflict between the New York statute, which barred a military orders defense, and the law of nations, which authorized such a defense, the court concluded that there was no conflict between the New York statute and the law of nations. Both Hamilton's brief and the court's opinion planted seeds for the later adoption of the Constitution's treaty supremacy rule.

III. JOHN JAY'S REPORT TO CONGRESS

This chapter referred above to Lord Carmarthen's diplomatic note summarizing British complaints about U.S. violations of the 1783 peace treaty. Britain's concerns focused on Articles 4, 5, and 6. In Article 4, the United States promised that American debtors would repay their debts to British creditors. Article 5 offered protection for land owned by British subjects in the United States. Article 6 prohibited punitive measures against those who supported Britain during the war.[37]

John Adams, the U.S. minister in London, forwarded Lord Carmarthen's note to John Jay, the U.S. secretary for foreign affairs. Jay undertook a detailed study to determine, among other things, "[w]hether any and which of the Acts

enumerated in the [British] List of Grievances do violate the treaty of peace between the United States and Great Britain?"[38] After completing an exhaustive
review of state laws and policies, Jay concluded: "From the aforegoing review of
the several Acts complained of, it is manifest, that the 4th and 6th Articles of the
treaty have been violated by certain of them."[39] Moreover, he added, "it is certain
that deviations on our part preceded any on the part of Britain; and therefore instead of being justified *by* them, afford excuse *to* them."[40] Thus, treaty violations
attributable to the acts of state governments provided a justification for Britain
to postpone removal of its troops from U.S. territory.

In light of his conclusions, Jay recommended that Congress adopt three resolutions to address the problem of state treaty violations. The first stipulated
"[t]hat the legislatures of the several States cannot of right pass any act or acts . . .
for restraining, limiting or in any manner impeding, retarding or counteracting
the operation or execution of" the peace treaty. The second added: "That all such
acts or parts of Acts as may be now existing in either of the States, repugnant to
the treaty of peace, ought to be forthwith repealed."[41]

Two other passages in Jay's proposed resolutions anticipated the future language of the Supremacy Clause. The first resolution stated that ratified treaties
"become, in virtue of the Confederation, part of the law of the land, and are not
only independent of the will and power of such [state] Legislatures, but also binding and obligatory on them."[42] Thus, even under the Articles of Confederation,
Jay asserted that treaties were supreme over state laws. Jay's third proposed resolution recommended that states pass laws stipulating "that the Courts of law and
equity in all Causes and questions cognizable by them respectively, and arising
from or touching the said treaty, shall decide and adjudge according to the true
intent and meaning of the same, any thing in the said Acts or parts of Acts to
the contrary thereof in any wise notwithstanding."[43] This language is similar
to the final clause of the Supremacy Clause, which directs state judges to apply
treaties, "any Thing in the Constitution or Laws of any State to the Contrary
notwithstanding." Thus, Jay's proposed resolutions anticipated both aspects of
the Constitution's treaty supremacy rule: that valid, ratified treaties supersede
conflicting state laws; and that state courts have a duty to apply the treaty when
there is a conflict between a treaty and state law.

The Continental Congress adopted Jay's proposed resolutions almost verbatim.[44] Congress then asked Jay to draft a letter to the states. Jay provided a seven-
page letter addressing violations of the 1783 peace treaty by state governments
and recommending measures to remedy those violations. Congress endorsed
Jay's letter and transmitted it to state governments.[45] That letter stated in part:

> Not only the obvious dictates of religion, morality and national honor, but
> also the first principles of good policy, demand a candid and punctual com-
> pliance with engagements constitutionally and fairly made . . . It is our duty
> to take care that all the rights which they [the British] ought to enjoy within
> our Jurisdiction by the laws of nations and the faith of treaties remain invio-
> late. And it is also our duty to provide that the essential interests and peace

of the whole confederacy be not impaired or endangered by deviations from the line of public faith into which any of its members may from whatever cause be unadvisedly drawn.[46]

Thus, Congress affirmed that treaty compliance was a matter of both national honor and national security.

The letter from Congress to the states also affirmed the crucial role of state courts in enforcing treaties:

> In cases between Individuals, all doubts respecting the meaning of a treaty, like all doubts respecting the meaning of a law, are in the first instance mere judicial questions, and are to be heard and decided in the Courts of Justice having cognizance of the causes in which they arise; and whose duty it is to determine them according to the rules and maxims established by the laws of Nations for the interpretation of treaties.[47]

However, state courts took a different view of the matter. Despite Congress's exhortations, state courts continued to apply state laws and disregard the peace treaty with Britain. The persistent refusal of state courts to apply the peace treaty was a key factor that led to the call for a constitutional convention.

IV. THE CONSTITUTIONAL CONVENTION

Representatives from twelve of the thirteen states met in Philadelphia for almost four months between May and September 1787 to draft a new Constitution for the United States. As Professor Ramsey notes, "there is general agreement [among historians] that foreign affairs difficulties were a root—if not the root— of the drive to replace the Articles" of Confederation with a new Constitution.[48] In April 1787, as he was preparing for the Constitutional Convention, James Madison drafted a famous essay entitled "Vices of the Political System of the United States." One key vice he identified was the repeated "violations of the law of nations and of treaties."[49] Similarly, near the very beginning of the Convention, Edmund Randolph identified the inability of Congress to prevent the infraction of treaties as one of the chief defects of the Articles of Confederation.[50]

Congress's inability to compel state compliance with international law can be viewed as one aspect of a larger problem: its inability to compel state compliance with national law. Under the Articles of Confederation, Alexander Hamilton observed, the laws enacted by Congress were "in theory ... constitutionally binding on the members of the Union, yet in practice they are mere recommendations which the States observe or disregard at their option."[51] Thus, when the Framers met to draft a new Constitution, they all agreed that the national government should have the power to compel state compliance with both national law and international obligations. State violations of national and international law were two aspects of the same underlying problem, and both required a similar solution.

During the Constitutional Convention, delegates discussed two competing proposals for remedying the problem of state violations of national and international law. The initial discussions focused on the "Virginia Plan." Under that proposal, Congress would have had the power "to negative all laws passed by the several States contravening, in the opinion of the national legislature, the articles of union, or any treaties subsisting under the authority of the union."[52] If the Convention had adopted this proposal, it would have given Congress a direct veto over all state laws that impeded accomplishment of the objectives embodied in national laws or treaties. Advocates of a stronger, centralized national authority generally favored the Virginia Plan.[53] However, delegates who favored greater state autonomy objected to the proposed power to "negative" state laws. Gouverneur Morris said, "The proposal of it would disgust all the States." Luther Martin "considered the power as improper and inadmissible." On July 17, the delegates voted to reject this particular feature of the Virginia Plan.[54]

The competing proposal was the "New Jersey" plan. In its initial formulation, the New Jersey Plan provided "that all Acts of the U. States . . . and all Treaties made & ratified under the authority of the U. States shall be the supreme law of the respective States . . . and that the Judiciary of the several States shall be bound thereby in their decisions, any thing in the respective laws of the Individual States to the contrary notwithstanding."[55] After a series of editorial changes, this provision ultimately became the Supremacy Clause.[56] Like the Virginia Plan, the New Jersey Plan provided a single mechanism for invalidating state laws that conflicted with federal statutes and treaties. Unlike the Virginia Plan, which would have empowered the *national legislature* to invalidate state laws, the New Jersey Plan required *state courts* to invalidate state laws that conflicted with federal statutes and treaties.

James Madison favored the Virginia Plan; he objected that "[c]onfidence cannot be put in the State Tribunals as guardians of the National authority and interests."[57] Despite his and others' objections, the delegates approved a variant of the New Jersey proposal immediately after they rejected the Virginia proposal for a legislative "negative" over state laws. The text they approved required state courts to invalidate state laws that conflicted with federal statutes or treaties.[58] Professor Rakove notes: "Here in seminal form was the supremacy clause of the Constitution—but ironically presented as a weak" alternative to the Virginia Plan.[59] Advocates of greater state autonomy favored this "weaker" alternative because it gave primary responsibility to state courts to enforce the supremacy of treaties (and federal statutes) over conflicting state laws. Notably, even the staunchest defenders of state autonomy agreed that the Constitution must include some mechanism to invalidate state laws that conflicted with treaties. Professor Vázquez notes: "The rejection of the Virginia plan thus reflects a decision not to make the legislature the primary interpreter and enforcer of treaties against the states, and the adoption of the Supremacy Clause represents a decision to vest this power and duty in the courts."[60]

I stated previously that the Framers agreed to address the problem of state treaty violations by vesting power over treaty compliance in the *national* government. One could argue that rejection of the Virginia Plan and adoption of the Supremacy Clause contradicts that claim, because the Supremacy Clause effectively makes state courts the first line of defense in addressing state treaty violations. However, state court decisions involving the interpretation or application of treaties can be appealed to the U.S. Supreme Court.[61] Moreover, the Constitution authorizes Congress to create lower federal courts and extends the federal judicial power to cases arising under treaties.[62] Thus, state courts are the first line of defense, but they are not the last. The Supreme Court has the power to review state court decisions involving treaties, and Congress has the power to channel treaty cases into lower federal courts if it decides that state courts are not sufficiently attentive to the federal interest in treaty compliance. In this way, the constitutional provisions involving courts and treaties ensured federal control over treaty compliance, while also respecting state autonomy.

V. THE CONSTITUTION'S TEXT

The Constitution includes several distinct provisions related to treaties. Article I provides: "No State shall enter into any Treaty, Alliance or Confederation." Article I further adds: "No State shall, without the Consent of Congress . . . enter into any Agreement or Compact . . . with a foreign Power."[63] By denying states the power to enter into international agreements, Article I manifests the Framers' agreement to centralize control over international agreements in the national government.

Article II grants the president the power to make treaties "by and with the Advice and Consent of the Senate . . . provided two-thirds of the Senators present concur."[64] Two points are evident from the text. First, Article II excludes the House of Representatives from the treaty-making process. Second, Article II imposes no explicit restriction on the subject matter of treaties. A third point is less obvious, but perhaps more important: Article II manifests the Framers' commitment to protect state interests. Under the original constitutional design, state legislatures selected senators to represent the states.[65] Thus, the decision to require Senate consent for treaties, combined with the requirement for a two-thirds majority vote in the Senate, gave states significant power to prevent the national government from concluding treaties contrary to state interests.

Whereas states retained some power to inhibit treaty ratification, the constitutional text and structure manifest a clear decision to deny states the power to obstruct compliance with valid, ratified treaties. Several constitutional provisions address treaty implementation, either implicitly or explicitly. The Executive Vesting Clause in Article II vests the "executive power . . . in a President of the United States." The Take Care Clause obligates the president to "take Care that the Laws be faithfully executed."[66] At the Founding, there was general agreement that the president's responsibility for executing "the Laws" included the power and duty to execute treaties.[67] The Necessary and Proper Clause in Article I grants Congress the power "[t]o make all Laws which shall be necessary and proper for carrying into Execution . . . all other Powers vested by this Constitution in the

Government of the United States."[68] As the Treaty Power is one of the powers vested by the Constitution in the federal government, the Necessary and Proper Clause has generally been understood to grant Congress the power to enact laws that are "necessary and proper" for implementing treaties.[69] Whether it is "proper" for Congress to use this power to regulate matters that would otherwise be subject to exclusive state control is contested, but the basic idea that Congress can enact legislation to implement treaties was not controversial until recently.[70]

Article III, Section 2 provides: "The judicial Power shall extend to all Cases, in Law and Equity, arising under this Constitution, the Laws of the United States, and Treaties made, or which shall be made, under their Authority."[71] The contrast with Article I and II is striking. Under Article I, Congress's role in implementing treaties is implicit, not explicit; the Necessary and Proper Clause does not mention treaties explicitly. Similarly, under Article II, the president's role in implementing treaties is implicit, not explicit. Article II grants the president an explicit power to make treaties, but the president's power to implement treaties is merely implicit in the Executive Vesting Clause and the Take Care Clause. In contrast, Article III grants the federal judiciary an explicit power to implement treaties by specifying that the judicial power extends "to all Cases . . . arising under . . . Treaties." This explicit constitutional text demonstrates that the Framers expected courts to play an important role in treaty enforcement.[72]

After the Senate consents to ratification, and the president ratifies a treaty, the Supremacy Clause specifies that the treaty becomes "the supreme Law of the Land; and the Judges in every State shall be bound thereby."[73] The Supremacy Clause applies equally to federal statutes and treaties. In Professor Nelson's terms, it establishes a "rule of applicability," specifying that federal statutes and treaties are applicable in state courts. "At least as far as the courts are concerned, then, federal statutes [and treaties] take effect automatically within each state and form part of the same body of jurisprudence as state statutes."[74] The word "automatically" is important here. Although many people in the Founding generation thought that congressional legislation was necessary for treaties to override federal statutes (see Chapter 3), the consensus view was that treaties automatically supersede conflicting state law, and no legislation was necessary for that purpose.

In addition to establishing a rule of applicability, the Supremacy Clause also creates a "rule of priority." By declaring that federal statutes and treaties are "supreme," the Constitution directs state courts to give precedence to federal law over state law whenever there is a conflict, "even if the state law had been enacted more recently."[75] Thus, by creating a constitutional duty for state courts to apply treaties when there is a conflict between a treaty and state law, the Constitution restricts the power of state legislatures to obstruct compliance with treaty obligations.

The final phrase of the Supremacy Clause reinforces the centrality of courts in the constitutional scheme to prevent states from obstructing compliance with valid, ratified treaties. That phrase adds: "any Thing in the Constitution or Laws of any State to the Contrary notwithstanding." As Professor Nelson explains, this phrase is a "*non obstante*" provision. Absent the non obstante provision, state courts might reasonably have applied the well-established presumption against implied repeals—an interpretive principle that directs courts to construe a later law in harmony with an earlier law, unless the lawmaker clearly intended to repeal the earlier law. If courts applied that presumption, they would construe federal statutes and treaties narrowly to avoid conflicts with previously enacted state laws. The non obstante provision directs state courts *not* to apply the presumption against implied repeals, and instead, to interpret federal statutes and treaties in accordance with their ordinary meaning, even if that results in the repeal of an otherwise valid state law.[76]

In sum, the Supremacy Clause, viewed as a whole, was crafted to ensure that valid, ratified treaties automatically repeal conflicting state laws, including state laws that were unknown to the treaty drafters at the time they wrote the treaty. According to the text of the Supremacy Clause, the key criterion for a treaty to repeal (or invalidate) a state law is not the "intent of the treaty drafters," but rather the existence of a conflict between federal and state law. Insofar as modern judicial doctrine emphasizes intent, rather than conflict, as the touchstone for self-execution analysis, that doctrine has strayed from the original understanding of the Supremacy Clause. (Chapter 8 discusses the origins of the "intent" doctrine.)

State Ratification Debates

James Madison said that the Constitution that emerged from the Federal Convention in Philadelphia "was nothing more than the draft of a plan, nothing but a dead letter, until life and validity were breathed into it by the voice of the people, speaking through the several State Conventions." Accordingly, Madison argued, insofar as the Constitution's text is ambiguous, we should seek the meaning of the Constitution "not in the General Convention, which proposed, but in the State Conventions, which accepted and ratified the Constitution."[1] Although Madison arguably understated the significance of the Federal Convention, scholars agree that the records of the state ratifying conventions are important sources to shed light on the original understanding of the Constitution. Accordingly, Chapter 2 examines state ratification debates to determine how participants in those debates understood the treaty supremacy rule. Before analyzing these debates, one point of clarification may be helpful. Throughout this book, I distinguish between the treaty supremacy rule and self-execution doctrine. The treaty supremacy rule, as traditionally understood, consisted of two elements. First, all treaties supersede conflicting state laws. Second, courts have a constitutional duty to apply treaties when there is a conflict between a treaty and state law. In contrast, self-execution doctrine before World War II generally addressed the relationship among treaties, federal statutes, and federal executive power. Many modern commentators have blurred the distinction between supremacy and self-execution issues. Although participants in the state ratification debates also occasionally blurred that distinction, they typically assumed a fairly sharp conceptual division between supremacy issues and self-execution issues.

Recent scholarship about the original understanding of the Treaty Power and the Supremacy Clause can be divided broadly into two sets of issues. One group of scholars has focused on the relationship between treaties and state law.[2] That debate has centered on the question of whether there are federalism limits on the Treaty Power, and if so, what are those limits. (The term "federalism limits" refers to constitutional limits on the Treaty Power whose purpose is to protect state autonomy from federal interference.) The federalism debate has largely ignored the self-execution question: that is, the question of whether federal legislation is needed to implement treaties. No scholar who advocates strong federalism limits on the Treaty Power contends that Congress can overcome those limits by enacting legislation to implement treaties.

A second group of scholars has focused on the original understanding of self-execution.[3] Scholars who advocate a broad doctrine of non-self-execution (NSE) have defended their positions on federal separation-of-powers grounds, not on federalism grounds. They argue, for example, that treaties cannot override federal statutes,[4] or that treaties cannot create domestic law in areas within the scope of Congress's legislative powers.[5] However, no contemporary scholar has argued that the Framers understood the Constitution to create a class of "non-self-executing" treaties that do not supersede conflicting state laws. No modern scholar has presented an originalist argument to support an NSE exception to the Constitution's treaty supremacy rule because the Founding materials provide no support for such an argument. As Jack Rakove has written: "[T]he framers were virtually of one mind [with respect to treaty supremacy] ... The imperative need to make treaties legally binding on both the states and their citizens was widely recognized by 1787. The major consequence of this perception was the ready adoption of the supremacy clause."[6] In sum, state ratification materials do not provide unambiguous answers to questions about self-execution, or about federalism limits on the Treaty Power, but those materials demonstrate a clear interpretive consensus supporting both elements of the treaty supremacy rule.[7]

This chapter is divided into three sections, corresponding to the three main objections to the Constitution's treaty provisions raised by anti-Federalists. First, anti-Federalists argued that the Article II Treaty Power enabled the federal government to bargain away navigation rights on the Mississippi River, which were vitally important to Virginia and other southern states. Second, they argued that the combination of the Treaty Power and the Supremacy Clause threatened to deprive citizens of individual rights protected by the Bill of Rights provisions in state constitutions. Third, they argued that the Constitution violated separation of powers principles by empowering the president and Senate to create federal law, in the form of treaties, without the participation of the House of Representatives. The following sections discuss the anti-Federalist objections and Federalist responses.

I. THE TREATY POWER, NAVIGATION RIGHTS, AND THE MISSISSIPPI RIVER

Based on available records, it appears that delegates to the Virginia ratifying convention spent more time debating treaty-related issues than did the delegates to any of the other state ratifying conventions. Charles Warren estimated that almost 10 percent of the published records from the Virginia Convention involved discussion of the Treaty Power and the Supremacy Clause.[8] Much of that debate concerned navigation rights on the Mississippi River.

In the 1780s, Spain controlled access to the Gulf of Mexico from the Mississippi River. As early as 1779, Congress sought a commercial treaty with Spain with a proviso "that the United States shall enjoy the free navigation of the River

Mississippi into and from the sea."[9] However, Spain was not inclined to grant the navigation rights that the United States wanted. In 1786, Secretary for Foreign Affairs John Jay concluded that Spain was unlikely to yield on this issue until the United States was strong enough to seize control forcibly. Hence, he recommended conclusion of a treaty in which Spain would grant the United States beneficial commercial concessions in exchange for a U.S. agreement to "forbear to press its claim to free navigation for a period of twenty-five years."[10] The proposal created a sharp regional divide within the country. The northeastern states generally supported the proposal because it would have promoted their commercial interests. The southern states were strongly opposed. Virginia, North Carolina, and Georgia claimed ownership of land between the Appalachian Mountains and the Mississippi River. They wanted to promote settlement in the region, but the economic viability of westward expansion depended on access to the Gulf of Mexico via the Mississippi River. They were able to block the so-called Jay-Gardoqui treaty because, under the Articles of Confederation, affirmative votes of nine states were necessary to approve a treaty.[11]

Virginia held its ratifying convention for the new Constitution in June 1788. Memories of the failed Jay-Gardoqui treaty were still fresh in the minds of the Virginia delegates when they convened to debate the merits of the proposed Constitution. Many delegates feared that the new Constitution provided inadequate protection against a northern plot to conclude a treaty that would sacrifice the southern interest in navigation on the Mississippi to gain favorable commercial concessions for the benefit of northern states. For example, Patrick Henry argued: "By the Confederation, the rights of territory are secured. No treaty can be made without the consent of nine States. . . . If it be put in the power of a less number, you will most infallibly lose the Mississippi. . . . This new Constitution will involve in its operation the loss of the navigation of that valuable river."[12] Similarly, William Grayson said: "If the Mississippi was yielded to Spain, the migration to the Western country would be stopped, and the Northern States would . . . preserve their superiority and influence over that of the Southern. . . . Is it not highly imprudent to vest a power in the generality, which will enable those States to relinquish that river?"[13] The problem, from the anti-Federalists' perspective, stemmed from Article II, Section 2 of the Constitution. That provision grants the president power to make treaties "by and with the Advice and Consent of the Senate . . . provided two thirds of the Senators *present* concur." Anti-Federalists emphasized the word "present." Article I, Section 5 stipulates that a majority of the Senate's members "shall constitute a Quorum to do Business." Thus, assuming a total of thirteen states, with two senators from each state, a total of fourteen senators from seven states would constitute a quorum, and ten senators from five states could provide the two-thirds majority necessary to approve a treaty.[14]

James Madison prepared a response to this argument even before the commencement of the Virginia Convention. In a letter to George Nicholas, Madison presented several reasons why, in his view, the danger posited by the anti-Federalists was more hypothetical than real.[15] First, he argued, adoption of the new Constitution would strengthen the United States significantly, thereby enhancing its leverage in future negotiations with Spain. Second, the two-thirds rule in the new Constitution was substantially equivalent to the two-thirds rule under the Articles. In his view, very few senators would be absent for important decisions, such as whether to approve a new treaty. Moreover, he asserted, "the circumstance most material to be remarked in a comparative examination of the two systems, is the security which the new one affords by making the concurrence of the President necessary to the validity of Treaties." He added: "At present the will of a single body can make a Treaty. If the new Government be established no treaty can be made without the joint consent of two distinct and independent wills."[16] Federalist delegates repeated these arguments throughout the Virginia Convention.[17]

The anti-Federalists were not persuaded. On June 25, the Virginia delegates voted 89 to 79 in favor of ratifying the new Constitution. The Federalists won an important victory, inasmuch as ratification was not contingent on acceptance of proposed amendments. However, the anti-Federalists persuaded the Virginia Convention to adopt a long list of recommended constitutional amendments, along with an exhortation to Virginia's "Representatives in Congress to exert all their influence and use all reasonable and legal methods to obtain a ratification of the foregoing alterations and provisions."[18] One proposed amendment dealt specifically with the Mississippi issue: "[N]o treaty ceding, contracting, restraining, or suspending the territorial rights or claims of the United States ... [to] navigating the American rivers, shall be made, but in cases of the most urgent and extreme necessity; nor shall any such treaty be ratified without the concurrence of three fourths of the whole number of the members of both houses respectively."[19] About one month later, the North Carolina Convention adopted a proposed amendment that was virtually identical to the Virginia proposal, except that North Carolina refused to ratify the new Constitution until Congress considered the proposed amendments.[20] By requiring a three-fourths majority in both Houses of Congress, the proposed amendment, if adopted, would have made it all but politically impossible to secure ratification of a treaty abandoning the U.S. claim to navigation rights on the Mississippi River.

It bears emphasis that the proposed amendment addressed treaty making, not treaty implementation. Thus, the amendment, if adopted, would not have affected the operation of the Constitution's treaty supremacy rule, because that rule addresses the application of treaties *after* they enter into force, whereas the proposed amendment addressed the conditions to be satisfied *before* a treaty enters into force. Ultimately, the amendment proposed by Virginia and North Carolina never passed. Hence, the current Constitution retains the rule that two-thirds of the senators *present* is a sufficient number to approve a treaty.

II. TREATY SUPREMACY AND STATE LAW

The state ratification debates are replete with statements by both Federalists and anti-Federalists affirming the treaty supremacy rule. To reiterate, the Constitution's treaty supremacy rule consists of two elements. First, valid, ratified treaties supersede conflicting state laws, including state constitutions. Second, courts have a constitutional duty to apply treaties when presented with a conflict between a treaty and state law. Participants in state ratification debates generally understood that the treaty supremacy rule constituted a correct interpretation of the Constitution. (The fact that they agreed on treaty supremacy does not mean that they agreed on self-execution. Self-execution is a separate issue, discussed below.) The anti-Federalists objected to the treaty supremacy rule on policy grounds because it meant that treaties could potentially deprive individuals of rights protected by state constitutions. To secure protection for individual rights, the Federalists ultimately accepted a federal Bill of Rights that limits the Treaty Power (as well as Congress's legislative powers). Inasmuch as adoption of the federal Bill of Rights addressed the main policy objection to the treaty supremacy rule, controversy about the merits of the rule largely disappeared after adoption of the Bill of Rights.

A. Anti-Federalist Objections

Many of the leading anti-Federalists affirmed the treaty supremacy rule. In that context, they expressed their fears that treaties would override state constitutional protections for individual rights. For example, the Federal Farmer wrote: "There are certain rights which we have always held sacred in the United States, and recognized in all our constitutions, and which, by the adoption of the new constitution, [in] its present form will be left unsecured." After quoting the Supremacy Clause, he added, "The president and two thirds of the senate will be empowered to make treaties indefinitely, and when these treaties shall be made, they will also abolish all laws and state constitutions incompatible with them."[21] Brutus wrote in the *New York Journal* "that the different state constitutions are repealed and entirely done away, so far as they are inconsistent with this [Constitution] ... or with treaties made, or which shall be made, under the authority of the United States; of what avail will the constitutions of the respective states be to preserve the rights of the citizens?"[22] Similarly, Cato wrote that the treaty "power is a very important one, and may be exercised in various ways, so as to affect your person and property." By means of treaties, he continued, "you may be transported to Europe, to fight the wars of ambitious princes ... and a thousand other obligations may be entered into; all which will become the supreme law of the land, and you are bound by it."[23]

Anti-Federalists made similar arguments in the state ratifying conventions. For example, in the North Carolina Convention, William Lancaster stated: "But if treaties are to be the supreme law of the land, it [sic] may repeal the laws of different states, and render nugatory our bill of rights."[24] In the Virginia Convention, Patrick Henry discussed the case of a Russian ambassador who was wrongfully arrested by a British man in England. "The Russian Emperor demanded [the surrender of] the [British] man at whose instance his Ambassador was arrested, to be given up to him [the Emperor], to be put to instant death."[25] The queen refused to surrender the guilty party, citing English law as a source of protection for the man's rights. Henry said: "Suppose the case of the Russian Ambassador here. The President can settle it by a treaty, and have the man arrested, and punished according to the Russian manner. The Constitutions of these States may be most flagrantly violated without remedy" because, under the proposed Constitution, "[t]reaties are binding, notwithstanding our [state] laws and Constitutions."[26] In sum, the anti-Federalists correctly recognized that, under the Constitution's treaty supremacy rule, treaties would supersede conflicting state laws, including provisions in state constitutions that protected individual rights. As discussed below, they suggested various amendments to remedy this problem, but the main solution involved adoption of a federal Bill of Rights to limit the Treaty Power and other federal powers.

B. The Federalist Response

Professor Yoo contends that anti-Federalist objections to self-execution persuaded Federalists to backpedal, thereby producing a shared understanding that many treaties would be non-self-executing.[27] I address that argument below. Here, the crucial point is that the Federalists did not backpedal at all on the treaty supremacy issue. To the contrary, they responded to anti-Federalist concerns by insisting that the treaty supremacy rule was vitally necessary to prevent treaty violations by the states.

For example, James Iredell responded to George Mason's objections to the Constitution as follows: "It seems to result unavoidably from the nature of the thing, that when the constitutional right to make treaties is exercised, the treaty so made should be binding upon those who delegated authority for that purpose. If it was not, what foreign power would trust us?"[28] Similarly, Alexander Hamilton, referring to government under the Articles of Confederation, wrote: "The treaties of the United States under the present Constitution are liable to the infractions of thirteen different legislatures ... The faith, the reputation, the peace of the whole Union are thus continually at the mercy of the prejudices, the passions, and the interests of every member of which it is composed."[29] The treaty supremacy rule, codified in Article VI of the new Constitution, was a necessary corrective to this problem. "The treaties of the United States," Hamilton wrote, "to have any force at all, must be considered as part of the law of the land."[30] Madison agreed entirely with Hamilton on this point. He wrote, "If we are to be one nation in any respect, it clearly ought to be in respect to other nations."[31] The Treaty Power, he added, is similar under the new Constitution and the Articles, "with this difference only." Under the Articles, "treaties might be substantially frustrated by regulations of the States," whereas under the new Constitution the Supremacy Clause ensured that the national government would no longer be embarrassed by state treaty violations.[32]

James Wilson advanced similar arguments during the Pennsylvania Convention. He asserted that "it cannot be controverted that when made, [treaties] ought to be observed. . . . I am sorry to say it, that in order to prevent the payment of British debts, and from other causes, our treaties have been violated,

and violated too by the express laws of several states in the Union." Then, referring to the Supremacy Clause, he added: "This clause, sir, will show the world
that we make the faith of treaties a constitutional part of the character of the
United States; that we secure its performance no longer nominally, for the judges
of the United States will be enabled to carry them into effect, let the legislatures
of the different states do what they may."[33] Wilson then addressed the case of a
"wicked law" enacted by one of the states "enabling a [domestic] debtor to pay
his [foreign] creditor" less than the full value of the debt. The foreigner, said
Wilson, "complains to his prince or sovereign, of the injustice that has been done
him." The sovereign, in turn, tells the United States: "My subject has received a
flagrant injury; do me justice, or I will do myself justice." As "the United States
are answerable for the injury, ought they not to possess the means of compelling the faulty state to repair it? They ought, and this is what is done" in the new
Constitution, which enables the foreigner to "apply to the General Court, where
the unequal and partial laws of a particular state would have . . . no force."[34]

Several Federalist delegates to the Virginia Convention also defended the
treaty supremacy rule. Francis Corbin's statement merits a lengthy quotation:

> But, say Gentlemen, all treaties made under this Constitution, are to be the
> supreme law of nations; that is, in their way of construction, paramount to
> the Constitution itself, and the laws of Congress. It is as clear, as that two
> and two make four, that the treaties made are to be binding on the States
> only. Is it not necessary that they should be binding on the States? Fatal
> experience has proved, that treaties would never be complied with, if their
> observance depended on the will of the States; and the consequences would
> be constant war. For, if any one State could counteract a treaty, how could
> the United States avoid hostility with foreign nations? Do not Gentlemen
> see the infinite dangers that would result from it, if a small part of the com-
> munity could drag the whole Confederacy into war?[35]

Thus, Corbin rejected the claim that treaties are supreme over the federal
Constitution and federal statutes, while simultaneously affirming the supremacy
of treaties over state law. Madison made a similar argument: "I think the argument of the Gentleman [Francis Corbin] who restrained the supremacy of these
to the laws of particular States, and not to Congress, is rational. Here the supremacy of a treaty is contrasted with the supremacy of the laws of the States."[36]

The Federalists also contended that the Constitution incorporated adequate
procedural safeguards to prevent abuse of the Treaty Power. For example, James
Wilson told the Pennsylvania Convention that the Senate's power to make treaties is "under a check, by a constituent part of the government, and nearly the
immediate representative of the people, I mean the President of the United
States."[37] In a letter to George Nicholas, Madison highlighted the need for a two-
thirds majority vote in the Senate to approve a treaty, the fact that the states
are represented in the Senate, and the need for presidential approval to ratify a
treaty. All these factors, Madison argued, made it unlikely that the United States

would approve a bad treaty.[38] Alexander Hamilton made a similar argument in the Federalist Papers,[39] as did George Nicholas in the Virginia Convention.[40] James Iredell told the North Carolina Convention that "the sovereignty of the states is particularly concerned" with treaty making, "and the great caution of giving the states an equality of suffrage in making treaties, was for the express purpose of taking care of that sovereignty, and attending to their interests, as political bodies, in foreign negotiations."[41]

In addition to highlighting the procedural safeguards that prevented abuse of the Treaty Power, and emphasizing the need to prevent treaty violations by the states, Federalists hinted at two potential limitations on the Treaty Power. First, they asserted that "[t]he exercise of the power must be consistent with the object of the delegation,"[42] and that the president and Senate could not make a treaty "inconsistent with the delegated powers."[43] Madison said that "[t]he object of treaties . . . is external," but he immediately added that it is not "possible to enumerate all the cases in which such external regulations would be necessary. . . . It is most safe therefore to leave it to be exercised as contingencies may arise."[44] Thus, the Federalists conceded that treaties may be used only to regulate matters that are proper subjects of negotiation with foreign powers, but they insisted that the Constitution must grant the president and Senate broad discretion to determine, "as contingencies arise," what is a proper subject of negotiation. This argument was not very reassuring to the anti-Federalists because the Federalists did not cite a single example of a treaty that would be inconsistent with "the object of the delegation."

Some Federalists also suggested that the Treaty Power could not be applied to infringe fundamental rights. For example, when Patrick Henry argued that the president and Senate "can make a treaty relinquishing our rights and inflicting punishments," George Nicholas replied "that they can do no such thing . . . [because they can] make no treaty which shall be repugnant to the spirit of the Constitution."[45] Similarly, Madison said: "I do not conceive that power is given to the President and Senate . . . to alienate any great essential right."[46] The central problem with this argument was that the federal Constitution did not enumerate the "great essential rights" to which Madison referred. The state constitutions enumerated those rights, but the Supremacy Clause made treaties supreme over state constitutions. Therefore, to protect fundamental rights from infringement by the Treaty Power, anti-Federalists insisted that a federal Bill of Rights was needed. Ultimately, the Federalists acceded to that demand because, absent a federal Bill of Rights, the Supremacy Clause meant that any treaty infringing individual rights would trump conflicting provisions in state constitutions designed to protect those rights.[47]

In reviewing the available records of state ratification debates, it is difficult to find a single statement in which a Federalist proponent of the Constitution sought to allay anti-Federalist concerns by suggesting that treaties would be non-self-executing with respect to state law—that is, that federal implementing legislation would be necessary to secure the supremacy of treaties over state law. One can identify two main reasons why Federalists did not make that argument.

First, a rule requiring federal legislation to grant treaties supremacy over state law would effectively have given the states a license to violate treaties in the absence of such legislation. Such a rule would have been contrary to the central purpose of the treaty portion of the Supremacy Clause: to preclude treaty violations by the states. Second, a rule requiring federal legislation to grant treaties supremacy over state law would have done very little to address the anti-Federalists' main concern. Anti-Federalists feared that the federal government would enact laws to trump state constitutional provisions protecting fundamental rights. They did not care whether such a federal law took the form of a treaty or a statute—either way, they objected to federal laws that threatened their fundamental rights.

C. Proposed Constitutional Amendments

By August 1788, twelve state ratifying conventions had voted on the Constitution.[48] Five states voted in favor of ratification and proposed amendments: Massachusetts, South Carolina, New Hampshire, Virginia, and New York. Four states voted in favor of ratification without proposing any amendments: Delaware, New Jersey, Georgia, and Connecticut. North Carolina voted in favor of a set of proposed amendments, but withheld its ratification pending a decision on possible amendments. Pennsylvania and Maryland voted in favor of ratification without amendments, but the anti-Federalists in both states proposed amendments that were not approved by the full Conventions.[49] Thus, a total of eight states proposed amendments to the Constitution. (For these purposes, I count the proposals by the anti-Federalists in Pennsylvania and Maryland as state proposals.) All eight states proposed one or more amendments that were substantially similar to amendments that would ultimately be included in the Bill of Rights.[50]

Five of the eight states proposed amendments other than individual rights provisions that, if adopted, would have affected the operation of the treaty supremacy rule: Pennsylvania, Maryland, Virginia, New York, and North Carolina. The Virginia and North Carolina proposals were designed specifically to address Article 4 of the 1783 peace treaty with Britain, which obligated the United States to ensure that American debtors repaid British creditors. Virginia's proposed amendment stated: "But the judicial power of the United States shall extend to no case where the cause of action shall have originated before the ratification of this Constitution, except in disputes ... [not relevant here]."[51] The language of the North Carolina proposal was identical.[52] As discussed in Chapter 1, one of the main reasons for including treaties in the Supremacy Clause was to ensure that British creditors could collect their debts from American debtors in accordance with Article 4 of the peace treaty, notwithstanding laws enacted by several states to bar debt collection.[53] The Virginia and North Carolina proposals to limit federal judicial power would have precluded federal judicial review of state court decisions implicating Article 4, because causes of action involving that treaty article originated before ratification of the Constitution. Thus, the proposed amendments would not have modified the treaty supremacy rule as such, but they would have precluded federal judicial review of state court decisions in one set of cases involving application of the treaty supremacy rule.

The New York Convention and the anti-Federalists in Pennsylvania and Maryland proposed amendments that would have modified the treaty supremacy rule by excluding state constitutions (but not other state laws) from the scope of the treaty supremacy rule. The three proposals differ from each other, so they merit separate treatment. The dissenters in Pennsylvania proposed a long list of "propositions" and stated their "willingness to agree to the [Constitution], provided it was so amended as to meet those propositions, or something similar to them."[54] Proposition 13 stated: "That no treaty which shall be directly opposed to the existing laws of the United States in Congress assembled shall be valid until such laws shall be repealed, or made conformable to such treaty; neither shall any treaties be valid which are in contradiction to the constitution of the United States, or the constitutions of the several states."[55] The proposed amendment, if adopted, would have done three things. First, it would have established a clear rule of non-self-execution for treaties that conflict with federal statutes. Second, it would have clarified that any treaty conflicting with the federal Constitution is invalid. Third, it would have modified the treaty supremacy rule so that treaties supersede conflicting state laws, but treaties do not take precedence over state constitutions. Notably, the dissenters believed that non-self-execution—that is, a requirement for federal implementing legislation—provided a good solution for conflicts between treaties and federal statutes, but they did not propose non-self-execution to address the problem of conflicts between treaties and state constitutions. Instead, they preferred to modify the treaty supremacy rule so that state constitutions (but not other state laws) would take precedence over treaties in the event of a conflict.

The anti-Federalists in Maryland proposed an amendment that would have modified the treaty supremacy rule in a similar fashion. The Maryland proposal stated: "No law of Congress, or treaties, shall be effectual to repeal or abrogate the constitutions, or bill of rights, of the states, or any of them, or any part of the said constitutions, or bills of rights."[56] The Maryland proposal makes clear that anti-Federalists feared that treaties and federal statutes would override state bills of rights. Their proposed solution was the same for treaties and statutes: to exempt state constitutions from the federal supremacy rule, so that federal statutes and treaties would be supreme over state statutes and common law, but not over state constitutions or bills of rights.

The proposed New York amendment stated: "That the senators and representatives, and all executive and judicial officers of the United States, shall be bound by oath or affirmation not to infringe or violate the constitutions or rights of the respective states."[57] The proposed amendment should be read in conjunction with a declaration by the New York Convention "that no treaty is to be construed, so to operate, as to alter the Constitution of any State."[58] Viewed together, these two provisions manifest the New York delegates' fear that, in light of the Supremacy Clause, federal officers might apply treaties in ways that would nullify state constitutions. If the proposed amendment had been adopted, it is not entirely clear how it would have affected the operation of the Supremacy Clause. One possible construction is that state court judges would still have been bound by treaties, because the Supremacy Clause states explicitly that "the judges in every state shall be bound thereby,"[59] but federal officers would have been barred from applying treaties to override state constitutions. Regardless, there is no evidence that this particular New York proposal garnered support outside of New York.

Notably, no state proposed an amendment to make treaties non-self-executing with respect to state law. In other words, no state proposed an amendment requiring federal legislation to grant treaties supremacy over state law. Moreover, three states proposed amendments implying that anti-Federalists did not think a rule of non-self-execution would solve the perceived problem posed by the treaty supremacy rule. The Pennsylvania dissenters proposed a non-self-execution rule to resolve conflicts between treaties and federal statutes, but not to resolve conflicts between treaties and state law.[60] The Maryland minority proposed an amendment that would effectively have granted state constitutions supremacy over treaties *and* federal statutes.[61] If that proposal had been adopted, federal legislation to implement treaties would be legally ineffective if it conflicted with state constitutional provisions. North Carolina proposed the following amendment: "That no treaties which shall be directly opposed to the existing laws of the United States in Congress assembled, shall be valid until such laws shall be repealed, or made conformable to such treaty; nor shall any treaty be valid which is contradictory to the Constitution of the United States."[62] The North Carolina proposal, if adopted, would have established a rule of non-self-execution to resolve conflicts between treaties and federal statutes, but it would not have affected the treaty supremacy rule.

The only evidence that any Founders considered non-self-execution to be a viable rule for addressing conflicts between treaties and state law comes from a meeting convened in Harrisburg, Pennsylvania, in September 1788.[63] This meeting was not a formal state convention; it was a conference "of the citizens of this state who conceive that a revision of the federal system ... is necessary."[64] Thirty-three anti-Federalists from thirteen Pennsylvania counties met to discuss possible amendments to address their fears about the new Constitution. They proposed the following language to be added to the Supremacy Clause: "Provided always that no treaty, which shall hereafter be made, shall be deemed or construed to alter or affect any law of the United States, or of any particular state, until such treaty shall have been laid before and assented to by the House of Representatives in Congress."[65] This proposal, if adopted as a constitutional amendment, would have made treaties non-self-executing with respect to both state laws and federal statutes. However, there is no evidence that the proposal garnered significant support within Pennsylvania, much less outside the state. The lack of support for this proposal is easy to explain: it did not address the anti-Federalists' primary concern. They feared that the national government would enact federal laws—in the form of treaties or statutes—that would override protections for individual rights codified in state constitutions. The Harrisburg proposal for modifying the Supremacy Clause did little to calm the anti-Federalists' fears because it did not constrain Congress's legislative power. In contrast, the Bill of Rights approved by Congress in September 1789 directly addressed the anti-Federalists' primary concern. Hence, proposals to modify the treaty supremacy rule largely disappeared after the United States amended the Constitution by adopting a federal Bill of Rights.

III. THE HOUSE OF REPRESENTATIVES AND TREATY IMPLEMENTATION

During state ratification debates, several leading anti-Federalists argued that the Constitution was flawed because Article II empowered the president and Senate to create federal law, in the form of treaties, without the participation of the House of Representatives. They advocated a House role either in treaty making or treaty implementation for at least some types of treaties,[66] and they advanced both formalist and functionalist arguments in support of their position. Formalists contended that treaties should have the form of law if they were going to have the effect of law. House participation was necessary to give treaties the form of law.[67] Functionalists emphasized that the Senate represented the states, whereas the House represented the people. House participation was necessary to secure the rights of the people.[68] The ensuing debate between Federalists and anti-Federalists supports three conclusions about the original understanding of self-execution. The Founders generally agreed that: (1) some treaties would require legislative implementation; (2) treaties requiring an expenditure of funds would require legislative implementation; and (3) the House of Representatives would probably exert some informal political influence over the treaty process. The next subsection briefly addresses these three points. The following subsection explains why, in my view, the ratification materials do not support the stronger non-self-execution claims advanced by John Yoo and Vasan Kesavan.

A. The Need for Legislative Implementation

State ratification materials include numerous statements by Federalists indicating that some treaties will require implementing legislation. At the Pennsylvania Convention, James Wilson made one such statement that merits lengthy quotation:

> It well deserves to be remarked, that though the House of Representatives possess no active part in making treaties, yet their legislative authority will be found to have strong restraining influence upon both President and Senate. In England, if the king and his ministers find themselves, during their negotiation, to be embarrassed, because an existing law is not repealed, or a new law is not enacted, they give notice to the legislature of their situation and inform them that it will be necessary, before the treaty

can operate, that some law be repealed or some be made. And will not the same thing take place here?[69]

Professor Yoo construes this statement to mean that "treaties would need implementing legislation, just as they did in Great Britain, before they could take direct effect at home."[70] Granted, Wilson's statement suggests that *some* treaties would require implementing legislation, but he neither stated nor implied that *all* treaties would require implementing legislation. Moreover, as discussed below, the practice in Britain at the time was that *some*, but not *all*, treaties required implementing legislation. Thus, Wilson's statement supports a conclusion that some treaties are non-self-executing, but it provides little guidance about which treaties are non-self-executing.

In Federalist 53, James Madison acknowledged that "the House of Representatives is not immediately to participate in foreign negotiations." Even so, he said, treaties "will frequently deserve [the House's] attention in the ordinary course of legislation and will sometimes demand particular legislative sanction and cooperation."[71] Similarly, Madison wrote in a letter to George Nicholas that the House's "approbation and cooperation may often be necessary in carrying treaties into full effect."[72] Like Wilson, Madison believed that the House would play a role in implementing some treaties, but he did not articulate criteria for distinguishing between self-executing and non-self-executing treaties.

In contrast, Federalist 69, written by Alexander Hamilton, provided fairly clear criteria for distinguishing between treaties that require legislative implementation and those that do not. Hamilton was describing British practice, but his essay strongly implies that treaty implementation under the new Constitution would likely conform to British practice. Hamilton first noted that "[t]he king of Great Britain is the sole and absolute representative of the nation in all foreign transactions. He can of his own accord make treaties of peace, commerce, alliance, and of every other description."[73] Hamilton explicitly rejected the claim that treaties made by the king "stand in need of the ratification, of Parliament," asserting that "compacts entered into by the royal authority have the most complete legal validity and perfection, independent of any other sanction." He continued:

The Parliament, it is true, is sometimes seen employing itself in altering the existing laws to conform them to the stipulations in a new treaty; and this may have possibly given birth to the imagination that its cooperation was necessary to the obligatory efficacy of the treaty. But this parliamentary interposition proceeds from a different cause: from the necessity of adjusting a most artificial and intricate system of revenue and commercial laws, to the changes made in them by the operation of the treaty; and of adapting new provisions and precautions to the new state of things, to keep the machine from running into disorder.[74]

Here, it is helpful to consider a concrete example to illustrate Hamilton's thinking. Assume that the United States enacts a federal statute imposing a penny-per-pound duty on imported wool. Later, the United States concludes a treaty with Britain, agreeing to permit duty-free imports of wool from Britain. If we apply Hamilton's explanation of British practice to the United States, the treaty itself has "obligatory efficacy," without any further legislative action. The "operation of the treaty," by itself, changes the "system of revenue and commercial laws." Nevertheless, to be prudent, it makes sense for Congress to enact legislation "to keep the machine from running into disorder." Absent such legislation, the executive officers charged with collection of import duties might have to consult numerous treaties, as well as federal statutes, to determine the correct import duty to be charged for a particular item. By modifying the legislation to conform to the treaty, Congress eases the burden on administrative officers by ensuring that all relevant rules are codified in a single statute, instead of being scattered among various treaties. In sum, legislation is not needed to give the treaty "obligatory efficacy," but it is needed for practical reasons "to keep the machine from running into disorder." Under this view, the distinction between self-executing and non-self-executing treaties—that is, the question whether a treaty requires legislative implementation—hinges on a pragmatic judgment based on the totality of the circumstances. The idea that the need for implementing legislation hinges on a pragmatic judgment of this type characterized Supreme Court jurisprudence on self-execution for much of the nineteenth century.[75]

Even so, the ratification materials do support one bright-line rule about self-execution: treaties that obligate the United States to spend money require legislative implementation. Article I, Section 9 of the Constitution states: "No money shall be drawn from the Treasury, but in consequence of appropriations made by law."[76] In theory, one could construe the word "law" to include treaties, as treaties are the "law of the land" under the Supremacy Clause. Under that construction, the president could invoke a treaty as a source of authority to withdraw money from the Treasury. However, neither Hamilton nor Jay—both of whom endorsed a broad view of executive power in foreign affairs—defended the position that a treaty by itself, without implementing legislation, could authorize the president to draw money from the Treasury. Moreover, James Iredell, James Madison, and others argued that bicameral legislation authorizing expenditure of federal funds is necessary before the president is permitted to withdraw money from the Treasury to pay for treaty implementation.[77] Post-ratification materials from the 1790s also support the conclusion that the Founders agreed on the need for bicameral legislation to implement treaties requiring an expenditure of funds.[78]

The ratification materials also manifest a widely shared assumption that the House of Representatives would likely exert significant political influence over treaty making, despite its lack of formal legal authority. For example, George Nicholas told the Virginia Convention: "Although the Representatives have no immediate agency in treaties, yet from their influence in the Government, they will direct everything. They will be a considerable check on the Senate and President."[79] Expanding on this theme a few days later, Nicholas analogized the House of Representatives to the British House of Commons. He said, "The King of Great Britain can make what treaties he pleases. But, Sir, do not the House of

Commons influence them? Will he make a treaty manifestly repugnant to their interests? Will they not tell him, he is mistaken in that respect as in many others? Will they not bring the Minister, who advises a bad treaty, to punishment? This gives them such influence that they can dictate in what manner they shall be made."[80] Nicholas argued that the House of Representatives would influence treaty making in the United States in a similar fashion. James Iredell sounded a similar theme in a statement to the North Carolina Convention.[81]

B. A Brief Response to Yoo and Kesavan

Professor Yoo contends that "the best reading of the Constitution" is that treaties "in areas that fall within Congress' Article I, Section 8 powers" require legislative "implementation by Congress."[82] Several other scholars have demonstrated persuasively that the evidence adduced by Yoo does not support his thesis.[83] I will not belabor the point here. Yoo quotes numerous sources supporting the proposition that *some* treaties require legislative implementation. He infers on that basis that all treaties within the scope of Congress's Article I, Section 8 powers require legislative implementation. (Many, but not all, of the powers granted to Congress under the Constitution are included in Article I, Section 8.) However, in a 140-page article on the subject, Yoo fails to cite a single statement from the ratification debates in which one of the Framers explicitly endorsed Yoo's preferred interpretation of the Constitution.[84]

Among the leading Federalists, Francis Corbin came closest to endorsing Yoo's position. During the Virginia Convention, Corbin said: "Treaties are generally of a commercial nature, being a regulation of commercial intercourse between different nations. In all commercial treaties it will be necessary to obtain the consent of the [House of] Representatives."[85] Several days later, he referred to "the difference between a commercial treaty and other treaties." In Britain, he said, "[a] commercial treaty must be submitted to the consideration of Parliament; because such treaties will render it necessary to alter some laws, add new clauses to some, and repeal others." He contended that similar factors supported the need for legislative implementation of commercial treaties in the United States.[86] Among the anti-Federalists, the Federal Farmer made a similar argument to support his view that commercial treaties should be non-self-executing.[87] Thus, it is clear that *some* influential Founders believed that commercial treaties would be (or should be) non-self-executing. However, neither Corbin nor the Federal Farmer defined the term "commercial treaty," so it is not entirely clear what that term includes. Regardless, the category of "commercial treaties" is certainly much narrower than Yoo's category of treaties "in areas that fall within Congress' Article I, Section 8 powers,"[88] and Yoo does not explain or justify the leap from the narrower to the broader category.

If we set aside Yoo's claim, there is an additional problem with the assertion that the Founders agreed that all "commercial treaties" are non-self-executing. Two states proposed constitutional amendments specifically designed to address the category of "commercial treaties." Virginia recommended an amendment stating "[t]hat no commercial treaty shall be ratified without the concurrence of two-thirds of the whole number of the members of the Senate."[89] North Carolina advocated an identical amendment.[90] Thus, the Virginia and North Carolina delegations were evidently concerned that the Constitution did not provide adequate safeguards for commercial treaties, but they did not propose a role for the House of Representatives. Instead, they suggested changing the Senate voting rule from "two-thirds of the Senators present"[91] to "two-thirds of the whole number of the members of the Senate." The lack of reference to the House of Representatives is especially striking because, in the very same amendment, both Virginia and North Carolina proposed a role for the House of Representatives in approving treaties "ceding, contracting, restraining or suspending the territorial rights or claims of the United States."[92] Thus, the Virginia and North Carolina delegates evidently believed that House participation was essential for treaties ceding territory, but not for commercial treaties. Granted, the recommended amendments addressed treaty making, not treaty implementation. Even so, the proposed amendments cast doubt on the claim that the Founders reached a consensus that bicameral legislation is needed to implement all commercial treaties.

Vasan Kesavan rejects Yoo's "total non-self-execution" thesis. He proposes, instead, a "partial non-self-execution" thesis. According to Kesavan, when the United States ratifies a treaty that conflicts with a previously enacted federal statute, "the treaty must be non-self-executing as a matter of domestic law. . . . In order for the treaty to have the force of domestic law, Congress must remove the conflict by amending or repealing the existing statute(s) so as to conform to the treaty."[93] Thus, whereas Yoo's analysis turns on the scope of Congress's Article I powers, Kesavan's analysis turns on the existence of a conflict between a treaty and a previously enacted federal statute. Kesavan acknowledges that his approach is inconsistent with the later-in-time rule, which has been an entrenched feature of Supreme Court jurisprudence since the late nineteenth century. However, he contends, the later-in-time rule is "wrong" because it is inconsistent with the original understanding of the Constitution.[94]

To his credit, Kesavan marshals a substantial body of evidence from the Federal Convention in Philadelphia and from the state ratifying conventions to support his thesis.[95] Taken as a whole, that evidence demonstrates that *some* members of the Founding generation believed that legislation would be necessary to implement treaties that conflicted with prior federal statutes. However, in my judgment, there is a sufficient body of conflicting evidence that it is not possible to identify a consensus view among the Founders about the proper rule for resolving conflicts between treaties and federal statutes. For example, John Jay wrote in Federalist 64:

[I]t would be impossible to find a nation who would make any bargain with us, which should be binding on them absolutely, but on us only so long and so far as we may think proper to be bound by it. They who make laws may, without doubt, amend or repeal them; and it will not be disputed that they who make treaties may alter or cancel them; but still let us not forget that treaties are made, not by only one of the contracting parties, but by both, and consequently, that as the consent of both was essential to their formation at first, so must it ever afterwards be to alter or cancel them. . . . [Treaties] are just as binding and just as far beyond the reach of legislative acts now as they will be at any future period, or under any form of government.[96]

This passage suggests that, in Jay's view, all conflicts between treaties and statutes must be resolved in favor of treaties because treaties are "beyond the reach of legislative acts." In contrast, Kesavan argues that all conflicts between treaties and statutes must be resolved in favor of statutes. The fact that John Jay, one of the most influential members of the Founding generation, explicitly rejected Kesavan's view casts doubt on his claim that the Founding materials establish a consensus view on this point.

Two state ratifying conventions proposed constitutional amendments to address conflicts between treaties and statutes. The Pennsylvania dissenters recommended an amendment stating "[t]hat no treaty which shall be directly opposed to the existing laws of the United States in Congress assembled shall be valid until such laws shall be repealed, or made conformable to such treaty."[97] The North Carolina Convention adopted almost identical language.[98] The proposed amendments, if adopted, would have codified Kesavan's preferred rule in the Constitution by requiring legislative implementation for all treaties that conflict with prior federal statutes. Kesavan contends that we should construe the proposed amendments as interpretive statements designed to clarify the correct interpretation of the unamended Constitution.[99] However, that is not how the Pennsylvania dissenters explained their suggested amendment. They said: "We offered our objections to the convention, and opposed those parts of the plan, which, in our opinion, would be injurious to you . . . and closed our arguments by offering the following propositions."[100] They then listed fourteen propositions, including the proposed amendment regarding treaties. After listing the propositions, they declared their "willingness to agree to the plan [i.e., the Constitution], provided that it was so amended as to meet those propositions, or something similar to them."[101] Thus, the Pennsylvania dissenters wanted to amend the Constitution because they believed that a rule of non-self-execution would be desirable to regulate conflicts between treaties and prior federal statutes, but they believed a constitutional amendment was needed to achieve that result. Similarly, the North Carolina Convention offered "amendments to the most ambiguous and exceptionable parts of the said Constitution"[102] and withheld its consent to ratification, pending further consideration of the suggested amendments. Thus, the North Carolina majority, like the Pennsylvania minority, favored Kesavan's proposed rule, but did not believe that the rule had been incorporated into the Constitution as initially drafted. Since the amendment recommended by the Pennsylvania dissenters and the North Carolina Convention was never adopted, the available evidence suggests that, as of 1789, there was no agreed rule for resolving conflicts between treaties and statutes.

* * *

In sum, the preceding analysis supports three main conclusions. First, those who participated in state ratification debates, including both Federalists and anti-Federalists, anticipated that *some* treaties would require legislation by Congress to be given practical effect. In other words, *some* treaties are non-self-executing (NSE). Second, many anti-Federalists objected to the treaty supremacy rule codified in the Supremacy Clause because it gave the treaty makers power to override the Bill of Rights protections in state constitutions. The nation addressed that objection by amending the Constitution to incorporate a Bill of Rights into the federal Constitution. Third, there is no evidence to support the proposition that the Constitution, as originally understood, incorporated an NSE exception to the treaty supremacy rule.

Treaty Supremacy in the 1790s

The Supremacy Clause provides a specific rule for resolving conflicts between treaties and state laws. But the Constitution's text leaves unanswered a set of related questions. Are there constitutional limits on the Article II power to make treaties? If so, what are those limits? How should conflicts between treaties and federal statutes be resolved? Under what circumstances is federal legislation necessary to implement treaties? Table One summarizes key issues that Congress, courts, and federal executive officers confronted in the first decade after adoption of the Constitution.

Consider, first, treaties that overlap with state law. During the 1790s, all agreed that a valid, ratified treaty supersedes conflicting state law. The Supremacy Clause said so, as did the Supreme Court in *Ware v. Hylton*. However, Article 9 of the Jay Treaty provoked a heated debate about constitutional limits on the Article II Treaty Power. Several commentators asserted that Article 9 was unconstitutional because it infringed the reserved powers of the states. (Although state law generally governed title to real property, Article 9 purported to grant British subjects property rights in the United States, notwithstanding contrary

Table One. SELF-EXECUTION AND TREATY SUPREMACY, CIRCA 1790

	Supremacy Issue: Does Treaty Supersede State Law?	Self-Execution Issue: Does Treaty Require Federal Implementing Legislation?
Treaty Overlaps with State Law	Treaty supersedes conflicting state law if it is valid. Debates about treaty validity	N.A.—Self-execution issue not relevant to overlap between treaty and state law
Treaty Overlaps with Federal Statute and/or Congress's Legislative Authority	N.A.—Supremacy issue not relevant to overlap between treaty and federal statute	Debates about which treaties require federal implementing legislation

state law.) Notably, though, no one suggested that the concept of self-execution was relevant to conflicts between treaties and state law. If a treaty conflicted with state law, it was either constitutionally invalid (because it infringed the reserved powers of the states) or it superseded conflicting state laws. In the constitutional discourse of the 1790s, no one had conceived of the idea that there might be an NSE exception to the treaty supremacy rule.

Consider, next, treaties that overlap with federal statutes. The Jay Treaty debates addressed several issues involving treaties that regulate matters within the scope of Congress's legislative authority. These include the question of whether a valid, ratified treaty supersedes a prior conflicting federal statute, and whether a valid federal statute supersedes a prior conflicting treaty.[1] The discussion here focused on two related issues that also emerged in the Jay Treaty debates. First, if the president ratifies a treaty whose execution requires an appropriation of money, is the House of Representatives constitutionally obligated to appropriate the funds? Second, aside from appropriation of money, are there other types of treaty obligations whose implementation requires federal legislation approved by both Houses of Congress? Using the rhetoric of self-execution, the second question can be rephrased as follows: What types of treaty provisions are constitutionally non-self-executing?

One note on terminology may be helpful here. In modern parlance, some commentators equate "self-executing" with "judicially enforceable," and "non-self-executing" with "not judicially enforceable."[2] This view is consistent with the political-judicial concept of self-execution. In the 1790s, though, debates about self-execution were framed in terms of the congressional-executive concept, not the political-judicial concept.[3] At that time, self-execution related to the House of Representatives' role in implementing treaties that overlapped with Congress's legislative authority. If a treaty was not self-executing, bicameral legislation was necessary to authorize federal executive officers to implement it. If it was self-executing, the treaty itself operated as a rule of conduct for federal executive officers, and implementing legislation was not required. This chapter uses the term "self-executing" in accordance with the congressional-executive concept of self-execution.

I. *WARE V. HYLTON*

Ware v. Hylton was the first important Supreme Court decision after adoption of the Constitution involving an alleged conflict between a treaty and state law.[4] The plaintiff, Ware, was the administrator of the estate of William Jones, a British citizen who loaned money to Virginia citizens in 1774. The Virginia legislature passed a law in 1777, in the midst of the Revolutionary War, to sequester British property. In accordance with that law, Hylton & Co. paid a portion of the debt to a state loan office established by the Commonwealth of Virginia. When Ware sued to collect the debt, defendants argued that "by virtue of the said act of Assembly, [we] are discharged from so much of the debt" as was paid to the state loan office.[5] In response, the plaintiff invoked Article 4 of the 1783 peace treaty between the United States and Britain.[6] During the war, several states passed laws to sequester or extinguish debts owed to British creditors. Article 4 was designed to help British creditors recover those debts. It specified "that creditors on either side shall meet with no lawful impediment to the recovery of the full value . . . of all bona fide debts heretofore contracted."[7]

In oral argument before the Supreme Court, counsel for the British creditor claimed: "[I]f any impediment ever existed to the recovery of the debt, it is removed by the operation of the treaty . . . [which is] the supreme law of the land."[8] On the other side, future chief justice John Marshall represented the Virginia debtors. Marshall argued that the Virginia legislature had the power to extinguish the debt, and it exercised that power when it passed the contested legislation.[9] Therefore, he concluded, "at the time of entering into the Treaty of 1783, the Defendant owed nothing to the Plaintiff."[10] The treaty, he noted, promises that "creditors" can recover "debts." However, he argued, when the treaty took effect in 1783, his clients did not owe a "debt," and the British plaintiff was no longer a "creditor," because the Virginia law had extinguished the debt.[11] Neither Marshall nor his co-counsel challenged opposing counsel's argument that, under the Supremacy Clause, the treaty superseded conflicting state law. He effectively conceded the constitutional point. He argued instead, based on a combination of treaty interpretation and state law, that there was no conflict between the treaty and state law.

Five Supreme Court justices issued separate opinions in *Ware*. Justices Chase, Paterson, Wilson, and Cushing agreed that Article 4 of the treaty secured the creditor's right to recover payment from the debtors. Justice Cushing said: "[B]y the constitution of the United States," the treaty was "sanctioned as the supreme law . . . paramount and controlling to all state laws, and even state constitutions, wheresoever they interfere or disagree." He added: "The treaty, then, as to the point in question, is of equal force with the constitution itself; and certainly, with any law whatsoever."[12] Justice Paterson agreed that the treaty "repeals the legislative act of Virginia,"[13] but his argument rested entirely on the treaty. He did not address the meaning of the Supremacy Clause. Similarly, Justice Wilson asserted that the treaty "[i]ndependent . . . of the Constitution of the United States . . . is sufficient to remove every impediment founded on the law of Virginia."[14]

Justice Chase thought the treaty might have superseded state law, even under the Articles of Confederation. But, he added, "[i]f doubts could exist before the establishment of the present national government, they must be entirely removed by the 6th article of the Constitution."[15] After quoting the Supremacy Clause, he offered the following analysis:

Four things are apparent on a view of this 6th article of the National Constitution. . . . 2nd. That the Constitution, or laws, of any of the States so far as either of them shall be found contrary to that treaty are by force of the said article, prostrated before the treaty. 3rd. That consequently the treaty of 1783 has superior power to the Legislature of any State, because no

Legislature of any State has any kind of power over the Constitution, which was its creator. 4thly. That it is the declared duty of the State Judges to determine any Constitution, or laws of any State, contrary to that treaty (or any other) made under the authority of the United States, null and void. National or Federal Judges are bound by duty and oath to the same conduct.[16]

In sum, Justice Chase affirmed both elements of the treaty supremacy rule: first, that valid, ratified treaties supersede conflicting state laws; and second, that state courts have a constitutional duty to apply the treaty if there is a conflict.

Justice Iredell was the sole dissenter in *Ware*,[17] but he agreed fully with Justice Chase's analysis of the Supremacy Clause. Justice Iredell said: "Under this Constitution therefore, so far as a treaty constitutionally is binding . . . it is also by the vigour of its own authority to be executed in fact. It would not otherwise be the supreme law in the new sense provided for." Moreover, he added, "I consider, therefore, that when this constitution was ratified, the case as to the treaty in question stood upon the same footing, as if every act constituting an impediment to a creditor's recovery had been expressly repealed, and any further act passed, which the public obligation had before required, if a repeal alone would not have been sufficient."[18] From his standpoint, though, Virginia, by enacting a law to sequester the debt, had effectively substituted itself as the proper debtor in the case. Therefore, plaintiff's claim should be dismissed because the plaintiff sued the wrong defendant.[19]

Ware is significant because it was the first major Supreme Court decision that involved an alleged conflict between a treaty and state law. Five justices wrote opinions in the case. Five attorneys presented oral arguments that are summarized in the published Supreme Court opinion. Most of those men had participated in either the Constitutional Convention, one of the state ratification debates, or both.[20] None of them challenged the proposition that the Constitution accords treaties supremacy over state law. No one contested the proposition that the Supremacy Clause requires courts to apply treaties when there is a conflict between a treaty and state law. John Marshall—whom some people (mistakenly) credit for inventing the doctrine of NSE treaties[21]—did not even hint at the possibility that there might be an NSE exception to the Constitution's treaty supremacy rule, even though his clients would have benefited from such an exception. Thus, *Ware* tends to refute the claim that the Founders recognized an NSE exception to the Constitution's treaty supremacy rule.

Ware is also significant for another reason. Justice Iredell's opinion provides a lucid explanation of the distinction between "executory" and "executed" treaty provisions:[22] a distinction that Marshall applied three decades later as chief justice in *Foster v. Neilson* (discussed in Chapter 4.) Iredell was the only justice who would have ruled in favor of Marshall's clients in *Ware*. Thus, Iredell's opinion provides an important benchmark for understanding Marshall's later thinking about self-execution.

Justice Iredell's analysis relied on Blackstone's distinction between executory and executed contracts.[23] Justice Iredell said that executed treaty provisions "require no further act to be done,"[24] because the goal to be accomplished is achieved immediately when the treaty takes effect. Iredell cited Britain's acknowledgment of U.S. independence as an example of an executed provision. In contrast, executory provisions require the nation to take action in the future, after the treaty becomes legally effective, to fulfill its treaty commitments. Iredell divided executory treaty provisions into three classes: legislative, executive, and judicial.[25] In his view, "when a nation promises to do a thing, it is to be understood, that this promise is to be carried into execution, in the manner which the Constitution of that nation prescribes."[26] Thus, Iredell's analytic framework involves a two-step analysis. In step one, the court analyzes the treaty to determine whether the provision is executory or executed. If it is executory, the second step entails a domestic separation-of-powers analysis to determine whether treaty implementation requires judicial, executive, or legislative action.

To understand Iredell's two-step approach, it is essential to grasp the conceptual distinction between an executory treaty provision and a non-self-executing provision. The statement that a treaty is "non-self-executing" means that congressional legislation is necessary to implement the treaty; if the treaty is "self-executing," no such legislation is needed.[27] The statement that a treaty is "executory" means that some future action is necessary to implement the treaty. If a treaty is "executed," no such action is required because the goal is accomplished immediately when the treaty takes effect. Thus, all non-self-executing treaty provisions are executory, but not all executory provisions are non-self-executing. Some executory treaty provisions can be implemented by executive or judicial action.

It bears emphasis that, under Iredell's two-step approach, Article 4 of the 1783 peace treaty was an executory treaty provision that required judicial implementation. Article 4 was executory because it required the United States to take action in the future to ensure that British creditors recovered their debts. Although Article 4 was executory, it did not require legislative implementation. The Court held that judicial action was the appropriate means to implement the treaty because the combination of the treaty and the Supremacy Clause obligated state courts to "execute" the U.S. treaty obligation by ordering American debtors to pay their debts to British creditors.

II. THE JAY TREATY DEBATES

While *Ware v. Hylton* was making its way to the Supreme Court, the Jay Treaty sparked a major political controversy that preoccupied the nation for almost one year in 1795–1796.[28] In the early 1790s, President Washington confronted numerous difficulties in the U.S. relationship with Britain. Britain maintained troops within the borders of the United States, despite the king's pledge in the 1783 peace treaty to "withdraw all his armies, garrisons, and fleets from the said United States."[29] The continued presence of British troops, amidst other sources of friction in U.S.-British relations, threatened a renewed outbreak of war. President Washington dispatched John Jay to Britain to negotiate a new treaty

to avert a potentially catastrophic war and settle other ongoing disputes.[30] Jay
and his British counterpart signed the Jay Treaty in London in November 1794.[31]

The Jay Treaty was one of the first treaties concluded by the United States after
adoption of the Constitution.[32] Decisions about treaty ratification and implementation sparked robust debates about various constitutional issues, which
occurred in a highly charged political atmosphere. The United States was just beginning to develop a two-party system at that time, with a growing rift between
Federalists (led by John Adams and Alexander Hamilton) and Republicans (led
by Thomas Jefferson and James Madison).[33] Meanwhile, France and Britain were
in the midst of a bitter war. Federalists favored the British; Republicans favored
the French. Republicans viewed the Jay Treaty as a misguided effort to align
the United States with Britain in its ongoing war with France.[34] In their zeal to
defeat the treaty, Republicans raised a wide variety of constitutional and policy
objections.

The Jay Treaty debates proceeded in three distinct phases. The Senate considered the treaty in June 1795, resulting in a Senate vote in favor of ratification
on June 24.[35] Unfortunately, the published records reveal very little about the
substance of Senate discussions. After the Senate voted, the public engaged in
a vigorous debate, which lasted from July 1795 until March 1796. Essays and
pamphlets published during this period contained detailed analyses of several
important constitutional issues.[36] The House of Representatives debated the Jay
Treaty for almost two months between March 7 and May 3, 1796.[37] The analysis
below focuses on three key issues that emerged from those debates: Article 9 and
states' rights, appropriation of funds for treaty implementation, and the need for
legislation to implement certain types of treaty provisions.

A. Article 9 and States' Rights

On June 24, 1795, Senator Henry Tazewell of Virginia submitted a motion stating that "the Senate will not consent to the ratification" of the Jay Treaty.[38] His
motion listed seven objections to the treaty, including the claim that "the rights
of individual States, are, by the ninth article of the Treaty, unconstitutionally
infringed." Article 9 states:

> It is agreed, that British Subjects who now hold Lands in the Territories of
> the United States . . . shall continue to hold them according to the nature
> and Tenure of their respective Estates and Titles therein, and may grant
> Sell or Devise the same to whom they please, in like manner as if they were
> Natives; and that neither they nor their Heirs or assigns shall, so far as may
> respect the said Lands . . . be regarded as Aliens.[39]

The official records of the Senate proceedings do not record any substantive argument in support of the claim that Article 9 was unconstitutional. Regardless,
the constitutional argument is straightforward. The Tenth Amendment to
the Constitution says: "The powers not delegated to the United States by the

Constitution, nor prohibited by it to the States, are reserved to the States respectively, or to the people."[40] Absent a treaty, the power to regulate estates and titles in real property belonged exclusively to the states, not the federal government. Thus, Tazewell's constitutional objection was founded on the assumption that the president and Senate may not use the Article II Treaty Power to regulate matters that would be beyond the scope of federal regulatory power in the absence of a treaty.[41]

The Senate defeated Tazewell's motion by a vote of 19-10. On the same day, the Senate voted 20-10 in support of ratifying the Jay Treaty.[42] President Washington ratified the treaty for the United States in August 1795. Given the Senate's consent and the president's ratification, one could infer that President Washington and at least twenty Senators believed Tazewell's constitutional objection was unfounded.[43]

After the Senate consented to ratification, a vigorous public debate ensued. Several prominent Republicans raised states' rights objections to Article 9. For example, Robert Livingston, writing under the pseudonym Cato, asserted that Article 9

> appears to infringe the constitutional independence of the respective states. . . . Neither congress, nor any member of the federal government, appear to me to have any right to declare the tenure by which lands shall be holden in the territories of the individual states . . . . This is an act of sovereignty which is confined to state legislatures, and which they have not ceded to congress, about which, therefore, I am led to doubt the right of the president and senate to treat . . . .[44]

Other prominent Republicans, including Alexander Dallas and Brockholst Livingston, advanced similar arguments.[45] One unidentified commentator, writing under the pseudonym Atticus, stated:

> By what part of the constitution have the president and senate the power of regulating the tenure of real estates? We look in vain for such a grant in the constitution, even to congress itself; this right then, not being delegated to the United States, nor "prohibited" by the constitution to the states, is "reserved to the states respectively, or to the people." Shall the president dare to invade the chartered rights of the states?[46]

It is not entirely clear whether Cato, Atticus, and others believed that Article 9 was void as a matter of international law, or merely void as a matter of domestic law. Regardless, one thing is clear. None of the Republican commentators who challenged Article 9 on constitutional grounds believed that the constitutional defect could be cured if the treaty was non-self-executing. The concept of non-self-execution, as it was understood at the time, meant that *Congress* had to enact implementing legislation to execute the treaty. The Republican commentators believed that Congress could not enact implementing legislation to execute

Article 9 because Article 9 addressed matters beyond the scope of Congress's legislative powers.[47]

Meanwhile, the Federalists who supported Article 9 uniformly assumed that implementing legislation was unnecessary because Article 9 superseded conflicting state laws by virtue of the Supremacy Clause.[48] In sum, the public debate over Article 9 divided cleanly into two opposing positions. On one side, Republicans asserted that Article 9 was unconstitutional, and the constitutional defect could not be cured by federal implementing legislation. On the other side, Federalists claimed that Article 9 was constitutionally valid and implementing legislation was unnecessary. In the extensive public debate, no one suggested that Article 9 was constitutionally valid, but Congress needed to enact legislation to "execute" it. No one suggested the possibility that there might be an NSE exception to the treaty supremacy rule.

B. Appropriation of Money for Treaty Implementation

The Jay Treaty included several provisions whose implementation required an appropriation of funds. The treaty itself did not purport to appropriate money. All agreed that legislation approved by both Houses of Congress was necessary to appropriate funds for treaty implementation. However, Federalists and Republicans disagreed about whether the House was constitutionally obligated to provide the necessary funding.[49] Republicans argued that the House had no constitutional duty to appropriate money for treaty implementation. For example, Edward Livingston said it was his "firm conviction that the House were vested with a discretionary power of carrying the Treaty into effect, or refusing it their sanction."[50] In response, Federalists asserted that the House had a duty "to make the necessary appropriations ... if they did not execute it, they violated the trust reposed in them."[51] After extended debate, the House voted 57-35, largely along partisan lines, to approve a resolution that stated in relevant part: "And it is the Constitutional right and duty of the House of Representatives, in all such cases, to deliberate on the expediency or inexpediency of carrying such Treaty into effect, and to determine and act thereon, as, in their judgment, may be most conducive to the public good."[52] (Call this the "House Treaty Resolution.") In short, the House affirmed its constitutional prerogative to refuse to appropriate funds needed to implement a treaty approved by the Senate and ratified by the president. Nevertheless, after asserting its constitutional prerogatives, the House joined the Senate in enacting legislation to appropriate money for treaty implementation.[53] Thus, as other commentators have suggested, "the episode ended in a standoff on the constitutional questions."[54]

C. Which Treaties Require Legislative Implementation?

Federalists and Republicans agreed that bicameral legislation to appropriate money was constitutionally required to execute a treaty provision that obligated the United States to spend money. Did the same principle require bicameral legislation to execute other treaty provisions addressing matters within the scope of Congress's legislative powers? Here, it is helpful to introduce some terminology. Modern commentators distinguish between "concurrent" and "exclusive" powers. The president and Senate cannot use the Article II Treaty Power to create domestic law in areas where the Constitution grants Congress "exclusive" lawmaking power. However, the president and Senate can use the Article II Treaty Power to create domestic law in areas where Congress exercises "concurrent" lawmaking authority. Therefore, treaties that address matters within the scope of Congress's exclusive powers are "constitutionally non-self-executing."[55]

In the Jay Treaty debates, House Republicans staked out a position that all of Congress's Article I legislative powers are "exclusive" ones. The House resolution quoted above also stated: "[W]hen a Treaty stipulates regulations on any of the subjects submitted by the Constitution to the power of Congress, it must depend, for its execution, as to such stipulations, on a law or laws to be passed by Congress."[56] In other words, House Republicans asserted that all treaty provisions obligating the United States to take affirmative steps within the scope of Congress's Article I legislative powers are constitutionally non-self-executing.[57] Therefore, the Constitution requires legislation approved by both Houses of Congress to implement such treaty provisions.

Federalists vigorously disputed this claim. Their views were not entirely uniform, and they did not use the "concurrent/exclusive" terminology, but they tended to say that all of Congress's legislative powers, except for the power to appropriate money, are "concurrent" rather than "exclusive" powers. For example, Alexander Hamilton said, "In our constitution, which gives *ipso facto* the force of law to Treaties, making them equally with Acts of Congress, the supreme law of the land, a treaty must necessarily repeal an antecedent law contrary to it; according to the legal maxim that *leges posteriores priores contrarias abrogant*."[58] (The Latin phrase means that a later-in-time law supersedes an earlier, conflicting law.) As a treaty could not be "contrary to" a federal statute unless the treaty addressed matters within the scope of Congress's legislative powers, Hamilton's statement implies that treaties within the scope of Congress's legislative powers do not require legislative implementation.

On March 14, Congressman Theophilus Bradbury presented a detailed explanation of the Federalist position. He began by summarizing his understanding of the opposing view: "Where any articles of a Treaty were repugnant to prior existing acts of Congress, those acts must first be repealed by Congress before such Treaty can become the law of the land."[59] He assumed, without conceding "the truth of the fact," that some articles of the Jay Treaty did conflict with prior federal statutes. Nevertheless, "he altogether denied the principle" that legislation was necessary to implement such treaty provisions. To the contrary, Bradbury asserted, "the [Jay] Treaty has already a legal existence; that it is now the law of the land; and that, therefore, no act of Congress is, or can be, necessary to make it so."[60]

Some commentators have asserted that the House debates ultimately vindicated the Republican position because the House approved the House Treaty Resolution by a significant majority.[61] Upon closer examination, though, this claim is untenable. While the House was discussing the Jay Treaty, it also discussed treaties with Algiers, Spain, and certain Native American tribes.[62] One week after the House voted for the House Treaty Resolution, Congressman Sedgwick introduced a resolution stating: "[t]hat provision ought to be made by law for carrying into effect, with good faith, the Treaties lately concluded between the Dey and Regency of Algiers, the King of Great Britain [i.e., the Jay Treaty], the King of Spain, and certain Indian tribes Northwest of the Ohio."[63] After extended procedural wrangling about whether the four treaties should be considered in one resolution or separate resolutions, the House chose to focus on the Spanish treaty. At that point, Congressman Goodhue made a statement that merits a lengthy quotation:

> [He] wished to inform the Committee, and particularly those who have held up this idea that whenever a Treaty provides an arrangement, running counter to an existing law, it becomes necessary, in order to give such arrangement validity, that a repealing law should be made: that, in the tenth article of the Spanish treaty, it is stipulated that [certain Spanish goods] ... shall not be subject to the payment of any greater dues or duties than they would be in a like case on board of an American vessel, which is annulling our revenue laws in this respect, which requires the payment of ten percent more. He mentioned this only to remind those gentlemen who had held up this idea, as intended to operate relative to the British Treaty, that if it be necessary in the one case, it must be in the other, and not that he held any such opinion, for he believed a Treaty was a law of the land, without any interference of theirs to make it so.[64]

In short, if the Republicans wished to remain faithful to the principle articulated in the House Treaty Resolution, then Congress would need to enact legislation to amend or repeal existing import laws to implement Article 10 of the Spanish treaty. Similarly, although Congressman Goodhue did not say so explicitly, Congress would have to amend or repeal existing import laws to implement Article 15 of the Jay Treaty, which promised that British imports would be subject to no higher duty "than are or shall be payable on the importation of the like articles ... of any other Foreign Country."[65] In fact, though, the only implementing legislation that was proposed or enacted for either treaty was legislation to appropriate money.[66] Thus, although the House resolution endorsed the principle that *all* treaty provisions within the scope of Congress's legislative powers require implementing legislation, Congress never enacted such legislation (except to appropriate money), even though both the Jay Treaty and the Spanish treaty included provisions addressing matters subject to Congress's legislative authority.[67]

In sum, arguments about the Jay Treaty stretched out for the better part of one year, including debates in the Senate, the public, and the House of Representatives. Partisans raised numerous constitutional issues, including

the states' rights objection to Article 9, the House's constitutional prerogative to refuse to appropriate money, and questions about whether implementing legislation was required to execute treaty provisions within the scope
of Congress's legislative powers. Despite vigorous partisan debate, though,
one proposition remained unchallenged. No one seriously contested the
Constitution's treaty supremacy rule—valid, ratified treaties supersede conflicting state laws, and courts are constitutionally bound to apply treaties in
the event of a conflict. No one proposed an NSE exception to the treaty supremacy rule. As Professor Parry observed, "nothing in the debates undermined the founding understanding that treaties would override state law and
bind the states, including through judicial enforcement in cases brought by or
against individuals."[68]

* * *

In sum, as of 1800, treaty supremacy and self-execution were distinct doctrines
that addressed two distinct sets of non-overlapping issues. Treaty supremacy
addressed the relationship between treaties and state law. Self-execution was a
federal separation-of-powers doctrine that addressed the relationship among the
Treaty Power, federal executive power, and Congress's legislative powers. Self-
execution was understood in terms of the congressional-executive concept, not
the political-judicial concept.

The conceptual firewall that separated treaty supremacy doctrine from
self-execution doctrine remained intact between 1800 and 1945. However,
self-execution doctrine became increasingly incoherent in the late nineteenth
and early twentieth centuries, as lawyers and judges began to muddle the distinction between the congressional-executive and political-judicial concepts
of self-execution. Growing incoherence in self-execution doctrine before
World War II sowed the seeds for the development of an NSE exception to the
treaty supremacy rule after World War II. Parts Two and Three explore these
developments.

PART TWO

Treaty Supremacy from 1800 to 1945

The Oxford English Dictionary defines "gibberish" as "unintelligible speech ... of arbitrary invention; inarticulate chatter, jargon."[1] Adapting this definition to the legal context, we can define "legal gibberish" as a legal term of art that is used to obfuscate legal issues. When lawyers and judges utilize legal gibberish, they create confusion because the gibberish functions as a substitute for rational legal analysis. Over time, the terms "self-executing" and "non-self-executing" acquired the characteristics of legal gibberish. The application of self-execution rhetoric as legal gibberish, which began in the late nineteenth century, helped ensure that the post–World War II transformation of the treaty supremacy rule remained largely invisible. Much of Part Two explores the development of self-execution doctrine from 1800 to 1945.

In reviewing legislative, executive, and judicial materials from 1800 to 1945, one is struck by the fact that lawyers and judges had an extremely bifurcated view of the relationship among treaties, state law, and federal law. Treaties that overlapped with state regulatory authority fit into one box. Treaties that overlapped with Congress's regulatory authority fit into a different box. The treaty supremacy rule governed the relationship between treaties and state law. The concept of self-execution applied almost exclusively to treaties that overlapped with federal statutes and/or Congress's regulatory authority. The NSE exception to the Constitution's treaty supremacy rule did not exist because the concepts of "self-execution" and "treaty supremacy" belonged in two entirely separate boxes. Table One on p. 47 summarizes the conceptual framework applied by legislative, executive, and judicial officials throughout this period.

When modern scholars read older cases involving treaties and state law, they sometimes say that the court assumed that the treaty at issue was "self-executing." That is a profound misreading of the case law. Between 1800 and 1945, the distinction between self-executing (SE) and non-self-executing (NSE) treaties had almost no relevance to cases involving treaties and state law. The treaty supremacy rule governed the relationship between treaties and state law, subject to disputes about the constitutional validity of treaties that interfered with state regulatory authority. In cases where one party alleged a conflict between a treaty and state law, the question of whether the treaty was self-executing was almost never raised, because the concept of self-execution applied to a discrete category of cases. As Quincy Wright stated in 1951, "the distinction between self-executing and non-self-executing treaties has been used in American constitutional law only with reference to the agency of the Federal Government competent to execute the treaty and has had no reference to the relations between the Federal Government and the States."[2] The strict conceptual division between self-execution and treaty supremacy meant that the treaty supremacy rule operated, in practice, as a mandatory rule. Moreover, the mandatory quality of the treaty supremacy rule ensured that the rule served its intended purpose: to prevent state government officers from undermining national policy by violating binding treaty obligations.

Despite the strict division between supremacy and self-execution, lawyers developed several distinct variants of NSE doctrine before World War II. The Introduction to this book referred to both the "congressional-executive" concept and the "political-judicial" concept of self-execution.[3] (The "federal-state" concept did not emerge until after 1945. Part Three addresses the "federal-state" concept.) Under the congressional-executive concept, an NSE treaty does not operate as a rule of conduct for federal executive officers unless Congress enacts implementing legislation, but federal executive officers apply SE treaties as law and need not await legislative authorization to do so. In contrast, under the political-judicial concept, SE treaty provisions are judicially enforceable, but courts may not apply NSE provisions unless Congress enacts implementing legislation. Beginning in the late nineteenth century, lawyers and judges used the terms "self-executing" and "non-self-executing" to express both the congressional-executive concept and the political-judicial concept, without distinguishing clearly between them. Their failure to distinguish between the two concepts meant that self-execution rhetoric began to function as legal gibberish.

The tendency to conflate the congressional-executive concept with the political-judicial concept created one layer of confusion. Professor Edwin Dickinson added a second layer when he published an influential law review article in 1926 that introduced the "one-step approach" to self-execution analysis.[4] Before that time, lawyers and judges generally applied a "two-step approach."[5] Emergence of the one-step approach in the period between World War I and World War II established an essential building block for creation of an NSE exception to the treaty supremacy rule after World War II. Therefore, it is crucial to understand the distinction between the one-step and two-step approaches.

The two-step approach distinguishes between international obligation questions and domestic implementation questions. "What does the treaty require the United States to do?" is an international obligation question. "Which government actors have the power and/or duty to carry out that treaty obligation?" is a domestic implementation question. Under the two-step approach, step one involves a treaty interpretation analysis to determine the content and scope of the international obligation. Step two involves a domestic separation-of-powers analysis to determine the respective roles of Congress, the president, and the courts in executing treaty requirements. The two-step approach makes sense because the appropriate division of authority over treaty implementation between Congress and the president (the congressional-executive concept), or between the political branches and the courts (the political-judicial concept), often hinges on the content and scope of the international obligation. For example, if a treaty requires the United States to pay money to an international organization, Congress must play a role in treaty implementation, because appropriation of funds is a congressional function. In contrast, if a treaty prohibits torture, the president does not need legislative authorization to issue orders to subordinate federal officers to prevent torture.

The one-step approach bypasses the international obligation question and focuses exclusively on the domestic implementation question.[6] Under the one-step approach, courts ask simply whether the treaty makers (i.e., the president and Senate, acting together under the Treaty Power) intended the treaty to be self-executing. If they intended it to be non-self-executing, then courts and federal executive officers must await congressional action before applying the treaty. But if the treaty makers intended the treaty to be self-executing, then courts (under the political-judicial concept) and federal executive officers (under the congressional-executive concept) are empowered to apply the treaty as law and need not await legislative authorization to do so. Under the one-step approach, courts perform a treaty interpretation analysis to determine the intent of the treaty makers. However, the content and scope of the international obligation is irrelevant. The crucial question is whether the treaty makers intended the treaty to be self-executing.

The distinction between one-step and two-step approaches raises a critical point that most courts and commentators have overlooked: the implicit constitutional assumptions underlying the one-step approach differ fundamentally from the implicit constitutional assumptions underlying the two-step approach. The two-step approach rests on two assumptions that are uncontested. First, Article II grants the treaty makers power to make decisions about the content and scope of the international obligation codified in a treaty. Second, the Constitution limits the power of certain government actors to execute treaties. Specifically, if the two-step approach is combined with the congressional-executive concept, NSE doctrine assumes that the *Constitution limits the power of federal executive officers* to implement certain types of treaty provisions. For example, federal executive officers do not have the legal authority to execute a treaty requiring appropriation of money. If the two-step approach is combined with the political-judicial concept, NSE doctrine assumes that the *Constitution limits the power of courts* to apply certain types of treaty provisions. For example, courts do not have authority to apply a treaty requiring the United States to "make best efforts to eliminate poverty," unless Congress first enacts implementing legislation, because decisions about how best to eliminate poverty are not the types of decisions that courts are authorized to make under our system of divided power. (*See* Table Two on p. 64.)

In contrast, the one-step approach tacitly assumes that Article II grants the treaty makers an affirmative power to make decisions about domestic treaty implementation that are not contingent upon the content of the international obligation. Specifically, if the one-step approach is combined with the congressional-executive concept, NSE doctrine assumes that *Article II grants the treaty makers an affirmative power to require congressional legislation as a prerequisite before federal executive officers can execute treaty provisions* that would otherwise fall within the scope of federal executive authority. For example, if a treaty prohibits torture, but the treaty makers specify that the treaty is not self-executing, the president must await federal legislation before he (or she) is authorized to issue regulations implementing the treaty. Similarly, if the one-step approach is combined with the political-judicial concept, NSE doctrine assumes that *Article II grants the treaty makers an affirmative power to require congressional legislation as a prerequisite before courts can apply treaty provisions* that would otherwise fall within the scope of judicial authority. For example, if a treaty prohibits racial discrimination, but the treaty makers specify that the treaty is not self-executing, courts must await legislative action before they are authorized to apply the treaty.

In sum, the two-step approach assumes that the treaty makers control domestic implementation *indirectly* by making decisions about the content and scope of the international obligation. In contrast, the one-step approach assumes that the treaty makers control domestic implementation *directly* by making decisions about domestic implementation that are not contingent upon the content of the international obligation. The implicit constitutional assumptions underlying the two-step approach are uncontested. However, certain implicit constitutional assumptions involving particular applications of the one-step approach are hotly contested, as discussed in Part Four.[7] Regardless, the key point for now is that development of the one-step approach in the first half of the twentieth century established an essential building block for the creation of an NSE exception to the treaty supremacy rule after World War II.

When Edwin Dickinson invented the one-step approach in 1926, he used the rhetoric of self-execution as legal gibberish, together with the authority of Chief Justice Marshall's opinion in *Foster v. Neilson*,[8] to mask the fact that he was creating a novel version of self-execution doctrine. Here, it is important to note a key difference between lawyers, on the one hand, and artists and scientists, on the other. Artists and scientists gain professional prestige by creating or inventing something truly novel. In contrast, a judge loses legitimacy if he or she is perceived to be creating new law. Thus, when lawyers want to persuade judges to create new law, they typically claim that they are merely applying an established legal principle to a new situation.[9] When Dickinson wrote his influential law review article in 1926, he probably believed that he was applying an established legal principle to a new situation. However, his novel version of NSE doctrine was based on unstated constitutional assumptions that differed substantially from the assumptions underlying prior doctrine. His success in masking those differences contributed to the process of invisible constitutional transformation.

Table Two summarizes different variants of NSE doctrine. For now, it is important to highlight four different versions of NSE doctrine.[10]

- The *constitutional doctrine* combines a two-step approach with the congressional-executive concept. The doctrine assumes that federal executive officers have the requisite authority to implement SE treaty provisions, but the Constitution limits their power to implement NSE provisions, absent congressional authorization. The doctrine can be traced to congressional debates about the Jay Treaty (discussed in Chapter 3).

- The *justiciability doctrine* combines a two-step approach with the political-judicial concept. The doctrine assumes that courts have the requisite authority to apply SE treaty provisions, but the Constitution limits their power to apply NSE provisions, absent congressional authorization. The doctrine is often associated with the Supreme Court decision in *The Head Money Cases*[11] (discussed in Chapter 7). However, Chief Justice Marshall also applied a variant of the justiciability doctrine in *Foster v. Neilson* (discussed in Chapter 4).

- The *intent doctrine* combines a one-step approach with the congressional-executive concept. The doctrine assumes that the Constitution grants the treaty makers an affirmative power to modify the default rules that would otherwise govern the division of power over treaty implementation between Congress and the president. The doctrine can be traced to a 1926 law review article by Professor Edwin Dickinson (discussed in Chapter 8).

- The *Fujii doctrine* combines a one-step approach with the federal-state concept. The doctrine assumes that the Constitution grants the treaty makers an affirmative power to opt out of the treaty supremacy rule by deciding that a particular treaty will not supersede conflicting state laws. The doctrine developed in the early 1950s in the context of debates about domestic application of international human rights treaties. (*See* Part Three.)

Table Two. VARIETIES OF NSE DOCTRINES, CIRCA 1945

	Two-Step Approach to Self-Execution Analysis	One-Step Approach to Self-Execution Analysis
Congressional-Executive Concept	Constitutional Doctrine (Origin: 1790s)	Intent Doctrine (Origin: 1920s)
Federal-State Concept		*Fujii* Doctrine developed after 1945. *See* Part Three.
Political-Judicial Concept	Justiciability Doctrine (Origin: 1880s or earlier)	Three variants of NSE doctrine developed after 1970. *See* Part Four.

A widely accepted myth holds that Chief Justice Marshall applied the one-step approach to self-execution analysis in *Foster v. Neilson* in 1829. That myth is utterly false, as explained in Chapter 4. Nevertheless, the use of self-execution rhetoric as legal gibberish obfuscated distinctions among different variants of NSE doctrine and helped perpetuate the mythical view of *Foster*. Widespread acceptance of the myth played an important role in the development of the intent doctrine between 1920 and 1945, as explained in Chapter 8. Moreover, the *Foster* myth also played a crucial role in the transformation of the treaty supremacy rule after World War II, as explained in Part Three. In brief, widespread acceptance of the *Foster* myth helped establish the legitimacy of the *Fujii* doctrine in the 1950s. Acceptance of the *Fujii* doctrine converted the treaty supremacy rule from a mandatory to an optional rule by creating an NSE exception to the treaty supremacy rule.

Despite the use of self-execution rhetoric as legal gibberish, legislative, executive, and judicial authorities before 1945 agreed on one point: self-execution doctrine did not affect the relationship between treaties and state law. In cases where a party alleged a conflict between a treaty and state law, no published judicial decision before 1945 held that the treaty was NSE. Moreover, in cases where a party alleged a conflict between a treaty and state law, no Supreme Court decision before 1945 included any significant analysis of self-execution. In sum, before 1945 the courts generally behaved as if they believed that the distinction between SE and NSE treaties was not relevant to cases in which parties alleged a conflict between a treaty and state law. The strict conceptual division between self-execution and treaty supremacy helped ensure that the treaty supremacy rule served its intended purpose: to prevent state government officers from undermining national policy by violating binding treaty obligations.

Part Two is divided into five chapters. Chapter 4 presents a detailed analysis of Chief Justice Marshall's opinion in *Foster v. Neilson*. Chapter 5 addresses the intersection between treaties and state law; it focuses on the treaty supremacy rule. Chapter 6 discusses the doctrine of self-executing treaties as it developed in Congress and the executive branch between 1800 and 1945. Chapter 7 then addresses self-execution doctrine as it developed in the federal courts during the same period. Chapter 8 examines legal, political, and historical developments in the early twentieth century that laid the groundwork for the constitutional transformation after 1945. Part Three demonstrates that the advent of modern international human rights law was the spark that triggered the creation of an NSE exception to the Constitution's treaty supremacy rule. However, the transformation of the treaty supremacy rule would not have occurred, at least not in the same way, if the legal profession had not been receptive to a constitutional change that departed radically from the original understanding of the Constitution. Chapter 8 examines developments in the early twentieth century that made the legal profession receptive to such a change.

Finally, let me issue a warning to readers. Chapters 6 and 7 are very technical; they explore the intricacies of self-execution doctrine. Readers who are not particularly interested in the technical details of self-execution doctrine may wish to skip those chapters. If you decide to do so, the summary provided in the preceding pages should give you sufficient information to follow the thread of the argument through the rest of the book.

4

Foster v. Neilson

Modern mythology holds that Chief Justice Marshall's opinion in *Foster v. Neilson* (1829) is the source of non-self-execution (NSE) doctrine. The mythical view of *Foster* is incorrect in several respects, but two points bear emphasis here. First, *Foster* says nothing about the relationship between treaties and state law. Therefore, lawyers and judges are wrong to cite *Foster* as authority for an NSE exception to the treaty supremacy rule. Second, Marshall applied a two-step approach in *Foster*, not a one-step approach. Therefore, lawyers and judges are wrong to cite *Foster* as authority for a one-step approach to self-execution analysis. Even so, modern reliance on *Foster* to support propositions that it does not actually support illustrates the process of invisible constitutional change. By citing *Foster* as authority to support novel claims about self-execution, lawyers and judges changed the law substantially, while claiming that they were merely applying established principles to new circumstances. To understand how later generations of lawyers used *Foster* to change the meaning of the Constitution we must begin by examining *Foster* itself.

In *Foster*, Marshall penned the following words, which have come to be associated with the doctrine of non-self-executing treaties:

> Our constitution declares a treaty to be the law of the land. It is, consequently, to be regarded in courts of justice as equivalent to an act of the legislature, whenever it operates of itself without the aid of any legislative provision. But when the terms of the stipulation import a contract, when either of the parties engages to perform a particular act, the treaty addresses itself to the political, not the judicial department; and the legislature must execute the contract before it can become a rule for the Court.[1]

This quote appears on the sixty-first page of a sixty-four-page decision. Marshall's entire NSE rationale fills only about three pages in that decision. Unfortunately, courts and commentators typically ignore most of the sixty pages preceding the quoted language. In contrast, the account presented here addresses the entire opinion, because one cannot fully understand Marshall's NSE rationale without understanding the rest of the opinion. This chapter is divided into four sections. The first section addresses the first two holdings in *Foster*. The next addresses

Foster and the treaty supremacy rule. The third section provides historical context that helps clarify Marshall's NSE rationale in *Foster*. The final section addresses Marshall's self-execution analysis.

I. THE FIRST TWO HOLDINGS IN *FOSTER*

Foster involved a dispute over title to land in what is now southeastern Louisiana.[2] James Foster and Pleasants Elam were the named plaintiffs in the case. However, the Supreme Court litigation was funded by land speculators who hoped to earn a profit by selling other land in the region. A decision in favor of Foster and Elam would have validated the speculators' title claims. Additionally, "several thousand families" were reportedly interested in the litigation because the validity of their titles also hinged on the outcome of the Supreme Court decision.[3] To understand the issues in dispute, it is helpful to recount the history of the surrounding area.

A. The Land at Issue

The land at issue in *Foster* is situated in an area bounded on the north by the 31st parallel, on the west by the Mississippi River and on the east by the Perdido River. In terms of contemporary geography, this area includes the southernmost portions of Alabama and Mississippi, and parts of southeastern Louisiana.[4] Let us call the area "Floriana." In the early nineteenth century, the United States and Spain disagreed about whether Floriana was part of Florida, which belonged to Spain, or part of Louisiana, which belonged to the United States.

As of 1760, Louisiana was French territory and Florida was Spanish territory. The Perdido River was the accepted boundary between Louisiana and Florida. Floriana, therefore, was part of Louisiana. In 1763, Great Britain, France, and Spain signed the Treaty of Paris. In the Treaty of Paris, Spain ceded Florida to Great Britain, and France ceded to Great Britain that portion of Louisiana lying east of the Mississippi River, except for New Orleans and the island on which it is situated. In a separate, secret treaty, France ceded the rest of Louisiana to Spain (including New Orleans). The king of England then divided his newly acquired territory into two provinces, which he called East and West Florida. By a royal proclamation in 1763, he established the 31st parallel as the northern border of the two Floridas. At that time, Floriana became part of West Florida.[5]

The United States declared its independence in 1776. Spain conquered Florida during the Revolutionary War, reclaiming the land from Britain. In September 1783, Great Britain signed peace treaties with both the United States and Spain. In the treaty with Spain, Britain ceded East and West Florida (including Floriana) to Spain, but the treaty did not specify the boundaries of Florida. The treaty between Britain and the United States established the Mississippi River as the western boundary of the United States, and the 31st parallel as the southern boundary between the United States and Florida.[6] Neither treaty established a boundary between Louisiana and Florida. The precise location of that boundary was not important at that time because Spain owned both Louisiana and Florida (having acquired Louisiana from France in 1763 and Florida from Britain in 1783).[7]

France and Spain concluded the Treaty of Saint Ildefonso in 1800. In that treaty, Spain agreed "to retrocede to the French republic ... the colony or province of Louisiana, with the same extent that it now has in the hands of Spain, and that it had when France possessed it ...."[8] This language was very ambiguous. The province of Louisiana "when France possessed it," prior to 1763, included Floriana—that is, the land east of the Mississippi, west of the Perdido, and south of the 31st parallel. But Britain had incorporated Floriana into Florida in 1763, and Spain had acquired Floriana (along with the rest of Florida) from Britain in 1783. Therefore, Spain insisted that Floriana remained part of Spanish Florida when Spain ceded Louisiana to France in 1800.[9]

The United States acquired Louisiana from France in the 1803 Louisiana treaty. That treaty did not specify the eastern boundary of Louisiana. Instead, it referred to the Treaty of Saint Ildefonso to define the boundary.[10] Beginning in 1803, Congress passed a series of acts to establish U.S. control over Louisiana. Congressional actions left no doubt that Congress believed the United States had acquired Floriana from France as part of the Louisiana Treaty.[11] Congress, therefore, asserted U.S. sovereignty over Floriana. Meanwhile, Spain continued to assert Spanish sovereignty over Floriana, claiming the territory as part of Florida. The United States and Spain did not finally resolve their boundary dispute until Spain ceded Florida to the United States in the 1819 Florida treaty.[12] In the interim, however, between 1803 and 1819, Spain had granted land in Floriana to hundreds or thousands of Spanish grantees, including the predecessor to the *Foster* plaintiffs.

B. The "Political Question" Holding in *Foster*

Foster involved a dispute over title to land in Floriana. Plaintiffs traced their title to an 1804 land grant from the Spanish governor of Florida.[13] Defendant alleged that, prior to 1804, the land had been "ceded by Spain to France, and by France to the United States; and the officer making said grant had not then and there any right [to grant the land], and the said grant is wholly null and void."[14] Thus, the first question presented was whether the 1804 Spanish land grant was valid. Resolution of that question, in turn, hinged on whether the United States had acquired the land from France in 1803 as part of the Louisiana Treaty—the very same issue that was the subject of a boundary dispute between the United States and Spain from 1803 to 1819.

The Court noted that the language of the relevant treaties—the Louisiana Treaty and the Treaty of St. Ildefonso—could plausibly be interpreted to support either the Spanish position (that the land was part of Spanish Florida in 1804), or the U.S. position (that it was part of the United States in 1804).[15] In this context, Marshall stated:

> In a controversy between two nations concerning national boundary, it
> is scarcely possible that the courts of either should refuse to abide by the

measures adopted by its own government. There being no common tribunal to decide between them, each determines for itself on its own rights, and if they cannot adjust their differences peaceably, the right remains with the strongest. The judiciary is not that department of the government, to which the assertion of its interests against foreign powers is confided . . . . [I]t is the province of the Court to conform its decisions to the will of the legislature, if that will has been clearly expressed.[16]

In short, the Court held "that the question of boundary between the United States and Spain, was a question for the political departments of the government . . . ."[17] As Congress had enacted numerous statutes asserting U.S. sovereignty over Floriana, the Court accepted that the United States had acquired the territory when it purchased Louisiana in 1803.[18] Consequently, plaintiffs could not establish a valid title on the basis of the 1804 Spanish grant because the Spanish governor had no authority to grant land in U.S. territory. Daniel Webster represented the plaintiffs in *Foster*. Shortly after the Supreme Court decision, Webster wrote that his clients lost "on the precise grounds which our fears had anticipated . . . that a question of boundaries, between us & a foreign State, is fit for the consideration of the other branches rather than the Judiciary."[19] The Court did not address the merits of another case involving land in Floriana until it decided *Garcia v. Lee* nine years after *Foster*.[20] By that time, Roger Taney was chief justice. In *Garcia*, Taney reaffirmed *Foster*'s political question holding, stating "that the boundary line determined on as the true one by the political departments of the government, must be recognised as the true one by the judicial department . . . ."[21]

Most modern scholarship on self-execution ignores *Foster*'s political question holding because the key self-execution passage in *Foster* examines Article 8 of the 1819 Florida treaty, whereas *Foster*'s political question holding was based on the 1803 Louisiana treaty and the Treaty of St. Ildefonso. Even so, the political question holding is important for several reasons. First, it was the only unanimous holding in *Foster*; the Court was divided on other issues. Second, Chief Justice Taney characterized the political question holding as the "leading principle"[22] in *Foster*. And, as noted above, Daniel Webster identified it as the "precise grounds" on which his clients lost. Finally, *Foster*'s political question holding was a precursor to the political-judicial concept of self-execution and the associated justiciability doctrine. (*See* Table Two, p. 64.) However, the *Foster* version of justiciability was much narrower than modern justiciability doctrine because, in Marshall's words, the principle applied only to cases involving "a controversy between two nations concerning national boundary."[23]

C. The Territorial Application of Article 8

Having held that the plaintiffs could not establish valid title on the basis of the 1804 Spanish land grant, the Court next considered whether they could establish valid title on the basis of Article 8 of the Florida Treaty. Article 8 said: "All the grants of land made before the 24th of January, 1818, by his Catholic Majesty [the King of Spain], or by his lawful authorities, in the said Territories ... shall be ratified and confirmed to the persons in possession of the lands, to the same extent that the same grants would be valid if the territories had remained under the dominion of" Spain.[24] Article 8 clearly created an obligation for the United States to protect the property rights of Spanish grantees. However, the justices disagreed about whether Floriana was part of the "Territories" covered in Article 8. "The majority of the Court," said Marshall, believed that the Article 8 duty to protect the property rights of Spanish grantees applied only to land grants in Florida proper, not to grants in Floriana.[25] Therefore, according to the majority, Spanish grants in Floriana after 1803 were simply "void."[26] In contrast, Marshall wrote, "one other judge and myself are inclined to adopt" the view that Spanish land grants in Floriana "were as obligatory on the United States, as on his catholic majesty."[27] Thus, Marshall and one other justice thought the United States had a duty under Article 8 to respect the property rights of individuals, such as the *Foster* plaintiffs, who received Spanish land grants in Floriana before January 1818.[28]

If Marshall had agreed with the majority that Article 8 did not apply to land in Floriana, it would not have been necessary for the Court to decide whether Article 8 was self-executing. The Court could have resolved the case on the grounds that: (1) the initial Spanish land grant was invalid (the Court's unanimous "political question" holding), and (2) plaintiffs had no rights under the Florida treaty because Article 8 did not apply to land in Floriana (the majority view on the territorial application issue). Indeed, the Court decided *Garcia v. Lee*, the next case involving land in Floriana, on precisely these grounds. Moreover, Chief Justice Taney, writing for the Court in *Garcia*, said that the Court had decided *Foster* on these grounds. Specifically, Taney said, *Foster* decided "that this grant [in Floriana] is not embraced by the eighth article of the treaty, which ceded the Floridas to the United States; *that the stipulations in that article are confined to the territory which belonged to Spain at the time of the cession, according to the American construction of the treaty* ...."[29]

Thus, from the perspective of Chief Justice Taney, writing nine years after *Foster*, Marshall's discussion of non-self-execution was not part of the majority rationale for the Court's decision in *Foster*. In an important sense, Taney was right. If the *Foster* Court had followed modern practice, individual justices would have written separate opinions. A different judge would have written the majority opinion, holding that Article 8 did not apply to land in Floriana. Marshall would have written a separate concurring opinion setting forth his view that Article 8 was not self-executing. But Marshall exercised tight discipline over "his" court, so justices rarely wrote separate opinions in the Marshall era.[30] Accordingly, Marshall's opinion for the Court presented the majority view,[31] and then presented his alternative non-self-execution rationale.[32] The majority view and Marshall's NSE rationale both yielded the same result: recipients of Spanish grants in Floriana had to petition Congress to obtain legal recognition of their land claims.

II. TREATY SUPREMACY IN *FOSTER*

The Constitution's treaty supremacy rule addresses conflicts, or alleged conflicts, between treaties and state law. If neither party in a lawsuit raises a claim based on state law, then the treaty supremacy rule is simply not relevant. The treaty supremacy rule was not relevant in *Foster* because neither party raised a claim based on state law.

Unfortunately, this fact has been obscured because the published version of the case does not specify the legal basis of defendant's claim. The plaintiffs in *Foster* brought a claim known as an "ejectment" action.[33] The goal of an ejectment action is to eject the defendant from property he occupies. As the defendant in an ejectment action always has actual possession of the property, the defendant is not required to establish the legal basis of his claim. The defendant can win based on actual possession if he can show that the plaintiffs' title claim is defective. Thus, the published decision in *Foster* does not specify the legal basis of defendant's claim because David Neilson, the defendant, did not need to establish the legal basis of his claim to win the lawsuit.

Although the Court's opinion in *Foster* does not specify the basis of Neilson's claim, we know from other sources that Neilson's asserted property right was based on federal law, not state law. As noted above, Daniel Webster represented the plaintiffs in *Foster*. Webster's papers specify that Neilson was "the occupant under a United States grant."[34] Additionally, in his argument to the Court, Webster summarized the issue as follows: "The question for the decision of the Court is, whether the lands sued for by the petitioners are a part of the province of Louisiana, as that province was ceded by France to the United States; or are a part of West Florida . . . . If a part of Louisiana; then the lands were public domain, *and now belonged to the United States or her grantees*. If a part of Florida; then the grant under which the plaintiff derives title is good, and he is entitled to recover."[35] Webster argued that the plaintiffs had good title because the land at issue was part of Spanish Florida before 1819. However, he conceded, if the Court disagreed with him on that point, then the land "belonged to the United States or her grantees." David Neilson was one of those grantees. As the recipient of a land grant from the federal government, his property claim was based on federal law, not state law.

This point is extremely important because it demonstrates that *Foster* did not endorse an NSE exception to the treaty supremacy rule. The treaty supremacy rule was not relevant to *Foster* because neither party raised a claim based on state law. Therefore, however one interprets the self-execution portion of Marshall's opinion in *Foster* (discussed below), it does not address the relationship between treaties and state law. Nevertheless, modern lawyers, judges, and scholars routinely cite *Foster* as authority for an NSE exception to the treaty supremacy rule.[36] In our common law system, judicial opinions are often reinterpreted by later generations of lawyers so that a judicial decision becomes accepted as a source of authority for a proposition that the court did not actually decide. In that process, the actual basis for the court's decision is slowly forgotten. That is the nature of invisible constitutional change.

III. HISTORICAL CONTEXT

We are slowly circling around the main issue: the self-execution portion of Marshall's opinion in *Foster*.[37] Before we tackle that portion of Marshall's opinion, some historical context is needed. This section first addresses the Jonathan Robbins affair, where Marshall, serving as a congressman from Virginia, made an important statement about the Constitution and treaty implementation. It then addresses a series of Supreme Court cases decided after *Foster* that involved land claims in Florida and Louisiana. Familiarity with these materials will help the reader understand Marshall's non-self-execution rationale in *Foster*.

Before addressing the Jonathan Robbins affair, it is helpful to recall some terminology introduced in Chapter 3. There, we saw that Justice Iredell distinguished between "executory" and "executed" treaty provisions. Executory provisions require the nation to take action in the future to fulfill its treaty commitments. In contrast, executed provisions "require no further act to be done"[38] because the goal to be accomplished is achieved immediately when the treaty takes effect. This distinction influenced the way that nineteenth century lawyers thought about the Constitution and treaty implementation.

A. The Jonathan Robbins Affair

We saw in Chapter 3 that Federalists and Republicans in Congress had a vigorous debate about treaties and the Constitution in 1795–1796, when George Washington presented the Jay Treaty to Congress. A few years later, Congress resumed the debate when Republicans introduced a formal resolution criticizing President Adams (a Federalist) for his handling of the so-called "Jonathan Robbins affair." In that context, John Marshall, serving as a Federalist congressman from Virginia before he became chief justice, delivered an important speech presenting a constitutional defense of President Adams's actions. Marshall's speech set forth his views about the allocation of responsibility for treaty implementation among the three branches of the federal government.[39]

The Robbins case arose when British authorities sought the extradition of Jonathan Robbins on the charge that he committed murder on a British warship. Under Article 27 of the Jay Treaty, the United States agreed to extradite fugitives to Britain if certain conditions were satisfied.[40] British authorities asked Thomas Bee, the federal district judge in South Carolina, to order Robbins's extradition. When Judge Bee refused, the British approached Secretary of State Timothy Pickering. After consulting with President Adams, Pickering sent Judge Bee a letter conveying the president's "advice and request, that [Robbins] may be delivered up to the consul or other agent of Great Britain."[41] After receiving Pickering's letter, Judge Bee ordered Robbins to be delivered to British authorities,[42] and the government proceeded to extradite him.

Consistent with Republican positions in the Jay Treaty debates, Republicans argued that President Adams acted improperly because he lacked the authority to extradite Robbins until Congress enacted legislation to implement Article 27.[43]

(In other words, Article 27 was NSE under the constitutional doctrine.) In response, Marshall explained the Federalist position as follows: "[The president] is charged to execute the laws. A treaty is declared to be a law. He must then execute a treaty, where he . . . possesses the means of executing it."[44] In Marshall's view, the president had a duty to execute Article 27 because the treaty had the force of law under the Supremacy Clause, and the president has the constitutional power and duty under Article II to "take Care that the Laws be faithfully executed."[45] (In other words, Article 27 was SE under the constitutional doctrine.) Marshall agreed that Congress "may prescribe the mode, and Congress may devolve on others the whole execution of the contract; but, till this be done, it seems the duty of the Executive department to execute the contract by any means it possesses."[46] Thus, Marshall applied a two-step approach to support his conclusion that Article 27 was self-executing under the congressional-executive concept. He did not argue that international law authorized the president to execute the treaty; he argued that the Constitution authorized the president to execute the treaty.

All congressional participants in the Robbins debate agreed that Article 27 was executory, meaning that it required some future action by the United States. But the fact that it was executory did not mean that Congress was the only branch of government authorized to execute the treaty. To the contrary, the congressional debate focused almost exclusively on the question of whether the judiciary or the executive was the appropriate branch to execute the treaty. Republicans argued that Article 27 required judicial implementation.[47] Federalists argued that Article 27 required executive implementation. Thus, consistent with Justice Iredell's two-step approach in *Ware v. Hylton* (see Chapter 3), the consensus view was that some executory treaty provisions require judicial implementation, and some executory provisions require executive implementation.

Finally, in accordance with the two-step approach to self-execution analysis, all participants in the Robbins debate agreed that constitutional law, not international law, determines which branch of government is responsible for treaty implementation. In Marshall's words, the distribution of power among the branches is governed by "the principles of the American Government."[48] Marshall acknowledged that explicit treaty language providing for a specific mode of treaty implementation would have controlling effect.[49] However, in the absence of such explicit treaty language, constitutional separation-of-powers principles determine which branch of government has the power and/or duty to implement a particular treaty provision.

B. Land Claims in Louisiana and Florida

By 1820, the United States had concluded two major treaties involving acquisition of land from foreign powers: the 1803 treaty acquiring Louisiana from France and the 1819 treaty acquiring Florida from Spain. Article 3 of the Louisiana Treaty and Article 8 of the Florida Treaty protected the property rights of individuals who owned land in the subject territories before the transfer of sovereignty.[50] The Court interpreted both provisions to provide identical protection for individual property rights. The NSE portion of Marshall's opinion in *Foster* involved Article 8 of the Florida treaty.

The Court decided *Foster* in 1829. Over the next three decades, the Court decided at least seventy-five other cases involving Article 8 of the Florida Treaty and/or Article 3 of the Louisiana Treaty.[51] Modern scholars who have written about the historical origins of self-execution doctrine have generally overlooked the Louisiana and Florida property cases.[52] However, one cannot properly interpret Marshall's NSE rationale in *Foster* without understanding those cases. The property claims presented in those cases can be divided into three groups: claims involving perfect titles; claims involving inchoate titles based on legally valid grants; and claims involving grants from a government representative who lacked authority to convey valid, legal title. (The Court used the terms "perfect," "complete," and "legal" title interchangeably, distinguishing sharply between this class of property rights and "inchoate," "incomplete," or "equitable" titles, terms it also used interchangeably.) The characterization of the relevant treaty provisions as "executory" or "executed" depended on the nature of the property interests at stake in a particular case.[53]

If a person held a perfect title to real property before the effective date of the treaty, he retained his title when sovereignty passed to the United States. The United States had no obligation to take affirmative steps to perfect such already-perfect titles.[54] As Justice Catron explained: "That the perfect titles, made by Spain, before the 24th January, 1818, within the ceded territory, are intrinsically valid ... is the established doctrine of this Court; and that they need no sanction from the legislative or judicial departments of this country."[55] Article 8 of the Florida Treaty and Article 3 of the Louisiana Treaty—as applied to perfect titles—were "executed," not "executory," because the United States did not have to take any future action to implement its treaty obligation to respect perfected property rights.[56]

The second class of cases under the Florida and Louisiana treaties involved inchoate titles based on legally valid grants. When Florida belonged to Spain, the Spanish government issued many "contingent" land grants, where the grant did not become effective until the grantee took some specified action. In one case, for example, the grant stated that the grantee "may build a water saw-mill in that creek, of the river St. John called M'Girt's; under the precise condition, however, that until he builds said mill, this grant will be considered null and void."[57] These types of grants created inchoate titles that could be converted into perfect titles when the specified action was completed. If a person held an inchoate title before the effective date of the treaty, "the fee [i.e., the legal title] was transferred to the United States by the treaty, with the equity [i.e., an inchoate title] attached in the claimant."[58] The relevant treaty provisions obligated the United States to convert such inchoate titles into perfect titles (i.e., legal titles), but only insofar as the prior sovereign (France or Spain) was obligated to perfect the title of that particular claimant.[59] With respect to these claimants, Article 8 of the Florida

Treaty and Article 3 of the Louisiana Treaty were executory, not executed, because the United States had to take future action to perfect these inchoate titles.

The Supreme Court stated in several cases that federal legislation was required to perfect the titles of claimants who held inchoate titles at the time sovereignty passed to the United States, because Congress was the only branch of government with the constitutional authority to convert inchoate titles into perfect titles.[60] It bears emphasis that such statements presuppose a two-step approach. First, the Court determined as a matter of treaty interpretation that a particular treaty required conversion of inchoate titles to perfect titles. Second, the Court decided as a matter of U.S. constitutional law that federal legislation was needed to implement that obligation. The Court did not clearly articulate this view until 1844,[61] fifteen years after its decision in *Foster*. Nevertheless, as explained in the next section, the doctrine that federal legislation was constitutionally required to convert inchoate titles into perfect titles helps clarify Marshall's NSE rationale in *Foster*.

The third class of cases involved grants made by government representatives who lacked authority to convey legal title because the grant was made after the date on which the grantor's government ceded the territory to a different sovereign. (*Foster* belongs in this category.) In some of these cases, the Court held that the grant was void because the government that issued the grant lacked authority to do so.[62] In other cases, though, the Court held that claimants had an equitable claim (i.e., an inchoate title) because they inhabited land on the basis of a good faith belief that the government granting the land had the authority to do so.[63] In several cases, Congress enacted legislation to validate the property claims of individuals in this group. The Court ruled in favor of claimants who could point to such legislation to support their claims,[64] but it never ruled in favor of any claimant who merely asserted an equitable claim unsupported by such legislation.

In sum, with respect to claimants who held perfect legal titles, Article 8 of the Florida Treaty and Article 3 of the Louisiana Treaty were executed, not executory. However, with respect to claimants who held inchoate titles, the same treaty provisions were executory, and Congress was the only institution with the domestic constitutional authority to execute U.S. treaty obligations. Finally, with respect to grants made by government representatives who lacked authority to convey legal title, the Court sometimes held that such grants were void, and sometimes held that such grants gave rise to equitable claims, which required congressional sanction before they could be enforced in court. In every case where the issue arose, the Court applied a two-step analysis, not a one-step analysis, to determine whether the treaty obligation required legislative implementation in that case.

IV. THE SELF-EXECUTION ISSUE IN *FOSTER*

As noted previously, Article 8 of the Florida treaty pledged that Spanish land grants "shall be ratified and confirmed to the persons in possession of the lands . . . ." In *Foster*, Marshall said that "the ratification and confirmation which are promised must be the act of the legislature."[65] However, just four years later, in *United States v. Percheman*, he said that Spanish grants were "ratified and confirmed by force of the instrument itself" [i.e., the treaty] and did not require "some future legislative act."[66] The modern interpretation of *Foster* and *Percheman* explains those decisions in terms of the one-step approach to self-execution analysis. (Recall that the one-step approach says that treaty interpretation determines which government actors in the United States are responsible for treaty implementation. In contrast, the two-step approach looks to domestic law to answer domestic separation-of-powers questions.) According to the modern interpretation, *Foster*'s conclusion that Article 8 was non-self-executing rested entirely on a treaty interpretation analysis.[67] Then, Marshall reversed himself in *Percheman* and decided that Article 8 was self-executing, again by applying a treaty interpretation analysis. In *Medellin v. Texas*—the most important Supreme Court decision on self-execution in the past century—Chief Justice Roberts relied on this "modern interpretation" to justify his view that the classification of a treaty provision as SE or NSE hinges entirely on treaty interpretation analysis.[68]

This section demonstrates that the modern interpretation of *Foster* and *Percheman* is mistaken in several respects. The one-step approach, which views self-execution purely as a treaty interpretation issue,[69] does not offer a convincing explanation of Marshall's opinions in *Foster* and *Percheman*. Instead, Marshall's rationale is best explained as an application of the two-step approach. Indeed, the first person to propose a one-step interpretation of *Foster* and *Percheman* was Edwin Dickinson, writing in 1926, almost one hundred years after *Foster* was decided.[70] Before that time, relevant authorities generally construed *Foster* in accordance with a two-step analysis.

A. The Property Interests at Stake in *Foster* and *Percheman*

In the early nineteenth century, the Supreme Court's docket was filled with cases involving disputes over title to land. From the perspective of the parties, *Foster* and *Percheman* were both cases about land ownership; treaty issues were incidental. Thus, it should come as no surprise that, from the perspective of nineteenth century lawyers (including Marshall), the key factor that distinguished *Percheman* from *Foster* was the nature of the property interest at stake. The land at issue in *Percheman* was in East Florida, an area subject to undisputed Spanish sovereignty from 1783 until 1819. Percheman traced his title to an 1815 grant from the Spanish governor of Florida, a grant made when Spain exercised complete sovereignty over East Florida. The Spanish governor conveyed title to Percheman "in absolute property."[71] Therefore, in terms of the tripartite division of cases discussed in the previous section, *Percheman* fits in the class of cases involving perfect titles. In Marshall's view, legislation was not necessary to validate Percheman's title because he already had a perfect title before Spain conveyed Florida to the United States.

In contrast, the land at issue in *Foster* was in Floriana, an area that was the subject of competing sovereignty claims between 1800 and 1819. The court held unanimously in *Foster* that the Spanish grant upon which the plaintiffs relied was invalid because the grantor lacked authority to convey title.[72] Therefore, *Foster* falls squarely within the class of cases involving grants made by government representatives who lacked authority to convey legal title.

As noted previously, cases where the grantor lacked authority to convey title can be further subdivided into two groups: those where the grant was simply void, and those where the grant gave rise to an equitable claim.[73] The *Foster* Court divided precisely along these lines. "The majority of the Court," said Marshall, believed that Spanish grants of land in Floriana after 1803 were simply "void."[74] In contrast, Marshall wrote, "[o]ne other judge and myself are inclined to adopt" the opinion that imperfect grants for land in Floriana "were as obligatory on the United States, as on his catholic majesty."[75] In other words, Marshall thought the *Foster* plaintiffs had some sort of inchoate title, which gave rise to an equitable claim. In a later case involving a Spanish land grant in Floriana, the Court expressed the idea as follows: "Although the United States disavowed that any right to the soil passed by such concessions; still they were not disregarded as giving no equity to the claimant."[76] The Court explained that an "inchoate" or "equitable" title was a property right that "had so attached to any piece or tract of land ... as to affect the conscience of the former sovereign, 'with a trust,' and make him a trustee for an individual."[77] Thus, in Marshall's view, under Article 8 of the Florida treaty, the United States inherited Spain's position as a "trustee" for individuals, like the plaintiffs in *Foster*, who had equitable claims to property based on Spanish grants. Those grants did not convey legal title, but they nevertheless affected "the conscience of the former sovereign with a trust."

B. The Law of Nations and Individual Property Rights

Before undertaking a treaty interpretation analysis in *Percheman*, Marshall explained the background principles of the law of nations (i.e., international law) that apply when territory is passed from one sovereign to another. In his view, the law of nations ensured that individuals who held perfect titles to land retained those titles when a sovereign conveyed the surrounding territory to a different sovereign.

> Had Florida changed its sovereign by an act containing no stipulation respecting the property of individuals, the right of property in all those who became subjects or citizens of the new government would have been unaffected by the change; it would have remained the same as under the ancient sovereign.... A cession of territory is never understood to be a cession of the property belonging to its inhabitants. The king cedes that only which belonged to him; lands he had previously granted, were not his to cede. Neither party could so understand the cession; neither party could consider itself as attempting a wrong to individuals, condemned by the practice of the whole civilized world. The cession of a territory, by its name, from one

sovereign to another ... would be necessarily understood to pass the sovereignty only, and not to interfere with private property.[78]

In Marshall's view, private property rights "remained the same" when one sovereign conveyed land to another. Marshall stated explicitly that these principles "ought to be kept in view, when we construe the eighth article of the treaty."[79] He then proceeded to analyze the treaty text.[80] Thus, in *Percheman*, Marshall construed Article 8 of the Florida Treaty in conformity with the principles of the law of nations.

Those principles applied to perfect titles differently than to inchoate titles. To appreciate this point, it is helpful to recall the distinction between executory and executed treaty provisions. Executory treaty provisions require the nation to take future action to fulfill its treaty commitments, whereas executed treaty provisions "require no further act to be done."[81] The Court held in *Percheman* that Article 8 was executed, as applied to Percheman's land, because Percheman held title "in absolute property." No future action was necessary to grant him legal title because he already held legal title before Spain ceded Florida to the United States. In Marshall's words, "that sense of justice and of right which is acknowledged and felt by the whole civilized world would be outraged"[82] if the treaty deprived him of preexisting property rights by requiring legislative action to grant him property that he already owned.

Conversely, if an individual held an inchoate title to property before the date of the treaty, the treaty did not magically convert that inchoate title into a perfect legal title. Under the law of nations, the property rights of individuals who held inchoate titles "remain[ed] undisturbed,"[83] just as the property rights of individuals who held perfect titles remained undisturbed. An individual with an inchoate title had an equitable claim against the sovereign, entitling him to insist that the sovereign take affirmative steps to convert that inchoate title into a perfect title.[84] When sovereignty transferred from Spain to the United States, "the fee [i.e., the legal title] was transferred to the United States by the treaty, with the equity attached in the claimant."[85] Accordingly, the equitable claim against Spain became an equitable claim against the United States. Inasmuch as future action was still needed to convert the inchoate title into a perfect title, Article 8 was executory as it applied to inchoate titles, including the title at issue in *Foster*.

Thus, contrary to the "modern interpretation," *Percheman* did not overrule *Foster*. In both cases, Marshall construed Article 8 in accordance with the law of nations principle that private property rights "remain undisturbed" when one sovereign conveys territory to another. Article 8 was executed as it applied to Percheman because he already held a perfect title before the treaty took effect. However, Article 8 was executory as it applied to the *Foster* plaintiffs because they had an inchoate title, not a perfect title.

The Court's decision in *United States v. Arredondo* confirms this view.[86] The Court decided *Arredondo* in 1832, three years after *Foster*, and one year before *Percheman*. *Arredondo* was the first Supreme Court decision involving a Spanish grant in East Florida.[87] *Arredondo*, like *Percheman*, held that a Spanish grant in

East Florida did not require legislative action because the grant was confirmed "simultaneously with the ratification and confirmation of the treaty."[88] This holding might appear to conflict with *Foster*, but the Court said its decision should be "distinctly understood as not in the least impairing, but affirming the principle of *Foster v. Nelson*."[89] Justice Baldwin, writing for the Court in *Arredondo*, explained why the need for legislation in *Foster* was entirely consistent with the conclusion that legislation was unnecessary in *Arredondo*.[90] He said: "The rules vary according to the kind of title set up; distinctions have been made in all the laws between perfect or complete grants, fully executed, or inchoate incomplete ones, ... [which] required some act of the government to be done to complete it."[91] In short, perfect titles did not require legislative confirmation because they were "fully executed" by the treaty. However, inchoate titles (such as the one in *Foster*) required "some act of government to be done to complete" the title.[92]

C. Textual Analysis in *Foster* and *Percheman*

According to the modern interpretation, Marshall's textual analysis of the Florida Treaty led him to conclude in *Foster* that Article 8 was non-self-executing. In *Percheman*, though, Marshall's analysis of the Spanish text led him to conclude that Article 8 was self-executing.[93] The modern interpretation is wrong. Marshall's textual analysis in both *Foster* and *Percheman* focused on the nineteenth century distinction between executory and executed treaty provisions, not the twentieth century distinction between self-executing and non-self-executing provisions. The SE/NSE distinction focuses on a "who" question: Is treaty implementation the responsibility of Congress, the president, or the courts? The executed/executory distinction focuses on a "when" question: Did the treaty accomplish its goal immediately upon entry into force, or is future action necessary to implement the treaty?

Article 8 of the Florida Treaty specified that land grants made by Spanish authorities prior to the date of the treaty "shall be ratified and confirmed to the persons in possession of the lands."[94] In *Foster*, Marshall distinguished this language from hypothetical language stating that land "grants are hereby confirmed."[95] "Had such been its language," said Marshall, "it would have acted directly on the subject."[96] In other words, it would have been executed, not executory, because no future action would be necessary to implement a provision stating that grants "are hereby confirmed." However, according to Marshall's analysis in *Foster*, because Article 8 specified that the land grants "shall be ratified and confirmed," the treaty merely "pledge[d] the faith of the United States to pass acts which shall ratify and confirm" the grants.[97] In other words, he concluded that Article 8 was executory, not executed, because it obligated the United States to take future action to confirm the grants. Indeed, Richard Smith Coxe, Daniel Webster's co-counsel in *Foster*, said shortly after the *Foster* decision that the Court construed "the treaty of 1819 as an *executory contract* between the two nations, which did not of itself confirm the existing titles, but merely stipulated that they should be confirmed."[98] Thus, Marshall's textual analysis in *Foster* focused on the distinction between executory and executed treaty provisions, not the modern distinction between self-executing and non-self-executing treaty provisions.

In *Arredondo*, Justice Baldwin analyzed the difference between the English and Spanish versions of the treaty. He noted that the Spanish verb *"quedan"* "means 'shall remain' . . . in the present tense." In contrast, "[i]n the English original, the words are 'shall be'—words in the future."[99] Justice Baldwin invoked the general principle that the terms of a land grant should be construed in accordance with the intention of the grantor. Inasmuch as the king of Spain granted Florida to the United States, and the Spanish text expressed his intention, the Court should construe the grant as a present grant (executed), not a stipulation for future action (executory). Therefore, the Spanish grants were confirmed "simultaneously with the ratification and confirmation of the treaty."[100] Baldwin's entire analysis in this portion of his opinion focused on a "when" question, not a "who" question.

Chief Justice Marshall wrote his opinion in *Percheman* one year after the Court decided *Arredondo*. *Percheman* reiterated what the Court had already said in *Arredondo*. Joseph White, the attorney who represented Percheman, compared the English and Spanish versions of Article 8. He argued that "[t]he English side of the treaty leaves the ratification of the grants *executory*—they shall be ratified; the Spanish, *executed*—they shall continue acknowledged and confirmed."[101] Marshall's analysis of the Spanish and English texts followed Justice Baldwin's analysis in *Arredondo* and White's argument in *Percheman*.[102] Marshall contrasted the Spanish version—which (as newly retranslated) specified that grants "shall remain ratified and confirmed"—with the original English version, which specified that grants "shall be ratified and confirmed."[103] He concluded that Article 8 was executed, not executory, as it applied to Percheman's land, because the United States did not need to take any future action to perfect Percheman's already-perfect title.[104] Although Marshall did not use the words "executed" and "executory," later nineteenth century Supreme Court opinions confirm that Marshall's analysis in *Foster* and *Percheman* relied on the distinction between executory and executed treaty provisions.[105]

Of course, Marshall said in *Foster* not only that the United States was obligated to take future action to implement Article 8 (i.e., it was executory), but also that *legislative* action was necessary (i.e., it was non-self-executing). The modern interpretation holds that, under Marshall's analysis in *Foster*, "the need for implementing legislation has its source in the treaty itself."[106] However, the modern interpretation is mistaken for three reasons.

First, the claim that Article 8 requires legislative implementation, as a matter of treaty interpretation, has no basis in the treaty text. The treaty specifies that the grants "shall be ratified and confirmed."[107] But as Marshall himself conceded, the text does not address the question "[b]y whom shall they be ratified and confirmed?"[108] Marshall analyzed the text in *Foster* and *Percheman* to address a "when" question, not a "who" question. Self-execution is a "who" question. Marshall had to look beyond the text to answer that question because the text did not provide an answer.

Second, it was well established in the early nineteenth century, as it is today, that international law does not govern the internal processes by which a nation implements its treaty obligations.[109] The question of who shall ratify and confirm the grants—Congress, the president, or the judiciary—is a question about the internal process through which the United States implements its treaty obligations. As Marshall said in his speech to Congress in the Jonathan Robbins case, the distribution of power among the branches is governed by "the principles of the American Government."[110] In short, Marshall recognized that self-execution—specifically, the "who" question—is not (usually) governed by treaty interpretation principles. Rather, it is a question governed by domestic law.

Third, if the modern interpretation is correct—and *Percheman* held as a matter of treaty interpretation that Article 8 was self-executing—then Article 8 would have to be self-executing for all property interests, including inchoate titles as well as perfect titles. However, after *Percheman*, the Supreme Court decided dozens of cases involving Article 8 of the Florida Treaty and Article 3 of the Louisiana Treaty. In those cases, the Court repeatedly affirmed that congressional legislation was necessary to perfect inchoate titles. Yet, no legislation was necessary to implement U.S. treaty obligations regarding already-perfect titles.[111] Therefore, treaty interpretation, without more, cannot answer the question of whether a particular treaty provision requires legislative implementation, because the Court's decisions in the Louisiana-Florida property cases established that the same treaty provision required legislative implementation in some cases but not others. Hence, it is necessary to shift from a one-step analysis (treaty interpretation alone) to a two-step analysis (treaty interpretation, plus a domestic separation-of-powers analysis) to understand why some treaties require legislative implementation. As the next section contends, Marshall's conclusion in *Foster* that Article 8 required legislative implementation probably rested on certain unstated assumptions about the Constitution's allocation of governmental power to regulate property.

D. The Need for Legislative Implementation

In *Foster*, Marshall stated clearly that legislation was necessary to implement Article 8 of the Florida Treaty.[112] Unfortunately, he did not explain why he thought so. The best explanation is that Marshall believed legislation was necessary because: (1) the plaintiffs held an inchoate title, (2) the treaty obligated the United States to perfect that inchoate title insofar as Spain had a pre-existing duty to perfect the title, and (3) for domestic separation-of-powers reasons, federal legislation was necessary to perfect inchoate titles.

Before I address these points directly, it is helpful to recall two points discussed previously. First, in *Ware v. Hylton*, Justice Iredell stated that executory treaty obligations can be divided into three classes—legislative, executive, and judicial—depending on which branch of government has the domestic constitutional authority to implement the treaty obligation.[113] Second, in his speech in the Jonathan Robbins case, Marshall applied Iredell's two-step approach to support his claim that the president had the domestic constitutional authority to execute Article 27 of the Jay Treaty.[114] Thus, it should come as no surprise that Marshall applied the same two-step approach to analyze the issues in *Foster*. Under Iredell's framework, the question whether a treaty is executed or executory involves treaty interpretation (step one), but the question whether an executory treaty requires legislative, executive, or judicial implementation involves a constitutional separation-of-powers analysis (step two).

Under Marshall's analysis in *Foster*, Article 8 merely granted the plaintiffs an inchoate title. Marshall wrote that this inchoate title was "as obligatory on the United States, as on his catholic majesty."[115] In other words, the United States had a treaty obligation to perfect the plaintiffs' inchoate title "to the same extent that the same grants would be valid if the territories had remained under the dominion of his catholic majesty."[116] Marshall's opinion makes clear that he thought this was an executory treaty obligation. Thus, step one of the two-step analysis is fairly clear. Unfortunately, though, step two of the analysis—the constitutional separation-of-powers analysis—is underdeveloped in *Foster*. In essence, Marshall stated his conclusion that legislative implementation was necessary (rather than judicial or executive implementation), but he did not provide the separation of powers analysis needed to support that conclusion.

Even so, other materials discussed previously help illuminate Marshall's unstated separation-of-powers rationale. Marshall's speech in the Jonathan Robbins case demonstrates that he believed all government actors have a constitutional duty to implement U.S. treaty obligations, insofar as they can do so by acting within the scope of their domestic legal authority.[117] Therefore, Marshall's conclusion in *Foster* that Article 8 required legislative implementation implies that he thought the president and the judiciary lacked the domestic legal authority to convert the plaintiff's inchoate title into a perfect legal title. This conclusion is consistent with later cases in which the Supreme Court held explicitly that Congress was the only institution with the domestic constitutional authority to convert inchoate titles into perfect titles.[118]

The Court never explained why Congress had exclusive constitutional authority to convert inchoate titles into perfect titles. However, Article IV of the Constitution provides textual support for this view. It states: "The Congress shall have Power to dispose of and make all needful Rules and Regulations respecting the Territory or other Property belonging to the United States; and nothing in this Constitution shall be so construed as to Prejudice any Claims of the United States."[119] Consider the situation of individuals who held inchoate titles to land in Louisiana or Florida before the United States acquired sovereignty over those territories. When the relevant treaty conveyed sovereignty over the land, the legal title "was transferred to the United States by the treaty, with the equity attached in the claimant."[120] Hence, upon entry into force of the treaty, the land became subject to Congress's Article IV power to regulate "[p]roperty belonging to the United States."[121] In contrast, if a person held a perfect title before the treaty entered into force, the land never became subject to Congress's Article IV power because the treaty did not disturb perfect titles.

The majority of cases arising under Article 3 of the Louisiana Treaty and Article 8 of the Florida Treaty pitted private claimants against the United States.[122] If the executive or judicial branches awarded legal titles to private claimants on the basis of the treaties themselves, without awaiting congressional guidance, the United States would have lost its legal title to the property. However, Article IV specifies that "nothing in this Constitution shall be so construed as to Prejudice any Claims of the United States,"[123] implying that the executive and judicial branches must exercise their constitutional powers so as not to interfere with Congress's Article IV Property Power. Therefore, if the executive or judicial branch attempted to convert equitable titles into legal titles without awaiting congressional action, they would have prejudiced claims of the United States in contravention of Article IV. This may explain why the Court consistently held that federal legislation was constitutionally required to implement Article 8 of the Florida Treaty and Article 3 of the Louisiana Treaty, as those articles applied to inchoate titles.

In sum, although Marshall's opinion in *Foster* is hardly a model of clarity, Marshall apparently believed that legislation was necessary to implement Article 8 because: the plaintiffs held an inchoate title, the treaty obligated the United States to perfect that inchoate title to the same extent that Spain was obligated to do so, and federal legislation was necessary to perfect the plaintiffs' inchoate title because Article IV granted Congress the exclusive power to dispose of territory belonging to the United States. More importantly, Marshall applied a two-step analysis in *Foster* and *Percheman*, not a one-step analysis. Therefore, insofar as modern lawyers and judges cite *Foster* as authority for a one-step approach, their reliance is misplaced.

Treaties and State Law

This chapter addresses the relationship between treaties and state law, as reflected in legislative, executive, and judicial materials from 1800 to 1945. The record shows that controversies about federalism limits on the Treaty Power arose episodically throughout the period, at least until the Supreme Court decided *Missouri v. Holland* in 1920.[1] Those controversies addressed the constitutional *validity* of treaties that allegedly infringed upon states' rights. Clearly, if a treaty is constitutionally invalid—for whatever reason—it cannot be the "supreme Law of the Land."[2] However, not even the most vehement advocates of states' rights proposed an exception to the treaty supremacy rule for non-self-executing (NSE) treaties. Those who sought to restrict the impact of treaties on state law did not contest the consensus view that the Supremacy Clause creates a mandatory rule—that all valid, ratified treaties supersede conflicting state laws, and that judges are constitutionally bound to apply valid, ratified treaties that conflict with state law. In sum, despite recurring debates about states' rights limitations on the Treaty Power, as of 1945 there was virtually no support for an NSE exception to the Constitution's treaty supremacy rule.

This chapter is divided into four sections. The first analyzes Supreme Court case law during the period. The next addresses judicial decisions in state courts. The third section reviews select congressional materials involving the relationship between treaties and state law. The final section discusses U.S. attorney general opinions concerning the relationship between treaties and state law, including the practice of "executive federalism"—that is, executive branch practice designed to mitigate the tension between treaty supremacy and state autonomy.[3]

I. U.S. SUPREME COURT CASES INVOLVING CONFLICTS BETWEEN TREATIES AND STATE LAW

This book uses the term "treaty supremacy cases" to refer to litigated cases in which one or more parties alleged a conflict between a treaty and state or local legislative or executive action. The Supreme Court decided about sixty treaty supremacy cases between 1800 and 1945. The sixty cases reviewed here constitute a reasonably complete set of all Supreme Court decisions in treaty supremacy cases during the period.[4] None of the sixty cases holds that a treaty is not self-executing.

None of the cases holds that a treaty requires implementing legislation. Perhaps the most surprising fact about these cases is that *none of them even mention the term "self-executing" or "non-self-executing"*! Apparently, during this period, the Court did not believe that the distinction between self-executing and non-self-executing treaties was relevant to treaty supremacy cases.[5]

The Court's standard mode of analysis was simply to address the question of whether there was a conflict between the treaty and state law. (For convenience, I refer simply to conflicts between treaties and state law, but the reader should understand that the term "state law" includes state and local legislative and executive action.) In twenty-six of sixty cases, the Court held that there was a conflict and the treaty prevailed.[6] In twenty-six other cases, the Court held that there was no conflict, so the state could apply its own law.[7] In no case did the Court state or imply that a state or local government would be free to apply its own law in the face of a conflicting NSE treaty.

The Court resolved eight of the sixty cases without specifically deciding whether there was a conflict between the treaty and state law. In all eight cases, the Court's rationale for avoiding the merits of the treaty claim would have applied equally to a statutory claim. For example, the Court dismissed one case for lack of jurisdiction and remanded another for additional fact-finding.[8] In two cases, the Court avoided ruling directly on the treaty claim because the party who invoked the treaty prevailed on other grounds.[9] In *Ward v. Race Horse*, where a defendant raised a treaty-based defense to a state criminal charge, the Court held that the treaty was no longer operative because it had been superseded by a later-enacted federal statute.[10] In *United States v. Texas*, the Court affirmed its jurisdiction over the case, but postponed consideration of the merits to a later date.[11] In *Oetjen v. Central Leather Co.*, the plaintiff invoked a treaty to overcome defendant's state law, contract claim. The Court invoked both the political question doctrine and the act of state doctrine to avoid ruling on the merits of plaintiff's treaty argument.[12] In *Spies v. Illinois*, petitioners sought Supreme Court review of state court convictions and death sentences. Petitioners raised mostly constitutional issues, but added "that they have been denied by the decision of the court below rights guaranteed to them by treaties."[13] The Court noted that the petitioners had failed to identify any particular treaty that applied. Moreover, it added, "no such questions were made and decided in either of the courts below, and they cannot be raised in this court for the first time."[14] None of these cases supports an NSE exception to the treaty supremacy rule. Moreover, no case suggests that there are any limitations on judicial enforcement of treaties that differ from the general limitations on judicial enforcement of federal statutes.

Several of the cases cited above explicitly affirm the principle of treaty supremacy without any caveat to exclude NSE treaties. For example, *Hines v. Davidowitz* affirmed the principle that treaties supersede conflicting state laws. The Court said: "When the national government by treaty or statute has established rules and regulations touching the rights, privileges, obligations or burdens of aliens as such, the treaty or statute is the supreme law of the land. No state can add to or take from the force and effect of such treaty or statute."[15] Many other cases include similar statements.[16] *Owings v. Norwood's Lessee* affirmed the principle that treaties are judicially enforceable. In that case, Chief Justice Marshall said: "Each treaty stipulates something respecting the citizens of the two nations, and gives them rights. Whenever a right grows out of, or is protected by, a treaty, it is sanctioned against all the laws and judicial decisions of the states; and whoever may have this right, it is to be protected."[17] Other cases include similar endorsements of the courts' power and duty to enforce treaties.[18] However, in the sixty cases under review, one searches in vain for even a single sentence suggesting that NSE treaties constitute an exception to the general principle that treaties are "binding alike [on] national and state courts . . . and must be enforced by them."[19] (It bears emphasis that these sixty cases involve alleged conflicts between treaties and state law. Treaties that overlap with federal statutes or Congress's legislative authority are addressed in Chapters 6 and 7.)

Modern commentators routinely cite *Foster v. Neilson* and *The Head Money Cases* to establish the nineteenth-century pedigree of NSE doctrine. Therefore, it is important to consider how the Supreme Court itself applied *Foster* and *Head Money* in the years preceding 1945. Ten of the sixty cases under review include citations to *Foster, Head Money,* or both.[20]

Four of those ten cases provide strong endorsements of the treaty supremacy rule. In *Asakura v. City of Seattle,* the Court cited both *Foster* and *Head Money* in support of this statement:

> The treaty is binding within the state of Washington. The rule of equality established by it cannot be rendered nugatory in any part of the United States by municipal ordinances or state laws. It stands on the same footing of supremacy as do the provisions of the Constitution and laws of the United States. It operates of itself without the aid of any legislation, state or national; and it will be applied and given authoritative effect by the courts.[21]

In *Maiorano v. Baltimore & Ohio R.R. Co.,* the Court cited both *Foster* and *Head Money* in support of the following statement: "We do not deem it necessary to consider the constitutional limits of the treaty-making power. A treaty, within those limits, by the express words of the Constitution, is the supreme law of the land, *binding alike national and state courts,* and is capable of enforcement, and *must be enforced by them* in the litigation of private rights."[22] Similarly, in *Bacardi Corp. v. Domenech,* the Court cited *Head Money* in support of the following statement: "This treaty on ratification became a part of our law. No special legislation in the United States was necessary to make it effective. The treaty bound Puerto Rico and could not be overriden by the Puerto Rican legislature."[23] Finally, in *Hauenstein v. Lynham,* the Court cited *Foster* in support of this statement: "It must always be borne in mind that the Constitution, laws, and treaties of the United States are as much a part of the law of every State as its own local laws and Constitution. This is a fundamental principle in our system of complex national polity. We have no doubt that this treaty is within the treaty-making power conferred by the Constitution. *And it is our duty to give it full effect.*"[24] Thus, *Asakura, Maiorano, Bacardi,* and *Hauenstein* all include emphatic endorsements of the treaty supremacy rule, and all four cases cite *Foster, Head Money,* or both in support of that rule. None of these cases states or implies that there is an exception to the treaty supremacy rule for NSE treaties.[25]

In both *Coffee v. Groover*[26] and *Davis v. Police Jury of Parish of Concordia,*[27] the Court cited *Foster* for the proposition that Spain had no authority to issue land grants in Louisiana after October 1, 1800, because Spain ceded sovereignty to France on that date in the treaty of St. Ildefonso.[28] In *Lattimer v. Poteet,* in a separate concurring opinion, Chief Justice Taney cited *Foster* for the proposition that courts are bound to follow the political branches in their construction of treaty provisions establishing territorial boundaries between sovereigns.[29] *United States v. Texas* involved a dispute over the boundary between the United States and Texas in an area near the Oklahoma border. Texas cited *Foster* for the proposition that determination of the boundary was a political question, not subject to judicial resolution, but the Court ruled that *Foster's* political question holding applied only to boundaries "between independent nations."[30] In *Oetjen v. Central Leather Co.,* the Court cited *Foster* in support of its political question holding.[31] Finally, in *Pigeon River Co. v. Charles W. Cox, Ltd.,* the Court cited *Head Money* in support of the later-in-time rule.[32] None of the cases discussed in this paragraph provide any support for the claim that there is an NSE exception to the Constitution's treaty supremacy rule.

In sum, between 1800 and 1945, Supreme Court decisions in treaty supremacy cases uniformly supported application of the Constitution's treaty supremacy rule, without any exception for NSE treaties.[33] However, it bears emphasis that the cases discussed above all involve alleged conflicts between treaties and state law. Thus, the fact that the Supreme Court cited *Foster* and *Head Money* in support of the principle of treaty supremacy does not mean that modern courts are wrong to cite those cases in support of non-self-execution. Rather, it shows that the Supreme Court before 1945 viewed treaty supremacy cases very differently than it did cases involving the intersection among treaties, federal statutes, and Congress's legislative power.[34] (See Table One, p. 47.)

Professor Bradley cites several Supreme Court decisions from this period that, in his view, support a federalism limitation on the Treaty Power.[35] I will assume, without endorsing his position, that he is correct. Even so, the cases he cites provide no support for an NSE exception to the treaty supremacy rule. *Holden v. Joy* and *Holmes v. Jennison* do not implicate the treaty supremacy rule because no party alleged a conflict between a treaty and state law.[36] *Geofroy v. Riggs* explicitly affirmed the treaty supremacy rule without any exception for NSE treaties.[37] *Prevost v. Greneaux* is best understood in relation to executive federalism; I address it below in that context.[38] Three other cases merit further discussion: *The Passenger Cases, The License Cases,* and *New Orleans v. United States.* All three include statements that, at a minimum, express sympathy for some type of federalism limit on the Treaty Power.[39] For that reason, one might expect to find therein a statement hinting at a possible exception to the treaty supremacy rule. There are no such statements.

In *New Orleans v. United States*,[40] the City of New Orleans tried to sell some vacant lots in the city. The United States sought an injunction "to restrain the city council from selling the land, or doing any other act which shall invade the rightful dominion of the United States over said land."[41] The U.S. government asserted "dominion" on the basis of an 1803 treaty with France. The outcome hinged on whether the king of France had the power to convey the land at issue to the United States. If the king had power to alienate the land, "there can be no doubt that it passed under the treaty to the United States, and they [the federal government] have a right to dispose of it, the same as other public lands."[42] However, after reviewing the history of New Orleans under both French and Spanish law, the Court concluded that the land at issue was not "part of the public domain or crown lands, which the king could sell and convey."[43] Because the city, not the king, had prior possession under French and Spanish law, the city retained possession when the king conveyed "crown lands" to the United States under the treaty. The Court upheld the city's right to sell the vacant lots because the treaty did not convey possession of those lots to the United States. If, however, the treaty had conveyed possession to the United States, the Court left no doubt that the federal government's claim would have prevailed over the city's claim.[44]

In *The License Cases*,[45] petitioners challenged the validity of state laws in Massachusetts, New Hampshire, and Rhode Island that regulated the sale of liquor. The case turned primarily on the Constitution's allocation of authority between state police power and the federal commerce power. However, counsel also argued that certain state laws were invalid because they violated "public treaties of the United States with Holland, France, and other countries, containing stipulations for the admission of spirits into the United States."[46] Six justices wrote opinions in the case; only three of those opinions mentioned the treaty issue. All three agreed that the state laws at issue did not conflict with any treaty cited by appellants.[47] Justice Catron, in a concurring opinion, noted that state law "could not be in violation of any treaty with any foreign power which had been referred to ... because the liquor in question here was proved to be American gin."[48] None of the justices ventured an opinion about how the case would be resolved if a state law did conflict with a treaty.

In *The Passenger Cases*,[49] petitioners challenged the validity of New York and Massachusetts laws that imposed taxes on foreign passengers arriving in their ports. In a 5-4 decision, the Court invalidated the state laws. All five majority justices wrote separate opinions; three of them relied partly on treaties to invalidate the state laws. Justice McLean relied specifically on the Jay Treaty to support his conclusion that the New York law was invalid.[50] Justice Wayne concluded "[t]hat the acts of Massachusetts and New York in question in these cases conflict with treaty stipulations existing between the United States and Great Britain ... and that said laws are therefore unconstitutional and void."[51] Justice Catron also said that the state taxes conflicted with "treaties expressly providing for [the] free and secure admission" of foreigners.[52]

In contrast, Chief Justice Taney's dissenting opinion provided a passionate defense of state sovereignty: "if the people of the several States of this Union

reserved to themselves the power [to tax arriving passengers] ... then any
treaty or law of Congress invading this right ... against the consent of the
State, would be an usurpation of power which this court could neither recognize nor enforce."[53] Shortly after this passage, though, Taney added: "If the
United States have the power, then any legislation by the State in conflict with
a treaty or act of Congress would be void."[54] In short, Chief Justice Taney accepted the strict, dualistic approach that prevailed from the Founding until
World War II. All conflicts between treaties and state law could be divided
into two, and only two, categories. Constitutionally invalid treaties are void.
Constitutionally valid treaties supersede conflicting state laws. From Taney's
perspective—and from the perspective of every other Supreme Court justice
who wrote an opinion on the subject before 1945—the Constitution does
not recognize a category of valid treaties that *do not* supersede conflicting
state laws.

II. STATE COURT CASES INVOLVING CONFLICTS
BETWEEN TREATIES AND STATE LAW

A review of state court decisions in treaty supremacy cases between 1800
and 1945 reveals a pattern that is broadly similar to the pattern for Supreme
Court cases. I reviewed seventy-eight published state court decisions in which
one or more parties alleged a conflict between a treaty and state law.[55] The
seventy-eight selected cases are not a complete set of treaty supremacy cases
before 1945, but there is good reason to believe that the selected cases are
fairly representative.[56] None of the seventy-eight cases holds that a treaty is
not self-executing. None of the cases holds that the treaty at issue requires
implementing legislation to make it operative. None of the seventy-eight cases
holds that the subject treaty is not judicially enforceable. Only one of the
seventy-eight cases actually uses the term "self-executing" anywhere in the
opinion.[57] Thus, subject to caveats discussed below, one could reasonably infer
that state courts before 1945 did not believe that the distinction between self-
executing and non-self-executing treaties was a relevant factor in evaluating
treaty supremacy cases.

   Like the Supreme Court, state courts addressed the vast majority of cases by
deciding whether there was a conflict between the treaty and state law, without regard to whether the treaty was self-executing or non-self-executing. The
data set includes forty-eight cases holding that the treaty superseded state law,[58]
twenty-eight cases holding that there was no conflict between the treaty and
state law,[59] and two cases that the courts resolved without specifically deciding
whether there was a conflict.[60] Both cases where courts refrained from deciding whether the treaty conflicted with state law affirmed the principle of treaty
supremacy. The Supreme Court of Nebraska stated in *Butschkowski v. Brecks*:
"When the facts brought the case within the provisions of this treaty it was the
duty of the court to enforce its terms just as fully as those of a statute of the state.
In so far as the local statutes are in conflict with the treaty, the provisions of

the treaty must govern."[61] Similarly, the Supreme Court of Minnesota stated in *Minnesota Canal & Power Co. v. Pratt*:

> Being the supreme law of the land, the treaty is obligatory upon all the courts and people of the nation. Its prohibitions recognize no state lines. Every citizen of the United States is under a duty to observe and respect the law of the treaty. The petitioner is proceeding to construct dams and reservoirs which it is claimed will result in a violation of the Webster-Ashburton treaty. If this result would follow the construction of such works, we are very clear that the courts of the state should not authorize any proceeding which would result in the violation of the treaty.[62]

Thus, although the courts in *Butschkowski* and *Minnesota Canal & Power Co.* refrained from deciding the merits of the treaty supremacy arguments, their avoidance of the merits did not stem from any reluctance to enforce treaties.[63]

More than half the state court cases include an explicit statement affirming the principle that treaties take precedence over conflicting state laws. For example, the Supreme Court of Appeals of West Virginia said in 1933: "The Constitution of the United States, article 6, makes this treaty a portion of 'the Supreme Law of the Land' ... Consequently the treaty must be given due significance in applying a state statute."[64] The Court of Civil Appeals of Texas said in 1921 that the Constitution grants treaties "the sacredness, dignity, and force of the Constitution ... [Although Texas] has the power and authority to enact any rules and regulations she deems necessary to safeguard the interests of her citizens ... those rules and regulations cannot antagonize and be given higher dignity and power than the Constitution of the United States."[65] The Supreme Court of Tennessee said in 1905: "In case of a conflict between the statutes of a state and the terms of a treaty, the latter must prevail."[66] The Supreme Court of California said in 1855 "that treaties are the supreme law of the land, and that State legislation must yield to them."[67] Notably, the cited cases do not state or imply that there is any exception for NSE treaties. Similarly, dozens of other cases affirm the principle of treaty supremacy without mentioning any exception for NSE treaties.[68]

In addition to affirming the principle that treaties supersede state law, many cases state explicitly that judges have a duty to apply treaties. For example, the Surrogate's Court in Kings County, New York, said in 1939 that treaties are "the supreme law of the land, which *this and every other court is under obligation to effectuate*, and in respect of which no authority for variation or modification exists by any judicial tribunal."[69] The Supreme Court of Errors of Connecticut said in 1922 that treaties "are a part of the supreme law of the land; and ... their *construction and application, whenever necessary, are, as with any other law, to be considered and determined by the courts*."[70] Similarly, the Supreme Court of North Dakota said in 1919 that a valid treaty "supersedes and renders nugatory all conflicting provisions in the laws or Constitution of any state, and in case such conflict arises *it is the duty of the judges of every state to uphold and enforce the treaty provisions*."[71] None of these cases mentions any exclusion for NSE treaties. Moreover, dozens of other cases affirm the principle that judges have a duty to apply treaties without distinguishing between self-executing and non-self-executing treaties.[72]

Thirteen of the seventy-eight cases cite either *Foster v. Neilson*[73] or *The Head Money Cases*,[74] or both.[75] I have already discussed two of those cases: *Butschkowski v. Brecks* and *Minnesota Canal & Power Co. v. Pratt*. Both endorse the treaty supremacy rule. Consider the other eleven cases that cite either *Foster* or *Head Money*. Some of those cases include dicta stating that some treaties require legislative implementation or that there are limitations on judicial enforcement of treaties.[76] Nevertheless, as a group, those eleven cases provide strong support for the principle of treaty supremacy. In eight of eleven cases, the courts applied the treaty to override state law;[77] in the other three cases, courts applied the treaty as a rule of decision, but concluded that the treaty did not conflict with state law.[78] Moreover, ten of the eleven cases include explicit statements endorsing the principle of treaty supremacy.[79] For example, an 1881 decision by the Court of Appeals of Texas that cites *Foster* said:

> [U]nder our Constitution, a public treaty is not merely a compact or bargain to be enforced by the executive and legislative departments of the Federal government, but living laws, operating and binding the judiciary of this State, as much as the Federal and State Constitutions, or the acts of Congress or those of the State Legislature. It follows, therefore, that the judicial tribunals of this State are required to take cognizance of, and give effect to the treaties made by the Federal government with other nations, just as if they composed a part of our Criminal Code. Indeed, they stand, if made in pursuance of the Constitution, upon higher ground than our State Constitution or any act of the Legislature of this State; for, if there be a conflict, the Federal Constitution being supreme, all treaties made in pursuance thereof must of necessity be supreme. Hence in case of conflict State Constitutions and acts of the Legislature must yield. In our opinion, then, the judiciary of this State is bound to take notice of and enforce treaties, treating them as if they composed a part of our Code.[80]

Inasmuch as modern courts routinely cite *Foster* and *Head Money* to support NSE doctrine, one might expect to find that older cases citing *Foster* and *Head Money* would support the proposition that there is an NSE exception to the treaty supremacy rule. However, none of the thirteen cases that cite *Foster* or *Head Money* provides any significant support for an optional treaty supremacy rule. State Supreme Courts in Washington and California cited *Foster* for the proposition that "the Constitution, laws, and treaties of the United States are as much a part of the law of every state as its own local laws and Constitution."[81] The Court of Appeals of Texas cited *Foster* to support the claim that treaties must "be regarded and enforced by the State judiciary as equivalent to acts of the Legislature, without the aid of legislative enactments."[82] A New York court cited *Foster* for the proposition that courts should interpret treaties in accordance with the shared understanding of the parties.[83] Three other courts cited *Foster* to support the idea that some treaties *do not* require implementing legislation;[84] none of those cases held that the treaty at issue *did* require implementing legislation.

Citations to *Head Money*, if anything, provide even less support for an NSE exception to the treaty supremacy rule. The New York Court of Appeals cited *Head Money* to support the claim that a treaty "is paramount to the Constitution and statutes of the state, but not to acts of Congress."[85] The Supreme Judicial Court of Massachusetts cited *Head Money* for the proposition that when "anything in the Constitution or laws of a state are in conflict with a treaty, the latter must prevail."[86] The Supreme Court of Minnesota cited *Head Money* for the idea that "the Constitution ... declares a treaty the law of the land supreme and paramount over state Constitutions and laws."[87] The Supreme Court of Nebraska cited *Head Money* as authority for the statement that "treaties are the supreme law of the land, and that a self-executing treaty requires no legislation to put it into operation."[88] The Supreme Courts of Vermont and Illinois both cited *Head Money* to support judicial enforcement of treaties to protect individual rights.[89] Finally, the New York Court of Appeals cited *Head Money* in support of the following statement: "A treaty has a twofold aspect. In its primary operation, it is a compact between independent states. In its secondary operation, it is a source of private rights for individuals within states."[90] It is difficult to find authority in any of these cases for an NSE exception to the treaty supremacy rule.

The case that comes closest to supporting such an exception is *Little v. Watson.*[91] *Little* involved a dispute over title to property along the border between Maine and Canada. Between 1783 and 1842, the United States and Great Britain had an ongoing dispute about the precise boundary line between Maine and New Brunswick (now part of Canada). The two countries finally settled their differences in the 1842 Webster-Ashburton treaty.[92] Before 1842, Little held a valid title to property in Maine, based on a grant from the State of Massachusetts (when Maine was part of Massachusetts). Watson held title to property in New Brunswick, based on a British grant. Unfortunately, they both held titles to the same property. The treaty made clear that the property would be part of the United States after entry into force of the treaty. Additionally, Article IV specified: "All grants of land heretofore made by either Party, within the limits of the territory which by this Treaty falls within the dominions of the other Party, shall be held valid, ratified, and confirmed to the persons in possession under such grants ...."[93] Inasmuch as Watson was "in possession" under a grant from the province of New Brunswick, the court construed Article IV to mean that the land was "ratified and confirmed" to Watson under the treaty.[94]

Little's attorneys "insisted, that the treaty does not operate upon the title or grant *proprio vigore*, but only as a contract requiring legislative interposition to carry it into effect."[95] In other words, they argued that the treaty was not self-executing. The Supreme Judicial Court of Maine rejected Little's argument. In doing so, the court cited Marshall's opinions in *Foster* and *Percheman* to support its conclusion that Article IV of the Webster-Ashburton treaty was "the supreme law and operative as such" because the treaty "does not contemplate any future act as necessary to the validity, ratification, or confirmation, of the grant."[96] Thus, although the court rejected Little's non-self-execution argument, its opinion arguably implies that self-execution doctrine is relevant to some cases involving alleged conflicts between treaties and state law.

Even so, one is hard pressed to construe *Little* to support an NSE exception to the treaty supremacy rule. The *Little* court stated emphatically that the judiciary had the power and duty to implement Article IV and need not await legislative action to do so. "It is the duty of this court to consider that treaty to be a law operating upon the grant made under the authority of the British government, and declaring, that it shall be held valid, ratified and confirmed."[97] Consequently, Little lost his land because the treaty trumped his state law property right. To add insult to injury, the court rejected his Fifth Amendment takings claim on the ground that the Takings Clause does not constrain the Article II Treaty Power.[98] Thus, on balance, *Little v. Watson* tends to support an expansive view of the Treaty Power and of the judiciary's role in enforcing treaties.

Before we conclude this analysis of state court cases, one other issue merits discussion. Three of the seventy-eight cases include language supporting some type of federalism limit on the Treaty Power: *Succession of Thompson*,[99] *Siemssen v. Bofer*,[100] and *People ex rel. Att'y Gen. v. Naglee*.[101] *Thompson* is a very short opinion that has one sentence supporting federalism limits: "The right claimed is incompatible with the sovereignty of the State whose jurisdiction extends over the property of foreigners as well as citizens found within its limits."[102]

The California Supreme Court decided *Siemssen* one year after *People v. Gerke*.[103] In *Gerke*, the court rejected a states' rights argument challenging the constitutional validity of a bilateral treaty with Prussia. In that context, the court defended a very broad view of the Article II Treaty Power that might be construed to reject any federalism limits on the Treaty Power. Writing separately, Chief Justice Murray said: "I neither concur nor dissent from the opinion of the Court, not having heard the argument or examined the questions sufficiently to arrive at any satisfactory conclusion."[104] Apparently, after further reflection, the chief justice wished he had dissented in *Gerke*. So, in *Siemssen v. Bofer*, he wrote the dissent that he did not write in *Gerke*. *Siemssen* identifies Murray's opinion as "the opinion of the Court."[105] However, Murray devoted most of his opinion in *Siemssen* to explaining why he had "great doubts" about the majority opinion in *Gerke*. In this portion of the opinion, Murray was clearly writing for himself and perhaps one other justice.[106] Finally, after devoting several paragraphs to explaining his disagreement with *Gerke*, Murray turned to the case at hand. Ultimately, the court held in *Siemssen* that there was no conflict between the treaty at issue and California law, so it did not need to decide any other questions.[107] Even so, Murray's critique of *Gerke* offers some ammunition for those who support a limited view of the Treaty Power, because he defended both federalism and separation of powers limits on the Treaty Power.

Naglee also provides some support for federalism limits on the Treaty Power. *Naglee* arose in the context of the California gold rush. The California legislature passed a law "requiring foreigners to pay a license fee of twenty dollars a month for the privilege of working the gold mines in this State."[108] Naglee challenged the validity of the law on both constitutional and treaty grounds. The court concluded that the state law was constitutional and "not repugnant to [the Jay] Treaty."[109] It then added:

> But even if the provisions of the statute did clash with the stipulations of that, or of any other treaty, the conclusion is not deducible that the treaty must, therefore, stand, and the State law give way. . . . When [a treaty] transcends these [constitutional] limits [on the Treaty Power], like an Act of Congress which transcends the constitutional authority of that body, it cannot supersede a State law which enforces or exercises any power of the State not granted away by the Constitution.[110]

The court also quoted Chief Justice Taney as follows: "If the United States have the power, then any legislation by the State in conflict with a treaty or Act of Congress, would be void. And if the States possess it, then any Act on the subject by the General Government, in conflict with the State law, would also be void."[111] As noted previously,[112] Taney's analysis is strictly bimodal. If a treaty is constitutionally invalid, it does not supersede state laws. But if a treaty is constitutionally valid, it does supersede conflicting state laws. Neither Taney nor the California Supreme Court in *Naglee* recognized a category of constitutionally valid treaties that *do not* supersede conflicting state laws.

III. CONGRESSIONAL DELIBERATIONS ABOUT TREATIES AND FEDERALISM

Congress enacted federal trademark legislation in 1881 that was designed primarily to implement U.S. obligations under bilateral trademark treaties. In that context, Congress considered potential federalism limits on treaty-implementing legislation. In 1892, the Senate debated but did not pass proposed criminal legislation to punish individuals who commit crimes against aliens in violation of U.S. treaty obligations. This section analyzes these two episodes from the latter half of the nineteenth century. The analysis sheds light on the nineteenth-century understanding of the relationship between treaty supremacy and self-execution.

A. Legislation to Punish Individuals Who Violate the Treaty Rights of Aliens

As of 1890, the United States was a party to numerous bilateral treaties that promised "protection and security" for foreign nationals in the United States.[113] For example, an 1871 treaty with Italy said: "The citizens of each of the high contracting parties shall receive, in the states and territories of the other, the most constant protection and security for their persons and property, and shall enjoy in this respect the same rights and privileges as are or shall be granted to the natives . . . ."[114] In 1891, in the City of New Orleans, an angry mob "led by the most influential citizens of that great city," broke into a city jail and murdered eleven prisoners who were detained there, including three Italian nationals.[115] Despite repeated protests by the Italian government, the perpetrators were never punished because the federal government lacked the power to prosecute them and the state government lacked the will to do so.

In response to this incident, President Benjamin Harrison urged Congress to enact legislation "to make offenses against the treaty rights of foreigners domiciled in the United States cognizable in the federal courts."[116] The Senate referred the matter to the Committee on Foreign Relations, and the Committee proposed the following legislation:

> That any act committed in any State or Territory of the United States in violation of the rights of a citizen or subject of a foreign country secured to such citizen or subject by treaty between the United States and such foreign country, which act constitutes a crime under the laws of such State or Territory, shall constitute a like crime against the peace and dignity of the United States, punishable in like manner as in the courts of said States or Territories . . . and may be prosecuted in the courts of the United States . . . .[117]

In essence, the proposed statute created a new federal crime consisting of two elements: (1) the act constituted a crime under the laws of the state where it was committed, and (2) the act violated the rights of a foreigner protected under a bilateral treaty.

The proposed legislation generated a lengthy debate in the Senate in which critics challenged the legislation on both constitutional and policy grounds.[118] Notably, both critics and proponents of the legislation shared two underlying assumptions. First, treaty provisions such as the above-quoted provision in the treaty with Italy would supersede any state criminal laws that discriminated against foreigners. No legislation was necessary to supersede such discriminatory state laws. Second, those very same treaty provisions were non-self-executing, in the sense that federal legislation was needed to authorize federal criminal punishment for treaty violations.

Consider, first, the principle of treaty supremacy. Senator Vilas (Wisconsin), an opponent of the legislation, claimed that federal legislation was "entirely unnecessary," because "every citizen of any foreign Government, enjoys now in each of the States of the Union the same measure of protection, the same rights and privileges that are enjoyed by the citizens of that State, so far as its criminal laws are concerned . . . . There has no instance been pointed out to the contrary."[119] Senator Gray (Delaware), another opponent of the legislation, added "that it is quite impossible that any such instance should occur, for no State could discriminate against the citizens or subjects of a foreign country in its penal laws." If it attempted to do so, "[a] treaty which secured to a citizen or subject of the contracting party all the rights of a native would be the supreme law of the land and would control and govern."[120] Senator Vilas agreed that if a state did try to discriminate against foreigners "the attempt would be void by virtue of the supremacy of the treaty law of the country."[121] Notably, no one mentioned the doctrine of self-execution in this context. No one said that the distinction between self-executing and non-self-executing treaties had any bearing on the supremacy of treaties over state law. All participants in the debate agreed that, by virtue of the Supremacy Clause, treaties guaranteeing equal protection for foreigners would supersede state criminal laws that discriminated against foreigners if states enacted such laws.

Senators who opposed the legislation argued that nothing more was necessary to comply with U.S. treaty obligations. The relevant treaties merely promised foreigners the same rights as citizens, and state laws already provided equal rights.[122] In contrast, proponents of the legislation argued that mere formal equality was not sufficient. In their view, the treaties promised protection and security. In the United States, there was an unfortunate history of violence against certain groups of foreigners motivated by anti-foreign sentiment.[123] In light of that history, the United States had a treaty obligation to take affirmative steps to provide meaningful protection for foreigners.[124] The treaties themselves did not authorize the federal executive to prosecute crimes of violence committed against foreigners, nor did the treaties authorize federal courts to exercise jurisdiction over such cases. Hence, supporters of the proposed legislation argued that federal legislation was necessary to confer the requisite authority on federal prosecutors and federal courts.[125]

Opponents of the legislation did not dispute the claim that legislation would be needed to authorize *federal* prosecution and punishment. However, they argued, *federal* prosecution and punishment was not necessary to comply with U.S. treaty obligations because state law already authorized prosecution and punishment for conduct violating the treaty rights of foreigners. The following exchange between Senator Morgan (Alabama) and Senator Gray (Delaware) is instructive. Senator Morgan, who supported the legislation, noted that Italy "had agreed with the Government of the United States that their citizens should have judicial protection, and when they sent their minister here to ask it at the hands of our government we said 'We cannot do it; we have no power in the matter . . . We cannot do anything at all. We have misled you.' "[126] He believed "that we owe it to ourselves, to the honor of our country," to follow through on our treaty commitments.[127] In response, Senator Gray said:

> I will ask the Senator what the situation would have been if the bill which is now before the Senate had been a law at the time of the occurrence in New Orleans? . . . [W]ould not the situation have been that the case would have been presented to a grand jury in a Federal court taken from the same vicinage as the grand jury of the State court, and that when the grand jury of the Federal court should refuse to act . . . as the State grand jury did, the same reply would be made to a foreign country as has already been made?[128]

As Senator Gray's comment illustrates, opponents of the legislation were not persuaded that expansion of federal criminal jurisdiction would enhance protection for the treaty rights of foreigners, given the protection already available under state criminal law. Moreover, several opponents objected to the expansion of federal criminal jurisdiction where such expansion was unnecessary.[129] Their objections were rooted in principles of federalism, but they generally framed those objections as policy arguments rather than constitutional ones.

No one used the term "self-executing" to frame his arguments about the need for implementing legislation. Regardless, it is fair to say that proponents of the legislation believed the relevant treaties were "non-self-executing," in the sense that federal legislation was necessary to ensure U.S. compliance with its treaty obligations. That conclusion was based on a combination of treaty interpretation (treaties require more than mere formal equality), practical policy judgment (we cannot trust the states), and constitutional separation-of-powers principles (legislation is necessary to authorize federal prosecution and punishment).[130] Opponents of the legislation believed that the relevant treaties were "self-executing," in the sense that federal legislation was not necessary to ensure treaty compliance. They did not dispute the relevant separation-of-powers principles, but they disagreed with the legislation's supporters with respect to treaty interpretation and practical policy judgment. Although proponents and critics disagreed about self-execution, they agreed fully on the principle of treaty supremacy. No one argued that legislation was necessary to supersede discriminatory state laws. They all agreed that the relevant treaties would supersede any discriminatory state legislation by virtue of the Supremacy Clause.

B. Legislation to Implement Trademark Treaties

State courts have enforced trademark rights under the common law since the eighteenth century. The first U.S. trademark treaty was an "additional Article" added to a prior commercial treaty with Russia, signed in January 1869.[131] Over the next decade, the United States concluded trademark treaties with Belgium, France, the Austro-Hungarian Empire, the German Empire, Great Britain, and Brazil.[132] Meanwhile, Congress enacted the first federal trademark statutes in 1870 and 1876.[133] However, those statutes had a short shelf life because the Supreme Court ruled in 1879 in the *Trademark Cases* that both statutes were unconstitutional.[134]

In the *Trademark Cases*, the Court considered three different potential sources of congressional power to enact federal trademark legislation. First, it held that the power "to promote the Progress of Science and useful Arts"[135] did not authorize Congress to enact trademark legislation, even though it did authorize Congress to regulate patents and copyrights.[136] Second, the Court ducked the question whether the Commerce Clause might authorize Congress to enact some trademark legislation. Instead, it held more narrowly that the Commerce Clause did not authorize the specific legislation at issue, because that legislation was not "limited to commerce with foreign nations, commerce among the States, and commerce with the Indian tribes."[137] Third, the Court noted in passing that it was "leaving untouched the whole question of the treaty-making power over trade-marks, and of the duty of Congress to pass any laws necessary to carry treaties into effect."[138] The Court's decision left the United States "without any [federal] statutory rules for registration and protection of trade-mark rights."[139]

However, the trademark treaties noted above remained in force. Broadly speaking, those treaties contained three types of provisions. First, the treaties promised that the citizens of U.S. treaty partners "shall enjoy in the United States, the same protection as native citizens" with respect to trademarks.[140] Even without such treaty provisions, courts ruled that aliens could enforce their trademark rights in U.S. courts in precisely the same way as U.S. citizens. For example, in a trademark case involving a British plaintiff, before there was a trademark treaty with Britain, Justice Story said: "There is no difference between the case of a citizen and that of an alien friend where his rights are openly violated."[141] Absent treaty stipulations, though, states could have enacted legislation to discriminate between citizens and noncitizens with respect to trademark rights. The treaties effectively barred such discriminatory state legislation. In this respect, Congressman Hammond, the key architect of federal trademark legislation, recognized that the treaties operated *"proprio vigore"* by virtue of the Supremacy Clause, and no legislation was necessary to grant foreigners equal rights, or to override discriminatory state laws.[142]

Second, some of the treaties included language specifying that foreigners who wanted to "secure" their trademark rights in the United States were required to register their trademarks with the U.S. Patent Office in Washington, DC.[143] The statute enacted by Congress in 1870 established an administrative procedure that foreigners could utilize to do so. However, the Supreme Court invalidated that statute in the *Trademark Cases.* Moreover, the registration provisions of the treaties were clearly non-self-executing, in the sense that the treaties themselves did not purport to create a federal administrative procedure for trademark registration. Thus, the Court's decision in the *Trademark Cases* left a gap in treaty implementation because the citizens of U.S. treaty partners no longer had an available mechanism to register their trademarks. Legislation enacted by Congress in 1881 was designed to fill that gap in order to ensure fulfillment of U.S. treaty obligations.[144] The House Committee Report makes clear that Congress relied expressly on its power under the Necessary and Proper Clause to implement treaties as the source of its constitutional authority to enact the legislation.[145]

To reiterate, there was broad consensus in Congress that *legislation was needed* to implement the treaties' trademark registration provisions (which operated exclusively at the federal level), and *legislation was not needed* to implement the treaties' non-discrimination provisions (which barred discriminatory state legislation). Issues regarding legislative implementation of a third type of treaty provision were more controversial. The trademark treaties typically included language obligating the United States to "prohibit" trademark counterfeiting, or specifying that "reproduction" of protected trademarks was "forbidden."[146] Prior statutes provided two types of remedies or sanctions for violations of those prohibitions. First, the 1870 statute authorized civil actions for damages and/or injunctive relief.[147] Second, the 1876 statute imposed federal criminal penalties for certain trademark violations.[148] However, the Supreme Court invalidated both statutes in the *Trademark Cases*. Hence, in its deliberations over new trademark legislation in 1879–1881, Congress had to decide how best to implement the treaties' prohibitions on counterfeiting and unauthorized reproduction. The minimalist option would have been for Congress to do nothing, leaving implementation entirely to the states. The maximalist option would have been to revive both the civil remedies from the 1870 statute and the criminal penalties from the 1876 statute. In assessing these and other options, Congress weighed both constitutional and treaty interpretation issues.

The House referred the matter to the Judiciary Committee, which in turn referred it to a subcommittee composed of Representatives Nathaniel Hammond, Edward Robertson, and Frank Hurd.[149] Representative Hammond, the former attorney general of Georgia and a recognized authority on constitutional law, took a leading role in drafting legislation.[150] Relying on his expertise, the House Judiciary Committee decided that Congress's Commerce Power could not support federal trademark legislation. In contrast, the Committee concluded that Congress's treaty-implementing power under the Necessary and Proper Clause did support legislation, provided that such legislation was restricted to trademarks used in commerce with foreign nations or with Indian tribes.[151] The legislation approved by Congress incorporated that restriction.[152]

Having chosen to rely on Congress's treaty-implementing power, the House Judiciary Committee also had to decide whether to revive the civil and criminal remedies contained in the prior statutes. The Committee bill reported to Congress included both.[153] However, when he presented the bill to the House, Representative Hammond proposed striking the criminal penalties. He argued that such penalties were not necessary to implement U.S. treaty obligations, and that "it is bad policy to increase the criminal jurisdiction of the United States courts, unless it be necessary to maintain the power, dignity, or purity of the Government or some of its departments."[154] The final legislation did not include criminal penalties, but it did authorize trademark owners harmed by the "wrongful use" of their trademarks to sue in federal court for both damages and injunctive relief.[155] Absent relevant treaty provisions, matters involving damages and injunctive relief for violations of trademark rights would have been left entirely to state law—at least if the Committee was right to conclude that the Commerce Clause, as construed in the nineteenth century, did not authorize federal trademark legislation. Therefore, Congress's decision to create a federal cause of action for trademark owners manifests its belief that the trademark treaties, combined with the Necessary and Proper Clause, provided a basis for Congress to enact federal legislation that would have exceeded the scope of its legislative powers in the absence of relevant treaty provisions.

In sum, congressional deliberations over trademark legislation and legislation to punish attacks against foreigners reveal important lessons about the nineteenth century conceptual framework for thinking about treaty supremacy and self-execution. In both cases, Congress assumed that legislation was not necessary to supersede conflicting state laws because the relevant treaties superseded conflicting state laws by the force of the Supremacy Clause. However, legislation was necessary to create a federal registration system for trademarks, to create a federal cause of action for trademark owners, and to create federal criminal penalties for individuals who violated the treaty rights of foreigners (although Congress chose not to enact such penalties). Thus, in the nineteenth-century conceptual framework, a treaty that was non-self-executing for some purposes still superseded conflicting state laws under the Supremacy Clause.

IV. EXECUTIVE BRANCH MATERIALS

A. U.S. Attorney General Opinions

During the nineteenth century, four different U.S. attorney generals issued a total of six official opinions concerning the relationship between treaties and state law.[156] Two of those opinions defended strict federalism limits on the Treaty Power. In 1819, Attorney General William Wirt concluded that an alien in the United States "cannot inherit real or fast property at all: nor is there any power in the general government, as I conceive, to alter, either by law or treaty, the provisions of the particular States in this respect."[157] In 1831, Attorney General Berrien decided that "an act of the legislature of South Carolina, which inhibits the entrance of free persons of color into that State, is . . . a justifiable exercise of the reserved powers of that State, and . . . that Congress are under a constitutional obligation to respect it in the formation of treaties, and in the enactment of laws."[158]

Three other opinions endorsed a strong nationalist view of the Treaty Power, with few (if any) federalism-based limits. Writing in 1824, Attorney General Wirt decided that the South Carolina law restricting entrance of free blacks into the state was void because, inter alia, it conflicted with a treaty with Great Britain.[159] Then, in the 1850s, Attorney General Cushing effectively overruled Wirt's prior view about alien inheritance rights, concluding that a bilateral treaty with Prussia that protected the right of aliens to inherit property superseded conflicting state laws.[160] Finally, in 1898, Attorney General Griggs decided "that the United States has power to enter into treaty stipulations with Great Britain for the regulation of the fisheries in the waters of the United States and Canada along the international boundary."[161] One opinion did not take a strong stand either way, but is best construed to be consistent with the nationalist view.[162]

The key point, for present purposes, is that none of the six opinions says anything about self-execution or non-self-execution. They all assume, at least implicitly, that the distinction between self-executing and non-self-executing treaties is simply not relevant to the question presented. Although the opinions express sharply contrasting views about federalism limits on the Treaty Power, they all agree, at least implicitly, that valid treaties supersede conflicting state laws, and invalid treaties do not supersede conflicting state laws. None of the opinions acknowledges the existence of a third category of valid, ratified treaties that *do not* supersede conflicting state laws. Thus, the attorney general opinions are consistent with the consensus view reflected in judicial opinions: before 1945, there was no NSE exception to the Constitution's treaty supremacy rule.

B. Executive Federalism

Although the courts routinely applied the treaty supremacy principle to override state laws, the executive branch developed creative approaches to treaty drafting that helped soften the impact of treaty supremacy on state autonomy. An 1853 Consular Convention with France provides a good example.[163] Article 7 protected the right of U.S. and French citizens to own property in the territory of the other country and "to dispose of it as they may please ... by donation, testament or otherwise."[164] The final text was the product of an extended negotiating process that involved the French ambassador in Washington, three U.S. secretaries of state, the U.S. Senate, and the French Minister of Foreign Affairs in Paris.[165] The French ambassador in Washington, Count Eugene de Sartiges, initially proposed the following language: "In those States of the Union where the laws forbid a foreigner to become the owner of real estate, a period of three years shall be given to the French heirs to dispose of the real property of the inheritances which may fall to them."[166] The draft language acknowledged the fact that many states had laws prohibiting noncitizens from owning real estate, but protected the ability of French heirs to collect the value of their inheritance by selling land they inherited. This was a fairly typical provision in treaties at that time.[167] Such provisions accommodated federalism concerns by framing international obligations in a way that incorporated state law as a limitation on the scope of the international obligation.

After Ambassador Sartiges proposed the language quoted above, the French Ministry of Foreign Affairs in Paris apparently decided that the proposed draft did not go far enough. Three months after submitting his initial draft to Secretary of State Daniel Webster, Sartiges wrote to Acting Secretary of State Charles Conrad, who had replaced Webster due to the latter's failing health, "that my Government had found insufficient the guaranties stipulated by Article 7" of the prior draft.[168] In its place, he proposed the following language: "French persons shall enjoy the right to own movable and immovable property in the United States on the same basis and in the same way as citizens of the United States. . . . Citizens of the United States shall reciprocally enjoy [the same rights] in France."[169] In explaining this proposal, Sartiges noted that France had changed its law in 1819 to repeal the old rule that prohibited foreigners from inheriting and owning land in France. Thus, he said, "[t]his new draft is based on the principle of an exact reciprocity." He added: "Distinctions of nationality have ... no longer any purpose. I would even say that they are as injurious as they are inequitable."[170]

A few weeks after Sartiges submitted his second draft, Edward Everett became secretary of state. The record of conversations between Everett and Sartiges is not available, but Everett may have told Sartiges that the United States could not or would not agree to the proposed second draft, because state law governed ownership of real property in the United States.[171] In any case, the following (third) draft emerged from their negotiations: "*In all the States of the Union whose existing laws permit it*, Frenchmen shall enjoy the right of possessing personal and real property by the same title and in the same manner as the citizens of the United States."[172] The agreed text also said: "In like manner, but with the reservation of the ulterior right of establishing reciprocity . . . the Government of France accords to the citizens of the United States the same rights within its territory in respect to real and personal property and to inheritance, as are enjoyed there by its own citizens."[173] Thus, Frenchmen in the United States would be granted the same rights as citizens, insofar as state law permitted, and U.S. citizens in France would be granted the same rights as French citizens. However, France reserved the right to retaliate against citizens of U.S. states that discriminated against foreigners.

The U.S. Senate was not fully satisfied with this solution. The Senate amended the language agreed between Everett and Sartiges so that the final version states: "In all the States of the Union whose existing laws permit it, *so long and to the same extent as the said laws shall remain in force*, Frenchmen shall enjoy the right of possessing personal and real property by the same title and in the same manner as the citizens of the United States."[174] Apparently, some senators were concerned that the prior draft might be construed as a constraint on the freedom of states to change their laws.[175] Thus, the final version effectively allows states that had abolished prohibitions on alien land ownership to reintroduce such prohibitions in the future without violating the treaty.[176] Several years after the treaty with France was consummated, the Supreme Court applied it in *Prevost v. Greneaux*.[177] After concluding that Louisiana law did not conflict with the treaty, Chief Justice Taney added: "In affirming this judgment, it is proper to say that the obligation of the treaty and its operation in the State, after it was made, depend upon the laws of Louisiana."[178]

One could argue that the language and history of the 1853 Consular Convention, together with Taney's comment in *Prevost*, provide an important precedent for the modern practice of attaching non-self-executing declarations ("NSE declarations") to treaties.[179] According to one interpretation, NSE declarations permit states to apply their own laws, notwithstanding conflicting treaty obligations.[180] Similarly, although the Supremacy Clause says that treaties supersede conflicting state laws, the 1853 Convention is cleverly drafted to preserve the continued operation of state laws, despite the treaty. Moreover, Taney's statement in *Prevost* clearly shows that the Supreme Court endorsed this practice.[181]

The preceding argument is unpersuasive. To understand why, it is helpful to compare the actual language of the 1853 Convention with modern NSE doctrine. The actual treaty language, with the words rearranged to facilitate comparison, says: "Frenchmen shall enjoy the right of possessing . . . real property . . . in the same manner as the citizens of the United States . . . [i]n all the States of the Union whose . . . laws permit it." Compare this language to the following hypothetical treaty provision: "Frenchmen shall enjoy the right of possessing real property in the same manner as the citizens of the United States. However, as a matter of domestic law, this treaty shall not supersede conflicting state laws in the United States." The second sentence of the hypothetical treaty provision is an NSE clause. The NSE clause differs from the 1853 Convention in three important respects. First, the actual treaty language—"in all the States of the Union . . . whose laws permit it"—operated on the international plane to limit the scope of the international obligation that the United States undertook in the treaty. In contrast, the hypothetical NSE clause does not operate on the international plane at all. It does not alter the nature of the international obligation in any way.[182]

The second point follows from the first. Under the actual treaty, if State A passed a law to prohibit ownership of property by French citizens, the United States would not be in violation of its treaty obligation. Indeed, the treaty language was drafted purposely to ensure that the United States would not be violating its treaty obligation in those circumstances. Thus, the actual treaty language is fully consistent with the Framers' primary goal when they drafted the Supremacy Clause—to prevent states from taking actions that trigger a breach of U.S. treaty obligations.[183] In contrast, under the hypothetical treaty language, if State A passed a law to prohibit ownership of property by French citizens, the United States would be in violation of its treaty obligation, because the second sentence does not limit the scope of the international obligation expressed in the first sentence. Thus, the hypothetical NSE clause impedes accomplishment of the primary goal underlying the Supremacy Clause by permitting states to engage in conduct that triggers a breach of U.S. treaty obligations.

Third, the actual treaty language does not conflict with the original understanding of the Supremacy Clause. As discussed in Chapter 1, the Supremacy Clause expresses a conflict of laws rule: *if there is a conflict* between the treaty and state law, the treaty takes precedence.[184] Article 7 of the 1853 Convention, as written, effectively eliminated the possibility of a conflict between the treaty obligation and state law by incorporating state law as a limitation on the scope of the international obligation. Inasmuch as the treaty language eliminated the possibility of a conflict, there was no conflict to which the Supremacy Clause could apply. In contrast, the hypothetical NSE clause does not eliminate conflicts between the treaty obligation and state law. If State A prohibited ownership of property by French citizens, then under the hypothetical treaty provision there would be a conflict between state law and the treaty obligation to grant Frenchmen equal property rights. In those circumstances, the treaty supremacy rule says that the treaty takes precedence over state law, but the NSE clause says that state law takes precedence over the treaty. Thus, the NSE clause conflicts directly with the original understanding of the Supremacy Clause.

In making this argument, I am not expressing a view about whether the hypothetical NSE clause is constitutionally valid. Rather, my purpose is to show that the type of executive treaty practice reflected in Article 7 of the 1853 Convention with France, and in other similar treaty provisions from that era, is quite different from the modern practice of attaching NSE declarations to treaties. Therefore, assuming that executive branch practice is an important source of precedent with respect to treaties, the type of federalism clause incorporated in Article 7 of the 1853 Convention does not provide a meaningful precedent for modern NSE declarations. More broadly, just as the judicial record before 1945 reveals a stark absence of precedents to support an NSE exception to the treaty supremacy rule, the record of executive branch practice before 1945 reveals an absence of precedents to support the modern practice of attaching NSE declarations to treaties (assuming that NSE declarations mean that treaties do not supersede conflicting state laws).

In sum, this chapter has presented a thorough review of legislative, executive, and judicial materials from 1800 to 1945 involving the relationship between treaties and state law. The historical materials demonstrate that, as of 1945, there was no significant support for an NSE exception to the Constitution's treaty supremacy rule.

6

Self-Execution in the Political Branches

The Supremacy Clause provides a specific rule for resolving conflicts between treaties and state law. However, the Constitution does not include any specific textual rule for resolving conflicts between treaties and federal statutes. In the early nineteenth century, members of Congress and others engaged in episodic debates about the proper rule for resolving conflicts between treaties and federal statutes.[1] The Supreme Court finally settled the matter in 1871 when it declared that "[a] treaty may supersede a prior act of Congress, and an act of Congress may supersede a prior treaty."[2] The so-called "later-in-time" rule has remained a fixed feature of U.S. foreign affairs law since that time.

One related question has proved to be more intractable: Who has the legal authority and/or legal duty to implement treaties that regulate matters within the scope of Congress's legislative powers? There are two distinct aspects to this question. First, to what extent does the Constitution itself assign the president the power and/or duty to implement such treaties, without awaiting specific legislative authorization? Second, what role do courts play in implementing such treaties? Over time, legislative, executive, and judicial officers developed the doctrine of self-executing and non-self-executing treaties to help address these questions. Unfortunately, lawyers, judges, and scholars have applied self-execution doctrine to address both aspects of the question, without always distinguishing clearly between the congressional-executive and political-judicial concepts of self-execution. The tendency to conflate these two concepts has been a persistent source of confusion in self-execution doctrine, at least since the late nineteenth century.

Before World II, though, debates about self-execution—in Congress, in the executive branch, and in the courts—dealt almost exclusively with treaties that regulated matters within the scope of Congress's legislative powers, *and outside the scope of the states' legislative powers*. Therefore, although the doctrine of self-execution was an ongoing source of confusion and disagreement, the disagreement did not extend to matters within the scope of the Constitution's treaty supremacy rule. Before World War II, the rule codified in the Supremacy Clause—that *all* valid, ratified treaties supersede conflicting state law—remained largely unaffected by various controversies surrounding self-execution doctrine.

Chapters 6 and 7 address the implementation and enforcement of treaties that regulate matters within the scope of Congress's legislative powers. This chapter summarizes key legislative and executive materials between 1800 and 1945. Chapter 7 analyzes relevant judicial decisions. Chapter 6 is divided into three sections. The first discusses congressional debates about self-execution. The second addresses the practice of incorporating "non-self-execution" clauses into treaties during this period. The final section analyzes attorney general opinions related to self-execution.

I. CONGRESSIONAL DEBATES ABOUT SELF-EXECUTION

We saw in Chapter 3 that during legislative debates about the Jay Treaty, Federalists and Republicans disagreed vehemently about which treaties are constitutionally non-self-executing. Republicans argued, in effect, that all treaties regulating matters within the scope of Congress's legislative powers are constitutionally non-self-executing. In contrast, Federalists argued that implementing legislation was not constitutionally required for any treaties, except insofar as treaty implementation required an appropriation of funds.[3]

Congress replayed a similar debate twenty years later when President James Madison asked Congress to enact legislation to implement portions of an 1815 commercial treaty with Great Britain.[4] (Recall that Madison was a leading Republican in the House of Representatives during the Jay Treaty debates.) The 1815 treaty included three substantive articles that required some domestic implementation in the United States: Articles 1, 2, and 4.[5] Notably, when Congressman John Forsyth introduced implementing legislation in the House of Representatives, his proposed legislation dealt solely with Article 2.[6] Articles 1 and 4 both addressed matters that intersected with state law.[7] In 1815–1816, nobody proposed legislation to implement the treaty provisions that overlapped with areas of state regulatory authority. The proposed legislation focused solely on Article 2, which concerned matters subject to exclusive federal control.

Article 2 addressed various types of charges—duties, bounties, and drawbacks—applied to imports of goods into the United States, and exports of goods from the United States. Article 2 also promised that British vessels in U.S. ports would not be charged higher tonnage fees than were charged for U.S. vessels in U.S. ports. (Reciprocal provisions addressed imports into and exports from Britain and its territories, as well as tonnage fees in British ports.) Article I of the Constitution expressly prohibits the states from laying "any Imposts or Duties on Imports or Exports," and from imposing "any duty of Tonnage," absent congressional consent.[8] Article I also grants Congress the "Power to lay and collect Taxes, Duties, Imposts and Excises."[9] Accordingly, all agreed that Article 2 addressed matters subject to exclusive national control. They disagreed, though, about whether implementing legislation was *constitutionally* required to implement Article 2.[10] Despite internal disagreements in both the House and the Senate, most senators believed that implementing legislation was not necessary because the treaty itself repealed any prior federal statutes inconsistent with the treaty.[11] Most House members, in contrast, endorsed the view that implementing legislation was constitutionally required.[12]

Representatives who advocated legislation offered at least three different arguments in support of their view that implementing legislation was constitutionally required. Representative Philip Barbour, who later became a Supreme Court justice, said: "whenever a treaty operates upon a subject, which . . . is amongst the enumerated powers of legislation, delegated by the Constitution to Congress—that in such case, the assent and cooperation of Congress are necessary to give effect to such treaty."[13] His position would deny the existence of any "concurrent" powers. Under his view, all of Congress's legislative powers are "exclusive" powers, meaning that no treaty has the force of law domestically if it concerns a matter within the scope of Congress's enumerated powers. (The terms "concurrent" and "exclusive" powers are explained in Chapter 3.[14]) Representative John Forsyth advocated a somewhat more moderate position. "Whenever a treaty contains anything contrary to . . . existing laws, the laws must be repealed by Congress before the engagement can be complied with; because . . . [a] law can be repealed only by the authority which enacted it."[15] His view admitted the possibility that some of Congress's legislative powers may be concurrent rather than exclusive. However, Forsyth's position rejected the later-in-time rule, at least insofar as that rule applies to a later treaty and an earlier statute.

Representative Henry St. George Tucker advanced a different argument. Although Tucker was inclined to agree with Barbour's view,[16] his statement offered a more moderate defense of the need for legislation in this particular case. First, he noted that many treaties promise future action by the government. In such a case, "the stipulations of the contract shall be carried into effect by that department of the Government within whose province they may respectively fall."[17] If the treaty promises action of an executive nature, "the Executive alone may carry the treaty into full and complete operation." However, "[i]f it be agreed that something shall be done, which falls within the province of the legislative power, then the legislative aid become[s] necessary."[18] Thus, Tucker clearly advocated a two-step approach to self-execution analysis, similar to the two-step approach endorsed by Justice Iredell in *Ware v. Hylton* and applied by Chief Justice Marshall in *Foster v. Neilson*.[19] Under the two-step approach, the conclusion that a treaty is executory—in the sense that future action is needed to implement it—*does not* mean that implementing legislation is required. Rather, the conclusion that a treaty is executory necessitates a domestic separation-of-powers analysis to determine which branch of government has the requisite authority to implement the treaty.

Tucker did not offer a comprehensive view about which types of treaty provisions require legislative action and which types require executive action. However, he took a strong stand on one point: matters involving taxation and revenue are inherently legislative.

> Is there, I will ask, any subject of legislation, Mr. Speaker, in which this House has greater interest or greater Constitutional control than that which is in anywise connected with taxation and revenue? . . . The treaty engages that a

part of our revenues, which were heretofore raised from taxes and duties on British ships, shall be taken from them, and of course shall be raised from other objects. As we must raise the amount, and can no longer derive it from British vessels, we must draw it ... from some other source .... A law in this case is, therefore, peculiarly necessary to remove those duties which the legislative body alone can impose, and alone can abrogate.[20]

Here was the seed of an idea for distinguishing between concurrent and exclusive powers. The treaty provision at issue fell on the "exclusive" side of the line because, as a practical matter, it required Congress to enact legislation to raise additional revenue to compensate for the revenue that would be lost as a result of the treaty. I refer below to the Tucker theory to express the idea that implementing legislation is constitutionally required for treaty provisions affecting taxation and revenue.

The Senate was not persuaded that legislation was necessary. Senator James Barbour, Representative Philip Barbour's brother, explained the dominant Senate view: "[T]he treaty, upon the exchange of its ratification, did, of itself, repeal any commercial regulation, incompatible with its provisions, existing in our municipal code."[21] Senator Barbour acknowledged that legislation is necessary to implement some treaties. However, he said, "[n]o legislative sanction is necessary, if the treaty be capable of self-execution."[22] (This appears to be the first recorded use of the term "self-execution" in conjunction with "treaty." Senator Barbour made this statement in January 1816, more than a decade before the Supreme Court decided *Foster*.) He then identified three types of treaty provisions for which implementing legislation is constitutionally necessary: those requiring criminal penalties,[23] those requiring an appropriation of money,[24] and any treaty that would commit the nation to war.[25] Barbour also endorsed the last-in-time rule: "If they have exercised their respective powers on the same subject, the last act, whether by the Legislature or the treaty-making power, abrogates a former one."[26]

Consistent with these competing views about whether Article 2 of the 1815 treaty required implementing legislation, the two chambers produced very different bills. The draft Senate bill said: "That so much of any act or acts as is contrary to the provisions of the Convention ... shall be deemed and taken to be of no force or effect."[27] The Senate bill merely declared the effect of the treaty; it did not purport to repeal any prior law because, in the Senate's view, the treaty had already repealed prior conflicting statutes. The House bill, by contrast, contained four discrete sections corresponding to four different paragraphs in Article 2 of the treaty, each of which addressed a different type of fee or charge on imports, exports, or vessels entering ports.[28] Eventually, the House and Senate appointed a conference committee to work out a compromise. In that context, the House conferees prepared a statement for their Senate colleagues. That statement said, in part:

[T]here is no irreconcilable difference between the two branches of the Legislature.... [The House] admit[s], that to some, nay many treaties, no legislative sanction is required, no legislative aid is necessary.... [The Senate] are believed to acknowledge the necessity of legislative enactment to carry into execution all treaties which contain stipulations requiring appropriations.... [T]here is no difference in principle between the Houses; the difference is only in the application of the principle.[29]

In light of disagreements about "the application of the principle," Congressman Forsyth, speaking on behalf of the House, argued that "it is safer, in every doubtful case, to legislate."[30] To understand Forsyth's argument, it is important to note that the specific treaty provisions at issue related to import duties. Prior federal statutes required customs collectors to collect duties on British imports; the treaty promised to reduce those duties. If Congress failed to enact legislation, the president would still need to instruct the customs collectors whether to collect higher duties, as required by the prior statute, or lower duties, as stipulated in the treaty. "[H]e would be reduced to the alternative of breaking the Constitution or the treaty. He must either set at naught the supreme law of the land, or jeopardize the national faith and the national peace."[31] From Forsyth's perspective, the president would be "breaking the Constitution" if he instructed customs collectors to violate the statute by reducing import duties. But he would be violating the treaty if he instructed them to continue collecting higher duties, as required by the statute. Therefore, Forsyth believed, legislation was needed to provide clear guidance to the president and subordinate executive officials so that they did not have to choose between "breaking the Constitution or the treaty."

Ultimately, the conferees agreed on a bill that was much closer to the original Senate version than the House version. In that respect, the Senate arguably scored an important victory for a narrow view of the scope of Congress's exclusive legislative powers and a correspondingly broad view of concurrent powers—and with that, a broad view of the category of self-executing treaties. On the other hand, the Senate agreed to enact legislation on a topic where senators "doubted whether any act of legislation was necessary."[32] Moreover, despite Senate warnings that the legislation should not be viewed as a precedent, it soon became a routine matter for Congress to enact implementing legislation for most treaties that had the effect of reducing revenues.[33] Hence, Congressman Tucker's view that implementing legislation was "peculiarly necessary" for treaties affecting taxation or revenue was vindicated to some extent.

The debate between the House and the Senate about which treaties require implementing legislation did not end in 1816. Instead, the controversy reappeared several times over the course of the nineteenth century. The two most notable episodes involved the 1867 treaty for the acquisition of Alaska from Russia,[34] and an 1884 convention with the Kingdom of Hawaii.[35] In the Alaska treaty, the United States agreed to pay "his Majesty the Emperor of all the Russias ... seven million two hundred thousand dollars in gold."[36] The treaty entered into force in June 1867. The House passed a bill one year later that said in relevant part:

Whereas ... the subjects thus embraced in the stipulations of said treaty are among the subjects which by the Constitution of the United States are submitted to the power of Congress and over which Congress has jurisdiction;

and it being for such reason necessary that the consent of Congress should be given to said stipulation before the same can have full force and effect . . . . Therefore, Be it enacted, That the assent of Congress is hereby given to the stipulations of said treaty.[37]

This statement in the House bill was largely symbolic. By the time the House passed the bill, the treaty had already been in force for more than one year, and the United States had already taken possession of Alaska. Regardless, the Senate would not agree to any law stipulating that Congress gave its "consent" to the treaty. Ultimately, the final legislation appropriated the money needed "to fulfil stipulations contained in the sixth article of the treaty with Russia,"[38] but Congress did not "consent" to the treaty, because the treaty had already entered into force.

The House and Senate reached a similar standoff two decades later concerning a commercial treaty with Hawaii. The controversial treaty, signed in December 1884, merely extended the duration of a prior treaty between the United States and Hawaii, signed in 1875. To understand the controversy that emerged in the 1880s, it is necessary first to discuss the earlier treaty. In Article I of the 1875 treaty, the United States agreed "to admit all the articles named in the following schedule, the same being the growth and manufacture or produce of the Hawaiian Islands, into all the ports of the United States free of duty."[39] Article V, however, stipulated that the treaty would not "take effect . . . until a law to carry it into operation shall have been passed by the Congress of the United States of America."[40] Congress passed the requisite legislation in August 1876,[41] and the two parties signed a Protocol on September 9, 1876, specifying that the treaty "will take effect on the date hereof."[42] The House of Representatives was quite satisfied with this arrangement, because it meant that the House voted to approve domestic implementing legislation before the treaty became legally effective on the international plane.

The 1875 treaty with Hawaii expired in 1883. To continue the arrangement for duty-free imports, the United States and Hawaii signed a new treaty in December 1884.[43] Unlike the earlier one, the 1884 treaty *did not* include a provision that required implementing legislation as a condition precedent for the treaty to take effect internationally. The Senate consented to ratification on January 20, 1887.[44] Shortly thereafter, the House adopted a resolution instructing the House Judiciary Committee to report "as soon as possible whether a treaty which involves the rate of duty to be imposed on any article or the admission of any article free of duty can be valid and binding without the concurrence of the House of Representatives, and how far the power conferred on the House by the Constitution . . . to originate measures to lay and collect duties can be controlled by the treaty-making power."[45] Two months later, Representative John Randolph Tucker—Chairman of the Judiciary Committee, and grandson of the congressman who participated in debates about the 1815 treaty with Britain—delivered the requested report to the House on behalf of the Judiciary Committee.[46] The report endorsed the Tucker theory first articulated by Representative Tucker's grandfather. It concluded "[t]hat the President, by and with the advice and consent of the Senate, cannot negotiate a treaty which shall be binding on the United States, whereby duties on imports are to be regulated ... without the sanction of an act of Congress."[47] Nevertheless, the treaty took effect later that year, and Congress never enacted legislation to implement it.[48] Thus, the controversy over the Hawaii treaty ultimately showed that the executive branch believed it had the authority to execute at least some treaties regulating import duties without awaiting implementing legislation.

The congressional debates about self-execution demonstrate that Congress—unlike the courts—was not at all confused about the theoretical basis for NSE doctrine. Members of Congress generally understood self-execution in terms of the congressional-executive concept. They recognized that NSE doctrine was a constitutional doctrine, not a treaty interpretation doctrine. Specifically, it was a federal separation-of-powers doctrine designed to accomplish two goals: to protect the lawmaking prerogatives of the House of Representatives and to limit the power of federal executive officers to implement treaties, especially treaties affecting import duties. Members of Congress disagreed among themselves about which of the Article I legislative powers were exclusive powers and which were concurrent powers. However, they agreed that treaties within the scope of Congress's exclusive powers were constitutionally non-self-executing.

It is instructive to compare the congressional debates discussed in this section with the congressional debates addressed in Chapter 5. The legislative materials discussed in Chapter 5 related to trademark treaties and treaties guaranteeing security and protection for foreigners—both areas that overlapped with state law. In that context, the characterization of treaty provisions as self-executing or non-self-executing was not controversial. Instead, the controversy focused on whether Congress had power to legislate in areas otherwise governed by state law, and if so whether Congress should refrain from enacting certain types of regulations out of respect for state autonomy.[49]

In contrast, the legislative materials discussed in this chapter relate to treaties addressing matters subject to exclusive federal control. Indeed, before World War II, the *only* types of treaty provisions that sparked major controversies about self-execution in Congress were those related to federal revenues and expenses. Debates over the Jay Treaty and the Alaska Treaty generated a lot of wide-ranging rhetoric, but the real point in controversy in both cases was whether the House was constitutionally obligated to appropriate money to implement treaty commitments. Similarly, debates over the 1884 Hawaii treaty and the 1815 treaty with Britain also produced a lot of speech-making, but the specific point at issue in both cases was whether a later-in-time treaty could supersede a previously enacted statute that raised revenue for the federal government. One can find isolated statements in these debates to the effect that NSE treaties are not "the law of the land." Taken out of context, one might construe such statements to mean that NSE treaties do not supersede state law. Viewed in context, though, it is clear that none of the congressional debates about self-execution discussed in this chapter are relevant to the relationship between treaties and state law, because the treaty provisions at issue all concerned matters outside the scope of state regulatory authority. Indeed, between 1800 and 1945, there are no recorded congressional debates about self-execution that involved treaties within the scope of state regulatory authority.

Thus, viewed together, the legislative materials discussed in Chapters 5 and 6 show that, before World War II, the doctrine of treaty supremacy addressed the relationship between treaties and state law (subject to federalism constraints), whereas the doctrine of self-execution addressed federal separation-of-powers issues. Under the agreed conceptual framework, the distinction between self-executing and non-self-executing treaties was not relevant to analysis of the relationship between treaties and state law.

II. EXECUTIVE BRANCH PRACTICE: NSE CLAUSES IN TREATIES

Between 1850 and 1905, the United States ratified six treaties with clauses that can reasonably be described as "non-self-execution" clauses: an 1854 treaty with Great Britain, an 1857 treaty with Denmark, an 1871 treaty with Great Britain, an 1875 treaty with the Kingdom of Hawaii, an 1883 treaty with Mexico, and a 1902 treaty with Cuba.[50] Nineteenth-century NSE clauses were used primarily for treaties involving import duties. The practice of attaching NSE clauses to such treaties largely disappeared after the 1902 treaty with Cuba. Two factors contributed to the demise of the nineteenth-century version of NSE clauses. First, in the late nineteenth century, the United States began using congressional-executive agreements, instead of treaties, to govern bilateral trade relations with other countries.[51] Second, the practice was rooted in the Tucker theory of concurrent and exclusive powers, which held that treaties affecting import duties were constitutionally non-self-executing. The Supreme Court rejected that theory, at least implicitly, in *De Lima v. Bidwell*, decided in 1901.[52]

This section first reviews the treaties with Denmark, Hawaii, Mexico, and Cuba. It then discusses the two treaties with Great Britain and concludes with comments about the differences between traditional and modern NSE clauses.

A. Treaties with Denmark, Hawaii, Mexico, and Cuba

The main purpose of the 1857 treaty with Denmark was "to terminate amicably the differences which have arisen between [the U.S. and Denmark] in regard to the tolls levied by Denmark on American vessels and their cargoes passing through the Sound and Belts."[53] For more than four centuries before 1857, Denmark had charged tolls to ships traversing channels between the North Sea and the Baltic Sea.[54] Several countries with shipping interests in the Baltic Sea region urged Denmark to abolish the so-called "sound dues." In March 1857, Denmark concluded a treaty with several European countries in which the other countries agreed to make lump-sum payments to Denmark in exchange for Denmark's agreement to abolish the dues. The United States concluded a separate treaty with Denmark, in which Denmark guaranteed "entire freedom of the navigation of the Sound and the Belts in favor of American vessels and their cargoes." In exchange, the United States agreed to pay the government of Denmark $393,011, plus interest.[55] In Article V, the two countries agreed to revive an 1826 treaty, which the United States had abrogated to gain leverage over Denmark in negotiations concerning the sound dues.[56] Article VI of the 1857 treaty contained an NSE clause. It said: "The present Convention shall take effect as soon as the laws to carry it into operation shall be passed by the governments of the contracting parties, and the sum stipulated to be paid by the United States shall be received by or tendered to Denmark."[57] Thus, legislation was a condition precedent for the Convention to "take effect."

Several points are noteworthy regarding the treaty with Denmark and the subsequent legislation. First, Congress enacted legislation "to fulfil the stipulations contained in the third and sixth articles of the treaty."[58] The legislation appropriated money to make payments of principal and interest. Second, the legislation did nothing to implement Article V, which revived the 1826 treaty. This point is significant because the 1826 treaty included various provisions that overlapped with state regulatory authority.[59] The decision to enact legislation to appropriate money, but not to implement Article V, manifests the shared view of the political branches that no legislation was needed to implement the treaty provisions that overlapped with state regulatory authority. The Supreme Court also shared that view, as evidenced by a subsequent Court decision applying the 1826 treaty to invalidate an Iowa state law.[60] Thus, even though the treaty contained a specific article that required legislation as a condition precedent for the treaty to "take effect," no such legislation was needed to give effect to the treaty provisions that overlapped with state law.[61]

The 1875 treaty with Hawaii was a typical reciprocal trade agreement. The United States promised to admit Hawaiian goods into U.S. ports without charging import duties, in exchange for Hawaii's agreement to admit U.S. goods duty free.[62] Both countries also agreed not to impose duties on exports to each other. Article V of the treaty, as initially drafted by the treaty negotiators, said:

> The present convention shall take effect as soon as it shall have been approved and proclaimed by his Majesty the King of the Hawaiian Islands, and shall have been ratified and duly proclaimed on the part of the Government of the United States, *and the laws required* to carry it into operation shall have been passed by the Congress of the United States of America.[63]

The negotiators signed the treaty on January 30, 1875. When the Senate consented to ratification on March 18, 1875, it amended the above-quoted language by striking the phrase "and the laws required" and replacing it with the phrase "but not until a law."[64] Thus, the Senate amendment makes clear that enactment of implementing legislation is a condition precedent for the convention to "take effect."

The United States and Hawaii exchanged ratifications on June 3, 1875, and the president proclaimed the treaty on that date. Ordinarily, the treaty would have "taken effect" on that date, but the condition precedent (the NSE clause) postponed the effective date of the treaty. Congress enacted the necessary implementing legislation on August 15, 1876. The legislation provided in relevant part: "That whenever the President ... shall receive satisfactory evidence that the legislature of the Hawaiian Islands have passed laws on their part to give full effect to the provisions of the convention ... he is hereby authorized to issue his proclamation declaring that he has such evidence; and thereupon, from the date of such proclamation" the articles specified in the treaty will be admitted free of duty into the United States.[65] The president delegated this statutory authority to the Acting Secretary of State. On September 9, 1876, the Acting Secretary and his Hawaiian counterpart signed a protocol declaring that the Convention "will take effect on the date hereof."[66] Thus, the NSE clause postponed the effective date of the treaty from June 3, 1875, until September 9, 1876.

Three points about the Hawaiian treaty are noteworthy. First, Congress enacted legislation to implement the treaty. Second, Congress and the president structured the process to ensure that the treaty became legally effective on the international plane at precisely the same moment that the legislation took effect domestically, so there was no gap between international obligation and domestic implementation. Third, the treaty had no impact whatsoever on state law, because the subject matter—import and export duties—is a matter that the Constitution places outside the scope of state regulatory authority.

U.S. negotiators signed a commercial treaty with Mexico on January 20, 1883.[67] Like the Hawaiian treaty, the 1883 treaty with Mexico was a typical reciprocal trade agreement in which each party agreed to admit specified goods from the other country duty free. Article VIII stated:

> The present convention shall take effect as soon as it has been approved and ratified by both contracting parties, according to their respective constitutions; but not until laws necessary to carry it into operation, shall have been passed both by the Congress of the United States and the Government of the United Mexican States, and regulations provided accordingly, which shall take place *within twelve months from the date of the exchange of ratifications* to which Article X refers.[68]

Article X stipulated that the ratifications "shall be duly exchanged" within twelve months from the date of signature. However, when the Senate did not consent to ratification within the twelve-month period specified in Article X, the parties signed a Protocol on January 17, 1884, extending the period for exchange of ratifications until May 20, 1884.[69] The Senate consented to ratification on March 11, 1884,[70] and the parties exchanged ratifications on May 20, 1884.

Exchange of ratifications started the clock for the twelve-month deadline in Article VIII (quoted above). When it became clear that the required implementing legislation would not be enacted within the twelve-month deadline, the parties signed an "Additional Article" to extend that deadline until May 20, 1886.[71] Another year passed and the requisite legislation still had not passed, so the parties signed a "Supplementary Article" to extend the deadline until May 20, 1887.[72] Ultimately, the parties never enacted the necessary legislation and the treaty never took effect. Thus, the net result of the NSE clause in Article VIII was that the treaty never became legally operative—either internationally or domestically—because Article VIII made enactment of legislation a condition precedent for the treaty to take effect, and the condition precedent was never satisfied.

The United States signed a reciprocal trade agreement with Cuba on December 11, 1902.[73] The agreement with Cuba was slightly more complicated than the aforementioned agreements with Hawaii and Mexico. Under the terms of the agreement, certain goods would be admitted duty free, whereas others would be admitted "at a reduction of twenty percentum" from the ordinary statutory rate.[74] There were also special provisions for U.S. tobacco exports to Cuba, and Cuban sugar exports to the United States.[75] Article XI specified that "the convention shall go into effect on the tenth day after the exchange of ratifications."[76] The Senate consented to ratification on February 16, 1903, subject to an amendment that added the following sentence to Article XI: "This convention shall not take effect until the same shall have been approved by the Congress."[77] The parties exchanged ratifications on March 31, 1903. Congress enacted the necessary implementing legislation on December 17, 1903.[78] The legislation provided, in part: "That whenever the President of the United States shall receive satisfactory evidence that the Republic of Cuba has made provision to give full effect to [the treaty] ... he is hereby authorized to issue his proclamation declaring that he has received such evidence," after which time Cuban goods shall be admitted into the United States in accordance with the terms of the treaty.[79] The president issued his proclamation on December 17, the same day the statute was enacted.

Absent the Senate amendment, the treaty would have become legally effective on April 10, 1903, in accordance with the original text of Article XI. What was the effect of the Senate amendment? The U.S. Supreme Court addressed that question in *United States v. American Sugar Refining Co.*[80] In *American Sugar*, a company imported sugar into the United States between June and September 1903. The customs collector assessed duties at the higher (statutory) rate. The importer paid under protest and filed for a refund, claiming that duties should have been charged under the lower (treaty) rate. The Court said that the correct rate "depends upon when the treaty went into effect."[81] The Court decided that the treaty took effect on December 27, 1903. Two facts were crucial in making this assessment. First, President Roosevelt issued a proclamation on December 17, declaring the Convention "to be in effect on the tenth day from the date of this my proclamation."[82] Second, the president of Cuba also issued a proclamation on December 17, "declaring that the treaty should take effect in Cuba on the day named in" President Roosevelt's proclamation.[83] From the Court's perspective, the agreement of the two presidents effectively settled the matter.

Several points about the Cuba treaty are noteworthy. First, Congress enacted legislation to implement the treaty. Second, the treaty became legally effective on the international plane at precisely the same moment the legislation took effect domestically, so that there was no gap between the international obligation and the domestic implementation of that obligation.[84] Third, in contrast to the agreements with Hawaii and Mexico—neither of which had any apparent overlap with state law—the Cuba treaty included one article that potentially overlapped with state or local law. In Article IX, the parties agreed that any tax "that may be imposed by the national or local authorities of either of the two countries upon the articles of merchandise embraced in ... this convention, subsequent to importation and prior to their entering into consumption ... shall be imposed and collected without discrimination upon like articles whencesoever imported."[85] Thus, under Article IX, if the United States imported raw materials from Cuba for use in a manufacturing process in Florida, for example, and Florida charged a value-added tax (VAT) to the manufacturer, the treaty prohibited discrimination against Cuban imports in assessing that tax.

In this hypothetical example, if Florida imposed a VAT that discriminated against Cuban imports, Article IX would ordinarily supersede the Florida law under the express terms of the Supremacy Clause. However, the Senate amendment stipulated that the treaty "shall not take effect until the same shall have been approved by the Congress."[86] Did the Senate amendment, which essentially added an NSE clause to the treaty, mean that Article IX did not supersede Florida law, absent implementing legislation? One could argue that Congress held that view, because the legislation enacted by Congress repeated, almost verbatim, the text of Article IX, and incorporated its terms into the statute.[87] Why would Congress repeat the terms of Article IX in the text of the statute if it believed that the treaty itself superseded conflicting state law under the terms of the Supremacy Clause? Two answers seem plausible. First, both Article IX and the statute refer to taxes "that may be imposed by the national or local authorities."[88] Congress may have thought that the reference to taxes imposed by "national ... authorities" required implementing legislation. Second, given that congressional drafters copied verbatim much of the treaty text into the statutory text, Congress may have incorporated this provision into the statute without giving the matter much thought. At least one other factor supports this conclusion. The statute enacted by Congress includes the following language: "nothing herein contained shall be held or construed as an admission on the part of the House of Representatives that customs duties can be changed otherwise than by an Act of Congress, originating in said House."[89] This language suggests that the House's main goal was to preserve its control over legislation involving customs duties. As Article IX did not address customs duties, the House drafters may not have paid much attention to Article IX.

Regardless, as a practical matter, the NSE clause in the Cuba treaty did not permit states to enact discriminatory tax laws in contravention of the treaty. As noted above, the federal statute and the treaty entered into force at precisely the same time, and the statute contained precisely the same prohibition on discriminatory taxes that was included in Article IX of the treaty. Therefore, a state tax law that discriminated against Cuban imports would have been invalid under the combined force of the statute, the treaty, and the Supremacy Clause. The precise role played by the statute, the treaty, and the Supremacy Clause in this equation seems relatively unimportant, because any state law in violation of Article IX would have been void. In the final analysis, the NSE clause was entirely consistent with the goals underlying the Supremacy Clause because it did not permit states to engage in conduct that would trigger a violation of U.S. treaty obligations.

B. Two Treaties with Great Britain

An 1854 treaty with the United Kingdom appears to be the first treaty ever concluded by the United States with an NSE clause in the treaty. Article V stated: "The present treaty shall take effect as soon as the laws required to carry it into operation shall have been passed by the Imperial Parliament of Great Britain and by the Provincial Parliaments of those British North American Colonies which are affected by this treaty on the one hand, and by the Congress of the United States on the other."[90] Negotiators signed the treaty in June 1854. The Senate provided its consent on August 2, 1854, and Congress enacted implementing legislation on August 5.[91] The United States and Great Britain exchanged instruments of ratification on September 9, and the president issued his proclamation on September 11, 1854. At that point, according to the U.S. attorney general, the treaty "became complete and perfect as a treaty."[92] However, Article V said that the treaty would not "take effect" until the British and provincial parliaments passed the necessary laws. The legislatures of Canada, Nova Scotia, New Brunswick, and Prince Edward Island did so between September 23 and December 13, 1854. The British Parliament enacted legislation on February 19, 1855.[93] Hence, the question arose: What was the status and effect of the treaty between the president's proclamation in September 1854 and the date in February 1855 when the final condition precedent for the treaty to "take effect" had been satisfied?

Attorney General Caleb Cushing provided a detailed analysis of that question in response to a request from Secretary of State William Marcy.[94] Cushing's analysis distinguished between treaty provisions that "may be contingent or executory only," and provisions that are "susceptible of execution . . . forthwith, by their own proper vigor, requiring no preliminary act to be performed on either side as antecedent to such execution, save mere formal orders of the executive authorities of each Government."[95] Cushing referred specifically to Article III of the 1854 treaty, in which the parties agreed reciprocally that imports from the other country "shall be admitted into each country free of duty."[96] In Cushing's view, the treaty commitment to admit goods free of duty was "contingent or executory." Therefore, U.S. customs collectors had a (statutory) obligation to continue to charge "duties of customs on the importation into the United States of any of the articles of merchandise enumerated in the treaty, until the requisite legislation should have been had."[97] According to Cushing, though, the provision on duty-free imports was the *only* treaty provision whose execution had to await implementing legislation.

Article II granted "British subjects . . . the liberty to take fish . . . on the Eastern sea coasts and shores of the United States . . . and in the bays, harbors, and creeks . . . with permission to land upon the said coasts of the United States . . . for the purpose of drying their nets and curing their fish."[98] Article IV granted British subjects "the right freely to navigate Lake Michigan with their vessels, boats, and crafts."[99] Cushing said that these provisions "are of such nature as to be susceptible of execution . . . forthwith, by their own proper vigor, requiring no preliminary act to be performed on either side as antecedent to such execution."[100] Thus, even though Article V stated explicitly that the treaty would not "take effect" until legislation had been enacted, Cushing said that Article V merely postponed the effective date of Article III (on duty-free imports), but did not preclude Articles II and IV from taking full effect on the date of the president's proclamation.

Not coincidentally, Cushing's analysis aligns perfectly with the division between state and federal regulatory authority. Article III relates to import duties, a matter that is subject to exclusive federal control. Even in the absence of a treaty, states would not have been free to impose duties on British imports, because the Constitution itself precludes states from imposing such duties without express congressional consent.[101] The NSE clause in the treaty, as interpreted by the attorney general, meant that treaty provisions dealing with matters subject to exclusive federal control had to await implementing legislation. In contrast, absent treaty stipulations, states would have been free to enact their own rules for coastal fishing, or for navigation on Lake Michigan.[102] Under Cushing's analysis, Articles II and IV of the treaty took effect immediately upon the president's proclamation, thereby superseding any state laws that conflicted with British fishing or navigation rights under Article II or IV.[103] Thus, even though the treaty contained an NSE clause specifying that enactment of legislation was a condition precedent for the treaty to "take effect," the attorney general's interpretation meant that, as a practical matter, treaty provisions that intersected with state regulatory authority took effect immediately. The NSE clause had no impact on the relationship between the treaty and state law. Under this approach, the NSE clause was entirely consistent with the goals of the Constitution's treaty supremacy rule.

The United States terminated the 1854 treaty with Great Britain in 1866. The two countries then signed a new treaty in 1871, known as the Treaty of Washington.[104] That treaty addressed a wide range of issues that had arisen in diplomatic relations between the United States and Britain. Articles 1–17 addressed the "Alabama claims" arbitration.[105] Articles 18–32 addressed navigation and fishing rights, and issues pertaining to duty-free imports and exports between the United States and Canada. Articles 34–42 concerned the western border with Canada. Article 33 included an NSE clause. It stipulated that Articles 18–25, inclusive, and Article 30 "shall take effect as soon as the laws required to carry them into operation shall have been passed by the Imperial Parliament of Great Britain, by the Parliament of Canada, and by the Legislature of Prince Edward's Island on the one hand, and by the Congress of the United States on the other."[106] Thus, the treaty established a two-tiered approach to entry into force. Most of the treaty became legally operative on June 17, 1871, when the parties exchanged ratifications. However, the NSE clause in Article 33 established a condition precedent, such that four different legislative bodies had to enact legislation before Articles 18–25 and Article 30 became legally operative. The requisite legislation was passed between June 1872 and March 1873 and the designated articles took effect on July 1, 1873, as specified in a special Protocol signed on June 7, 1873.[107]

It is instructive to compare treaty Articles 18–32 with the legislation that Congress enacted to implement the treaty.[108] Articles 18–20 addressed coastal fishing rights for U.S. fishermen along the shores of Quebec, Nova Scotia, New Brunswick, and Prince Edward's Island, and reciprocal rights for British subjects to take fish "on the eastern sea-coasts of the United States north of the thirty-ninth parallel."[109] The legislation enacted by Congress did not include any provisions to implement these articles. The NSE clause in Article 33 stipulated that legislation was a precondition for Articles 18–20 to take effect, apparently because the drafters believed that the legislatures of Canada and Prince Edward's Island had to enact legislation to grant rights to U.S. fisherman, and the United States did not want to grant reciprocal rights to British subjects until that legislation had been enacted. But Congress did not believe that legislation was necessary to implement Articles 18–20 in the United States—notwithstanding the NSE clause in Article 33—because Congress recognized that the combined effect of the treaty and the Supremacy Clause would invalidate any state laws inconsistent with the treaty.

Articles 21, 29, 30, and 31 addressed duties on imports and exports between the United States and Canada, as well as duties on transshipment of goods through the United States and Canada. Article 32 extended key provisions to the territory of Newfoundland. The NSE clause in Article 33 stipulated that legislation was a condition precedent for Articles 21 and 30 to take effect, but the NSE clause said nothing about Articles 29, 31, or 32. Nevertheless, Congress enacted legislation to implement Articles 21 and 29–32.[110] Thus, Congress determined for itself that Articles 29, 31, and 32 required legislative implementation—even though they were not mentioned in the NSE clause—because those articles addressed duties on exports and duties on transshipment of goods.[111] Conversely, the NSE clause expressly required legislation as a precondition for Articles 22–25 to take effect, but Congress did not enact legislation to implement those articles. Articles 22–25 established modalities for an arbitration commission to resolve disputes between the United States and Great Britain related to fishing rights and import duties. Congress apparently believed that the president had sufficient authority to implement these provisions himself and did not need additional legislative authorization.[112]

In sum, it appears that the precise language of the NSE clause in Article 33 had very little influence on Congress's decision about which treaty provisions required legislative implementation. Treaty provisions that overlapped with state law (Articles 18–20) did not require legislative implementation, despite the express reference in Article 33.[113] Similarly, treaty provisions related to international arbitration (Articles 22–25) did not require legislative implementation, despite the express reference in Article 33. However, treaty provisions relating to import and export duties (Articles 21 and 29–32) did require legislative implementation, even though Article 33 did not specify that legislation was needed to implement Article 29, 31, or 32. The record suggests that Congress believed it was important to enact legislation to implement treaty provisions that affected U.S. revenue collection, but other types of treaty provisions did not require legislative implementation.

C. Comparing "Traditional" NSE Clauses to Modern NSE Declarations

In all the treaties discussed in the previous section, the treaty drafters applied the "condition precedent" version of NSE doctrine. (*See* Table Three, p. 128.) The *condition precedent doctrine* assumes that a treaty will not take effect on the international plane until after implementing legislation is enacted if the treaty itself specifies that implementing legislation is a condition precedent for the international entry into force of the treaty. In the past few decades, it has become common practice for the president and Senate to ratify treaties subject to "NSE declarations."[114] In certain respects, the nineteenth-century practice of drafting treaties with NSE clauses set a precedent for the modern practice of ratifying treaties subject to NSE declarations. However, if one compares modern NSE declarations to nineteenth-century NSE clauses, several differences are apparent.

First, the treaty makers who adopted traditional NSE clauses intended for Congress to enact legislation to make the treaties legally operative. In contrast, modern NSE declarations are typically accompanied by a statement that the treaty makers do not believe any implementing legislation is needed.[115] Second, the traditional NSE clauses had no impact on the relationship between treaties and state law. In contrast, modern NSE declarations are commonly understood to mean that the treaties to which they are attached do not supersede conflicting state laws, or that judges are not bound by NSE treaty provisions that conflict with state laws.[116] Thus, traditional NSE clauses were entirely consistent with the original understanding of the Supremacy Clause. In contrast, modern NSE declarations are in tension with the original understanding. Moreover, traditional NSE clauses were entirely consistent with the central goal of the Constitution's treaty supremacy rule: to ensure that states do not engage in conduct that triggers U.S. treaty violations. In contrast, modern NSE declarations may conflict with that goal, insofar as they are construed to permit states to violate U.S. treaty obligations.

Additionally, traditional NSE clauses promoted harmony between U.S. international obligations and the domestic implementation of those obligations. Those clauses typically postponed international entry into force of treaty provisions that affected import and export duties until after Congress enacted implementing legislation. At the time when the provisions were being negotiated, many people believed that implementing legislation was *constitutionally* required for treaty provisions affecting import and export duties.[117] Thus, the NSE clauses ensured that the treaty did not become legally operative on the international plane until after the United States adopted legislation necessary to implement the treaty domestically. In contrast, modern NSE declarations drive a wedge between the nation's international obligations and the domestic implementation of those obligations. Modern NSE declarations do not affect the time at which the treaty becomes legally operative on the international plane. However, the declarations constrain, and are intended to constrain, the domestic application of treaty obligations after they become legally binding on the international plane.

III. ATTORNEY GENERAL OPINIONS

Between 1800 and 1945, nine different U.S. attorney generals issued a total of ten official opinions addressing the distinction between self-executing and non-self-executing treaties. Those opinions generally manifest an understanding of self-execution that is consistent with the congressional-executive concept, not the political-judicial concept. Subject to minor caveats noted below, all ten opinions are concerned exclusively with questions of federal law, not state law. Thus, the attorney general opinions generally confirm the conclusion that the concept of self-execution, as understood before 1945, was not relevant to issues involving the relationship between treaties and state law.

Three opinions address conflicts between an 1894 treaty with China and prior federal statutes regulating Chinese immigration. In an 1896 opinion, Acting Attorney-General Conrad concluded that Article III of the 1894 treaty with China was self-executing and therefore superseded Section 6 of an 1884 federal statute.[118] Two years later, Acting Attorney-General Boyd reaffirmed this conclusion, stating that "the treaty being subsequent to the act of 1884 has modified the requirements thereof."[119] Similarly, a 1901 opinion by Attorney General Knox held that Article II of the 1894 treaty was self-executing and therefore superseded Section 7 of an 1888 federal statute.[120] All three opinions dealt exclusively with matters of federal law; no state law was at issue in any of the opinions. All three opinions direct federal executive officials to conform their conduct to the requirements of the 1894 treaty, rather than conflicting requirements of older federal statutes.

Two other attorney general opinions addressed a 1909 treaty with Great Britain that regulated waters on the border between the United States and Canada.[121] A 1913 opinion by Attorney General McReynolds stated: "That the subject matter of this treaty, namely, the regulation of the boundary waters between this country and Canada, being, by its very nature, beyond the competency either of Congress or the States, is one peculiarly within the treaty making power."[122] He concluded that Article V of the treaty was self-executing and therefore authorized the president to supervise "diversion within the State of New York of the waters of the Niagara River ... in the absence of legislation by Congress to the contrary."[123] Two years later, Attorney General Gregory concluded that Article I of the same treaty was self-executing and superseded Section 3109 of the Revised Statutes, because the statute "is in my opinion so clearly incompatible with the provisions of the later treaty."[124] Therefore, he said, it is "the duty of the officials, whose function it is to administer the laws and regulations relating to commerce upon the Great Lakes, to fulfil, by proper administrative action, the requirements of the treaty."[125] Like the opinions concerning the treaty with China, these two opinions dealt exclusively with matters of federal law. No state law was at issue.

In 1854, Attorney General Caleb Cushing authored two opinions related to self-execution, involving two different bilateral treaties with Britain. As discussed previously, one of those opinions addressed an 1854 treaty that contained an NSE clause.[126] Cushing concluded that the NSE clause postponed the effective date of the treaty provision that overlapped with federal law, but the provisions that intersected with state law took effect immediately "by their own proper vigor, requiring no preliminary act to be performed,"[127] despite the explicit NSE clause in the treaty. The other opinion addressed a bilateral copyright convention. Cushing concluded that "the first article of the convention ... [had] the legal effect of so far repealing or modifying the first section of the act of Congress, as to annul anything therein, which might be construed otherwise to deprive a British subject in the United States of the rights defined by the convention ...."[128] However, he added, "the question of remedies to secure and enforce those rights is a different and independent one."[129] In his opinion, the treaty itself conferred "on British subjects, not only the rights, but also the remedies of our own law." But he acknowledged that the courts may not agree with his assessment regarding the sufficiency of available judicial remedies, in which case "it is not to be doubted that any law, necessary for the purpose, would be duly enacted by Congress."[130] The central point for present purposes is that his analysis of the copyright convention focused exclusively on federal law. No state law was at issue.

Similarly, the other three attorney general opinions addressing self-execution dealt exclusively with matters of federal law. An 1870 opinion by Attorney General Akerman held that an 1866 treaty with the Choctaw and Chickasaw Indians was self-executing, and therefore no legislation was needed to authorize the secretary of the treasury to issue bonds to the Choctaw Indians.[131] An 1889 opinion by Attorney General Miller concluded that Article II of the 1883 Paris Convention—a multilateral treaty related to patents and trademarks—did not supersede a federal patent statute because the treaty was not self-executing.[132] Finally, a 1913 opinion by Attorney General Wickersham concluded that Article XI of the Service Regulations that formed part of a radiotelegraphic convention "was not designed to be self-executing" and therefore did "not effect a modification of the terms of" a 1912 federal statute.[133] The 1889 opinion by Attorney General Miller and the 1913 opinion by Attorney General Wickersham are the only two opinions to hold that a treaty is not self-executing. Both opinions merit further analysis.

Consider, first, the 1889 opinion by Attorney General Miller. A Swiss citizen, Ferdinand Bourquin, claimed the right to file a patent application with the U.S. Patent Office. Federal statutes limited that right to U.S. citizens and a narrow class of noncitizens that did not include Bourquin. Even so, he claimed that the 1883 Paris Convention granted him the same rights as U.S. citizens. The treaty said: "The subjects or citizens of each of the contracting States shall enjoy, in all the other States" that are parties to the treaty "so far as concerns patents for inventions ... the advantages that the respective laws thereof at present accord ... to subjects or citizens."[134] Thus, the treaty clearly obligated the United States to grant Bourquin the same rights that the United States granted to its own citizens. But the patent examiners in the Patent Office needed to know whether they should be guided by the statute (which precluded Bourquin from filing his application) or the treaty (which granted him the same rights as U.S. citizens). In Attorney General Miller's view, the answer turned on whether the treaty was self-executing. Miller's opinion addressed two different theories of self-execution. First, he considered whether the Article I power to secure to "Inventors the exclusive Right to their ... Discoveries"[135] granted Congress exclusive power over patents, thereby precluding the treaty makers from using the Article II Treaty Power to regulate patents.[136] In other words, he considered whether the Paris Convention was constitutionally non-self-executing because it purported to regulate a subject within the scope of Congress's exclusive legislative powers. Ultimately, he concluded that he did not need to answer that constitutional question because he rested his decision on the "contract version" of NSE doctrine. (See Table Three, p. 128.)

The *contract doctrine* is founded on a misinterpretation of Chief Justice Marshall's opinion in *Foster v. Neilson*. Marshall said: "[W]hen the terms of the stipulation import a contract, when either of the parties engages to perform a particular act, the treaty addresses itself to the political, not the judicial department; and the legislature must execute the contract before it can become a rule for the Court."[137] As discussed in Chapter 4, Marshall envisioned a two-step analysis. In step one, courts engage in treaty interpretation to answer an international law question: whether the provision at issue is *executed* or *executory*. For executory provisions, step two involves a separation-of-powers analysis to answer a domestic law question: Which branch of government has the legal authority and/or legal duty to implement the treaty? The *contract doctrine* conflates international law issues with domestic law issues by adopting a conclusive presumption that Congress is the only branch of government with the domestic legal authority to implement executory treaty provisions. Attorney General Miller's 1889 opinion was the first authoritative legal document to apply the contract doctrine.

Miller held that the Paris Convention was "a contract operative in the future infraterritorially" because each party "covenants to grant in the future to the subjects and citizens of the other parties certain special rights."[138] In other words, he held on treaty interpretation grounds that the treaty was executory. That portion of his reasoning is sound. But Miller also construed Marshall's opinion in *Foster* (incorrectly) to mean that all executory treaty provisions are non-self-executing. He said: "[The treaty] is a contract operative in the future infraterritorially. It is therefore not self-executing, but requires legislation to render it effective for the modification of existing laws."[139] Miller's opinion is about five pages long, but the core of his rationale is contained in these two sentences. In essence, he reasoned that the treaty was not self-executing (i.e., not a rule of conduct for U.S. patent examiners) *because it was executory.* Miller's inference is valid only if one assumes that all executory treaty provisions are non-self-executing. However, the assumption that all executory treaty provisions require implementing legislation is impossible to reconcile with the vast majority of legislative, executive, and judicial materials dating back to the Founding. Even so, between about 1890 and 1920, courts often relied on Attorney General Miller's opinion and the associated *contract version* of NSE doctrine, especially in patent cases.[140] By 1945, though, courts and executive officials had effectively abandoned the contract doctrine because they recognized that it was based on a faulty assumption.

Attorney General Wickersham's 1913 opinion addressed a conflict between a 1912 statute and a 1913 treaty, both of which concerned equipment for transmitting radio signals between ships and coastal stations.[141] The treaty obligated the United States "to apply the provisions of the present convention to all radio stations ... which are established or worked by the contracting parties ... between the coast and vessels at sea." It also obligated the United States "to make the observance of these provisions obligatory upon private enterprises."[142] To implement the treaty, the secretary of commerce and labor needed to enact new federal regulations. The question was whether the secretary could invoke the treaty as authority for enacting those regulations, or whether federal legislation was necessary to authorize him to enact regulations to implement the treaty. Wickersham concluded that legislation was needed because the treaty was not self-executing. He cited *Foster* for the following proposition: "When the terms of a treaty import a contract on the part of the United States to do something, it is said that the treaty addresses itself to the political department, and in that event Congress must enact the necessary legislation to make it operative."[143] This rationale is difficult to defend. Virtually all treaties "import a contract on the part of the United States to do something." If all such treaties were non-self-executing, then the vast majority of treaties ratified by the United States would be NSE. But that conclusion is at odds with the bulk of legislative, executive, and judicial authorities since the Founding.

Wickersham relied on the following text to support his conclusion that the treaty was not self-executing: "The high contracting parties bind themselves to take, or propose to their respective legislatures, the necessary measures for insuring the execution of the present convention."[144] Quite clearly, the quoted language does not require states to enact legislation to implement the treaty. It requires them to take the necessary measures to execute the treaty, either by enacting legislation, or by some other means. Even so, Wickersham misinterpreted this language to mean that the treaty itself required the United States to enact legislation.[145]

The 1889 opinion by Attorney General Miller and the 1913 opinion by Attorney General Wickersham are important because they established precedents for the future use of NSE doctrine as legal gibberish. Nevertheless, neither opinion supports an NSE exception to the treaty supremacy rule, because both opinions addressed matters governed exclusively by federal law. Indeed, it is instructive to compare the attorney general opinions discussed in this section with the attorney general opinions on treaties and federalism (discussed in Chapter 5). The attorney general opinions on federalism do not mention self-execution, and the attorney general opinions on self-execution generally do not mention state law. Therefore, viewed together, the two sets of opinions reinforce the conclusion that, before 1945, the doctrine of self-execution had no relevance to questions involving the relationship between treaties and state law.

* * *

In sum, analysis of legislative and executive materials between 1800 and 1945 supports several conclusions. Congress consistently applied the *constitutional version* of NSE doctrine throughout the period. Accordingly, Congress was not at all confused about the meaning of "self-execution." Congress understood self-execution in accordance with the congressional-executive concept. Congress viewed self-execution as a domestic separation-of-powers doctrine designed to preserve the House of Representatives' legislative prerogatives and limit the power of federal executive officers to implement treaties. The executive branch practice of drafting and negotiating treaties was generally consistent with the congressional view of self-execution. The executive branch sometimes added NSE clauses to treaties during this period. Such clauses stipulated that bicameral legislation was a condition precedent for the international entry into force of the subject treaties (the *condition precedent version* of NSE doctrine). The NSE clauses were also designed to preserve the House of Representatives' legislative prerogatives; such clauses applied only to treaty provisions regulating matters that were arguably within the scope of Congress's exclusive legislative powers.

Finally, attorney general opinions on self-execution introduced a significant degree of confusion into NSE doctrine. The 1889 opinion by Attorney General Miller introduced the *contract version* of NSE doctrine. The contract version is theoretically incoherent because it is based on the untenable assumption that all executory treaty provisions are non-self-executing. The next chapter shows that some U.S. courts in the late nineteenth and early twentieth centuries were misled by the contract version of NSE doctrine. However, as of 1945 there was no significant legislative, executive, or judicial authority to support an NSE exception to the Constitution's treaty supremacy rule. Table Three summarizes the distinct variants of NSE doctrine that existed circa 1900.

Table Three. Varieties of NSE Doctrines, Circa 1900

	Two-Step Approach to Self-Execution Analysis	One-Step Approach to Self-Execution Analysis
Congressional-Executive Concept	*Constitutional Doctrine*: assumes that Constitution limits power of federal executive officers to implement treaties. *See* pp. 108–13. *Condition Precedent Doctrine*: assumes that treaty makers have power to require legislation as a precondition for treaty to take effect internationally. *See* pp. 122–23. *Contract Doctrine*: assumes that all executory treaty provisions are constitutionally non-self-executing. *See* pp. 125–26.	Did not exist as of 1900
Political-Judicial Concept	*Justiciability Doctrine*: assumes that Constitution limits power of courts to apply treaties. *See* Chapter 7, pp. 132–34.	Did not exist as of 1900

7

Self-Execution in the Federal Courts

Between 1800 and 1945, the Supreme Court decided approximately 550 cases involving the judicial application of treaties.[1] In exactly eleven of those cases, the Court used the term "self-executing" or "non-self-executing" as an adjective to modify the word "treaty." If one expands the search to include cases that do not use the term "self-executing," but that say something at least marginally relevant to self-execution doctrine, the Court decided about twenty-five or thirty cases between 1800 and 1945 that are relevant to self-execution doctrine. Analysis of those cases yields three main conclusions. First, self-execution doctrine had virtually no impact on the Court's application of treaties before 1945. The Court's dominant approach in treaty cases was simply to apply the treaty, without pausing to consider whether the treaty at issue was self-executing or non-self-executing. Second, the Court never articulated a coherent self-execution doctrine. At best, decisions in individual cases that a particular treaty was self-executing or non-self-executing lacked a clear rationale. At worst, such conclusions were supported by analysis that obfuscated more than it clarified. Third, the self-execution cases discussed in this chapter reinforce the primary conclusion of Chapter 5: the issue of self-execution generally did not arise in treaty supremacy cases. Thus, Supreme Court decisions before 1945 provide no support for an NSE exception to the Constitution's treaty supremacy rule.

This chapter is divided into five sections. The first focuses on the eleven Supreme Court cases that use the term "self-executing" to modify the word "treaty." The next presents a detailed analysis of six landmark cases that define the parameters of self-execution doctrine. Inasmuch as contemporary courts and commentators typically identify *Foster v. Neilson*[2] and *The Head Money Cases*[3] as the primary authorities for modern NSE doctrine, the third section analyzes Supreme Court decisions before 1945 in which one or more parties raised a treaty-based argument and the Court cited *Foster, Head Money,* or both. The next section analyzes decisions by lower federal appellate courts that are relevant to self-execution doctrine. These lower court decisions reinforce the conclusion that, before 1945, there was no NSE exception to the Constitution's treaty supremacy rule.

The final section of this chapter addresses a potential objection. Chapters 5–7 divide treaties into two categories: those that overlap with state regulatory authority (Chapter 5) and those that overlap with federal regulatory authority (Chapters 6–7). Hence, one might object, the analysis fails to account for cases involving treaties that overlap with both state and federal regulatory authority. The final section of this chapter discusses cases in that category. The analysis reinforces the main conclusions summarized above.

I. SUPREME COURT CASES THAT USE THE TERM "SELF-EXECUTING"

Between 1800 and 1945, the Court decided eleven cases in which a majority, concurring, or dissenting opinion used the term "self-executing" or "non-self-executing" to modify "treaty." In reverse chronological order, those eleven cases are: *Aguilar v. Standard Oil Co., Factor v. Laubenheimer, Cook v. United States, Maul v. United States, Cameron Septic Tank Co. v. City of Knoxville, Fok Young Yo v. United States, United States v. Lee Yen Tai, De Lima v. Bidwell, Mitchell v. Furman, Whitney v. Robertson,* and *Bartram v. Robertson.*[4] In *Whitney,* the Court defined "self-executing" to mean that treaty provisions "require no legislation to make them operative."[5] It added that self-executing provisions "have the force and effect of a legislative enactment." Conversely, non-self-executing provisions "can only be enforced pursuant to legislation to carry them into effect."[6] In *De Lima,* the Court quoted *Whitney* as follows: "By the Constitution a treaty is placed on the same footing, and made of like obligation, with an act of legislation . . . but if the two are inconsistent, the one last in date will control the other, provided always that the stipulation of the treaty on the subject is self-executing."[7] These passages explain the consequences that follow from a conclusion that a treaty is self-executing or non-self-executing. Self-executing provisions have the force of law and supersede prior conflicting statutes, but NSE provisions do not supersede prior federal statutes and are not enforceable in the absence of legislation. In both *Whitney* and *De Lima,* the Court clearly understood self-execution in accordance with the congressional-executive concept: the question in both cases was whether customs collectors should apply a treaty or a conflicting statute to determine the correct amount of import duty to be charged. However, neither *Whitney* nor *De Lima* explicitly identifies criteria that courts can apply to determine which treaty provisions are self-executing.

Other cases that use the term "self-executing" or "non-self-executing" are equally unhelpful. In *Factor v. Laubenheimer,* the Court said: "Under the laws of Great Britain extradition treaties are not self-executing, and effect must be given to them by an act of Parliament designating the crimes."[8] However, the Court did not provide criteria for distinguishing between self-executing and non-self-executing treaties in the United States. In *United States v. Lee Yen Tai,*[9] *Mitchell v. Furman,*[10] and *Bartram v. Robertson,*[11] the Court used the term "self-executing" to modify "treaty." However, the Court did not reach a definite conclusion about whether a particular treaty was self-executing. Moreover, it did not define the term "self-executing" or identify criteria for distinguishing between self-executing and non-self-executing treaties. In *Fok Young Yo v. United States*, the Court noted in passing that an 1880 treaty with China "was not self-executing."[12] However, the key treaty at issue in *Fok Young Yo* was an 1894 agreement with China. In regard to that treaty, the Court said: "But the provision of this treaty applicable here ... proceeded on the ground of its existence and continuance under governmental regulations, and no act of Congress was required."[13] Unfortunately, the Court did not explain why the 1880 treaty was non-self-executing, nor did it explain why the 1894 treaty was self-executing.

In *Aguilar v. Standard Oil Co., Cook v. United States, Maul v. United States*, and *Cameron Septic Tank Co. v. City of Knoxville*, the Court or individual justices cited the views of the federal political branches as authority for the proposition that a particular treaty provision was self-executing or non-self-executing. In *Aguilar*, Chief Justice Stone cited a letter written by Secretary of State Cordell Hull to support the conclusion that Article 2 of the Shipowners' Liability Convention was partially self-executing and partially non-self-executing.[14] In both *Cook* and *Maul*, Justice Brandeis cited a letter from Secretary of State Charles Evans Hughes to the Chairman of the House Foreign Affairs Committee to support his view that bilateral liquor treaties were self-executing.[15] In *Cameron Septic*, Justice McKenna said that "[t]he action of Congress must be taken into account" and cited a statement by "the member in charge of [a bill] in the House of Representatives" to support his conclusion that it was "the sense of Congress" that the treaty of Brussels of December 14, 1900, was not self-executing.[16] Taken together, these cases suggest that courts should accord significant weight to views expressed by Congress and the federal executive branch in assessing whether a particular treaty provision is self-executing or non-self-executing. However, in *De Lima v. Bidwell*, the Court specifically rejected the government's argument that an 1899 treaty with Spain was not self-executing.[17] Overall, the Supreme Court cases that use the term "self-executing" in conjunction with "treaty" do not provide clear, analytical criteria to guide the lower courts in evaluating whether a particular treaty provision is self-executing or non-self-executing.

None of the Supreme Court cases from 1800 to 1945 that used the term "self-executing" in conjunction with "treaty" involved any state law issues. *Whitney, Bartram*, and *De Lima* involved import duties. *Aguilar, Cook*, and *Maul* involved admiralty and maritime law. *Lee Yen Tai* and *Fok Young Yo* involved Chinese immigration. *Factor v. Laubenheimer* was an international extradition case. *Cameron Septic* was a patent case. These are all areas governed exclusively by federal law. *Mitchell v. Furman* involved a dispute over title to real property in Florida, a matter that is ordinarily governed by state law. However, state law had no bearing on the case because the Court concluded that appellees' title "must stand or fall by their contention that" a 1795 Spanish land grant gave them "a complete and perfect title" before the 1819 treaty with Spain took effect.[18] In sum, this brief survey reinforces the conclusion that self-execution doctrine before 1945 was generally not relevant to treaty supremacy cases.

II. SIX LANDMARK CASES ON SELF-EXECUTION

The preceding section focused narrowly on cases that used the term "self-executing" or "non-self-executing." This section widens the aperture to consider other cases that address the question of whether, and in what circumstances, legislation is needed to implement a treaty. Chapter 4 discussed *Foster v. Neilson* and *United States v. Percheman*, which are arguably the two most important cases before 1945 on self-execution doctrine. This section addresses six other landmark cases that establish the parameters of NSE doctrine as that doctrine was developed by the Supreme Court between 1800 and 1945. In chronological order, they are: *The Head Money Cases, Whitney v. Robertson, De Lima v. Bidwell, Downes v. Bidwell, Cameron Septic Tank Co. v. City of Knoxville,* and *Cook v. United States.*[19]

A. The Head Money Cases

In *The Head Money Cases,*[20] plaintiffs were transporting immigrants from Europe to the United States. Acting pursuant to an 1882 federal statute, the collector at the port of New York charged the shipping company a fee of fifty cents for each person brought into the United States. The plaintiffs paid under protest and sued for a refund. After rebuffing a constitutional challenge to the 1882 statute, the Court addressed the plaintiffs' argument that the statute "violates provisions contained in numerous treaties of our government with friendly nations." The Court stated that the 1882 statute did not violate "any of these treaties, on any just construction of them."[21] However, the Court rested its decision primarily on the later-in-time rule. If there was a conflict between the 1882 statute and prior treaties, the Court said, that conflict would have to be resolved in favor of the later-in-time statute.[22] In the course of his later-in-time analysis, Justice Samuel Miller made the following statement, which subsequently came to be associated with NSE doctrine:

> A treaty is primarily a compact between independent nations. It depends for the enforcement of its provisions on the interest and the honor of the governments which are parties to it. . . . It is obvious that with all this the judicial courts have nothing to do and can give no redress. But a treaty may also contain provisions which confer certain rights upon the citizens or subjects of one of the nations residing in the territorial limits of the other, which partake of the nature of municipal law, and which are capable of enforcement as between private parties in the courts of the country. . . . A treaty, then, is a law of the land as an act of congress is, whenever its provisions prescribe a rule by which the rights of the private citizen or subject may be determined. And when such rights are of a nature to be enforced in a court of justice, that court resorts to the treaty for a rule of decision for the case before it as it would to a statute.[23]

This passage from *Head Money* is often said to be the origin of the "justiciability" version of NSE doctrine. The constitutional doctrine, the condition precedent doctrine, and the contract doctrine all involve the congressional-executive concept of self-execution. Those doctrines focus on whether legislation is necessary for the treaty to function as a rule of conduct for federal executive officials. In contrast, the justiciability doctrine involves the political-judicial concept of self-execution. It focuses on whether the treaty is "of a nature to be enforced in a court of justice." Unlike the attorney general opinions discussed in Chapter 6, *Head Money* is not concerned with whether executive officers must conform their conduct to treaty requirements. Rather, *Head Money* is concerned with whether judges are competent to apply the treaty. Justice Miller's opinion in *Head Money* did not use the term "self-executing" to denote treaty provisions that courts are competent to enforce. Nevertheless, courts and commentators subsequently cited *Head Money* to support a distinction between self-executing treaty provisions (which courts are competent to apply) and NSE provisions (which courts are not competent to apply). Table Three on page 128 summarizes four different versions of NSE doctrine that had emerged by 1900.

The passage quoted above from *Head Money* hints at two different reasons why courts may not be competent to apply certain types of treaty provisions. First, some treaty provisions operate merely as a "compact between independent nations."[24] I refer to these as "horizontal" treaty provisions because they regulate horizontal relations between nations. Such provisions differ from "vertical" treaty provisions, which regulate relations between states and private parties, and "transnational" treaty provisions, which regulate cross-border relationships between private parties.[25] *Head Money* refers jointly to vertical and transnational treaty provisions when it speaks of provisions that "confer certain rights upon the citizens or subjects of one of the nations residing in the territorial limits of the other."[26] Thus, *Head Money* suggests that domestic courts are competent to apply vertical and transnational treaty provisions, but they are not competent to apply horizontal treaty provisions. Although one can identify exceptions to this general principle, it is rare to find a case in which a domestic court in any country applies a horizontal treaty provision.[27]

Apart from the distinctions among horizontal, vertical, and transnational treaty provisions, *Head Money* also suggests another reason why some treaty provisions are beyond judicial competence to enforce. Justice Miller refers to provisions that "prescribe a rule by which the rights of the private citizen or subject may be determined."[28] Sometimes, a vertical or transnational treaty provision is so vague or indeterminate that courts are not capable of determining the rights of private parties by applying the treaty to the facts at hand. In this respect, a vague or indeterminate treaty provision is not judicially enforceable for the same reason that a vague or indeterminate statute is not judicially enforceable: the party who asks the court to enforce the treaty or statute is effectively asking the court to "make" law, rather than "apply" the law. In particular cases, reasonable people may disagree about whether a particular treaty provision is beyond judicial competence. Nevertheless, the principle that there are limits on judicial competence to apply treaties is not controversial.[29]

The introduction to Part Two asserted that the term "non-self-executing" functions as legal gibberish because courts and commentators apply the term as a substitute for rational legal analysis. As discussed in Chapter 6, application of the contract doctrine tended to obfuscate critical distinctions between international and domestic legal issues because the doctrine was based on a faulty premise.[30] In contrast to the contract doctrine, the justiciability doctrine can be used to clarify, rather than obfuscate, important legal issues. However, use of the terms "self-executing" and "non-self-executing" to refer both to the congressional-executive concept and the political-judicial concept tends to generate confusion. For that reason, even though the justiciability doctrine associated with *Head Money* is based on sound premises (unlike the contract doctrine), the justiciability doctrine has added another element of confusion to NSE doctrine.

B. *Whitney v. Robertson*

Whitney v. Robertson is the only nineteenth-century case in which the Supreme Court may have held that a treaty required implementing legislation,[31] but *Whitney* is subject to conflicting interpretations on this point. In *Whitney*, plaintiffs sued to recover duties paid on sugar imported from the Dominican Republic. The defendant customs collector had imposed duties pursuant to an 1870 statute.[32] Plaintiffs claimed that the goods should have been admitted duty free. Their argument rested on the combined effect of two treaties: an 1867 treaty with the Dominican Republic and an 1875 treaty with the Kingdom of Hawaii.[33] Article IX of the Dominican treaty stated: "No higher or other duty shall be imposed on the importation into the United States of any article the growth, produce, or manufacture of the Dominican Republic . . . than are or shall be payable on the like articles the growth, produce, or manufacture of any other foreign country."[34] By itself, the Dominican treaty did not entitle plaintiffs to import Dominican sugar duty free because in 1867 there was no treaty or statute that authorized duty-free imports of Hawaiian sugar. However, plaintiffs contended that the 1875 treaty with Hawaii (which provided for duty-free imports of Hawaiian sugar), read together with the 1867 treaty with the Dominican Republic (which prohibited higher duties for Dominican sugar than for other sugar), obligated the United States to permit duty-free imports of Dominican sugar.[35]

The Court rejected plaintiffs' argument on two grounds. First, the Court held as a matter of treaty interpretation that the treaty with the Dominican Republic merely obligated the United States to refrain from enacting tariff legislation that discriminated against Dominican imports. It did not obligate the United States to extend automatically to the Dominican Republic special tariff reductions such as the duty-free provision in the Hawaiian treaty. In the alternative, the Court held that, under the later-in-time rule, even if the treaties did create an international obligation to permit duty-free imports of Dominican sugar, the 1870 tariff statute superseded the 1867 Dominican treaty as a matter of domestic law.[36]

At first blush, the Court's later-in-time analysis appears to be seriously flawed because the plaintiffs claimed a right to duty-free imports under the 1875 Hawaiian treaty, which should have trumped the 1870 statute under the later-in-time rule. In light of this apparent anomaly, there are two possible explanations for the Court's later-in-time holding. Professor Hollis argues that, from the Court's perspective, the 1875 treaty with Hawaii "was irrelevant."[37] Under his view, the Court believed that any treaty rights the plaintiffs could legitimately claim must be derived from the 1867 treaty with the Dominican Republic because plaintiffs had imported sugar from the Dominican Republic, not from Hawaii. Under the later-in-time rule, the 1870 statute trumped the 1867 treaty, regardless of whether the treaty was self-executing or non-self-executing. Thus, under this interpretation of *Whitney*, the Court's statement about non-self-execution was mere dicta that had no effect on its application of the later-in-time rule.[38]

An alternative interpretation of *Whitney*, which I have defended elsewhere,[39] contends that the Court's later-in-time analysis incorporated an implicit holding that the 1875 Hawaiian treaty was not self-executing. This interpretation emphasizes the Court's statement that when a treaty and a statute "are inconsistent, the one last in date will control the other, provided the stipulation of the treaty on the subject is self-executing."[40] Under this interpretation, *Whitney* might be construed to mean that even if the 1875 Hawaiian treaty conflicted with the 1870 statute, the statute still applied because the Hawaiian treaty was not self-executing. However, one problem with this interpretation is that the Court never explained why the Hawaiian treaty was not self-executing.[41]

In sum, the Court's decision in *Whitney* is subject to two different interpretations. Under the first, its statements about self-execution were merely dicta. Under the second, the later-in-time analysis includes an implicit (but unexplained) holding that the 1875 Hawaiian treaty was not self-executing. Under the latter view, the non-self-execution holding is an alternative one, because the Court also held that the importers lost on treaty interpretation grounds. Under either interpretation, *Whitney* provides very little guidance for lower courts about how to determine whether a particular treaty provision is self-executing, because the Court never explained why the 1875 treaty was not self-executing—if that is, indeed, what the Court held.

C. *Downes* and *De Lima*

In *De Lima v. Bidwell*, an importer sued to recover duties paid under protest for items imported from Puerto Rico. The United States acquired Puerto Rico from Spain pursuant to a treaty that ended the Spanish-American War.[42] The treaty entered into force on April 11, 1899. The firm of De Lima & Co. "imported" sugar from Puerto Rico to New York in Autumn 1899. The Court said, "Whether these cargoes of sugar were subject to duty depends solely upon the question whether Porto Rico was a 'foreign country' at the time the sugars were shipped."[43] The answer to that question turned on whether the treaty with Spain converted Puerto Rico from a "foreign country" to U.S. territory for the purpose of U.S. tariff laws. The government insisted that "while the island may be to a certain extent domestic territory, it still remains a 'foreign country' under the tariff laws, until Congress has embraced it within the general revenue system."[44] In other words, the government argued that the treaty with Spain was not self-executing because legislation was needed to convert Puerto Rico from "foreign" to "domestic" for the purpose of U.S. tariff laws. The Court rejected the government's argument, concluding "that by the ratification of the treaty of Paris the island became territory of the United States, although not an organized territory in the technical sense of the word."[45] The Court did not state specifically that the treaty with Spain was "self-executing," but it held that legislation was not necessary to convert Puerto Rico from "foreign" to "domestic" for the purpose of U.S. tariff laws. Therefore, even though the Tariff Act of 1897 imposed duties on sugar imported from Puerto Rico, the treaty with Spain superseded the earlier statute and exempted De Lima's sugar from import duties.

The Court reached this conclusion by performing a detailed analysis of legislative, executive, and judicial precedents for the prior hundred years.[46] However, the Court did not analyze precedents related to self-execution, per se. Instead, it analyzed precedents related to the acquisition of territory, concluding that once a territory is "ceded to and in the possession of the United States . . . [the combination of cession and possession] produce[s] a change of nationality for revenue purposes."[47] In contrast to *Aguilar, Cook, Maul,* and *Cameron Septic*—all of which accepted at face value the government's view that a particular treaty provision was self-executing or non-self-executing[48]—the Court in *De Lima* rejected the government's view that legislation was necessary to exempt Puerto Rican sugar from import duties. The Court supported its conclusion by conducting a detailed analysis of legislative, executive, and judicial practice. Thus, the Court's opinion in *De Lima* could potentially have provided an analytical methodology for lower courts to follow in performing self-execution analysis. However, later decisions rarely cite *De Lima* as authority for self-execution doctrine.[49] Therefore, self-execution doctrine from 1900 to 1945 remained devoid of any useful analytical criteria for distinguishing between self-executing and non-self-executing treaties. As stated in a 1948 memorandum to the Department of State Legal Adviser, "An examination of adjudicated cases and of some treatises and of some of the law reviews has failed to disclose a clear definition of the term 'Self-Executing Treaty.' "[50]

Downes v. Bidwell[51] was a companion case to *De Lima v. Bidwell.* Like *De Lima, Downes* involved the question of whether merchandise imported from Puerto Rico was subject to import duties. However, the goods at issue in *De Lima* were imported in 1899, whereas the goods at issue in *Downes* were imported after Congress passed the Foraker Act in April 1900.[52] The Foraker Act required "the payment of 15 per centum of the duties which are required to be levied, collected, and paid upon like articles of merchandise imported from foreign countries."[53] The importer in *Downes* argued that the Foraker Act was unconstitutional, because the Constitution stipulates that "all Duties, Imposts and Excises shall be uniform throughout the United States."[54] If Puerto Rico was part of the

United States, within the meaning of the Uniformity Clause, then the Foraker Act would be unconstitutional. However, the Court held that the Foraker Act was constitutional. The majority held that the treaty for acquisition of Puerto Rico from Spain did not automatically make Puerto Rico part of the United States for the purpose of the Constitution's revenue clauses.[55]

Reading *De Lima* and *Downes* together, the Court held that the 1898 treaty with Spain was "self-executing" in that the treaty itself made Puerto Rico part of the United States for the purpose of the Tariff Act of 1897 (*De Lima*), but it was "non-self-executing" in that federal legislation was needed to make Puerto Rico part of the United States for the purpose of the Constitution's revenue clauses (*Downes*). In short, the Court held that a single treaty provision—Article II of the 1898 treaty with Spain, which says that "Spain cedes to the United States the island of Porto Rico"[56]—was self-executing for some purposes but not for others. Thus, *De Lima* and *Downes* teach that the answer to the question of whether a treaty requires implementing legislation depends on the context in which one seeks to apply the treaty. This is an important lesson that is entirely consistent with the Court's context-specific application of the Louisiana and Florida treaties in *Foster, Percheman*, and subsequent Louisiana/Florida property cases. Unfortunately, the idea that a single treaty provision can be self-executing for some purposes and non-self-executing for others has been largely forgotten in the subsequent development of self-execution doctrine.[57]

D. *Cameron Septic*

Cameron Septic Tank Co. v. City of Knoxville is the only case before 1945 in which the Supreme Court unambiguously held that a treaty required implementing legislation. (Marshall's statement in *Foster* was a minority view, and *Whitney*'s statements about self-execution were arguably dicta.) In *Cameron Septic*, plaintiff sued defendant for patent infringement. Defendant argued that the patent had expired. In response, plaintiff argued that Article 4 *bis* of the 1900 Treaty of Brussels[58] extended the life of the patent beyond its initial term.[59] The Court said: "Two propositions are involved in the [plaintiff's] contentions: (1) that the treaty applies to the Cameron patent; (2) that the treaty is self-executing."[60] The Court ruled against plaintiff on both points. First, it examined the text and negotiating history of the treaty, concluding as a matter of treaty interpretation that the treaty did "not extend the term of . . . the patent beyond that which was given by the law under which the patent had been issued."[61] The Court could have stopped there, without addressing the self-execution issue, because the Court's holding that the treaty did not extend the term of the patent provided a sufficient basis for ruling in favor of defendant.

However, the Court chose to address the self-execution issue as well. Its alternative holding that Article 4 *bis* was not self-executing provided an independent ground to support the ruling in favor of the defendant. Unfortunately, though, Justice McKenna's opinion for the Court did not present a coherent rationale to support the conclusion that Article 4 *bis* was not self-executing.

Justice McKenna relied partly on the 1889 opinion by Attorney General Miller discussed in Chapter 6.[62] As explained previously, Miller's opinion was based on the untenable premise that all executory treaty provisions are NSE, so Miller's opinion provides little analytical support for the Court's NSE holding in *Cameron Septic*. Justice McKenna also asserted that any doubt as to whether Article 4 *bis* was self-executing "would be entirely removed by the legislative action of other states ... [that] adopted legislation giving full force and effect to the provisions of" the treaty.[63] With due respect for Justice McKenna, the fact that other countries have enacted legislation to implement a treaty has no relevance to the question of whether legislation is needed to implement the treaty in the United States. It is well settled that a treaty provision can be self-executing in one country, even if it requires implementing legislation in another country.[64]

Justice McKenna also relied on Congress's views to support the conclusion that Article 4 *bis* was not self-executing. In 1903, Congress enacted a statute entitled "An Act to Effectuate the Provisions of the ... International Convention for the Protection of Industrial Property."[65] The "international convention" in the title of the statute was the 1900 Treaty of Brussels, so there is no question that the legislation was designed to implement the treaty. Accordingly, Justice McKenna noted that the legislation "expressed the sense of Congress and those concerned with the treaty that it required legislation to become effective."[66] Plaintiff conceded that *some* treaty provisions required legislative implementation. However, the plaintiff argued, Congress chose not to enact legislation to implement Article 4 *bis* because that article "accomplished all that it could accomplish the instant the treaty went into effect, and there was nothing further to be done."[67] In other words, plaintiff argued that some treaty provisions (including Article 4 *bis*) were self-executing and others were non-self-executing. The fact that Congress enacted legislation to implement *some* treaty provisions does not logically support an inference that provisions such as Article 4 *bis*, which the legislation did not implement, are also NSE. Justice McKenna responded to this argument by reiterating that "it is certainly the sense of Congress that" the treaty is not-self-executing. He added that "we are unable to accept the distinction" made by plaintiff.[68] It remains unclear why the Court was unable to accept that distinction. Regardless, Justice McKenna correctly relied on Congress to support his view that *some* of the treaty provisions were NSE, but he failed to offer a coherent rationale to support his conclusion that Article 4 *bis* was NSE.

E. *Cook v. United States*

In *Cook v. United States*,[69] U.S. Coast Guard officers boarded a British vessel about 11.5 miles from the coast that was allegedly engaged in liquor smuggling. The government filed a libel to enforce a penalty against the ship's master, Frank Cook. Cook claimed that the seizure was unlawful because it violated a bilateral treaty with Britain.[70] The government claimed that the seizure was authorized by

Section 581 of the Tariff Act.[71] Section 581 authorized seizures up to twelve miles from shore. If that was the relevant rule, then the seizure was lawful. However, the treaty limited the government's seizure authority to the "distance which can be traversed in one hour by the vessel suspected of endeavoring to commit the offense."[72] If the treaty rule was applicable in *Cook*, it limited the government's seizure authority to a distance of ten miles, given the speed of the vessel at issue. Hence, if the treaty rule applied, the seizure was unlawful and the libel would have to be dismissed.

The Court held that the treaty provided the applicable rule because the 1924 treaty superseded the 1922 statute under the later-in-time rule.[73] The Court said: "[I]n a strict sense the Treaty was self-executing, in that no legislation was necessary to authorize executive action pursuant to its provisions."[74] Justice Brandeis cited a letter from Secretary of State Charles Evans Hughes to the Chairman of the House Foreign Affairs Committee to support his view that the treaty was self-executing.[75] (Interestingly, the very same Charles Evans Hughes was serving as chief justice when the Court decided *Cook*. He joined Justice Brandeis's opinion in *Cook*.) Brandeis added that "[t]his conclusion is supported by the course of administrative practice." In that context, he cited Treasury Department instructions to the Coast Guard, which made clear that "seizing officers should be instructed to produce evidence, not that the vessel was found within the [twelve-mile] limit, but that she was apprehended within one hour's sailing distance from the coast."[76] The Court concluded on this basis that the liquor treaty with Britain was self-executing. Therefore, the treaty superseded the 1922 statute.

That was not the end of the matter because Congress had re-enacted "section 581 in the Tariff Act of 1930 in the identical terms of the act of 1922."[77] Hence, the government argued that the 1930 statute superseded the 1924 treaty under the later-in-time rule. The Court rejected this argument. Justice Brandeis invoked the presumption against implied repeals, stating: "A treaty will not be deemed to have been abrogated or modified by a later statute, unless such purpose on the part of Congress has been clearly expressed."[78] He found no evidence that Congress intended to abrogate or modify the 1924 treaty when it enacted the 1930 statute. He referred to committee reports, congressional debates, and "consistent departmental practice" to support his conclusion that "[s]earches and seizures in the enforcement of the laws prohibiting alcoholic liquors are governed, since the 1930 act, as they were before, by the provisions of the Treaty."[79] In sum, the Court found a conflict between the 1924 treaty and the 1922 statute and applied the later-in-time rule to resolve that conflict. However, it applied the presumption against implied repeals to support its holding that there was no conflict between the 1930 statute and the 1924 treaty, even though the 1930 statute was identical to the 1922 statute.

Chapter 8 addresses the intent version of NSE doctrine. In brief, the intent doctrine holds that the intent of the (executive) treaty makers determines whether a particular treaty provision is self-executing or non-self-executing.

Like the intent doctrine, Justice Brandeis's analysis in *Cook* placed great weight on the views of the executive branch. However, Brandeis's analysis differed from the intent doctrine in two key respects. First, Justice Brandeis gave considerable weight to the executive's application of the treaty ex post, after the treaty entered into force. In contrast, the intent doctrine focuses on the executive's intent ex ante, when the treaty was being negotiated. Second, Brandeis treated the executive's views as persuasive, but not dispositive; indeed, the Court ruled against the executive in *Cook*. In contrast, the intent doctrine treats the executive's views as dispositive because, under the intent doctrine, the intent of the treaty makers determines whether a treaty is self-executing.

III. SUPREME COURT CASES THAT CITE *FOSTER*, *HEAD MONEY*, OR BOTH

The cases discussed so far in this chapter are not the only Supreme Court decisions relevant to NSE doctrine. The modern doctrine of self-execution is generally traced to two nineteenth-century Supreme Court cases: *Foster v. Neilson* and *The Head Money Cases*. Accordingly, I searched for all Supreme Court decisions before 1946 that cited either *Foster* or *Head Money*. Excluding the cases discussed previously in this chapter, and excluding cases in which neither party asserted a treaty-based right,[80] the searches identified a total of forty-five Supreme Court decisions that cited *Foster*, *Head Money*, or both.[81]

Surprisingly, most of those forty-five cases do not say anything relevant to NSE doctrine. Seventeen cases involving disputes about title to real property cited *Foster* either to support the proposition that old Spanish grants were void, or to support the conclusion that disputes about territorial boundaries between sovereigns are political questions.[82] (As discussed in Chapter 4, the first two holdings in *Foster* involved the validity of Spanish grants and the political question doctrine.) Two cases not involving real property cited *Foster* as authority for the political question doctrine.[83] Twelve cases cited *Head Money*, *Foster*, or both as authority for the later-in-time rule.[84] Four cases cited *Head Money*, *Foster*, or both to support the principle of treaty supremacy.[85] Two cases cited *Head Money* to support other claims that it does not actually support.[86] Thus, in the final analysis, only twelve of the forty-five cases cited *Foster* or *Head Money* to support a proposition relevant to NSE doctrine.[87] The following paragraphs discuss those twelve cases.

In *United States v. Rauscher*, *Chew Heong v. United States*, and *United States v. Brooks*, the Court applied treaties as constraints on federal authority. In *Rauscher*, defendant invoked a bilateral extradition treaty with Britain as a bar to federal criminal prosecution. Absent the treaty, Section 5347 of the Revised Statutes clearly authorized the prosecution. Nevertheless, the Court held that the treaty required dismissal of the criminal charges. The Court cited both *Foster* and *Head Money* in support of its view that the treaty was "the supreme law of the land, of which the courts are bound to take judicial notice, and to enforce in any appropriate proceeding the rights of persons growing out of that treaty."[88]

Thus, *Rauscher* applied a treaty to override a previously enacted federal statute, thereby preventing the government from exercising its statutory authority to prosecute Rauscher.

In *Chew Heong*, petitioner filed a writ of habeas corpus to challenge an administrative decision that denied him permission to enter the United States. The Court cited *Foster* to support its view that an 1880 treaty with China was "a part of the supreme law of the land" and invoked "the duty imposed by the Constitution to respect treaty stipulations when they become the subject of judicial proceedings."[89] The Court held that the treaty granted petitioner the right "to return to, and remain in, the United States."[90] Despite an apparent conflict between the 1880 treaty and an 1882 federal statute, the Court invoked the presumption against implied repeals to support its holding that the later-in-time statute did not deprive petitioner of his treaty-based right to enter and remain in the United States.[91]

In *United States v. Brooks*, Brooks claimed title to property in Louisiana on the basis of an 1835 treaty with the Caddo Indians. Brooks's attorney cited *Foster* to support his argument that the treaty, "being ratified and confirmed by the President and Senate, becomes the supreme law, and cannot be set aside by the courts, on any ground whatever."[92] The Court held that the treaty granted Brooks's predecessor "a fee simple title to all the rights which the Caddoes had in these lands" and that implementing legislation was not necessary because "[n]othing further was contemplated by the treaty to perfect the title."[93] *Brooks* is interesting because Congress passed a statute in 1842, several years after the treaty was ratified, that was intended to confirm the titles of other private claimants who asserted title in opposition to Brooks. By affirming the validity of Brooks's title, the Court's decision implied that the 1842 statute was invalid. Thus, *Brooks* applied the "vested property rights" exception to the later-in-time rule, which holds that a later-in-time statute cannot deprive individuals of vested property rights derived from a treaty.[94]

In *Terlinden v. Ames*, *Baldwin v. Franks*, *United States v. Forty-Three Gallons of Whiskey*, and *Holden v. Joy*, the government invoked treaties to support the exercise of federal executive authority. In *Baldwin*, the federal government charged defendants with a conspiracy to expel Chinese persons from their lawful residences.[95] The majority acknowledged that a bilateral treaty granted certain rights to Chinese nationals residing in the United States. However, the majority held that the criminal statutes invoked by the government did not create federal criminal penalties for violations of treaty rights.[96] The majority left open the possibility that defendants could be prosecuted under state law.

Justice Field dissented. He argued that Section 5336 of the Revised Statutes authorized federal criminal punishment for violations of the treaty with China. Specifically, "section 5336 declares that if two or more persons . . . conspire by force to prevent, hinder, or delay the execution of any law of the United States, each of them shall be punished" by fine, imprisonment, or both.[97] Justice Field cited both *Foster* and *Head Money* to support the claim that "in many instances a treaty operates by its own force—that is, without the aid of any legislative enactment."[98] He noted that the treaty granted Chinese nationals a right to reside in the United States. Moreover, he said:

> A treaty, in conferring a right of residence, requires no congressional legisla-
> tion for the enforcement of that right. The treaty in that particular is executed
> by the intended beneficiaries. They select their residence. . . . A conspiracy
> to prevent by force a residence in the town or county selected by them ap-
> pears to me, therefore, to be a conspiracy to prevent the operation-that is,
> the execution-of a law of the United States, and to be within the letter and
> spirit of the third clause of section 5336.[99]

Thus, in Justice Field's view, the treaty with China executed a "non-self-executing" federal statute. Section 5336 was "non-self-executing" in the sense that it depended for its operation on the enactment of other federal laws, because the statute prohibited conspiracies to "hinder . . . the execution of any law of the United States," but the statute had no field of application unless the federal government enacted other laws whose execution could potentially be obstructed by private actors. In Justice Field's view, the treaty with China was such a "law." If the treaty with China did not exist, Section 5336 would not authorize federal criminal penalties for defendants' conduct. Because the treaty did exist, and be-cause defendants' conduct hindered the operation of that treaty, Section 5336 authorized federal criminal prosecution (according to Justice Field).[100]

Justice Field's dissent in *Baldwin* provides a helpful framework for analyz-ing the relationship between treaties and federal executive authority in cases where the government invokes a treaty to support federal executive authority. In many such cases, the government is arguing, in essence, that a treaty executes a "non-self-executing" federal statute. For example, in *Terlinden v. Ames* the gov-ernment sought extradition of a fugitive to Prussia in accordance with an 1852 treaty with Prussia.[101] The Court rejected petitioner's challenge to the govern-ment's authority to extradite him, invoking the extradition treaty as the primary basis for the government's legal authority to extradite.[102] *Terlinden* also impli-cated an 1848 federal statute that established procedures for international extra-dition cases.[103] The statute authorized the secretary of state to extradite fugitives in cases where there "may exist [in the future], any treaty or convention for ex-tradition between the government of the United States" and the relevant foreign government.[104] Thus, the federal extradition statute was "non-self-executing," in the sense that the statute depended upon the conclusion of subsequent treaties to trigger the secretary of state's legal authority to extradite. In *Terlinden*, the Court held—without using these words—that the treaty "executed" the statute, thereby making legally operative the secretary's latent authority to extradite the individual fugitive. The Court applied a similar analytical framework, relying on specific treaties to execute the "non-self-executing" statute, in numerous extradi-tion cases decided between 1848 and 1945.[105]

United States v. Forty-Three Gallons of Whiskey can also be described as a case where a treaty executed a "non-self-executing" federal statute. In *Forty-Three*

Gallons, the government sought forfeiture of property seized under a federal statute that prohibited introduction of liquor into Indian country. Defendant argued that the statute did not apply to him because the seizure occurred in Minnesota, outside the bounds of any Indian reservation. Thus, in his view, his conduct was governed exclusively by state law. The federal statute, by its own force, applied to territory within Indian reservations, but did not apply to other territory within the State of Minnesota. In May 1864, President Lincoln proclaimed a treaty with the Chippewa Indians, in which the Chippewa ceded to the United States a large tract of land in Minnesota. Article VII stipulated: "The laws of the United States now in force . . . prohibiting the introduction and sale of spirituous liquors in the Indian country, shall be in full force and effect throughout the country hereby ceded."[106] The Court cited *Foster* for the proposition "[t]hat a treaty is to be regarded, in courts of justice, as equivalent to an act of the legislature, whenever it operates of itself, without the aid of any legislative provision." It then added, "No legislation is required to put the seventh article in force; and it must become a rule of action."[107] Thus, the Court held that Article VII of the Chippewa treaty augmented the government's enforcement authority by extending federal liquor laws into ceded territory within the State of Minnesota, but outside the boundaries of any Indian reservation.[108]

Holden v. Joy involved a dispute over title to real property in Kansas. The outcome hinged on "whether the title claimed by the respondent [Joy] is a valid one."[109] Joy's title was founded on a patent issued by the secretary of the interior. The secretary's authority to issue the patent was based on an 1866 treaty with the Cherokee tribe, and an 1868 supplemental treaty. Holden argued "that the President and Senate, in concluding such a treaty, could not lawfully covenant that a patent should issue to convey lands which belonged to the United States without the consent of Congress."[110] The Court rejected this argument. It cited *Foster* for the proposition that "there are many authorities where it is held that a treaty may convey to a grantee a good title to such lands without an act of Congress conferring it."[111] Thus, the Court ruled in favor of Joy because the treaties authorized the secretary to issue a patent for the land, and no further legislation was needed to supplement the secretary's authority.[112]

The Court cited *Foster* in both *Pollard's Heirs v. Kibbe* and *United States v. Arredondo*, primarily for the purpose of distinguishing *Foster*. I addressed *Arredondo* in Chapter 4,[113] so I focus here on *Kibbe. Kibbe,* like *Foster,* involved land west of the Perdido River, in the area subject to a territorial dispute with Spain between 1803 and 1819. Counsel for defendants cited *Foster* for the proposition that "Spanish grants, made for any part of the territory west of the Perdido, after the treaty of 1803 . . . are declared void."[114] The Court ruled against defendants. It held that claims based on Spanish grants after 1803 "are certainly not beyond the reach of Congress to confirm, although it may require a special act of Congress for that purpose; and the present claim being founded upon such act, distinguishes it from the doctrine of this Court" in *Foster.*[115] Thus, in contrast to the plaintiffs in *Foster,* the plaintiffs in *Kibbe* prevailed because Congress had passed a special act to confirm their titles (which derived from Spanish grants).[116]

In *In re Metzger*, an international extradition case, the attorney general's argument cited *Foster* in support of the proposition that the District Court "had competent authority, under the provisions of the treaty and the laws of the United States now in force, to take jurisdiction of this case, and to order the apprehension of the accused ... pursuant to the stipulations of the treaty."[117] The Court decided *Metzger* before Congress enacted the 1848 extradition statute (discussed previously with reference to *Terlinden*). Nevertheless, the Court held that it was proper for a judicial officer to decide "[w]hether the crime charged is sufficiently proved, and comes within the treaty."[118] Thus, the Court held that the extradition treaty was self-executing, in the sense that the judicial officer had authority to apply the treaty, even without specific legislative authorization.[119]

The other two cases referenced above merely cite or quote the relevant passage from *Foster* or *Head Money*, without analyzing the question of whether the particular treaty at issue was self-executing. In *Valentine v. U.S. ex rel. Neidecker*, the Court quoted *Foster* for the proposition that a treaty is "to be regarded in courts of justice as equivalent to an act of the legislature, whenever it operates of itself, without the aid of any legislative provision."[120] In *Ex parte Cooper*, Chief Justice Fuller quoted the passage from *Head Money* associated with the justiciability version of NSE doctrine, but the *Head Money* quote was not part of the Court's rationale for deciding the case.[121]

* * *

Thus far, this chapter and Chapter 4 have focused on twenty-seven Supreme Court decisions between 1800 and 1945 that shed light on the Court's application of self-execution doctrine. These include: *Foster* and *Percheman*; six other cases identified as "landmark" cases; seven other cases that use the term "self-executing" in conjunction with "treaty"; and twelve cases that cited *Foster, Head Money*, or both for some proposition relevant to self-execution doctrine. Before we turn to an analysis of lower federal court decisions, it may be helpful to summarize the main conclusions that arise from the preceding analysis.

First, self-execution doctrine had very little impact on the Supreme Court's application of treaties before 1945. As noted at the beginning of this chapter, between 1800 and 1945 the Court decided approximately 550 cases involving the judicial application of treaties. Apart from the twenty-seven cases analyzed above, the Court said almost nothing about self-execution in the other 500-plus treaty cases decided during the period. Rather, the Court's dominant approach was simply to apply the treaty, without pausing to consider whether the treaty at issue was self-executing or non-self-executing.[122]

Second, the Court failed to articulate a coherent NSE doctrine. *De Lima* and *Downes* could have provided the basis for a coherent doctrine, but courts and commentators rarely cited either case as authority for NSE doctrine. Justice Field's dissenting opinion in *Baldwin v. Franks* presented insightful analysis of relevant issues, but his opinion had almost no impact on the subsequent evolution of judicial doctrine. Justice Miller introduced the justiciability version of NSE doctrine in *Head Money*, but the Court never applied the justiciability doctrine to decide a case before 1945. *Whitney* is helpful in that it defines the term "self-executing," but it does not provide criteria to guide lower courts in determining which treaties are SE or NSE. The best that can be said about the Court's NSE doctrine before 1945 is that the doctrine did little harm because it was rarely applied.

Finally, twenty-five of the twenty-seven cases analyzed above dealt exclusively with questions of federal law. *De Lima, Downes, Whitney,* and *Bartram* involved federal import duties.[123] *Lee Yen Tai, Fok Young Yo, Chew Heong,* and *Head Money* involved immigration.[124] *Valentine, Factor, Terlinden,* and *Metzger* were international extradition cases.[125] *Aguilar, Cook, Maul,* and *Cooper* were admiralty/maritime cases.[126] *Mitchell, Holden, Brooks, Kibbe, Percheman, Arredondo,* and *Foster* were real property cases that did not present any state law questions.[127] *Cameron Septic* was a patent case, and *Rauscher* was a federal criminal case.[128] Inasmuch as no question of state law was presented in any of these cases, they tend to reinforce the conclusion that self-execution doctrine before 1945 was generally not relevant to treaty supremacy cases. Two of the twenty-seven cases—*Baldwin v. Franks* and *United States v. Forty-Three Gallons of Whiskey*—did implicate some state law issues.[129] I will say more about these two cases later in this chapter. At present, it suffices to note that no Supreme Court decision before 1945 either stated or implied that there is an NSE exception to the Constitution's treaty supremacy rule.

IV. FEDERAL APPELLATE CASES RELATED TO SELF-EXECUTION

To test the relationship between treaty supremacy and self-execution, I searched for all federal appellate opinions between 1800 and 1945, other than Supreme Court opinions, that used the term "self-executing" in conjunction with "treaty." I also searched for all federal appellate opinions during the relevant time period that cited *Foster, Head Money,* or both, where at least one party raised a treaty-based claim or defense. These searches identified a total of thirty-six published appellate opinions, other than Supreme Court opinions, that say something relevant to self-execution doctrine.[130]

Thirty-three of the thirty-six cases dealt with matters governed exclusively by federal law, not state law. Those thirty-three cases include twelve cases involving import duties,[131] five patent cases,[132] four immigration cases,[133] four cases involving Native Americans,[134] three admiralty/maritime cases,[135] two cases related to international arbitration,[136] two real property cases,[137] and one case involving a trial by military commission.[138] None of these cases involved any substantive claim or defense based on state law. Therefore, they do not support the claim that there is an NSE exception to the Constitution's treaty supremacy rule. Moreover, these thirty-three cases are consistent with the conclusion that self-execution doctrine before 1945 was generally not relevant to treaty supremacy cases.

Three of the thirty-six cases implicated some state law issues: *O'Donnell v. United States,*[139] *Turner v. American Baptist Missionary Union,*[140] and *United States v. New Bedford Bridge.*[141] For the reasons explained below, none of these cases supports an NSE exception to the Constitution's treaty supremacy rule.

O'Donnell involved a dispute over title to land on Mare Island in San Francisco Bay. When the Ninth Circuit decided the case in 1936, the United States had been using the land as a navy yard for about eighty years. O'Donnell traced his title to a patent issued by the State of California in 1857, after California became a state.[142] The United States purchased the land in 1853 from Bissell and Aspinwall, who traced their title to a grant from the Mexican Governor of California in 1841, when California was part of Mexico. The Bissell/Aspinwall title was protected by the Treaty of Guadalupe Hidalgo, the 1848 treaty in which Mexico ceded California to the United States.[143] Thus, the case pitted the government's treaty-based claim against the individual's state law claim. In the course of its analysis, the Ninth Circuit said that the relevant provisions of the Treaty of Guadalupe Hidalgo "are not self-executing."[144] The fact that the court used the term "self-executing" in a case involving an alleged conflict between a treaty and state law suggests that self-execution doctrine may be marginally relevant to treaty supremacy cases.

In the final analysis, though, the categorization of the treaty as non-self-executing was immaterial. After the United States acquired California from Mexico, Congress established a Board of Land Commissioners ("Board") to process land claims by individuals who asserted titles protected by the treaty. "Bissell and Aspinwall ... filed their petition before the Board, seeking confirmation of their title ... [and] the Board confirmed their title by decree of May 8, 1855."[145] The Board proceeding was supposed to be an adversary proceeding between Bissell and Aspinwall, on one side, and the federal government, on the other side. However, the U.S. government had purchased Bissell and Aspinwall's property interest in 1853. Hence, the Ninth Circuit held that the Board's decision did not establish the U.S. government's property right "because it was given in a nonadversary action in which the claimant and defendant were one, and hence no justiciable issue existed upon which adjudication could be had."[146] The Ninth Circuit ruled against the government, primarily on this basis. The Supreme Court reversed, holding in favor of the government on the grounds that "the decree of the Board ... must be taken as conclusive."[147] The Supreme Court opinion says nothing about self-execution. From the Supreme Court's perspective, it was immaterial whether the Treaty of Guadalupe Hidalgo was self-executing. Ultimately, the outcome of the case hinged on the validity of the Board decision, and the Board's authority derived from a statute designed to implement the treaty.

Turner v. American Baptist Missionary Union involved a dispute over title to land in Michigan.[148] The Missionary Union (ABMU) had built a church and occupied the land for many years when it belonged to Native Americans, before Michigan became a state. In March 1836, the United States concluded a treaty with the Ottawa and Chippewa Indians. The treaty said: "The net proceeds of the sale of the one hundred and sixty acres of land, upon the Grand River upon which the missionary society have erected their buildings, shall be paid to the said society, in lieu of the value of their said improvements."[149] Thus, ABMU had a treaty-based right to the proceeds from sale of the land. Turner settled on the land in July 1836 and built a house the following year. His asserted title depended partly on an 1838 federal preemption statute (which granted rights to settlers in possession of land), and partly on a Michigan state law enacted in 1842. ABMU filed an ejectment action in state court to recover possession of the land. In response, Turner sued in federal court, seeking an injunction to block the state court action. Associate Justice John McLean, sitting as a Circuit Justice, held for ABMU.[150]

Justice McLean first held that "[t]he state of Michigan can exercise no power whatever over the *public lands* within her limits. She is expressly prohibited from doing this by a compact agreed to in the admission of the state into the Union."[151] Accordingly, the justice had to determine whether the land at issue was "public land"—that is, land to which the United States held title. Congress passed a law in June 1836 authorizing the Michigan legislature to select and locate "five entire sections of land . . . from any of the *unappropriated* lands belonging to the United States within the said State."[152] Acting pursuant to this federal statute, the Michigan legislature selected the land in controversy. Justice McLean held that "[t]he part of the land entered had been specially appropriated by the treaty. . . . It was not, therefore, open to location by the agent of the state."[153] Because the federal statute merely authorized Michigan to select "unappropriated lands," and because the land at issue was specially appropriated by the treaty, Michigan acted unlawfully when it selected the land at issue. Therefore, insofar as Turner's title depended on Michigan state law, Turner lost because Michigan lacked authority to grant him the land. In this respect, *Turner* appears to be a straightforward treaty supremacy case in which the treaty claim prevailed over the state law claim.

Turner's claim also hinged partly on a federal preemption statute, enacted in June 1838, which granted property rights to "every actual settler of the public lands . . . who was in possession and a housekeeper, by personal residence thereon, at the time of the passage of this act."[154] The president proclaimed the disputed land for sale in July 1838, and Turner "proved his pre-emption claim" in October of that year.[155] Hence, he appeared to have a valid property right based on federal law. However, Justice McLean said: "Without a law the president is not authorized to sell the public lands, so that this treaty, though so far as the Indians were concerned, was the supreme law of the land, yet, as regards the right to the proceeds of the above tract, an act of congress is required."[156] In other words, the treaty provision requiring payment of money to ABMU was constitutionally non-self-executing, because "money cannot be appropriated by the treaty-making power."[157] Congress had not yet appropriated money to make the payment to ABMU required by the treaty. Until Congress did so, the president lacked authority to sell the land to a third party, because the federal preemption statute "declares that its provisions should not apply to lands which had been reserved."[158] Justice McLean held that the land at issue had been reserved by the treaty in 1836. Therefore, the president acted unlawfully when he proclaimed the land for sale in July 1838, because the preemption statute did not authorize him to sell land that had been reserved by the treaty until Congress appropriated money to pay ABMU.

Turner is one of the few nineteenth-century decisions addressing both treaty supremacy and self-execution in a single case. However, the two sets of issues are analytically distinct. Justice McLean applied treaty supremacy doctrine to reject Turner's asserted state law property right. He applied self-execution doctrine to reject Turner's argument that he had a valid property right based on federal law. In short, the self-execution analysis had no bearing on the treaty supremacy issue. Justice McLean understood self-execution as a federal separation-of-powers doctrine that required the president to obtain congressional authorization before he could sell public land reserved by treaty.

United States v. New Bedford Bridge was a federal criminal case. The indictment charged a corporation with erecting a bridge across a river "so that navigators and citizens cannot pass to and from the sea . . . as they before did and of right ought to do, thus injuring the coasting and foreign trade of other nations."[159] Defendant moved to quash the indictment on the grounds that "congress has not declared the act charged in the indictment to be an offence against the United States." Associate Justice Levi Woodbury, sitting as a Circuit Justice, granted the motion to quash on the grounds that no act of Congress created criminal penalties for defendant's conduct. The government argued, among other things, that the Massachusetts law authorizing the corporation to erect a bridge violated certain treaties promising freedom of navigation to U.S. treaty partners. Justice Woodbury agreed that the obstruction to navigation created by the bridge "seems to violate the spirit of the [Jay Treaty] with England." He said: "Sometimes treaties may . . . be enforced without any new or additional provision, and in such case, it may be the duty of the judicial tribunals to execute them without any act of Congress. In other cases . . . laws will be first necessary."[160] Thus, he recognized the distinction between self-executing and non-self-executing treaties, without using those terms.

Justice Woodbury held, in essence, that treaties promising freedom of navigation were self-executing for some purposes, but not for other purposes. Referring to obstructions to navigation created by the bridge, he said "it would be difficult to try them as crimes, when nowhere declared to be so, or to try them by this court, unless jurisdiction over them is in some appropriate manner clearly conferred on it."[161] Thus, for the purpose of creating federal criminal jurisdiction, the freedom of navigation provisions in the Jay Treaty and other similar treaties were non-self-executing. Legislation was necessary to create federal criminal jurisdiction.[162] However, he said, "even now any individual, suffering by this obstruction in his rights to free navigation, is not probably without redress." He continued: "[V]essels which from their size cannot pass through the draw, or as high up the harbor . . . as they used to; and the owners of such, when actually obstructed and delayed by means of this bridge, might probably have redress in damages, or by way of injunction . . . ."[163] Moreover, he added, "Civil redress . . . in the cases before described, seems obtainable in the courts both of the states and United States, notwithstanding the decision in *Foster v. Neilson*."[164] Thus, the freedom of navigation provisions in the Jay Treaty and other similar treaties were self-executing, in the sense that injured parties could (probably) bring civil suits for damages or an injunction, even without legislation specifically authorizing such suits.

New Bedford Bridge could be described, in some sense, as a treaty supremacy case, because Massachusetts law authorized construction of a bridge that arguably violated navigation rights protected by treaties. However, because the case came to him as a federal criminal indictment, Justice Woodbury's opinion focused almost entirely on federal separation-of-powers issues. The central question was whether the court had jurisdiction to adjudicate the criminal charges. He concluded that the court lacked jurisdiction because Congress had not granted the court jurisdiction. Most of his opinion is unrelated to either self-execution or treaty supremacy. Nevertheless his conclusion that treaties granting navigation rights are self-executing for some purposes, but not others, was entirely consistent with the dominant nineteenth-century understanding that a particular treaty provision might be self-executing for some purposes, while requiring legislation for other purposes.

In sum, the decisions by lower federal appellate courts are broadly consistent with Supreme Court decisions. Self-execution doctrine, as applied by federal appellate courts before 1945, had almost no relevance to treaty supremacy issues. Self-execution doctrine and treaty supremacy doctrine were two independent doctrines that rarely arose in the same case. There was not a single published federal court decision before 1945 that endorsed or applied an NSE exception to the Constitution's treaty supremacy rule.

V. THE PROBLEM OF OVERLAPPING JURISDICTION

Chapter 5 analyzed application of the treaty supremacy rule in circumstances where treaties intersected with state law. This chapter has analyzed application of self-execution doctrine in situations where treaties intersected with federal law. The question arises, "how did the Supreme Court handle cases where treaties intersected with both state and federal regulatory authority?" In such cases, one might expect to see some connection between treaty supremacy doctrine and self-execution doctrine. In fact, though, even in cases where state and federal jurisdiction overlapped, the doctrines of treaty supremacy and self-execution tended to operate independently. This section analyzes six illustrative judicial decisions where treaties addressed matters subject to both state and federal regulatory authority: *Hines v. Davidowitz, Pigeon River Co. v. Charles W. Cox, Ltd., Oetjen v. Central Leather Co., Thomas v. Gay, Baldwin v. Franks*, and *United States v. Forty-Three Gallons of Whiskey*.[165] The cases divide broadly into two groups. *Hines, Pigeon River, Oetjen* and *Thomas* involved "legal conflicts." *Baldwin* and *Forty-Three Gallons* involved "jurisdictional conflicts." The Court or individual justices sometimes applied self-execution doctrine to cases involving jurisdictional conflicts between state and federal regulatory authority, but it did not apply self-execution doctrine to cases involving legal conflicts between treaties and state law.

In *Hines v. Davidowitz*, individual plaintiffs sued to enjoin enforcement of a Pennsylvania statute that required aliens to register with the state Department of Labor. The United States contended that "the subject of alien registration is reserved exclusively for federal regulation" because it "concerns our international relations, in regard to which foreign nations ought to be considered and their rights respected, whether the rule be established by treaty or by legislation."[166] Neither the plaintiffs nor the United States identified a specific treaty with which the Pennsylvania law conflicted. Even so, the Supreme Court affirmed the principle of treaty supremacy: "When the national government by treaty or statute has established rules and regulations touching the rights, privileges, obligations or burdens of aliens as such, the treaty or statute is the supreme law of the land. No state can add to or take from the force and effect of such treaty or statute."[167] Ultimately, the Court did not decide whether the Pennsylvania law conflicted with U.S. treaty obligations, preferring instead to rest its holding on statutory preemption grounds. The Court held that Congress, by "its adoption of a comprehensive, integrated scheme for regulation of aliens—including its 1940 registration act—. . . has precluded state action like that taken by Pennsylvania."[168]

In *Pigeon River Co. v. Charles W. Cox, Ltd.*, a Minnesota corporation had made improvements to a river that flows along the border between Minnesota and Canada. The Minnesota company sued a Canadian defendant to collect tolls for its use of the river. The lower court ruled that Article 2 of the Webster-Ashburton Treaty prohibited collection of such tolls.[169] The case involved an alleged conflict between the treaty and state law because defendant invoked the treaty and plaintiff invoked a Minnesota law that "authorized the erection of these improvements and the charging of reasonable tolls."[170] Congress had also enacted legislation in 1901 authorizing the plaintiff to make improvements on the river and to impose "a reasonable charge therefor."[171] The Court said: "We think that it is proper to infer that the Congress . . . did not consider the authority to make [improvements] and to impose a reasonable charge for their use, as being inconsistent with the treaty stipulation. We regard the action of the Congress . . . as a practical construction of the treaty as permitting these works and justifying the charge."[172] Thus, in the Court's view, both state and federal law supported the company's right to charge a toll, and the treaty did not prohibit such a toll.

Oetjen v. Central Leather Co. involved a dispute over title to two consignments of hides. Oetjen claimed title as the assignee of a Mexican partnership. Central Leather had purchased the goods from a Texas corporation, which in turn purchased them from General Villa. Oetjen argued that General Villa never held valid title because he confiscated the goods in violation of the Hague Convention of 1907.[173] Thus, both parties asserted state law contract claims, but Oetjen challenged Central Leather's claim by raising a treaty supremacy argument. Confiscation of the goods in Mexico occurred in the context of a civil war. After the war, "the government of the United States recognized the government of Carranza as the *de facto* government of the Republic of Mexico," and later as the de jure government.[174] General Villa fought for Carranza during the civil war. The Court offered two different rationales for avoiding a decision on the merits of the treaty supremacy issue. First, "when a government which originates in revolution or revolt is recognized by the political department of our government as the *de jure* government of the country in which it is established, such recognition ... validates all the actions and conduct of the government so recognized from the commencement of its existence."[175] Second, the Court applied the act-of-state doctrine, stating: "Every sovereign state is bound to respect the independence of every other sovereign state, and the courts of one country will not sit in judgment on the acts of the government of another done within its own territory."[176] Because the Court refused to decide the merits of the treaty supremacy issue, Central Leather prevailed on the basis of actual possession, plus a (state law) contractual right supported by the federal act of recognition.

In *Thomas v. Gay*,[177] the Osage Indians leased land in the Oklahoma Territory to Caucasian ranchers for cattle grazing. (Oklahoma was not yet a state.) Oklahoma levied taxes on the cattle ranchers. The ranchers challenged the validity of the taxes on several grounds, two of which are relevant here. First, the ranchers argued that the United States violated treaty rights of the Osage Indians by incorporating Osage land into the Oklahoma Territory without their consent. The Court invoked the later-in-time rule to reject that argument, stating "that an act of congress may supersede a prior treaty, and that any questions that may arise are beyond the sphere of judicial cognizance."[178] As Congress had enacted a law making Osage lands part of Oklahoma, the ranchers could not successfully challenge that law by invoking a prior conflicting treaty. Second, the federal law creating the Oklahoma Territory granted legislative power to the territorial government, but stipulated that "[n]othing in this act shall be construed to impair any right now pertaining to any Indians or Indian tribe in said territory."[179] The ranchers argued that the tax impaired the rights of the Osage by diminishing the value of their land, because ranchers would not pay as much for grazing rights if they knew they would be taxed. The Court said "that a tax put upon the cattle of the lessees is too remote and indirect to be deemed a tax upon the lands or privileges of the Indians."[180] Thus, from the Court's perspective, federal law supported the territorial government's taxing power, despite the economic harm to the Osage.

The four cases addressed in the preceding paragraphs—*Hines, Pigeon River, Oetjen,* and *Thomas*—all involved alleged conflicts between treaties and state law. *Hines* referred to treaties generally without identifying a particular treaty. The other three cases identified specific treaties. In *Oetjen*, the state law at issue was common law. In *Thomas*, the "state law" was the law of a territorial government. The other cases involved state statutes. *Pigeon River* was the only case where the Court decided the merits of the treaty supremacy issue; it held that there was no conflict between the treaty and state law. The Court invalidated state law in *Hines* on statutory preemption grounds, without deciding whether state law conflicted with any particular treaty. It upheld state common law in *Oetjen,* invoking the act of state doctrine and the political question doctrine to avoid the merits of the treaty supremacy argument. It also upheld state law in *Thomas,* avoiding the merits of the treaty supremacy argument by invoking a later-in-time federal statute to override the treaty. Thus, it appears that the Court had some tendency to avoid the merits of treaty supremacy arguments in cases involving overlapping state and federal jurisdiction.

The other two cases in the (small) illustrative sample are *Baldwin v. Franks* and *United States v. Forty-Three Gallons of Whiskey*. The central facts of both are summarized above.[181] Here, I highlight three salient features of these cases. First, like the four other cases discussed in this section, both *Baldwin* and *Forty-Three Gallons* involved issues of overlapping state and federal jurisdiction. In both cases, the government argued that the combined effect of a treaty and a federal statute authorized the federal government to penalize conduct that, absent the treaty, would be regulated exclusively by state law.[182] Second, unlike the other four cases in this section, neither *Baldwin* nor *Forty-Three Gallons* implicated the treaty supremacy rule, because neither involved an alleged conflict between a treaty and state law. In fact, neither *Baldwin* nor *Forty-Three Gallons* mentioned any particular state law. The only federal-state "conflicts" in those cases were disputes about whether the defendants' conduct fell within the scope of federal penal laws. If not, state penal laws would apply.

Third, both *Baldwin* and *Whiskey* contained some explicit discussion of self-execution issues, although in *Baldwin* the issue arose only in Justice Field's dissent. Here, too, *Baldwin* and *Whiskey* differ from the other four cases discussed in this section, none of which said anything about self-execution doctrine in the United States. (The Court in *Pigeon River* noted that "the rights and privileges given by a treaty are, *under Canadian law*, enforceable by the courts only where the treaty has been implemented or sanctioned by legislation."[183]) In sum, all six cases discussed in this section involved some type of overlap between state and federal regulatory authority. However, only four of the cases implicated the Constitution's treaty supremacy rule. Those four—*Hines, Pigeon River, Oetjen*, and *Thomas*—did not include any explicit discussion of self-execution. In contrast, the two cases that did not implicate treaty supremacy—*Baldwin* and *Forty-Three Gallons*—both contained some explicit discussion of self-execution. Hence, even the jurisdictional overlap cases tend to support the proposition that, before 1945, self-execution and treaty supremacy were two independent, non-overlapping doctrines. The fact that the two doctrines operated independently helps explain why, before 1945, there was no NSE exception to the Constitution's treaty supremacy rule.

Seeds of Change

Chapters 4 to 7 demonstrated that legislative, executive, and judicial authorities from 1800 to 1945 provide virtually no support for an NSE exception to the Constitution's treaty supremacy rule. Even so, certain developments during this period planted seeds for the revolution that followed after 1945. As discussed in Part Three, the advent of modern international human rights law sparked an invisible constitutional change that converted the treaty supremacy rule from a mandatory to an optional rule. This chapter examines developments in the early twentieth century that laid the groundwork for subsequent constitutional change.

Two such developments merit only brief mention because they have been analyzed in detail elsewhere. First, U.S. geopolitical power grew steadily from the Spanish-American War in 1898 until the end of World War II. As discussed in Chapter 1, one of the Framers' key goals in adopting the Supremacy Clause was to promote compliance with U.S. treaty obligations. Treaty compliance mattered to the Framers partly for reasons of national honor, but also because the United States was a weak nation that lived in fear of more powerful European nations.[1] Thus, as of 1789, treaty violations posed a significant threat to national survival. By 1945, however, the United States had become the most powerful nation in the world.[2] Regardless of one's views about national honor, the United States could now violate treaties without fear that retaliation would threaten the nation's survival. Therefore, from a pragmatic standpoint, treaty compliance was not as important in 1945 as it had been in 1789. The compliance rationale underlying the Constitution's treaty supremacy rule had not disappeared completely by 1945, but that rationale was not as compelling in the late twentieth century as it had been in the eighteenth century.

Second, in the late nineteenth and early twentieth centuries, positivism replaced natural law as the dominant jurisprudential paradigm for thinking about international law. The older, natural law paradigm encompassed transnational relations between private parties, vertical relations between states and private parties, and horizontal relations between states. In contrast, the newer, positivist paradigm focused narrowly on horizontal relations between states as the proper subject of international law.[3] The positivists' narrow focus on horizontal relations had significant implications for the treaty supremacy rule. Recall that there are two distinct aspects to that rule: (1) treaties supersede conflicting state laws, and (2) courts have a constitutional duty to apply treaties in the event of a conflict. If one adopts a positivist presumption that international law deals exclusively with horizontal relations between nation-states, it is rarely appropriate for domestic courts to apply international law, because domestic courts rarely have jurisdiction over horizontal disputes between nation-states. Parties in domestic litigation continued to raise treaty-based claims long after the emergence of the positivist paradigm, and domestic courts continued to adjudicate those claims. Nevertheless, American lawyers and judges who viewed international law through a positivist lens tended to approach treaty-based claims with greater skepticism than did their natural law predecessors. For example, as discussed in Chapters 10 and 11, Manley Hudson exerted significant influence over the California Supreme Court decision in the landmark *Fujii* case,[4] and Hudson's positivist (statist) perspective on international law influenced his interpretation of the U.N. Charter's human rights provisions.[5]

This chapter focuses on three other developments in the early twentieth century that sowed the seeds for the transformation of the treaty supremacy rule, which occurred after World War II. First, the nation's ill-fated experiment with Prohibition had a surprising effect on NSE doctrine. To help enforce Prohibition, the United States concluded numerous bilateral "liquor treaties" with various countries. U.S. courts decided dozens of cases in which parties urged courts to apply the liquor treaties. In that context, Professor Edwin Dickinson published an article in the *American Journal of International Law* that created a new "intent version" of NSE doctrine, which quickly became the accepted orthodoxy.[6] Second, the growth of executive discretion in foreign affairs was one of the most significant constitutional developments in the United States in the period between the two World Wars. Dickinson's intent doctrine gained rapid acceptance within the federal executive branch because it supported the rise of executive discretion in foreign affairs. Finally, as Professor Gardbaum has demonstrated, the Supreme Court in the early twentieth century began to conflate the concepts of supremacy and preemption.[7] Widespread confusion about the distinction between supremacy and preemption in the statutory context probably magnified confusion about the distinction between supremacy and self-execution in the treaty context. Indeed, the creation of an NSE exception to the Constitution's treaty supremacy rule after 1945 had much in common with the conversion of the Constitution's statutory supremacy rule into statutory preemption doctrine earlier in the twentieth century. The remainder of this chapter analyzes these three developments in greater detail.

I. EDWIN DICKINSON AND THE LIQUOR TREATIES

The Eighteenth Amendment was ratified in January 1919. The amendment prohibited "the manufacture, sale, or transportation of intoxicating liquors within, [and] the importation thereof into . . . the United States."[8] Congress enacted the National Prohibition Act later that year to implement the amendment.[9] Federal efforts to enforce prohibition set in motion a chain of events that ultimately helped transform the treaty supremacy rule. Shortly after the Prohibition Act took effect, the attorney general reported that "rum-running vessels of American and foreign registry, carrying liquor from foreign ports to our shores, have swarmed along our seaboards, smuggling liquors into the United States in violation of our laws." He added, "The liquor smuggling business is the most gigantic criminal problem the United States has ever faced on the high seas."[10] International law recognized U.S. territorial jurisdiction over waters within three miles of the coast.[11] Federal statutes granted government officers authority to enforce U.S. laws extraterritorially by boarding non-U.S. vessels within twelve miles of the coast.[12] (Government officers could board U.S. vessels anywhere on the high seas.) However, the "rum-runners" evaded federal enforcement efforts by stationing a vessel with large stores of liquor beyond the twelve-mile limit and using small, fast boats to ferry small batches of contraband to shore. If the Coast Guard caught a small boat, federal agents had no authority to search or seize the larger vessel hovering beyond the twelve-mile limit unless it was a U.S. ship.

Between 1924 and 1930, the United States concluded bilateral treaties with sixteen countries that authorized federal officers to search and seize non-U.S. vessels beyond the twelve-mile limit.[13] To understand how the treaties operated, it is helpful to consider a hypothetical case before the treaties took effect. Assume that a British vessel was engaged in liquor smuggling. The ship hovered about fifteen miles from the coast, carrying large stores of prohibited liquor. The captain conspired with partners on shore who operated a fleet of small, fast boats that cruised back and forth between the hovering vessel and land. The onshore partners were clearly guilty of violating the Prohibition Act by importing liquor into the United States. The small boats were subject to forfeiture, provided that government agents seized the boats within the twelve-mile limit.[14] However, federal agents could not lawfully seize the British vessel while it remained outside the twelve-mile limit. If the government seized the British vessel illegally and filed criminal charges against the captain, non-U.S. defendants could successfully challenge the court's jurisdiction by arguing that the seizure was unlawful.[15] Under this hypothetical scenario, the captain of the British vessel was guilty of conspiracy.[16] Nevertheless, he could successfully evade prosecution if he did not voluntarily enter U.S. territory. (If he entered voluntarily, he would effectively waive his jurisdictional defense.)

The treaties altered the rule governing search-and-seizure outside U.S. territorial waters. The treaty with Britain is illustrative. Under that treaty, the United States affirmed "the principle that 3 marine miles extending from the coast-line outwards ... constitute the proper limits of territorial waters."[17] Britain agreed that it would "raise no objection to the boarding of private vessels under the British flag outside the limits of" U.S. territorial waters. This provision addressed the diplomatic protests that had arisen when U.S. agents searched British ships outside the three-mile limit. But the treaty did not merely address the diplomatic dispute; it permitted U.S. officers to search British vessels outside U.S. territorial waters. If the search revealed that "there is reasonable cause for belief that the vessel has committed or is committing ... an offense against the laws of the United States ... prohibiting the importation of alcoholic beverages, the vessel may be seized and taken into a port of the United States."[18] However, "[t]he rights conferred by this article *shall not be exercised at a greater distance from the coast ... than can be traversed in one hour*" by the hovering vessel or by the vessel "in which the liquor is intended to be conveyed to the" shore.[19] In sum, the treaties authorized search-and-seizure operations outside U.S. territorial waters with respect to foreign-flagged vessels from relevant countries. The treaties also replaced the previous twelve-mile limit with a rule based on the distance from the coast that can be traversed in one hour. The one-hour rule expanded the geographic scope of the government's search-and-seizure authority beyond the previous twelve-mile limit in some cases, but constrained that authority in others, depending on the speed of the boats involved.

With this background in mind, this section addresses Chief Justice Taft's construction of the liquor treaties in *Ford v. United States* (1927) and Professor Dickinson's analysis in a 1926 law review article. Dickinson's analysis was less cogent, but more influential.

A. Chief Justice Taft's Analysis in *Ford*

Ford v. United States[20] was a criminal case arising from the seizure of a British vessel off the coast of California. At trial, the parties presented conflicting evidence about whether the seizure occurred within the treaty's one-hour rule. Defendants filed a "motion to exclude and suppress the evidence of the ship and cargo" because the seizure was "not within the zone of the high seas prescribed by the treaty."[21] The trial court denied the motion and defendants were convicted. On appeal, the government cited *Ker v. Illinois* to support its argument "that an illegal seizure would not have ousted the jurisdiction of the court to try the defendants." The Supreme Court distinguished *Ker* on the grounds that *Ker* involved an alleged violation of customary international law, not a treaty. Chief Justice Taft said "that the illegal seizure of the defendant [in *Ker*] violated neither the federal Constitution, nor a federal law, nor a treaty of the United States." Therefore, the unlawful seizure in *Ker* "was not a matter of federal cognizance." In *Ford*, though, "a treaty of the United States is directly involved and the question is quite different."[22] The Court continued: "The issue whether the ship was seized within the prescribed limit did not affect the question of the defendants' guilt or innocence. It only affected the right of the court to hold their persons for trial."[23] In sum, if the government seized the British vessel in violation of the treaty, such an illegal seizure would not affect the defendants' guilt or innocence, but it would deprive the court of jurisdiction over the defendants.

Nevertheless, the Court affirmed the convictions because the attorneys representing the defendants committed a serious error. They objected to the allegedly unlawful seizure by filing a motion to exclude evidence. The Court said: "The proper way of raising the issue of fact of the place of seizure was by a plea to the jurisdiction. A plea to the jurisdiction must precede that plea of not guilty. Such a plea was not filed. The effect of the failure to file it was to waive the question of the jurisdiction of the persons of the defendants."[24] Thus, if the government seized the British vessel in violation of the one-hour rule codified in the treaty, the defendants could invoke the treaty as the basis for a jurisdictional defense. However, the defendants waived that defense by failing to raise it. Notably, the Court's analysis tacitly assumed that the treaty was self-executing (SE), in the sense that no legislation was necessary to authorize criminal defendants to invoke the treaty in support of a jurisdictional defense. The Court's unstated assumption that trial courts did not need legislative authorization to apply the treaty to decide a contested jurisdictional issue was consistent with the large body of precedent that had developed since the 1790s, wherein courts applied treaties to decide litigated issues without pausing to consider whether the treaties were self-executing.[25]

The defendants in *Ford* were tried in California. Trial judges and criminal defense attorneys in California quickly learned the lesson of *Ford*. In the same year that the Supreme Court decided *Ford*, two federal district courts in California ruled that they lacked jurisdiction over criminal defendants because government agents seized the defendants on the high seas beyond the geographic limits of the government's seizure authority, as prescribed by the relevant treaties.[26] Both cases involved federal criminal charges related to liquor smuggling. Both cases involved the bilateral liquor treaty with Panama, because both cases involved Panamanian vessels. Both courts relied on *Ford* as authority. In *Ferris*, the court said: "Hence, as the instant seizure was far outside the [treaty] limit, it is sheer aggression and trespass . . . contrary to the treaty, not to be sanctioned by any court, and cannot be the basis of any proceeding adverse to defendants."[27] In *Schouweiler*, the court said: "As jurisdiction cannot be justified, except by showing that the facts of restraint committed by the government were within the extended privileges allowed by that treaty, it follows necessarily that the plea to the jurisdiction must be held good."[28] Consistent with Chief Justice Taft's opinion in *Ford*, neither court analyzed the question of whether the treaty with Panama was self-executing.[29] From their perspective, the fact that the government seized defendants in violation of treaty rules establishing the geographic limits of the government's seizure authority was sufficient to deprive the courts of jurisdiction. Analysis of self-execution was not necessary because a violation of the one-hour rule codified in the treaty had precisely the same effect as a violation of the twelve-mile (statutory) rule that predated the treaty.

B. Dickinson and the Intent Doctrine

In 1926, Professor Edwin Dickinson published an article in the *American Journal of International Law* entitled "Are the Liquor Treaties Self-Executing?"[30] In it he stated: "If the treaty was intended to be self-executing, it has immediately the effect of law. If not, it requires legislation before it can become a rule for the courts."[31] With these two sentences, Dickinson created the intent version of NSE doctrine.[32] The proposition that the intent of the treaty makers is the touchstone of self-execution analysis is a central tenet of modern doctrine.[33] Hence, it is no exaggeration to say that Dickinson created modern NSE doctrine, although it bears emphasis that Dickinson was thinking solely in federal separation-of powers-terms—not in terms of the supremacy of treaties over state law—when he wrote the words quoted above.

It was no accident that Dickinson created modern NSE doctrine in an article addressing the liquor treaties. From his perspective, the self-execution issue boiled down "to the question whether legislation is required to make Article II of the [liquor] treaties effective."[34] He did not explain fully what he meant by the term "effective," but the overall tenor of his article—and of a separate article published contemporaneously in *Harvard Law Review*[35]—suggests that he sought to demonstrate that the executive branch and the courts could give practical effect to the liquor treaties without awaiting legislative implementation. The issue was important, in his view, because several lower courts had held that the liquor treaties were not self-executing.[36] If their views prevailed, the courts might well frustrate the executive's enforcement efforts.

Unfortunately, Dickinson misinterpreted the liquor treaties. His erroneous interpretation had significant implications for his self-execution analysis. He said, quite correctly, that executive officers "may go ahead, in reliance upon the treaties, to visit, search, and seize" foreign vessels within the distance determined by the one-hour rule prescribed by the treaties. He then argued that "the treaties make the inhibitions of United States revenue and prohibition laws effective in the one-hour zone." In other words, he argued that the treaties expanded the geographic reach of federal penal laws. If the treaties did not have this effect, he said, they would merely authorize the executive "to search and seize foreign vessels which are guilty of no offense."[37] On this point, he was clearly mistaken. As Chief Justice Taft made clear in *Ford*, "[t]he issue whether the ship was seized within the prescribed limit did not affect the question of the defendants' guilt or innocence."[38] However, the Supreme Court decided *Ford* one year after Dickinson wrote his article, so Dickinson did not have the benefit of Taft's analysis. Accordingly, Dickinson analyzed self-execution on the basis of the mistaken assumption that a finding of non-self-execution, coupled with the fact that Congress had not enacted implementing legislation, would mean that people seized under the liquor treaties were "guilty of no offense." Before Dickinson published his article, at least one lower court had held that a vessel seized under the British treaty was not guilty of any offense because the treaty was not self-executing.[39] Thus, Dickinson aimed to demonstrate that the liquor treaties were self-executing, in the sense that they expanded the geographic reach of substantive penal laws beyond prior territorial limits.

Dickinson faced an uphill battle in this respect. He acknowledged that leading authorities, including Quincy Wright, "suggested that treaties defining crimes and extending criminal jurisdiction . . . require legislation to make them effective because of historical traditions and constitutional interpretation."[40] In response, Dickinson argued that "the evidence in support of such historical traditions seems meager; and really authoritative constitutional interpretation is lacking."[41] However, Dickinson was an international law scholar, not a constitutional law scholar. He may have been reluctant to confront Wright, a leading constitutional expert, directly on a question of constitutional law. So, he attempted to shift the terms of the debate by arguing that self-execution was properly viewed as a treaty interpretation question, rather than a constitutional law question.[42]

Dickinson's article set forth a tripartite approach to self-execution analysis. First, he said, "Treaties not infrequently stipulate in terms that they shall be put into effect by legislative enactment."[43] Thus, Dickinson's first category included treaties containing an express NSE clause in the text of the treaty (similar to a condition precedent clause).[44] The examples he cited in footnotes indicate that he construed certain treaty provisions as express NSE clauses that, in my view, are not properly classified as such.[45] Regardless, his main goal here was sensible: to bracket treaties with express NSE clauses in order to focus on treaties lacking such provisions. Dickinson's second category included treaties whose "nature . . . [is] such that legislative action is required before [they] can become effective."[46] His explanation of this category made clear that he was referring to treaties that are constitutionally non-self-executing. But he did not include treaties "extending criminal jurisdiction" in this category.

Dickinson then addressed treaties that did not fit into either of his first two categories. With respect to such treaties, he said, "it would appear that the question [of self-execution] is simply one of construction."[47] In other words, apart from constitutionally NSE treaties and treaties with express NSE clauses, self-execution should be analyzed as a treaty interpretation issue. Then he added: "If the treaty was intended to be self-executing, it has immediately the effect of law. If not, it requires legislation before it can become a rule for the courts."[48] Thus, according to Dickinson, courts should perform the requisite treaty interpretation analysis by searching for the intent of the treaty makers to determine whether they intended the treaty to be self-executing. Under this approach, the intent of the treaty makers is dispositive.

Dickinson's *intent doctrine* is similar to the *contract doctrine* in that both versions of NSE doctrine encourage courts to engage in treaty interpretation analysis to determine whether the treaty is self-executing. However, the contract doctrine involves a two-step approach, whereas the intent doctrine involves a one-step approach. Under the contract doctrine, courts examine the treaty text to determine whether the particular treaty provision is executory or executed (step one). If the provision is executory, then it necessarily follows (according to the contract doctrine) that legislation is required to implement the treaty.[49] Thus, under the contract doctrine, step two follows automatically from step one, but step two is still an analytically distinct step. In contrast, Dickinson's intent doctrine involves a one-step approach: courts engage in treaty interpretation to determine whether the treaty makers intended the treaty to be self-executing, not to determine whether the treaty is executory.

Dickinson conceived of self-execution in terms of the congressional-executive concept. If the liquor treaties were self-executing, then implementing legislation was not necessary, because the treaties themselves altered the geographic reach of federal criminal laws. However, if the liquor treaties were NSE, then separate legislation would be needed to expand the geographic reach of federal criminal statutes.[50] One problem with Dickinson's intent doctrine is that treaty makers rarely express any specific intention as to whether legislation is required to accomplish the treaty's purpose. Treaties that do contain an explicit requirement for legislation fit into Dickinson's first category, not the third category. Hence, Dickinson's intent doctrine makes the "intent of the treaty makers" dispositive with respect to self-execution in precisely those cases where the treaty makers have not expressed their intentions in the treaty text. Therefore, as a practical matter, the doctrine encourages courts to create a fictitious intent, because they must find some "intent" to answer the question whether the treaty is self-executing.[51] The contract doctrine does not suffer from this problem because courts can readily distinguish between executory and executed treaty provisions by applying the ordinary tools of treaty interpretation, as Chief Justice Marshall did in *Foster* and *Percheman*.[52]

Aside from the problem of fictitious intent, Dickinson's intent doctrine raises an important constitutional question. To illustrate this point, consider the following hypothetical treaty. "Article 1: U.S. government officers are authorized to seize vessels within one hour's sailing distance from the coast. Article 2: After the treaty enters into force internationally, Article 1 shall have no legal effect within the United States until Congress enacts implementing legislation." I will refer to treaty provisions such as Article 2 as "no legal effect" clauses, or simply NLE clauses.[53] Assume that the treaty enters into force internationally, but Congress does not enact implementing legislation. Do federal officers have the authority to seize a vessel beyond the twelve-mile statutory limit if that vessel is within the one-hour limit prescribed by the treaty? Prior doctrine suggested that the president's power to "take Care that the Laws be faithfully executed" (the "Take Care Clause"), combined with the fact that treaties have the status of "law" under the Supremacy Clause, meant that federal officers could execute Article 1 by seizing vessels beyond the twelve-mile limit. However, Dickinson would presumably say that Article 2 overrides Article 1 because the NLE clause expresses the treaty makers' intention to make Article 1 non-self-executing. Hence, there is some tension between the NLE clause and the president's power under the Take Care Clause. Even so, there are plausible arguments to support the constitutional validity of NLE clauses. I address those arguments below.[54] At present, the critical point is that Dickinson did not address those constitutional arguments. Thus, his intent doctrine rests on the unexamined premise that Article II of the Constitution grants the treaty makers an affirmative power to adopt a valid treaty provision that bars the treaty from having any domestic legal effect after it enters into force internationally.

Here, it is important to distinguish the intent doctrine from the condition precedent doctrine. The two doctrines are similar in that both doctrines assume that Article II grants the treaty makers (i.e., the president and Senate) the power to require legislation as a condition precedent for the treaty to take effect. However, there are important differences between the hypothetical NLE clause at issue here (which is associated with the intent doctrine) and the condition precedent clauses discussed in Chapter 6 (which are associated with the condition precedent doctrine). When the treaty makers adopt an NLE clause, they regulate domestic law *directly* by requiring legislation *as a precondition for the treaty to take effect domestically,* even after it has entered into force internationally. In contrast, when the treaty makers adopt a condition precedent clause of the type discussed in Chapter 6, they regulate domestic law *indirectly* by requiring legislation *as a precondition for the treaty to take effect internationally.* Article II of the Constitution unquestionably grants the treaty makers an affirmative power to adopt treaty provisions that establish conditions for the international entry into force of the treaty. Before Dickinson wrote his article, though, there was little or no authority to support the claim that Article II grants the treaty makers an affirmative power to adopt treaty provisions that establish preconditions for a treaty to take effect domestically after it has already entered into force internationally.

To elucidate this point, it is helpful to distinguish between the intent doctrine and the constitutional doctrine. The constitutional doctrine rests on the assumption that the Article II power to create federal law by means of treaties is subject to constitutional limitations.[55] If the treaty makers attempt to use the Article II Treaty Power to create federal law in violation of those constitutional limitations, the resultant treaty is not the "Law of the Land" within the meaning of the Supremacy Clause for precisely the same reason that an unconstitutional statute is not the "Law of the Land." If federal lawmakers act beyond the scope of their constitutionally delegated lawmaking powers, the product of their illicit lawmaking attempt is not a valid law. The intent doctrine differs fundamentally from the constitutional doctrine. The constitutional doctrine rests on the uncontroversial premise that the Article II Treaty Power is *subject to constitutional limitations.* In contrast, the intent doctrine rests on the unstated premise that Article II *grants the treaty makers an affirmative power* to adopt a valid treaty provision that bars the treaty from having any domestic legal effect after it enters into force internationally. When Dickinson wrote his article in 1926, there was very little authority, if any, to support the proposition that Article II grants the treaty makers that type of affirmative power.[56] Table Four summarizes the key differences among the intent doctrine, the constitutional doctrine, and the condition precedent doctrine.

In sum, the preceding analysis supports three key points. First, the intent doctrine is problematic because it encourages courts to create a fictitious "intent of the treaty makers" to decide whether a treaty is self-executing. Second, the intent doctrine was a novel doctrine when Dickinson created it in 1926; it differs significantly from the constitutional doctrine, the condition precedent doctrine, the contract doctrine, and the justiciability doctrine.[57] Third, when Dickinson created the intent doctrine he was thinking about treaties that addressed matters governed exclusively by federal law; he was not thinking about treaties that could potentially give rise to a conflict between federal (treaty) law and state law.

Table Four. IMPLICIT ASSUMPTIONS UNDERLYING DIFFERENT NSE DOCTRINES

	Article II Grants Treaty Makers (TMs) Affirmative Power	Constitution Limits Article II Treaty Power
Legislation Is Necessary for Treaty to Take Effect Internationally	*Condition Precedent Doctrine*: Art. II grants TMs affirmative power to require legislation as precondition for treaty to enter into force internationally.	
Legislation Is Necessary for Treaty to Take Effect Domestically	*Intent Doctrine*: Art. II grants TMs affirmative power to require legislation as precondition for treaty to have domestic legal effect, even after international entry into force.	*Constitutional Doctrine*: Constitution requires legislation as precondition for domestic implementation of treaty within scope of Congress's exclusive Article I powers.

Dickinson's article was extremely influential for two independent reasons. First, as discussed in the next section, Green Hackworth, the State Department legal adviser, adopted Dickinson's intent doctrine and incorporated it into his *Digest of International Law*.[58] Second, as discussed in Chapter 13, Dickinson played a key role in shaping the ALI's *Restatement of Foreign Relations Law*, which also adopted Dickinson's intent doctrine.[59] In light of the problems associated with the intent doctrine, the question arises: Why was the doctrine so readily accepted? A partial answer is that the intent doctrine fit well with contemporaneous developments that supported the growth of executive discretion in foreign affairs. The next section explores the relationship between the intent doctrine and the rise of executive discretion. A more complete answer must explain the transplantation of the intent doctrine from the federal separation-of-powers context (as in the liquor treaties) to the federal supremacy context (as in human rights treaties). The final section of this chapter discusses changes in federal preemption doctrine that helped lay the groundwork for the subsequent transformation of the treaty supremacy rule from a mandatory to an optional rule.

II. THE RISE OF EXECUTIVE DISCRETION IN FOREIGN AFFAIRS

The growth of executive discretion in foreign affairs was one of the most significant constitutional developments in the United States in the period between the two World Wars. Professor Edward White has demonstrated that Supreme Court decisions between 1936 and 1945 promoted the emergence of a new constitutional foreign affairs regime that concentrated increased power in the federal executive branch.[60] His account emphasizes three features of the new regime. First, in *United States v. Curtiss-Wright Export Corp.*, the Court said in dicta that the president exercises "plenary and exclusive power ... as the sole organ of the federal government in the field of international relations."[61] Second, in *United States v. Belmont* and *United States v. Pink*, the Court held that sole executive agreements supersede conflicting state laws in the same way that a treaty supersedes conflicting state laws.[62] Third, the Court effectively rewrote the rules governing foreign sovereign immunity in the 1930s and 1940s. ("Foreign sovereign immunity" means that foreign states are immune from the jurisdiction of U.S. courts.) Before 1930, courts decided sovereign immunity issues by applying customary international law as the controlling rule of decision. However, the Court held in *Ex parte Peru* and *Mexico v. Hoffman* that courts owe absolute deference to the executive branch's political judgment as to which defendants are entitled to sovereign immunity.[63]

The entrenchment of the intent version of NSE doctrine in the 1930s and 1940s both supported, and was supported by, the rise of executive discretion in foreign affairs. Green Hackworth published his influential eight-volume *Digest of International Law* between 1940 and 1944.[64] Hackworth's *Digest* was an updated version of John Bassett Moore's *Digest*, published in 1906.[65] These two publications provide good indicators of State Department views about international law in the first half of the twentieth century. It is instructive to compare the discussion of treaty supremacy and self-execution in the two *Digests*. Both Moore's *Digest* and Hackworth's *Digest* include emphatic endorsements of the treaty supremacy rule, without any exception for NSE treaties.[66] Hence, State Department views about treaty supremacy did not change significantly between 1906 and 1944.

In contrast, State Department views about self-execution changed substantially during this period. Hackworth's *Digest* devoted an entire section of about ten pages to the topic of self-executing treaties.[67] There was no comparable section in Moore's *Digest*. Instead, the term "self-executing" appeared a total of five times in five discrete sections of Moore's 230-page discussion of treaties.[68] Hackworth's decision to devote an entire section to self-execution indicates that the topic gained greater importance between 1906 and 1944.

Hackworth's *Digest* included a lengthy quotation from Dickinson's 1926 law review article, leaving the reader with little doubt that Hackworth approved Dickinson's intent doctrine.[69] In contrast, none of Moore's various references to self-execution indicated that "intent" is a relevant criterion in assessing whether a treaty is self-executing. In one passage, Moore quoted a letter from Secretary of State Bayard that distinguished between two types of treaty provisions: those where "the authoritative construction is that of the political branch of the government," and those where "the courts act with entire independence of the Executive."[70] This passage is consistent with the justiciability doctrine.[71] A separate passage discussed the 1883 treaty with Mexico, addressed in Chapter 6, which involved application of the condition precedent doctrine.[72] A third passage summarized congressional debates about the 1815 commercial treaty with Great Britain (also discussed in Chapter 6), which involved the con-stitutional doctrine.[73] Thus, Moore's *Digest* accurately reflected the fact that, at the turn of the century, various sources supported the constitutional doctrine, the condition precedent doctrine, and the justiciability doctrine. Moore also quoted the critical passage from *Foster v. Neilson* that modern commentators have identified as the source of the intent doctrine. After quoting *Foster*, Moore added a single sentence of his own commentary, which is somewhat ambigu-ous, but which is best construed in accordance with the contract version of NSE doctrine.[74] Although Moore's chapter on treaties filled about 230 pages, one is hard-pressed to find even a single sentence that can reasonably be construed to support the intent doctrine. Thus, Hackworth's evident endorsement of the intent doctrine was a significant departure from Moore's *Digest*.

Why did Hackworth endorse Dickinson's novel intent doctrine? The most plausible answer is that the intent doctrine both supported, and was sup-ported by, the then-emerging regime of executive discretion in foreign affairs. Hackworth served as legal adviser in the Department of State from 1931 to 1946. Before that, he served as the solicitor for the Department of State, which was roughly the equivalent position before the Department created the legal adviser position. Hackworth's long career in the State Department probably made him predisposed to favor an executive-centered vision of U.S. foreign policy. The intent doctrine fit well with that vision.

To appreciate this point, it is helpful to consider two cases that Hackworth cited in his discussion of self-executing treaties: *Ex parte Toscano* and *Robertson v. General Electric Co.*[75] In *Toscano*, defeated troops who were fighting a civil war in Mexico "fled with their arms across the boundary line between the United States and Mexico, and sought refuge and asylum from the pursuing enemy."[76] The United States detained them, claiming detention authority under article XI of the 1907 Hague Convention. The detainees filed habeas petitions, alleging that their detention violated the Fifth Amendment Due Process Clause and that the Hague Convention was not self-executing.[77] The court rejected their due process argument, stating that "here 'due process of law' is found in the Hague Treaty, its execution by the President, and the admitted facts which bring petitioners under its operation."[78] The court also held that the treaty was self-executing, reasoning that "the duty devolves upon the President" to execute treaties unless Congress "expressly designated someone [else] for that purpose."[79] Two points bear empha-sis. First, the Hague Convention operated in this context as a power-enhancing treaty: it allowed the government to detain Mexican nationals without violat-ing international law. (Absent the treaty, their detention would probably have violated international legal obligations that the United States owed to Mexico.) Second, the court effectively applied a presumption in favor of self-execution. Its rationale implies that the president has the power to execute treaties unless Congress directs otherwise.

In *Robertson*, General Electric Co. applied for a patent covering an inven-tion previously patented in Germany. The United States and Germany were parties to treaties providing "that the owner of a foreign patent may obtain a

patent for his invention in this country, if" he files an application within specified time limits.[80] The Patent Office denied the application, ruling that the time
limit had expired. General Electric argued that its application was timely because the Treaty of Berlin had extended "the time for filing such application for a
period of six months after the date upon which it became effective."[81] The Fourth
Circuit ruled against General Electric on two grounds. First, it held on treaty
interpretation grounds that the Treaty of Berlin did not provide the six-month
extension claimed by General Electric.[82] Second, it held that "complainants are
not entitled to the patent applied for, because the [treaty] is not self-executing
and no legislation has been enacted to carry it into effect."[83] The Fourth Circuit
relied heavily on Attorney General Miller's 1889 opinion, discussed in Chapter 6,
which applied the contract doctrine to hold that a different patent treaty was
NSE because it "was a contract operating in the future infraterritorially."[84] Thus,
consistent with the contract doctrine, the rationale in *Robertson* implies that all
treaties that operate in the future infraterritorially are non-self-executing. If the
court in *Toscano* applied the same rationale, it would have held that the Hague
Convention was NSE, because it was a "contract operating in the future infraterritorially." Conversely, if the *Robertson* court had applied the *Toscano* rationale,
it would have held that the Treaty of Berlin was self-executing, because Congress
had not designated anyone outside the executive branch to execute the treaty.
Despite this apparent contradiction, Hackworth cited both cases approvingly in
his *Digest*.[85]

From Hackworth's perspective, *Toscano* and *Robertson* probably appeared to
be entirely consistent with each other because both cases supported executive
discretion in treaty implementation. The holding in *Toscano*—that Article XI
of the Hague Convention was self-executing—supported executive discretion
because Article XI was a power-enhancing provision. It authorized detention
of Mexican nationals in circumstances where their detention would probably
have been illegal, absent the treaty. The holding in *Robertson* that the treaty was
not self-executing supported executive discretion because that was a power-
constraining treaty. It obligated the United States to grant owners of foreign patents additional time for filing their patent applications.

Broadly speaking, a power-enhancing treaty augments executive discretion if
it is self-executing (as in *Toscano*), but does not augment executive discretion if
it is NSE, because in that case the executive must await congressional authorization to implement the treaty. Conversely, a power-constraining treaty restricts
executive discretion if it is self-executing (e.g., by requiring the Patent Office to
extend the deadline for filing a patent application), but does not restrict executive discretion if it is NSE, because the executive can invoke Congress's failure
to enact legislation as a reason for not implementing the treaty (as in *Robertson*).
Therefore, if one favors executive discretion in foreign affairs, the "best" doctrine is one that makes power-enhancing treaties self-executing (to maximize
executive discretion), but makes power-constraining treaties non-self-executing
(to avoid restricting executive discretion). The intent doctrine is ideally suited for
this purpose because, under the intent doctrine, the executive has the power in

its treaty-making capacity to decide authoritatively that a particular treaty provision is self-executing or non-self-executing, merely by manifesting its intent
to that effect. Thus, the intent doctrine gives the executive branch virtually unlimited discretion to make power-enhancing treaties self-executing and to make
power-constraining treaties non-self-executing.[86] Given this feature of the intent
doctrine, it is not surprising that Hackworth, in his capacity as State Department
legal adviser, endorsed the doctrine. Hackworth's approval of the doctrine was
significant because his *Digest* was the "bible" for an entire generation of State
Department lawyers.[87]

Compare this feature of the intent doctrine to the other versions of NSE
doctrine that had developed before 1900. The constitutional doctrine generally limits executive discretion by preventing the executive from implementing
treaties for which legislation is constitutionally required. The contract doctrine
also tends to limit executive discretion because that doctrine requires legislative implementation for all treaty provisions that "operate in the future infraterritorially."[88] Inasmuch as most treaties operate in the future infraterritorially,
consistent application of the contract doctrine would mean that implementing
legislation is required for almost all treaty provisions. The condition precedent
doctrine supports executive flexibility at the treaty drafting stage, but the decision to include a condition precedent clause in the treaty text limits executive
discretion in the implementation phase, because the president may not execute
the treaty until Congress enacts implementing legislation.[89] The justiciability
doctrine supports executive discretion with respect to treaties classified as non-
justiciable. However, under the justiciability doctrine it is the courts, not the
executive, who decide whether a particular treaty-related issue is justiciable. In
contrast, under the intent doctrine, the executive branch has virtually unlimited
discretion to decide which treaties are self-executing. Thus, the intent doctrine
supports greater executive discretion than any prior version of NSE doctrine.

III. IS THE INTENT DOCTRINE CONSTITUTIONAL?

The fact that the intent doctrine promotes executive discretion in foreign affairs
helps explain why Hackworth and the executive branch endorsed the doctrine.
However, we must still consider whether the implicit assumptions underlying
the intent doctrine had constitutional support before Hackworth published his
Digest in the 1940s. Recall the hypothetical treaty discussed above. Article 1 authorizes government officers to seize vessels at sea. Article 2 is an NLE (no legal
effect) clause, which stipulates that Article 1 "shall not have the effect of law" domestically, absent implementing legislation. The intent doctrine rests on the unstated assumption that the Constitution grants the treaty makers an affirmative
power to adopt NLE clauses: clauses that preclude particular treaty provisions
from having domestic legal effect even after they enter into force internationally.
That assumption is arguably in tension with the Supremacy Clause, which specifies that all treaties are the "supreme law of the land." How can a treaty be the
"supreme law of the land" if it does not have any "domestic legal effect"?

Professor Vazquez defends the constitutional validity of provisions similar to NLE clauses by invoking the authority of *Foster* and *Percheman*.[90] His argument rests on the premise that Marshall applied a one-step approach in *Foster* and *Percheman*. However, as explained in Chapter 4, the better view is that Marshall applied a two-step approach.[91] Marshall's two-step approach does not support the intent doctrine because Marshall did not suggest that Article II grants the treaty makers an affirmative power to make decisions about domestic implementation that are not contingent upon the international obligation embodied in the treaty. Aside from *Foster* and *Percheman*, the Supreme Court did not issue any decisions before 1945 whose rationale supports the claim that the Constitution grants the treaty makers the power to adopt NLE clauses.

In addition to judicial precedent, one must also consider the practice of the political branches. As Justice Frankfurter said:

> [A] systematic, unbroken, executive practice, long pursued to the knowledge of the Congress and never before questioned, engaged in by Presidents who have also sworn to uphold the Constitution, making as it were such exercise of power part of the structure of our government, may be treated as a gloss on "executive Power" vested in the President by [section] 1 of Art. II.[92]

The practice of the political branches is an important criterion for assessing constitutional separation-of-powers questions, especially in the field of foreign affairs. Dickinson's article cited four examples of treaties that "stipulate in terms that they shall be put into effect by legislative enactment."[93] If that claim is correct, then executive branch practice would support the validity of NLE clauses. However, Dickinson's examples do not support his claim.

Dickinson cited an 1824 treaty with Russia, in which the parties agreed to prohibit their citizens from selling liquor and firearms "to the natives." The parties reserved "to themselves to determine upon the penalties to be incurred, and to inflict the punishments in case of the contravention of this article by their respective citizens or subjects."[94] In the United States, there is probably a *constitutional requirement* for Congress to enact implementing legislation before the courts can impose penalties on individuals for violating the treaty. However, the subject provision is not an NLE clause, because it does not, *as a matter of international law*, require legislation as a precondition for the treaty to take effect domestically.

Dickinson also cited an 1884 Convention for Protection of Submarine Cables.[95] Article XII of that treaty states: "The High Contracting Parties engage to take or to propose to their respective legislative bodies the measures necessary in order to secure the execution of this Convention, and especially in order to cause the punishment, either by fine or imprisonment, or both, of such persons as may violate the provisions of articles II, V and VI."[96] Insofar as the treaty envisions criminal punishment, it probably requires legislative implementation in the United States *as a matter of constitutional law*. However, *as a matter of international law*, this provision does not require legislation as a precondition for the treaty to have domestic legal effect. Therefore, the provision does not constitute executive practice supporting the constitutional validity of NLE clauses.

The other two treaty provisions that Dickinson cited are similar to the 1884 convention in that they grant the parties discretion to decide for themselves whether legislation is necessary to implement the treaty. A 1916 treaty with Britain on migratory birds said: "The High Contracting Powers agree themselves to take, or propose to their respective appropriate law-making bodies, the necessary measures for insuring the execution of the present Convention."[97] Similarly, in a 1911 convention on fur seals, the parties agreed "to enact and enforce such legislation as may be necessary to make effective the foregoing provisions with appropriate penalties for violations thereof."[98] Both treaties obligate the parties to take the necessary measures to execute or "make effective" the treaty obligations. However, both treaties give the parties discretion to decide for themselves whether legislation is necessary to implement the treaty obligations. Hence, these treaty provisions do not constitute executive practice supporting the constitutional validity of NLE clauses. As of 1945, one could certainly find isolated statements in executive branch documents supporting the intent doctrine.[99] However, before 1945 no official attorney general opinion (with the possible exception of Attorney General Wickersham's 1913 opinion) had endorsed or applied the intent doctrine.[100] Moreover, although the United States had concluded several treaties with condition precedent clauses, there is no evidence that the United States had ever concluded a treaty with an NLE clause.[101] Therefore, as of 1945, neither executive practice nor judicial precedent supported the claim that the Constitution grants the treaty makers the power to adopt a valid treaty clause that precludes the treaty from having domestic legal effect after it enters into force internationally.

Nevertheless, there is a plausible textual, originalist argument in support of the constitutional validity of the intent doctrine, as Dickinson and Hackworth understood that doctrine. The argument depends critically on two points. First, the Supremacy Clause was not originally intended to regulate the relationship between federal legislative and executive power. It was drafted as a conflict of laws rule to regulate conflicts between federal law and state law.[102] Second, when Hackworth published his Digest in 1940–1944, NSE doctrine had almost no relevance to conflicts between treaties and state law. At that time, treaty supremacy doctrine governed conflicts between treaties and state law, and self-execution doctrine operated solely on a federal separation-of-powers level. Therefore, if one construes the phrase "Law of the Land" in the Supremacy Clause not as an isolated phrase, but rather as an integral part of a constitutional provision governing the relationship between federal law and state law, the tension between the intent doctrine and the Supremacy Clause dissolves. The intent doctrine (as conceived by Dickinson and Hackworth) addressed the relationship between federal executive and legislative power, whereas the Supremacy Clause addressed the relationship between federal law and state law.

Moreover, from a functional separation-of-powers standpoint, the intent doctrine does not threaten any important structural constitutional principles because the treaty makers' intentions operate as a "one-way ratchet." Under the intent doctrine, the treaty makers can choose to make a treaty NSE that would otherwise be self-executing (SE), but they cannot choose to make a treaty SE if it is constitutionally NSE. For example, a treaty that ostensibly authorizes the president to raise revenue is NSE, regardless of the treaty makers' intentions, because the Constitution itself requires that "all Bills for raising Revenue shall originate in the House of Representatives."[103] Conversely, suppose that a treaty authorizes seizure of foreign vessels beyond the twelve-mile statutory limit, but the treaty makers adopt an NLE clause specifying that the treaty will not take effect domestically until Congress enacts implementing legislation. The net effect would be that the executive, in its treaty-making capacity, imposed a limitation on the executive, in its treaty-implementing capacity. It is difficult to see why this type of self-limitation is constitutionally problematic, at least in cases where non-self-execution does not operate as an exception to the treaty supremacy rule.[104]

In sum, structural and functional arguments support the conclusion that the intent doctrine is constitutionally valid, provided that: (1) the Supremacy Clause functions as a conflict of laws rule to regulate conflicts between federal and state law, and (2) NSE doctrine functions as a federal separation-of-powers doctrine that does not affect conflicts between federal and state law. However, the Supreme Court reinterpreted the Supremacy Clause in the first half of the twentieth century so that, by 1947, the first condition was no longer true. The next section discusses that development. Part Three addresses the transformation of NSE doctrine from a federal separation-of-powers doctrine to a doctrine that converted the treaty supremacy rule from a mandatory to an optional rule.

IV. PREEMPTION DOCTRINE, SELF-EXECUTION, AND TREATY SUPREMACY

Modern Supreme Court doctrine links the concept of preemption to the Supremacy Clause. For example, the Court stated recently that "[p]re-emption of state law . . . occurs through the 'direct operation of the Supremacy Clause.'"[105] As Professor Stephen Gardbaum has explained, though, the claim that preemption doctrine is rooted in the Supremacy Clause is founded upon confusion about the conceptual distinction between preemption and supremacy. Gardbaum says: "The supremacy of federal law means that valid federal law overrides otherwise valid state law in cases of conflict between the two. . . . Preemption, by contrast, means (a) that states are deprived of their power to act at all in a given area, and (b) that this is so whether or not state law is in conflict with federal law."[106] Whereas the principle of federal supremacy is clearly expressed in the Supremacy Clause, Gardbaum contends, Congress's power to preempt state law derives from Article I of the Constitution. In his words, "the power of preemption . . . has nothing to do with the Supremacy Clause."[107]

In accordance with the principle of federal supremacy, the Supreme Court has applied federal statutes and treaties to override *conflicting* state laws since the 1790s.[108] However, as Gardbaum has demonstrated, the Court did not clearly hold that a federal statute preempted a *non-conflicting* state law until it decided *Southern Railway Co. v. Reid* in 1912.[109] Two other cases decided in 1913 and 1915 solidified the notion that Congress has an affirmative power to enact legislation that "occupies a field," thereby precluding states from regulating in that field— even if states had concurrent power to regulate absent federal legislation, and even if the state regulation did not conflict with federal law.[110] The conceptual shift from federal supremacy over conflicting state laws to federal preemption of non-conflicting state laws supported a significant expansion of federal power. To curb that expansion, the Court in the 1930s and 1940s developed a presumption against preemption. Applying that presumption, the Court (at least in theory) would not hold that federal law preempted state law unless Congress clearly manifested its intent to preempt state law.[111] Thus, whereas "conflict" was the touchstone of traditional supremacy doctrine, "intent" became the touchstone of modern preemption doctrine.

The shift from a conflict-based doctrine to an intent-based one occurred between 1912 and 1947. According to Gardbaum's account, there were two steps in that process. First, between 1912 and 1915, the Court decided that Congress had a discretionary power to preempt state laws that did not conflict with federal law. Second, in the 1930s and 1940s, the Court established that lower courts should perform an intent-based analysis to determine whether, in a particular case, Congress intended to exercise its power to preempt state law. The doctrines of treaty supremacy and self-execution evolved in a similar way during roughly the same time period, but the steps in the process were different. The intent version of NSE doctrine gained acceptance within the executive branch between the 1926 publication of Dickinson's article and the 1943 publication of the treaty chapter of Hackworth's *Digest*.[112] Then, after World War II, lawyers and judges transplanted Dickinson's intent doctrine from the separation of powers sphere to the treaty supremacy sphere.[113]

Professor Gardbaum identifies three key distinctions between traditional supremacy doctrine and modern preemption doctrine:

> First, whereas conflict is essential to the application of supremacy, it is largely irrelevant to the issue of preemption. Second, whereas preemption is a discretionary power depending on the intent of Congress for its exercise, the principle of supremacy operates *automatically*, without regard to such intent, to trump conflicting state laws. Third, determining whether or not a state law conflicts with a federal law is an *ex post* judicial matter, involving first the interpretation of the state law in question and then an evaluation of its compatibility with the federal law. Preemption, by contrast, is an *ex ante* legislative exercise that does not involve the interpretation of state laws.[114]

The parallels with modern NSE doctrine are striking. First, whereas conflict was the touchstone of traditional supremacy doctrine, intent is the touchstone of both modern preemption doctrine and modern NSE doctrine. Second, the traditional supremacy rule operated automatically so that treaties and statutes superseded conflicting state laws, regardless of the intent of the federal lawmakers. In contrast, under modern doctrine, Congress has the discretionary power under Article I to *preempt non-conflicting state laws*, and the treaty makers have the discretionary power under Article II to decide that *a treaty does not supersede conflicting state laws*. Third, under traditional supremacy doctrine, courts decided ex post whether a treaty or statute conflicted with state law. In contrast, under modern doctrine, Congress decides ex ante whether to preempt state law, and the treaty makers decide ex ante whether a treaty is self-executing or non-self-executing. Finally, traditional supremacy doctrine was firmly rooted in the text and original understanding of the Supremacy Clause. In contrast, although modern preemption doctrine and modern self-execution doctrine are mistakenly linked to the Supremacy Clause, the better view is that Congress's power to preempt non-conflicting state laws is derived from Article I, and the treaty makers' power to decide that a particular treaty is self-executing or non-self-executing is rooted in Article II. In light of these parallels, the conversion of traditional supremacy doctrine into modern preemption doctrine between 1912 and 1947 was clearly an important precursor for the creation of an NSE exception to the Constitution's treaty supremacy rule—an exception that developed between 1948 and 1965. Table Five summarizes the results of these transformative processes.

Table Five. Supremacy, Preemption, and Self-Execution

Traditional Supremacy Doctrine (for both treaties and statutes)	Modern Preemption Doctrine (for statutes)	Modern Self-Execution Doctrine (for treaties)
Touchstone is conflict	Touchstone is intent	Touchstone is intent
Conflict of laws rule	Discretionary power of Congress under Article I	Discretionary power of president and Senate under Article II
Judges decide ex post whether there is conflict with state law	Congress decides ex ante whether to preempt state law	Treaty makers decide ex ante whether treaty is self-executing
Rooted in Supremacy Clause	Mistakenly linked to Supremacy Clause	Mistakenly linked to Supremacy Clause

Before we conclude this discussion, one additional point merits comment. Modern NSE doctrine holds that an NSE treaty does not supersede conflicting state laws. This feature of modern NSE doctrine has no parallel in modern preemption doctrine. The Supreme Court has never held that Article I grants Congress a discretionary power to decide that a particular federal statute does not supersede conflicting state laws.[115] However, modern NSE doctrine assumes implicitly that Article II grants the treaty makers a discretionary power to decide that a particular treaty does not supersede conflicting state laws. This aspect of modern NSE doctrine creates a tension between the doctrine and the original understanding of the Supremacy Clause that is not present in preemption doctrine and was not present in NSE doctrine before 1945. Part Three analyzes the development of an NSE exception to the treaty supremacy rule between 1945 and 1965.

The Human Rights Revolution

From the Founding until World War II, the treaty supremacy rule was a mandatory rule consisting of two elements. First, all valid, ratified treaties supersede conflicting state laws. Second, courts have a constitutional duty to apply treaties when they have jurisdiction over a justiciable claim involving a conflict between a treaty and state law. There was no exception for NSE treaties because self-execution doctrine was not relevant to treaty supremacy cases.[1]

The American Law Institute (ALI) published its Restatement (Second) of Foreign Relations Law in 1965. The Restatement asserted that non-self-executing (NSE) treaties do not supersede conflicting state laws. The NSE exception to the treaty supremacy rule (the optional supremacy rule) was potentially problematic because it allowed state and local governments to violate U.S. treaty obligations. Thus, the optional supremacy rule was in tension with the Framers' goal of designing a Constitution that precluded state governments from breaching national treaty obligations.[2] What changed between 1945 and 1965? Why did the ALI endorse a doctrine that is at odds with the original understanding of the treaty supremacy rule and with the vast weight of legislative, executive, and judicial authority from the Founding until World War II? Part Three addresses these questions.

The central story line can be summarized as follows. With the adoption of the U.N. Charter in 1945 and the Universal Declaration of Human Rights in 1948, the norms of universality and non-discrimination were incorporated into modern international law. Universality means that all human beings have certain fundamental rights. Non-discrimination means that governments may not discriminate on the basis of race, gender, or other prohibited factors in making decisions about the scope of protection to be accorded for human rights. The new international norms exerted a powerful magnetic pull, sparking an explosion of human rights activism in the United States. Between 1945 and 1954, human rights activists litigated dozens of cases in which claimants asked U.S. courts to apply the U.N. Charter's human rights provisions in conjunction with the treaty supremacy rule to invalidate discriminatory state laws. In 1950, in *Fujii v. California*, a California court applied the U.N. Charter and the treaty supremacy rule to invalidate a state law that discriminated against Japanese nationals.[3] The potential implications were shocking. If *Fujii* was right, the United States had effectively abrogated Jim Crow laws throughout the South by ratifying the U.N. Charter.

The explosion of human rights activism produced a conservative reaction. Activists gathered support within the American Bar Association (ABA) for a proposed constitutional amendment to abolish the treaty supremacy rule. Senator John Bricker, working closely with the ABA, rallied support within the U.S. Senate for a similar amendment, known as the Bricker Amendment. Conservatives in the ABA and the Senate cited *Fujii* repeatedly as "exhibit number one" in support of the proposed Bricker Amendment. Bricker's supporters feared that application of human rights norms in conjunction with the treaty supremacy rule would produce a fundamental change in the balance of power between state governments and the federal government. They argued that a constitutional amendment to abolish the treaty supremacy rule was necessary to avert that danger.

The Eisenhower administration opposed the Bricker Amendment on the grounds that it would erode the federal government's control over the conduct of foreign policy. Internationalists within the ABA shared that concern. Opponents of the Bricker Amendment argued that a constitutional amendment was unnecessary because Bricker's fears could be addressed by including language in human rights treaties, or in unilateral declarations attached to those treaties, stipulating that the treaties would not supersede state laws unless Congress enacted implementing legislation. Implicit in this argument was an unstated assumption that the treaty supremacy rule is optional—that is, that Article II grants the treaty makers an affirmative power to opt out of the treaty supremacy rule by declaring that the treaty is not self-executing. In the early 1950s, when Bricker's opponents first introduced this argument, the proposition that the treaty supremacy rule is optional was a novel idea. Even so, the optional supremacy rule rapidly gained acceptance as settled law.

The idea that there is an NSE exception to the treaty supremacy rule was the result of a four-stage evolution of self-execution doctrine. In brief, the four stages were:

- Stage one: The *constitutional doctrine* originated in the 1790s. It assumes that the Constitution limits the power of federal executive officials to implement treaties. Federal executive officials have the power to implement self-executing treaties, but legislation is necessary to authorize implementation of NSE treaties.[4]
- Stage two: The *condition precedent doctrine* originated in the 1850s. It assumes that Article II grants the treaty makers an affirmative power to decide that a treaty is non-self-executing. The treaty makers exercise that power by inserting a clause in the treaty, or in a unilateral reservation, that requires federal legislation as a precondition for the treaty to enter into force internationally. Such condition precedent clauses postpone international entry into force, but they have no domestic effect after the treaty enters into force.[5]
- Stage three: The *intent doctrine* originated in the 1920s. It also assumes that Article II grants the treaty makers an affirmative power to decide that a treaty is non-self-executing. The treaty makers exercise that power by adopting a clause that requires federal legislation as a precondition for the treaty to "take effect" domestically after it enters into force internationally. Like the constitutional doctrine, this type of NSE clause bars federal executive officers from implementing the treaty until Congress enacts authorizing legislation. However, the NSE clause does not affect the relationship between treaties and state law.[6]
- Stage four: The *Fujii doctrine* originated in the 1950s in the context of the Bricker Amendment controversy. It also assumes that Article II grants the treaty makers an affirmative power to decide that a treaty is non-self-executing. The treaty makers exercise that power by adopting a clause that requires federal legislation as a precondition for the treaty to supersede conflicting state laws. Like the intent doctrine, but unlike the condition precedent doctrine, the effect of an NSE clause under the *Fujii* doctrine is purely domestic: it does not modify the nation's international legal obligations.[7]

The California Supreme Court endorsed the optional treaty supremacy rule in its 1952 decision in *Fujii v. State*,[8] the appeal from the lower court decision in *Fujii*.

I refer to the NSE exception to the treaty supremacy rule as "the *Fujii* doctrine" because the California Supreme Court decision in *Fujii* was the first published judicial decision in U.S. history to hold that NSE treaties do not supersede conflicting state laws. Senior members of the Eisenhower administration issued a series of statements in 1953—in Senate testimony during the Bricker Amendment hearings—in which they also endorsed the NSE exception to the treaty supremacy rule.[9] However, statements by senior executive officials were not readily accessible to courts, so most courts continued to apply the traditional treaty supremacy rule until the ALI published its Restatement of Foreign Relations Law in 1965.[10] As a practical matter, the ALI codified the new constitutional understanding that developed within the Eisenhower administration during the Bricker Amendment debates.[11] Once that new understanding was codified in the Restatement, state courts and lower federal courts began to apply the optional supremacy rule. Table Six summarizes the various NSE doctrines that existed in 1965, when the ALI published the Restatement.

Table Six. VARIETIES OF NSE DOCTRINES, CIRCA 1965

	Two-Step Approach to Self-Execution Analysis	One-Step Approach to Self-Execution Analysis
Congressional-Executive Concept	Constitutional Doctrine (Origin: 1790s) Condition Precedent Doctrine (Origin: 1850s)	Intent Doctrine (Origin: 1920s)
Federal-State Concept		*Fujii* Doctrine (Origin: 1950s)
Political-Judicial Concept	Justiciability Doctrine (Origin: 1880s or earlier)	Three variants of NSE doctrine developed after 1970. *See* Part Four.

Notes to Table Six:

- Under the two-step approach, the president and Senate make decisions about the content and scope of the international obligation; those decisions affect domestic implementation indirectly. Under the one-step approach, the president and Senate make decisions about domestic implementation directly; those decisions are not contingent upon the content of the international obligation.

- Under the federal-state concept, an NSE treaty does not supersede conflicting state laws. Under the congressional-executive concept, an NSE treaty does not provide a rule of conduct for federal executive officers. Under the political-judicial concept, an NSE treaty does provide a rule of conduct for federal executive officers, but there are constraints on judicial enforcement of NSE treaties.
- Table Six omits the contract doctrine because this doctrine had effectively disappeared by about 1940.

I refer to the transformative process that gave rise to a new constitutional understanding as the "de facto Bricker Amendment." Other scholars have written about the "de facto ERA."[12] In the ERA example, advocates of women's equality pursued their goals by means of a constitutional amendment (the ERA). The amendment was not approved, but ERA supporters achieved some of their goals by triggering a transformative process that yielded a new constitutional understanding. In the Bricker example, human rights advocates pursued their goals by litigating claims based on the U.N. Charter and the treaty supremacy rule. Their political adversaries mobilized support for the proposed Bricker Amendment in an attempt to abolish the treaty supremacy rule. As in the case of the de facto ERA, the proposed amendment was never approved, but Bricker's supporters achieved some of their goals by triggering a transformative process that effectively converted the treaty supremacy rule from a mandatory to an optional rule.

Several factors help explain why the optional treaty supremacy rule gained general acceptance between 1950 and 1965. One such factor was the widespread belief in "American exceptionalism"—a view that the United States has the best constitutional system in the world. In cases where human rights claimants raised treaty supremacy arguments based on the U.N. Charter, they also raised Fourteenth Amendment equal protection claims. The lower court in *Fujii* held that a discriminatory California law violated the U.N. Charter, but did not violate the Equal Protection Clause. In the eyes of many people, that decision was tantamount to an admission that our Constitution is fundamentally flawed because it does not satisfy international human rights standards. The lower court decision in *Fujii* was impossible to reconcile with the public faith in American exceptionalism. The NSE exception to the treaty supremacy rule helped preserve the faith in American exceptionalism by providing a legal rationale that enabled courts to avoid the uncomfortable question whether international human rights standards provided more robust protection against racial discrimination than did the Equal Protection Clause.

Two key events in 1954 helped solidify the new constitutional understanding manifested in the *Fujii* doctrine. On February 26, the Senate voted 60-31 in favor of one version of the Bricker Amendment. The tally was one vote short of the requisite two-thirds majority, but it was sufficiently close to convince any remaining doubters that Bricker's supporters constituted a potent political force. Then, on May 17, the Supreme Court issued its landmark decision in *Brown v. Board of Education*,[13] which revolutionized constitutional equal protection doctrine. In *Bolling v. Sharpe*,[14] a companion case to *Brown*, petitioners argued forcefully that racial segregation in the District of Columbia public schools violated U.S. treaty obligations under the U.N. Charter, and that the Charter superseded local law under the Supremacy Clause. The Supreme Court ducked the treaty supremacy argument in *Bolling*, relying instead on equal protection doctrine to support its holding that racial segregation was unconstitutional.

By applying equal protection doctrine to invalidate discriminatory state laws, instead of applying the U.N. Charter and the treaty supremacy rule, the Supreme Court helped preserve the public faith in American exceptionalism. U.S. diplomats supported domestic civil rights reform because racial discrimination at home was undermining the nation's Cold War foreign policy by providing ammunition for foreign critics who condemned the United States' racist policies and practices. The executive branch supported application of equal protection doctrine, rather than the treaty supremacy rule, because expanded human rights protection under the Equal Protection Clause promoted the goals of Cold War foreign policy by helping U.S. diplomats sell the virtues of our constitutional system to a skeptical global audience.

In light of the Senate vote on the Bricker Amendment and the Supreme Court decisions in *Brown* and *Bolling*, human rights activists who had previously invoked the U.N. Charter and the treaty supremacy rule in domestic civil rights litigation changed their strategy. They abandoned international human rights claims and focused, instead, on constitutional equal protection claims. *Brown* and *Bolling* meant that their constitutional claims were more likely to succeed. And the Senate vote on the Bricker Amendment persuaded them that judicial decisions applying the U.N. Charter and the treaty supremacy rule would have the unwanted effect of mobilizing support for their political adversaries. Consequently, international human rights litigation in U.S. courts largely disappeared after 1954. Even so, the human rights litigation of the late 1940s and early 1950s had a powerful impact on constitutional history. The U.N. Charter's anti-discrimination norm had been a part of the "paper Constitution" in the United States since adoption of the Fourteenth Amendment in 1868. That norm did not become a part of the "living Constitution" until after the Fourteenth Amendment was subjected to the magnetic pull of international human rights law.[15]

Part Three presents this story in greater detail. Chapters 9 to 11 are organized chronologically. Chapter 9 covers events in 1946–1948. Chapters 10 and 11, respectively, cover developments in 1949–1951, and 1952–1954. Chapter 12 surveys U.S. judicial decisions in treaty supremacy cases between 1945 and 1965. The record shows that, during this period, courts continued to handle treaty supremacy cases by applying the traditional treaty supremacy rule, except in cases where litigants raised claims based on the U.N. Charter's human rights provisions. Prior to 1965, when the ALI published the Restatement, cases involving judicial application of the Charter's human rights provisions were the only ones in which courts endorsed an NSE exception to the treaty supremacy rule.

Chapter 13 addresses the drafting and adoption of the Restatement (Second) of Foreign Relations Law. The ALI began preliminary work on the Restatement in 1951, but the work did not begin in earnest until the ALI assembled a team of Reporters in 1956. The main drafting work occurred between 1957 and 1962. The Reporters generally shared a belief in American exceptionalism. They were also committed to supporting the U.S. foreign policy agenda in the Cold War. The optional treaty supremacy rule promoted these goals and beliefs. The *Fujii* doctrine enabled lawyers and judges to preserve their faith in American exceptionalism by ducking the uncomfortable question of whether international human rights law provides stronger protection for human rights than does the U.S. Constitution. It also supported U.S. foreign policy by helping to avoid the diplomatic embarrassment that would ensue if a U.S. court held that a state or local law violated international human rights norms.

Human Rights Activism in the United States: 1946–1948

This chapter examines the magnetic pull of international human rights norms on the United States in the years immediately after World War II, and the early signs of a powerful conservative reaction. The analysis is divided into seven sections: the creation of modern international human rights law, the impact of international human rights on the conduct of U.S. diplomacy, the NAACP petition to the United Nations concerning race discrimination in the United States, domestic human rights litigation, the Truman administration's response, the Supreme Court's response, and conservative reaction in the American Bar Association. There is very little evidence of any fundamental change in thinking about the treaty supremacy rule during this period. Even so, the creation of modern international human rights law unleashed powerful political forces in the years 1946–1948 that would begin to tear at the fabric of the traditional treaty supremacy rule in the period from 1949 to 1954.

I. THE ADVENT OF MODERN INTERNATIONAL HUMAN RIGHTS LAW

Modern international human rights law was born in 1945 with the adoption of the U.N. Charter. The Preamble to the Charter proclaims "faith in fundamental human rights, in the dignity and worth of the human person, [and] in the equal rights of men and women." Article 1 identifies promotion of human rights as one of the main purposes of the United Nations. Article 55 specifies that the United Nations "shall promote . . . universal respect for, and observance of, human rights and fundamental freedoms for all *without distinction as to race, sex, language, or religion.*" In Article 56, Member States "pledge themselves to take joint and separate action . . . for the achievement of the purposes set forth in Article 55."

When the U.N. General Assembly (UNGA) met in Paris, France, in Fall 1948 it adopted two documents that provided cornerstones for the future development of international human rights law: the Convention on the Prevention and Punishment of the Crime of Genocide[1] and the Universal Declaration of Human Rights.[2] The United Nation's ability to complete work rapidly on both documents indicates that, with the horrors of World War II still fresh in their minds, States were willing to set aside the usual bickering that often leads to lengthy delays in multilateral negotiations. Ernest Gross, a U.S. delegate to the United Nations, expressed the prevailing attitude succinctly: "Having regard to the troubled state of the world, it was essential that the [Genocide] convention should be adopted as soon as possible, before the memory of the barbarous crimes which had been committed faded from the minds of men."[3]

The United States played a central role in drafting and negotiating both the Genocide Convention and the Universal Declaration, but the drafting process for the two documents differed considerably. The Commission on Human Rights— a permanent U.N. Commission created by the Economic and Social Council (ECOSOC)—took the lead in drafting the Universal Declaration. Under the chairmanship of Eleanor Roosevelt, the Commission worked on the Declaration from January 1947 until June 1948, when it produced a text substantially similar to the final version. At the UNGA meeting in Fall 1948, the Third Committee of the General Assembly (the Social, Humanitarian, and Cultural Committee) scrutinized the draft declaration closely and made several minor revisions. The General Assembly adopted the final text of the Universal Declaration on December 10, 1948.[4]

In contrast to the Universal Declaration, the Commission on Human Rights had almost no role in drafting the Genocide Convention. Instead, the U.N. Secretariat produced an initial draft of the Convention with the aid of three expert consultants who served in their individual capacities. Later, ECOSOC created an ad hoc drafting committee with representatives from China, France, Lebanon, Poland, the Soviet Union, the United States, and Venezuela. The ad hoc committee submitted a draft to the General Assembly, which referred the matter to the Sixth Committee (the Legal Affairs Committee). The Sixth Committee revised and finalized the text of the Genocide Convention while the Third Committee completed its work on the Universal Declaration. The General Assembly adopted the final text of the Genocide Convention on December 9, 1948.[5]

The Genocide Convention and the Universal Declaration differ considerably from each other. The Convention is a legally binding treaty; the Declaration is a non-binding statement of principles.[6] The Convention focuses narrowly on a single issue: genocide. The Declaration addresses a broad range of civil, political, social, economic, and cultural rights. The main goal of the Convention is to ensure that certain especially heinous conduct is subjected to criminal punishment. The Declaration says very little about criminal punishment; it establishes "a common standard of achievement for all peoples and all nations," with the goal of securing "universal and effective recognition and observance" of the enumerated rights.[7] Despite these differences, the common thread that links the two documents is a condemnation of conduct rooted in racial, ethnic, or religious prejudice. Hence, the Universal Declaration proclaims: "Everyone is entitled to all the rights and freedoms set forth in this Declaration, without distinction of any kind, such as race, colour, sex, language, religion . . . or other status."[8] The

Genocide Convention defines genocide as "acts committed with intent to destroy . . . a national, ethnical, racial or religious group, as such."[9]

The Universal Declaration and the Genocide Convention signaled that a prohibition on racial discrimination would be one of the foundational norms of the postwar international order. However, legally sanctioned racial discrimination was still pervasive in the United States in 1948. Hence, the international community's condemnation of racial prejudice was destined to produce a collision between international human rights law and U.S. domestic laws and practices. The remainder of this chapter examines the dynamics of that collision in both foreign and domestic affairs during the latter part of Harry Truman's first term as president.

II. INTERNATIONAL HUMAN RIGHTS AND U.S. DIPLOMACY

Three statements by senior executive officials show that the practice of racial discrimination in the United States was a serious liability for the Truman administration's conduct of U.S. foreign policy. In a letter to the Fair Employment Practice Committee on May 8, 1946, Acting Secretary of State Dean Acheson stated:

[T]he existence of discrimination against minority groups in this country has an adverse effect upon our relations with other countries. We are reminded over and over by some foreign newspapers and spokesmen, that our treatment of various minorities leaves much to be desired. . . . Frequently we find it next to impossible to formulate a satisfactory answer to our critics in other countries; the gap between the things we stand for in principle and the facts of a particular situation may be too wide to be bridged. . . . The Department of State, therefore, has good reason to hope for the continued and increased effectiveness of public and private efforts to do away with these discriminations.[10]

In October 1947, when the National Association for the Advancement of Colored People (NAACP) submitted a human rights petition to the United Nations on behalf of African Americans, Attorney General Tom Clark told the National Association of Attorneys General "he was humiliated that African Americans had to seek redress of their grievances from the UN."[11] In a brief submitted to the U.S. Supreme Court in December 1947, the government stated: "The fact that racial restrictive covenants are being enforced by instrumentalities of government has become a source of serious embarrassment to agencies of the Federal Government in the performance of many essential functions, including . . . the conduct of foreign affairs."[12] Other scholars have demonstrated that the adverse effect of race discrimination on the conduct of U.S. foreign policy was a key factor supporting civil rights reform in the United States in the decades after World War II.[13] However, prior accounts have understated the significance of international human rights law as a critical factor linking race discrimination in the United States to the conduct of U.S. foreign policy.

Racial discrimination—including lynching, Jim Crow laws, and restrictions on political participation by African Americans—was a fact of life in the United States from the end of Reconstruction until World War II.[14] During that period, "the gap between the things we stand for in principle and the facts of a particular situation," in Acheson's words, was as wide, if not wider, than the gap that existed after World War II. Nevertheless, in the early twentieth century, racial discrimination was generally not perceived as a handicap in our relations with other countries. Why not? One possible answer is that U.S. foreign policy before World War II focused primarily on relationships with European countries whose population was primarily white. In contrast, after World War II, relationships with non-European countries became increasingly important. But that is surely not the whole story.

In the late nineteenth and early twentieth centuries, the United States maintained diplomatic relations with various Asian, African, and Latin American countries. Racial discrimination against Chinese nationals, for example, was sometimes an irritant in the U.S. relationship with China.[15] Before World War II, though, discrimination against Chinese nationals was a bilateral issue with China, not a multilateral issue that affected U.S. relationships with a broader range of countries. Adoption of the U.N. Charter and the Universal Declaration of Human Rights signaled a change in the conduct of international diplomacy by creating a new international norm against racial discrimination that effectively multilateralized the problem of race discrimination. Before adoption of the Charter, the obligation not to discriminate against Chinese nationals was an obligation owed to China. After adoption of the Charter, the obligation not to discriminate on the basis of race or nationality became an obligation *erga omnes*—that is, an obligation owed to the entire international community.[16] This helps explain why discrimination against African Americans in the United States became a subject of intense media interest throughout the world in the late 1940s,[17] even though foreign media generally ignored the problem before the Charter created a new international norm.

To be clear, I am not claiming that the Charter itself caused a change in the conduct of international diplomacy. Rather, the decision by States to include human rights provisions in the U.N. Charter, and to adopt the Genocide Convention and the Universal Declaration, manifested a changed attitude about "domestic" racial discrimination. Before World War II, diplomats typically did not criticize other countries for their treatment of their own racial minorities, unless the complaining country shared a national, ethnic, or religious affiliation with the persecuted minority. Unspoken rules of diplomatic protocol dictated that a country's treatment of its own racial minorities was a purely domestic matter, not a proper subject of international diplomacy. Thus, before World War II, if an Asian or European state criticized the United States for its treatment of African Americans, it was a sufficient response to say, "That's none of your business." After adoption of the U.N. Charter, though, that response was no longer sufficient. Revelations about Nazi atrocities prompted States to create modern international human rights law. The new international law manifested a shared belief that a nation's treatment of its own minorities was no longer a purely domestic matter; it had become a matter of international concern. By codifying the norm against racial discrimination in various international instruments, States converted "domestic" race discrimination into a subject of international diplomacy.[18] Human rights law provided an international standard that countries could use to judge the behavior of other countries. Hence, the creation of new, international anti-discrimination norms transformed Jim Crow from a domestic matter into a foreign policy issue.

III. INTERNATIONAL HUMAN RIGHTS ACTIVISM: PETITIONING THE UNITED NATIONS

The years 1946–1947 were the high point in the NAACP's effort to utilize the United Nations' international human rights machinery to press for improved conditions for African Americans in the United States. At the San Francisco conference in 1945, where final drafting of the U.N. Charter was completed, NAACP leaders had lobbied for strong human rights language in the Charter. Although they were disappointed with the results,[19] the Charter's human rights provisions did provide a helpful platform for further human rights activism.

The National Negro Congress (NNC) sought to take advantage of the Charter's human rights provisions by filing a petition with the United Nations. "At the NNC's request, historian Herbert Aptheker drafted an eight-page report ... that outlined African Americans' economic, political, and social oppression." The report addressed continued lynching, sub-standard housing, inferior educational facilities, restrictions on voting rights, and more. The NNC presented its petition to the U.N. Secretary General's office in June 1946, asking the United Nations to "end the oppression of the American Negro."[20]

Initially, the NAACP leadership was divided as to whether petitioning the United Nations was a good idea. Roy Wilkins dismissed the NNC petition as a "publicity stunt." However, Walter White and W.E.B. Du Bois disagreed with Wilkins. Accordingly, White asked Du Bois to prepare a detailed petition to the United Nations on behalf of the NAACP. White believed that Eleanor Roosevelt— as chair of the Commission on Human Rights, and an NAACP Board member— would be a powerful ally "to champion the cause of African Americans before the international body." Du Bois was less optimistic about Roosevelt's willingness to use her position to advance their cause. Nevertheless, he concluded "that the United States, because of the emerging Cold War, was vulnerable to a skillfully publicized expose on American racism. This publicity would force the nation to address the needs of its 13 million African Americans, regardless of what the UN could or would do."[21] Thus, Du Bois's politically astute strategy anticipated the subsequent development of "naming and shaming" campaigns by other international human rights organizations.[22] Even if the United Nations itself would not or could not fix the problems, Du Bois thought that it provided an excellent forum for pressuring the United States to remedy problems of racial discrimination at home.

Du Bois devoted most of his time from Summer 1946 to Fall 1947 preparing a 200-page petition to the United Nations "that documented both the effects of human rights abuses on America's black population and the UN's obliga- tion to intervene." Du Bois recruited a stellar team of scholars and attorneys to work with him on the petition.[23] By the fall of 1947, the petition was sufficiently polished to present to the United Nations. The problem, at that point, was how to get someone in the United Nations to act on the petition. The Commission on Human Rights had decided in February 1947 that it had "no power to take any action in regard to any complaints regarding human rights."[24] Undaunted, NAACP representatives "contacted all of the UN delegations, as well as Secretary General Trygve Lie, asking for their support in bringing the NAACP's petition before the General Assembly." In response, Lie "suggested that Du Bois con- tact John Humphrey," the head of the United Nation's Human Rights Division. Humphrey, in turn, "told Du Bois that only member states could place a petition before the UN."[25]

Recognizing that he was being stonewalled, Du Bois decided to enlist the media as an ally. Within the NAACP, Du Bois reported to Walter White. However, acting without White's consent, Du Bois leaked copies of the petition to newspapers.[26] On October 12, 1947, the New York Times published a story about the NAACP petition. The *Times* quoted Du Bois as saying that it "is not the Soviet Union that threatens the United States so much as Mississippi: Not Stalin and Molotov but Bilbo and Rankin."[27] (John Rankin and Theodore Bilbo were senators from Mississippi.) Other papers also highlighted the NAACP human rights petition. The ensuing media pressure forced Humphrey to receive the NAACP petition on behalf of the United Nations. The NAACP hoped to stage an elaborate ceremony with maximum press coverage to publicize the filing of its petition. However, "Humphrey insisted on limiting those coming ... to 12 or 15 of the leaders of the Association."[28] Humphrey met with a small group of the NAACP's leaders on October 23, 1947. White and Du Bois both delivered powerful speeches, urging the United Nations to remedy the problems of racial discrimination in the United States. In response, Humphrey advised them that "the Commission ... has no power to take any action ... concerning human rights."[29]

After meeting with Humphrey, the NAACP shifted its focus to the upcoming meeting of the U.N. Subcommission on the Prevention of Discrimination and Protection of Minorities (MINDIS). MINDIS was scheduled to meet in Geneva in November and December 1947. Before the meeting, Du Bois conducted a skillful public relations campaign to generate media attention for the NAACP petition. The media response was mostly favorable. The *Chicago Defender* called the NAACP petition "a searing indictment" of the nation's "failure to practice what it preaches."[30] Journalist Saul Padover wrote: "[I]f there is not much de- mocracy in Hungary and Bulgaria, there is possibly even less of it ... in South Carolina and Mississippi."[31] This was precisely the type of publicity that Du Bois hoped would shame the U.S. government into taking action to remedy problems of race discrimination. Du Bois's "name and shame" strategy met with limited success. Attorney General Tom Clark told the National Association of Attorneys General that he was "humiliated" that African Americans had to seek redress of their grievances from the United Nations.[32] However, Clark did not translate his humiliation into concrete, effective action.

When MINDIS met in Geneva in late 1947, the Soviet delegation, with the NAACP petition "strapped in its holster, went gunning for the United States." The Soviet delegate, Alexander Borisov, "exploited every opportunity to launch into a severe attack on U.S. discrimination practices."[33] He pushed hard, but without success, to include the NAACP petition on the agenda of the U.N. Commission on Human Rights. Borisov's attempt to use the NAACP petition to embarrass the United States was precisely what the NAACP's detractors had feared. One U.S. newspaper criticized the NAACP for furnishing "Soviet Russia with new ammunition."[34] Jonathan Daniels, the U.S. representative to MINDIS, who was generally supportive of the NAACP's policies and programs, was "absolutely furious with Walter White" for submitting a petition to the United Nations that "was used as a political weapon" by the Soviets.[35] Eleanor Roosevelt, who was a member of the NAACP Board of Directors, suggested that White and Du Bois "had erred in going to the UN because the only petitions the Soviets ever supported were those authored by known communist dominated groups."[36]

The critical response from Daniels and Roosevelt created a split between White and Du Bois. White held a very high opinion of Roosevelt and sought her approval. Accordingly, he wanted to shift the NAACP's focus away from the petition, and focus instead on strengthening the Universal Declaration of Human Rights and the Covenant on Human Rights. Du Bois, on the other hand, wanted to continue deploying the NAACP petition to support a "name and shame" strategy, with the goal of prodding the U.S. government to take concrete steps to remedy problems of racial discrimination. White feared that a continuation of the shaming campaign would lead to accusations that the NAACP was aligning itself with communists. Given the general anti-communist climate of the times, his fears were not unfounded. Ultimately, continued infighting between White and Du Bois led to an NAACP Board decision to terminate Du Bois's employment in September 1948. Disagreement over human rights strategy was not the only reason that the Board fired Du Bois, but it was a key element in the chain of events leading to that decision.[37]

After firing Du Bois, the NAACP reduced its engagement with the U.N.'s international human rights machinery. But the NAACP did not abandon its international human rights activism. Instead, the organization chose to focus on domestic litigation as a vehicle for human rights activism.

IV. DOMESTIC HUMAN RIGHTS LITIGATION

Between January and June 1948, the U.S. Supreme Court published five decisions addressing seven cases in which litigants raised arguments based on the U.N. Charter's human rights provisions. *Shelley v. Kraemer* involved two joined cases in which petitioners challenged state court decisions affirming the validity of racially restrictive covenants in Missouri and Michigan.[38] (Racially restrictive covenants are private contracts intended to preclude people of certain racial groups from buying and/or leasing homes in designated neighborhoods.) *Hurd v. Hodge* involved two joined cases in which petitioners challenged racially restrictive covenants in the District of Columbia.[39] *Oyama v. California* and *Takahashi v. Fish & Game Commission* involved challenges to California laws that discriminated against Japanese nationals. The statute in *Oyama* prevented Japanese nationals from owning land in California; the one in *Takahashi* barred Japanese from securing a commercial fishing license from the State of California.[40] *Bob-Lo Excursion Company v. Michigan* involved a corporate defendant who appealed a criminal conviction under a state civil rights statute.[41] The briefs in these cases are interesting for several reasons.

First, the list of individual attorneys who made Charter-based human rights arguments in these cases is impressive. Thurgood Marshall, the future Supreme Court justice, represented the petitioners in *McGhee v. Sipes*, the companion case to *Shelley v. Kraemer*. Marshall also filed amicus briefs on behalf of the NAACP in support of the petitioner in *Takahashi* and the appellee in *Bob-Lo Excursion Co.* Dean Acheson, the future secretary of state, represented the petitioner in *Takahashi*. Spottswood Robinson, the future D.C. Circuit judge, represented the petitioner in *Hurd v. Hodge*. Edwin Borchard (Yale law professor), Zechariah Chafee, Jr. (Harvard law professor) and others co-signed an amicus brief on behalf of the ACLU in *Oyama*. Myres McDougal (Yale law professor), Philip Jessup (future judge on the International Court of Justice) and others co-signed an amicus brief on behalf of the American Association for the United Nations in *Shelley v. Kraemer* and the other restrictive covenant cases. All of their briefs made legal arguments based partly on the U.N. Charter's human rights provisions.[42] Thus, the lawyers who supported judicial application of the Charter to invalidate racially discriminatory laws and practices included mainstream, establishment lawyers, not just naive "one-worlders."

Second, the range of organizations that supported Charter-based, human rights arguments is also impressive. The ACLU advanced a Charter-based argument in its amicus brief supporting the petitioners in *Oyama*.[43] The NAACP, the ACLU, and the National Lawyers Guild made a Charter-based argument in a joint amicus brief supporting the appellee in *Bob-Lo Excursion Co.*[44] The ACLU, the American Jewish Congress, the American Veterans Committee, the NAACP, and the National Lawyers Guild all raised Charter-based arguments in separate amicus briefs supporting the petitioner in *Takahashi*.[45] The ACLU, the American Association for the United Nations, the American Indian Citizens League of California, the Congress of Industrial Organizations and affiliated organizations, the Japanese-American Citizens League, the Non-Sectarian Anti-Nazi League to Champion Human Rights, and the St. Louis Civil Liberties Committee all advanced Charter-based human rights arguments in their amicus briefs supporting petitioners in *Shelley* and/or other restrictive covenant cases.[46] The list of organizations is significant because it demonstrates that, in the late 1940s, there was no split between "civil rights" organizations and "human rights" organizations. The leading domestic civil rights organizations were human rights organizations. The leaders of key organizations defined their institutional missions in terms of human rights.[47] This helps explain why so many organizations that would be classified today as "civil rights" organizations invoked the human rights provisions of the U.N. Charter to support their preferred outcomes in domestic "civil rights" litigation.

Not all the briefs referenced above invoked the U.N. Charter in support of treaty supremacy arguments. For example, the amicus brief submitted by the Japanese-American Citizens League in *Hurd v. Hodge* cited, among other things, the U.N. Charter and the Act of Chapultepec (a resolution adopted by the Pan American Union in 1945) to support the assertion that judicial enforcement of racially restrictive covenants "is contrary to the public policy of the United States."[48] The petitioner's brief in *Takahashi* cited the U.N. Charter, the draft Universal Declaration of Human Rights, and the draft American Declaration of the Rights and Duties of Man (subsequently adopted by the Ninth International Conference of American States) to support an argument that the federal government—by adopting laws and treaties "aimed at preventing injurious discriminations against aliens"—had "occupied the field" with respect to regulation of aliens, thereby precluding states from passing their own laws regulating aliens.[49]

On the other hand, many of the briefs argued expressly that the Supremacy Clause required domestic courts to apply the Charter's human rights provisions to invalidate racially discriminatory laws and practices. For example, Thurgood Marshall, lead counsel for petitioner in *McGhee v. Sipes*, wrote: "The human rights provisions of the United Nations Charter, as treaty provisions, are the supreme law of the land and no citizen may lawfully enter into a contract in subversion of their purposes. The restrictive agreement here presented for enforcement falls within this proscription."[50] Similarly, the petitioner's brief in *Hurd v. Hodge* stated:

When the judicial arm of the Government of the United States . . . enforces a restrictive covenant which, solely on the basis of race, forbids a person to purchase and occupy land for residential purposes, such action clearly violates the Government's obligation under the Charter not to lend its aid to such racial discriminations. The supremacy of this Treaty precludes the specific enforcement in any court of the United States of a covenant whose objective is contrary to the objectives of the Treaty.[51]

An amicus brief submitted by the ACLU in *Oyama v. California*, after quoting Article 55 of the U.N. Charter, stated: "It seems clear that the California Alien Land Law is invalid by virtue of this treaty provision, for State laws must be consistent with, and in conformity to, the treaties of the United States."[52] The brief cited the Supremacy Clause as authority. The NAACP amicus brief in *Takahashi* stated:

The United Nations Charter is a treaty, duly executed by the President and ratified by the Senate. Under Article VI, Section 2 of the Constitution such a treaty is the "supreme Law of the Land" and specifically, "the Judges in

every State shall be bound thereby, any Thing in the Constitution or Laws
of any State to the Contrary notwithstanding." The right to work has long
been recognized as a fundamental human right in American law. The laws
of California attempt to deny to Japanese this fundamental right in contravention of the international obligations of the United States.[53]

These are just a few examples of briefs where parties or amici invoked the U.N.
Charter together with the Constitution's treaty supremacy rule to support arguments for invalidating discriminatory laws or practices.[54]

Interestingly, despite the prevalence of Charter-based treaty supremacy arguments in cases decided by the Supreme Court in the October 1947 term, no opposing party in any case argued that the Charter's human rights provisions were not
self-executing. Appellee's brief in *Bob-Lo* did not even mention the U.N. Charter.[55]
In *Oyama*, respondent addressed the U.N. Charter argument on the merits, contending that the statutory classification in California's Alien Land Law was not
"based on race" and that the Charter did not apply because the state had taken possession of the land at issue before the Charter existed.[56] In *Takahashi*, respondents
acknowledged that the U.N. Charter provided "that everyone is entitled to human
rights and freedoms without distinction as to race, sex, language or religion," but
argued that the Charter did not preclude California from conserving its "fisheries
by prohibiting fishing entirely or by limiting the privilege to its own citizens," or to
select groups of noncitizens.[57] The respondent briefs in *Oyama* and *Takahashi* did
not address the question of whether the Charter was self-executing.[58]

The petitioners' briefs in *Hurd v. Hodge* and *McGhee v. Sipes* presented very
explicit, fairly detailed treaty supremacy arguments.[59] Even so, neither respondent addressed the question of whether the U.N. Charter's human rights provisions were self-executing. Respondent in *McGhee* argued that the Charter "does
not affect the subjects of one of the member nations in their private contractual
relations; it specifically excludes from its operation matters which are within
the domestic, as distinguished from international, jurisdiction of the member
nations."[60] Respondent added that the Charter "does no more than pledge this
Nation to encourage and assist *other nations,* not fortunate enough to have our
form of government. As a treaty it refers only to matters *between* nations involved, and cannot be applied to private rights among the citizens of any member
nation."[61] The respondent brief in *Hurd v. Hodge* contained almost identical language.[62] None of the party briefs in *McGhee* or *Hurd* mentioned the distinction
between self-executing and non-self-executing treaties. Thus, the party briefs in
the restrictive covenant cases indicate that sophisticated Supreme Court litiga-
tors circa 1948 did not believe that the distinction between self-executing and
non-self-executing treaties was relevant to treaty supremacy claims. As demonstrated in Parts One and Two, that belief was well founded: from 1789 to 1945,
the distinction between self-executing and non-self-executing treaties was generally not relevant to treaty supremacy claims.

Lawyers filed more than a dozen amicus briefs in the Supreme Court in
the October 1947 term invoking the U.N. Charter's human rights provisions.

Only two such briefs provided any indication that the distinction between self-executing and non-self-executing treaties might be relevant to treaty supremacy claims based on the Charter's human rights provisions. In *Takahashi*, the NAACP and the National Lawyers Guild (NLG) filed a joint brief supporting the petitioner. The brief devoted several pages to an argument that "a state law denying to a racial group the right to engage in a common occupation violates the obligations of the United States under the United Nations Charter." At the end of that argument, the brief included two sentences on self-execution. "Within the framework of a federal form of government there may be many fields in which the United Nations Charter will require specific enabling legislation before it becomes an effective obligation upon the people of the United States. Yet certain aspects of the Charter are by force of American law sufficiently clear to constitute the supreme law of the land as a self-executing obligation and thus to supersede state laws which violate them."[63]

Similarly, the American Association for the United Nations (AAUN) filed an amicus brief in *Shelley* and related cases. The thirty-page brief argued that racially restrictive covenants violate the U.N. Charter's human rights provisions and that the Charter supersedes conflicting state laws under the Supremacy Clause.[64] The brief addressed the self-execution issue in a single sentence. "Even conceding, *arguendo*, that Articles 55(c) and 56 of the United Nations Charter are not self-executing, they nevertheless constitute an authoritative declaration of the foreign policy of the United States as committing this Government to the elimination of racial discrimination."[65] To reiterate, the NAACP/NLG brief in *Takahashi* and the AAUN brief in *Shelley* were the only two briefs that even addressed the question of whether the Charter's human rights provisions were self-executing. The rather cursory treatment of self-execution in both briefs indicates that their authors thought the issue was perhaps relevant, but not very important. In contrast, numerous other briefs filed in the Supreme Court in the October 1947 term invoked the Charter's human rights provisions without even mentioning the self-execution issue. The authors of those briefs apparently believed that the distinction between self-executing and non-self-executing treaties was not relevant to Charter-based treaty supremacy claims.

In sum, as of 1948 the conceptual firewall that insulated treaty supremacy doctrine from self-execution doctrine remained largely intact. However, as discussed in Chapters 10 and 11, that firewall would experience substantial degradation over the next few years. The erosion of that conceptual firewall ultimately transformed the Constitution's treaty supremacy rule from a mandatory to an optional rule.

V. THE TRUMAN ADMINISTRATION CHARTS A MIDDLE PATH

In the years 1946 to 1948, the Truman administration supported efforts to end racial discrimination in the United States. In December 1946, President Truman established the President's Committee on Civil Rights, directing the Committee to develop recommendations for legislative or other measures to promote "more adequate and effective means and procedures for the protection of the civil rights of the people of the United States."[66] The Committee delivered its report the next year. The report identified "a moral reason, an economic reason, and an international reason for believing that the time" was ripe for taking affirmative steps to end racial discrimination in the United States. The moral reason related to the shocking "difference between what we preach about civil rights and what we practice." The economic reason involved the "loss of a huge, potential market for goods [as] a direct result of the economic discrimination which is practiced against many of our minority groups."[67]

The Committee explained the international reason for domestic civil rights reform as follows: "Our foreign policy is designed to make the United States an enormous, positive influence for peace and progress throughout the world. We have tried to let nothing, not even extreme political differences between ourselves and foreign nations, stand in the way of this goal. But our domestic civil rights shortcomings are a serious obstacle" to the accomplishment of our foreign policy objectives.[68] The Committee explained why race discrimination at home had become a foreign policy problem. "We cannot escape the fact that our civil rights record has been an issue in world politics. The world's press and radio are full of it. . . . We and our friends have been, and are, stressing our achievements. Those with competing philosophies . . . have tried to prove our democracy an empty fraud, and our nation a consistent oppressor of underprivileged people."[69] In other words, "domestic" racial discrimination had become a foreign policy issue because the Soviet Union exploited the issue in its effort to persuade Third World countries that Soviet-style socialism offered greater hope for oppressed people than did American-style capitalism. Additionally, the Committee added:

> [O]ur civil rights record has growing international implications. . . . Many of
> man's problems, we have been learning, are capable of ultimate solution only
> through international cooperation and action. The subject of human rights,
> itself, has been made a major concern of the United Nations. . . . A lynching
> in a rural American community is not a challenge to that community's con-
> science alone. The repercussions of such a crime are heard not only in the
> locality, or indeed only in our own nation. They echo from one end of the
> globe to the other . . . . Similarly, interference with the right of a qualified
> citizen to vote locally cannot today remain a local problem. An American
> diplomat cannot forcefully argue for free elections in foreign lands without
> meeting the challenge that in many sections of America qualified voters do
> not have free access to the polls.[70]

In sum, by creating the United Nations, and establishing promotion of human rights as one of its primary goals, the nations of the world had determined that lynching and free elections would henceforth be matters of international concern. Thus, race discrimination in the United States was a foreign policy issue because the nations of the world made it one.

President Truman was apparently persuaded that civil rights reform at home was necessary to advance U.S. foreign policy interests abroad. In February 1948, he delivered a special message to Congress proposing enactment of civil rights laws to "establish a permanent civil rights commission, outlaw lynching, and protect the right to vote, among other proposals."[71] In support of these proposals, the president stated: "If we wish to inspire the peoples of the world whose freedom is in jeopardy, if we wish to restore hope to those who have already lost their civil liberties, if we wish to fulfill the promise that is ours, we must correct the remaining imperfections in our practice of democracy."[72] Thus, Truman told Congress that the United States needed civil rights legislation to promote its foreign policy interests. Historians débate whether he was sincere about pursuing civil rights legislation or whether the proposed legislation was an election-year gambit to win the black vote.[73] Regardless, Southern Democrats who controlled key committees in Congress ensured that no significant civil rights legislation would be passed during Truman's presidency.

Unable to secure legislative support for civil rights reform, Truman pursued his civil rights agenda by promulgating executive orders. In July 1948 he issued Executive Order 9981, declaring a policy "that there shall be equality of treatment and opportunity for all persons in the armed services without regard to race, color, religion, or national origin."[74] The order specified that the policy should be implemented "as rapidly as possible, having due regard to the time required to effectuate any necessary changes without impairing efficiency or morale." However, the order did not establish a specific timeline for achieving full equality.[75]

Apart from the failed attempt to enact civil rights legislation, and the half measure of an executive order addressing racial discrimination in the military, the Truman administration sought to promote civil rights by filing amicus briefs supporting petitioners in the major human rights cases discussed previously.[76] The executive branch filed a single amicus brief supporting petitioners in all four restrictive covenant cases.[77] It also filed an amicus brief supporting the petitioner in *Takahashi*.[78] Attorney General Tom Clark signed both briefs on behalf of the government. As Professor Dudziak has explained, the attorney general's decision to sign his own name on the briefs, rather than delegating that task to subordinate officials, signaled that the Truman administration was committed at the highest levels to ending racially discriminatory laws and practices.[79]

The government's brief in the restrictive covenant cases contended that "enforcement of racial restrictive covenants is contrary to the public policy of the United States."[80] In that context, the brief noted that the United States has a treaty obligation under the U.N. Charter to promote "universal respect for, and observance of, human rights and fundamental freedoms, for all without distinction as to race, sex, language, or religion." The brief also cited a resolution adopted by the U.N. General Assembly calling on governments "to put an immediate end to religious and so-called racial persecutions and discrimination." Additionally, the brief cited a resolution adopted by the Inter-American Conference on Problems of War and Peace that urged governments to "make every effort to prevent in their respective countries all acts which may provoke discrimination among individuals because of race or religion." The government concluded this portion of its brief as follows: "The legislative, executive, and international pronouncements set out above reflect a public policy wholly inconsistent with the enforcement of racial restrictive covenants. . . . [E]ven if the decrees below are not stricken on specific constitutional grounds, they may properly be set aside as being inconsistent with the public policy of the United States."[81] Thus, the government did not endorse a treaty supremacy argument, but it did cite the Charter and other international instruments in support of its argument that courts may not enforce racially restrictive covenants, because such covenants contravene the public policy of the United States.

The Truman administration also filed an amicus brief supporting the petitioner in *Takahashi*. In that case, the petitioner challenged the validity of a California law that barred Japanese nationals from obtaining commercial fishing licenses.[82] The government brief in support of petitioner did not mention the U.N. Charter or other international human rights instruments, but it did offer a foreign policy rationale for invalidating the California law. The brief quoted the Supreme Court decision in *Hines v. Davidowitz* as follows:

> It is of importance that this legislation is in a field which affects international relations, the one aspect of our government that from the first has been most generally conceded imperatively to demand broad national authority. Any concurrent state power that may exist is restricted to the narrowest of limits; the state's power here is not bottomed on the same broad base as is its power to tax.[83]

The brief did not explain why denial of a fishing license to a Japanese national "affects international relations"—perhaps because the point was sufficiently obvious that no explanation was required. In the political/diplomatic context of the late 1940s, every incident of racial discrimination in the United States affected international relations.

President Truman said in his State of the Union address in early 1948: "Our first goal is to secure fully the essential human rights of our citizens."[84] As president, Truman's power to accomplish that goal was constrained by Congress's unwillingness to enact major civil rights legislation. However, the Supreme Court had substantial power to promote human rights, so the Truman administration filed amicus briefs urging the Court to exercise that power. One way the Court could have exercised its power to promote human rights would have been to apply the U.N. Charter in conjunction with the Supremacy Clause to invalidate discriminatory state laws. However, briefs submitted by the Truman administration did not advocate a treaty supremacy rationale. Instead, the government raised a combination of constitutional, public policy, and foreign policy arguments to support outcomes in civil rights cases that would, as a practical matter, enhance U.S. compliance with international human rights norms.

VI. THE COURTS AND HUMAN RIGHTS

In cases where parties and/or amici invoked the U.N. Charter's human rights provisions, the Supreme Court invariably ruled in favor of human rights claimants, but rarely relied on the Charter to support its judgment. Instead, the Court preferred to apply a constitutional or statutory rationale to support results consistent with the Charter's anti-discrimination norm.

In *Bob-Lo Excursion Co. v. Michigan*, the State of Michigan prosecuted a corporate defendant under the Michigan Civil Rights Act.[85] The Act made it a misdemeanor for a company to discriminate on the basis of race in the provision of public accommodations. The defendant ran an amusement park in Canada; it operated two steamships that transported patrons between Detroit and the amusement park. The company challenged the Michigan statute on constitutional grounds, arguing that the statute interfered with its conduct of international commerce. Neither party invoked the Charter, but the NAACP and ACLU did so in their amicus brief. They argued that the Michigan law was valid because, inter alia, it merely required the defendant "to cooperate in carrying out the obligations of this country under the United Nations Charter."[86] The Supreme Court agreed with the state court's conclusion that the Commerce Clause "does not forbid applying the Michigan civil rights act to sustain appellant's conviction."[87] The Court did not mention the Charter, but its decision promoted U.S. compliance with emerging international human rights norms by affirming the power of state governments to prohibit racial discrimination by private parties.

In *Takahashi v. Fish & Game Commission*, Torao Takahashi sought a court order compelling the Commission to grant him a commercial fishing license.[88] He held a license and worked as a commercial fisherman from 1915 to 1942. However, California enacted a law in 1943 that prohibited issuance of a fishing license to "alien Japanese." Takahashi challenged the validity of the California law, relying in part on the Charter's human rights provisions. Several amicus briefs also raised Charter-based human rights arguments.[89] The Court held that the state law was invalid because it interfered with the federal government's exclusive control over immigration and because it discriminated on the basis of race in violation of the Fourteenth Amendment.[90] The Court's opinion did not mention the U.N. Charter, but *Takahashi* was broadly consistent with international anti-discrimination norms because the decision constrained the power of state governments to discriminate on the basis of race or nationality.

In *Oyama v. California*, the state claimed that land escheated to the state under the California Alien Land Law when Kajiro Oyama, a Japanese national, purchased two parcels of land in California as a gift for his son Fred, who was a U.S. citizen. The California statute prohibited Kajiro from owning land in California, but permitted Fred, as a U.S. citizen, to own land. Even so, under state law, Fred faced "the necessity of overcoming a statutory presumption that conveyances financed by his father and recorded in Fred's name were not" actually intended as gifts.[91] In addition, the state imposed other obstacles that made it very difficult for Fred to prove his rightful ownership of the land.

"The cumulative effect," the Court said, "was clearly to discriminate against Fred Oyama. He was saddled with an onerous burden of proof which need not be borne by California children generally."[92] Hence, the Court held "that the Alien Land Law, as applied in this case, deprives Fred Oyama of the equal protection" of the laws.[93] Chief Justice Vinson's majority opinion did not mention the U.N. Charter, nor did it challenge the validity of the statutory provision that barred Japanese nationals from owning land in California.

In contrast, four justices joined two separate concurring opinions that would have invalidated the Alien Land Law on its face. Both concurring opinions relied partly on the U.N. Charter. Justice Black wrote an opinion for himself and Justice Douglas. His opinion relied primarily on the Equal Protection Clause as a basis for invalidating the Alien Land Law,[94] but he viewed the Charter as an independent ground for invalidating the statute.

> There are additional reasons now why that [California] law stands as an obstacle to the free accomplishment of our policy in the international field. One of these reasons is that we have recently pledged ourselves to cooperate with the United Nations to "promote ... universal respect for, and observance of, human rights and fundamental freedoms for all without distinction as to race, sex, language, or religion." How can this nation be faithful to this international pledge if state laws which bar land ownership and occupancy by aliens on account of race are permitted to be enforced?[95]

Justice Murphy wrote an opinion for himself and Justice Rutledge. Like Justices Black and Douglas, they would have held that the statutory provision barring Japanese nationals from owning land in California was invalid. Justice Murphy wrote that the Alien Land Law violated the Equal Protection Clause because it "was designed to effectuate a purely racial discrimination, to prohibit a Japanese alien from owning or using agricultural land solely because he is a Japanese alien."[96] He also explained in detail how "the Alien Land Law from its inception has proved an embarrassment to the United States Government. This statute has ... overflowed into the realm of foreign policy; it has had direct and unfortunate consequences on this country's relations with Japan."[97] Then he added:

> Moreover, this nation has recently pledged itself, through the United Nations Charter, to promote respect for, and observance of, human rights and fundamental freedoms for all without distinction as to race, sex, language and religion. The Alien Land Law stands as a barrier to the fulfillment of that national pledge. Its inconsistency with the Charter, which has been duly ratified and adopted by the United States, is but one more reason why the statute must be condemned.[98]

Thus, four of nine justices would have invalidated California's Alien Land Law, in part because it conflicted with the nation's human rights obligations under the U.N. Charter.

The parties and amici in *Shelley* and the other restrictive covenant cases relied heavily on Charter-based human rights arguments to support their view that courts may not enforce racially restrictive covenants.[99] The Supreme Court agreed that courts may not enforce racially restrictive covenants, but it chose not to rely on the U.N. Charter to support that conclusion. *Shelley v. Kraemer* involved judicial enforcement of restrictive covenants by state courts. The Court held "that in granting judicial enforcement of the restrictive agreements in these cases, the States have denied petitioners the equal protection of the laws [in violation of the Fourteenth Amendment] and that, therefore, the action of the state courts cannot stand."[100] *Hurd v. Hodge* involved judicial enforcement by federal courts of restrictive covenants in the District of Columbia. The Court held "that the action of the District Court directed against the Negro purchasers and the white sellers denies rights intended by Congress to be protected by the Civil Rights Act [of 1866] and that, consequently, the action cannot stand."[101]

In sum, the Supreme Court ruled in favor of human rights claimants in every case where one or more briefs raised arguments based on the Charter's human rights provisions. However, the Court preferred to apply a constitutional or statutory rationale to support its decisions, rather than relying directly on the Charter. The Court's decisions promoted U.S. compliance with emerging international human rights norms by expanding incrementally the scope of constitutional and statutory protections against racial discrimination, without challenging the overarching legal framework that permitted Southern states to continue applying Jim Crow laws. The Court's decisions in these cases were not foreordained. Dissenting opinions in *Oyama* and *Takahashi* indicated that some justices were still committed to a traditional view of states' rights, even where states invoked state sovereignty to help justify racially discriminatory laws.[102] Justices Reed, Jackson, and Rutledge recused themselves in the restrictive covenant cases, perhaps because they were parties to such restrictive covenants themselves.[103] In the 1940s, the Charter's anti-discrimination norm had not penetrated far enough into American culture to make it politically untenable for the Senate to confirm a Supreme Court nominee who owned a home subject to a racially restrictive covenant.[104] However, the magnetic pull of the Charter's anti-discrimination norm would soon change that situation.

Before we conclude this section, the decision by a New York state court in *Curran v. City of New York* merits discussion.[105] Curran was a New York taxpayer who sought a declaratory judgment to set aside a series of actions by the City related to establishment of the U.N. headquarters site in Manhattan. Curran objected, among other things, to the City's decision that "the headquarters site of the United Nations will be exempted from taxation on the tax rolls of the City of New York."[106] The court cited Article 105 of the U.N. Charter, which states: "The Organization shall enjoy in the territory of each of its Members such privileges and immunities as are necessary for the fulfilment of its purposes." The court then added: "*Even without further action by Congress or by the State . . .* the immunities 'necessary for the fulfillment of its purposes,' conferred upon the United Nations by Article 105, includes immunity from taxation."[107] In other words, the court held that Article 105 of the U.N. Charter is self-executing. *Curran* is one of the few decisions by any U.S. court holding that a particular provision of the U.N. Charter is self-executing. Ironically, though, in his official report to the president on the U.N. Charter, Secretary of State Stettinius stated explicitly that "legislation will be needed to ... afford all of the appropriate privileges and immunities due the Organization and its officials under" Article 105.[108] Thus, the Court in *Curran* adopted a view on self-execution that was precisely the opposite of the view expressed by the secretary of state.

Moreover, in his official report to the president, Article 105 was the only article that Secretary Stettinius identified specifically as a provision that required implementing legislation. In particular, Stettinius's report said nothing about whether the Charter's human rights provisions were self-executing.[109] Nevertheless, courts in the United States would soon decide that the Charter's human rights provisions were not self-executing, and they would invoke the ostensible "intent of the treaty makers" to support that conclusion.[110] Thus, *Curran* initiated a trend in which judicial decisions about the self-executing character of various Charter provisions pay lip service to the "intent of the treaty makers," while ignoring the views expressed by the secretary of state in his official report to the President.[111]

VII. CONSERVATIVE REACTION: THE AMERICAN BAR ASSOCIATION

Frank Holman served as President of the American Bar Association (ABA) in 1948–1949. He was one of the original members of the ABA Special Committee on Peace and Law Through United Nations (the "Special Committee"), created in 1944. The Special Committee effectively controlled ABA policymaking on international human rights issues in the late 1940s and early 1950s, despite opposition from the Section on International and Comparative Law. Moreover, the Special Committee, guided by Holman and like-minded attorneys, was implacably hostile to international human rights law.[112]

In September 1948, the ABA House of Delegates approved a set of resolutions relating to the Universal Declaration of Human Rights and a draft Covenant on Human Rights.[113] To understand those resolutions, some background information regarding the work of the Commission on Human Rights may be helpful. The Commission met in Lake Success, New York, in May and June 1948.[114] At that meeting, the Commission adopted a draft Declaration of Human Rights for submission to the General Assembly. However, the Commission did not have sufficient time to examine in detail the draft Covenant on Human Rights. (Recall that the Declaration was intended to be a non-binding statement of principles, whereas the Covenant was supposed to be a legally binding treaty.) Therefore, in its final report on the meeting in May/June 1948, the Commission expressed its intention to resume work on the Covenant at its next session.[115]

The Special Committee, in preparation for the ABA House of Delegates meeting in September, adopted resolutions attacking both the Declaration and the Covenant, even though the Commission had not yet approved the Covenant.

The Special Committee proposed a resolution stating that "the American Bar Association is of the opinion that the Draft Declaration on Human Rights ... and the Draft Covenant on Human Rights are not in such contents or form as to be suitable for approval and adoption by the General Assembly of the United Nations."[116] The Commission on Human Rights had expressed the view that the Declaration was ready for consideration by the General Assembly, but the Covenant was not yet ready. Even so, the Special Committee did not distinguish between the two documents.

The Special Committee also proposed a resolution stating that "the American Bar Association is of the opinion that action upon the Draft Declaration ... and upon the Draft Covenant ... should be deferred by the General Assembly ... until its regular session in 1949."[117] As above, the Special Committee's insistence on linking the two documents is puzzling. The U.S. government favored prompt action on the Declaration, but preferred to defer action on the Covenant. The Commission, acting under the chairmanship of Eleanor Roosevelt, had effectively adopted the U.S. government views on the proper timetable for acting on the Declaration and Covenant, respectively.[118] Even so, the Special Committee was trying to throw a wrench in the works by delaying action on the document that the U.S. government approved.

The Special Committee proposed an additional resolution stating that "the American Bar Association is of the opinion that any Declaration on Human Rights should not be in any manner approved, accepted or promulgated by or in behalf of the Government of the United States except upon ... approval of it by, the Congress of the United States."[119] Again, this resolution was contrary to the strategy adopted by the Commission and favored by the U.S. government. Under that strategy, the Declaration did not require congressional approval precisely because it was not intended to be a legally binding instrument. In contrast, the Covenant would ultimately require Senate approval because it was intended to be a legally binding treaty. The resolutions proposed by the Special Committee were apparently intended to delay progress on the Human Rights Commission's program of work.[120]

At the ABA House of Delegates meeting in September, a member of the ABA Section of International and Comparative Law (the "Section") "moved that the [Special] Committee on Peace and Law be abolished."[121] He proposed, instead, that the Special Committee should be reconstituted as a subcommittee of the Section. His motion was merely one tactical move in an ongoing battle between the Special Committee and the Section. The Section generally supported the work of the Commission on Human Rights, whereas the Special Committee was strongly opposed to most of the proposals emanating from the Commission. Frank Holman was the ABA president at the time, and he was firmly on the side of the Special Committee. Not surprisingly, the motion to abolish the Special Committee failed. Shortly thereafter, the ABA House of Delegates approved all of the human rights resolutions proposed by the Special Committee.[122] The resolutions approved by the House of Delegates established a pattern of opposition between the ABA and the Commission on Human Rights that would persist for the next several years. As the Commission pressed ahead in its effort to create new international human rights instruments, the ABA resolutely opposed the Commission's work.

Frank Holman explained the rationale behind the ABA resolutions in an article published in the *ABA Journal* in November 1948.[123] He argued that the draft Declaration and draft Covenant were "at variance with our fundamental concept of individual rights and freedoms." The U.N. documents did not give adequate protection for private property or for "conducting business under a free enterprise system." He derided the Declaration and Covenant as "a proposal for world-wide socialism to be imposed through the United Nations on the United States." In order to enforce the Covenant, he argued, "the United Nations will have to interfere continually and minutely into the internal affairs of member nations."[124] From a contemporary perspective, Holman's fears appear to be largely unfounded. Regardless, his articulation of those fears persuaded the leading association of American lawyers to adopt resolutions opposing the work of the U.N. Commission on Human Rights.

Interestingly, the relevant ABA documents demonstrate that, as of November 1948, the leading opponents of the Declaration and Covenant had not yet conceived of the idea that the allegedly harmful effects of ratifying the Covenant could be mitigated by declaring the Covenant to be non-self-executing. Holman wrote that the Covenant "is to be ratified as a treaty and under our Constitution is to become the supreme law of the land and in due course implemented against all of us."[125] The report of the Special Committee stated: "The proposed Covenant would be a treaty; under our Constitution (Article VI), a treaty becomes 'the supreme law of the land,' binding the judges of every state and superior to the Constitution and laws of every state."[126] Holman and other Committee members were surely aware of the doctrine of non-self-executing treaties. However, under the established doctrine that had prevailed for more than 150 years, the classification of a treaty as self-executing or non-self-executing did not affect the operation of the Constitution's treaty supremacy rule. Hence, Holman and the Special Committee had good reason to assume that the treaty supremacy rule would govern the relationship between the Covenant and state law, even if the Covenant was "non-self-executing" in some other sense of that term.

In sum, at the end of 1948 the conceptual firewall that separated treaty supremacy doctrine from self-execution doctrine remained largely intact. However, as discussed in the next chapter, that firewall would soon begin to erode as the legal gibberish of "self-execution" spread from the federal separation-of-powers sphere to the treaty supremacy sphere. Expansion of the "intent doctrine"—which makes the "intent of the treaty makers" the touchstone of self-execution analysis—to encompass treaty supremacy issues would ultimately transform the Constitution's treaty supremacy rule from a mandatory to an optional rule.

The Nationalists Strike Back: 1949–1951

Whereas President Truman's first term in office was a period of intense human rights activism, both domestically and internationally, conservative forces in the American Bar Association (ABA) and the U.S. Senate launched a significant counterattack during his second term, which began with his inauguration in January 1949. I use the term "nationalist" to describe those who led the counterattack against domestic application of international human rights law. They were "nationalist" in that they adopted a very rigid view of the separation between international and domestic affairs. They viewed human rights as a purely domestic matter that was not a proper subject of international law or diplomacy. Hence, they sought to isolate the domestic legal system from what they perceived to be the pernicious influence of international human rights law.

This chapter begins with a brief discussion of key developments in the U.N. Commission on Human Rights. It then analyzes the Truman administration's failed effort to obtain Senate consent for ratification of the Genocide Convention. The next two sections present a detailed analysis of the California Court of Appeal's decision in *Fujii v. California*. *Fujii* is significant because it is one of the few cases in which a U.S. court applied the Charter's human rights provisions in conjunction with the Constitution's treaty supremacy rule to invalidate a state law.[1] *Fujii* also triggered alarm bells in both the Senate and the ABA, leading to proposals for a constitutional amendment. The next section analyzes early moves toward development of the Bricker Amendment in 1950 and 1951. The final section examines three key civil rights cases decided by the U.S. Supreme Court in June 1950.

The overall story is that efforts to incorporate international human rights norms into U.S. law began to diverge onto two separate tracks. The "civil rights" track yielded important victories in Supreme Court decisions that became key precedents for the Court's landmark 1954 decision in *Brown v. Board of Education*, but the Court did not mention the Charter or the Universal Declaration in those cases. The nationalists' counterattack dominated the "human rights" track, effectively killing the Genocide Convention in the Senate and building momentum in support of the proposed Bricker Amendment.

I. THE U.N. COMMISSION ON HUMAN RIGHTS

In the years 1949–1951, the U.N. Commission on Human Rights continued working on a draft Covenant on Human Rights, acting under the supervision of ECOSOC and the General Assembly. The primary goal was to translate the norms embodied in the Universal Declaration into specific, legally binding treaty commitments. The Commission held its fifth, sixth, and seventh sessions, respectively, in Spring 1949, Spring 1950, and Spring 1951.[2]

At the 1949 meeting, the United States proposed an amendment to the draft Covenant that provided in part: "The provisions of this Covenant shall not themselves become effective as domestic law."[3] Eleanor Roosevelt explained that in some States, such as the United States, "a ratified treaty became the highest law of the country," but in other States "a treaty was not automatically incorporated in the national legislation." The proposed amendment "was designed to place those two categories of States on the same footing."[4] Her statement tacitly assumed that the Constitution's treaty supremacy rule placed the United States at an unfair disadvantage relative to other countries. Those who opposed U.S. ratification of human rights treaties generally shared that assumption, but Mrs. Roosevelt did not explain why the treaty supremacy rule should be considered a disadvantage for the United States.

The representative from the Philippines objected to the U.S. proposal. He explained that, in the Philippines, "all international treaties and conventions, when ratified were incorporated without further formalities in domestic law." The U.S. proposal, even if adopted, "could not change the constitutional rule of the Philippines."[5] The Lebanese representative added that the appropriate mechanism for incorporating the Covenant into domestic law "was entirely a question of the constitutional law of States; there was no reason why the Covenant should interfere with the application of that law."[6] After further discussion, the Commission voted against the U.S. proposal.[7] The Commission's rejection of the proposed U.S. amendment manifested a shared understanding that the question whether the Covenant would be directly applicable as domestic law would be governed by the domestic law of individual States, not by the terms of the Covenant. This point is highly significant. During this time frame, the idea was beginning to take root in the United States that the issue of whether a treaty is "effective as domestic law" is a treaty interpretation question. However, delegates from other nations believed that the self-execution question was governed by domestic constitutional law. Thus, there was an emerging gulf between the nascent U.S. view that self-execution is an international law question and the prevailing view in other countries that self-execution is a domestic law question.

At the end of the session, Mrs. Roosevelt stated for the record that "the Covenant would not be self-operative as far as United States domestic law was concerned."[8] She did not explain precisely what she meant by the term "self-operative," but she probably meant that the Covenant would not become effective as domestic law in the United States, absent implementing legislation. If that is what she meant, her statement reflected a very different understanding of the Supremacy Clause than the one that had prevailed from the Founding until World War II. Under the traditional view—the mandatory treaty supremacy rule—the Covenant would automatically supersede conflicting state laws in the United States, even if Congress did not enact implementing legislation.[9] Roosevelt's statement was the earliest recorded statement by any government official in the legislative, executive, or judicial branch to hint at the idea that the treaty supremacy rule might be optional, rather than mandatory. She was almost certainly reading a statement prepared by State Department lawyers.[10] Therefore, her statement demonstrates that, by June 1949, government lawyers had begun to think about transplanting NSE doctrine from the separation of powers sphere to the treaty supremacy sphere. It is unclear, though, whether they recognized that application of NSE doctrine as an exception to the treaty supremacy rule would constitute a sharp departure from prior constitutional practice.

During this period, various U.N. organs debated whether to include economic and social rights in the same treaty with civil and political rights. "The Commission initially prepared a draft covering civil and political rights only."[11] However, at its 1950 meeting, the General Assembly adopted a resolution instructing the Commission "to include in the draft covenant a clear expression of economic, social and cultural rights in a manner which relates them to the civil and political freedoms proclaimed by the draft covenant."[12] The General Assembly later reversed itself, deciding in 1952 that the Commission should draft two separate covenants: one for civil and political rights and a separate one for economic, social, and cultural rights.[13] In the interim, though, the Commission worked diligently in 1950 and 1951 to prepare a single Covenant to address the full panoply of rights. The Commission's effort to incorporate the full range of rights into a single Covenant provoked alarm among ABA leaders. Frank Holman warned that U.S. ratification of the proposed Covenant would transform "the Federal Government . . . into a completely socialistic and centralized state."[14] Holman's views had significant political force at a time when the nation was immersed in a communist witch-hunt at home and a Cold War battle with the Soviet Union overseas.

Aside from its work on the Covenant, the Commission on Human Rights continued to receive human rights petitions from aggrieved individuals around the world. Despite the Commission's prior decision that it had no power to act on individual petitions, some civil rights groups in the United States continued to believe that petitioning the United Nations was a worthwhile endeavor. The Civil Rights Congress (CRC), a leading civil rights organization in the United States, "was on the attorney general's list of subversive organizations."[15] In late 1951, the CRC released a petition to the United Nations entitled *We Charge Genocide*."[16] The petition was framed as an indictment of the United States. It alleged "that public officials of certain states, and certain officials of the Government of the United States of America, are guilty of conspiring to commit genocide, of complicity in genocide, of inciting to genocide, and of other offenses forbidden by the Genocide Convention."[17] The petition was more than two hundred pages long. It included a detailed analysis of the Genocide Convention and a mountain of evidence designed to support the charges in the indictment. William Patterson, the national secretary of the CRC, was the document's principal author. He acted "with encouragement and support from the Communist Party."[18] The Commission on Human Rights would not accept the petition unless it came from a national government. Patterson recognized that the document "would lose its impact if it was seen as just another propaganda blast from the Soviet Union or its allies,"[19] so he sought a government sponsor from outside the Soviet bloc. In January 1952 he persuaded two "countries from outside the Soviet bloc ... to place the *Genocide* petition on the agenda of the Commission on Human Rights."[20] Given the CRC's links to the Communist Party, the *Genocide* petition probably reinforced the growing belief among American conservatives that the United Nation's human rights agenda was really "a Communist plan for destroying the American way of life."[21]

II. THE GENOCIDE CONVENTION

President Truman transmitted the Genocide Convention to the Senate in June 1949; he urged the Senate to provide its advice and consent for ratification.[22] The president's message included a letter signed by Acting Secretary of State James Webb, which presented a detailed analysis of the Convention. Webb's letter did not specifically address the question of whether the Convention as a whole was self-executing. However, he noted that Article VII obligates parties to extradite individuals charged with genocide by other states. He added: "Only after Congress has defined, and provided for the punishment of, the crime of genocide, and authorized surrender therefor, will it be possible to give effect to the provisions of article VII."[23] Thus, the executive branch determined that legislation was necessary to implement Article VII, but it did not specify whether legislation was needed to implement other treaty provisions.

The ABA responded quickly to the president's message. The July 1949 issue of the *ABA Journal* included an article by Carl Rix, then chairman of the ABA Special Committee on Peace and Law Through United Nations (the "Special Committee"). Rix's essay addressed both the Genocide Convention and the Covenant on Human Rights. He said:

> It seems to be plain that the essential portions of the genocide treaty and the proposed human rights treaty are self-executing. ... Thus there may be created, as law, a third body of treaty law in this country with no constitutional basis whatsoever, of equal dignity with our Constitution, as supreme law of the land, superseding all state constitutions, decisions and laws of the states covering the same subjects. ... The effect in this country ... in a field which has been almost exclusive in the states, is so far-reaching in its consequence that the word revolutionary is not fully descriptive. ... I leave to your imagination as to what would happen ... if subversive elements should teach minorities that the field of civil rights and laws had been removed to the field of international law.[24]

Rix referred to the "sinister and cynical suggestion" by the President's Committee on Civil Rights that, in light of *Missouri v. Holland*, human rights treaties could become "a possible basis for civil rights legislation." He concluded that "[t]he road to federal absolutism is being made very, very easy."[25]

Rix's essay was rhetorically effective but analytically flawed. First, his assertion that "the genocide treaty and the proposed human rights treaty are self-executing" mixed apples and oranges, because the draft Covenant and the Genocide Convention were very different types of treaties. Many of the Covenant's obligations would clearly have been self-executing under then-existing doctrine. In contrast, the primary obligation under the Genocide Convention was to punish genocide. Assuming that treaty ratification would have obligated the United States to create a new federal crime of genocide, it was fairly clear in 1949 under established constitutional precedents that federal officers could not actually prosecute anyone for genocide unless Congress enacted legislation to authorize such federal prosecutions.[26] Thus, the Genocide Convention was non-self-executing in the sense that implementing legislation was constitutionally required before the federal government could prosecute anyone for genocide.

Rix's main constitutional concern involved federal encroachment on states' rights. In this respect, also, the Genocide Convention and the draft Covenant raised very different issues. The Constitution's treaty supremacy rule means that treaties supersede *conflicting* state laws. The only type of state law that would present a genuine conflict with the Genocide Convention would be one authorizing genocide. Obviously, no such law existed, so the specter of a true conflict between the Genocide Convention and state law was purely hypothetical. In contrast, the proposed Covenant, which was still in draft form at that time, might well have superseded state laws authorizing racial segregation, because Article 20 of the 1949 draft prohibited racial discrimination.[27] By linking the Genocide Convention with the Covenant, without distinguishing between the two, Rix implied that the Genocide Convention might supersede state laws. That was never a valid concern.

However, the Genocide Convention did raise a different type of federalism concern. The Supreme Court held in *Missouri v. Holland* that the combination of a valid, ratified treaty with the Necessary and Proper Clause empowered Congress to regulate matters that would otherwise fall within the exclusive jurisdiction of the states.[28] As of 1949, one could have plausibly argued that ratification of the Genocide Convention would empower Congress to enact federal anti-lynching legislation, although it was doubtful at the time whether Congress had authority to enact such legislation in the absence of a treaty. Even so, Rix's claim that ratification of the Genocide Convention would expand federal power at the expense of states' rights was contestable. The Truman administration argued that reliance on *Missouri v. Holland* was unnecessary because Congress had the power under the Define and Punish Clause to enact legislation authorizing federal criminal punishment for genocide.[29] Regardless, by linking the Genocide Convention to the draft Covenant and invoking the specter of federal interference with states' rights, Rix and other members of the Special Committee successfully mobilized opposition to the Genocide Convention within the ABA.

At a meeting of the ABA House of Delegates in September 1949, the Special Committee and the Section on International and Comparative Law (the "Section") submitted competing resolutions on the Genocide Convention for approval by the House of Delegates. The Special Committee proposed a resolution stating that "the Genocide Convention, as submitted, shall not be ratified by the United States."[30] The Special Committee also prepared a twenty-page report highlighting the many alleged defects of the Convention.[31] The Committee's report referred to "the problems which arise in the constitutional system of the United States if a treaty deals with what have always been regarded as domestic questions." The Committee expressed concern that ratification of the Convention would bring about "a tremendous change in the structure of the relation of states and the federal government under our Constitution, of doubtful constitutionality." In the Committee's view, such a change would be "truly revolutionary" and should not "be effected without amendment of our Constitution."[32]

The Special Committee's report placed the Section on the defensive. Most of the Section's members supported ratification of the Genocide Convention, but they believed they had to respond to the Special Committee's objections. Hence, the Section submitted a draft resolution stating that the ABA approves ratification of the Genocide Convention, subject to seven specific reservations designed to address the concerns raised by the Special Committee.[33] One of the proposed reservations stated "[t]hat Articles I through VII of the Convention are not self-executing in the U.S." and "that Federal legislation will be necessary to carry out the provisions of these articles."[34] The proposed NSE reservation was effectively window dressing, designed to reassure the Convention's critics. Federal legislation was necessary to carry out most of the provisions in Articles I through VII, even without the NSE reservation, because those provisions were constitutionally NSE.[35] The only obligation for which implementing legislation was not necessary was the one under Article I to "prevent" genocide. Moreover, if the United States had ratified the treaty with the NSE reservation, the president would clearly have had the authority to take some steps to prevent genocide, even without federal legislation specifically authorizing him to do so. In short, the proposed NSE reservation was probably not intended to have any practical effect on the president's authority to implement the Convention or on the courts' authority to enforce the Convention. In this respect, the proposed NSE reservation for the Genocide Convention was quite different from the proposal advanced the following year to attach an NSE reservation to the Covenant (discussed later in this chapter).

Frank Holman, speaking both as ABA president and as a member of the Special Committee, criticized the Section's proposed resolution. He argued that the reservations proposed by the Section "were the result of too brief study and were phrased in language too loose to accomplish a satisfactory result." He noted that the Special Committee had "attempted to formulate reservations which would protect the constitutional rights of the United States and its citizens without being able to reach a satisfactory solution." (The Special Committee could

not find a "satisfactory solution" because most of its members were nationalists: they believed that crimes committed in the United States should be regulated exclusively by domestic law, not by international law.) Accordingly, Holman
urged adoption of the "compromise resolution" drafted by an ad hoc committee
during the House of Delegates meeting.[36] The so-called compromise resolution,
like the resolution proposed by the Special Committee, included a clause recommending that the Senate should not consent to ratification of the Genocide
Convention.[37] After extended debate, the ABA House of Delegates rejected the
Section's proposed resolution and approved the compromise resolution.[38] Thus,
as of September 1949, the ABA was officially on record opposing ratification of
the Genocide Convention.

A subcommittee of the Senate Foreign Relations Committee held four days
of hearings on the Genocide Convention in January and February 1950.[39] The
Subcommittee heard testimony from two State Department officials and one
Justice Department official, all of whom supported ratification. One of the gov-
ernment witnesses was Adrian Fisher, who was then serving as legal adviser in
the Department of State. A few years later, the American Law Institute selected
Fisher to be the Chief Reporter for the Restatement (Second) of Foreign Relations
Law. (Chapter 13 discusses the Restatement and Fisher's role in drafting it.)

The Subcommittee also heard oral testimony from approximately forty private witnesses and received written submissions from about fifty other individuals and organizations.[40] Most of the individuals and organizations who testified
orally or in writing supported treaty ratification. However, three members of the
ABA Special Committee testified against ratification: Alfred J. Schweppe (then
serving as chairman of the Special Committee), Carl B. Rix (prior chairman of
the Special Committee and a past ABA president), and George A. Finch.[41] Those
who opposed ratification generally repeated arguments that Rix and others had
made previously.[42]

Apparently troubled by the criticisms raised by treaty opponents, the Senate
delayed action for several months. In August 1950, the House Foreign Affairs
Committee staff prepared a detailed memorandum addressing various legal and
constitutional objections to the Genocide Convention.[43] The memo asserted that
Congress had authority under the Define and Punish Clause, "even in the absence of the Genocide Convention [to] define genocide as an offense against the
law of nations and provide for its punishment by statute."[44] Therefore, the memo
stated, the Convention "does not enlarge the present constitutional jurisdiction
of the Federal Government."[45] Additionally, the memo stated that the Genocide
Convention "is not self-executing in character." Therefore, "[i]t will be necessary
for the Congress to enact implementing legislation before the courts of this country will give effect to the Genocide Convention."[46] The memo explained: "[W]hile
the convention defines the conduct which is to be punished, it does not attempt
to prescribe penalties and procedures but leaves this up to each contracting
state. . . . In this connection, it should be noted that penal conventions in general
are not regarded as self-executing in character."[47] The legal and constitutional
analysis prepared by the Foreign Affairs Committee staff generally supported

the Truman administration's position and helped rebut arguments made by the ABA Special Committee.

On September 6, 1950, the Senate Foreign Relations Committee met in executive session to consider the Genocide Convention. Senator Brien McMahon (D-CT), who chaired the Subcommittee on the Genocide Convention, moved to report the treaty out of committee and present it to the full Senate for a vote. Senator Henry Cabot Lodge (R-MA) seconded the motion. However, Senator Tom Connally (D-TX) used his power as committee chairman to delay action. Connally noted that Senator Walter George (D-GA) and others opposed ratification;[48] he expressed concerns about provoking a "floor fight." Connally quoted the ABA resolution discussed above, including the ABA's recommendation that the Senate should not approve the Convention. He added, "In the face of that [ABA resolution] I do not see how the committee could proceed with any peace and not avoid a bitter controversy on the floor."[49] The Convention never made it out of Committee in 1950, thanks to the successful lobbying effort by members of the ABA Special Committee. After the 81st Congress, the Senate did not take any significant action on the Convention until 1970, when, for the first time, the Senate Foreign Relations Committee recommended ratification.[50] The United States finally became a party to the Genocide Convention in 1988. Despite opposition in the United States, the Convention entered into force internationally in January 1951.

III. STATE COURT LITIGATION: THE *FUJII* CASE

In the years after World War II, state courts handled numerous cases in which civil rights claimants raised arguments based on the U.N. Charter's human rights provisions.[51] This section focuses on the *Fujii* decision because it was the most significant such case, both legally and politically. In July 1948, Mr. Sei Fujii paid $200 to purchase a plot of land in Los Angeles County. He sought to provoke a legal confrontation with the State of California to challenge the validity of California's Alien Land Law. Fujii was a sixty-five-year-old Japanese citizen who had lived in the United States since 1903. He was a graduate of the University of Southern California Law School and publisher of the *Kashu Mainichi*, a bilingual Japanese-American newspaper that he founded in the 1930s. Fujii hired his longtime friend and law school classmate J. Marion Wright to represent him. Shortly after Fujii purchased the land, Wright filed a complaint in California Superior Court in *Fujii v. California*.[52] The complaint sought a declaration that Fujii held a valid title to the land. California's Alien Land Law clearly prohibited Fujii from owning land in California. So, to win the case, Wright would have to persuade the court that the Alien Land Law was invalid.[53]

Fujii made a wise choice by hiring Wright to represent him. Wright had been representing Japanese clients in legal matters for more than thirty years before he filed the complaint in *Fujii*. In the 1920s, Wright scored an important victory for Japanese-Americans in *Jordan v. Tashiro*, a landmark case that he argued successfully before the U.S. Supreme Court.[54] In *Tashiro*, the Court applied a bilateral treaty between the United States and Japan to protect the rights of Japanese citizens. However, the bilateral treaty with Japan did not apply to Fujii's case because the United States terminated the treaty in 1940.

California's Alien Land Law did not, by its terms, single out Japanese for discriminatory treatment. Instead, the statute barred all noncitizens from owning land in California, unless they were eligible to become naturalized citizens.[55] Federal law, not California law, determined who was eligible for naturalization. California adopted the Alien Land Law in 1920. At that time, only "free white persons, aliens of African nativity, persons of African descent and [some] native born Filipinos were eligible to become naturalized citizens."[56] By the time Fujii bought his land in 1948, Congress had expanded eligibility to include "persons who are descendants of races indigenous to the continents of North or South America or adjacent islands, Filipino persons or persons of Filipino descent, Chinese persons and persons of Chinese descent, and persons of races indigenous to India."[57] Thus, as of 1948, Japanese were one of the few remaining national groups still ineligible for citizenship because of their nationality. Moreover, of those national groups who were ineligible for citizenship, Japanese nationals were the only group with a sizeable population residing in California. Therefore, the main practical effect of the Alien Land Law was to preclude Japanese from owning land in California. Fujii and Wright were well aware of these facts; they were determined to end California's long-standing practice of discriminating against Japanese people.

The California Superior Court held a hearing in *Fujii v. California* in March 1949. The court issued its decision six weeks later, upholding the validity of the Alien Land Law. The court relied on established legal authorities granting states broad discretion to make rules for disposition of real property within the state. As of 1949, many states in the United States had laws that discriminated against blacks, Asians, and other groups on the basis of race or nationality. Federal law did not prohibit such discrimination. That, at least, was the trial court's view. And the court could cite ample legal authority to support that view. Fujii appealed the trial court decision. Wright devoted most of his appellate brief to the argument that the Alien Land Law violated the Fourteenth Amendment Equal Protection Clause. In response, the state's brief cited numerous decisions by the U.S. Supreme Court and the California Supreme Court holding that the Alien Land Law did not violate the Fourteenth Amendment.[58] Thus, in terms of controlling legal precedent, Wright and Fujii faced an uphill battle.

Perhaps recognizing the weakness of his equal protection argument, Wright added a short section at the end of his brief arguing that the Alien Land Law was inconsistent with "the exalted principles and high resolutions of our nation as expressed in the United Nations Charter."[59] Two Charter provisions are especially relevant for *Fujii*. Article 55 states: "the United Nations shall promote ... universal respect for, and observance of, human rights and fundamental freedoms for all without distinction as to race, sex, language, or religion." Under Article 56, the United States and other Member States "pledge themselves to take joint and separate action ... for the achievement of the purposes set forth in

Article 55."[60] Viewed together, Articles 55 and 56 obligate the United States to take "separate action" to promote "human rights . . . for all without distinction as to race." This general statement raises a host of questions. Is the right to own property a "human right"? If so, what type of "separate action" must the United States take to promote that right? Is a statutory distinction between citizens and noncitizens a "distinction as to race" within the meaning of Article 55 if, in practice, the statute has a disproportionate negative impact on Japanese nationals? Finally, assuming that there is an actual conflict between the Alien Land Law and the U.N. Charter, should a California court apply the Alien Land Law to decide the case, or should it apply the Charter?

The California Court of Appeal issued its decision in *Fujii* in April 1950.[61] The court easily dismissed Wright's equal protection argument, citing a long string of decisions by the U.S. Supreme Court and the California Supreme Court upholding the constitutional validity of the Alien Land Law. The court concluded this portion of its opinion with the following observation:

> [T]his opinion might well be terminated under the doctrine of *stare decisis* with a reaffirmation of the former decisions, since upon constitutional questions we deem ourselves obliged to follow the decisions of the Supreme Courts of the United States and of this State until one of those courts should announce the overruling of its own decisions.[62]

The court then addressed Wright's argument based on the Charter's human rights provisions. It held that California's Alien Land Law was invalid because California law discriminated on the basis of race in contravention of the U.N. Charter, and the Supremacy Clause required state courts to resolve the conflict between the Charter and California law in favor of the treaty.[63] We will examine the legal issues raised by the court's opinion in more detail below. For now, the political reaction to the Court of Appeal's decision is more significant than its legal rationale. The decision sent shock waves through the U.S. political system whose effects are still felt today.

The Court of Appeal issued its decision on April 24, 1950. An article the next day in the *Los Angeles Times* described *Fujii* as a "precedent-setting decision." The *Los Angeles Daily Journal*, a newspaper written primarily for the legal profession, correctly described *Fujii* as "the first decision in which the Charter of the United Nations has been invoked to invalidate a law of a State."[64] The *New York Times* also published a short story about the case.[65]

On April 28, 1950, four days after the Court of Appeal's decision, Senator Forrest Donnell, a Republican from Missouri, warned his colleagues in the U.S. Senate about the dangers of the *Fujii* decision. The fact that the Senate devoted time in floor debate to a discussion of the *Fujii* case is extremely unusual. U.S. Supreme Court decisions routinely attract the Senate's attention. The Senate sometimes heeds decisions by state supreme courts and lower federal courts. However, this was a decision by an intermediate appellate court in California: a state court, not a federal court. Intermediate appellate courts in the fifty states of the United States issue hundreds or thousands of decisions every day. The U.S. Senate rarely notices any of them. Even so, the Senate spent approximately one hour of its valuable time on April 28, 1950, discussing the implications of the *Fujii* decision.[66]

Senator Donnell read a lengthy statement in which he quoted several paragraphs from the Court of Appeal's decision. He summarized the decision as follows: "Mr. President, the opinion from which I have just read holds . . . that a valid treaty, which is, by the Constitution of the United States, the supreme law of the land, invalidates the law of a state which is in conflict with said treaty." Senator Homer Ferguson (R-MI) was not prepared to concede that the California court's decision was correct. However, if the decision was correct, he noted, the effect of the U.N. Charter "may be to nullify or make void all statutes in any State in relation to distinctions made between the sexes; and, in addition, we may find that by that means equal rights have already been established in the United States."[67] He did not need to state explicitly—because it was obvious to everyone present—that the Charter would also invalidate Jim Crow laws throughout the South.

Senator Donnell also reminded his colleagues about the 1920 U.S. Supreme Court decision in *Missouri v. Holland*.[68] Donnell explained that *Holland* held that "the adoption of a treaty on a given subject matter which is within the Treaty Power and as to which subject matter there had been no previous grant to Congress of legislative power causes Congress . . . to be possessed of power to legislate to carry into effect such treaty." Senator George Malone (R-NV) responded: "If I correctly understand the Senator's interpretation . . . it does open the door to Congress to legislate on subjects which were never given by the States through the Constitution of the United States to the Congress in the first place." Donnell said, "That is precisely correct." Malone replied, "To that extent, it is dangerous." Donnell agreed: "To my mind, it is highly dangerous" because "the effect of a treaty may possibly be to vest in the Congress of the United States a vast reservoir of power to legislate on matters which perhaps previously had been confined to the States."[69]

The danger to which they referred did not stem from the *Fujii* decision, as such. From Donnell's perspective, the real danger lay in the Constitution's Supremacy Clause, which meant that treaties ratified by the United States automatically superseded conflicting state laws. Additionally, the Supreme Court's prior decision in *Missouri v. Holland* was dangerous because it meant that the federal government could utilize the Treaty Power to extend Congress's legislative powers into areas that had previously been the exclusive province of state legislation. Still, the *Fujii* decision was a dramatic reminder that U.S. ratification of the U.N. Charter opened the door to legal arguments by various aggrieved groups and individuals who sought to invalidate state laws that allegedly discriminated on the basis of "race, sex, language, or religion."[70] The Senate debate on *Fujii* in April 1950 laid the groundwork for future Senate deliberations on the Bricker Amendment, which began the following year.

While U.S. senators discussed the implications of the *Fujii* decision, the State of California was preparing its next move in the litigation. Two weeks after the

Court of Appeal's decision, the California attorney general filed a Petition for Rehearing in the Court of Appeal.[71] The Petition for Rehearing contended that the Court of Appeal was mistaken because the human rights provisions of the U.N. Charter are not self-executing, and therefore the Charter "does not supersede" the Alien Land Law. We will address the merits of that argument below. The more salient point for now is the fact that the attorney general apparently received a good deal of informal assistance from Judge Manley Hudson. Judge Hudson was one of the most respected international law experts in the United States at that time. Hudson held the Bemis Chair of International Law at Harvard Law School, a position to which he was appointed in 1924.[72] He had served as a judge on the Permanent Court of International Justice for ten years in the 1930s and 1940s. In 1950, when the Court of Appeal issued its decision in *Fujii*, Hudson was serving as the president of the American Society of International Law,[73] and a member of the United Nations International Law Commission.[74]

As noted above, it was quite unusual for the U.S. Senate to devote time during floor debate to discussion of a decision by an intermediate-level state court. It was, if anything, even more unusual for a person of Manley Hudson's stature to intervene personally in litigation pending before an intermediate-level state court. Regardless, on April 28, 1950, just four days after the Court of Appeal's decision, Judge Hudson sent a telegram to "counsel for the State of California" expressing his view that the court's decision was mistaken.[75] Soon afterward, Hudson provided the California attorney general's office a prepublication version of an essay that would later be published in the *American Journal of International Law*.[76] The essay explained in detail why Hudson believed the Court of Appeal's decision was wrong. The attorney general included Hudson's essay as Appendix A to the Petition for Rehearing.[77] The attorney general's legal argument in the Petition relied heavily on Hudson's analysis.

At first blush, it is very surprising that Judge Hudson intervened at his own initiative in the *Fujii* case in an attempt to reverse a judicial decision giving effect to the U.N. Charter. Hudson had devoted his entire professional life to promoting the development of international law. Why was he so strongly opposed to a judicial decision applying international law? One can find a partial answer to this question in the records of ABA proceedings. In 1949, the ABA Special Committee obtained a grant to convene a series of regional conferences "in many cities of the United States to study and consider the proposed International Covenant on Human Rights and the Genocide Convention."[78] Under the grant, the Special Committee convened meetings in more than a dozen cities between February and September 1949. The moderators for those meetings were "President Frank E. Holman, Judge Manley O. Hudson, Judge Orie L. Phillips, George A. Finch, Alfred J. Schweppe and Carl Rix."[79] Except for Judge Hudson, every one of the moderators was a member of the Special Committee and an outspoken critic of U.S. ratification of human rights treaties.[80] Thus, Hudson's decision to participate as a moderator is a strong indicator that he, too, opposed ratification of human rights treaties. His published writings make clear that he opposed judicial enforcement of the Charter's human rights provisions.[81]

Apparently, then, Hudson saw the *Fujii* case as an excellent opportunity to promote his view that the Charter's human rights provisions did not supersede California law because they were not self-executing. In that respect, Hudson was a remarkably successful advocate. When the California Supreme Court finally decided *Fujii* in 1952, it adopted Hudson's rationale.[82] In doing so, the California Supreme Court became the first court in U.S. history to hold that a non-self-executing treaty does not supersede conflicting state law. Thus, Hudson's essay had a decisive impact on the California Supreme Court, and *Fujii* was a landmark decision in the process of transformation that converted the treaty supremacy rule from a mandatory to an optional rule. Before discussing the California Supreme Court decision, though, let us return to the year 1950.

The California attorney general filed his petition for rehearing on May 9. Three days later, on May 12, the American Civil Liberties Union (ACLU) and the American Jewish Congress (AJC) filed a joint amicus curiae brief opposing the petition for rehearing.[83] Their brief contended that the Court of Appeal's decision was correct: the Alien Land Law was invalid because it conflicted with the U.N. Charter's human rights provisions. A few days after the ACLU and AJC filed their joint brief, the Japanese American Citizens' League and the National Association for the Advancement of Colored People (NAACP) filed an Application for Leave to Join with Brief Amici Curiae, stating that the ACLU/AJC brief "is in accordance with the views of these petitioning amici curiae and petitioning amici curiae join therein."[84] As discussed in Chapter 9, *Fujii* was one of many cases during this period where groups that we now identify as "domestic civil rights" organizations filed legal briefs invoking the U.N. Charter to support their preferred outcomes in domestic civil rights cases.

The California Court of Appeal denied the Petition for Rehearing on May 22, 1950.[85] The denial of the State's petition effectively closed the first chapter of the *Fujii* litigation. By that time the battle lines were drawn. The ACLU, the NAACP, and other civil rights organizations supported judicial application of the U.N. Charter to invalidate discriminatory state laws. Senate Republicans, state governments and others feared that judicial application of the U.N. Charter would disrupt the racial status quo in the Jim Crow South and upset the constitutional balance between the federal government and state governments.

IV. SCHOLARLY COMMENTARY ON *FUJII*

The Court of Appeal's decision in *Fujii* unleashed a flood of scholarly commentary.[86] This section focuses on articles published in 1950–1951 by three of the nation's leading scholars: Manley Hudson, Quincy Wright, and Oscar Schachter.[87] Quincy Wright was a leading expert on constitutional foreign affairs law.[88] In contrast, Hudson and Schachter were international law scholars, not constitutional law scholars. In 1950, Hudson was nearing the end of a long, distinguished career. For most of Hudson's career, the dominant international law paradigm focused on horizontal relations between States, not vertical relations between States and individuals. In 1950, Schachter was still in the early stages of his career.[89] Unlike Hudson, he eagerly embraced the new paradigm of international human rights law, which addressed legal relationships between States and their citizens. These differences undoubtedly shaped the way these three men viewed the issues raised by the *Fujii* case. The following analysis divides the relevant issues into constitutional law issues, international law issues, and issues involving the overlap between constitutional and international law.

A. The Constitutional Law Issue

Hudson wrote: "a provision in a treaty may be incorporated in the national law of the United States, so as to supersede . . . inconsistent State legislation. It has long been established, however, that this is true only of self-executing provisions." He cited *Foster v. Neilson* as authority for this proposition. He concluded that "the Charter's provisions on human rights have not been incorporated into the municipal law of the United States so as to supersede inconsistent State legislation, because they are not self-executing."[90] Thus, in his view, the *Fujii* decision was wrong because the court overlooked the distinction between self-executing and non-self-executing treaties.

Hudson was an international law scholar, not a constitutional law scholar. Quincy Wright, who was a constitutional law scholar, explained that Hudson's analysis was flawed because Hudson conflated the concepts of self-execution and treaty supremacy. Wright first claimed that the *Fujii* decision "follows a long and unbroken tradition that if State legislation conflicts with obligations undertaken by the United States in a treaty, the legislation will not be applied by the courts." He noted that this unbroken tradition was firmly rooted in the text and original understanding of the Supremacy Clause.[91] Thus, in Wright's view, the *Fujii* decision was correct because *Fujii* was a treaty supremacy case, not a self-execution case. Wright then introduced the concept of non-self-executing treaties.

> [T]he distinction between self-executing and non-self-executing treaties has been used in American constitutional law only with reference to the agency of the Federal Government competent to execute the treaty and has had no reference to the relations between the Federal Government and the States, except in those rare instances where the treaty itself makes execution contingent upon State action. One, therefore, finds little judicial discussion of this distinction in cases involving the compatibility of State legislation with treaty provisions.[92]

In short, Wright argued that self-execution is a federal separation-of-powers doctrine, but the principle of treaty supremacy governs the relationship between treaties and state law. As demonstrated in Part Two, Wright's statement was an accurate description of the constitutional law of the United States, circa 1950. However, Hudson's effort to transplant NSE doctrine from the separation of powers sphere to the treaty supremacy sphere soon attracted other adherents.

By expanding the concept of self-execution to encompass the previously distinct doctrine of treaty supremacy, Hudson played a key role in the process of invisible constitutional change.

Given Hudson's mistaken reliance on *Foster v. Neilson* to support his position, Wright devoted several pages of his article to an analysis of Marshall's opinion in *Foster*. Wright said that "the opinion in *Foster v. Neilson* is of no value for interpreting the relation of a treaty provision concerning individual rights to State legislation. On that question the record of the Supreme Court is clear. Rights protected by treaty overrule conflicting State legislation *ex proprio vigore*."[93] On this point, Wright was clearly correct. Hudson's claim that NSE treaties do not supersede inconsistent state law finds no support in *Foster* because there was no state law at issue in *Foster*.[94] To highlight the distinction between self-execution and treaty supremacy, Wright added: "In practice, the doctrine of non-self-executing treaties has been applied only to preserve the constitutional rights of the political organs of the Federal Government—the President, the Congress, and especially the House of Representatives ... in matters which for historical or practical reasons have been considered peculiarly within the competence of these organs."[95]

In his debate with Hudson, Wright's position was supported by the original understanding of the Constitution, dozens of consistent judicial precedents, and a sophisticated understanding of the crucial constitutional distinction between federal supremacy and federal separation-of-powers issues. In contrast, Hudson tended to conflate the distinction between supremacy and separation-of-powers issues. Moreover, his position was at odds with the original understanding and lacked support in judicial precedent. However, Hudson's position was supported by members of the ABA Special Committee who were vehemently opposed to domestic application of international human rights law. Ultimately, the ABA prevailed because they overcame Wright's cogent legal analysis with the force of constitutional politics.

B. The International Law Issues

In their separate essays, both Wright and Shachter argued that Article 56 of the U.N. Charter imposed legal obligations on Member States. To some extent, they were attacking a straw man, because Hudson conceded that Article 56 imposed legal obligations on the United States. Nevertheless, analysis of this question is relevant because it is related to a distinct concept of non-self-execution. Wright stated "that the term 'non-self-executing treaties' may have a meaning in international law different from that in American constitutional law." Under this concept, "the term may refer to treaty provisions which do not impose obligations upon the parties."[96] Similarly, Shachter acknowledged that "the human rights provisions cannot be considered as rules of law by American courts" if they do not impose legal obligations on the United States.[97] Thus, although Article VI of the Constitution specifies that "the Judges in every State shall be bound thereby," Wright and Shachter agreed that judges are not bound by treaty provisions that do not impose legal obligations on the United States. They also agreed that one could plausibly use the "non-self-execution" label to describe such treaty provisions. But they argued that the Charter's human rights provisions did impose legal obligations on the United States, so they were "self-executing" in that sense of the term.[98]

Hudson, of course, was a very sophisticated international lawyer. He agreed that Article 56 of the U.N. Charter imposed binding obligations on Member States, but he advocated a particular interpretation of that article. Article 56 states: "*All Members pledge themselves to take joint and separate action in co-operation with the Organization* for the achievement of the purposes set forth in Article 55." One of those purposes is to promote "universal respect for, and observance of, human rights and fundamental freedoms for all without distinction as to race, sex, language, or religion."[99] The text of Article 56 is somewhat ambiguous. What does it mean to take "separate action in cooperation with the Organization"? In Hudson's view, "The obligation imposed by Article 56 is limited to cooperation with the United Nations."[100] In other words, Article 56 did not obligate states to take action *domestically* to achieve the purposes set forth in Article 55. It merely obligated them to act on the international plane in cooperation with the United Nations to promote the goals articulated in Article 55. Hudson defended this view in his published writings and in his role as chairman of the International Law Commission.[101] Hudson's interpretation was undoubtedly influenced by his positivist vision of international law, which emphasized state-to-state relations rather than individual rights.

Both Wright and Schachter disagreed with Hudson's interpretation of Article 56. Wright argued that "the reference to 'separate' action as distinct from 'joint' action indicates that the Members are individually bound to act" to promote observance of human rights.[102] Wright attributed to Hudson the view that the treaty pledge to take separate action is not an obligation "to treat persons under their jurisdiction with respect for human rights but to promote international cooperation to that end."[103] However, Wright argued, "[w]ith this construction Article 56 adds little, if anything, to Article 55 and is, therefore, meaningless and redundant." To avoid the conclusion that the term "separate action" in Article 56 is meaningless, Wright said, one must construe it to mean "as a minimum, abstention from separate action, such as enforcement of racially discriminating land laws, which would oppose the purposes of the organization." Therefore, he concluded, "the terms of Article 56 amply support the opinion of the court in the *Fujii* case."[104]

Schachter's analysis of the negotiating history supported Wright's textual analysis.[105] An early draft of Article 56 included a threefold pledge to take "joint action," to take "separate action," and to cooperate with the United Nations. "The U.S. delegation then expressed doubt concerning the pledge to take separate action; it preferred simply a pledge to cooperate. But the Australian delegation . . . continued to urge inclusion of a pledge to take separate action as distinguished from cooperation." Hence, Schachter concluded that the draftsmen "rejected a text which provided merely for a pledge to cooperate with the Organization . . .

they attached importance to the words 'separate action'."[106] Thus, in his view, the obligation to take "separate action in cooperation with the Organization" meant that U.N. Member States were obligated to act independently, within their respective domestic legal and political systems, to achieve the goals articulated in the U.N. Charter, including the goal of promoting human rights.

C. Judicial Competence and the Nexus between International and Domestic Issues

The dispute over the correct interpretation of Article 56 was intimately connected to a dispute about self-execution. If Hudson's interpretation was correct, Article 56 merely obligated the United States to act internationally; it did not obligate the United States to act domestically to promote the human rights goals articulated in Article 55. Under this view, domestic courts are not competent to enforce Article 56 because courts cannot act for the United States on the international plane. As Hudson said, "a court is not the appropriate agency to determine for the Government of the United States the particular way in which it should cooperate with the United Nations."[107] In Hudson's view, the conclusion that courts are "not the appropriate agency" was linked to the justiciability version of NSE doctrine. He said, "[T]he Charter's provisions on human rights ... are not self-executing. They state general purposes and create for the United States only obligations to cooperate in promoting certain ends. Insofar as the United States is concerned, they address themselves to the political, not to the judicial department."[108] Here, Hudson's claim that Article 56 was "not self-executing" meant that Charter-based human rights claims were not justiciable, because domestic courts were not competent to enforce Article 56. The conclusion that domestic courts were not competent to enforce the treaty followed inexorably from Hudson's view that Article 56 merely obligates the United States to cooperate with the United Nations on the international plane.

As noted above, Wright and Schachter both construed Article 56 to mean that the United States had a legally binding treaty obligation to take separate action *domestically* to promote human rights "without distinction as to race." Under that interpretation, there is no apparent reason why domestic courts are not competent to apply Article 56. As Wright said, "[W]henever a treaty has been duly concluded and ratified by the acknowledged authorities ... an obligation is thereby imposed upon each and every department of the government [including the judiciary] to carry it into complete effect according to its terms."[109] Additionally, Wright added, "The principle of Federal supremacy and the explicit terms of Article 6 of the Constitution make it clear that if a treaty provision establishes obligations of the United States without specification of any particular organ or procedure for carrying it out, courts must apply it in preference to conflicting State legislation."[110]

Although Hudson's primary argument against judicial enforcement of the Charter's human rights provisions relied on his interpretation of Article 56, he also suggested another possible argument against judicial enforcement. "The 'human rights and fundamental freedoms' referred to in Articles 1(3) and 55(c), 62(2), and 76(c) are not defined in the Charter of the United Nations."[111] Hudson did not elaborate, but he probably thought that a treaty obligation to promote human rights, without additional provisions defining the specific content of those rights, was simply too vague for domestic courts to apply. Note that this argument also applies the justiciability version of NSE doctrine, but it differs from the justiciability argument discussed above.

Schachter's article specifically addressed this argument. He said: "[I]t has been asserted that the pledge to take action to promote respect for and observation of human rights is too vague and indefinite to enable a court to give it practical effect." Schachter conceded "that the supremacy clause of the Constitution does not compel a court to enforce a treaty provision which is so incomplete or indefinite that it cannot be applied in a particular case."[112] But he argued that this principle did not preclude judicial application of the Charter's human rights provisions in cases like *Fujii*. He noted that Article 55(c) "contains the significant prohibition against discrimination because of race, sex, language or religion, a theme which is recurrent throughout the Charter and which in itself furnishes considerable content to the notion of human rights."[113] He argued that the Charter's human rights provisions "are no vaguer than any number of well-known constitutional and statutory expressions which have been left to the courts to apply." And he added, "It cannot be said that a greater degree of precision is required in a treaty provision than in an act of Congress."[114] Finally, referring specifically to *Fujii* and other cases involving California's Alien Land Law, he concluded: "In these cases the statute denying persons the right to own land because of race was held to be inconsistent with the pledge undertaken in the Charter; it obviously followed that, under the supremacy clause, the statute would have to yield to the treaty and hence be declared invalid."[115] Thus, in Schachter's view, application of Article 56 in *Fujii* was within the scope of judicial competence because: (1) the right to own land is clearly a "human right," even if the outer boundaries of that concept are fuzzy, and (2) California was discriminating on the basis of race, which is clearly prohibited by the U.N. Charter.[116]

In conclusion, Hudson, Wright, and Schachter agreed that there are limits on the judiciary's competence to enforce treaties and that one can reasonably apply the jargon of non-self-execution to describe those limits. However, non-self-execution as a doctrine of judicial competence differs considerably from Hudson's claim that Article 56 does not "supersede inconsistent State legislation."[117] In any case, Hudson's attempt to stretch the concept of non-self-execution to create an exception to the treaty supremacy rule helped lay the groundwork for subsequent acceptance of the idea that an NSE treaty does not supersede inconsistent state laws. That idea—which I refer to as the "*Fujii* doctrine," or the "optional supremacy rule"—gained acceptance because it helped mediate the tension between human rights and states' rights, and it enabled the U.S. political system to accommodate the demands of Bricker and his supporters without adopting a formal constitutional amendment.

V. EARLY STEPS TOWARD A CONSTITUTIONAL AMENDMENT

In 1950–1951, Senator John Bricker and the ABA worked independently to develop proposals for constitutional amendments designed to address the perceived threat posed by *Fujii* and the draft Covenant on Human Rights. This section first analyzes developments in the ABA and then discusses action by Bricker in the Senate.

A. The American Bar Association

A few months after the California Court of Appeal issued its decision in *Fujii*, Frank Holman published an essay in the *ABA Journal* in which he warned of the dangers of "treaty law-making."[118] Holman said: "The *Fujii* decision means that our right to self-government, both state and national, and our right to determine for ourselves what kinds of laws we want to live under, can be nullified whenever the President and two-thirds of the members of the Senate present at the time approve a treaty on a particular subject." He argued that "treaty law can result in changing our form of government from a republic to a socialistic and centralized state—with such increase in the power of the Federal Government at the expense of the states that the doctrine of states' rights and local self-government can become . . . nonexistent in the United States." Additionally, he claimed: "It is not an overstatement to say that the Republic is threatened to its very foundations." Finally, he concluded: "It may be that a full and impartial study of the disturbing implications and legal effects of Article VI of our Constitution will indicate the necessity of a constitutional amendment" to guard against "the inherent dangers to the rights of individuals and to the rights of the states."[119]

At around the same time, the Special Committee for Peace and Law Through United Nations issued a detailed analysis of the dangers posed by the draft Covenant on Human Rights.[120] The Committee report also highlighted the dangerous implications of the *Fujii* decision. If *Fujii* is affirmed, the report said, "[i]t will furnish a treaty basis without need of any other constitutional sanction, for claiming invalidation of state laws that make any distinction or classification on account of sex, race, color, language, property, birth, status, political, or other opinion."[121] The report added that numerous state laws could be invalidated, including "laws relating to women, to miscegenation, to citizenship or property qualifications for numerous purposes . . . possibly even state laws undertaking to outlaw the Communist party as a political party."[122] (Within the next two decades, much of what the Committee feared had transpired—not through treaty law, but through a combination of federal legislation and constitutional interpretation. For example, the Supreme Court invalidated state miscegenation laws in *Loving v. Virginia*,[123] and it invalidated state laws requiring payment of a fee to vote in state elections in *Harper v. Virginia Board of Elections*.[124] Thus, the Special Committee accurately predicted that federalization of human rights law would lead to invalidation of many state laws, but they mistakenly believed that treaties would be the primary mechanism for federalization of human rights.)

Based on its analysis of the dangers posed by human rights treaties, the Special Committee prepared a draft resolution, which the ABA House of Delegates approved at its annual meeting in September 1950.[125] In that resolution, the ABA expressed its formal opinion "that the Draft International Covenant on Human Rights . . . is not in such form nor of such content as to be suitable for . . . ratification by the United States." The resolution also authorized a study of the Treaty Power with the goal of developing a recommended set of constitutional amendments. In particular, the resolution suggested possible amendments providing that (1) "a *treaty shall not become the supreme law of the land upon ratification except* to the extent that it shall thereafter be made so by act of Congress", and (2) "in legislating to give effect to treaties Congress shall make no law not otherwise authorized by the Constitution."[126] The first proposed amendment, if adopted, would have abolished the treaty supremacy rule. The second proposed amendment would have reversed the Supreme Court's decision in *Missouri v. Holland*. It bears emphasis that the Committee developed both proposals to address the perceived threat posed by the Covenant on Human Rights and other potential human rights treaties.[127] As of September 1950, though, the ABA had not actually proposed a constitutional amendment. It merely authorized a study to consider possible amendments.

While the Special Committee was preparing its report, the Section of International and Comparative Law was working on a competing proposal. The Section reported at the ABA's midyear meeting in February 1950 that it had created a committee on Constitutional Aspects of International Agreements to study the effect on the Constitution of the draft Covenant on Human Rights.[128] Harold Stassen—the former governor of Minnesota, then president of the University of Pennsylvania, and perennial presidential candidate—chaired the committee within the Section. Stassen presented the Section's draft resolution to the ABA House of Delegates in September 1950, which the ABA also approved with minor amendments.[129] That resolution authorized a study to consider a proposal "that every multi-partite agreement to which the United States becomes a party in social and economic areas, such as those involved in the Covenant on Human Rights and in the Genocide Pact" should contain either a treaty article or a unilateral reservation conforming substantially to the following text: "*It is expressly stipulated that none of the provisions of this instrument shall be regarded as a part of the domestic law of any of the contracting parties by virtue of the coming into force of this instrument as an international agreement.*"[130] For convenience, I will refer to this proposal as the "Stassen proposal," although it is unclear whether Stassen personally devised it. Regardless, the ABA House of Delegates approved both the Section's resolution and the Special Committee's resolution. Hence, the ABA authorized two concurrent studies to consider competing proposals to address the perceived danger posed by human rights treaties.

Stassen claimed that a treaty provision or a unilateral reservation along the lines of the Stassen proposal "would better accomplish the purpose than amendment to the Constitution."[131] That claim is contestable because it is unclear whether the Stassen proposal, if adopted, would have been legally effective.

To assess that question, consider the following hypothetical. Assume that the United States ratified the Covenant on Human Rights, as it existed in 1950, with the addition of a treaty article identical to the Stassen proposal. In that case, the United States would be party to a treaty stipulating that "none of the provisions of this instrument shall be regarded as a part of the domestic law" of the United States "by virtue of the coming into force of this instrument as an international agreement." However, the Constitution's Supremacy Clause states that "all treaties made . . . under the Authority of the United States, shall be the supreme Law of the Land." There appears to be a conflict between the treaty language and the constitutional text. To defend his proposal, Stassen would presumably have argued that there is no conflict because the treaty supremacy rule is optional, not mandatory. Thus, the Stassen proposal tacitly assumed that the Constitution creates an optional treaty supremacy rule. In 1950, that was a very novel assumption.

Note that application of the Stassen proposal to the draft Covenant was very different than its application to the Genocide Convention. There was a broad consensus in 1950 that the main substantive obligation of the Genocide Convention—the obligation to punish individuals who commit genocide—was constitutionally non-self-executing. As the solicitor general stated in his Senate testimony, "It is not the function of treaties to enact the fiscal or criminal law of a nation. For this purpose no treaty is self-executing."[132] Thus, even without the Stassen proposal, the Genocide Convention's obligation to punish people would not be legally operative as domestic law unless Congress enacted implementing legislation. The Covenant differed from the Genocide Convention in this respect because the Covenant did not create an obligation to impose criminal penalties for specified conduct. Thus, unlike the Genocide Convention, the Covenant was not constitutionally NSE. Moreover, the Genocide Convention's obligation to prohibit genocide did not conflict with any state law in the United States because no state law authorized genocide. In contrast, the Covenant directly implicated the treaty supremacy rule because the Covenant obligation to ban racial discrimination conflicted with then-existing laws in many states.

The Covenant also differed significantly from the U.N. Charter's human rights provisions, insofar as self-execution is concerned. Recall that Manley Hudson presented two main arguments in support of his view that the Charter's human rights provisions did not create justiciable rights.[133] First, he argued that the Article 56 obligation to cooperate with the United Nations operated purely on the international plane, but did not obligate the United States to take action domestically to promote human rights. Assuming that Hudson's position was a plausible interpretation of the Charter, it was not a plausible interpretation of the Covenant. The draft Covenant in 1950 stated: "Each State Party hereto undertakes to respect and to ensure to all individuals within its territory and subject to its jurisdiction the rights recognized in this Covenant, without distinction of any kind, such as race . . . ."[134] This language clearly obligates States to protect human rights domestically. Second, Hudson argued that the Charter's human rights provisions were too vague to be enforceable by a domestic court. That argument may have been persuasive for some of the articles in the draft Covenant, but it was certainly not true for all of the Covenant's provisions. For example, Article 7 of the 1950 draft Covenant stated: "No one shall be imprisoned merely on the ground of inability to fulfill a contractual obligation."[135] It is difficult to imagine that any state or federal judge in 1950 would have held that Article 7 was too vague to be judicially enforceable. Thus, even if one agrees with Hudson's argument that the Charter's human rights provisions did not create justiciable rights, many of the Covenant's provisions would have been justiciable under Hudson's analysis.

It is also instructive to compare the Stassen proposal to the condition precedent clauses discussed in Chapter 6. Recall that nineteenth-century condition precedent clauses were treaty provisions that postponed international entry into force of a treaty until after implementing legislation had been enacted.[136] In contrast, the Stassen proposal, as applied to the Covenant, would have deprived the Covenant of domestic legal force even after the treaty took effect internationally. (The proposal stated expressly that "none of the provisions of this instrument shall be regarded as a part of the domestic law ... by virtue of the coming into force of this instrument as an international agreement."[137]) Given that Article II empowers the president and Senate to adopt a treaty provision that postpones international entry into force until after implementing legislation is enacted, it does not follow that Article II also empowers them to adopt a provision depriving the treaty of domestic legal effect after the treaty becomes internationally operative. Moreover, nineteenth-century condition precedent clauses did not affect the relationship between treaties and state law; they operated exclusively on a federal separation of powers level to protect the legislative prerogatives of the House of Representatives. Indeed, even when a specific treaty clause was drafted more broadly, the U.S. attorney general construed it so that the clause did not affect the relationship between the treaty and state law.[138] In contrast, Stassen defended his proposal by saying that "the treaty clause must not be allowed to take effect so as to change the structure of the federal-state system in the United States."[139] Thus, the Stassen proposal was clearly intended to preclude the Covenant from superseding conflicting state laws.

Like the great Manley Hudson, Stassen and his colleagues in the Section on International and Comparative Law were trying to stretch the concept of self-execution to encompass the previously distinct doctrine of treaty supremacy. They began with the premise that Article II grants the treaty makers the power to stipulate that a treaty is non-self-executing at the federal separation-of-powers level. (As explained in Chapter 8, that premise gained acceptance in the period between 1920 and 1945 when the intent doctrine became accepted as State Department orthodoxy.[140]) They then inferred that Article II also grants the treaty makers the power to stipulate that a treaty does not supersede conflicting state laws. The conclusion does not follow from the premise because the constitutional principles governing federal separation of powers differ from the constitutional principles governing the relationship between federal and state law. Even so, Manley Hudson and Harold Stassen were not the only lawyers who were stretching the concept of self-execution to encompass the previously distinct doctrine of treaty supremacy. Recall that Eleanor Roosevelt, during the 1949 session of the U.N. Commission on Human Rights, proposed the following language for insertion in the draft Covenant: "The provisions of this Covenant shall not themselves become effective as domestic law."[141] State Department lawyers presumably drafted this language and provided it to Mrs. Roosevelt.[142] Given the similarity between the Stassen proposal and the State Department proposal, it seems likely that State Department lawyers in 1949 also believed that NSE doctrine could be expanded to encompass the relationship between treaties and state law. Thus, despite 150 years of consistent practice whereby self-execution and treaty supremacy were treated as distinct issues, the idea was beginning to emerge circa 1949–1950 that Article II grants the treaty makers an affirmative power to insert an NSE clause in a treaty, or in a unilateral reservation, that would have the legal effect of precluding the treaty from superseding inconsistent state laws. The unstated assumption that Article II grants the treaty makers such an affirmative power—that is, that the treaty supremacy rule is optional—is the core constitutional premise underlying the *Fujii* doctrine.[143]

Stassen's proposal was clearly intended to be a more "international law friendly" alternative to the constitutional amendment favored by the Special Committee. Whereas the Special Committee's proposed amendment would have overruled *Missouri v. Holland*, the Section's proposal would have left *Holland* largely intact.[144] Additionally, the Special Committee's proposed amendment would have affected all treaties ratified by the United States. In contrast, the Section's proposal would have affected only multilateral treaties "in social and economic areas." However, if the Section's proposal was more "international law friendly," the Special Committee's proposal may have been more "constitutional law friendly," at least from a formalist perspective. The Special Committee sought to amend the Constitution overtly by employing the formal amendment process provided in Article V of the Constitution. In contrast, the Stassen proposal was based on an unstated constitutional premise that was never debated in an open, transparent manner. That premise—the idea that the treaty supremacy rule is optional, not mandatory—gained broad acceptance because it served certain political purposes.[145] However, proponents of the optional supremacy rule never acknowledged publicly that the switch from a mandatory to an optional rule constituted a dramatic change from the traditional understanding of the Supremacy Clause. In short, the optional treaty supremacy rule emerged from a process of invisible constitutional change. As explained in Chapter 15, the lack of transparency creates significant tension between the transformative process and principles of democratic legitimacy.

B. John Bricker and the Senate

Senator John Bricker served as a Republican senator from Ohio between 1947 and 1959. He had previously served as governor of Ohio from 1939 to 1945. He ran unsuccessfully for vice president as Thomas Dewey's running mate in the 1944 presidential election. Bricker was a staunch conservative who opposed expansion of the federal government's power and believed strongly in states' rights. He was a member of the isolationist wing of the Republican Party, unlike President Eisenhower (also a Republican), whose tendencies were much more internationalist. Bricker objected strongly to what he perceived as an attempt by the United Nations to interfere with the national sovereignty of the United States.[146]

On July 17, 1951, Bricker proposed a "sense of the Senate" resolution expressing opposition to the draft Covenant on Human Rights prepared by the U.N. Commission on Human Rights. That resolution, S. Res. 177, stated that the draft Covenant "is not acceptable to the United States." It urged the president to "instruct United States representatives at the United Nations to withdraw from further negotiations with respect to the Covenant on Human Rights." The resolution also expressed concern that the Covenant, if ratified, would "prejudice those rights of the American people which are now protected by the" Constitution's Bill of Rights.[147] Other scholars have analyzed Bricker's opposition to the draft Covenant.[148] Of more immediate interest, here, is the link between S. Res. 177 and subsequent proposals to amend the Constitution.

Bricker's speech on the Senate floor caught the attention of ABA leaders who were exploring a possible constitutional amendment to address the perceived danger posed by the Covenant and other potential human rights treaties. Within a few days after Bricker gave his speech, both Frank Holman and Alfred Schweppe wrote to Bricker and praised his strong stance against the Covenant. (Schweppe was then serving as the chairman of the ABA Committee on Peace and Law Through United Nations.) Schweppe's letter, in particular, "raised the possibility of amending the Constitution to eliminate the problems posed by the covenant on human rights." In his written responses to Holman and Schweppe, "Bricker agreed that a constitutional amendment might be the best way to protect against the perils presented by" the draft Covenant.[149] At that time, the ABA Special Committee was studying a possible constitutional amendment, as authorized by the ABA House of Delegates the previous year.

Bricker was impatient, though, and did not want to wait for the ABA to complete its work, so he introduced S.J. Res. 102 on the Senate floor in September 1951.[150] S.J. Res. 102 contained the text of a proposed constitutional amendment; it was the first of several distinct versions of the so-called Bricker Amendment. The amendment was motivated by two main concerns: opposition to the Covenant on Human Rights and concern about the president's use of executive agreements to evade the constitutional requirement to obtain Senate advice and consent for treaties.

S.J. Res. 102 did not modify the Constitution's treaty supremacy rule. Indeed, under S.J. Res. 102, the Constitution would still have stated explicitly that treaties are "the supreme law of the land" and that "judges in every State shall be bound thereby."[151] Rather than modifying the treaty supremacy rule, S.J. Res. 102 would have imposed subject matter limits on the Treaty Power. Thus, Bricker's proposed amendment stated: "No treaty shall be made abridging any of the rights and freedoms recognized in this Constitution." Similarly, it stated: "No treaty or executive agreements shall be made respecting the rights and freedoms of citizens of the United States recognized in this Constitution . . . or any other matters essentially within the domestic jurisdiction of the United States."[152] From Bricker's perspective, all matters pertaining to the protection of human rights were essentially within the domestic jurisdiction of the United States. Therefore, his proposed amendment was designed to prevent the United States from becoming a party to any human rights treaty. As he said, his purpose was "to bury the so-called covenant on human rights so deep that no one holding high public office will ever dare to attempt its resurrection."[153] To reiterate, though, S.J. Res. 102 would not have altered the Constitution's treaty supremacy rule as it applied to other types of treaties.

Aside from blocking U.S. participation in human rights treaties, S.J. Res. 102 was also designed to constrain the president's use of sole executive agreements. A "sole executive agreement" is a binding international agreement that the president concludes on the basis of his own constitutional authority, without obtaining Senate advice and consent. In *United States v. Belmont* (1937) and *United States v. Pink* (1942), the Supreme Court held that the president could use sole executive agreements to override state law.[154] Bricker's proposed amendment was designed to overrule *Belmont* and *Pink*. Thus, the draft amendment stipulated that "[e]xecutive agreements shall not be made in lieu of treaties." Moreover, it said: "Executive agreements, other than those expressly authorized by the Congress, shall, if not sooner terminated, expire automatically six months after the end of the term of office for which the President making the agreement shall have been elected . . . ."[155]

If one compares S.J. Res. 102 to the language recommended by the ABA Special Committee the previous year,[156] several differences are apparent. First, Bricker wanted to limit the president's use of executive agreements, whereas the ABA Special Committee was not focused on the problems posed by executive agreements. Second, the Special Committee's text was designed to overrule *Missouri v. Holland*, whereas Bricker's proposal did not specifically address *Holland*. (Bricker was concerned about the combination of *Holland* and human rights treaties,[157] but he wanted to address the problem by preventing the United States from entering into human rights treaties.) Third, the Special Committee's proposed text would have abolished the Constitution's treaty supremacy rule. In contrast, Bricker's proposal would not have altered the treaty supremacy rule. He preferred to tackle the problem by preventing use of the Treaty Power to enter into human rights treaties. Chapter 11 examines further developments in the ABA and the Senate related to the Bricker Amendment in 1952–1954.

VI. MAJOR CIVIL RIGHTS CASES DECIDED IN JUNE 1950

The Supreme Court decided three important civil rights cases in June 1950: *Henderson v. United States, Sweatt v. Painter,* and *McLaurin v. Oklahoma State Regents.*[158] In all three cases, parties invoked the U.N. Charter in support of their civil rights claims. In all three cases, the U.S. government filed briefs in support of civil rights claimants. In all three, the Supreme Court decided in favor of the civil rights claimants without referencing the U.N. Charter. Thus, the Court continued the process it had begun two years earlier—laying the ground-work for its subsequent decision in *Brown v. Board of Education* and incorpo-rating the Charter's anti-discrimination norm into the Fourteenth Amendment and other provisions of U.S. domestic law. This section first addresses *Henderson*. It then discusses *Sweatt* and *McLaurin* together.

A. *Henderson v. United States*

In *Henderson*, appellant filed a complaint with the Interstate Commerce Commission (ICC) against the Southern Railway Co. to challenge the compa-ny's rule requiring racially segregated dining cars on its trains. The ICC ruled in favor of the company, holding that its policy of racial segregation did not violate the Interstate Commerce Act. A federal district court upheld that decision, and Henderson appealed to the Supreme Court.[159] Henderson's brief argued that the railroad company had violated the federal statute and the ICC had violated the Fifth Amendment. Additionally, his brief made the following argument:

> The [U.N.] Charter is a treaty ratified by the Senate and like all treaties so ratified is the supreme law of the land. . . . This "supreme law of the land" and pledge of our government prevents it from any wise aiding, sanction-ing, or condoning the kind of racial segregation involved in the case at bar. On the contrary it compels the Federal government and all Federal agencies to respect, observe, and promote human rights without racial distinction. The Commission and court below in validating the Commission's finding have condoned the respondent's discriminatory regulation thereby violat-ing the Federal government's obligation under the [U.N.] Charter.[160]

The federal government was technically an opposing party in the case before the Supreme Court because Henderson's appeal challenged the conduct of the ICC, a federal agency. Nevertheless, the government filed a brief supporting Henderson's argument that the railroad's racial segregation policy was unlaw-ful. The government contended that racial segregation has a deleterious effect on the nation as a whole.[161] In that context, the brief noted that remarks of foreign diplomats "in a subcommittee of the United Nations General Assembly typify the manner in which racial discrimination in this country is turned against us in the international field," thereby impairing accomplishment of our foreign policy goals. The brief also added:

> Our opposition to racial discrimination has been affirmed in treaties and international agreements. The Charter of the United Nations has been approved as a treaty. By Article 55, the United Nations agree to promote "universal respect for, and observance of, human rights and fundamental freedoms for all without distinction as to race, sex, language, or religion."

... Racial segregation enforced by law hardly comports with the high principles to which, in the international field, we have subscribed. Our position and standing before the critical bar of world opinion are weakened if
segregation not only is practiced in this country but also is condoned by
federal law.[162]

Several civil rights organizations filed amicus briefs supporting Henderson. The
American Veterans Committee's brief cited the U.N. Charter in support of its
claim that the railroad's policy contravened the "national policy of the United
States."[163] Although Henderson's brief, the government's brief, and one amicus
brief cited the U.N. Charter, none of them presented a treaty supremacy argument because no state law was implicated in *Henderson*.

The Supreme Court decided *Henderson* on statutory grounds. It held unanimously that the rules and practices adopted by the railroad company violated
Section 3(1) of the Interstate Commerce Act. The statute at the time made it unlawful for a railroad in interstate commerce "to subject any particular person ...
to any undue or unreasonable prejudice or disadvantage in any respect whatsoever."[164] The Southern Railway Co. argued that its policies did not violate the Act
because it provided equal treatment to white and Negro passengers. The company's brief cited numerous Supreme Court decisions holding that racial segregation was lawful if people of different races received equal treatment.[165] The
justices were not persuaded. They concluded that "the railroad's current rules
and practices cause passengers to be subjected to undue or unreasonable prejudice or disadvantage in violation of s 3(1)."[166] The Court did not cite the U.N.
Charter or refer explicitly to the foreign policy arguments raised by the government. However, the justices were undoubtedly aware that a contrary decision
would have undermined the government's effort to persuade world opinion that
the United States honored its human rights obligations under the U.N. Charter.[167]

B. *Sweatt* and *McLaurin*

Sweatt and *McLaurin* both involved racial segregation in graduate programs operated by state universities. When Herman Sweatt applied for admission to the
University of Texas Law School, he was denied admission because he was black.
He sued the school officials, seeking a court order to compel his admission. In
response, the university decided to open a new law school for Negroes the following year, but Sweatt argued that the new school did not satisfy the Constitution's
equality rule.[168] G.W. McLaurin applied to the University of Oklahoma to pursue
a doctoral degree in education. The university accepted him into the doctoral
program, but "he was required to sit apart at a designated desk in an anteroom
adjoining the classroom; to sit at a designated desk on the mezzanine floor of the
library, but not to use the desks in the regular reading room; and to sit at a designated table and to eat at a different time from the other students in the school
cafeteria."[169] McLaurin sued to challenge the Oklahoma law that required racial
segregation.

Thurgood Marshall acted as co-counsel for both Sweatt and McLaurin. Appellant's brief in *McLaurin* contended that Oklahoma violated the Fourteenth Amendment Equal Protection Clause by requiring racial segregation in a graduate education program. The brief quoted Justice Black's concurring opinion in *Oyama v. California* as follows: "We have recently pledged ourselves to cooperate with the United Nations to promote . . . universal respect for, and observance of, human rights and fundamental freedoms for all without distinction as to race, sex, language, or religion. How can this nation be faithful to this international pledge if state laws which bar land ownership and occupancy by aliens on account of race are permitted to be enforced?"[170]

Similarly, petitioner's brief in *Sweatt* argued that Texas violated the Equal Protection Clause by denying him admission to the University of Texas School of Law. The brief also urged the Court to overrule *Plessy v. Ferguson*. Petitioner argued in that context:

> Since *Plessy v. Ferguson*, we have fought two World Wars for the preservation and maintenance of democracy, and have become a signatory of the United Nations Charter which provides that there shall be no discrimination based on race, creed or color. This Court now recognizes and accepts as one of its primary responsibilities the protection of minority groups against governmental discrimination based upon considerations of race or color.[171]

Petitioner's claim that the Court "now recognizes" protection of racial minorities "as one of its primary responsibilities" was more aspirational than real at that point in time, but the Court was clearly moving in that direction in 1950. Equally important, the justices probably recognized that the Court shared responsibility "for the preservation and maintenance of democracy." Moreover, as the quotation from Justice Black's opinion in *Oyama* suggests, they recognized that they could help promote that goal by issuing decisions consistent with the Charter's anti-discrimination norm.

The United States filed a single amicus brief in *Sweatt* and *McLaurin*.[172] The government's brief argued that the two cases "test the vitality and strength of the democratic ideals to which the United States is dedicated."[173] Moreover, the government added:

> The Court is here asked to place the seal of constitutional approval upon an undisguised species of racial discrimination. If the imprimatur of constitutionality should be put on such a denial of equality . . . the ideals embodied in our Bill of Rights would be ridiculed as empty words. . . . The lag between what Americans profess and what we practice would be used to support the charges of hypocrisy and the decadence of democratic society.

The brief cross-referenced the government's brief in *Henderson* to support the claim that "the existence of racial discrimination in this country embarrasses the United States in the conduct of foreign affairs." Additionally, the brief said: "It is in the context of a world in which freedom and equality must become living realities, if the democratic way of life is to survive, that the issues in these cases should be viewed."[174] The Cold War context virtually jumps from the pages of the government's brief. The Truman administration recognized that racial discrimination at home undermined the nation's goal of persuading a skeptical Third World audience that the U.S. democratic system was superior to the Soviet communist system. Unfortunately, because Southern Democrats controlled key committees in Congress, President Truman could not persuade Congress to help him eliminate racial segregation.[175] So, instead, the Truman administration enlisted the support of the Supreme Court in its effort to persuade the world that the United States had a system of government worth emulating.

Although several briefs in *Sweatt* and *McLaurin* urged the Court to overrule *Plessy*,[176] the Court was not (yet) prepared to do so. Not until its 1954 decision in *Brown* would the Court overrule *Plessy* and finally repudiate the "separate but equal" doctrine that perpetuated racial segregation in the United States. In *Sweatt* and *McLaurin*—both decided on the same day in June 1950—the Court adopted a more cautious approach. The Court focused narrowly on the specific facts in each case, holding that Texas and Oklahoma both violated the Equal Protection Clause because the educational programs offered to Sweatt and McLaurin were not substantially equal to the programs offered to white students.[177] The Court declined to issue a broader pronouncement about the legality of racially segregated schools in other factual contexts.

* * *

In an insightful essay on the process of constitutional change, Professors Jack Balkin and Reva Siegel contend that a constitutional "principle always comes with an imagined regulatory scene that makes the meaning of the principle coherent to us. When that background understanding is disturbed the principle becomes 'unstuck' from its hermeneutic moorings; it no longer seems clear how the principle applies or even whether it should apply." Moreover, they add: "[P]olitical contestation plays an important role in shaping understandings about the meaning and application of constitutional principles."[178] The imagined regulatory scene that made the treaty supremacy rule coherent for more than 150 years did not account for the advent of modern international human rights law. Codification of human rights principles in the U.N. Charter and the Universal Declaration gave rise to intense political contestation in the United States. As a result of that contestation, the treaty supremacy rule became "unstuck" from its traditional moorings. In the period from 1949 to 1951, the idea that the treaty supremacy rule might be optional, rather than mandatory, began to emerge in diplomatic practice (Eleanor Roosevelt's proposed treaty language), in scholarly writing (Manley Hudson), and in the ABA (the Stassen proposal). However, the optional treaty supremacy rule did not appear in any judicial decision until 1952—a topic to be considered in the next chapter.

Meanwhile, the same political contestation that caused the treaty supremacy rule to become unstuck also caused the equal protection principle to become unstuck. Professors Balkin and Siegel say: "Groups with competing interests may avail themselves of the opportunity presented by social, economic, and technological change to try to push the law in their favored direction."[179] The advent of modern international human rights law presented different opportunities for different groups. While Senator Bricker and his allies pressed to limit the scope of the treaty supremacy rule, human rights advocates pressed to expand the scope of the Equal Protection Clause by challenging discriminatory practices that had existed for decades. As the treaty supremacy rule was contracting, the equal protection principle was expanding. These processes continued in the period from 1952 to 1954, as explained in the next chapter.

Fujii, Brown, and Bricker: 1952–1954

This chapter addresses three key developments in the period from 1952 to 1954: the California Supreme Court decision in *Fujii v. State* in April 1952; the Senate vote on the Bricker Amendment in February 1954; and the U.S. Supreme Court decisions in *Brown* and *Bolling* in May 1954. *Fujii* was the first judicial decision by any state or federal court to hold that a non-self-executing (NSE) treaty does not supersede conflicting state laws. The Senate vote on the Bricker Amendment persuaded human rights advocates that it would be politically dangerous to continue arguing that courts should apply the U.N. Charter and the Supremacy Clause to invalidate discriminatory state laws. The Supreme Court decisions in *Brown* and *Bolling* persuaded human rights advocates that they could achieve their political objectives without relying directly on the U.N. Charter. The combination of *Fujii, Brown*, and Bricker effectively terminated the explosion of Charter-based human rights litigation in domestic courts that prevailed from about 1947 to 1954. Additionally, the Senate debates on the Bricker Amendment helped solidify a consensus within the federal political branches supporting an NSE exception to the treaty supremacy rule. Given the politics of the Bricker Amendment controversy, virtually no one acknowledged that the optional supremacy rule was a novel constitutional doctrine that was directly at odds with the traditional understanding of the Supremacy Clause.

I. THE *FUJII* CASE IN THE CALIFORNIA SUPREME COURT

The California Supreme Court issued its decision in *Fujii v. State* in April 1952.[1] *Fujii* marks a critical turning point in the transformation of the Constitution's treaty supremacy rule. This section analyzes the parties' briefs and the court's decision in *Fujii*. The next explains why the *Fujii* court adopted an opinion that departed sharply from the original understanding of the Supremacy Clause, and from 150 years of legislative, executive, and judicial precedent supporting a mandatory treaty supremacy rule.

The California attorney general filed a Petition for Hearing in the California Supreme Court in June 1950.[2] The attorney general wrapped himself in the cloak of Manley Hudson's authority. The brief provided a detailed account of Hudson's credentials along with a lengthy quotation from the telegram that Hudson sent to the attorney general (AG) shortly after the Court of Appeal issued its decision.[3] An Appendix to the brief reproduced a prepublication version of Hudson's forthcoming essay in the *American Journal of International Law*. As discussed in Chapter 10, Hudson's essay expanded the concept of self-execution to encompass the previously separate doctrine of treaty supremacy. Hudson effectively re-conceptualized treaty supremacy as an adjunct of self-execution doctrine, rather than an independent doctrine. The AG's brief followed precisely the same approach. Ultimately, the expansion of the self-execution concept to encompass treaty supremacy was a critical factor in the process of invisible constitutional change.

The AG's brief asserted that it is "well established and axiomatic that a United States treaty . . . supersedes municipal law only when the provisions of the treaty are self-executing."[4] This statement is highly misleading. As of 1950, it was well established that an NSE treaty does not supersede a prior conflicting *federal statute* under the later-in-time rule.[5] However, as of 1950, there was almost no legal authority for the proposition that an NSE treaty does not supersede conflicting *state law*. To the contrary, Article VI of the Constitution provides explicitly that valid, ratified treaties supersede conflicting state law; 150 years of legislative, executive, and judicial precedent confirmed that there was no exception for NSE treaties. Thus, as of 1950, there was ample support for an NSE exception to the later-in-time rule, but there was virtually no support for an NSE exception to the treaty supremacy rule.

Nevertheless, the AG's brief adopted the premise that an NSE treaty does not supersede conflicting state laws. Opposing counsel did not challenge that premise. Instead, they argued that Articles 55 and 56 are self-executing.[6] If Fujii's attorneys had consulted Quincy Wright, Professor Wright might have told them that the question whether Articles 55 and 56 are self-executing was not relevant to Fujii's claim, because the "distinction between self-executing and non-self-executing treaties has been used in American constitutional law only with reference to the agency of the Federal Government competent to execute the treaty and has had no reference to the relations between the Federal Government and the States."[7] Instead, by framing their argument in terms of self-execution, Fujii's lawyers tacitly conceded that Articles 55 and 56 would not supersede California law unless they were self-executing. As the point appeared to be uncontested, the California Supreme Court said in its decision that a treaty "does not automatically supersede local laws which are inconsistent with it unless the treaty provisions are self-executing."[8] Hence was born the "*Fujii* doctrine": the doctrine that an NSE treaty does not supersede conflicting state laws.

Before the California Supreme Court decided *Fujii* in 1952, the leading authorities supporting the *Fujii* doctrine were: (1) draft treaty language that the United States proposed to the Commission on Human Rights in 1949, which other states firmly rejected;[9] (2) Manley Hudson's essay in the *American Journal of International Law* in 1950;[10] and (3) the "Stassen proposal" adopted by an ABA committee in 1950.[11] *Fujii* was the first decision by any state or federal court to endorse the proposition that an NSE treaty does not supersede conflicting state laws. Hence, the California Supreme Court effectively converted self-execution from a federal separation-of-powers doctrine into a novel exception to the Constitution's treaty supremacy rule. Moreover, the court did so without acknowledging that it was endorsing a fundamental change in the relationship between treaties and state law.

Apart from the treaty supremacy issues, the California AG also argued that Articles 55 and 56 are not self-executing because they are "vague, and wholly wanting in definition."[12] We considered this argument in Chapter 10 in the discussion of articles by Hudson, Wright, and Schachter, but the point merits reconsideration because it is the AG's strongest argument. The argument can be summarized as follows. Articles 55 and 56 do not prohibit all forms of racial discrimination: they merely prohibit racial discrimination with respect to "human rights and fundamental freedoms." The Charter itself does not define the term "human rights and fundamental freedoms." Therefore, absent further international agreement, each state has discretion to decide for itself the specific content to be given to that phrase. Within the United States, in our system of divided government, the task of giving specific content to that general phrase is properly viewed as a legislative or executive task, not a judicial one. Therefore, the judiciary is not competent to enforce Articles 55 and 56 unless the legislative or executive branch enacts legislation or regulations to clarify the content of the phrase "human rights and fundamental freedoms." Thus, in accordance with the justiciability version of NSE doctrine, Articles 55 and 56 are not self-executing because they are too vague for the judiciary to enforce. The California Supreme Court arguably applied this version of NSE doctrine when it said that treaties held to be self-executing "prescribed in detail the rules governing rights and obligations of individuals," but the Charter's human rights provisions "lack the mandatory quality and definiteness which would indicate an intent to create justiciable rights in private persons."[13]

Reasonable people may disagree about the conclusion that Articles 55 and 56 are too vague for judicial enforcement. There is a strong counterargument that the judiciary is competent to determine that the right at issue in *Fujii*—that is, the right to own real property—is a human right, even if the judiciary is not competent to determine, for example, that the right to social security is a human right.[14] Regardless, two points are clear. First, in accordance with the justiciability version of NSE doctrine, "the supremacy clause of the Constitution does not compel a court to enforce a treaty provision which is so incomplete or indefinite that it cannot be applied in a particular case."[15] Second, assuming that a court is not competent to enforce a particular treaty provision in a particular case, one may not reasonably infer, on that basis alone, that the treaty does not supersede conflicting state laws. The California Supreme Court's rationale in *Fujii* seems to be: (1) Articles 55 and 56 are too vague to be judicially enforceable; (2) therefore, they are not self-executing; and (3) therefore, they do not supersede conflicting state laws. The second proposition follows from the first under the political-judicial concept of self-execution. However, the third proposition does not follow from either of the first two, because the third is based on the federal-state concept of self-execution, which is very different from the political-judicial concept.[16]

Fujii is also significant because it applied a one-step approach to self-execution analysis. Recall that, under a two-step approach, lawyers perform a treaty interpretation analysis to answer questions about the content and scope of the international obligation (step one), followed by a domestic separation-of-powers analysis to answer domestic implementation questions (step two). In contrast, under a one-step approach, lawyers perform a treaty interpretation analysis to answer domestic implementation questions.[17] In *Fujii*, the key domestic implementation question was whether the U.N. Charter has the status of supreme federal law in the United States (that is, whether it supersedes conflicting state laws). The U.N. Charter says nothing whatsoever about that question. Nevertheless, the AG framed his analysis of self-execution as a treaty interpretation analysis. The AG's brief analyzed the Charter's text and the "intent of the draftsmen and signatories."[18] Based on that treaty interpretation analysis, the brief asserted that Articles 55 and 56 of the U.N. Charter are not self-executing because the drafters intended those articles to be non-self-executing. However, the ostensible "intent" of the Charter's drafters is a purely fictitious intent. The AG's brief defined "not self-executing" to mean that a treaty does not supersede conflicting state laws. Given that definition, the Charter's drafters had no intent with respect to self-execution because they recognized that the relationship between treaties and state law is governed by domestic constitutional law.

To be fair, the AG's brief in *Fujii* was not the first legal analysis of self-execution that applied a fictitious intent test. By 1950, the tendency to apply a fictitious "intent of the treaty makers" had become fairly common in self-execution analysis.[19] However, prior cases that relied on fictitious intent involved federal separation-of-powers issues, not treaty supremacy issues. The AG's brief in *Fujii* may have been the first legal brief to transplant that particular feature of self-execution doctrine from the federal separation-of-powers context to the treaty supremacy context. Unfortunately, the opposing brief made precisely the same mistake. Opposing counsel said: "Whether or not a treaty shall be self-executing involves a question of intent. . . . To determine whether [the treaty is self-executing], the intent of the parties, reflected primarily in the terms of the treaty itself, must be examined."[20] Inasmuch as both parties seemingly agreed upon the correct mode of analysis, the California Supreme Court adopted that mode of analysis in its decision. For example, the court said: "In determining whether a treaty is self-executing courts look to the intent of the signatory parties as manifested by the language of the instrument, and, if the instrument is uncertain, recourse may be had to the circumstances surrounding its execution."[21] Moreover, the court concluded its analysis of self-execution by saying: "[T]he charter provisions relied on by plaintiff were not intended to supersede existing domestic legislation."[22] Thus, the court's self-execution holding relied heavily on an ostensible "intent of the treaty makers" that was purely fictitious. To reiterate, the asserted "intent" is fictitious because the Charter's drafters had no intention to alter the constitutional rules governing the relationship between treaties and state law in the United States.[23]

Finally, it bears emphasis that *Fujii*'s combination of the intent test (the one-step approach) with the proposition that an NSE treaty does not supersede conflicting state laws (the federal-state concept of self-execution) is based on a key, unstated assumption about the nature of the treaty supremacy rule. The rule holds that treaties supersede conflicting state laws. If the operation of the rule is contingent on the "intent of the treaty makers"—as *Fujii* implies—then the tacit assumption must be that Article II grants the treaty makers an affirmative power to opt out of the treaty supremacy rule. If the treaty makers did not have that power, then their intent would be irrelevant. Thus, *Fujii* implicitly assumes that the treaty supremacy rule is optional, not mandatory. *Fujii's* tacit approval of the optional supremacy rule was a dramatic departure from the original understanding of the Supremacy Clause and from 150 years of legislative, executive, and judicial precedent supporting a mandatory rule. The next section explains why the California Supreme Court implicitly endorsed a novel NSE exception to the treaty supremacy rule.

II. THE POLITICS OF THE *FUJII* DECISION

Although the briefs submitted to the California Supreme Court focused on the U.N. Charter, the court devoted most of its analysis to the equal protection issue. The court held in a 4-3 decision that the Alien Land Law violated the Fourteenth Amendment because it "is obviously designed and administered as an instrument for effectuating racial discrimination."[24] The majority decision was directly contrary to controlling precedent. The U.S. Supreme Court had upheld the validity of the Alien Land Law against a Fourteenth Amendment challenge in 1923 in *Porterfield v. Webb.*[25] Moreover, in its 1948 decision in *Oyama v. California,* the Court expressly declined to reconsider *Porterfield* when invited to do so.[26] Thus, the dissent in *Fujii* remarked: "It is, indeed, an unusual procedure when a state court holds unconstitutional on federal grounds a state act which the United States Supreme Court holds to be constitutional as against the same attack."[27]

The California Supreme Court decision in *Fujii* presents a puzzle. Why did the Court refuse to follow controlling precedent and uphold the validity of the Alien Land Law? Or, if the California court wanted to invalidate the statute, why not do so on the basis of the California Constitution, or on the basis of the U.N. Charter, to avoid the accusation that it was willfully disregarding U.S. Supreme Court precedent? I suggest that the California Supreme Court applied the Fourteenth Amendment to invalidate the Alien Land Law because the majority believed there were no good options, but its Fourteenth Amendment holding was the best available option. In essence, the court had four choices: affirm the validity of the Alien Land Law, invalidate the law on the basis of the California Constitution, invalidate the law on the basis of the U.N. Charter, or invalidate the law on the basis of the Fourteenth Amendment. Let us consider each of these options.

A. Affirm the Validity of the Alien Land Law

Justice Schauer, writing for the dissent in *Fujii,* accused the majority of invalidating the Alien Land Law because the statute was "obnoxious to their personal social views and to their concepts of desirable international relations."[28]

In a separate concurring opinion, Justice Carter defended the majority against Schauer's charge.[29] However, to paraphrase Shakespeare, "the justice doth protest too much, methinks." Justice Schauer's criticism was directly on target. By 1952, when the California Supreme Court issued its decision, the United States was engaged in a global public relations campaign to persuade the world that its democratic system was superior to the Soviet communist system. In that context, the United States was subject to mounting criticism—in the United Nations and elsewhere—that its racially discriminatory practices were inconsistent with its stated commitment to the anti-discrimination principles enshrined in the U.N. Charter and the Universal Declaration.[30] A decision to affirm the validity of the Alien Land Law would have undermined the federal government's effort to sell the virtues of American democracy to a skeptical global audience. The California Supreme Court justices were surely aware of these developments.[31]

Foreign policy considerations aside, the majority was clearly sympathetic to Fujii's claim. The court dutifully recited the state's assertion that "the purpose of the alien land law is to restrict the use and ownership of land to persons who are loyal and have an interest in the welfare of the state."[32] In several prior decisions, both the U.S. Supreme Court and the California Supreme Court had agreed that the stated goal was a valid purpose and that California's statutory classifications were reasonably related to that purpose.[33] In contrast, the *Fujii* majority asserted "that the real purpose of the legislation was the elimination of competition by alien Japanese in farming California land."[34] Moreover, they said, even if one accepts at face value the state's alleged purpose, "there is no reasonable relationship between that asserted purpose and the classification on the basis of eligibility to citizenship."[35] These and other passages from the majority opinion suggest that four of the seven justices were strongly inclined to invalidate the Alien Land Law. The question was whether they could articulate a persuasive legal rationale to support their preferred outcome.

B. Apply the California Constitution

In his initial brief filed with the Court of Appeal, Fujii argued that "the Alien Land Law is invalid special legislation prohibited by the California Constitution."[36] His argument relied on prior California Supreme Court decisions stating that "the test for determining the validity of a statute where a claim is made that it unlawfully discriminates against any class is substantially the same under the state [constitutional] prohibitions against special legislation and the equal protection clause of the federal Constitution."[37] In light of those precedents, the California Supreme Court could have articulated a plausible rationale to support a holding that the Alien Land Law violated the California Constitution. However, the court ignored Fujii's state law constitutional argument and focused on his federal constitutional argument. The court's decision to rely on federal constitutional law is surprising because the California Supreme Court has the power to decide the proper interpretation of the California Constitution, but its decisions applying the federal Constitution are subject to reversal by the U.S. Supreme Court.

Why did the California Supreme Court apply federal constitutional law, instead of state constitutional law? Any attempt to answer that question is speculative, but the following explanation seems plausible. The animating principle guiding the court's decision was the idea that human rights are *universal*: all human beings are entitled to human rights because they are human beings. That, of course, is also the animating principle behind the Universal Declaration of Human Rights and the human rights provisions of the U.N. Charter. The Charter and the Universal Declaration exerted "normative pull" on the *Fujii* majority.[38] The court endorsed the Charter's human rights principles in the following passage: "[T]he United Nations Charter ... expresses the universal desire of thinking men for peace and for equality of rights and opportunities. The charter represents a moral commitment of foremost importance, and we must not permit the spirit of our pledge to be compromised or disparaged in either our domestic or foreign affairs."[39] The majority may have thought that a decision based on the California Constitution would have been at odds with the Charter's principled commitment to universality. If the California Constitution bans racial discrimination, but the federal Constitution does not, then the nation's commitment to human rights could hardly be deemed "universal." In contrast, a holding based on the federal Constitution would affirm "the spirit of our pledge" in the U.N. Charter.

C. Apply the U.N. Charter

As explained previously, in its discussion of the U.N. Charter the California Supreme Court applied a fictitious "intent of the treaty makers" test to decide the self-execution question. When a court indulges in a fictitious intent test, one can safely assume that other, unspoken factors guided the court's decision. In this case, two different explanations seem plausible. First, the majority justices in *Fujii* might have concluded that it would be politically dangerous to base their holding on the U.N. Charter. After almost three years of internal bureaucratic skirmishing within the ABA, the ABA House of Delegates approved a proposed constitutional amendment in February 1952,[40] just two months before the California Supreme Court issued its decision in *Fujii.* The justices had been explicitly informed about the mounting pressure from the ABA for a constitutional amendment to address the perceived threat posed by human rights treaties.[41] Moreover, the justices knew that the lower court decision in *Fujii* had provoked expressions of alarm in the United States Senate. The very fact that the Senate devoted time in floor debate to a decision by an intermediate-level state court was sufficiently anomalous that it could not have gone unnoticed by the California Supreme Court.[42] In short, the justices may reasonably have feared that a holding based on the U.N. Charter would have provoked an undesirable political response from the Senate, the ABA, or both. The court's non-self-execution holding enabled it to dodge this potential minefield.

Politics aside, there is another reason why the justices may have preferred to base their decision on the Fourteenth Amendment, rather than the U.N. Charter.

In the aftermath of World War II, and still today, many of the political and intellectual elite in the United States shared an attitude of "American exceptionalism"—a belief that the United States has the best constitutional system in the world. If the court held that the Alien Land Law violated the U.N. Charter, but did not violate the Fourteenth Amendment, its opinion would imply that international law provided stronger protection against racial discrimination than did the U.S. Constitution. An admission of that type, even if only implicit in the court's decision, would be impossible to reconcile with the public faith in American exceptionalism. As one commentator noted shortly after the California Supreme Court decision in *Fujii*, it would be "a reproach to our constitutional system to confess that the values it establishes fall below any requirement of the Charter."[43]

Thus, the juxtaposition of the U.N. Charter argument with the equal protection argument created cognitive dissonance for the majority justices in *Fujii*.[44] Accordingly, they could not bring themselves to admit, even implicitly, that international law provided stronger protection from racial discrimination than did the Fourteenth Amendment. To avoid confronting that uncomfortable proposition, they reinterpreted the Constitution and incorporated into the Fourteenth Amendment the strong anti-discrimination principle embodied in the U.N. Charter and the Universal Declaration. Indeed, Frank Holman said in testimony before a Senate subcommittee:

> Thus, though in a technical legal sense the California Supreme Court holds the charter is not a self-executing treaty, the charter is allowed to produce the same effect by projecting itself into the thinking of the court in a new construction of the equal protection clause of the 14th amendment to the Constitution of the United States to the extent that earlier statutes and decisions of years' standing, even of the Supreme Court of the United States, are overruled by the Supreme Court of California upon the identical issue because of the influence of this international thinking.[45]

D. Apply the Fourteenth Amendment

The U.S. Supreme Court decided in *Porterfield v. Webb* that the Alien Land Law *did not* violate the Fourteenth Amendment.[46] Despite what appeared to be controlling precedent, the California Supreme Court held in *Fujii* that the Alien Land Law *did* violate the Fourteenth Amendment. The *Fujii* court justified its departure from *Porterfield* by invoking two U.S. Supreme Court cases decided in 1948: *Oyama v. California*,[47] and *Takahashi v. Fish and Game Commission*.[48] In both *Oyama* and *Takahashi*, the U.S. Supreme Court reversed California Supreme Court decisions involving the rights of California residents of Japanese descent.[49] The *Fujii* court said that *Oyama*, *Takahashi*, "and other recent decisions of the United States Supreme Court ... state and apply concepts of rights under the Fourteenth Amendment that are at variance with the opinions in the earlier cases," such as *Porterfield*.[50] However, the *Fujii* court's claim that *Oyama* and *Takahashi* weakened the precedential force of *Porterfield* is not persuasive.

Torao Takahashi was a California resident of Japanese descent. From 1915 to 1942 he earned his livelihood as a fisherman, operating with a commercial fishing license granted by the State of California. California amended its licensing law in 1945, rendering Takahashi ineligible for a commercial fishing license. The U.S. Supreme Court held that the amended California law violated the Fourteenth Amendment.[51] The Court said: "[H]aving been lawfully admitted into the country under federal law, [Takahashi] had a federal privilege to enter and abide in any state in the Union and thereafter under the Fourteenth Amendment . . . this privilege . . . carried with it the right to work for a living in the common occupations of the community."[52] The Court distinguished explicitly between the right to work for a living and the right to own real property. The Court affirmed the states' power to restrict land ownership by noncitizens as an incident of the "power of states to control the devolution and ownership of land within their borders."[53] Thus, *Takahashi* does not support the California court's decision in *Fujii* because *Takahashi* distinguished expressly between the right to own land (at issue in *Fujii*) and the right to earn a livelihood as a fisherman.

Fred Oyama was a U.S. citizen who was born in the United States. His father, Kajiro, was a Japanese national who was not eligible for citizenship. Kajiro purchased two parcels of land in California in the 1930s, when Fred was less than ten years old. The deeds for both parcels were in Fred's name because the Alien Land Law barred Kajiro from owning land in California. In 1944, when Fred was sixteen, "the State filed a petition to declare an escheat of the two parcels on the ground that the conveyances . . . had been with intent to violate and evade the Alien Land Law."[54] The California courts ruled in favor of the state; they relied heavily on Section 9(a) of the Alien Land Law, which created a "statutory presumption that any conveyance is with 'intent to prevent, evade or avoid' escheat if an ineligible alien pays the consideration."[55]

The U.S. Supreme Court reversed. The Court compared Fred's case to the situation of other children in California whose parents buy land as a gift for their minor children. In the ordinary case, "where a parent pays for a conveyance to his child there is a presumption that a gift is intended."[56] In contrast, Fred faced "the necessity of overcoming a statutory presumption that conveyances financed by his father and recorded in Fred's name were not gifts at all."[57] In addition, the state imposed other obstacles that made it difficult, if not impossible, for Fred to prove his rightful ownership of the land. "The cumulative effect," the Court said, "was clearly to discriminate against Fred Oyama. He was saddled with an onerous burden of proof which need not be borne by California children generally."[58] Hence, the Court held "that the Alien Land Law, as applied in this case, deprives Fred Oyama of the equal protection" of the laws.[59] Even so, *Oyama* provides little support for the California court's decision in *Fujii* because *Oyama* addressed the rights of U.S.-citizen children of Japanese nationals, whereas *Fujii* implicated the rights of a Japanese national who was not eligible for citizenship. Moreover, although the petitioner in *Oyama* urged the U.S. Supreme Court to reconsider its earlier holding in *Porterfield v. Webb*, the Court expressly declined to do so.[60]

In sum, the Fourteenth Amendment holding in *Fujii* stood on shaky doctrinal ground because it contravened the earlier decision in *Porterfield*, and the Supreme Court's later decisions in *Takahashi* and *Oyama* did not really undermine the rationale of *Porterfield* (despite the *Fujii* court's claim to the contrary). The *Fujii* court apparently based its decision on the Fourteenth Amendment because the other options were even less attractive. The *Fujii* majority did not want to uphold the validity of the Alien Land Law because they objected to the law's discriminatory effects, and they probably recognized that a decision upholding the law would undermine the nation's foreign policy objectives. They did not want to base their decision on the California Constitution because a holding based on state law would have been in tension with the commitment to universal human rights that animated their decision. If they applied the U.N. Charter to invalidate the Alien Land Law, they would have been stepping into a political minefield. Additionally, a holding based on the U.N. Charter would have been inconsistent with their faith in American exceptionalism. So, the Court opted for the least unsatisfactory alternative. Despite apparently conflicting precedent, the California Supreme Court reinterpreted the Constitution and incorporated into the Fourteenth Amendment the strong anti-discrimination principle embodied in the U.N. Charter and the Universal Declaration. In this respect, the California Supreme Court decision in *Fujii* foreshadowed the U.S. Supreme Court decisions in *Brown* and *Bolling* two years later.

III. *BROWN* AND *BOLLING*

The U.S. Supreme Court issued its landmark decisions in *Brown v. Board of Education* and *Bolling v. Sharpe* in May 1954.[61] *Brown* involved four consolidated cases from Kansas, South Carolina, Virginia, and Delaware. Plaintiffs in all four cases alleged that racially segregated public schools violated the Fourteenth Amendment Equal Protection Clause. *Bolling* involved a single case challenging the legality of racially segregated public schools in the District of Columbia. Petitioners raised arguments based on the Fifth Amendment and the U.N. Charter.[62] The Court first heard oral argument in the school segregation cases in December 1952; it then requested additional argument and deferred final decision until the following term. Ultimately, the Court held that racial segregation in state-run public schools violated the Fourteenth Amendment, and racial segregation in District of Columbia public schools violated the Fifth Amendment. The Court's decisions in *Brown* and *Bolling* did not mention the U.N. Charter. Several scholars have analyzed the sociolegal context to help explain why the Court held that racial segregation was unconstitutional,[63] despite the dearth of support from constitutional text, precedent, or original understanding to support that holding. This section focuses on a somewhat different question: Why did the Court choose to rely on the Fifth and Fourteenth Amendments, rather than the U.N. Charter, to support its conclusions?

This section first examines the U.N. Charter argument in *Bolling*, focusing on the self-execution issue. It then presents a legal analysis of the issues in *Brown* and *Bolling*, examining arguments based on text, precedent, and the original understanding of the Fifth Amendment, the Fourteenth Amendment, and the U.N. Charter. The analysis suggests that the Charter-based argument for desegregation was legally sound—probably stronger than the constitutional arguments. I then consider various extralegal factors that may have induced the Court to disregard the Charter-based arguments and base its decision on the Fifth and Fourteenth Amendments.

A. The Charter and Self-Execution in *Bolling*

The petitioners' brief in *Bolling* raised several distinct arguments, but counsel devoted a substantial portion of the brief to the claim that "respondents' refusal to admit minor petitioners to Sousa Junior High School solely because of race deprives them of fundamental freedoms in violation of . . . the Charter of the United Nations."[64] After quoting several provisions of the U.N. Charter, the brief asserted "that these articles give to minor petitioners rights which the respondents have violated because: (1) the United Nations Charter is a treaty of the United States, (2) the Articles of the Charter here in issue are capable of judicial enforcement, and (3) properly constructed, they prohibit the segregation of races in free public education."[65] The brief acknowledged the distinction between self-executing and non-self-executing treaties, asserting that "the sole distinction between self-executing and non-self-executing treaties has been used in American Constitutional Law only with reference to the agency of the Federal Government competent to execute that treaty. All other factors are irrelevant."[66] This language is almost a verbatim quote from Quincy Wright's 1951 article in the *American Journal of International Law*,[67] but the brief did not cite Wright. *Bolling's* attorneys argued that Articles 55 and 56 of the U.N. Charter "are capable of judicial interpretation and application without further legislative or executive action . . . and it thus becomes the duty of the courts, both state and federal, to give effect to its provisions."[68] The brief cited the Supremacy Clause as authority. Overall, petitioners devoted about eight pages of their brief to the U.N. Charter argument, urging the Court to hold that "government enforced racial segregation in the public schools of the District of Columbia does violence to the high ideals of the Constitution of the United States and the Charter of the United Nations."[69]

Respondents in *Bolling* devoted about sixteen pages of their brief to the U.N. Charter issue. They argued that the Charter's human rights provisions are not self-executing and that an NSE treaty "does not supersede local laws which are inconsistent with it."[70] Respondents' self-execution argument relied heavily on the California Supreme Court decision in *Fujii* and Manley Hudson's article in the *American Journal of International Law*.[71] Like the Court in *Fujii*, and like Judge Hudson, counsel for respondents in *Bolling* were stretching the concept of self-execution to encompass the previously distinct doctrine of treaty supremacy. Respondents' U.N. Charter argument tended to conflate international law questions with constitutional law ones. For example, respondents' brief said: "It is fundamental *in international law* that there are two kinds of treaties—self-executing and non-self-executing. The latter does not supersede local laws which are inconsistent with it."[72] In fact, from an international law perspective, the question whether a treaty is self-executing or non-self-executing is generally seen as a domestic law question. Moreover, even if some aspects of the self-execution issue might properly be viewed as an international law question, the U.N. Charter certainly does not purport to answer the particular question of whether Articles 55 and 56 supersede local laws in the United States.

In sum, the parties devoted a significant portion of their briefs in *Bolling* to analysis of self-execution, without saying anything very novel or insightful. Petitioners presented a respectable argument to support their view that the Charter's human rights provisions are "capable of judicial enforcement."[73] Respondents' argument followed the growing tendency to expand the concept of self-execution to encompass treaty supremacy issues. Neither brief said much about the merits of the Charter issue: whether maintenance of racially segregated schools violated the nation's treaty obligations under the U.N. Charter. The next section addresses that question.

B. The Merits of Legal Arguments Based on the Charter and the Constitution

As of 1952–1954, if one viewed the issue from a narrow, legalistic perspective, the argument that racially segregated public schools violated the Fourteenth Amendment was not very strong. When the justices met privately to discuss the school segregation cases in December 1952, Justice Robert Jackson reportedly assessed the arguments roughly as follows: "I find nothing in the text that says this [racial segregation in public schools] is unconstitutional. Nothing in the opinions of the courts say that it is unconstitutional. Nothing in the history of the Fourteenth Amendment says that it is unconstitutional. On the basis of precedents, I would have to say that it is constitutional."[74]

The text of the Constitution provided some support for the anti-segregation position. Under the Fourteenth Amendment, a state may not "deny to any person within its jurisdiction the equal protection of the laws."[75] Thurgood Marshall and his associates argued that racially segregated public schools were inherently unequal. Therefore, states that maintained such schools denied black children the equal protection guaranteed by the Fourteenth Amendment.[76] As a litigation tactic, the NAACP chose to argue that segregation itself was unconstitutional, even if the state provided physically comparable facilities for white and black children.[77] That approach forced the Court to address the constitutionality of segregation per se. In 1866, the very same Congress that proposed the Fourteenth Amendment enacted legislation "providing for separate schooling for the white and colored children in the District of Columbia."[78] Hence, the historical evidence demonstrated persuasively that the drafters of the Fourteenth Amendment did not believe that racially segregated schools were per se unconstitutional. Moreover, the Court held in *Plessy v. Ferguson*[79] and in a long line of subsequent cases that racial segregation was permissible, provided that the separate facilities were substantially equal. Additionally, Justice Harlan, the sole dissenter in *Plessy*, apparently believed that segregated schools were permissible.[80] Thus, although the text of the Fourteenth Amendment could reasonably be construed to prohibit racial segregation, the Court's own precedents and the original understanding of the Fourteenth Amendment weighed heavily against that interpretation. Accordingly, Justice Jackson "ridiculed the NAACP's brief as sociology, not law."[81]

The Fifth Amendment argument for desegregation of District of Columbia public schools was even weaker. The text of the amendment provides only that people shall not "be deprived of life, liberty, or property, without due process of law."[82] It says nothing about equality or racial discrimination. Moreover, the Fifth Amendment took effect in 1791, at a time when the Constitution treated slaves as property and the courts protected the property rights of slave-owners. Hence, none of the briefs in *Bolling* contended that the drafters of the Fifth Amendment intended to guarantee black children a right to attend racially integrated schools. Although *Plessy* did not technically control the Fifth Amendment, because it was a Fourteenth Amendment case, both the Supreme Court and the lower courts had relied on *Plessy* in the past to uphold racial segregation in the District of Columbia.[83] In sum, text, precedent and original understanding all weighed against the petitioners' Fifth Amendment claim in *Bolling*. (This may help explain why the petitioners in *Bolling* relied heavily on the U.N. Charter argument.)

When the justices met initially to discuss the segregation cases in December 1952, they did not follow their usual practice of voting on the cases. However, it is possible to reconstruct the justices' likely positions based on available conference notes. Justices Black, Douglas, Burton, and Minton were the only justices who expressed clear support for a holding that racial segregation in public schools is per se unconstitutional.[84] Frankfurter was prepared to join them to invalidate racial segregation in District of Columbia public schools, but he found the state cases more troubling, in part because the problem of crafting an appropriate remedy was more difficult.[85] Justice Reed spoke clearly in favor of affirming *Plessy*, and Chief Justice Vinson was probably inclined to join him in that position. Justices Jackson and Clark were apparently undecided.[86] In the end, the Court avoided a decision by ordering reargument for the following term. Surprisingly, given the prominence of the U.N. Charter argument in the *Bolling* briefs, the available records suggest that the justices hardly even considered the Charter rationale as an alternative to the Fifth and Fourteenth Amendment rationales.[87]

In contrast to arguments based on the Fifth and Fourteenth Amendments, the Charter-based argument for holding that racial segregation was unlawful was fairly strong. Articles 55 and 56 of the U.N. Charter obligate the United States to take "separate action" to promote "universal respect for, and observance of, human rights and fundamental freedoms *for all without distinction as to race*."[88] Whereas the Fourteenth Amendment, by its terms, focuses on "equal protection," the text of the Charter expresses a particularized rule condemning race-based distinctions. Therefore, even if the *Plessy* doctrine of "separate but equal" is a textually plausible interpretation of the Fourteenth Amendment, *Plessy* is not a textually plausible interpretation of the Charter. That is no accident. States drafted the human rights provisions of the Charter against the historical background of race-based classifications in Nazi Germany. Representatives of several civil rights groups served as advisors to the U.S. delegation in San Francisco when the Charter was drafted. They lobbied hard to add strong human rights language to the Charter, as did representatives from several Latin American countries.[89] Those who favored strong human rights provisions agreed that racial classifications, in general, were obnoxious and offensive.

The major powers were not enthusiastic about the human rights language supported by civil rights groups and non-European countries. John Foster Dulles, a member of the United States delegation and future secretary of state, devised a compromise solution. The United States would accept "an unequivocal statement guaranteeing freedom from discrimination on account of race, language, religion, or sex," but would insist on inserting a "domestic jurisdiction clause" in Article 2.[90] That clause said: "Nothing contained in the present Charter shall authorize the United Nations to intervene in matters which are essentially within the domestic jurisdiction of any state."[91] The major powers were satisfied with this solution because the domestic jurisdiction clause limited the authority of the United Nations to adopt coercive measures to compel States to abolish discriminatory laws and practices.

However, the domestic jurisdiction clause did not limit the scope of States' treaty obligations under Articles 55 and 56. Clearly, Articles 55 and 56 did not obligate the United States to abolish all forms of racial segregation immediately. However, the Charter did obligate the United States to take concrete steps to promote human rights "for all without distinction as to race." Thus, the petitioners in *Bolling* could argue persuasively that a judicial decision perpetuating racial segregation in public schools would have been inconsistent with that treaty obligation.[92] Respondents' primary counterargument emphasized that the Charter itself did not specify which "human rights and fundamental freedoms" required protection.[93] Even so, it would not have required a huge leap for the Court to hold that the right to public education was one of the rights encompassed within the phrase "human rights and fundamental freedoms" in Article 55 of the Charter.[94]

If the Court based its holdings in *Brown* and *Bolling* on the U.N. Charter, it could have ruled against the school districts without overruling any of its own precedents, thereby avoiding the *Plessy* problem. The Court could have cited the concurring opinions in *Oyama v. California* as authority for judicial application of the U.N. Charter.[95] Such a holding would have been inconsistent with the California Supreme Court decision in *Fujii*, but that decision had limited precedential force for the U.S. Supreme Court. Moreover, as of 1954, no other state or federal court had followed the California court's decision in *Fujii*; it was an isolated precedent. Additionally, insofar as the *Fujii* decision approved a novel NSE exception to the Constitution's treaty supremacy rule, *Fujii* was a dramatic departure from 150 years of legislative, executive, and judicial practice supporting application of the treaty supremacy rule without any NSE exception.

In sum, a holding that racially segregated public schools violated the U.N. Charter would have been legally defensible on the basis of treaty text, legal precedent, and the original understanding of the diplomats who drafted and negotiated the Charter. Even so, the Court's opinions in *Brown* and *Bolling* did not mention the U.N. Charter, and the available evidence suggests that the Court did not consider the Charter argument seriously in its internal deliberations. Hence, the question arises, why did the Court disregard the Charter argument and focus exclusively on the Fifth and Fourteenth Amendments? To answer that question, we must consider extralegal factors.

C. Extralegal Factors in *Brown* and *Bolling*

The Court's decision to rest its judgments on the Fifth and Fourteenth Amendments, instead of the U.N. Charter, was probably driven by a combination of foreign policy, domestic politics, and psychological factors. Two briefs filed in the October 1952 term in *Brown* and *Bolling* emphasized the foreign policy aspects of segregation. The American Civil Liberties Union (ACLU) and five other nongovernmental organizations filed a joint amicus brief in *Brown*.[96] The brief said:

> The United States is now engaged in an ideological world conflict in which the practices of our democracy are the subject of close scrutiny abroad. . . . We know that our enemies seize eagerly upon the weaknesses of our democracy and, for propaganda purposes, magnify, exaggerate and distort happenings in the United States. . . . Our discriminatory practices in education, in employment, in housing, have all been the subject of much adverse press comment in those foreign countries which we are trying to keep in the democratic camp.[97]

The brief quoted a series of newspaper articles from France, Austria, Germany, and Belgium that were highly critical of American racism. It concluded that "legally imposed segregation in our country, in any shape, manner or form, weakens our program to build and strengthen world democracy and combat totalitarianism."[98]

Shortly after Eisenhower's election, the lame-duck Truman administration filed a single amicus brief for all five segregation cases.[99] The brief highlighted the special problems posed by racial discrimination in the District of Columbia.

> This city is the window through which the world looks into our house. The embassies, legations, and representatives of all nations are here, at the seat of the Federal Government. Foreign officials and visitors naturally judge this country and our people by their experiences and observations in the nation's capital . . . . The shamefulness and absurdity of Washington's treatment of Negro Americans is highlighted by the presence of many dark-skinned

foreign visitors. Capital custom not only humiliates colored citizens, but is a source of considerable embarrassment to these visitors. Foreign officials are often mistaken for American Negroes and refused food, lodging and entertainment.[100]

Although the government brief emphasized the unique problems caused by racial discrimination in the nation's capital, it also placed those concerns in a broader, global context.

It is in the context of the present world struggle between freedom and tyranny that the problem of racial discrimination must be viewed. The United States is trying to prove to the people of the world, of every nationality, race, and color, that a free democracy is the most civilized and most secure form of government yet devised by man. We must set an example for others by showing firm determination to remove existing flaws in our democracy.... Racial discrimination furnishes grist for the Communist propaganda mills ... The continuance of racial discrimination in the United States remains a source of constant embarrassment to this Government in the day-to-day conduct of its foreign relations; and it jeopardizes the effective maintenance of our moral leadership of the free and democratic nations of the world.[101]

The message was not lost on the justices: nothing less than the United States' leadership of the free world was at stake. Justices Burton and Minton, in particular, were probably swayed by "the Cold War imperative for racial change."[102] The Cold War imperative helps explain why the justices voted to end racial segregation in public schools, but it does not explain why they chose to base their decision on the Fifth and Fourteenth Amendments, rather than the U.N. Charter. In fact, a decision based on the U.N. Charter might have better served the purpose of conveying a message to the world that the United States was truly committed to the *international* norm prohibiting racial discrimination.

Two distinct domestic political factors may have helped persuade the justices to base their decisions on the Fifth and Fourteenth Amendments, rather than the U.N. Charter. First, the Bricker Amendment controversy reached its peak intensity in the Senate between February 1953 and February 1954.[103] The Supreme Court's deliberations on *Brown* and *Bolling* lasted from December 1952 to May 1954. Thus, the Court was weighing its options in *Brown* and *Bolling* at a time when controversy over the proposed Bricker Amendment was headline news in Washington.[104] The justices surely recognized that a holding based on the U.N. Charter might have tipped the political scales in favor of the amendment. Even if individual justices were personally supportive of Bricker's agenda, the Court as a whole would probably have been reluctant to issue a decision that fanned the flames of a movement for a constitutional amendment.

The second domestic political factor relates to the problem of remedies. The justices were deeply concerned that a judicial order mandating desegregation would confront massive resistance in the Deep South. Indeed, Governor Byrnes of South Carolina had threatened to abolish public schools in the state if the Court ordered desegregation of public schools.[105] Justice Frankfurter, in particular, invoked concerns about the sensitivity of remedial issues as the main reason for the Court to refrain from issuing a decision in the 1952–1953 term and to hold the case over for an additional term.[106] Given the Court's fears about potential resistance to a judicial order based on the Fourteenth Amendment, the prospect of ordering states to desegregate schools to achieve compliance with the U.N. Charter was virtually unthinkable. Such an order would have created a powerful coalition between white supremacists in the South and the anti-U.N. forces in the ABA and the Senate, who were already concerned about U.N. intervention in matters of national sovereignty. As it happened, the Court's Fourteenth Amendment decision in *Brown* contributed to substantial political turmoil in the South;[107] the level of domestic political unrest might have been much worse if the Court had relied on the U.N. Charter as a legal hook to support a desegregation order.

The foregoing analysis might be construed to imply that the justices consciously weighed the costs and benefits of judicial reliance on the U.N. Charter versus the Fifth and Fourteenth Amendments. However, the available evidence suggests that they did not seriously consider the U.N. Charter argument. Why not? The parties devoted a substantial portion of their briefs in *Bolling* to the Charter issue, so one cannot blame the parties for failing to raise it. For the reasons explained previously, the Charter argument was at least as strong on the merits as the Fifth and Fourteenth Amendment arguments, so the Court could not dismiss the Charter argument as frivolous. I suggest that the best explanation is psychological. Professors Goodman and Jinks note that human behavior can sometimes be explained as an attempt "to avoid the unpleasant state of cognitive dissonance between what [people] profess in public and what they believe in private."[108] The Charter argument in *Bolling* created severe cognitive dissonance for the justices. They believed privately in American exceptionalism—that is, they believed that the United States has the best Constitution in the world. The arguments in *Brown* and *Bolling* forced them to confront the unpleasant fact that the Constitution, as it had been previously interpreted, was seriously deficient, because it permitted a form of racial discrimination that was inconsistent with the international human rights standards embodied in the U.N. Charter and the Universal Declaration. A judicial decision based on the U.N. Charter would have implicitly, if not explicitly, acknowledged that deficiency. As Professor Charles Fairman wrote, "It would seem, indeed, a reproach to our constitutional system to confess that the values it establishes fall below any requirement of the Charter. One should think very seriously before admitting such a deficiency."[109] The justices were not psychologically prepared to admit such a deficiency because that admission would have been inconsistent with their faith in American exceptionalism. Hence, I suggest, the justices applied the Fifth and Fourteenth Amendments, rather than the U.N. Charter, "to avoid the unpleasant state of cognitive dissonance between what they profess in public and what they believe in private."[110] By reinterpreting the Fifth and Fourteenth Amendments to ban racial segregation in public schools, the Court was able to reconcile its public pronouncements about the meaning of the Constitution with the justices' private faith in American exceptionalism.

On this view, the U.N. Charter influenced the outcome in *Brown* and *Bolling* in two distinct ways, even though the published decisions do not reference the Charter. First, the moral force of the Charter's anti-discrimination norm helped persuade the justices to reinterpret the Fifth and Fourteenth Amendments to address the cognitive dissonance problem. Second, as other commentators have noted, the Cold War foreign policy context influenced the Court's decisions.[111] Prior accounts that emphasize the Cold War have overlooked the fact that the advent of modern international human rights law, as codified in the U.N. Charter, shaped the foreign policy context. As discussed in Chapter 9, before adoption of the U.N. Charter the United States could easily have brushed off foreign criticism of racial discrimination in the United States by saying "it's none of your business." After adoption of the Charter's human rights provisions, that answer was no longer sufficient. Codification of international human rights norms in the U.N. Charter manifested a broad-based international agreement that domestic racial discrimination was now a proper subject of international diplomacy. The government brief in *Brown* and *Bolling* noted that "continuance of racial discrimination in the United States remains a source of constant embarrassment to this Government in the day-to-day conduct of its foreign relations."[112] That was true, in part, because codification of human rights norms in the Charter transformed race discrimination in the United States from a purely domestic issue to a foreign policy issue.

IV. THE BRICKER AMENDMENT

Senator Bricker introduced an early version of the Bricker Amendment in the Senate in February 1952, supported by fifty-eight co-sponsors.[113] The ABA House of Delegates approved its own version of a constitutional amendment later that month.[114] Over the next two years, various senators introduced about ten different versions of the so-called Bricker Amendment. The Senate Judiciary Committee held two sets of hearings on the proposed amendments: in May to June 1952, when Truman was president; and in February to April 1953, when Eisenhower was president.[115] The Judiciary Committee reported a proposed amendment to the full Senate in June 1953.[116] The decisive vote in the Senate came in February 1954, when the Senate voted 60-31 in favor of the "George substitute," falling one vote short of the required two-thirds majority.[117] Between 1952 and 1954, the Senate, the executive branch, the ABA, and others devoted substantial time and energy to the Bricker Amendment controversy.[118]

Proponents of the Bricker Amendment sought to accomplish four distinct goals: (1) to clarify that the Constitution takes precedence over a treaty in the event of a conflict, (2) to restrict the president's power to use executive agreements as a substitute for Article II treaties, (3) to overrule *Missouri v. Holland,*

and (4) to abolish the treaty supremacy rule or limit its scope so that most treaties affecting state law would not have any domestic legal effect unless Congress enacted implementing legislation. Goals 1, 3, and 4 constituted responses to the perceived threat posed by human rights treaties. Goal 2, by contrast, addressed the perceived threat posed by the rise of executive power in foreign affairs. The fourth goal is the most significant for the purpose of this book, but some commentary on the other three is necessary to understand the full scope of the Bricker Amendment controversy. Below, I first address proposals that would not have amended the treaty supremacy rule and then consider in more detail proposals that would have amended the treaty supremacy rule.

A. Proposals That Would Not Have Amended the Treaty Supremacy Rule

The Eisenhower administration supported the "Knowland substitute," introduced by acting Senate majority leader William Knowland (R-CA) in July 1953. Among other things, the Knowland substitute stipulated: "A provision of a treaty or other international agreement which conflicts with the Constitution shall not be of any force or effect."[119] Substantially identical language was included in the "George substitute," introduced by Senator Walter George (D-GA) in January 1954.[120] The proposition that any conflict between a treaty and the Constitution should be resolved in favor of the Constitution was not controversial. Many people believed that the quoted language merely restated the existing constitutional rule. However, Bricker and his supporters insisted that the matter was not settled and that a constitutional amendment was necessary to do so.[121] President Eisenhower was willing to support this provision, even though his advisors said it was not legally necessary, because he agreed that it was not harmful, and he thought he needed to support some version of the Bricker Amendment for political reasons.[122] Although the amendment never passed, the Supreme Court finally resolved the issue in 1957, deciding in *Reid v. Covert* that all conflicts between treaties and the Constitution must be resolved in favor of the Constitution.[123]

The ABA supported S.J. Res. 43, introduced by Senator Watkins in February 1953. That version of the amendment stated: "A treaty shall become effective as internal law in the United States only through legislation *which would be valid in the absence of a treaty.*" (emphasis added).[124] The highlighted language was commonly known as the "which clause." Recall that the Supreme Court decided in *Missouri v. Holland* that the combination of the Treaty Power and the Necessary and Proper Clause grants Congress the power to enact treaty-implementing legislation that would exceed the scope of Congress's Article I powers in the absence of a treaty.[125] The "which clause" would have limited Congress's power to implement treaties by overruling *Missouri v. Holland,* leaving the federal government dependent upon the states to implement treaties beyond the scope of Congress's Article I powers. Both the Truman and Eisenhower administrations strongly opposed the "which clause." They argued that the clause would severely constrain the federal government's power to implement treaties, thereby

reviving the problems that the United States experienced under the Articles of
Confederation.[126] Senator Bricker initially opposed the "which clause" because
he did not wish to impose undue constraints on Congress's legislative powers.
Later, he endorsed the clause to preserve his political alliance with ABA leaders.[127] The version of the Bricker Amendment reported to the full Senate by the
Judiciary Committee included the "which clause," despite strenuous objections
voiced by a minority on the committee.[128] The Senate as a whole never voted on
an amendment containing the "which clause." Ongoing consultations between
the Senate and the Eisenhower administration in late 1953 and early 1954 ultimately persuaded Senator Bricker to abandon the "which clause" because he
recognized that the Senate would vote against any version of the amendment
containing such a clause.[129]

Senator Bricker and ABA leaders disagreed about executive agreements. The
Supreme Court decided in *Belmont* and *Pink* that sole executive agreements—
that is, international agreements concluded by the president without Senate
consent—can supersede conflicting state laws, just as treaties supersede conflicting state laws.[130] Senator Bricker wanted to reverse or limit *Belmont* and *Pink*. The
ABA was less concerned about executive agreements. Hence, the amendment
proposed by Senator Bricker in February 1952 stated: "Executive agreements
shall not be made in lieu of treaties."[131] In contrast, the amendment approved by
the ABA House of Delegates in February 1952 was silent on the question of executive agreements.[132] The Eisenhower administration strenuously opposed limits
on the domestic effects of sole executive agreements.[133] On this point, though, the
president almost lost. The George substitute stated: "An international agreement
other than a treaty shall become effective as internal law in the United States
only by an act of the Congress."[134] The George substitute would have overruled
Belmont and *Pink* by making clear that sole executive agreements are not effective as domestic law unless Congress enacts legislation to give them domestic
legal effect. As noted previously, the Senate voted 60-31 in favor of the George
substitute, just one vote short of the necessary two-thirds majority.[135] Although
the amendment did not pass, the vote manifested substantial bipartisan support for a constitutional amendment constraining the president's power to create
domestic law by means of sole executive agreements.[136]

B. Proposals That Would Have Amended the Treaty Supremacy Rule

In June 1953, the Senate Judiciary Committee approved the following language
for consideration by the Senate: "A treaty shall become effective as internal law
in the United States only through legislation which would be valid in the absence of treaty."[137] This apparently simple sentence, if adopted as a constitutional amendment, would have accomplished three very different things. The
first part of the sentence, through the word "legislation," would have: (1) abolished the Constitution's treaty supremacy rule, and (2) made all treaties non-
self-executing (with respect to both state law and federal law). The second
part of the sentence, the "which clause," would have constrained Congress's

treaty implementing power by overruling *Missouri v. Holland.* The Judiciary
Committee's report distinguished clearly between the "which clause" and the
first half of the sentence.[138] However, neither the majority report nor the minority report distinguished clearly between the treaty supremacy issue and the self-
execution issue.[139] Indeed, almost all participants in the Bricker Amendment
debate tacitly assumed that treaty supremacy was a subset of self-execution
doctrine, rather than an independent doctrine that addressed discrete issues.
The tendency to view treaty supremacy as a subset of self-execution meant that
debates over the Bricker Amendment were clouded by a good deal of confusion. That confusion persisted, in part, because it served the political interests
of Bricker's opponents.

The Judiciary Committee report defended the proposed amendment as follows: "[W]ith respect to many treaties, it is a matter of judicial guess whether their
provisions are self-executing or not."[140] Supporters of the Bricker Amendment
contended that uncertainty about whether treaties would be classified as self-
executing or non-self-executing was a major problem because the Senate might
not know the effect of treaty ratification until several years after it consented to
ratification. Alfred Schweppe, Chairman of the ABA Committee on Peace and
Law Through the United Nations, testified:

The purpose of that [proposed amendment] is to take the Trojan-horse
element out of the treaty clause. Today a treaty is made. Two or three or
five years from now the several States find out that while everybody was
asleep, including probably Congress and the States, a provision was put in
the treaty which has the effect of invalidating a State constitutional provision or a State law. That comes about by reason of the supreme-law clause in
the sixth article, which makes treaties automatically domestic law.... What
this sentence [in the proposed constitutional amendment] does is to render
all treaties non-self-executing.[141]

Similarly, Senator Bricker testified: "The celebrated *Fujii* case in California is a
more recent reminder that treaties may have far-reaching and unintended consequences as a result of the American Constitution's unique treaty supremacy
clause."[142] The Judiciary Committee report added: "It seems reasonably certain
that if articles 55 and 56 [of the U.N. Charter] represent self-executing legal obligations, thousands of Federal and State laws have been superseded. No such
possibility would exist if the proposed amendment had been in effect at the
time the Senate gave its consent to ratification of the United Nations Charter."[143]
Therefore, the Committee concluded, the proposed amendment would eliminate the "Trojan-horse element" by removing "the question of the self-executing
nature of a treaty from the realm of judicial speculation and mak[ing] the internal effectiveness of the treaty within the United States depend exclusively on
statutes passed by" Congress or state legislatures.[144]

The Eisenhower administration opposed the proposal to make all treaties
non-self-executing, but it was prepared to compromise on the self-execution

issue. (In contrast, it refused to compromise on the "which clause" or executive agreements.) After the Judiciary Committee issued its report, the administration persuaded Senator Knowland to introduce a competing amendment (the "Knowland substitute").[145] On the same day that Senator Knowland introduced his substitute amendment in the Senate, "the White House released a statement by President Eisenhower in which he gave his 'unqualified support' to the Knowland substitute resolution."[146] Section 3 of the Knowland substitute stated: "When the Senate so provides in its consent to ratification, a treaty shall become effective as internal law in the United States only through enactment of appropriate legislation by the Congress."[147] Section 3 effectively created a presumption that treaties are both self-executing and supreme over state law, while permitting the Senate to reverse that presumption by adopting an appropriate condition when it consents to ratification. The Eisenhower administration was prepared to accept Section 3 of the Knowland substitute because it gave the president and Senate the flexibility to decide, on a case-by-case basis, whether a particular treaty would be self-executing and whether it would be supreme over state law. Thus, the Eisenhower administration supported an optional treaty supremacy rule.

Bricker and his supporters opposed the Knowland substitute because, in their view, it did not provide sufficient safeguards against the unanticipated domestic consequences of treaty ratification. Commenting on a similar proposal advanced by the ABA section on international law,[148] Alfred Schweppe said:

> We have been engaged in this study jointly for a period of time with the section on international law of the American Bar Association. ... The gentlemen of the international law section ... were of the view that you can control this thing sufficiently by putting clauses in the treaties, or by making reservations to treaties. The committee on peace and law ... does not believe that there is an effective answer to the extension of Federal power over the internal affairs of the States by the treaty method. We think that the appropriate remedy is a constitutional amendment which will take us over and above the language of anything that anybody can write into a treaty, or fail to get written into a treaty.[149]

Schweppe's comment related to a proposal that differed slightly from the Knowland substitute, but the underlying concern was the same. Schweppe, Bricker, and others were troubled by the "Trojan-horse element" of treaty ratification. In light of the *Fujii* case, they worried that—if the United States adopted a constitutional amendment along the lines of the Knowland substitute—the Senate could still consent to ratification of a treaty based on one set of expectations, only to learn later that courts applied the treaty in unexpected ways.

Senator Knowland introduced his substitute amendment in July 1953, but the Senate adjourned for the rest of the year in August without taking action on any proposed amendment.[150] When the Bricker Amendment finally came to the Senate floor in February 1954, three different versions of the amendment were presented for Senate consideration: the "Knowland-Ferguson" proposal, the "George substitute," and the Bricker proposal.[151] President Eisenhower supported the Knowland-Ferguson proposal. That text stated: "A provision of a treaty or other international agreement which conflicts with this Constitution shall not be of any force or effect."[152] The Knowland-Ferguson proposal said nothing about self-execution, executive agreements, or *Missouri v. Holland*; it merely reaffirmed the supremacy of the Constitution over treaties. The Senate never voted on the merits of Knowland-Ferguson because the Senate voted, instead, to replace Knowland-Ferguson with the George substitute.[153] (The vote to replace Knowland-Ferguson with the George substitute was a major political coup for Lyndon Johnson, the Senate minority leader.[154]) As noted previously, the George substitute did not address treaties, but it would have made all sole executive agreements non-self-executing.

Only one of the three proposals presented to the full Senate in February 1954 addressed the self-executing character of treaties.[155] The version supported by Senator Bricker at that time said: "A treaty or other international agreement shall become effective as internal law in the United States only through legislation by the Congress unless in advising and consenting to a treaty the Senate ... shall provide that such treaty may become effective as internal law without legislation by the Congress."[156] The Bricker proposal was similar to the Knowland substitute introduced in July 1953, but the two proposals differed in two key respects. First, whereas the Knowland substitute created a rebuttable presumption in favor of both self-execution and treaty supremacy, the Bricker proposal introduced in February 1954 created a rebuttable presumption against both self-execution and treaty supremacy. Second, the Bricker proposal made all executive agreements non-self-executing (like the George substitute), whereas the Knowland substitute was silent on the self-executing character of executive agreements. The Senate voted on Bricker's proposal on February 25. The final tally was forty-two votes in favor and fifty votes against.[157] Thus, Bricker failed to gain majority support for his proposal to make treaties presumptively non-self-executing. Nevertheless, as discussed in the next section, the Bricker Amendment controversy had a decisive impact on the process of invisible constitutional change.

C. Unexamined Constitutional Assumptions

Throughout the Bricker Amendment debates, virtually all the participants—with the notable exception of Quincy Wright—framed their arguments in a way that viewed treaty supremacy as a subset of self-execution issues. Various proposed amendments stated that treaties or executive agreements would not "become effective as internal law without legislation by the Congress."[158] The phrase "effective as internal law" appeared in the resolution approved by the ABA House of Delegates in February 1952, the amendment introduced by Senator Bricker in January 1953, the amendment approved by the Senate Judiciary Committee in June 1953, the Knowland substitute introduced in July 1953, the George substitute introduced in January 1954, and the text proposed by Senator Bricker in

February 1954.[159] Participants in the debate used the phrase "effective as internal law" to express both the idea of treaty supremacy (i.e., treaties supersede conflicting state laws) and the idea of self-execution (i.e., treaties operate as law for federal executive officials and supersede conflicting federal statutes).[160] From the Founding until 1945, legislative, executive, and judicial authorities consistently treated self-execution and treaty supremacy as distinct concepts. The Bricker Amendment debates expanded the concept of self-execution to absorb the previously distinct treaty supremacy rule.

The merger of self-execution and treaty supremacy served the political objectives of Bricker's opponents. To understand why, recall that opposition to human rights treaties was the primary factor motivating Bricker and his allies.[161] Many of those who opposed the Bricker Amendment shared Bricker's view that human rights treaties posed a threat to the United States' constitutional system.[162] However, they argued, a constitutional amendment was not necessary to address that threat because *Article II already granted the president and Senate the power to render treaties non-self-executing*, either by including appropriate language in the treaty itself, or by adopting a unilateral reservation at the time of ratification. Attorney General Brownell, Secretary of State Dulles, and Harold Stassen (whom Eisenhower had appointed as the Director of the Mutual Security Administration) all presented variants of this argument in their official Senate testimony.[163] The New York City Bar Association made a similar argument.[164] The minority view in the Senate Judiciary Committee report advanced this argument.[165] Senator George presented the argument during floor debate.[166] President Eisenhower, himself, made a similar argument in a private letter to John McCloy.[167] They all articulated a similar message: "We recognize that human rights treaties pose a potential threat, but we can address that threat by adopting treaty language or unilateral reservations to ensure that such treaties are not self-executing. Therefore, a constitutional amendment is unnecessary." The repeated assertion of this message was instrumental in defeating the Bricker Amendment.

Let us examine the claim that Article II grants the president and Senate the power to render treaties non-self-executing. Consider three different variants of that claim, which correspond to the condition precedent doctrine, the intent doctrine, and the *Fujii* doctrine. The *condition precedent doctrine* holds that the executive branch has the power to render treaties non-self-executing by inserting language in the treaty that makes federal legislation a precondition for the treaty to enter into force internationally. That doctrine is supported by executive treaty-making practice since at least 1854.[168] The claim that Article II grants the treaty makers such a power is not controversial.

The *intent doctrine* holds that Article II grants the treaty makers an affirmative power to make decisions about domestic law that are not contingent on the content or scope of the international obligation—specifically, that a treaty will not supersede federal statutes, and will not operate as law for federal executive officials, even after the treaty enters into force internationally.[169] The treaty makers can exercise that power either by inserting appropriate language in the treaty or by adopting a unilateral reservation. By 1944, when Green Hackworth published his *Digest of International Law,* the doctrine had gained broad acceptance within the executive branch because it facilitated the rise of executive power in foreign affairs.[170] The intent doctrine does not constitute an exception to the Constitution's treaty supremacy rule because the doctrine does not address the relationship between treaties and state law.

Neither the condition precedent doctrine nor the intent doctrine served the political objectives of Bricker's opponents because neither doctrine addressed the relationship between treaties and state law. To assuage the fears of Bricker and his supporters, it was essential to claim that Article II granted the treaty makers the power to render *human rights treaties* non-self-executing. Human rights treaties posed a threat, from Bricker's standpoint, precisely because such treaties could supersede conflicting state laws. Hence, Bricker's opponents advanced the *Fujii doctrine.* That doctrine holds that Article II grants the treaty makers an affirmative power to make decisions about domestic law that are not contingent on the content or scope of the international obligation. Specifically, the treaty makers have the power to adopt treaty text or unilateral reservations whose legal effect is to prevent treaties from superseding conflicting state laws.[171] The *Fujii* doctrine is directly contrary to the original understanding of the Supremacy Clause: that all treaties supersede conflicting state laws, and that the treaty supremacy rule operates automatically as a conflict of laws rule that is binding on the judiciary.[172] Almost all legislative, executive, and judicial authorities from the Founding until World War II were consistent with the original understanding of the treaty supremacy rule.[173] As of 1954, the California Supreme Court decision in *Fujii* was the only published judicial decision that supported the *Fujii* doctrine. As of 1954, the United States had not ratified any treaty in which the executive branch relied on the *Fujii* doctrine in its treaty-making capacity.[174] Nevertheless, Bricker's opponents consistently maintained that Article II empowered the treaty makers to adopt treaty text or unilateral reservations to exclude particular treaties or treaty provisions from the ordinary operation of the Constitution's treaty supremacy rule. In short, they contended that the treaty supremacy rule is optional, not mandatory. That argument helped persuade previously undecided senators to vote against Bricker's proposed amendment, which would have rendered all treaties presumptively non-self-executing.

Chapter 14 contends that a "changed circumstances" argument supports the conclusion that the *Fujii* doctrine is a defensible interpretation of the Constitution. At present, three points bear emphasis. First, the implicit constitutional assumption underlying the *Fujii* doctrine is very different from the assumptions underlying either the condition precedent doctrine or the intent doctrine. Second, when Bricker's opponents asserted repeatedly that Article II grants the treaty makers the power to render treaties non-self-executing, they consistently obfuscated the distinctions among the *Fujii* doctrine, the intent doctrine, and the condition precedent doctrine. By obfuscating those distinctions, they effectively expanded the concept of self-execution to swallow the previously distinct treaty supremacy rule. Third, there is no evidence that any

of the major players on either side of the debate—with the notable exception
of Quincy Wright—recognized that the expansion of self-execution doctrine to
encompass treaty supremacy heralded a dramatic change in the constitutional
rules governing the relationship between treaties and state law. Thus, the Bricker
Amendment debate gave rise to a new constitutional understanding through a
process of invisible constitutional change.

12

Business as Usual in the Courts: 1946–1965

Parts One and Two demonstrated that, before 1945, NSE doctrine had no significant impact on the relationship between treaties and state law. In treaty supremacy cases—that is, cases in which one or more parties alleged a conflict between a treaty and state law—the courts uniformly applied the treaty supremacy rule, without any exception for NSE treaties. Chapter 13 focuses on the Restatement (Second) of Foreign Relations Law, which the ALI published in 1965. The Restatement endorsed an NSE exception to the treaty supremacy rule: the proposition that NSE treaties do not supersede conflicting state laws.

This chapter analyzes judicial decisions between 1946 and 1965 to determine whether those decisions support an NSE exception to the treaty supremacy rule. The short answer is that U.S. Supreme Court decisions from this period provide no support whatsoever for an NSE exception to the treaty supremacy rule. In contrast, decisions by state courts and lower federal courts present a more mixed record. Most of those cases are consistent with the traditional conceptual firewall that separated treaty supremacy cases from self-execution cases. However, a few judicial decisions by state courts and lower federal courts in the 1950s and early 1960s show that the traditional firewall was beginning to erode during this period. Even so, the California Supreme Court decision in *Fujii* (in 1952) and a federal district court decision in 1961 are the only two published decisions from this period that clearly support an NSE exception to the treaty supremacy rule.[1] Both cases involved claims based on the human rights provisions of the U.N. Charter. Therefore, when the ALI published its Restatement in 1965, it could have endorsed the position that all treaties supersede conflicting state laws, except for the human rights provisions of the U.N. Charter. That position would be difficult to defend on a principled basis, but it would have been entirely consistent with every published judicial decision since the Founding. Instead, the ALI endorsed a much broader NSE exception to the treaty supremacy rule. The next chapter will examine the Restatement in more detail. This chapter reviews judicial decisions in treaty cases in the period after World War II.

This chapter is divided into three sections. The first addresses U.S. Supreme Court decisions in treaty cases between 1946 and 1965. The second analyzes decisions by state courts in treaty supremacy cases between 1949 and 1962. The final section discusses judicial decisions between 1949 and 1962 in which courts used the term "self-executing" in reference to a treaty or international agreement. (*See* p. 260 for an explanation of the choice of starting and ending dates.)

I. U.S. SUPREME COURT DECISIONS IN TREATY CASES

The Supreme Court issued sixteen decisions between 1946 and 1965 in which a party raised a treaty-based claim or defense and one or more justices relied expressly on a treaty to support his opinion.[2] In only two of those cases—*Clark v. Allen*[3] and *Kolovrat v. Oregon*[4]—did the Court squarely address an alleged conflict between a treaty and state law.[5] In both cases, the Court applied the treaty supremacy rule to override state law, without even hinting at a possible exception for NSE treaties.

In *Clark*, a California resident died in 1942, leaving real and personal property in the state. In her will, she bequeathed her entire estate to four relatives who were nationals and residents of Germany. The German nationals were not eligible legatees under the California Probate Code. Accordingly, six California residents contested the will, claiming that they were the rightful heirs under California law.[6] The Alien Property Custodian, a federal administrator charged with administering the Trading with the Enemy Act, intervened on behalf of the German nationals. He invoked Article IV of a 1923 treaty with Germany, which protected the right of German nationals to inherit real property in the United States. The Court said that if "the provisions of the treaty have not been superseded or abrogated they prevail over any requirements of California law which conflict with them."[7] In making this statement, the Court did not include any caveat for NSE treaties. Thus, the statement implies that the treaty would prevail over conflicting provisions of California law, regardless of whether the treaty is self-executing or non-self-executing. The Court concluded that the Trading with the Enemy Act, a federal statute, had not superseded or abrogated Article IV of the 1923 treaty with Germany.[8] Accordingly, Article IV was still good law. The Court noted that "[r]ights of succession to property are determined by local law." However, it added: "Those rights may be affected by an overriding federal policy, as where a treaty makes different or conflicting arrangements. . . . Then the state policy must give way."[9] The Court held expressly that the treaty trumped state law with respect to real property.[10] In so holding, the Court did not even mention the distinction between self-executing and non-self-executing treaties. Thus, the Court's opinion implies that the doctrine of self-execution is simply not relevant to cases involving alleged conflicts between treaties and state law. In this respect, the Court's opinion was entirely consistent with judicial precedent from the Founding until World War II.

The Court decided *Clark* in 1947, before the Bricker Amendment controversy had emerged. It decided *Kolovrat v. Oregon* in 1961,[11] several years after the controversy had subsided. One might surmise that the Bricker Amendment debate in the 1950s would influence the Court's application of the treaty supremacy rule in *Kolovrat*. In fact, the Court applied the treaty supremacy rule in *Kolovrat* without any exception for NSE treaties, just as it had in dozens of other treaty supremacy cases since the Founding. *Kolovrat* involved two consolidated cases in which Yugoslav nationals claimed the right to inherit property from individuals who died intestate in Oregon. The state claimed that the property escheated to the state, because Oregon law "severely limits the rights of aliens not living in the United States to take either real or personal property or its proceeds in Oregon by succession or testamentary disposition."[12] The foreign nationals invoked an 1881 treaty with Serbia that, in their view, protected their right to inherit their relatives' personal property. The Court held "that the 1881 Treaty does entitle petitioners to inherit personal property located in Oregon on the same basis as American next of kin."[13] In so holding, the Court explained that "state policies as to the rights of aliens to inherit must give way under our Constitution's Supremacy Clause to overriding federal treaties."[14] As in *Clark*, the Court said nothing whatsoever about the distinction between self-executing and non-self-executing treaties. Thus, the Court's rationale in *Kolovrat* is consistent with the proposition that all treaties supersede conflicting state laws, regardless of whether the treaty at issue is self-executing or non-self-executing. As of 1961, no Supreme Court decision had ever suggested otherwise.

Between 1946 and 1965, the Supreme Court decided only one case that includes any discussion of self-execution. In *Warren v. United States*,[15] a seaman filed a libel against the United States as the owner of the steamship *Anna Howard Shaw*. The seaman sought "maintenance and cure" for injuries he suffered by falling off a balcony while he was on shore leave.[16] Article 2, paragraph 1 of the Shipowners' Liability Convention, a multilateral treaty, imposed liability on shipowners for injuries sustained by seamen. Paragraph 2 of Article 2 authorized states to adopt national laws or regulations creating exceptions to the liability rule in paragraph 1 for injuries caused by "the wilful act, default or misbehaviour of the" injured person.[17] Warren, the seaman, argued "that under paragraph 1 a shipowner's duty to provide maintenance and cure is absolute and that the exceptions specified in paragraph 2 are not operative until a statute is enacted which puts them in force."[18] In other words, he claimed that paragraph 1 was self-executing, but paragraph 2 was not self-executing.[19] The Court rejected this view. It said: "Our conclusion is that the exceptions permitted by paragraph 2 are operative by virtue of the general maritime law and that no Act of Congress is necessary to give them force."[20] In short, paragraph 2 was self-executing because no legislation was necessary to give it effect. Even so, the Court ruled in favor of Warren on the grounds that his negligent conduct that caused the injury was not "wilful misbehavior within the meaning of the Convention."[21] Hence, the government was liable to Warren for maintenance and cure.

Warren is the only Supreme Court case between 1946 and 1965 that includes any explicit discussion of self-execution.[22] No issue of state law was present in *Warren*; the disputed issues were governed entirely by the treaty and federal maritime law. *Warren* is important because it is consistent with the traditional understanding of self-execution doctrine: that the distinction between self-executing and non-self-executing treaties has no bearing on the relationship between treaties and state law. Given that the Court decided sixteen treaty cases during this period, and *Warren* was the only one that explicitly addressed self-execution, one might infer that the justices during this time frame did not think the distinction between SE and NSE treaties was very important. Regardless, the doctrine of self-execution gained greater importance after the ALI published the Second Restatement.

II. TREATY SUPREMACY CASES IN STATE COURTS

"Treaty supremacy cases" are cases in which one or more parties alleged a conflict between a treaty and state law. Identifying treaty supremacy cases is challenging. Any single electronic search yields a set of cases that is both under and overinclusive. Accordingly, I conducted a series of electronic searches to identify published state court decisions in treaty supremacy cases. Those searches identified twenty-nine such cases between 1949 and 1962.[23] The searches may have missed a few cases, but the set of twenty-nine cases addressed here is a reasonably complete set of published state court decisions in treaty supremacy cases in the relevant time period.

I chose 1949 as the starting date because that was the first year in which lawyers initiated efforts outside the courts to create an NSE exception to the treaty supremacy rule.[24] I chose 1962 as the ending date because the ALI published a Proposed Official Draft of the Restatement in 1962.[25] The Proposed Official Draft was widely disseminated; courts began citing it as authority as early as 1962.[26] Moreover, the ALI did not make any substantive changes in the sections related to treaty supremacy or self-execution between publication of the Proposed Official Draft and publication of the final version in 1965. Therefore, analysis of state court decisions between 1949 and 1962 shows the extent to which political controversies surrounding international human rights law and the Bricker Amendment influenced state court decisions in run-of-the-mill treaty supremacy cases before the ALI published its Restatement.

In many treaty supremacy cases, state courts expressly affirmed the Constitution's treaty supremacy rule without mentioning any exception for NSE treaties. For example, in a case involving distribution of a decedent's assets to foreign nationals, the Appellate Division of the New York Supreme Court stated: "It is true, under general principles too familiar to require the citation of authorities, that a treaty between this country and a foreign power becomes the supreme law of the land and any local statute must yield if there is a conflict between the two."[27] Similarly, in a case involving criminal prosecution of Native Americans for violating state fishing laws, the Washington Supreme Court said: "The [United States] supreme court has consistently held that Indian treaties have the same force and effect as treaties with foreign nations, and consequently are the supreme law of the land and are binding upon state courts and state legislatures notwithstanding state laws to the contrary."[28] In a dispute over title to land in Mississippi, the Mississippi Supreme Court stated: "[E]very treaty made by the authority of the United States is superior to the constitution or laws of any individual state. If the law of a state is contrary to a treaty, it is void."[29] And in a case involving local government taxation of foreign aircraft, the California Supreme Court stated: "The international treaties upon which plaintiff relies . . . are not the Congressional action contemplated by the commerce clause . . . . But they are equally binding on the states. Treaties are the supreme law of the land, binding upon the courts of every state (art. VI, clause 2). If the tax here under review is repugnant to the terms of any such treaty, the tax must be declared invalid."[30] In these and other cases, state courts applied the Constitution's treaty supremacy rule without mentioning any exception for NSE treaties.[31] If courts believed that there was an NSE exception to the treaty supremacy rule, they would presumably have decided explicitly that the treaty at issue was self-executing before applying the treaty to override state law. Their persistent silence with respect to self-execution provides strong evidence that most state courts in the 1950s and early 1960s did not believe there was an NSE exception to the treaty supremacy rule.

Courts reached the merits of the treaty supremacy issue in twenty-seven of the twenty-nine treaty supremacy cases under review.[32] Consider, first, the two cases in which courts declined to reach the merits. The California Supreme Court decision in *Fujii v. California*,[33] discussed extensively in Chapter 11, was the only state court decision between 1949 and 1962 in which a state court invoked NSE doctrine as a rationale for declining to reach the merits of a claim that a treaty superseded conflicting state law. In the only other case where a court declined to reach the merits of the treaty supremacy issue, a prisoner filed a habeas petition challenging his extradition from California to Mississippi. The California court invoked well-established principles limiting the scope of habeas review in extradition cases to justify its refusal to address the merits of petitioner's constitutional or treaty-based claims.[34]

The twenty-seven cases where courts addressed the merits of treaty supremacy issues can be divided into two groups. In eighteen of twenty-seven cases, courts held that the treaty superseded conflicting state law.[35] In the other nine cases, courts determined that there was no conflict between the treaty and state law.[36]

Consider, first, the eighteen cases where courts held that a treaty superseded conflicting state law. In only two of those cases did the court hold that the treaty at issue was self-executing. In *Salamon v. Royal Dutch Airlines*,[37] plaintiff sued the airline for the wrongful death of her testator. She claimed that the airline's willful misconduct caused the death of the decedent when he was traveling from Amsterdam to New York City. The Court held that she had a valid cause of action against the airline under the Warsaw Convention. It said that the "Convention, as a treaty, constitutes part of the law of this land, overriding state law and policies . . . its provisions supersede the usual doctrine that the right and measure of recovery are governed by the *lex loci*."[38] It also added that the Convention was self-executing "and that its provisions do not require implementation and may be enforced in the same manner as if enacted by statute."[39] In *Iannone v. Radory Construction Corp.*,[40] a state workmen's compensation board awarded death benefits to the widow and daughter of a U.S. resident who sustained fatal injuries in an industrial accident. Under state law, non-resident aliens received reduced benefits. Hence, the board granted claimants only half the usual award because they were residents and nationals of Italy. The claimants argued that they were entitled to full benefits because a bilateral treaty with Italy superseded New York law. The court ruled in favor of the claimants. It quoted the Supremacy Clause and said: "[A]s the treaty is self-executing, it operates without the need of any legislation. Hence, it must be applied and given authoritative effect by the courts of this State."[41] *Salamon* and *Iannone* show that some state courts in the 1950s believed that self-execution doctrine was relevant to treaty supremacy cases. However, neither case supports an NSE exception to the treaty supremacy rule, because the courts in both cases held expressly that the treaty at issue superseded state law.

Apart from *Salamon* and *Iannone*, the data set includes sixteen other cases where state courts applied treaties to override conflicting state laws.[42] None of those cases say anything about self-execution. In all sixteen cases, courts applied the relevant treaties to override conflicting state laws without pausing to consider whether the treaty at issue was self-executing or non-self-executing. If, between 1949 and 1962, courts believed that NSE treaties do not supersede conflicting state laws, then they should have determined whether the treaties at issue were self-executing *before* deciding that the treaties superseded conflicting state laws. The fact that courts did not even consider the self-execution issue in sixteen of eighteen cases provides strong evidence that most state courts during this period did not believe there was an NSE exception to the Constitution's treaty supremacy rule.[43]

Consider, next, the nine cases where courts held that there was no conflict between the relevant treaty and state law. In eight of those nine cases, courts addressed the merits of the treaty supremacy claim without pausing to consider whether the treaty at issue was self-executing.[44] Those eight cases neither support nor refute the proposition that there is an NSE exception to the Constitution's treaty supremacy rule. The fact that courts decided the merits of the treaty supremacy claims without addressing the self-execution issue might mean that courts did not believe the self-execution issue was relevant. However, the courts' silence with respect to self-execution might also mean that they did not believe it was necessary to discuss self-execution in a case where there was no conflict between the treaty and state law.

Milliken v. State is the only case in this group where the court said something about self-execution.[45] In *Milliken*, the State of Florida prosecuted Milliken for violating a state statute that regulated the taking of shrimp in the Tortugas shrimp bed. Milliken argued that the statute was invalid because it conflicted with a treaty between the United States and Cuba. The treaty called for establishment of a commission composed of U.S. and Cuban nationals. The commission was charged with "obtaining scientific information concerning shrimp in the convention area, publishing its findings and adopting such regulations as are necessary to effectuate the purposes of the convention."[46] Milliken offered no evidence that the commission envisioned by the treaty had ever been constituted, or that it had adopted any regulations. Even so, he argued that the treaty "serves to preempt the field of shrimp conservation in the subject area and that therefore any Florida statute purporting to regulate the taking of shrimp in the Tortugas Shrimp Beds is inoperative and unenforceable."[47] The Court conceded that "the laws of the state relating to the same subject-matter shall be abrogated" if and when the commission actually adopted regulations.[48] However, it said: "Until the regulations and restrictions contemplated by the treaty shall be agreed upon and until the date of their being put into operation shall be proclaimed, the treaty is of no effect in displacing or superseding the authority of the State laws."[49] In this context, the court said that "a treaty provision will not operate to supersede or suspend a state statute if the treaty is not self-executing and if no implementing legislation has been enacted."[50] Given that Congress had not enacted legislation to implement the treaty with Cuba, and that the commission envisioned by the treaty had never promulgated any regulations related to shrimping in the Tortugas shrimp bed, the State of Florida remained free to enforce its own laws.

The statement in *Milliken* to the effect that a treaty does not supersede a state law "if the treaty is not self-executing" clearly provides some support for the proposition that an NSE treaty does not supersede conflicting state laws. However, *Milliken* provides only weak support for the *Fujii* doctrine because the treaty at issue did not contain any substantive rule governing shrimping in the Tortugas shrimp bed. The treaty merely called for the creation of a commission that would be empowered to adopt substantive rules. Until the commission actually promulgated such rules, there was simply no conflict to which the treaty supremacy rule could apply. Thus, although *Milliken* is somewhat ambiguous, it is best construed as a case in which the Court held that the state law was valid because there was no conflict between the treaty and state law.

In sum, state court decisions during this period were generally consistent with the traditional treaty supremacy rule. However, four of the twenty-nine cases under review—*Milliken, Salamon, Iannone, and Fujii*—show that the conceptual firewall that had previously separated treaty supremacy doctrine from self-execution doctrine began to erode in the 1950s. Even so, *Fujii* is the only one of the four cases that unambiguously supports an NSE exception to the Constitution's treaty supremacy rule. Conversely, the fifteen cases where courts applied treaties to override state laws without discussing the self-execution issue provide strong evidence that most state courts during this period did not believe there was an NSE exception to the treaty supremacy rule.

III. SELF-EXECUTION CASES IN LOWER FEDERAL COURTS

Between 1949 and 1962, inclusive, state and federal courts in the United States issued only nineteen published judicial opinions that use the word "self-executing" in conjunction with "treaty."[51] Five of those cases have already been discussed earlier in this chapter: the U.S. Supreme Court decision in *Warren v. United States*, and state court decisions in *Salamon v. Royal Dutch Airlines*,

Iannone v. Radory Construction Corp., Fujii v. California, and *Milliken v. State.*
This section addresses the other fourteen published opinions during this period
that explicitly discuss self-execution. Those fourteen cases include five federal
appellate opinions,[52] seven federal district court opinions,[53] and two Court of
Claims opinions.[54]

Before we address the substance of those cases, one point merits brief comment. It is difficult, if not impossible, to determine the precise number of "treaty
cases" in which state and federal courts issued published opinions between 1949
and 1962, but there were probably hundreds of such cases during the relevant time
period.[55] The fact that only nineteen of those cases use the word "self-executing"
in conjunction with "treaty" is significant. The dearth of cases involving self-
execution suggests that state and federal courts before 1962 did not believe that
self-execution doctrine was very important. In contrast, self-execution doctrine
became more salient after the ALI published the Restatement (Second).

Ten of the fourteen cases under review raised only questions of federal law,
not state law. Those ten cases include one international extradition case,[56] one
suit to enjoin federal government action,[57] one deportation case,[58] two federal
criminal prosecutions,[59] two suits in the Court of Claims seeking compensation
from the United States,[60] and three cases involving federal admiralty or maritime law.[61] Those ten cases are consistent with the vast majority of self-execution
cases before World War II, inasmuch as no state law issues were implicated.

The other four cases merit more extended discussion. In *Bowater S.S. Co.
v. Patterson,* the British owner of a vessel sued a longshoremen's union because
the union members refused to unload plaintiff's cargo at the port in Buffalo,
New York.[62] Plaintiff raised a claim under an 1815 treaty with Great Britain. The
court held that the relevant treaty provision was self-executing.[63] Moreover, the
court added that "the treaty must be interpreted as meaning that the specified
foreigners will be protected from interference with their rights to use American
ports when that interference constitutes a tort under either federal or state law."[64]
The Second Circuit remanded the case to the district court to determine whether
the union's conduct was tortious under state law. Thus, although *Bowater* implicated some state law issues, it was not a treaty supremacy case because no party
alleged a conflict between a treaty and state law.

In *Vanity Fair Mills, Inc. v. T. Eaton Co.,* a U.S. manufacturer sued a Canadian
company for trademark infringement.[65] The plaintiff also raised a state law claim
for unfair competition. Plaintiff contended that the 1883 Paris Convention, a
multilateral trademark treaty, as revised in 1934, was self-executing. The court
agreed with plaintiff's view that "no special legislation in the United States was
necessary to make the International Convention effective here."[66] However, the
court held that the Convention did not create "private rights under American
law for acts of unfair competition occurring in foreign countries."[67] Although
the plaintiff in *Vanity Fair Mills* raised a state law claim for unfair competition,
it was not a treaty supremacy case because no party alleged a conflict between a
treaty and state law. Therefore, both *Vanity Fair Mills* and *Bowater* are consistent with the proposition that, before the ALI published its Restatement, courts

generally behaved as if they believed that self-execution doctrine was not relevant to treaty supremacy cases.

However, the two other cases in this group—*Camacho v. Rogers*[68] and *Aerovias Interamericanas de Panama v. Dade County Port Authority*[69]—show that the conceptual firewall that had previously separated self-execution cases from treaty supremacy cases was beginning to erode during this period. In *Camacho*, plaintiffs sued to enjoin enforcement of New York statutory and constitutional provisions that required English language literacy as a precondition for eligibility to vote. They raised several distinct claims, including one claim based on the human rights provisions of the U.N. Charter. The district court rejected plaintiffs' treaty supremacy claim on the grounds that the Charter's human rights provisions are not self-executing.[70] In so holding, the district court relied heavily on the California Supreme Court's prior opinion in *Fujii*.

In *Aerovias Interamericanas*, a group of twelve foreign airlines sued the Dade County Port Authority, a political subdivision of the State of Florida that operated the international airport in Miami. Defendant charged higher rates to foreign airlines than to domestic ones. Plaintiffs claimed that the discriminatory rate schedule violated applicable provisions of the Chicago Convention, a multilateral treaty, and of certain bilateral air transport treaties. The District Court held that Article 15 "of the Chicago Convention, and the corresponding article of the various Air Transport Service Agreements, are self-executing, requiring no legislation in order to effect their command by this Court."[71] The District Court ruled in favor of the foreign airlines, holding that defendant's rate schedule was inconsistent with controlling treaty provisions, which took precedence over regulations promulgated by a state agency. The Fifth Circuit reversed. The Fifth Circuit did not discuss the self-execution issue, holding instead that the Port Authority's rate schedule did not conflict with U.S. treaty obligations.[72] Both *Camacho* and *Aerovias Interamericanas* show that, circa 1950 to 1960, at least some federal district courts believed that self-execution doctrine was relevant to treaty supremacy cases. However, only *Camacho* supports an NSE exception to the treaty supremacy rule, because the court in *Aerovias Interamericanas* held explicitly that the subject treaties were self-executing.

In sum, most cases during the period under review in which courts explicitly addressed self-execution doctrine did not involve any state law issues. As in earlier periods, most courts continued to behave as if they believed that self-execution doctrine was a federal separation-of-powers doctrine that had no bearing on the relationship between treaties and state law.

* * *

Judicial decisions tend to follow well-worn paths, at least until some outside shock diverts the course of judicial decision-making onto a new one. From the Founding until World War II, treaty supremacy cases and self-execution cases proceeded along two independent, non-intersecting paths. The controversy over human rights law and the Bricker Amendment created a shock to the system. Surprisingly, though, that outside shock had relatively little impact on judicial decision-making in treaty supremacy cases before the ALI published the Proposed

Official Draft of the Second Restatement in 1962. Between 1946 and 1962, the majority of treaty supremacy cases and self-execution cases continued along their well-trodden, non-intersecting paths, although the paths intersected in a handful of decisions by state courts and lower federal courts. Even so, the Bricker Amendment controversy exerted significant influence over the ALI Reporters who drafted the Second Restatement. Operating in the shadow of the Bricker Amendment, the Reporters codified an NSE exception to the Constitution's treaty supremacy rule. The next chapter addresses the Restatement.

The American Law Institute and the Restatement of Foreign Relations Law

The American Law Institute (ALI) published the Restatement (Second) of Foreign Relations Law in 1965. Section 141 says that a non-self-executing (NSE) treaty does not "supersede inconsistent provisions ... of the law of the several states." Section 154(2) says that a treaty is self-executing only if it "manifests an intention that its provisions shall be effective under the domestic law of the parties at the time it" enters into force internationally. The two provisions together express an optional treaty supremacy rule. A treaty is supreme over state law only if the drafters intended its provisions to be "effective under the domestic law" of the United States in the absence of implementing legislation. As a practical matter, the Restatement consolidated the transformation of the treaty supremacy rule from a mandatory to an optional rule. Before publication of the Restatement in 1965, no federal appellate court had endorsed the NSE exception to the treaty supremacy rule.[1] The leading authorities supporting the NSE exception were the California Supreme Court decision in *Fujii*, the federal district court decision in *Camacho v. Rogers*,[2] and statements by various government officials in the context of the Bricker Amendment debate.[3] *Fujii* was a state court decision, *Camacho* was a lower court decision, and the records of the Bricker Amendment debates were not easily accessible to courts. The Restatement provided an easily accessible, authoritative source that courts could cite to support the optional supremacy rule.

This chapter reviews the drafting history of the Restatement between 1951 and 1965 to shed light on the ALI's role in consolidating the transformation of the treaty supremacy rule. The first section presents short biographies of the main people responsible for producing the Restatement. The next provides a brief chronology of events to give the reader an overview of the process. The third carefully reviews successive drafts that ultimately produced Section 141 and related provisions. The final two sections address two central questions. First, why did the ALI endorse the optional treaty supremacy rule? Second, what impact did the Restatement have on the subsequent development of the law?

I. THE PRINCIPAL ACTORS

Judge Herbert Goodrich served as a judge on the U.S. Court of Appeals for the Third Circuit from 1940 until his death in 1962. President Roosevelt planned to nominate him for a position as an associate justice on the U.S. Supreme Court. However, the nomination was sitting on Roosevelt's desk when he died in 1945; it was never transmitted to the Senate. While serving as a federal judge, Goodrich also served as the director of the ALI from 1947 until 1962, and as the assistant director of the ALI from 1944 to 1947. Before his appointment to the Third Circuit, Goodrich was the dean of the University of Pennsylvania Law School. He also worked as a law professor at the University of Iowa and University of Michigan law schools. Goodrich was a leading expert in the conflict of laws, but he had no special expertise in U.S. foreign relations law. Nevertheless, he played a key role in launching the ALI project that ultimately produced the Restatement on Foreign Relations Law. Goodrich secured funding for the project, helped assemble the team of reporters and advisers who worked on it, and maintained steady pressure on the reporters to complete their work until his untimely death in June 1962.[4]

At the request of Judge Goodrich, Edwin Dickinson prepared a memo in January 1951 that sketched the outlines of a proposal for a "project in international law."[5] By 1951, Dickinson and Goodrich had known each other for many years. They were colleagues on the University of Michigan law faculty from 1922 to 1929. They both attended Carleton College in Minnesota, but it is unclear whether they knew each other at Carleton, because Dickinson graduated two years before Goodrich. After leaving the University of Michigan faculty in 1933, Dickinson taught at U.C. Berkeley (1933–1948) and the University of Pennsylvania (1948–1956). He served as the dean of the School of Jurisprudence at Berkeley for several years. Dickinson held several prominent positions in professional associations, including president of the Association of American Law Schools and president of the American Society of International Law. He also held numerous positions in the U.S. government, including appointments as special assistant to Attorney General Francis Biddle (1941–1943), general counsel to the American-Mexican Claims Commission (1943–1944), and Chairman of the Alien Enemy Repatriation Hearing Board (1945–1946). Dickinson was a member of the Permanent Court of Arbitration in The Hague from 1951 to 1960. He died of a heart attack on March 26, 1961, at the age of seventy-three.[6]

Dickinson was one of the leading international law scholars of his generation. He wrote numerous books and articles over the course of his distinguished career, including the 1926 article in the *American Journal of International Law* that created the intent version of self-execution doctrine. (*See* Chapter 8.) When Goodrich submitted a detailed proposal to the Ford Foundation in November 1951, seeking financial support for a "project in international law," he named Edwin Dickinson as the ideal candidate to be the Chief Reporter.[7] However, funding for the project did not materialize until 1954. By that time, Dickinson was almost ready to retire. He believed that the ALI would be better served by hiring a younger person to serve as Chief Reporter. Nevertheless, Dickinson played a central role in framing the initial study that ultimately led to the Restatement (Second). He worked closely with Goodrich to assemble the team of Reporters and Advisors and he served as "Chief Advisor" to the Reporters from 1955 until 1958, when much of the early drafting work was completed. Dickinson wrote to Goodrich in March 1958, asking to be removed from the payroll.[8] At about that time, Dickinson moved back to Northern California, where he lived for the remainder of his life. Dickinson remained active as an Advisor for the Restatement until his death in 1961.

In May 1954, the ALI Council—the chief governing body of the Institute—voted to approve Adrian Fisher as the Chief Reporter for the foreign relations project.[9] (At that point, it was unclear whether the project would take the form of a Restatement.) Fisher was then a partner at Covington & Burling. He was only forty years old, but he had already had a very distinguished legal career. Fisher clerked for Justices Brandeis and Frankfurter on the U.S. Supreme Court after he graduated from Harvard Law School. Between 1941 and 1952, he held several senior positions in the federal government, including appointments as a legal advisor to the U.S. judges in the Nuremberg Tribunal, solicitor and general counsel in the Commerce Department under Averell Harriman, general counsel to the Atomic Energy Commission, and legal advisor in the Department of State under Dean Acheson. Fisher served as the Chief Reporter for the Restatement from 1954 until completion of the project in 1965. During that time, he worked as a partner at Covington & Burling (until 1955) and served as vice president and general counsel for the *Washington Post* (1955–1961). Fisher returned to government in 1961, where he served for several years as the deputy director of the U.S. Arms Control and Disarmament Agency. He later served as dean of Georgetown Law School. Fisher died in 1983 at age sixty-nine.[10]

In October 1955, the Ford Foundation awarded the ALI a $300,000 grant to work on a project on foreign relations law.[11] Shortly thereafter, Goodrich, Dickinson, and Fisher began to consult among themselves about potential candidates to serve as Reporters. Goodrich wrote to Dickinson in December 1955 to inform him that the ALI Executive Committee "fully approved our recommendations for reporter, chief adviser and associate reporters." He named Kingman Brewster, Covey Oliver, and Cecil Olmstead as Associate Reporters.[12] Brewster declined the invitation, but Oliver and Olmstead eagerly accepted their appointments. Over the next several months, the ALI added Joseph Sweeney and I.N.P Stokes as Associate Reporters. Documents from the ALI archives indicate that Oliver and Olmstead drafted the key provisions on treaties and other international agreements,[13] so I focus here on Oliver and Olmstead.

Covey Oliver began his academic career as a professor at the University of Texas Law School; he taught there from 1936 to 1941. He left Texas to work in the State Department. From 1941 to 1949, Oliver served with the Department of State's Bureau of Economic and Business Affairs and the Board of Economic Warfare. Oliver returned to academia in 1949, following in the footsteps of Edwin Dickinson. Oliver joined the law faculty at U.C. Berkeley in 1949 (shortly after Dickinson left Berkeley for Penn) and then moved from Berkeley to Penn in 1956, at about the same time that Dickinson retired from Penn. Given the timing and their overlapping areas of expertise, one could surmise that both Berkeley and Penn may have hired Oliver to replace Dickinson. In an essay honoring Oliver's life and work, Oscar Schachter identified Dickinson as one of the key people who influenced Oliver's views on international law.[14] Oliver continued to teach at Penn until he retired in 1978, but he also held several government jobs during the same period. Oliver served as the U.S. ambassador to Colombia from 1964 to 1966, and then as assistant secretary of state for Inter-American Affairs from 1967 to 1969. Covey Oliver died in 2007 at the ripe old age of ninety-three.[15]

After receiving his LLB from University of Georgia School of Law, Cecil Olmstead studied at Yale Law School as a Sterling Graduate Fellow. When he graduated from Yale, he went to work in the Department of State as an assistant to the State Department legal advisor, Adrian Fisher. Shortly after Olmstead left government, Fisher recruited him to serve as an associate reporter on the Restatement. Olmstead taught at New York University Law School from 1953 to 1961. He left academia to take an in-house counsel position with Texaco Inc., where he later became an executive vice president. After leaving Texaco, Olmstead worked as a partner with Steptoe & Johnson LLP in Washington, DC. Throughout his career, Olmstead remained active in the American Law Institute and the American Branch of the International Law Association. Olmstead died in 2013 at the age of ninety-two.[16]

In addition to the people discussed above, the ALI recruited a small group to advise the Reporters who were drafting the Restatement. The only meeting of the advisory group that focused specifically on treaties was held in January 1959. The following individuals were present for all or part of that meeting: Robert Amory, Jr. (deputy director of the CIA); R. Ammi Cutter (justice on the Supreme Judicial Court of Massachusetts); Eli Whitney Debevoise (cofounder of Debevoise & Plimpton); Alwyn Freeman (staff member, Senate Foreign Relations Committee); John Howard; Philip Jessup (Columbia law professor and future judge on the ICJ); Nicholas Katzenbach (Yale law professor and future U.S. attorney general); Colonel Archibald King; Monroe Leigh (then a lawyer in the Defense Department, but soon to be a partner with Steptoe & Johnson); Brunson MacChesney (law professor at Northwestern University); and Jack Tate (Yale law professor who previously served as deputy legal adviser in the State Department).[17]

Noticeably absent from this list is Quincy Wright. In the 1950s, Wright was probably the leading scholar in the country in the field of U.S. foreign relations law. If he had served on the advisory group, the Restatement may well have adopted a different position on self-execution and treaty supremacy, because Wright had written extensively on those topics and his views were starkly at odds with the position adopted in the Restatement.[18] It remains unclear why Wright was excluded from the advisory group. One possible explanation is that Wright was trained as a political scientist, not a lawyer. It would be ironic, though, if the ALI excluded Wright for that reason. In February 1947, Edwin Dickinson had written a short note to Herbert Goodrich suggesting that it might be worthwhile for the ALI to undertake a project on the codification of international law. In that note, Dickinson acknowledged that his proposed project on international law was "quite unlike anything which the Institute has ever tackled hitherto." He recommended that the ALI "should be prepared to consult not only experts in law, but experts in history, politics, economics, comparative cultures," and more.[19] If Goodrich had followed this recommendation, the ALI might have recruited Wright to work on the Restatement, and the final product might have been very different.

II. EARLY WORK ON THE RESTATEMENT

Goodrich and Dickinson first prepared a proposal for a project on international law in 1951. Goodrich wrote to the Ford Foundation, the Carnegie Corporation, and the American Philosophical Society to seek funding for the project, but with little success.[20] The initial breakthrough came in April 1954, when Dean Rusk—the future secretary of state who was then president of the Rockefeller Foundation—told Goodrich informally that the Foundation would soon provide $10,000 for "exploratory work" in the field of "foreign relations law."[21] ALI received the grant in June of that year for a "preliminary survey" to be performed by Dickinson and Fisher; the work was to be completed by June 1955.[22] When Fisher's name was first suggested for the project in Spring 1954, Goodrich was not enthusiastic. He said: "I can think of no one who would be more crowded and give us less of his time than Adrian Fisher even though Fisher's time would be worth a great deal if we could get it."[23] These words proved to be prophetic. Over the next decade, Fisher's responsibilities as general counsel to the *Washington Post* and deputy director of the U.S. Arms Control and Disarmament Agency distracted him from his work as Chief Reporter. Fisher's tendency to prioritize other commitments over his work on the Restatement created an ongoing source of tension between Fisher and Goodrich.[24]

In 1954, though, Fisher persuaded his partners at Covington & Burling to support the ALI project by giving him time to work on it.[25] Fisher devoted substantial time and effort to the project over the next year. In March 1955, the ALI circulated a ninety-page document, written by Fisher, entitled an agenda for "discussion of possible work on project in the field of foreign relations law."[26] (Although the grant named Fisher and Dickinson as coauthors, Fisher did the bulk of the drafting, with Dickinson serving as a consultant.) The ALI convened a three-day conference in New York City in Spring 1955 to discuss "possible work on a project in the field of Foreign Relations Law." Approximately twenty men attended the conference, including Goodrich, Dickinson, Fisher, Cecil Olmstead, Judge Learned Hand, Philip Jessup (future judge on the ICJ), Herman Phleger (then the State Department legal adviser), and Nicholas Katzenbach (future U.S. attorney general). Based on the discussion at that conference, Goodrich and the ALI leadership decided that the ALI should produce a Restatement on Foreign Relations Law, if funding could be secured to support the project.

The conference records show that the Bricker Amendment controversy cast a long shadow over the ALI's deliberations. Before the conference, Dickinson informed Goodrich that the Rockefeller Foundation would not provide additional funding for a "major project." He added: "There is probably no point in speculating further about the Rockefeller people, but I cannot help wondering whether they are fearful that we might get them into a tangle with the 'Brickerites.' "[27] During the conference, at the very beginning of the discussion about treaties, Goodrich said: "Mr. Tweed [the ALI President] has been getting—and I have to a less extent—voices of apprehension ... lest we be suggesting that the Institute, which tries to be an objective, scholarly body, now plunge itself into a field of political controversy by even mentioning the name 'treaty.' "[28] Ammi Cutter (who would soon be appointed as a judge on the Supreme Judicial Court of Massachusetts) commented "that any fears that have been expressed about "stirring up the animals on the Bricker Amendment issue" are probably exaggerated." Harvey Bundy—Chairman of the Carnegie Endowment for International Peace, a potential donor for the Restatement project—disagreed. He said that any "prospectus" for a possible Restatement project would have to be crafted in a way to address "the fears of the donor organization" so that "members of the Board of Trustees ... might not approach it with a jaundiced eye."[29] The paper that Fisher prepared for the conference addressed treaties as the first of six possible topics to be covered in a potential Restatement.[30] Fisher pointedly asked Bundy: "What is your feeling about having the Treaties section coming first in terms of both the prospectus and various appendices?" Bundy replied, "I think the trustees only read the first three pages. I would like to have it come second or third.... Don't hit them in the face at the start with something which their enemies can attack them on."[31] Fisher heeded Bundy's advice. The revised draft that he prepared after the conference, which Goodrich later circulated to prospective donors, began with a section on territory and jurisdiction (less politically charged topics), followed by a section on treaties and international agreements.[32]

After the conference, Fisher prepared a lengthy report on the foreign relations law project. Goodrich used this report to seek funding for a Restatement on Foreign Relations Law. In October 1955, the Ford Foundation granted the ALI $300,000 to work on the Restatement, with a stipulation that the work should be completed within five years. The grant also specified that the Restatement would address four topics: jurisdiction and immunities, treaties and international agreements, recognition of states and governments, and protection of aliens and foreign investment.[33] After receipt of the grant, Goodrich, Dickinson, and Fisher spent several months assembling a team of Associate Reporters. The Reporters did not hold their first meeting to review initial drafts until October 1956.[34] Progress was slow, in part, because Fisher accepted a position as general counsel of the *Washington Post* in late 1955, which diverted his attention from the Restatement.

III. DRAFTING THE TREATY RULES

This section analyzes the drafting history of the Restatement provisions on three interrelated issues: the scope of the Treaty Power, the treaty supremacy rule, and self-execution doctrine. Before analyzing those three issues separately, it may be helpful to summarize the drafting process for ALI Restatements. The typical process—which was followed for the Restatement (Second) of Foreign Relations Law—involves several layers of review. First, the Reporters prepare "Preliminary Drafts" to be reviewed by the Advisory Committee. The Advisory Committee for the Restatement (Second) included about twenty people, all or most of whom had significant expertise in the field of foreign relations law. After the Advisory Committee comments on the Preliminary Draft, the Reporters make revisions and submit a "Council Draft" to the ALI Council. The ALI Council is a group of generalists, not specialists. The Council includes a group of fairly senior lawyers, judges, and scholars with a wide range of backgrounds in the legal profession. After the Council comments on the draft, the reporters make further revisions and submit a "Tentative Draft" to the ALI membership for review and comment at the ALI annual meeting. The ALI membership includes a few thousand lawyers, judges, and scholars. In any given year, several hundred members—perhaps even more than a thousand—will attend the annual meeting. It is not unusual for members at the ALI meeting to provide substantive comments that persuade the Reporters to make further revisions.

In the case of the Restatement on Foreign Relations Law, the Reporters, the Advisory Committee, and the Council focused primarily on issues related to jurisdiction and immunities from 1956 until the annual meeting in May 1958. The Reporters circulated Preliminary Drafts 4 and 5 in December 1958 and January 1959, respectively.[35] Those documents were the first drafts on treaty-related issues because the earlier numbered drafts addressed jurisdiction and immunities. The Advisory Committee met to discuss Preliminary Drafts 4 and 5 in January 1959.[36] Goodrich reported that there was "not very much difference of opinion among the group," although matters involving the "balance of power between the President and the Senate" were contentious.[37] The Reporters then prepared "Council Drafts" 4 and 5 in February and March 1959, incorporating comments received from the Advisory Committee.[38] The Council met in March 1959 to review those drafts. The Reporters incorporated their comments into Tentative Draft 3, which was circulated to the membership for discussion at the annual meeting in May 1959.[39] After the 1959 annual meeting, there were few substantive changes to the provisions on international agreements. Thus, although the drafting process for the Restatement as a whole stretched from 1956 to 1965, the key work on treaties was done between December 1958 and May 1959. Table Seven summarizes the key documents related to treaties. I refer to these documents below in analyzing the various drafts.

Table Seven. KEY ALI DOCUMENTS ON INTERNATIONAL AGREEMENTS

Document	Date	Scope
Agenda for Discussion	March 1955	All subjects
Transcript of Conference	March/April 1955	All subjects
Report on Foreign Relations Law Project	August 1955	All subjects
Preliminary Draft 4	December 1958	International agreements only
Preliminary Draft 5	January 1959	International agreements only
Council Draft 4	February 1959	International agreements only
Council Draft 5	March 1959	International agreements only
Tentative Draft 3	May 1959	International agreements only
Proposed Official Draft	May 1962	All subjects
Final	1965	All subjects

A. The Scope of the Treaty Power

The final version of the Restatement codifies five key principles involving the scope of the Article II Treaty Power. First, "the United States has the power under the Constitution to make an international agreement if . . . the matter is of international concern," but the federal government may not use the Treaty Power to regulate "matters of a purely internal nature."[40] Second, the Treaty Power is limited by express limitations in the Bill of Rights.[41] Third, the Treaty Power is not limited by the Tenth Amendment because it is a power "delegated to the United States within the meaning of the Tenth Amendment."[42] Fourth, the federal government may use treaties to regulate matters beyond the scope of Congress's Article I powers because the Treaty Power "is not limited by the extent of [legislative] powers delegated to the Congress" under Article I.[43] Fifth, treaties relating to human rights are arguably matters of international concern, but the Restatement hedges slightly on this point.[44] Preliminary Draft 4—the first draft of the treaty portion of the Restatement—expressed the first four principles in terms that were substantially similar to the final version.[45] Subsequent drafts made changes in wording and numbering,[46] but the first four principles were largely uncontested after the ALI circulated Preliminary Draft 4 in December 1958.

The "Agenda for Discussion" that Fisher circulated in March 1955 identified two possible tests for constitutional limits on the Treaty Power. The first test stated that the subject matter of treaties must be "within the delegated powers of the Federal Government in the absence of a treaty." If accepted, this test would effectively have overruled *Missouri v. Holland*, just as the ABA had proposed in the context of the Bricker Amendment.[47] The second test stated that treaties must address a proper subject "for international concern."[48] At the conference in Spring 1955, Fisher effectively rejected the first test and endorsed the second. He said: "I have found no confusion in the last six years as to whether or not there is authority to enter a treaty on a subject matter proper for international concern which is outside the delegated powers of the Federal Government, absent a treaty. All sides agree there is such power. The difference is in the respective note of enthusiasm or lack of enthusiasm with which they recognize the existence of that power."[49] Conference participants agreed that the "international concern" test was the proper test for constitutional limits on the Treaty Power and that the Treaty Power could be used to regulate matters that would be beyond the scope of Congress's delegated powers in the absence of a treaty. This agreement was reflected in the "Report on the Foreign Relations Law Project" that Fisher prepared after the conference.[50]

Judge John Parker, chief judge of the U.S. Court of Appeals for the Fourth Circuit, had some reservations about this approach. He said: "There is a problem that is troublesome; that is, the function of the treaty dealing with a nation's own nationals. We have had one or two cases where they have come up and claimed to us that ... they had certain rights under the Charter of the United Nations.... But that is just the sort of thing that these Brickerites are afraid of."[51] In response, Fisher contended that there was general agreement that the "international concern" test was the proper test for determining the constitutional limits on the Treaty Power. In his view, though, there was no consensus about whether "a treaty making promises as to the way you treat your own nationals" satisfied the "international concern" test. He added: "I don't think you want to exclude, certainly in a prospectus, the concept that it might be proper." Moreover, he said: "By and large we feel it is a proper matter for international concern what the Hungarians did to Cardinal Mindszehty. We have not said it is none of our business. He is an Hungarian National."[52] This interchange highlights the dilemma posed by human rights treaties. Fisher maintained that Hungary's treatment of its nationals was a proper subject of international concern, but he did not want to concede that the United States' treatment of its own nationals was a proper subject of international concern. Accordingly, Fisher's 1955 "Report on the Foreign Relations Law Project" remained agnostic on the question of whether "the way in which a government treats its own citizens is a matter 'of international concern' and hence a proper subject for a treaty."[53]

The Associate Reporters may have shared Fisher's ambivalence on the question of whether human rights treaties address matters of international concern. Preliminary Draft 4 (December 1958) and Council Draft 4 (February 1959) remained silent on that question. However, some members of the ALI Council apparently believed that the Restatement should address the question directly,[54] because Tentative Draft 3 (May 1959)—which was written after the Council meeting and before the annual meeting—added a Reporters' Note, as follows:

> Proposed treaties dealing with civil and human rights, such as the Genocide Convention, have raised questions in the United States, and indeed, in other countries as to whether or not they deal with matters that are appropriate for settlement by agreements between nations. The issues are not unlike those presented by Narcotics Conventions or Conventions on the Suppression of White Slavery. The problems are of nature [sic] whereby they cross national boundaries and cannot be effectively dealt with by unilateral national action. . . . In the case of genocide and other serious deprivations of human and civil rights, which past experience indicates may have results across national boundaries, if the United States wishes to participate in their international control, it must itself submit to the mechanisms of international control even though the problems are not serious in the United States. This is the *quid pro quo* necessary for international cooperative action and it also indicates the international nature of the subject.[55]

The final version of the Restatement includes similar language.[56] Note that the text carefully avoids the question whether racial discrimination is a matter of international concern, although it does say that genocide is an international issue.

The ALI's decision to take a strong stand in support of *Missouri v. Holland*[57]—combined with its decision to adopt language indicating that at least some human rights issues are matters of international concern—had significant implications for the treaty supremacy rule. If the federal government can use the Article II Treaty Power to address human rights issues, and if the Treaty Power can address matters beyond the scope of Congress's legislative powers, then perhaps the lower court decision in *Fujii* (holding that the U.N. Charter's human rights provisions trump California law) was correct. However, if the ALI's Restatement endorsed the lower court decision in *Fujii*, even implicitly, the Restatement might well revive political support for the Bricker Amendment—an outcome that almost all the Reporters, Advisors, and Council members wanted to avoid. Hence, the Reporters had an incentive to find some way to soften the impact of the treaty supremacy rule to avoid sparking a revival of the Bricker Amendment debate. The Restatement provisions on self-execution and treaty supremacy should be viewed in that context.

B. Treaty Supremacy in the Second Restatement

Section 141 of the Restatement provides: "A treaty made on behalf of the United States . . . that manifests an intention that it shall become effective as domestic law of the United States at the time it becomes binding on the United States: (a) is self-executing in that it is effective as domestic law of the United States, and (b) supersedes inconsistent provisions of earlier acts of Congress or of the law of the several states of the United States."[58] In contrast, a treaty "that does not manifest the intention referred to in Subsection (1) . . . is not self-executing and does not have the effect stated in Subsection (1)."[59] Thus, the Restatement endorses the optional treaty supremacy rule because an NSE treaty does not supersede conflicting state law, and the classification of a treaty as SE or NSE hinges on the intention of the treaty makers. Section 141 also raises other important issues related to self-execution doctrine, which are addressed in the next section. This section focuses on the optional treaty supremacy rule.

Neither the "Agenda for Discussion" that Fisher drafted in March 1955 nor the "Report on Foreign Relations Law" that Fisher prepared in Summer 1955 specifically addressed the treaty supremacy rule. Neither document stated or implied that there is an exception to the treaty supremacy rule for NSE treaties. At the ALI conference in Spring 1955, Fisher had a brief discussion of treaty supremacy with Herman Phleger (Fisher's successor as the State Department legal advisor) and Brunson MacChesney (a law professor at Northwestern University). That discussion was somewhat ambiguous, but could be construed to imply that there is no NSE exception to the treaty supremacy rule. The issue arose in the context of a discussion about the correct application of the principle that the Treaty Power is limited to subjects that are "a proper matter for international concern."[60] Fisher suggested that the Report should "start out with the test . . . that the subject is proper for international concern, and analyze how that test is applied." Goodrich endorsed this approach. Professor MacChesney then added that "in all the American Bar Association argumentation they always put in the companion question, that it overrules state law. Even when it is a proper matter for negotiation, it still overrules state law." Fisher replied: "It seems to me there can be no blinking of the fact in a scholarly treatment of this that if it is a proper matter for international negotiation . . . that entirely overrides state law." Phleger interjected: "That is right."[61]

At the Spring 1955 conference, this interchange was the only reference to the treaty supremacy rule in the course of a lengthy discussion of treaties. During this interchange, no one said anything about self-execution. It is significant that the issue of treaty supremacy arose in the context of a discussion about limits on the scope of the Treaty Power, not in the context of a discussion about self-execution. The conceptual linkage between treaty supremacy and the scope of the Treaty Power reflected the traditional doctrine of treaty supremacy that prevailed from the Founding until World War II. Under that doctrine, all treaties within the scope of the Treaty Power supersede conflicting state law; the question of self-execution was simply not relevant.[62] Fisher's statement, quoted above, appears to endorse the traditional treaty supremacy doctrine, although it is not entirely unambiguous.

The Reporters first addressed the treaty supremacy rule in Preliminary Draft 5 (PD 5), which was circulated to Advisers in January 1959. PD 5 abandoned the traditional treaty supremacy doctrine. It presented the treaty supremacy rule as an aspect of self-execution doctrine, not an independent doctrine. Section 3.04 states:

The provisions of Art. VI, § 2 of the Constitution under which treaties may be self-executing are in effect, permissive rather than mandatory.

Therefore, not all treaties concluded on behalf of the United States are self-executing.... [A non-self-executing] treaty does not operate as a rule for the executive branch, the judicial branch, *or the States* nor does an individual acquire rights under it until Congress has taken appropriate action to implement it.[63]

This statement appears in a comment, not in the black letter law. The corresponding black letter rule distinguishes between self-executing treaties—which are "effective as domestic law in the United States"—and NSE treaties, which are "not effective as domestic law in the United States."[64] The Reporters added in a comment that a self-executing treaty "furnishes a rule for the executive branch, the courts, *the states,* and private individuals by operation of its own terms."[65] In contrast, a non-self-executing treaty does not provide a rule for the executive, the courts, the states, or private parties. In sum, the Reporters conceptualized treaty supremacy as a subset of self-execution doctrine, rather than an independent doctrine. In this respect, PD 5 differed markedly from dozens, perhaps hundreds, of treaty supremacy cases decided by state and federal courts—dating back to the eighteenth century and continuing until the early 1960s—that applied the Constitution's treaty supremacy rule without any exception for NSE treaties.[66] However, PD 5 was consistent with the position articulated by government officials in the Bricker Amendment debates and with the California Supreme Court decision in *Fujii.*

After committing themselves in PD 5 to the proposition that NSE treaties do not "operate as a rule for ... the States," the Reporters adhered firmly to this position in subsequent drafts of the Restatement. Section 124 of Council Draft 4 repeated the claim that an NSE treaty "does not operate as a rule for the executive branch, the judicial branch, or the States nor does an individual acquire rights under it." Tentative Draft 3 (TD 3) repeats the same language.[67] In all three versions, the quoted language appeared only in a comment, not in the black letter law. However, TD 3 began the process of incorporating the NSE exception to the treaty supremacy rule into black letter law. Section 124(3) of TD 3 specifies that a *self-executing* treaty "may supersede inconsistent provisions of the law of the several States." The black letter provision does not explicitly address the relationship between NSE treaties and state law, but it does suggest, by negative implication, that an NSE treaty does not supersede conflicting state law. The Proposed Official Draft, published three years after TD 3, spells out the NSE exception to the treaty supremacy rule explicitly as part of the black letter rule. Subsection (1) of Section 144 says that a self-executing treaty "supersedes inconsistent provisions of ... the law of the several states." Subsection (2) adds that an NSE treaty "does not have the effect stated in Subsection (1)."[68] Thus, by the time the ALI published the Proposed Official Draft in 1962, the transformation was essentially complete. During the preliminary conference in 1955, Fisher seemed to endorse the traditional treaty supremacy rule, without any exception for NSE treaties. Both Phleger and MacChesney seemed to agree with him. PD 5, published in January 1959, endorsed an NSE exception to the treaty supremacy rule, but did not include the NSE exception as part of black letter law. The Proposed Official Draft, published in May 1962, codified the NSE exception to the treaty supremacy rule as an element of black letter law.

Records in the ALI archives demonstrate that Cecil Olmstead drafted the key language in PD 5 stipulating that NSE treaties do not "operate as a rule for . . . the States."[69] That language was included in Section 3.04 of PD 5, entitled "Treaties as Law of the United States." Section 3.04 operated in tandem with Section 4.09, entitled "Self-Executing and Non-Self-Executing International Agreements." Covey Oliver drafted Section 4.09. Thus, Olmstead and Oliver probably worked together closely to craft the NSE exception to the treaty supremacy rule. However, the role of the other Reporters is less clear. During the key period from December 1958 to May 1959, Adrian Fisher was apparently preoccupied with his duties as general counsel of the *Washington Post*. He may not have paid too much attention to the material on international agreements.[70] Goodrich had removed Dickinson from the ALI payroll in March 1958 (at Dickinson's request). Dickinson had retired and moved to California before the Reporters did any significant drafting work on treaties. Sweeney and Stokes, the other Reporters, may have been preoccupied with drafting the sections for which they had primary responsibility. There is no evidence that any of the Advisors or Council members contested the proposition that NSE treaties do not supersede conflicting state laws. Moreover, there is no evidence that any of the key participants acknowledged publicly that the NSE exception to the treaty supremacy rule constituted a fundamental change from the treaty supremacy doctrine that applied from the Founding until World War II.

Viewed together, Sections 3.04 and 4.09 of PD 5 cited a total of nine decisions by U.S. courts to support the Restatement's claims about treaty supremacy and self-execution. The corresponding provisions of Council Drafts 4 and 5 and Tentative Draft 3 cite the same set of nine cases.[71] Eight of those nine cases dealt exclusively with matters of federal law, not state law.[72] The California Supreme Court decision in *Fujii* was the only cited case that actually addressed the relationship between treaties and state law.[73] Moreover, as of 1959, when the Council and the ALI membership reviewed Council Drafts 4 and 5 and Tentative Draft 3, respectively, *Fujii* was the only published decision by any state or federal court that had endorsed an NSE exception to the treaty supremacy rule.

The Proposed Official Draft, published in 1962, cited five additional cases in the section on treaty supremacy: *Bacardi Corp. v. Domenech, Santovincenzo v. Egan, Asakura v. City of Seattle, Chirac v. Chirac,* and *Ware v. Hylton.* The final version of the Restatement cites the same five cases. In all five, the Supreme Court applied a treaty to override state or local law, without pausing to consider whether the treaty at issue was self-executing or non-self-executing.[74] Thus, all five cases support application of the treaty supremacy rule without any exception for NSE treaties. Therefore, although the Restatement endorsed an NSE exception to the treaty supremacy rule, the cases cited by the Reporters (apart from *Fujii*) are either: (1) not relevant to the treaty supremacy rule because they deal exclusively with matters of federal law, or (2) support application of the treaty supremacy rule without any exception for NSE treaties.

Interestingly, the Reporters did not cite testimony by government officials during the Bricker Amendment hearings, although that testimony provided strong support for the NSE exception to the supremacy rule. The three
Reporters who probably played the most significant role in crafting the relevant
rules—Adrian Fisher, Covey Oliver, and Cecil Olmstead—all served in the State
Department in the late 1940s or early 1950s, during the early stages of the Bricker
Amendment controversy.[75] It seems reasonable to infer that their views on treaty
supremacy and self-execution were influenced by their State Department service.
Thus, one is left with the impression that the Reporters' views on treaty supremacy were shaped by the Bricker Amendment debates, but the Reporters were reluctant to cite testimony from the Senate hearings on the Bricker Amendment to
support the positions they adopted in the Restatement.

C. Self-Execution in the Second Restatement

The documents that Fisher drafted in 1955 said very little about self-execution,
beyond noting that the Restatement should address the topic.[76] However, Fisher's
memoranda did emphasize "the practical reasons why a treaty should be self-
executing."[77] He added: "This is important in view of the suggestions which are
occasionally made that the Senate in giving its advice and consent to a treaty
should insert an understanding or reservation that the treaty should not be the
supreme law of the land until further action is taken by the Congress. The study
would analyze what the effect of such a practice would be."[78] Thus, in his initial
memoranda, Fisher did not take a firm stand on the question of whether an NSE
reservation would deprive a treaty of its status as supreme federal law.

In contrast, Preliminary Draft 5 (January 1959) was quite explicit on this point.
PD 5 said that the Senate "has used its power to condition its consent (usually by
a reservation) to specify whether the treaty is consented to as self-executing or
as non-self-executing."[79] This statement was simply false. As of 1959, the United
States had adopted numerous treaties with condition precedent clauses,[80] and
an ABA committee had endorsed the idea of adopting NSE reservations,[81] but
the Senate had never adopted an NSE reservation as a condition of its consent to
treaty ratification. (See Chapter 10, pp. 220–22 for analysis of the distinction between a condition precedent clause and an NSE reservation.) PD 5 also said: "A
treaty drafted as self-executing cannot be given effect as the supreme law of the
land . . . if the Senate has conditioned its consent by stating that the treaty is not
to be self-executing."[82] This statement was certainly defensible, but unsupported,
because the Senate's power to deprive a treaty of its status as supreme federal
law by adopting an NSE reservation had never been tested. Similar statements
about Senate practice and Senate power were repeated, with only slight modifications, in Council Draft 5, Tentative Draft 3, and the Proposed Official Draft.[83]
However, the final version of the Restatement does not specifically address the
Senate's power to adopt an NSE reservation, nor does it make any claims about
past Senate practice. It is unclear why the Reporters chose not to address this
issue in the final version.

PD 5 also adopted a mistaken view about the international legal principles related to self-execution. PD 5 stated: "General international law recognizes ... the power to make a binding international commitment that an international agreement shall have internal effect as law in the promising state without the necessity of implementing legislation."[84] The Reporters repeated this language, almost verbatim, in Council Draft 5, Tentative Draft 3, and the Proposed Official Draft (but not in the final version).[85] The claim is simply wrong, because it conflates questions of international law with questions of domestic law. It would be correct to say that international law recognizes "the power to make a binding international commitment that an international agreement shall have internal effect as law in the promising state." However, addition of the final clause—"without the necessity of implementing legislation"—converted a true statement into a false one. General international law does not address the question of whether implementing legislation is necessary to accord "internal effect" to a treaty. To the contrary, general international law recognizes that the question whether an international agreement has internal effect as law in a particular state in the absence of implementing legislation is governed by the domestic law of that state, not by international law.[86] Indeed, when the United States attempted to insert language into the draft Covenant on Human Rights stipulating that the "provisions of this Covenant shall not themselves become effective as domestic law," other states rejected the proposed text on the grounds that the domestic effect of the Covenant in their countries was governed by domestic constitutional law, and language in the Covenant could not alter their domestic constitutional rules.[87]

The final version of the Restatement did not repeat the language quoted in the previous paragraph.[88] Nevertheless, the Reporters' unfortunate tendency to conflate questions of international and domestic law persisted. Section 154(2) of the final version states: "When an international agreement to which the United States is a party manifests an intention that its provisions shall be effective under the domestic law of the parties at the time it comes into effect [internationally], the agreement is normally interpreted by the courts as self-executing under the law of the United States."[89] To appreciate the significance of this statement, it is important to distinguish between two hypothetical treaty provisions: (A) "this treaty shall not enter into force internationally until after the parties have taken the steps necessary to give effect to the treaty domestically"; and (B) "this treaty shall have domestic legal force immediately upon international entry into force of the treaty, regardless of whether the states parties enact domestic legislation to implement the treaty." Many treaties include language similar to hypothetical provision (A).[90] Such treaty provisions are not problematic.

However, Section 154(2) seems to envision treaty language similar to hypothetical (B). Specifically, Section 154(2) directs courts to examine treaties in search of language along the lines of hypothetical (B) to determine whether the treaty is self-executing. The problem with this approach is that treaties rarely, if ever, contain language like (B). Strict dualist states, such as Canada and the United Kingdom, would not agree to a treaty provision like (B). In dualist states, a provision like (B) would be legally invalid as a matter of domestic law because, under their domestic constitutional systems, no treaties have domestic legal force in the absence of implementing legislation.[91] Granted, it would be possible for the United States to conclude a treaty with the Netherlands, for example, that included language similar to hypothetical (B), because both countries have domestic legal systems that grant domestic legal force to at least some treaties.[92] However, to the best of my knowledge, the United States has never actually consummated a treaty with a provision like (B) because most diplomats who draft and negotiate treaties understand that constitutional law governs the legal effect of treaties within particular domestic legal systems, and negotiators cannot use treaties to alter domestic constitutional rules. Regardless, Section 154(2) encourages courts in the United States to examine treaties in search of language that does not exist to find evidence of an intention that does not exist. When courts are unable to find relevant language in the treaty, they create a fictitious "intent of the treaty makers" and claim, mistakenly, that the treaty language provides evidence of that intent.[93]

In sum, one problem with the Restatement's approach to self-execution is that the Restatement endorsed a one-step approach to SE analysis. The one-step approach conceives of the distinction between SE and NSE treaties as a treaty interpretation issue. In contrast, the two-step approach recognizes that classification of a treaty as SE or NSE involves two separate questions: an international obligation question and a domestic implementation question. The international obligation question is: "What does the treaty obligate the United States to do?" The answer to that question requires a treaty interpretation analysis. The domestic implementation question is: "Which government actor or actors have the domestic legal authority and/or the domestic legal duty to implement the treaty?" The answer to that question generally requires an analysis of domestic constitutional and statutory provisions governing the allocation of powers and duties among various actors within the domestic legal system. The Restatement encourages courts to undertake a treaty interpretation analysis to answer the domestic implementation question: a question that treaties almost never address. By encouraging courts to engage in a treaty interpretation analysis to answer a question that treaties typically do not address, the Restatement encouraged courts to decide treaty cases by inventing a fictitious, judicially created "intent of the treaty makers."

Ultimately, the "fictitious intent" test had its origins in Edwin Dickinson's 1926 law review article, which gave birth to the one-step approach. (The modern mythology that Chief Justice Marshall applied the one-step approach in *Foster v. Neilson* is false. *See* Chapter 4. Regarding Dickinson's role in creating the one-step approach, see Chapter 8.) Since publication of the Second Restatement in 1965, most judicial opinions addressing the SE/NSE dichotomy have applied some variant of the one-step approach, which typically involves some version of the fictitious intent test.[94] Therefore, although Dickinson did not play an active role in drafting the treaty rules in the Second Restatement, his intellectual legacy—in the form of the one-step approach to SE analysis—cast a long shadow over the Restatement and the subsequent evolution of self-execution doctrine.

IV. WHY DID THE ALI ENDORSE AN OPTIONAL TREATY SUPREMACY RULE?

Why did the ALI endorse the NSE exception to the treaty supremacy rule? The answer must account for several interrelated factors. First, the three Reporters who played the most significant role in crafting the Restatement's treaty rules—Adrian Fisher, Covey Oliver, and Cecil Olmstead—all served in the State Department in the late 1940s and/or early 1950s. During that time frame, the ABA and Senator Bricker were developing their proposals to amend the Constitution. In response to the Bricker Amendment proposals, the view that the Constitution's treaty supremacy rule is optional, not mandatory, gained widespread support within the executive branch.[95] The Reporters' views on treaty supremacy and self-execution were undoubtedly shaped by their government service. The available evidence suggests that the Reporters probably did not realize that the NSE exception to the treaty supremacy rule was a dramatic departure from the law that prevailed in the United States from the Founding until World War II. The mythological account of *Foster* (which Dickinson perpetrated in the 1920s), combined with the use of self-execution rhetoric as legal gibberish, helped obscure the fact that the ALI's version of NSE doctrine was starkly at odds with traditional treaty supremacy doctrine.

The optional treaty supremacy rule also advanced U.S. foreign policy interests in the Cold War. During the relevant time period, the Soviet Union was exploiting every available opportunity to criticize racist policies and practices in the United States. In cases such as *Bolling* and *Fujii*, a judicial holding that state or local law did not comply with the Charter's human rights provisions would have caused a major diplomatic embarrassment for the nation. The NSE exception to the treaty supremacy rule allowed the courts to avoid that embarrassment by ducking the question of whether state or local law complied with the Charter. Moreover, even if the ALI Reporters recognized the conflict between the traditional treaty supremacy rule and the NSE exception they endorsed, they had good reason to believe that affirmation of the traditional treaty supremacy rule would revive political support for the Bricker Amendment. Thus, the Reporters may have drafted the self-execution provision with the goal of avoiding revival of the Bricker Amendment controversy.

Finally, the combination of international pressure and domestic civil rights litigation sparked a process of "acculturation" in the United States. Professors Goodman and Jinks define acculturation as "the general process by which actors adopt the beliefs and behavioral patterns of the surrounding culture." The touchstone of acculturation, they say, "is that varying degrees of identification with a reference group generate varying degrees of cognitive and social pressures to conform." Goodman and Jinks claim that "acculturation narrows the gap between public acts and private preferences through internal cognitive processes: Under certain conditions people change their beliefs to avoid the unpleasant state of cognitive dissonance between what they profess in public and what they believe in private."[96] Cognitive dissonance was a key factor driving constitutional transformation in the United States between 1946 and 1965. Cases such as *Bolling* and *Fujii* created severe cognitive dissonance for American lawyers. If courts applied the U.N. Charter and traditional treaty supremacy doctrine to invalidate discriminatory state laws, they would have been tacitly admitting that the Charter provided stronger protection against racial discrimination than did the Fourteenth Amendment. Such an admission would have been contrary to their faith in American exceptionalism. To address that cognitive dissonance, the California Supreme Court in *Fujii* endorsed an NSE exception to the treaty supremacy rule. The NSE exception helped judges preserve their faith in American exceptionalism by ducking the uncomfortable question of whether international human rights law provides stronger protection for human rights than does the U.S. Constitution. In cases where it appears that the answer is yes, U.S. courts preferred to reinterpret the Fourteenth Amendment to satisfy international human rights standards, rather than applying the treaty supremacy rule. The ALI members who approved the Second Restatement were apparently comfortable with that resolution of the cognitive dissonance problem.

V. THE AFTERMATH OF THE SECOND RESTATEMENT

A central claim of this book is that publication of the Second Restatement effectively consolidated the process of invisible constitutional change that began in the late 1940s. This section provides evidence of consolidation by presenting "before and after" pictures from three types of sources: State Department digests of international law, leading treatises on U.S. foreign relations law, and leading casebooks on international law. The "before pictures" draw on materials published between 1922 and 1944. The "after pictures" present materials published between 1969 and 1973. The contrast between the two sets of pictures is striking. Materials published after 1965 typically presented treaty supremacy as an appendage of self-execution doctrine. In contrast, materials published before 1945 applied a conceptual framework in which treaty supremacy and self-execution were two distinct doctrines that addressed different issues.

A. State Department Digests

The *Digests of International Law* compiled by the Department of State provide the best evidence of executive branch views on issues pertaining to international law and U.S. foreign relations law. The Department published an eight-volume *Digest* in the early 1940s, edited by Green Heywood Hackworth, which includes a volume on treaties, published in 1943. The Department published a fifteen-volume *Digest* between 1963 and 1973, edited by Marjorie M. Whiteman, which includes a volume on treaties, published in 1970.[97]

Both Hackworth's *Digest* and Whiteman's *Digest* include one section on treaties as "Law of the Land" and a separate section on self-execution. The treatment of self-execution is markedly different in the two *Digests*. Hackworth's discussion of self-execution says nothing about the relationship between treaties and state law. Under the rubric of self-execution, Hackworth addressed treaties involving internment of prisoners of war, seizure of vessels on the high seas, patents, import duties, and boundary waters on the Canadian border.[98] None of these matters implicate the treaty supremacy rule because they are all matters governed exclusively by federal law, not state law.[99] (Hackworth's *Digest* includes an excerpt from an attorney general opinion stating that "the regulation of the boundary waters between this country and Canada . . . [is] beyond the competency . . . [of] the States.") In contrast, Hackworth's section on treaties as "Law of the Land" expressly affirms the treaty supremacy rule and cites approximately two dozen cases that applied the rule.[100] Thus, Hackworth's organization of the material manifests a conceptual framework in which the treaty supremacy rule governs the relationship between treaties and state law, whereas self-execution doctrine applies only to treaties involving matters outside the scope of state regulatory authority.

Whiteman's section on treaties as "Law of the Land," like Hackworth's, affirms the treaty supremacy rule.[101] However, in contrast to Hackworth, Whiteman cites only one judicial decision to support the rule. In Whiteman's Digest, most of the section on treaties as "Law of the Land" discusses matters beyond the scope of state regulatory power that are governed exclusively by federal law.[102] Whiteman's decision to include this material in a section on treaties as "Law of the Land" shows that the traditional conceptual firewall that separated treaty supremacy issues from self-execution issues had essentially disappeared by 1970 (at least, within the State Department).

More importantly, Whiteman's section on self-execution begins with the following statement: "Cases giving effect to treaties as against state statutes of course hold that the former are the supreme law of the land before which contrary local regulations cannot stand. However, in *Foster v. Neilson*, the Supreme Court developed an important distinction between what are now called self-executing and non-self-executing treaties, which determines the procedures whereby treaties become the law of the land."[103] The linkage of these two sentences with the word "however" is highly significant. The first sentence affirms the treaty supremacy rule. The second sentence, in essence, affirms the NSE exception to the treaty supremacy rule and cites *Foster* as authority for that exception. (As explained in Chapter 4, *Foster* did not endorse an NSE exception to the treaty supremacy rule because no state law was at issue in *Foster*.) Shortly after the quoted passage, Whiteman discusses the California Supreme Court decision in *Fujii*, noting that the court "held the human rights clauses [of the Charter] to be non-self-executing and not intended to supersede existing domestic legislation." She concludes that the result in *Fujii* "seems consistent with the criteria developed in earlier cases."[104] Thus, Whiteman's *Digest* shows that, by 1970, lawyers within the executive branch accepted the NSE exception to the treaty supremacy rule as settled law. In less than three decades, between publication of Hackworth's *Digest* (in 1943) and Whiteman's *Digest* (in 1970), the official executive branch position changed dramatically. In 1943, the NSE exception to the treaty supremacy rule did not exist. By 1970, though, the NSE exception to the treaty supremacy rule was settled law.

B. Leading Treatises on Foreign Relations Law

Professors Quincy Wright and Charles Cheney Hyde both published important treatises on U.S. foreign relations law in 1922.[105] After that, five decades elapsed before Louis Henkin published the next important treatise on foreign relations law in 1972.[106] A comparison between Henkin's treatise and the treatises by Wright and Hyde confirms that the law related to self-execution and treaty supremacy underwent a major transformation between 1922 and 1972.

Hyde says that "a treaty, constitutionally concluded and ratified, abrogates all State laws inconsistent therewith," adding that this "is necessarily accepted doctrine." Moreover, he states, "private alien litigants have constantly invoked the aid of the courts for the purpose of securing recognition of rights claimed under treaties . . ., and with full assurance that the supremacy of such agreements over any inconsistent local enactments would be recognized."[107] Hyde's treatise does not mention the term "self-executing" or "non-self-executing," but it does include a short section entitled "Absence of Necessary Legislation." In that section, Hyde cites *Foster* for the principle that if a treaty requires "a legislative enactment in order to make its provisions effective, the courts of the United States do not regard the agreement as one to be enforced by them until the requisite legislative action is taken."[108] Elsewhere, he notes that treaties requiring an appropriation of money, extradition treaties, and treaties "contemplating the modification of existing revenue laws" require legislative implementation.[109] However, nowhere does Hyde suggest that treaties addressing matters within the scope of state regulatory authority require legislative implementation. Thus, Hyde's treatise does not support the view that *Foster* created an NSE exception to the treaty supremacy rule.

Wright's treatise also supports application of the treaty supremacy rule without any exception for NSE treaties. For example, Wright says that "the jurisdiction of state courts usually extends to many cases involving the enforcement of treaty provisions . . . and in such cases, under the Federal Constitution they are obliged to apply the treaty as the supreme law of the land."[110] This passage does not mention any caveat or exclusion for NSE treaties. Similarly, in several other passages Wright presents a ringing endorsement of the treaty supremacy rule without mentioning any exception for NSE treaties.[111] Moreover, the key passages addressing self-execution doctrine say nothing about the relationship between treaties and state law.[112] Wright's 400-page book does include two short passages that might be construed to imply a degree of overlap between treaty supremacy doctrine and self-execution doctrine.[113] However, his other publications make it quite clear that he did not endorse an NSE exception to the treaty supremacy rule. For example, just three years before he published his treatise, Wright wrote an article in which he said: "all treaties might be called 'self-executing' in the sense that their formal conclusion imposes an immediate responsibility upon every governmental authority whose action may be necessary to give it complete effect."[114] Moreover, as discussed in Chapter 10, during debates about *Fujii* and the Bricker Amendment in the early 1950s Wright was the most outspoken critic of the movement to create an optional treaty supremacy rule.

Henkin's book includes a section on "Treaties as Law of the Land" with a sub-section entitled "Self-Executing and Non-Self-Executing Treaties."[115] The text makes it abundantly clear that Henkin endorsed the NSE exception to the treaty supremacy rule. Henkin notes that the Supremacy Clause was "designed princi-pally to assure the supremacy of treaties to state law." Shortly after this statement, he includes a lengthy quotation from Marshall's opinion in *Foster v. Neilson*. Henkin construes *Foster* to stand for the following proposition: "Not all treaties, however, are in fact law of the land of their own accord," because some trea-ties require "an act of Congress to carry out the international obligation." He says that Marshall's position "is established law." Finally, he adds that a non-self-executing treaty "supersedes state law" only "when implemented by Congress."[116] In sum, although the Constitution was originally designed to ensure the suprem-acy of treaties over state law, in Henkin's view, Marshall's opinion in *Foster* estab-lished an exception for NSE treaties that is now established law. Like Whiteman's *Digest*, Henkin's treatise accepted the myth that *Foster* created an NSE exception to the treaty supremacy rule, even though *Foster* did not actually address the re-lationship between treaties and state law.[117]

C. Leading International Law Casebooks

Legal casebooks in the 1920s and 1930s were written in a particular style. The books typically included lengthy excerpts from judicial decisions, with virtually no commentary by the casebook author. Authors assumed that students (the pri-mary audience for casebooks) would learn the relevant law simply by reading the cases. Accordingly, deducing the author's views from the contents of the case-book is a hazardous venture. Even so, the available evidence suggests that leading casebook authors in the 1920s and 1930s had not yet conceived of the idea that there is an NSE exception to the treaty supremacy rule. I focus here on two of the leading casebooks from this era: a book by Edwin Dickinson published in 1929 and one by Manley Hudson published in 1936.[118] As explained in previous chapters, Dickinson and Hudson were two of the key figures who helped create an NSE exception to the treaty supremacy rule after World War II. Hence, if one wanted to find support for such an NSE exception before World War II, case-books by Dickinson and Hudson would be a good place to look. However, one finds almost no support for an NSE exception in their books.

Dickinson's book has a chapter on treaties, including a section of about eight-een pages on the "legal effect of treaties." That section includes excerpts from two British cases and five American ones.[119] The five American cases are: *Foster v. Neilson, United States v. Schooner Peggy, The Pictonian, Asakura v. City of Seattle*, and *The Head Money Cases*.[120] *Head Money* is clearly included to teach students that a later-enacted statute trumps a prior conflicting treaty.[121] *Asakura* is included to illustrate application of the treaty supremacy rule: the Court held that a bilateral treaty with Japan superseded a local ordinance. At the end of the *Asakura* excerpt, Dickinson added the following footnote: "[T]reaties, made under the authority of the United States, operate by virtue of Article VI of the

Constitution, *proprio vigore*, as laws, and, without the aid of State legislation, supersede conflicting State acts."[122] The excerpt from *Asakura* does not mention the term "self-executing." *Foster, Schooner Peggy,* and *The Pictonian* are apparently included to illustrate application of self-execution doctrine. Readers are presumably familiar with *Foster. The Pictonian* was a Prohibition-era liquor smuggling case in which the court held that a bilateral liquor treaty with Great Britain was self-executing.[123] *Schooner Peggy* involved a wartime seizure of a French vessel. In that case—one of John Marshall's earliest opinions as chief justice—the Court effectively held that a bilateral treaty with France was self-executing, although it did not use the term "self-executing."[124] It bears emphasis that no question of state law was present in *Foster, Schooner Peggy,* or *The Pictonian.* Thus, by pairing *Asakura* (a treaty supremacy case) with the trio of *Foster, Schooner Peggy,* and *The Pictonian,* Dickinson's book likely left students with the impression that treaty supremacy doctrine governed the relationship between treaties and state law, whereas self-execution doctrine addressed federal separation-of-powers issues.

Hudson's book has a chapter on "agreements between states," which includes a section of about forty pages on the "form and effect" of international agreements.[125] That section includes excerpts from two British cases, one decision by the Permanent Court of International Justice, and seven American cases. The American ones are: *People v. Gerke, Milliken v. Stone, Missouri v. Holland, Davis v. Police Jury, Haver v. Yaker, Taylor v. Morton,* and *Robertson v. General Electric Co.*[126] *Davis* and *Haver* raised questions about the time at which a treaty becomes legally effective. In *Davis,* the U.S. Supreme Court held that a treaty conveying territory from one sovereign to another is legally effective between the two sovereigns from the date of signature.[127] In *Haver,* by contrast, the Court held that where a "treaty operates on individual rights," it is not legally effective (as a matter of domestic law) "until there is an exchange of ratifications," which typically occurs months or years after the date of signature.[128] *Taylor v. Morton* was an early case endorsing the later-in-time rule. The circuit court held that a later-enacted statute trumped a bilateral treaty with Russia in which the United States promised to reduce import duties on Russian hemp.[129] *Holland* raised questions about limits on Congress's power to implement treaties; *Gerke and Milliken* raised issues involving constitutional limits on the president's power to make treaties. In *Holland,* the U.S. Supreme Court held that the combination of a treaty and the Necessary and Proper Clause empowers Congress to enact legislation that would be beyond the scope of Congress's legislative powers in the absence of a treaty.[130] In *Milliken,* the Second Circuit dodged the constitutional question and resolved the case on other grounds.[131] In *Gerke,* the California Supreme Court held that a treaty was constitutionally valid and superseded conflicting state law. Hence, the treaty controlled the disposition of real estate in California that belonged to a Prussian citizen who died without a will.[132]

Robertson v. General Electric Co. is the only case in Hudson's book that addresses self-execution.[133] As discussed in Chapter 8, *Robertson* was a patent case in which the Fourth Circuit held that "complainants are not entitled to the patent applied for, because the [treaty] is not self-executing and no legislation has been enacted to carry it into effect."[134] The juxtaposition of *Robertson* and *Gerke* would probably have left student readers with the impression that the treaty supremacy rule governs conflicts between treaties and state law, whereas self-execution doctrine addresses federal separation-of-powers issues. Interestingly, Hudson chose not to include excerpts from *Foster v. Neilson* in the portion of his casebook addressing the domestic effects of treaties. Apparently, as of 1936, *Foster* had not yet achieved canonical status.

In contrast to casebooks published in the 1920s and 1930s, leading casebooks published between 1969 and 1973 either say nothing about the treaty supremacy rule[135] or they endorse the NSE exception. The two books providing the most extensive treatment are a 1969 casebook by Friedmann, Lissitzyn, and Pugh, and a 1973 book by Leech, Oliver, and Sweeney.[136] (Covey Oliver and Joseph Sweeney were both Associate Reporters for the Second Restatement. Noyes Leech also worked on the Restatement in an editorial capacity.[137])

The book by Friedmann et al. has a chapter on "international agreements." Within that chapter, there is no separate section on treaty supremacy. Instead, treaty supremacy issues are addressed in a section on "self-executing agreements and the need for implementing legislation."[138] Thus, the organization of the material suggests that the casebook authors conceived of treaty supremacy as an appendage of self-execution doctrine, not as an independent doctrine. The self-execution section reproduces excerpts from Marshall's opinion in *Foster*, followed by several notes. The notes include excerpts from the Second Restatement and a short discussion of the California Supreme Court decision in *Fujii*. (Citations to law review articles commenting on *Fujii* suggest that the casebook authors were not entirely persuaded that *Fujii* was correctly decided.) Also included is a fairly long excerpt from *Aerovias Interamericanas de Panama, S.A. v. Board of County Commissioners*,[139] where a federal district court held that a treaty superseded conflicting regulations promulgated by a state agency because the treaty was self-executing. As noted in Chapter 12, although *Aerovias Interamericanas* applied the treaty supremacy rule, the court's rationale tacitly assumed that only self-executing treaties supersede conflicting state law.[140] Therefore, the decision by the casebook authors to include a long excerpt from *Aerovias Interamericanas* reinforces the conclusion that the authors conceived of treaty supremacy as an appendage of self-execution doctrine.

The book by Leech et al. has two chapters on international agreements: one chapter on "international law" and a second one on international agreements as "law of the United States."[141] The second chapter includes a section of about ten pages on "self-execution of international agreements."[142] That section includes excerpts from *Asakura v. City of Seattle*,[143] the California Supreme Court decision in *Fujii*, and the Second Restatement. As discussed previously, *Asakura* was a treaty supremacy case that did not mention the term "self-executing" or "non-self-executing." The decision to include *Asakura* as one of the main cases in a section on self-execution shows the degree to which treaty supremacy doctrine had been subsumed within self-execution doctrine by the 1970s. The decision to include *Fujii* as one of the main cases demonstrates the influence of the California Supreme Court decision in that case. Overall, it appears that Leech and his co-authors were unaware that the treaty supremacy rule had ever functioned as an independent constitutional rule, unrelated to self-execution doctrine.

* * *

The preceding discussion shows that Whiteman's *Digest*, Henkin's treatise, and leading casebooks published in the late 1960s and early 1970s endorsed the NSE exception to the treaty supremacy rule, even though there was virtually no support for such an exception before 1945. Hence, the question arises: Did the law change as a result of the Restatement? Or did the Restatement and later works simply express the results of legal changes that occurred in the 1950s in the context of the Bricker Amendment controversy? The best answer is that the key changes occurred in the 1950s, but the Restatement played an important role in consolidating those changes.

As shown in Chapter 12, judicial decisions in the 1950s and early 1960s were generally consistent with prior doctrine. Most treaty supremacy cases during this period did not mention self-execution. Most self-execution cases during this period did not implicate any state law issues.[144] Courts may have been hesitant to cite *Fujii* as an authority on a question of federal law because *Fujii* was a state court decision. Courts were probably not familiar with the details of testimony by executive branch officials during the Bricker hearings because that testimony was not readily accessible to them. The *Fujii* doctrine—that is, the optional treaty supremacy rule—did not really become entrenched in judicial decision-making during this period because the courts needed a single, easily accessible source that they could cite as authority to support the proposition that an NSE treaty does not supersede conflicting state law. The Restatement provided such an authoritative source.

For example, in *In re Alien Children Education Litigation*,[145] plaintiffs challenged the validity of a Texas statute that prohibited use of state funds to educate persons who were not citizens of the United States or lawfully admitted aliens. Among other things, plaintiffs argued that the Texas law violated U.S. treaty obligations under Article 47 of the Charter of the Organization of American States. The court cited the Restatement for the proposition that "a treaty becomes the internal law of the United States and has the effect of domestic law only when that treaty is given effect by congressional legislation or is, by its nature, self-executing."[146] The court concluded "that Article 47 of the amended Charter of the Organization of American States is a non-self-executing treaty and that it does not invalidate inconsistent state laws."[147] In sum, the court justified its decision by citing the Restatement to support an NSE exception to the treaty supremacy rule. If the ALI had never published the Restatement, the court might have reached a similar result for different reasons.[148] However, the Restatement supported the court's conclusion that an NSE treaty "does not invalidate inconsistent state laws."

Treaty Supremacy and Constitutional Change

This Part addresses two main questions. First, how has treaty supremacy doctrine changed since 1965? Second, what does the evolution of treaty supremacy doctrine teach us about the process of constitutional change? Chapter 14 addresses treaty supremacy doctrine in the twenty-first century. Chapter 15 discusses the process of constitutional change.

In reviewing changes in treaty supremacy doctrine over the past half century, two key developments stand out. First, it has become a common practice for the political branches to ratify treaties with an attached declaration specifying that the treaty is not self-executing (NSE declarations). Second, in 2008 the Supreme Court decided *Medellín v. Texas*,[1] the most important judicial decision on treaty supremacy in the past century. Meanwhile, three new versions of NSE doctrine have developed since 1970: the "private right of action" doctrine, the "no private enforcement" (NPE) doctrine, and the "no judicial enforcement" (NJE) doctrine. Chapter 14 explains these doctrines. Viewing these three doctrines together with other variants of NSE doctrine that developed before 1965, one can identify eight distinct versions of NSE doctrine,[2] each of which is associated with a different assumption regarding the distribution of constitutional power over treaties. The table on the next page summarizes those eight doctrines and their corresponding constitutional assumptions.

Any account of treaty supremacy in the twenty-first century must explain the Supreme Court's decision in *Medellín* and the political branch practice associated with NSE declarations. Professor Curtis Bradley, one of the leading contemporary scholars of U.S. foreign relations law, contends that the NJE doctrine explains and justifies these recent developments.[3] In contrast, Chapter 14 contends that the NJE doctrine is constitutionally flawed and that the *Fujii* doctrine does a better job of explaining and justifying both *Medellín* and political branch practice.

Chapter 15 discusses the implications of this case study for broader theories of constitutional change. In the past two decades, several leading scholars have contributed to a burgeoning literature on social movements and constitutional change.[4] The story told in Part Three of this book is broadly consistent with social movement theories of constitutional transformation. In particular, the transformation of the treaty supremacy rule, which I call the "de facto Bricker Amendment," has much in common with the de facto ERA.[5] In both cases, a failed movement for a formal constitutional amendment gave rise to a new constitutional understanding that accomplished some of the objectives the amendment's proponents hoped to achieve. Chapter 15 compares the de facto Bricker Amendment to the de facto ERA. It also analyzes particular features of the de facto Bricker Amendment that tended to make the process of constitutional change invisible. The final section addresses the broader implications of the de facto Bricker Amendment for contemporary constitutional theory. In particular, I suggest that the phenomenon of invisible constitutional change is a distinct type of transformative process that merits additional scholarly research.

Table Eight. Constitutional Assumptions Underlying Eight
Versions of NSE Doctrine

Doctrine	Origin	Implicit Constitutional Assumption
Constitutional Doctrine	1790s	The Constitution limits the power of federal executive officers to implement treaties. Federal executive officers have the power to implement SE treaties, but not NSE treaties. *See* pp. 54–56, 108–13.
Justiciability Doctrine	1880s or earlier	The Constitution limits the power of state and federal courts to enforce treaties. Courts have the power to enforce SE treaties, but not NSE treaties. *See* pp. 132–34.
Condition Precedent Doctrine	1850s	Article II grants TMs affirmative power to decide that a treaty is NSE. They exercise power by adopting a clause requiring legislation as a precondition for the treaty to enter into force internationally. Such condition precedent clauses postpone international entry into force, but they have no domestic effect after the treaty enters into force. *See* pp. 122–23.

Doctrine	Origin	Implicit Constitutional Assumption
Intent Doctrine	1920s	Article II grants TMs affirmative power to decide that a treaty is NSE. They exercise power by adopting a clause requiring legislation as a precondition for the treaty to "take effect" domestically after it enters into force internationally. NSE clause bars federal executive officers from implementing the treaty until Congress enacts authorizing legislation, but does not affect the relationship between treaties and state law. *See* pp. 157–62.
Fujii Doctrine	1950s	Article II grants TMs affirmative power to decide that a treaty is NSE. They exercise power by adopting a clause requiring legislation as a precondition for the treaty to supersede state laws. NSE treaty is not the supreme law of the land. Like the intent doctrine, but unlike the condition precedent doctrine, the effect of an NSE clause is purely domestic: it does not modify the nation's international legal obligations. *See* pp. 220–23.
Private Right of Action Doctrine	1970s	Article II grants TMs affirmative power to decide that a treaty is NSE. They exercise power by adopting a clause requiring legislation as a precondition for the treaty to create a private right of action. SE treaties create a private right of action. NSE treaties do not. *See* pp. 297–98.
No Private Enforcement (NPE) Doctrine	1990s	Article II grants TMs affirmative power to decide that a treaty is NSE. They exercise power by adopting a clause requiring legislation as a precondition for private litigants to raise treaty-based claims and defenses. Private litigants can raise claims/defenses on the basis of SE treaties, but not on the basis of NSE treaties. *See* p. 298.
No Judicial Enforcement (NJE) Doctrine	After 2000???	Article II grants TMs affirmative power to decide that a treaty is NSE. They exercise power by adopting a clause requiring legislation as a precondition for state and federal courts to apply the treaty. An NSE treaty is the supreme law of land, but judges are powerless to enforce it, even if it would be judicially enforceable under the justiciability doctrine. *See* pp. 298–99.

* TMs = president and Senate, acting together in their Article II treaty-making capacity.

** SE = self-executing. NSE = non-self-executing.

*** The modern practice of attaching NSE declarations to treaties can potentially be explained as an application of the intent doctrine, the *Fujii* doctrine, the private right of action doctrine, the NPE doctrine, or the NJE doctrine. The political branches have not distinguished clearly among these five doctrines.

14

Treaty Supremacy in the Twenty-First Century

We saw at the end of the previous chapter that—by about 1970, if not earlier—treaty supremacy doctrine had become completely subsumed within self-execution doctrine, so that it was no longer accurate to speak about treaty supremacy as an independent doctrine. Therefore, the story of treaty supremacy after 1970 is inseparable from the story of self-execution doctrine. This chapter assesses important developments related to self-execution and treaty supremacy in the past few decades.

Recall that the traditional treaty supremacy rule consisted of two elements. First, treaties supersede conflicting state laws. Second, courts have a constitutional duty to apply treaties when there is an actual conflict between a treaty and state law. The first element of the treaty supremacy rule is rooted in the first half of the Supremacy Clause, which says that treaties are "the supreme Law of the Land." The second element is based on the second half of the clause, which says that "Judges in every State shall be bound thereby." The *Fujii* doctrine holds that Article II grants the treaty makers an affirmative power to opt out of the first part of the treaty supremacy rule by deciding that a particular treaty provision will not supersede conflicting state laws. Under the *Fujii* doctrine, an NSE treaty is not the "supreme Law of the Land." The NJE doctrine holds that Article II grants the treaty makers an affirmative power to opt out of the second part of the treaty supremacy rule by directing state and federal courts to refuse to enforce a treaty provision that has the status of supreme federal law. Under the NJE doctrine, an NSE treaty is the "supreme Law of the Land," but judges are not "bound thereby," even if—absent a political decision to bar judicial enforcement—the specific treaty provision at issue would be judicially enforceable under the justiciability doctrine. (*See* Table Nine on p. 296.)

The central claim I will defend in this chapter can be stated simply. The *Fujii* doctrine is constitutionally valid because our current, living Constitution grants the treaty makers the power to opt out of the first element of the treaty supremacy rule. In contrast, the NJE doctrine is not constitutionally valid because the Constitution, properly construed, does not grant the treaty makers the power to opt out of the second element of the treaty supremacy rule. However, two caveats are necessary at the outset. First, from a purely textual standpoint, both the *Fujii* doctrine and the NJE doctrine are problematic because both doctrines are difficult to square with the text of the Supremacy Clause. Second, there is very little practical difference between the two doctrines: the pros and cons of the two doctrines turn primarily on issues of theoretical coherence.

The argument proceeds in six steps. The first section summarizes the three new versions of NSE doctrine that developed after 1970. The next section presents a brief constitutional defense of the *Fujii* doctrine. The third presents a critique of the NJE doctrine. The next two sections, respectively, examine political branch practice related to NSE declarations and the Supreme Court decision in *Medellín v. Texas*.[1] Leading scholarly proponents of the NJE doctrine claim that *Medellín* and political branch practice support the NJE doctrine. In truth, neither the political branches nor the Supreme Court has articulated a coherent vision of NSE doctrine, so the relevant sources are open to conflicting interpretations. Even so, the following analysis contends that both *Medellín* and political branch practice are more consistent with the *Fujii* doctrine than the NJE doctrine. The final section considers whether the NPE doctrine presents a normatively desirable alternative to both the *Fujii* doctrine and the NJE doctrine.

I. THREE NEW VERSIONS OF NSE DOCTRINE

Table Nine presents eight distinct versions of NSE doctrine that feature in modern judicial and/or political branch practice. The chart is organized in accordance with the now-familiar division between one-step and two-step approaches and the distinction among the congressional-executive, federal-state, and political-judicial concepts. Five of the eight doctrines have been discussed previously: the constitutional doctrine, the condition precedent doctrine, the justiciability doctrine, the intent doctrine, and the *Fujii* doctrine. Readers may wish to consult

Table Nine. VARIETIES OF NSE DOCTRINES, CIRCA 2016

	Two-Step Approach	One-Step Approach
Congressional-Executive Concept	Constitutional Doctrine (Origin: 1790s) Condition Precedent Doctrine (Origin: 1850s)	Intent Doctrine (Origin: 1920s)
Federal-State Concept		*Fujii* Doctrine (Origin: 1950s)
Political-Judicial Concept	Justiciability Doctrine (Origin: 1880s or earlier)	Private Right of Action Doctrine (Origin: 1970s) No Private Enforcement Doctrine (Origin: 1990s) No Judicial Enforcement Doctrine (Origin: After 2000???)

prior chapters for detailed discussion of those doctrines.[2] The three new doctrines that emerged after 1970 are the private right of action doctrine, the "no
private enforcement" (NPE) doctrine, and the "no judicial enforcement" (NJE)
doctrine. This section summarizes those three doctrines.

Before addressing the three new doctrines, it may be helpful to remind readers about the categories used to organize Table Nine. Under the congressional-
executive concept, the SE/NSE distinction turns on whether a treaty operates
as a rule of conduct for federal executive officials. Under the federal-state concept, the SE/NSE distinction turns on whether a treaty supersedes conflicting
state laws. Under the political-judicial concept, the SE/NSE distinction turns on
whether and how treaties are enforceable in courts.[3] The two-step approach assumes that the treaty makers control domestic implementation of treaties *indirectly* by making decisions about the content and scope of the international
obligation. Accordingly, when courts apply a two-step approach to SE analysis,
they perform a treaty interpretation analysis to answer questions of international
law, followed by a domestic allocation-of-power analysis to answer domestic legal
questions.[4] In contrast, the one-step approach assumes that the treaty makers
control domestic implementation *directly* by making decisions about domestic
implementation that are not contingent upon the content of the international
obligation. Accordingly, when courts apply a one-step approach, they perform a
treaty interpretation analysis to answer domestic legal questions.[5]

The *private right of action doctrine* distinguishes between SE treaties, which
create a private right of action, and NSE treaties, which do not. (If a treaty creates
a "private right of action," or "private cause of action," then the treaty authorizes
a private plaintiff to file a lawsuit to enforce the treaty.) Like the justiciability
doctrine, the private right of action doctrine is based on the political-judicial
concept of self-execution. However, unlike the justiciability doctrine, the private
right of action doctrine applies a one-step approach. (See Table Nine, p. 296.)
When courts apply the private right of action doctrine, they do not analyze the
treaty to determine the content and scope of the international obligation (an international law question). Instead, they perform a treaty interpretation analysis
to ascertain whether the U.S. treaty makers intended to authorize private plaintiffs to file suits in U.S. courts to enforce the treaty (a domestic law question).

Many federal statutes do not create private rights of action. Instead, they
create administrative enforcement mechanisms and/or vest responsibility for
enforcement in the federal executive branch. The Supreme Court decided a series
of cases in the 1970s establishing an interpretive presumption against finding
implied private rights of action in federal statutes.[6] The Court's decisions establish that congressional intent is the dispositive factor in determining whether a
federal statute creates a private right of action. Beginning in 1979, lower federal
courts borrowed the Supreme Court's private-right-of-action doctrine from the
federal statutory context and applied it to self-execution analysis. For example,
in an influential opinion published in 1984, D.C. Circuit Judge Robert Bork
wrote: "Absent authorizing legislation, an individual has access to courts for enforcement of a treaty's provisions only when the treaty is self-executing, that is,

when it expressly or impliedly provides a private right of action."[7] Inasmuch as self-execution doctrine establishes that the "intent of the treaty makers" is the key factor in self-execution analysis (under a one-step approach), and Supreme Court doctrine establishes that congressional intent is the key factor in a private-right-of-action analysis, it made sense for lower courts to link the concept of self-execution with the concept of private rights of action.

The *no private enforcement (NPE) doctrine* is similar to the private right of action doctrine, in that both doctrines apply the political-judicial concept of self-execution, and both involve a one-step approach to SE analysis. (See Table Nine, p. 296.) When courts apply the NPE doctrine, they perform a treaty interpretation analysis to ascertain whether the U.S. treaty makers intended to authorize private parties to enforce the treaty. If a treaty is non-self-executing under the NPE doctrine, individual litigants are barred from raising treaty-based claims either offensively or defensively. In contrast, under the private right of action doctrine, the conclusion that a treaty is non-self-executing precludes plaintiffs from raising (at least some) offensive claims, but it does not preclude defendants in civil or criminal proceedings from invoking the treaty defensively.[8] Therefore, the NPE doctrine imposes more severe restrictions on private judicial enforcement than does the private right of action doctrine.

The NPE doctrine arose in the 1990s in the context of congressional action on free-trade agreements, including NAFTA and the WTO. Section 3312(c) of the NAFTA Implementation Act states: "No person other than the United States . . . shall have any cause of action *or defense* under the Agreement or by virtue of Congressional approval thereof."[9] Section 3312(b)(2), however, makes clear that NAFTA is judicially enforceable "in an action brought by the United States for the purpose of declaring" that NAFTA preempts a particular state law.[10] Congress adopted similar provisions in statutes implementing the WTO Agreement[11] and other free-trade agreements.[12] These statutes manifest Congress's intent to bar private enforcement of free-trade agreements in U.S. courts, but to permit judicial enforcement in actions initiated by the federal government. Similarly, the Senate has adopted resolutions of ratification for several treaties in the past decade with declarations specifying that the treaties do not "confer private rights enforceable in United States courts."[13] Like the statutes implementing free-trade agreements, these Senate declarations manifest an intention to bar private judicial enforcement of the subject treaties.[14]

The *no judicial enforcement (NJE) doctrine* is similar to both the NPE and private right of action doctrines, in that all three doctrines apply the political-judicial concept of self-execution, and all three involve a one-step approach to SE analysis. The NJE doctrine differs from the NPE doctrine in that the NPE doctrine restricts the power of private litigants to invoke treaties, whereas the NJE doctrine restricts the power of courts to enforce them. Moreover, the NPE doctrine merely limits judicial enforcement at the behest of private parties, whereas the NJE doctrine bars judicial enforcement in all cases, including those where the federal government sues to enforce a treaty. Therefore, the NJE doctrine imposes more severe restrictions on judicial enforcement than does the NPE doctrine.

The NJE doctrine is similar to the justiciability doctrine in that both doctrines bar the enforcement of some treaty provisions in all cases. However, when courts apply the justiciability doctrine, they perform a treaty interpretation analysis to determine the content and scope of the international obligation, followed by a domestic separation-of-powers analysis to determine whether courts are competent to enforce the treaty obligation (consistent with the two-step approach.) Thus, under justiciability doctrine, the conclusion that a treaty is not judicially enforceable results from a constitutional separation-of-powers analysis that emphasizes *constitutional limits on judicial power.*[15] In contrast, under the NJE doctrine, courts perform a treaty interpretation analysis to ascertain whether the U.S. treaty makers intended the treaty to be judicially enforceable (consistent with the one-step approach). Thus, the NJE doctrine rests on the implicit constitutional assumption that *Article II grants the treaty makers an affirmative power* to adopt a unilateral declaration to prevent courts from applying treaty provisions that have the status of supreme federal law and that are within the scope of judicial competence under a justiciability analysis. (See Table Eight on p. 292.)

The historical origins of the NJE doctrine are contested. Professor Curtis Bradley is the leading academic proponent of the NJE doctrine; he presented a detailed defense of the doctrine in an important law review article published in 2008.[16] (The term "NJE doctrine" is mine, not his). Professor Bradley's work is very influential, in part because he is a widely respected scholar, and in part because he is serving as a Reporter for the treaty portion of an ongoing ALI project to produce a new (Fourth) Restatement on U.S. Foreign Relations Law.[17] Professor Bradley's article cites a wide variety of sources that, in his view, support the NJE doctrine. In my view, though, no U.S. court has ever endorsed the key constitutional assumption underlying the NJE doctrine. Moreover, neither Congress nor the federal executive branch has ever endorsed that assumption. The next section of this chapter defends the constitutional validity of the *Fujii* doctrine. Later sections assess the constitutional validity of the NJE doctrine.

II. A DEFENSE OF THE *FUJII* DOCTRINE

The Supremacy Clause establishes the hierarchical superiority of federal law over state law. However, one could argue that the Supremacy Clause merely establishes an optional rule, rather than a mandatory one. According to this view, Article I grants Congress the power to opt out of the federal supremacy rule by stipulating that a particular federal statute will not preempt state law.[18] Similarly, Article II grants the treaty makers the power to opt out of the treaty supremacy rule by stipulating that a particular treaty or treaty provision will not supersede conflicting state law. The authors of the Second Restatement endorsed this view in an early draft. They said: "The provisions of Art. VI, § 2 of the Constitution . . . are in effect, permissive rather than mandatory."[19] The final version of the Second Restatement specifies that a treaty supersedes conflicting state law only if the treaty "manifests an intention that it shall become effective as domestic law of the United States at the time it becomes binding on the United States."[20] By making treaty supremacy contingent upon the intent of the treaty makers, the *Fujii* doctrine rests on an implicit assumption that Article II grants the treaty makers an affirmative power to decide that a particular treaty provision will not supersede conflicting state law. In short, the *Fujii* doctrine rests on the assumption that the treaty supremacy rule is an optional rule, subject to an exception for NSE treaties.

This section defends the constitutionality of the *Fujii* doctrine. It bears emphasis that the analysis focuses on treaty supremacy, not self-execution. The question is *not* whether the Supremacy Clause establishes a mandatory rule of self-execution. The question is whether the Supremacy Clause establishes a mandatory rule of treaty supremacy. Although reasonable minds could differ on this question, I contend that the best reading of the Constitution in the twenty-first century is that the *Fujii* doctrine is constitutional because the Supremacy Clause establishes an optional treaty supremacy rule.

The Supremacy Clause specifies that "all Treaties made, or which shall be made, under the Authority of the United States, shall be the supreme Law of the Land . . . any Thing in the Constitution or Laws of any State to the Contrary notwithstanding."[21] The words "all Treaties" and "shall be" are difficult to reconcile with the view that the Supremacy Clause permits an exception for NSE treaties. If the Framers of the Constitution wanted to permit an exception for NSE treaties, they could have used the phrase "some Treaties," instead of "all Treaties." If they wanted to establish an optional rule, they could have used the phrase "may be" or "could be," rather than "shall be." Thus, the text of the Supremacy Clause tends to support the view that the treaty supremacy rule is mandatory. However, one must not read particular constitutional provisions in isolation. Read in conjunction with Article II, the text does not foreclose the view that Article II grants the treaty makers an affirmative power to opt out of the treaty supremacy rule on a case-by-case basis. Just as the Fourteenth Amendment grants Congress an affirmative power to abrogate the state sovereign immunity protected by the Eleventh Amendment,[22] Article II could be construed to grant the treaty makers an affirmative power to opt out of the treaty supremacy rule codified in the Supremacy Clause. As a textual matter, the claim that Article II grants the treaty makers an affirmative power to opt out of the treaty supremacy rule is more easily defensible than the claim that the Supremacy Clause, standing alone, should be construed to support an optional supremacy rule.

Part One demonstrated that Founding era materials provide virtually no support for the claim that there is an NSE exception to the treaty supremacy rule.[23] Thus, if one gives controlling weight to the original understanding, one would have to conclude that the treaty supremacy rule is mandatory, not optional. Similarly, as shown in Part Two, legislative, executive, and judicial materials from 1800 to 1945 demonstrate that there was no NSE exception to the treaty supremacy rule before 1945.[24] Even so, a persuasive "changed circumstances" argument supports the view that the Constitution today is best construed to include an NSE exception to the treaty supremacy rule.

In the words of Justice Frankfurter: "[A] systematic, unbroken, executive practice, long pursued to the knowledge of the Congress and never before questioned, engaged in by Presidents who have also sworn to uphold the Constitution, making as it were such exercise of power part of the structure of our government, may be treated as a gloss on 'executive Power' vested in the President by s 1 of Art. II."[25] Under Frankfurter's view, which is now widely accepted, a presidential assertion of executive power combined with congressional acquiescence in the exercise of that power provides evidence that Article II grants the president the power he claims.

As of 2016, there is a substantial body of legislative and executive practice supporting the claim that Article II grants the president an affirmative power to opt out of the treaty supremacy rule. First, at the 1949 session of the Commission on Human Rights, the United States proposed the following amendment to the draft Covenant on Human Rights: "The provisions of this Covenant shall not themselves become effective as domestic law."[26] One must assume that this language was vetted with executive branch lawyers before Eleanor Roosevelt presented it to other delegations. (See Chapter 10, pp. 202–03.) Executive branch lawyers would not have approved the language unless they believed it was constitutionally valid. Given that the draft Covenant addressed numerous issues governed by state law in the United States, the validity of the proposed treaty language hinges on the assumption that Article II grants the president an affirmative power to opt out of the treaty supremacy rule. Thus, the proposed language indicates that there may have been an emerging consensus within the executive branch as early as 1949 supporting the president's power to opt out of the treaty supremacy rule. However, there is no evidence of congressional acquiescence at that time.

Before 1960, the best evidence of congressional acquiescence comes from debates over the Bricker Amendment in 1952–1954. Bricker's supporters argued that a constitutional amendment was necessary to avert the threat posed by human rights treaties. In response, Bricker's opponents contended that a constitutional amendment was not necessary because Article II already granted the president the power to opt out of the treaty supremacy rule, either by including appropriate language in the treaty itself, or by adopting a unilateral reservation at the time of ratification. Attorney General Brownell, Secretary of State Dulles, and Harold Stassen (director of the Mutual Security Administration) all presented variants of this argument in their official Senate testimony on behalf of the Eisenhower administration.[27] The minority view in the Senate Judiciary Committee report advanced this argument.[28] Senator George presented the argument during floor debate.[29] And President Eisenhower, himself, made a similar argument in a private letter to John McCloy.[30] They all articulated a similar message: "We recognize that human rights treaties pose a potential threat, but we can address that threat by adopting treaty language or unilateral reservations to ensure that such treaties do not supersede conflicting state laws. Therefore, a constitutional amendment is unnecessary." Meanwhile lawyers outside of government advanced similar arguments within the American Bar Association[31] and the New York City Bar Association.[32] In sum, the Bricker Amendment controversy gave rise to a new constitutional understanding—both within and outside of government—that the treaty supremacy rule is optional, and that Article II grants the president the power to opt out of the treaty supremacy rule on a case-by-case basis. (*See* Chapter 11.)

Here, it is important to recall that the traditional treaty supremacy rule consisted of two elements. First, treaties supersede conflicting state laws. Second, judges have a constitutional duty to apply treaties in cases presenting a conflict between a treaty and state law.[33] The *Fujii* doctrine is based on the assumption that the first element is optional: the treaty makers have the power to decide that a particular treaty will not be the "supreme law of the land," absent implementing legislation. In contrast, the NJE doctrine is based on the assumption that all treaties are the supreme law of the land, but the second element is optional: the treaty makers have the power to decide that a particular treaty will not be judicially enforceable.

The new constitutional understanding that emerged from the Bricker Amendment controversy was based on the *Fujii* doctrine, not the NJE doctrine. Indeed, the NJE doctrine would not have served the political purposes of Bricker's opponents. A key difference between the two doctrines relates to the president's power and duty to execute the law. Under the *Fujii* doctrine, the president has neither the power nor the duty to execute an NSE treaty, because an NSE treaty is not law. Under the NJE doctrine, though, the president has both the power and the duty to execute an NSE treaty because an NSE treaty is law. Bricker's supporters feared that the president would use his Article II powers to invalidate state laws. Indeed, one of the primary goals of the Bricker Amendment was to constrain the president's ability to use his foreign affairs powers to override state laws.[34] Thus, to counter the political momentum supporting the Bricker Amendment, it would not have been sufficient for Bricker's opponents to argue that the Constitution grants the treaty makers the power to opt out of the second element of the treaty supremacy rule. They needed to argue—and did argue— that the Constitution grants the treaty makers the power to opt out of the first element of the treaty supremacy rule by declaring that a treaty is not supreme federal law. Thus, the new constitutional understanding that emerged from the Bricker Amendment controversy shows that the core assumption underlying the *Fujii* doctrine was widely accepted by the end of the 1950s. In contrast, there is virtually no evidence to suggest that the main assumption underlying the NJE doctrine was accepted at that time.

Key documents published in the 1960s and 1970s provide additional evidence that lawyers at that time generally understood the optional treaty supremacy rule in accordance with the *Fujii* doctrine, not the NJE doctrine. The Second Restatement, published in 1965, said that "a treaty has immediate domestic effect as the supreme law of the land under Article VI, Clause 2 of the Constitution only if it is self-executing."[35] Whiteman's *Digest of International Law*, published in 1970, said that the distinction between SE and NSE treaties "determines the procedures whereby treaties become the law of the land."[36] Professor Henkin's leading treatise on foreign relations law, published in 1972, said: "Not all treaties, however, are in fact law of the land of their own accord."[37] All these statements are consistent with the *Fujii* doctrine, not the NJE doctrine, because they manifest an understanding that an NSE treaty is not the "law of the land."

Finally, as discussed in more detail later in this chapter, beginning in the 1990s the president and Senate have established a fairly routine practice of adopting treaties subject to NSE declarations. The meaning of NSE declarations is ambiguous, and the correct interpretation of those declarations is hotly contested. Even so, the practice of adopting treaties subject to NSE declarations provides additional evidence that the president and Senate accept the constitutional validity of the *Fujii* doctrine. Moreover, in light of political branch practice, and in light of relevant Supreme Court decisions, it would be difficult at this point in time to contend that NSE declarations are unconstitutional.

III. TWO VIEWS OF OPTIONAL SUPREMACY

The *Fujii* doctrine holds that the first element of the treaty supremacy rule is optional: the treaty makers have the power to decide that a particular treaty is not the "Law of the Land." The NJE doctrine holds that the second element of the rule is optional: the treaty makers have the power to decide that judges are not bound by a particular treaty, even though it is the Law of the Land. Thus, under the *Fujii* doctrine, neither courts nor federal executive officers have the power to enforce NSE treaties, absent implementing legislation, because NSE treaties are not part of domestic law. In contrast, under the NJE doctrine, NSE treaties are not judicially enforceable, but federal executive officers have both the power and the duty to implement NSE treaties because they are part of domestic law. (*See* Tables Eight and Nine, pp. 292 and 296.)

To appreciate the differences between the *Fujii* doctrine and the NJE doctrine, it is helpful to consider a hypothetical case. Assume that the United States ratifies the Convention on the Rights of the Child. Article 37(a) states: "Neither capital punishment nor life imprisonment without possibility of release shall be imposed for offences committed by persons below eighteen years of age."[38] Assume, further, that the United States does not adopt a reservation to Article 37, but it does adopt an NSE declaration. (These assumptions are admittedly unrealistic. Nevertheless, they are useful for clarifying the differences between the *Fujii* and NJE doctrines.) What is the effect of that declaration? Consider a criminal defendant in Florida who is charged with murder. Defendant was a seventeen-year-old when he committed the crime. The state seeks a life without parole (LWOP) sentence, which is authorized under state law. (In *Miller v. Alabama*,[39] the Supreme Court established constitutional limits on the power of state governments to impose LWOP sentences on juvenile offenders, but such sentences are constitutionally permissible in some cases.) Defendant invokes the treaty as a defense. Article 37(a) clearly bars the LWOP sentence. Should the court apply the treaty to bar the sentence? Or does the NSE declaration preclude the court from applying the treaty? To address this question, consider two different variants of an NSE declaration, which correspond, respectively, to the NJE doctrine and the

Fujii doctrine. Both variants share one feature in common: they do not alter the content or scope of the international obligation; their effects are purely domestic. (The political branches have consistently maintained that NSE declarations do not alter the content or scope of treaty-based international obligations.[40])

Under the first variant, the NSE declaration states: "This treaty supersedes conflicting state laws. However, state and federal courts shall not apply the treaty to override state law unless Congress enacts legislation authorizing judicial enforcement." Call this an "NJE declaration." This declaration applies the *NJE doctrine,* which assumes that the treaty makers have the power to decide that judges are not bound by a particular treaty, even though it is the Law of the Land. If we apply the NJE declaration to the hypothetical Florida case, the LWOP sentence is illegal as a matter of federal law because Article 37 supersedes conflicting state laws. Nevertheless, the judge is permitted to impose an LWOP sentence because the NJE declaration precludes courts from applying the treaty to invalidate state law. In short, under the NJE doctrine, a court may impose an illegal sentence on a criminal defendant. That result is deeply troubling. One should be very reluctant to conclude that the Constitution allows a court to impose an illegal sentence on a criminal defendant.

Under the second variant, the NSE declaration states: "This treaty shall not supersede conflicting state laws unless Congress enacts legislation stipulating that the treaty supersedes conflicting state laws." Call this a "*Fujii* declaration." This declaration applies the *Fujii* doctrine, which assumes that the treaty makers have the power to decide that a particular treaty is not the Law of the Land. If the assumption underlying the *Fujii* doctrine is correct, then the declaration is valid. In the hypothetical Florida case, the court would presumably impose an LWOP sentence (if Congress has not enacted relevant legislation) because the declaration stipulates that the treaty does not supersede state law. Thus, both the *Fujii* declaration and the NJE declaration yield the same result: in both cases, the court is permitted to impose the LWOP sentence. Under the *Fujii* doctrine, though, the LWOP sentence is legal because the treaty does not supersede Florida law. Therefore, the *Fujii* doctrine avoids the central constitutional difficulty inherent in the NJE doctrine. The NJE doctrine permits a court to impose a criminal sentence that violates federal law. Under the *Fujii* doctrine, though, courts are not permitted to impose illegal sentences on criminal defendants.

Inasmuch as the NJE declaration precludes a criminal defendant from raising a meritorious defense to a criminal charge, it violates the established rule that "a State must afford all individuals a meaningful opportunity to be heard if it is to fulfill the promise of the Due Process Clause."[41] The opportunity to be heard is an essential procedural right of both civil and criminal defendants.[42] Although the Due Process Clause does not guarantee plaintiffs a right of access to courts, "due process of law signifies a right to be heard in one's defence [*sic*]."[43] The distinction between plaintiffs and defendants is fundamental because plaintiffs have the option of resolving their disputes through "private structuring of individual relationships," but defendants are "forced to settle their claims of right and duty through the judicial process."[44]

Yakus v. United States is the closest that the Supreme Court has ever come to approving something like an NJE declaration.[45] In *Yakus*, two defendants had been convicted for violations of the Emergency Price Control Act (EPCA). The EPCA was a wartime measure, adopted in the midst of World War II, and designed to prevent inflation. The statute created an Office of Price Administration, headed by the Price Administrator, who had broad authority to enact regulations to stabilize prices. The defendants in *Yakus* were prosecuted for violating a regulation promulgated by the Price Administrator. In the course of their criminal trials, they tried to challenge the legality of that regulation. They argued that they could not be convicted for violating the regulation because the regulation itself was illegal. The trial court convicted them without addressing the merits of their argument that the regulation was illegal. When Congress enacted the statute, it had "deprive[d] the district court of power to consider the validity of the Administrator's regulation ... as a defense to a criminal prosecution for its violation."[46] The Supreme Court affirmed the convictions, despite the fact that the district court had not ruled on the legality of the regulation. The NJE declaration is similar to the statute at issue in *Yakus*. Just as the EPCA barred the court from deciding upon the legality of the regulation, the NJE declaration bars the court in the hypothetical Florida case from deciding upon the legality of the Florida law that authorizes an LWOP sentence. (More precisely, the NJE declaration bars the court from applying the treaty as a standard to judge the legality of the Florida law.)

Even so, there are critical differences between the NJE declaration and the EPCA. Under the EPCA, any person who wanted to challenge the legality of a regulation enacted by the Price Administrator could "within 60 days after it is issued file a protest specifically setting forth objections" to the regulation.[47] The statute granted the Price Administrator the authority to decide the merits of such a challenge. If the Price Administrator upheld the validity of the regulation, the aggrieved party could appeal to a federal appellate court and ultimately to the U.S. Supreme Court.[48] In sum, the EPCA barred individuals from challenging the validity of a regulation by way of a defense to a criminal prosecution, but it provided an alternative mechanism for obtaining a judicial ruling on the validity of that regulation. The availability of that alternative mechanism was crucial for the Supreme Court's decision in *Yakus*. The statutory provision that barred the trial court from deciding upon the legality of the regulation was valid precisely because it did not "deny, to those charged with violations, an adequate opportunity to be heard on the question of validity."[49] In *United States v. Mendoza-Lopez*, the Court cited *Yakus* for the proposition that it is permissible to impose a "criminal conviction for violation of an administrative regulation where the validity of the regulation could not be challenged in the criminal proceeding." However, the Court said, the decision in *Yakus* "turned on the fact that adequate judicial review of the validity of the regulation was available in another forum."[50] Applying that standard, the Court in *Mendoza-Lopez* held that a federal statute did "not comport with the constitutional requirement of due process" because it did not offer the defendant "an alternative means of obtaining judicial review."[51]

In sum, *Yakus* and *Mendoza-Lopez* demonstrate that Congress has the power to prevent a court, in the context of a criminal trial, from deciding the merits of an argument challenging the validity of the law that authorizes the government to impose criminal sanctions. However, if Congress wishes to exercise that power, it must provide an alternative procedural mechanism that gives the defendant an adequate opportunity to challenge the law's validity. Failure to do so violates the Due Process Clause. Measured by this standard, the NJE declaration is unconstitutional because it does not provide the defendant in the hypothetical Florida case any opportunity whatsoever to challenge the validity of the Florida law as a violation of the treaty. In contrast, the *Fujii* doctrine is not constitutionally problematic because the *Fujii* declaration would not prevent a court from deciding the merits of a criminal defendant's treaty-based defense.

One additional factor distinguishes the hypothetical Florida case from both *Yakus* and *Mendoza-Lopez*. Both *Yakus* and *Mendoza-Lopez* were federal prosecutions under federal criminal statutes. Neither case implicated the Supremacy Clause because no state law was at issue in either case. In contrast, the hypothetical Florida case does implicate the Supremacy Clause because the defendant alleges a conflict between the treaty (which is federal law under the NJE doctrine) and state law. The Supreme Court held in *Testa v. Katt* that the Supremacy Clause means that state courts may not "deny enforcement to claims growing out of a valid federal law."[52] More recently, in *Armstrong v. Exceptional Child Center, Inc.*, the Court said that the Supremacy "Clause creates a rule of decision: Courts . . . must not give effect to state laws that conflict with federal laws."[53] Moreover, the Court added: "[O]nce a case or controversy properly comes before a court, judges are bound by federal law. Thus, a court may not convict a criminal defendant of violating a state law that federal law prohibits."[54] Given that courts may not convict a defendant for violating a state law that federal law prohibits, it is difficult to see why a court should be permitted to impose a sentence on a criminal defendant that federal law prohibits. Thus, *Testa* and *Armstrong* suggest that the NJE declaration violates the Supremacy Clause as well as the Due Process Clause. In contrast, the *Fujii* declaration does not suffer from these problems because, under the *Fujii* declaration, the treaty is not federal law.

Professor Bradley's defense of the NJE doctrine relies heavily on political branch practice related to NSE declarations and the Supreme Court decision in *Medellín*. The next two sections address those topics. Neither the political branches nor the Supreme Court has articulated a clear, consistent understanding of NSE doctrine. Even so, despite the ambiguity of primary materials, I conclude that neither political branch practice nor *Medellín* offers much support for the NJE doctrine. In contrast, both *Medellín* and political branch practice lend at least some support for the constitutional validity of the *Fujii* doctrine.

IV. POLITICAL BRANCH PRACTICE AND NSE DECLARATIONS

In the past twenty-five years,[55] the Senate has provided its consent for approximately two dozen treaties subject to a declaration that the treaty is not-self-executing (NSE declarations).[56] This section shows that political branch practice related to NSE declarations tends to support the private right of action doctrine, the intent doctrine, and the *Fujii* doctrine, but provides very little support for the NJE doctrine.

The United States first ratified a treaty with an NSE declaration in 1992. Official explanations of those declarations have changed over time, but legislative and executive authorities have been consistent on two points. First, when the president and Senate adopt a treaty subject to an NSE declaration, that declaration does not alter the content or scope of the international obligation. For example, the Senate Foreign Relations Committee report for the Convention on Racial Discrimination stated: "Declaring the Convention to be non-self-executing in no way lessens the obligation of the United States to comply with its provisions as a matter of international law."[57]

The second point is related to the first: NSE declarations are founded on the expectation that courts will apply a one-step approach to self-execution analysis, in which the classification of a treaty as SE or NSE hinges on the unilateral intent of the U.S. treaty makers. For example, one government official explained the purpose of the NSE declarations as follows: "In broadly based multilateral treaties such as these, it is difficult to infer a common intent among the parties since nations have different practices on this subject .... In such a situation, the intent of the Executive and Senate at the time of ratification become significant and it is their duty to make that intention clear."[58] The asserted "duty" to make that intention clear is evidently one owed to courts to assist them in analyzing self-execution issues. The statement assumes that the courts will apply a one-step approach to self-execution analysis, focusing on the unilateral intent of the U.S. treaty makers. Of course, the political branches consider the first step of a two-step approach—the content and scope of the international obligation—when they decide whether implementing legislation is necessary. However, the goal of the NSE declaration is to assist courts in making a self-execution determination without having to consider the content of the international obligation. Although political branch explanations of NSE declarations have changed over time, the expectation that courts will apply a one-step approach has not changed.

President Carter transmitted four human rights treaties to the Senate in 1978.[59] The executive branch proposed NSE declarations for all four treaties. The secretary of state's official explanation of the NSE declarations said: "With such declarations, the substantive provisions of the treaties would not of themselves become effective as domestic law."[60] This explanation is consistent with the concept of self-execution embodied in the Second Restatement and the *Fujii doctrine*. If NSE treaties are not "effective as domestic law," then they are simply not the "Law of the Land." However, it appears that executive branch lawyers became uncomfortable with the notion that NSE treaties lack any domestic legal effect. During testimony before the Senate Foreign Relations Committee in 1979, Roberts Owen, the State Department legal adviser, offered a different explanation of the NSE declarations. He said: "A treaty is self-executing, and thus automatically the law of the land upon entry into force, or non-self-executing, requiring implementing legislation before it becomes a rule for the courts."[61] Owen equated self-executing with "Law of the Land," but he was apparently hesitant to say that an NSE treaty is not the "Law of the Land." Instead, he said, an NSE treaty is not a "rule for the courts," without specifying whether it might be "effective as domestic law" in some other way. Thus, Owen's statement could be construed to support the *NJE doctrine*.

The United States ratified the Genocide Convention in 1988 without an NSE declaration. The Senate resolution of ratification for the Genocide Convention included a declaration that "the President will not deposit the instrument of ratification until after the implementing legislation ... has been enacted."[62] The Senate Foreign Relations Committee explained this declaration as follows: "The Committee's declaration reinforces the fact that the Convention is not self-executing. In other words, no part of the Convention becomes law by itself."[63] As a matter of international law, a treaty does not become binding on the United States until after the president deposits the instrument of ratification. Thus, the Committee's explanation is consistent with the *condition precedent doctrine*— the Senate adopted a unilateral condition requiring federal legislation as a condition precedent before the treaty could become binding on the United States under international law.[64]

The United States ratified the International Covenant on Civil and Political Rights (ICCPR) in 1992, subject to a declaration "that the provisions of Articles 1 through 27 of the ICCPR are not self-executing."[65] The ICCPR was the first treaty in U.S. history that contained an express NSE declaration.[66] The executive branch explained that the NSE declaration was intended "to clarify that the Covenant will not create a private cause of action in U.S. courts," and the Senate Foreign Relations Committee adopted this language in its official report.[67] Thus, the first treaty that the United States ratified subject to an NSE declaration expressed the shared understanding of the president and Senate that the declaration should be construed in accordance with the *private right of action doctrine*. As I have explained elsewhere, the legislative and executive materials associated with three human rights treaties that the United States ratified in 1992 and 1994 show that the president and Senate understood the NSE declarations attached to those three treaties in accordance with the private right of action doctrine.[68]

However, more recent Senate actions on treaties manifest a different understanding of NSE declarations. Since the turn of the century, the Senate has provided its consent for approximately twenty treaties with NSE declarations attached.[69] In September 2008, in an unprecedented burst of treaty activity, the Senate consented to seventy-eight treaties in just four days.[70] The Senate's unusual flurry of activity was a response to the Court's March 2008 decision in *Medellín v. Texas*.[71] Senate treaty actions in September 2008 demonstrate that the Senate, at that time, understood the terms "self-executing" and "non-self-executing" in accordance with the *intent doctrine*.

The Senate adopted NSE declarations for seven of the seventy-eight treaties.[72] For sixty-nine other treaties, it adopted declarations specifying that the treaty is either wholly or partially self-executing.[73] The Senate did not explicitly define the terms "self-executing" and "non-self-executing." However, Senate resolutions for eight treaties (the "eight key treaties") shed light on its apparent understanding of those terms. For three of the eight key treaties, the Senate adopted declarations substantially equivalent to the following: "*This Protocol is self-executing. This Protocol does not confer private rights enforceable in United States courts.*"[74] For the other five treaties, the Senate declarations specified that the treaty was partially SE and partially NSE. Those declarations included language substantially equivalent to the following: "*None of the provisions in the Convention . . . confer private rights enforceable in United States courts.*"[75]

The Senate clearly did not conceive of self-execution in terms of the federal-state concept, because all of the eight key treaties address matters governed exclusively by federal law, not state law.[76] Hence, the *Fujii* doctrine is not applicable to those treaties. Moreover, the Senate did not conceive of self-execution in terms of the political-judicial concept. For the eight key treaties, it declared in a single paragraph that the treaty was wholly or partially self-executing *and* that it was not "enforceable in United States courts." If the Senate understood self-execution in terms of the political-judicial concept, those two statements would be mutually contradictory because, under the political-judicial concept, "self-executing" means "enforceable in courts." In contrast, there is no contradiction under the congressional-executive concept because "self-executing" means that legislation is not needed to authorize federal executive action pursuant to the treaty. Therefore, the declarations for the eight key treaties make it abundantly clear that the Senate understood self-execution in terms of the congressional-executive concept, not the political-judicial concept.[77] As explained above, NSE declarations are premised on the one-step approach, not the two-step approach. Moreover, as illustrated in Table Nine at the beginning of this chapter, the intent doctrine combines the one-step approach with the congressional-executive concept. Thus, the declarations for the eight key treaties provide powerful evidence that the Senate understood self-execution, at that time, in accordance with the *intent doctrine*.

In contrast, Senate deliberations on the Convention on the Rights of Persons with Disabilities in 2012–2014 suggest that the Senate, at that time, understood self-execution in accordance with the *Fujii doctrine*. President Obama transmitted the Convention to the Senate in May 2012. He proposed the following NSE declaration: "The United States declares that the provisions of the convention are not self-executing, and thus would not be directly enforced by U.S. courts or of itself give rise to individually enforceable rights."[78] This statement is ambiguous. It could be construed in accordance with the NJE doctrine. Under that interpretation, the statement that the treaty "would not be directly enforced" by courts is intended to define the meaning of the term "not self-executing." On the other hand, the statement could also be construed in accordance with the *Fujii* doctrine. Under that interpretation, the term "not self-executing" means "not the Law of the Land," and the statement that the treaty "would not be directly enforced" by courts follows as a logical consequence from the fact that the treaty is not the Law of the Land.

The Senate Committee Report for the Disabilities Convention removed this ambiguity. The Committee Report explains the NSE declaration as follows: "This [declaration] reflects the shared understanding of the committee and the executive branch that the provisions of the Treaty are not self-executing, are not directly enforceable in U.S. courts, and do not confer private rights of action enforceable in the United States."[79] If the political branches understood self-execution in accordance with the NJE doctrine, the statements that the treaty provisions "are not self-executing" and "not directly enforceable in U.S. courts" would be entirely redundant. In contrast, the redundancy is eliminated if one construes "not self-executing" to mean not "supreme Law of the Land," as in the *Fujii doctrine.*[80] Under the *Fujii* doctrine, the statements that the treaty provisions are "not directly enforceable" and "do not confer private rights of action" are not redundant because they both follow as a logical consequence from the statement that the provisions are "not self-executing" (i.e., not supreme Law of the Land).

It is important, here, to highlight a key difference between the Disabilities Convention and the "eight key treaties" discussed previously. Whereas those eight treaties address matters governed exclusively by federal law, the Disabilities Convention also addresses matters governed by state law. Hence, the political branches wanted to clarify that the Disabilities Convention will not operate as a rule of conduct for federal executive officers (per the intent doctrine) *and* that it will not supersede conflicting state laws (per the *Fujii* doctrine). If the NSE declaration attached to the Disabilities Convention is construed in accordance with the *Fujii* doctrine, it expresses both ideas simultaneously. Because an NSE treaty is not the "supreme Law of the Land" under the *Fujii* doctrine, it necessarily follows that it does not operate as a rule of conduct for federal executive officers.

In sum, Senate actions since 1990 demonstrate that the political branches have not expressed a clear, consistent understanding of self-execution. NSE declarations attached to human rights treaties that the United States ratified in 1992–1994 are best construed in accordance with the private right of action doctrine. Senate treaty actions in September 2008 manifest an understanding of self-execution rooted in the intent doctrine. The Senate Committee Report for the Disabilities Convention is best construed in accordance with the *Fujii* doctrine. One can find occasional testimony by executive branch officials and statements in executive branch documents that are arguably consistent with the NJE doctrine. However, there does not appear to be any evidence that the Senate itself has endorsed the NJE doctrine. This fact is highly significant because, under Frankfurter's political branch practice theory, congressional acquiescence is necessary to establish the constitutional validity of an executive branch practice. Moreover, in light of the constitutional problems inherent in the NJE doctrine (discussed in the previous section), the few scattered statements that might be construed to support the NJE doctrine constitute a very flimsy foundation on which to defend the constitutional validity of the doctrine.

V. *MEDELLÍN V. TEXAS*

In *Medellín v. Texas,*[81] the Supreme Court held that Article 94 of the U.N. Charter is not self-executing. The Court's decision is open to several competing interpretations. This section first summarizes the facts and procedural history of the case. The remainder of the analysis addresses three competing interpretations of the Court's decision. In brief, those three interpretations are: (1) the Court held that the United States did not violate international law by executing Medellín; (2) the Court held that the United States violated international law, but Texas did not violate federal law because Article 94 of the U.N. Charter is not federal law; and (3) the Court held that Article 94 is federal law, and Texas violated federal law, but the courts were powerless to halt that violation. The second interpretation is consistent with the *Fujii* doctrine. The third interpretation is consistent with the NJE doctrine. Leading scholars have defended both the first and third interpretations.[82] In contrast, I contend that the second interpretation provides the best explanation of the Court's decision. Therefore, *Medellín* is best construed in accordance with the *Fujii* doctrine, not the NJE doctrine.

A. The Facts and Procedural History

José Ernesto Medellín was a Mexican national convicted of murder in Texas state court and sentenced to death.[83] At the time of his initial arrest, Texas officials violated U.S. treaty obligations under the Vienna Convention on Consular Relations (VCCR) by failing to advise him of his right to consult with a consular officer. After an unsuccessful appeal, Medellín filed his first habeas corpus petition in state court in 1998, raising a claim for violation of the VCCR. The trial court denied that petition, and the Texas Court of Criminal Appeals affirmed.[84] Mexico then brought a claim against the United States in the International Court of Justice (ICJ) on behalf of Medellín and other Mexican nationals who were on death row in the United States (the *Avena* case).[85] The ICJ issued its *Avena* judgment in March 2004. It held that the United States violated the VCCR. To remedy the violation, the ICJ ordered the United States to provide judicial hearings for fifty-one Mexican nationals, including Medellín.[86]

After the ICJ decision, President Bush issued a memorandum (the "President's memorandum") stating "that the United States will discharge its international obligations under the [*Avena*] decision ... by having State courts give effect to the decision ... in cases filed by the 51 Mexican nationals addressed in that decision."[87] Meanwhile, Medellín filed a second habeas petition in Texas state court in 2005. He argued that it would be illegal for Texas to subject him to capital punishment without first providing the judicial hearing mandated by *Avena*. Specifically, he claimed that Article 94 of the U.N. Charter created a legally binding obligation for the United States to comply with the ICJ judgment in *Avena*, and that treaty obligation was directly binding on Texas courts and government officials under the Supremacy Clause.[88] The United States intervened on behalf of Medellín, arguing that the President's memorandum required Texas courts to grant him a judicial hearing.

Although state law restricts the right of prisoners to file more than one habeas petition, Medellín raised his Article 94 claim in accordance with state procedural rules. Section 5(a)(1) of the Texas Code of Criminal Procedure permits convicted prisoners to file a second habeas petition in cases where "the current claims and issues . . . could not have been presented previously in a timely initial application . . . because the factual or *legal basis for the claim was unavailable on the date the applicant filed the previous application.*"[89] The Texas Court of Criminal Appeals conceded that Medellín's U.N. Charter claim was unavailable when he filed his first habeas petition in 1998 because the ICJ did not decide *Avena* until 2004. Nevertheless, the Texas court denied Medellín's second habeas petition. It held that the *Avena* judgment did not provide a "legal basis for the claim" because the *Avena* judgment was not federal law.[90] The court was surely correct to hold that the *Avena* judgment itself was not federal law. However, the court simply ignored the far more compelling argument that Article 94 of the U.N. Charter is federal law.

The U.S. Supreme Court affirmed the Texas court's decision in March 2008. In Part II of his opinion for the Court, Chief Justice Roberts rejected Medellín's argument that Article 94, read in conjunction with the Supremacy Clause, required Texas courts to grant him a judicial hearing.[91] In Part III, Roberts rejected the U.S. government's argument that the President's memorandum required Texas courts to grant Medellín a judicial hearing.[92] Texas subsequently executed Medellín in August 2008. The State of Texas never provided Medellín the judicial hearing mandated by *Avena*.[93]

B. First Interpretation: No International Violation

Under the first interpretation of the Supreme Court's decision in *Medellín*, the Court held that Article 94 of the U.N. Charter did not create a binding obligation for the United States to comply with the ICJ judgment in *Avena*. Some language in the Court's opinion supports this interpretation. Article 94 states: "Each Member of the United Nations *undertakes to comply* with the decision of the International Court of Justice in any case to which it is a party."[94] The Court emphasized the phrase "undertakes to comply," and noted that Article 94 "does not provide that the United States 'shall' or 'must' comply with an ICJ decision."[95] Moreover, it said: "Noncompliance with an ICJ judgment . . . [was] always regarded as an option by the Executive and ratifying Senate during and after consideration of the UN Charter."[96] Additionally, the Court contended that Medellín's interpretation of Article 94 "would eliminate the option of noncompliance contemplated by Article 94(2)."[97] Professor Vázquez cites these and other passages in support of his view that the Court's decision in *Medellín* is best construed to mean that Article 94 does not actually obligate the United States, as a matter of international law, to comply with ICJ decisions.[98]

Professor Vázquez's interpretation of *Medellín* is attractive because, if he is right, *Medellín* is not at all problematic from a constitutional law standpoint. Under this interpretation, Chief Justice Roberts applied a two-step approach to self-execution analysis in *Medellín* in accordance with traditional justiciability doctrine. In step one, Roberts performed a treaty interpretation analysis and decided, as a matter of international law, that Article 94 gives the United States discretion to decide whether to comply with the ICJ judgment in *Avena*. In step two, he performed a domestic separation-of-powers analysis and concluded, as a matter of domestic law, that the judiciary is not the appropriate branch of government to make that discretionary decision on behalf of the United States.[99] If step one is correct as a matter of international law, then step two is surely correct as a matter of domestic law. No one contends that the Constitution grants the courts, rather than the political branches, the power to decide whether to follow a non-binding directive from an international institution.

Unfortunately, there are two significant problems with this interpretation of *Medellín*. First, the Court stated in several passages that the ICJ decision in *Avena* is binding on the United States as a matter of international law. For example, Chief Justice Roberts wrote: "No one disputes that the *Avena* decision . . . constitutes an international law obligation on the part of the United States."[100] Additionally, Roberts wrote: "The obligation on the part of signatory nations to comply with ICJ judgments derives . . . from Article 94 of the United Nations Charter."[101] In a separate concurring opinion, Justice Stevens said: "Even though the ICJ's judgment in *Avena* is not 'the supreme Law of the Land,' no one disputes that it constitutes an international law obligation on the part of the United States."[102] These and other statements show that the Court acknowledged that Article 94 creates a binding international legal obligation for the United States to comply with the *Avena* judgment.

Second, the claim that Article 94 does not create a binding obligation for the United States to comply with *Avena* is simply wrong as a matter of international law. Granted, Article 94 gives states discretion to determine *how* to implement ICJ decisions, but it does not give them discretion to *refuse to comply* with such decisions. The U.S. government has consistently maintained that Article 94 creates a binding obligation for the United States to comply with valid ICJ judgments.[103] No commentator has seriously contested this proposition. Although Professor Vázquez defends the first interpretation of the Court's opinion in *Medellín*, he agrees that, under this interpretation, the Court's opinion is incorrect as a matter of international law.[104] One should be hesitant to conclude that the Court's decision in *Medellín* was based on a mistaken view of international law, especially when the Court itself affirmed the (correct) view that *Avena* is binding on the United States as a matter of international law.

C. Second and Third Interpretations: *Fujii* Doctrine or NJE Doctrine?

Under the second interpretation of *Medellín*, the Court recognized that the United States has an international obligation to comply with *Avena*. However, the Court held that Texas was not obligated to comply with *Avena*, as a matter of domestic law, because Article 94 of the U.N. Charter lacks the force of law within our domestic legal system. The second interpretation provides the best explanation of what the Court actually said in *Medellín*.

Near the beginning of his opinion, Chief Justice Roberts offered the following definition of self-execution. "What we mean by 'self-executing' is that the treaty has automatic domestic effect as federal law upon ratification. Conversely, a 'non-self-executing' treaty does not by itself give rise to domestically enforceable federal law. Whether such a treaty has domestic effect depends upon implementing legislation passed by Congress."[105] Similarly, the Court said that treaties "are not domestic law unless Congress has either enacted implementing statutes or the treaty itself conveys an intention that it be 'self-executing' and is ratified on these terms."[106] Elsewhere, the Court distinguished "between treaties that automatically have effect as domestic law, and those that . . . do not by themselves function as binding federal law."[107] These statements indicate that, in the Court's view, an NSE treaty is not federal law (even though it has the force of law internationally). Inasmuch as the key distinction between the *Fujii* doctrine and the NJE doctrine turns on whether an NSE treaty is federal law, these statements suggest that the Court's conception of self-execution corresponds with the *Fujii* doctrine, not the NJE doctrine.

On the other hand, several passages in the Court's opinion could be construed to mean that an NSE treaty is federal law, but it is not judicially enforceable. For example, the Court said that Article 94 "is not a directive to domestic courts," and "that ICJ judgments were not meant to be enforceable in domestic courts."[108] Elsewhere, the Court said that the U.N. Charter does "not provide for implementation of ICJ judgments through direct enforcement in domestic courts."[109] Professor Bradley cites these and other passages to support his view that an NSE treaty is federal law, but that it is not judicially enforceable federal law.[110] In other words, he cites these passages to support his argument that we should construe *Medellín* in accordance with the NJE doctrine, not the *Fujii* doctrine.

Professor Bradley concedes that his interpretation of the Supremacy Clause is in tension with the Court's statements to the effect that NSE "treaties do not have any status as domestic law." However, he defends the NJE doctrine on the grounds that it "is easier to reconcile with the text of the Supremacy Clause."[111] Granted, the conclusion that NSE treaties are not domestic law is difficult to reconcile with the first half of the Supremacy Clause, which says that treaties are "the supreme Law of the Land." However, Bradley's claim that NSE treaties are a species of federal law that is not binding on courts is equally difficult to reconcile with the second half of the Supremacy Clause, which says that "Judges in every State shall be bound thereby." In a contest between the *Fujii* doctrine and the NJE doctrine, the text of the Supremacy Clause does not support either side.

Here, the key question is whether the actual language of the Court's opinion in *Medellín* supports the view that NSE treaties have the status of federal law. The answer is a resounding no. Nowhere in his opinion does Chief Justice Roberts say that NSE treaties are federal law, or that they have domestic legal effect. His various statements to the effect that NSE treaties are not judicially enforceable are entirely consistent with the proposition that NSE treaties are not federal law. Indeed, virtually all the language in Roberts's opinion can be explained by saying that NSE treaties are not judicially enforceable *because* they are not federal law. In contrast, the Court's various statements to the effect that NSE treaties "are not domestic law" and do not "have effect as domestic law" are difficult to reconcile with Professor Bradley's view that NSE treaties are federal law.

Moreover, the claim that NSE treaties are federal law is at odds with the main rationale in Part III of the Court's opinion in *Medellín*. In Part III, the Court rejected the U.S. government's argument that the President's memorandum required Texas courts to grant Medellín a judicial hearing. In that context, the Court said: "A non-self-executing treaty, by definition, is one that was ratified with the understanding that it is not to have domestic effect of its own force."[112] Since an NSE treaty is not domestic law, "[t]he responsibility for transforming an international obligation arising from a non-self-executing treaty into domestic law falls to Congress."[113] The conclusion that congressional action is necessary follows from "the fundamental constitutional principle that the power to make the necessary laws is in Congress; the power to execute in the President."[114] In the Court's view, the President's memorandum could not be justified as a valid exercise of the president's power to execute the law because Article 94 of the U.N. Charter is not federal law.[115] Thus, the president's memorandum was an invalid attempt "to enforce a non-self-executing treaty by unilaterally creating domestic law."[116] In sum, the Court's primary rationale for rejecting the federal government's argument rests on the premise that an NSE treaty is not federal law. Without that premise, Part III of the Court's opinion would simply be a naked conclusion without any supporting rationale.

Proponents of the NJE doctrine might argue that the "lawmaking" act at issue in Part III of *Medellín* was the act of converting an NSE treaty obligation into a judicially enforceable obligation. According to this view, the Article 94 obligation to comply with the *Avena* judgment is federal law, but it is not judicially enforceable law. Moreover, the president's attempt to convert that treaty obligation into judicially enforceable law was itself an illegitimate attempt to engage in presidential lawmaking. If this interpretation of *Medellín* is correct, it follows that the State of Texas violated supreme federal law when it executed *Medellín*, because Article 94 is supreme federal law, Article 94 mandates compliance with ICJ decisions, and the ICJ decision in *Avena* prohibited the United States from executing *Medellín* without first providing him a judicial hearing. This interpretation of *Medellín* is consistent with Justice Stevens's separate concurring opinion,[117] but no other justice joined his concurrence. Moreover, the conduct of both state and federal officers at the time of Medellín's execution suggests that they construed the Court's opinion to mean that his execution was entirely lawful as a matter of federal law. The conclusion that Medellín's execution was lawful is consistent with the *Fujii* doctrine because that doctrine holds that an NSE treaty *is not* federal law. However, that conclusion is squarely at odds with the NJE doctrine, which holds that an NSE treaty *is* supreme federal law.

Therefore, assuming that the Court's decision means that Medellín's execution did not violate federal law—as those directly affected by the decision apparently believed—*Medellín* tends to support the constitutional validity of the *Fujii* doctrine, but it does not support Professor Bradley's claim that the NJE doctrine is constitutionally valid.

I have argued elsewhere that *Medellín* was not correctly decided.[118] That argument hinges on two propositions. First, the Court's conclusion that Article 94 of the U.N. Charter is NSE depends upon the (empirical) claim that the U.S. treaty makers responsible for ratification intended the U.N. Charter to be NSE. Second, there is not a shred of evidence to support the Court's empirical claim about the intentions of the U.S. treaty makers.[119] The Court's willingness in *Medellín* to draw empirical conclusions without any supporting evidence highlights the need for a clear statement rule in applying the *Fujii* doctrine. Regardless, arguments about the constitutional validity of the *Fujii* doctrine do not depend upon specific, empirical claims about the intentions of the government officials responsible for ratification of the U.N. Charter.

VI. THE NPE DOCTRINE

So far, this chapter has painted a picture in which there is a stark choice between the *Fujii* doctrine and the NJE doctrine. The final section considers the NPE doctrine as a potential middle ground. The NPE doctrine is a close cousin of the NJE doctrine, but they differ in two key respects. First, under the NJE doctrine, the treaty makers use their Article II power to regulate courts by restricting the types of law that courts can apply to decide cases. In contrast, under the NPE doctrine, the treaty makers use their Article II power to regulate private litigants by restricting the types of law that they can invoke in legal arguments before courts. Second, the NJE doctrine restricts the federal government's use of courts to enforce treaties, whereas the NPE doctrine merely limits private judicial enforcement. (*See* Table Eight on p. 292.)

As noted earlier in this chapter, Congress has enacted several statutes implementing free-trade agreements that rely, at least implicitly, on something like the NPE doctrine. Consider NAFTA as an example. Section 3312(c) of the NAFTA Implementation Act states: "No person other than the United States . . . shall have any cause of action *or defense* under the Agreement or by virtue of Congressional approval thereof."[120] Section 3312(b)(2) adds: "No State law . . . may be declared invalid as to any person or circumstance on the ground that the provision or application is inconsistent with the Agreement, except in an action brought by the United States for the purpose of declaring such law or application invalid."[121] The statute clearly authorizes suits by the federal government to enforce NAFTA against the states. However, as a practical matter, the statute permits courts to disregard federal law in cases where individual defendants argue that state law conflicts with NAFTA.[122] Congress has enacted statutes for several other free-trade agreements that are substantially identical.[123] These statutes constitute persuasive evidence that the legislators who adopted them and the presidents who signed them believed that the Constitution authorized them to adopt laws barring *private* judicial enforcement of international agreements *both offensively and defensively*. If Article I grants Congress the power to enact such laws, it is reasonable to infer that Article II grants the treaty makers the power to adopt similar conditions in the context of treaty ratification. That, of course, is the core premise underlying the NPE doctrine. Therefore, political branch practice related to free-trade agreements supports the constitutional validity of the NPE doctrine. Similarly, Senate treaty actions in September 2008 are premised on an underlying assumption that Article II grants the treaty makers the power to adopt declarations barring private judicial enforcement.[124]

Of course, the fact that the political branches believe that the Constitution authorizes them to enact a particular law does not mean that their belief is correct. Moreover, no court has ever decided whether the "no private enforcement" provisions in free-trade agreements are constitutionally valid. To test the validity of these types of provisions, let us return to the hypothetical Florida case discussed earlier in this chapter. (In that case, a criminal defendant tries to invoke Article 37 of the Convention on the Rights of the Child (CRC) as the basis for a criminal defense.) Assume that the president and Senate adopt an NSE declaration for the CRC modeled on NAFTA. The declaration says: "This treaty supersedes conflicting state laws and is enforceable in an action brought by the United States for the purpose of declaring that a state law is invalid. However, no private party may invoke the treaty as the basis for a claim or defense in any state or federal court unless Congress enacts legislation authorizing private judicial enforcement." We will call this an "NPE declaration" to distinguish it from the NJE declaration discussed previously.[125] Under the standard established in *Yakus* and *Mendoza-Lopez*, the constitutional validity of the NPE declaration, as applied to the hypothetical Florida case, turns on whether "adequate judicial review of the validity of the [Florida law is] available in another forum."[126]

Inasmuch as the NPE declaration envisions government enforcement, the defendant in the hypothetical Florida case could petition the United States Department of Justice (DOJ) to file suit to challenge the validity of the Florida law. Specifically, the DOJ could sue to obtain a declaratory judgment that the Florida law authorizing LWOP sentences is invalid—as applied to criminal defendants who were less than eighteen years old when they committed their crimes—because it conflicts with the CRC. Additionally, the defendant in the Florida case could ask the Florida court to stay the proceedings in the criminal case while the government-initiated suit is pending. Finally, if the DOJ refuses to file suit to invalidate the Florida law, the defendant could file suit against an appropriate DOJ officer under the Administrative Procedure Act (APA) in an effort to compel the federal government to enforce the treaty against Florida.[127] The APA provides that a person who is "adversely affected or aggrieved by agency action . . . is entitled to judicial review thereof."[128] To prevail in an APA action, the Florida defendant (now federal plaintiff) would have to show that the DOJ's refusal to file suit to invalidate the Florida law was "arbitrary, capricious, [or] an abuse of discretion."[129]

Under the standard established in *Yakus* and *Mendoza-Lopez*, it is unclear whether the possibility of government enforcement action to invalidate the Florida law, combined with the possibility of an APA action to compel government enforcement, constitutes an "adequate opportunity" for judicial review of the validity of the Florida law. Regardless, analysis of the hypothetical Florida case shows that the NPE declaration has a better chance of surviving constitutional scrutiny under the Due Process Clause than does the NJE declaration. *Yakus* and *Mendoza-Lopez* require an "adequate opportunity" for judicial review in cases like the hypothetical Florida case. The NJE declaration provides *no opportunity whatsoever* for judicial review because it bars both government enforcement and private enforcement. In contrast, the NPE declaration permits *some opportunity* for judicial review in accordance with the process outlined above.[130]

From a policy standpoint, the NPE doctrine is attractive because there are various situations in which the political branches might wish to bar private enforcement of international agreements, while still preserving the option of government enforcement. The statutes implementing free-trade agreements show that the political branches have preferred this approach in the free-trade context. Similarly, Senate treaty actions in September 2008 regarding the "eight key treaties" manifest a similar policy judgment.[131] Thus, the NPE doctrine potentially offers an attractive middle ground between the *Fujii* doctrine and the NJE doctrine. The NPE doctrine is less problematic than the NJE doctrine from a constitutional standpoint. And, unlike the *Fujii* doctrine, it allows the treaty to operate as law for the federal executive branch, thereby permitting federal executive action to enforce the treaty.

From an interpretive standpoint, though, it is difficult to reconcile either *Medellín* or political branch practice with the NPE doctrine. Suppose that the term "not self-executing," as used in *Medellín*, means that the U.N. Charter is not privately enforceable, but it is enforceable in an action initiated by the federal government. In that case, President Bush could have filed suit against the State of Texas to block Medellín's execution. However, that result appears to be inconsistent with the rationale in Part III of the Court's opinion. Similarly, as noted above, the Senate adopted declarations for eight treaties in September 2008 specifying that the treaty is self-executing but "does not confer private rights enforceable in the United States courts." Those declarations demonstrate that, in the past, the Senate has not employed self-execution terminology in a manner that is consistent with the NPE doctrine, because those declarations are based upon the congressional-executive concept of self-execution,[132] whereas the NPE doctrine is based upon the political-judicial concept. Regardless, the political branches could refine their use of terminology in NSE declarations in the future to make clear that they intend to permit government enforcement, while barring private enforcement.[133]

∗ ∗ ∗

Self-execution doctrine continues to be a source of confusion for courts, commentators, and the political branches. Analysis of judicial decisions and political branch practice shows that "self-execution doctrine" is best understood as a set of eight distinct doctrines that are bundled together under the rubric of self-execution. Leading commentators have defended the NJE doctrine. However, that particular version of NSE doctrine violates the due process rights of criminal defendants, as articulated by the Supreme Court in *Yakus* and *Mendoza-Lopez*. In contrast, the *Fujii* doctrine avoids the central constitutional difficulty inherent in the NJE doctrine. Moreover, compared to the NJE doctrine, the *Fujii* doctrine does a better job of explaining the Supreme Court decision in *Medellín* and political branch practice related to NSE declarations.

Invisible Constitutional Change

Constitutional change happens in many different ways. Occasionally, "We the People" use the process specified in Article V to adopt a formal constitutional amendment.[1] At a few critical junctures in American history, the American people have become exceptionally politically mobilized and engaged in "higher lawmaking" without adopting a formal Article V amendment.[2] On a more routine basis, the meaning of particular constitutional provisions evolves incrementally as courts engage in common law constitutional interpretation.[3] Moreover, as numerous scholars have observed in recent years, social movements play a very significant role in influencing constitutional change.[4] Most leading theories of constitutional change share one feature in common. They assume that constitutional change is visible—that informed participants and observers know that it is happening when it is happening.[5]

I agree that most important constitutional changes are visible in this sense. However, Part Three described a very important constitutional change that happened almost imperceptibly. From the Founding until World War II, the Supremacy Clause was uniformly construed to mean that *all* conflicts between valid treaties and state law must be resolved in favor of the treaties. Between 1945 and 1965, though, a new constitutional consensus emerged. According to the new consensus, conflicts between non-self-executing treaties and state law must be resolved in favor of state law. For reasons to be explained shortly, I will refer to the transformation of the treaty supremacy rule as the "de facto Bricker Amendment." Before the de facto amendment, all valid treaties addressing matters within the scope of state regulatory authority were directly binding on state and local government actors, absent a decision by the federal political branches to authorize conduct inconsistent with the treaty.[6] Now, though, under our modern Constitution, state and local officers may act in contravention of non-self-executing treaty provisions, even without authorization from the federal political branches.[7] Before the transformation, the treaty supremacy rule was an independent constitutional rule. As a result of the de facto Bricker Amendment, the treaty supremacy rule has become an appendage of self-execution doctrine.

The key people responsible for the de facto Bricker Amendment—lawyers in the ABA, the executive branch, and the ALI—never publicly acknowledged that they were adopting a novel construction of the Supremacy Clause that departed sharply from the traditional constitutional understanding that prevailed from the Founding until World War II. They successfully concealed the novelty of the de facto Bricker Amendment by invoking the authority of Chief Justice Marshall's opinion in *Foster v. Neilson*,[8] and claiming (falsely) that their novel interpretation was merely a straightforward application of the key principle articulated in *Foster*. Indeed, they were so successful in perpetrating the mythical account of *Foster* that—judging by outward appearances—it seems that most of the key players honestly believed they were merely following established precedent, rather than creating a novel construction of an important constitutional rule.

I suspect that this type of "invisible" constitutional change happens more frequently than constitutional theorists have previously acknowledged. Certain entrenched features of our legal culture encourage lawyers to frame constitutional arguments as straightforward applications of established precedent, rather than framing their arguments as impassioned pleas for radical reform. Indeed—whether one is making a constitutional argument to a court, a legislature, an executive official, or in the broader arena of public debate—part of what makes the argument "legal," rather than "political," is the fact that the argument is presented as an application of accepted principles, rather than a plea for radical reform.[9] Moreover, in certain circumstances, proponents of radical reform are more likely to succeed if they can disguise their revolutionary agenda as an argument for application of established precedent. When that strategy succeeds—that is, when lawyers, judges, government officers, and the broader public accept the new rule as a simple application (or minor extension) of an established rule—the result is invisible constitutional transformation. The larger the gap between the magnitude of the perceived change and the magnitude of the actual change, the less visible is the transformative process. In the case of the de facto Bricker Amendment, that gap was exceptionally wide, because the actual change was dramatic but the perceived change was very slight.

This chapter explores the dynamics of invisible constitutional transformation. The analysis is divided into three sections. The first section compares the de facto Bricker Amendment to the de facto ERA. Here, I rely heavily on Professor Reva Siegel's excellent case study of the de facto ERA to provide a baseline for comparison.[10] The second section addresses the factors that tend to make constitutional change invisible, using the Bricker example to illustrate more general points. The final section addresses the broader lessons for constitutional theory.

I. COMPARING BRICKER TO THE ERA

As Professor Siegel notes in her seminal article, "movements regularly succeed in changing the Constitution without amending it—the de facto ERA is by no means the only such case."[11] This type of constitutional change is often the product of a clash between opposing social movements. Professors Balkin and Siegel note: "[P]olitical contestation plays an important role in shaping understandings about the meaning and application of constitutional principles.... When movements succeed in contesting the application of constitutional principles, they can help change the social meaning of constitutional principles and the practices they regulate."[12]

In the 1960s, lawyers in the women's movement decided to pursue a dual strategy to advance the cause of women's equality. They litigated claims based on the Equal Protection Clause, while also mobilizing politically to build support for a constitutional amendment (the ERA).[13] Similarly, in the late 1940s and early 1950s, human rights advocates pursued a dual strategy to advance the cause of racial equality. They litigated claims based on the U.N. Charter and the treaty supremacy rule, while simultaneously litigating claims based on the Equal Protection Clause.[14] Unlike the women's movement, though, the human rights advocates did not pursue their agenda by means of a formal constitutional amendment. Instead, when a state court applied the Supremacy Clause to invalidate a California law that conflicted with the U.N. Charter's human rights provisions,[15] leaders of the American Bar Association (ABA) responded by mobilizing support for a constitutional amendment to abolish the treaty supremacy rule (the Bricker Amendment).[16]

In both cases, political mobilization led to counter-mobilization.[17] Advocates of gender equality scored an important victory when Congress voted in favor of the ERA in 1972.[18] However, that victory provided a rallying point for defenders of "traditional values" who opposed the ERA. Led by Phyllis Schlafly, STOP ERA launched a successful campaign to block ratification of the ERA in key southern and western states whose votes were needed to enact the amendment.[19] In contrast to the ERA, Congress never voted in favor of the proposed Bricker Amendment. The decisive vote in the Senate came in February 1954, when the Senate voted 60-31 in favor of one version of the amendment, falling one vote short of the required two-thirds majority.[20] Whereas the ERA battle can be described as a conflict between two opposing forces (the women's movement versus STOP ERA), the Bricker battle is best described as a triangular relationship among three groups. First, human rights activists urged courts to apply the treaty supremacy rule in conjunction with the U.N. Charter's human rights provisions to promote their anti-discrimination goals. Second, Senator Bricker and his allies in the ABA advocated a constitutional amendment to abolish the treaty supremacy rule, because they perceived the combination of treaty supremacy and human rights as a threat to states' rights. Third, lawyers inside and outside the federal executive branch who sought to maintain federal control over foreign affairs mobilized to defeat the proposed Bricker Amendment in the Senate.[21]

In both cases, the new constitutional understanding that arose from the attempt to secure a formal constitutional amendment accomplished at least some of what the amendment's supporters hoped to achieve. Political contestation between opposing groups leads partisan advocates "to qualify their arguments in ways that recognize each other's claims, and, in this process ... internalize at least in part their opponents' normative concerns."[22] In the case of the ERA, the "feminist movement's claims on the equal citizenship principle were sufficiently compelling to the American public that ERA's opponents were constrained to affirm them."[23] On the other hand, "the women's movement gave up ... its robust understanding of what equality and citizenship require: universal child care, access to contraception, and available, safe abortion."[24] The de facto ERA that emerged from the clash between opposing political forces was a compromise that incorporated elements of both views.[25]

Similarly, the de facto Bricker Amendment was a compromise between the normative preferences of competing groups. Human rights advocates scored a crucial victory in *Brown v. Board of Education*.[26] However, just as the women's movement gave up its more robust claims for gender equality, advocates of racial equality effectively abandoned international human rights treaties as a source of enforceable norms in the United States. Senator Bricker and his allies in the ABA scored an important victory by persuading their adversaries to recognize a novel exception to the treaty supremacy rule for NSE treaties. Moreover, as Professor Henkin noted,[27] Bricker largely succeeded in his effort "to bury the so-called covenant on human rights so deep that no one holding high public office will ever dare to attempt its resurrection."[28] Sixty years after the "failed" Bricker Amendment, the United States still refuses to ratify most major international human rights treaties. Moreover, the human rights treaties that the United States has ratified include reservations, understandings, and declarations (RUDs) that effectively preclude the treaties from making any meaningful contribution to the protection of human rights in the United States.[29] Even so, Bricker's opponents also won important victories. They preserved a broad view of federal executive power in foreign affairs by defeating a proposed amendment that would have severely limited the reach of the Supreme Court's holdings in *Belmont* and *Pink*.[30] Additionally, they preserved Congress's power to implement treaties beyond the scope of Article I by defeating the ABA's attempt to enact a constitutional amendment that would have overruled *Missouri v. Holland*.[31]

Despite the similarities between the de facto ERA and the de facto Bricker Amendment, there are significant differences between the two cases. One important difference relates to tactics. When feminist lawyers and activists made their case for the ERA, Phyllis Schlafly and others argued that the ERA was dangerous because it threatened traditional family values.[32] In contrast, Senator Bricker's opponents rarely argued that his attempt to abolish the treaty supremacy rule was dangerous.[33] To the contrary, most of his's opponents conceded his central argument: that the combination of human rights treaties with the treaty supremacy rule was dangerous, and "must not be allowed to take effect so as to change the structure of the federal-state system in the United States."[34] Instead of arguing that Bricker's proposal to abolish the treaty supremacy rule was dangerous,[35] they argued that a constitutional amendment was not necessary to avert the danger posed by human rights treaties.[36] In the course of defending that argument, they advanced a novel construction of the treaty supremacy rule that gave rise to a new constitutional understanding—namely, that there is an NSE exception to the treaty supremacy rule.[37] Proponents of the NSE exception concealed the novelty of their construction of the Supremacy Clause by claiming continuity with established precedent.

Another key difference between Bricker and the ERA relates to the branch of the federal government that performed the critical "settlement function."[38] The Supreme Court effectively settled the parameters of the de facto ERA in a series of cases decided in the 1970s.[39] In contrast, the Court played almost no role in establishing the contours of the de facto Bricker Amendment. In the Bricker case, the federal executive branch performed the key settlement function by determining the parameters of the new constitutional understanding. Specifically, senior members of the Eisenhower administration issued a series of statements—in the context of Senate testimony during the Bricker Amendment hearings in 1953—in which they endorsed the new NSE exception to the treaty supremacy rule.[40] As statements by senior executive officials were not readily accessible to courts, courts continued to apply the traditional treaty supremacy rule until the American Law Institute published its Restatement (Second) of Foreign Relations Law in 1965.[41] As a practical matter, the ALI consolidated the new constitutional understanding that developed within the Eisenhower administration during the Bricker Amendment debates.[42] Once that new understanding was codified in the form of the Restatement, state courts and lower federal courts began to apply the NSE exception to the treaty supremacy rule. The Supreme Court finally endorsed the NSE exception to the treaty supremacy rule in its 2008 decision in *Medellín v. Texas*,[43] several decades after the de facto Bricker Amendment had become settled law. The Court in *Medellín* claimed that it was applying the rule from *Foster v. Neilson*, but *Foster* addressed self-execution, not treaty supremacy, which was understood at the time as an entirely separate issue.[44]

The central role played by the Eisenhower administration in creating the de facto Bricker Amendment, and the peripheral role of the Supreme Court, implicates an important issue in contemporary constitutional theory. Professor Kramer's leading work on popular constitutionalism raises both normative and historical questions related to judicial supremacy.[45] As a historical matter, Kramer claims that judicial supremacy did not become firmly established until after the Supreme Court's landmark decision in *Cooper v. Aaron* in 1958.[46] The Bricker Amendment story is consistent with Kramer's historical account in that the federal executive branch, not the Supreme Court, performed the key settlement function to resolve a major constitutional issue in 1952–1954, several years before *Cooper v. Aaron*. Moreover, analysis of the de facto Bricker Amendment suggests that judicial supremacy may not be quite as firmly entrenched today as Kramer and other scholars tend to assume. In particular, there may be a range of constitutional issues related to the conduct of foreign affairs where, even in the twenty-first century, the actual practice of constitutional interpretation is consistent with a departmentalist model, or perhaps a model of executive supremacy, rather than judicial supremacy. I return to this point below. First, though, let us consider the factors that tend to make constitutional change invisible.

II. WHAT MAKES CONSTITUTIONAL CHANGE INVISIBLE?

Several factors related to the transformation of the treaty supremacy rule in the 1950s combined to make that particular constitutional change less visible than many others. Analysis of those factors provides clues about where scholars might look for evidence of other invisible constitutional changes.

First, the transformation of the treaty supremacy rule relied heavily on the use of technical, legal jargon that was not widely understood. As documented in Parts One and Two, before 1945 self-execution doctrine and treaty supremacy doctrine were two independent, non-overlapping doctrines. In the early 1950s, lawyers in the ABA and the executive branch reinterpreted the treaty supremacy rule by importing self-execution rhetoric from the federal separation-of-powers realm to address the relationship between treaties and state law.[47] Even before this change occurred, though, self-execution doctrine was sufficiently arcane that, in retrospect, one can identify at least five distinct versions of the doctrine that existed before 1945, each of which was based on a different implicit assumption about the distribution of constitutional power over treaty implementation.[48] The fact that self-execution doctrine was already very complex and technical before 1945 meant that self-execution rhetoric was a helpful tool for concealing the change in treaty supremacy doctrine after 1945.

The second point is related to the first. Reliance on Chief Justice Marshall's opinion in *Foster v. Neilson* as the primary authority for the novel construction of the treaty supremacy rule also helped make the constitutional change invisible. As Professor West notes in a different context, "it is not precedent that the popular constitutional claim must fit with so much as it is constitutional myth."[49] Twentieth century lawyers created a mythical account of *Foster* that is closely linked to the modern understanding of treaty supremacy. Creation of the *Foster* myth evolved in two stages. First, Professor Edwin Dickinson wrote an influential article in the 1920s that reinterpreted *Foster* in the context of disputes about Prohibition-era treaties designed to block illegal liquor imports.[50] Dickinson's article laid the groundwork for the later reinterpretation of *Foster* in the 1950s that ultimately transformed the treaty supremacy rule.[51] The mythical account of *Foster* associated with modern self-execution doctrine preserves an appearance of historical continuity that conceals the dramatic constitutional transformation that occurred in the 1950s.

Third, as noted previously, federal executive officials performed the critical settlement function to establish the contours of the de facto Bricker Amendment. The fact that key interpretive decisions were made by executive officers, rather than courts, also contributed to the invisibility of the constitutional transformation. Judicial decisions on constitutional issues are usually the product of adversarial litigation in which the main issues are openly contested. Judicial decisions are published in a form that is easily accessible to the legal community; every lawyer is trained to analyze those decisions to identify the court's holding. Congressional testimony by senior executive officials is also published, but that congressional testimony is not as readily accessible to the average lawyer. Moreover, insofar as congressional testimony is the product of an adversarial contest between opposing views within the executive branch,[52] the official who testifies before Congress is unlikely to disclose internal executive branch conflicts, and the documents providing evidence of such internal conflicts are rarely accessible to the public. Consequently, in cases where a senior executive official announces a novel legal position in congressional testimony,[53] a lawyer who studies the relevant congressional testimony may not recognize that the speaker is announcing an innovative construction of a venerable constitutional rule. Therefore, in cases where the executive branch plays a central role in constitutional transformation, the resultant changes may be less visible than constitutional changes resulting from adversarial litigation and judicial decisions.

Lawyers within the executive branch are more likely to perform the critical settlement function when the contested constitutional issue relates to foreign affairs—as did the treaty supremacy rule at issue in the Bricker debates. Executive branch lawyers routinely engage in constitutional interpretation in both domestic and foreign affairs. In both domestic and foreign policy arenas, executive branch views on constitutional issues are potentially subject to judicial review, giving courts the final say on matters of constitutional construction.[54] However, the prevalence of judicial avoidance doctrines in the foreign affairs realm means that the executive branch is more likely to get the final say on constitutional foreign affairs questions than it does on domestic constitutional issues.[55] For example, it is well known that the Supreme Court has done very little to check the steady expansion of presidential war powers.[56] Similarly, a recent article by Professor Curtis Bradley shows how the executive branch, acting with very little judicial oversight, developed a novel construction of the constitutional rules related to treaty termination.[57] Since executive branch settlement tends to be less visible than judicial settlement, and since the executive branch is more likely to perform the settlement function with respect to constitutional foreign affairs matters, other examples of invisible constitutional transformation are likely to involve constitutional foreign affairs issues.

Another factor that probably contributed to the invisibility of the de facto Bricker Amendment was the fact that the crucial constitutional changes were countercyclical. In the early-to-mid 1950s, when the Bricker Amendment controversy was at its peak, the dominant trend of constitutional change involved a transfer of power from the states to the federal government.[58] In contrast, the de facto Bricker Amendment shifted power over treaty implementation from the federal government to the states by creating an exception to the treaty supremacy rule for non-self-executing treaties. Similarly, in the first half of the 1950s, the Supreme Court was initiating a major campaign to expand the scope of individual rights.[59] In contrast, the de facto Bricker Amendment tended to restrict protection for individual rights by removing human rights treaties as a potential source of enforceable rights. It is not surprising that scholars interested in the broad sweep of constitutional history might overlook important constitutional changes that tend to cut against the dominant narrative.

Finally, the point about cognitive dissonance that I have discussed previously bears emphasis in this context. "The holding of two or more inconsistent cognitions arouses the state of cognitive dissonance, which is experienced as uncomfortable tension. . . . Once dissonance is aroused, it needs to be reduced."[60] The California Court of Appeal's opinion in *Fujii* in 1950 created severe cognitive dissonance for Americans because the decision was tantamount to a proclamation that international human rights law provided more robust protection against racial discrimination than did the Fourteenth Amendment Equal Protection Clause.[61] As of 1950, that conclusion was legally sound, but politically unacceptable. Our national identity as Americans is rooted in the secular dogma that our Constitution is the best constitution in the world, sometimes called "American exceptionalism."[62] The *Fujii* decision created severe cognitive dissonance for many Americans by presenting a simple comparison: human rights protection under the U.N. Charter is greater than human rights protection under the Constitution. The de facto Bricker Amendment alleviated that cognitive dissonance by eliminating the U.N. Charter as a reference point. If the treaty supremacy rule does not apply to NSE treaties, and the U.N. Charter is an NSE treaty, then we are free to ignore the Charter in our national discussions about racial discrimination. In short, the de facto Bricker Amendment promoted an important social psychology objective: it helped make international human rights norms invisible so that we, as Americans, could avoid confronting the uncomfortable tension between our faith in American exceptionalism and the strong anti-discrimination norm expressed in the newly emergent body of international human rights law.

To accomplish that social psychology objective, the de facto Bricker Amendment, itself, had to be invisible. If the American public knew that lawyers were manipulating constitutional rules to hide certain uncomfortable truths, those truths could not remain hidden. Thus, the central constitutional change that defines the de facto Bricker Amendment—the creation of an NSE exception to the treaty supremacy rule—remained invisible because the legal profession and the American public wanted to shield their psyches from certain unpleasant truths that were impossible to reconcile with the public faith in American exceptionalism.

III. IMPLICATIONS FOR CONSTITUTIONAL THEORY

The story of the de facto Bricker Amendment has several implications for both positive and normative constitutional theory. Begin with positive theory, the main goal of which is to describe and explain the process of constitutional change. The leading positive theories of constitutional change tend to focus primarily, if not exclusively, on domestic factors that influence constitutional change.[63] However, foreign and transnational factors played a central role in the de facto Bricker Amendment. In the late 1940s and early 1950s, the domestic civil rights movement was very closely linked with the international human rights movement—so much so that it is a mistake to think of them as two separate movements.[64] Proponents of the Bricker Amendment were propelled by fear that the emerging body of international human rights law would transform the U.S. Constitution in ways they deemed undesirable.[65] Although their attempt to amend the Constitution through the Article V process failed, political contestation over the Bricker Amendment transformed the treaty supremacy rule. This example is not unique. New constitutional constructions often emerge from a battle of ideas; ideas travel freely across national borders. As Professor Resnik has urged, future scholarship in the field of positive constitutional theory should pay greater attention to foreign and transnational influences on domestic constitutional change.[66]

Much of the work on popular constitutionalism emphasizes the division between "the people" and the courts. According to this framework, "the people" shape constitutional change outside the courts, whereas lawyers and judges shape constitutional change by the judiciary.[67] In the case of the de facto Bricker Amendment, though, lawyers played a central role in shaping constitutional change outside the courts. The American Bar Association initiated the push for a constitutional amendment. A minority group within the ABA developed the key arguments against a constitutional amendment; in the process, they proposed a novel construction of the Supremacy Clause that ultimately gained broader acceptance. Lawyers within the executive branch legitimated the novel construction of the Supremacy Clause by drafting statements for senior officials who endorsed that construction in their congressional testimony.[68] Lawyers in the American Law Institute codified the new understanding of the treaty supremacy rule in a form that was readily accessible to judges and other lawyers.[69]

Social movement theories emphasize the importance of social movements in directing constitutional change.[70] In my view, social movement theory offers many important insights, but there is a tendency to understate the significance of lawyers as a group in directing the process of constitutional change. Lawyers use political processes to promote their agendas in much the same way that they use litigation to do so. There is no a priori reason to think that lawyers who make constitutional arguments in the political arena are more representative of "the people" than lawyers who make constitutional arguments in courts. Either way, lawyers play a critical role in driving the process of constitutional change.[71]

For the past few decades, political scientists and legal scholars have written extensively about the problem of "regulatory capture." Although there is no single agreed definition of the term, it generally refers to situations where "organized groups successfully act to vindicate their interests through government policy at the expense of the public interest."[72] The case of the de facto Bricker Amendment suggests that social movement theory may not have paid sufficient attention to a problem I will call "reverse capture." Reverse capture occurs when a social movement representing a broad public interest applies pressure on government actors who redirect the political momentum supporting that social movement and channel it in a direction that is more compatible with their narrow bureaucratic interests. That is precisely what happened with the de facto Bricker Amendment.

The movement in favor of the Bricker Amendment began as a response to the human rights movement—a movement that represented a broad public interest in anti-discrimination and racial equality. The Eisenhower administration formed a tactical alliance with human rights advocates in a joint effort to defeat the Bricker Amendment. However, in the course of political contestation over the proposed amendment, the interests of human rights advocates were effectively shoved aside because the Eisenhower administration was pursuing a different agenda, and its agenda dominated the response to the proposed amendment.[73] The episode illustrates a persistent problem confronting social movements that favor constitutional change. Activists outside government need allies within one or more branches of government to accomplish their goals. However, any alliance with legislative or executive officials poses a potential risk of reverse capture because those officials invariably have their own agendas, which may not align well with the movement's agenda.

If we turn from positive theory to normative theory, the case of the de facto Bricker Amendment raises questions about the democratic legitimacy of popular constitutionalism. Larry Kramer defines "judicial supremacy" as a system in which "the Court ... tells us what the Constitution means."[74] He contrasts judicial supremacy with popular constitutionalism, a system in which the "people themselves" decide what the Constitution means. Kramer contends that—measured by the yardstick of democratic legitimacy—popular constitutionalism is superior to judicial supremacy. I am sympathetic to Kramer's argument that the accumulation of power by unelected judges is at odds with principles of popular sovereignty. However, his case for the superiority of popular constitutionalism requires an explanation of how the "people themselves" make decisions about constitutional meaning. When pressed on that question, Kramer's answer is essentially that the people make those decisions through their elected representatives in the legislative and executive branches.[75]

In the eighteenth and nineteenth centuries, Congress made a significant contribution to the process of constitutional construction.[76] However, it is questionable whether the twenty-first century Congress has either the will or the ability to play the role that Kramer envisions for Congress as the peoples' representative in the construction of constitutional meaning. If Congress abdicates its role in constitutional construction, the executive branch would be left to serve as the primary governmental check on judicial supremacy. The case of the de facto Bricker Amendment suggests that executive decision-making on questions of constitutional construction may be less democratically legitimate than judicial decision-making. Although the people elect the president, presidents rely on unelected lawyers within the executive branch to advise them on questions of constitutional law. Executive decision-making is generally more secretive and less open to public scrutiny than judicial decision-making. For reasons discussed previously, the executive branch is likely to play a greater role in constitutional construction when the contested issue relates to foreign affairs. The culture of secrecy surrounding the conduct of U.S. foreign policy means that executive decision-making in foreign affairs is less transparent than executive decision-making on purely domestic issues.[77] Thus, in practice, there is a risk that "popular constitutionalism" in the modern era may entail constitutional construction by unelected executive branch lawyers whose conduct is shielded from public scrutiny by entrenched policies and practices that protect the secrecy of executive decision-making. Insofar as constitutional theory seeks to justify constitutional change as an expression of popular sovereignty, published opinions by unelected judges are preferable to classified, unpublished opinions by unelected executive branch attorneys.

Professor Balkin's theory of "living originalism" presents an elegant defense of the democratic legitimacy of our living Constitution.[78] Balkin says:

> Constitutional construction is either directly produced by the political branches . . . or is in the long run responsive to them because of institutional constraints on the federal judiciary. Thus, popular sovereignty is exercised directly through the creation of the constitutional framework . . . and either directly or indirectly through constitutional construction. The processes of living constitutionalism are consistent with and promote democratic legitimacy in the medium to long run because they allow political and social mobilizations to change the Constitution-in-practice through constitutional construction . . . .[79]

I find Balkin's account persuasive. However, the story of the de facto Bricker Amendment requires a cautionary note: some constitutional changes are largely invisible. Invisible constitutional transformation is difficult to reconcile with principles of democratic legitimacy because "the people" cannot easily mobilize to resist constitutional constructions that are shielded from public view.

Balkin contends that "legitimacy is not a property of individual constructions or interpretations but rather of the constitutional and political system as a whole."[80] However, in the general discourse of legal and political theory, "legitimacy" is a term that applies both to individual constructions and to the system as a whole. Legitimacy requires transparency. One can challenge the legitimacy of specific constructions that result from invisible constitutional transformation on the grounds that the process of invisible change lacks transparency. Moreover, Balkin's conclusion about the legitimacy of the system as a whole necessarily assumes that most constitutional change is visible, not invisible. That assumption may well be correct. Nevertheless, it is worthwhile for constitutional scholars to devote additional research to identifying other examples of invisible constitutional transformation. Until that research is completed, we cannot say with confidence whether the phenomenon of invisible constitutional change is a rare aberration, or a systemic feature that we have previously overlooked.

List of Abbreviations Used in Endnotes

ALI Archives	Archives of the American Law Institute for the Restatement (Second) of the Foreign Relations Law of the United States
Ann. Cong.	Annals of Congress
Ann. Rep. ABA	Annual Report of the American Bar Association
Bevans	Charles I. Bevans ed., Treaties and Other International Agreements of the United States of America, 1776–1949 (1968) (13 vols.)
Cong. Globe	Congressional Globe
Cong. Rec.	Congressional Record
DHRC	Merrill Jensen, John Kaminski, and Gaspare Saladino, eds., The Documentary History of the Ratification of the Constitution (1983–2013) (26 vols.)
Elliott's Debates	Jonathan Elliot, ed., The Debates in the Several State Conventions on the Adoption of the Federal Constitution, 2d ed. (1836) (4 vols.)
Federalist Papers	Benjamin Wright, ed., The Federalist Papers (1961)
FRUS	Department of State, Foreign Relations of the United States: 1952–1954 (1979–1989) (16 vols.)
Fujii Case File	California Supreme Court Archives, 2nd Civ. No. 17309, L.A. 21149, Fujii v. California
Hackworth	Green Haywood Hackworth, Digest of International Law (1940–1944) (8 vols.)
Hamilton Papers	Harold C. Syrett ed., The Papers of Alexander Hamilton (1961–1987) (27 vols.)
Hamilton Practice	Julius Goebel Jr. ed., The Law Practice of Alexander Hamilton (1964–1980) (4 vols.)

J. Cont. Cong.	Journals of the Continental Congress: 1774–1789
Madison Papers	William Hutchinson et al. eds., The Papers of James Madison (1962–1991) (17 vols.)
Malloy	William M. Malloy ed., Treaties, Conventions, International Acts, Protocols and Agreements (1910–1938) (4 vols.)
Miller	Hunter Miller ed., Treaties and Other International Acts of the United States of America (1931–1948) (8 vols.)
Moore	John Bassett Moore ed., A Digest of International Law (1906) (8 vols.)
Records	Max Farrand ed., Records of the Federal Convention of 1787 (1911) (4 vols.)
Restatement (Second)	American Law Institute, Restatement of the Law (Second): The Foreign Relations Law of the United States (1965)
Restatement (Third)	American Law Institute, Restatement of the Law (Third): The Foreign Relations Law of the United States (1987)
Wharton	Francis Wharton, A Digest of the International Law of the United States (1886) (3 vols.)
Whiteman	Marjorie M. Whiteman, Digest of International Law (1963–1973) (15 vols.)

Endnotes

Preface to the Paperback Edition (Oct. 30, 2021)

1. U.S. Const. art VI, cl. 2.
2. 217 P.2d 481 (Cal. App. 2d 1950).
3. U.S. Const. art VI, cl. 2.
4. 27 U.S. 253 (1829).
5. American Law Institute, Restatement of the Law (Second): The Foreign Relations Law of the United States (1965).
6. Medellín v. Texas, 552 U.S. 491, 505 n.2 (2008).
7. *See generally* Restatement (Fourth) of Foreign Relations Law of the United States § 310 (Am. Law Inst. 2018).
8. State v. Ball, 305 So.3d 90 (La. 2020); State v. Dressner, 255 So.3d 537 (La. 2018); Turrubiartes v. Olvera, No. 01-16-00322-CV, 2017 WL 2375787 (Tex. App. June 1, 2017); State v. Horton, No. 1 CA-CR 15-0179, 2016 WL 1742989 (Ariz. Ct. App. May 3, 2016).
9. *See Ball*, 305 So.3d at 98 ("[I]nsofar as international treaties apply, these treaties, either the ICCPR or the CERD, are not self-executing, meaning the courts may not enforce them in the absence of corresponding state or federal legislation."); *Dressner*, 255 So.3d at 543 ("Insofar as Dressner argues the ICCPR should apply, the treaty is not self-executing, meaning the Court may not enforce it in the absence of corresponding state or federal legislation."); *Turrubiartes*, 2017 WL 2375787, at *5 ("Treaties automatically have effect as domestic law only if the treaty is "self-executing" and is ratified on those terms (citing *Medellín*). The Covenant that Maria invokes is not a self-executing treaty and did not create a domestic private right of enforcement."); *Horton*, 2016 WL 1742989, at *6 ("The ICCPR does not create judicially-enforceable individual rights, is not self-executing, and has not been given effect by congressional legislation. Accordingly, the ICCPR is not binding on courts of the United States.") (citations omitted).
10. *See Ball*, 305 So.3d at 98 ("Ball introduces no authority showing that his execution is prohibited by international law."); *Dressner*, 255 So.3d at 543 ("Dressner introduces no authority for the idea that his execution is prohibited by international law."); *Horton*, 2016 WL 1742989, at *6 ("even assuming Appellant may invoke [the ICCPR], he has raised no issues constituting reversible error.")

11. *See* In re: State Question No. 807, Initiative Petition No. 423, 468 P.3d 383 (Ok 2020); Daskin v. Knowles, 193 A.3d 717 (Del. 2018); State v. Montgomery, 71 N.E.3d 180 (Ohio 2016); Savage v. Allstate Insurance Co., 2021 WL 137261 (Ky. Ct. App. 2021); Estate of Herzog v. Herzog, 33 Cal.App.5th 894 (Cal. Ct. App. 2019); Interest of T.M.E., 565 S.W.3d 383 (Tex. App. 2018); Rockefeller Technology Investments v. Changzhou Sinotype Technology Co., Ltd., 24 Cal.App.5th 115 (Cal. Ct. App. 2018); Tadross v. Tadross, 86 N.E.3d 827 (Ohio Ct. App. 2017); Gandy v. Raemisch, 405 P.3d 480 (Colo. App. 2017); El Zoobi v. United Airlines, Inc., 50 N.E.3d 1150 (Ill. App. Ct. 2016); Bevilacqua v. U.S. Bank, 194 So.3d 461 (Fla. Dist. Ct. App. 2016); Ingeneria y Exportacion de Tecnologia S.L. v. Freytech, Inc., 210 So.3d 211 (Fla. Dist. Ct. App. 2016); Delex, Inc. v. Sukhoi Civil Aircraft Co., 372 P.3d 797 (Wash. Ct. App. 2016); Gregor v. Otuorimuo, 2016 WL 2728135 (Conn. Super. Ct. April 19, 2016).

12. *Herzog*, 33 Cal.App.5th at 907-10 (concluding that "[t]he requirements of the Hague Convention certificate appear to be consistent with the final statement requirements of [California] Evidence Code section 1530").

13. *Daskin*, 193 A.3d at 723-25 (reversing Family Court decision in a divorce case because husband was not properly served under the Hague Service Convention); *Savage*, 2021 WL 137261 at *7-8 (affirming lower court decision to quash service of process for failure to comply with the Hague Service Convention); *Interest of T.M.E.*, 565 S.W.3d at 391-92 (reversing lower court decision in a child custody case because the father was not properly served under the Hague Service Convention); *Rockefeller Technology Investments*, 24 Cal.App.5th at 129-33 (reversing decision confirming arbitration award because Chinese company was not properly served under the Hague Service Convention); *Tadross*, 86 N.E.3d at 829-30 (reversing lower court decision in divorce case because wife was not properly served under the Hague Service Convention); *El Zoobi*, 50 N.E.3d at 1154-57 (holding that state tort law claims against airline company were preempted by the Montreal Convention).

14. *In re: State Question No. 807*, 468 P.3d at 391 (rejecting treaty preemption argument based on the Vienna Convention on Psychotropic Substances because "[p]etitioner makes no argument as to how exactly SQ 807 prevents the U.S. from complying with its treaty obligations"); *Montgomery*, 71 N.E.3d at 214 (Court rejected argument by death row prisoner that Ohio's death penalty statute violates "international law and treaties"); *Gandy*, 405 P.3d at 483-87 (holding that Colorado Department of Corrections regulation did not conflict with bilateral treaty between Canada and the United States on the execution of penal sentences); *Bevilacqua*, 194 So.3d at 464-65 (holding, in a foreclosure action, that mortgagee was properly served under the Hague Service Convention); *Ingeneria y Exportacion de Tecnologia S.L.*, 210 So.3d at 212-13 (where plaintiff sent documents to defendant as provided in Article 10(a) of the Hague Service Convention, service of process on Spanish company was deficient because plaintiff failed to serve defendant with a summons as required by state law, and Hague Convention does not eliminate requirement to serve summons); *Delex, Inc.*, 372 P.3d at 799-802 (holding that creditor who sought payment from Russian debtor was not required to follow the procedures in the Hague Service Convention to effectuate service of process); *Gregor*, 2016 WL 2728135, at *3-5 (holding that Hague Service Convention did not apply to service of process on defendant in Nigeria because Nigeria is not a party to the treaty).

15. *See* Daskin v. Knowles, 193 A.3d 717 (Del. 2018); Savage v. Allstate Insurance Co., 2021 WL 137261 (Ky. Ct. App. 2021); Interest of T.M.E., 565 S.W.3d 383 (Tex. App. 2018); Rockefeller Technology Investments v. Changzhou Sinotype Technology Co., Ltd., 24 Cal.App.5th 115 (Cal. Ct. App. 2018); Tadross v. Tadross, 86 N.E.3d 827 (Ohio Ct. App. 2017); Bevilacqua v. U.S. Bank, 194 So.3d 461 (Fla. Dist. Ct. App. 2016); Ingeneria y Exportacion de Tecnologia S.L. v. Freytech, Inc., 210 So.3d 211 (Fla. Dist. Ct. App. 2016); Delex, Inc. v. Sukhoi Civil Aircraft Co., 372 P.3d 797 (Wash. Ct. App. 2016); Gregor v. Otuorimuo, 2016 WL 2728135 (Conn. Super. Ct. April 19, 2016).

16. In *Canadian Lumber Trade Alliance v. U.S.*, 425 F.Supp.2d 1321, 1362 (Ct. Int'l Trade 2006), the Court of International Trade stated mistakenly that the Supreme Court held in *Volkswagenwerk Aktiengesellschaft v. Schlunk*, 486 U.S. 694 (1988), that the Hague Service Convention is self-executing. However, that statement is incorrect. The Supreme Court held in *Volkswagenwerk Aktiengesellschaft* that the Hague Service Convention preempts inconsistent state law, *id.* at 699, but did not explicitly decide whether the Convention is self-executing.

17. *See, e.g.*, Petmas Investors, Ltd. v. Sameiet Holbergs Gate 19, No. CIV.A. 13-6807, 2014 WL 6886028, at *6 (D. N.J. 2014); Randolph v. Hendry, 50 F.Supp.2d 572, 575 (S.D.W. Va. 1999); Fox v. Regie Nationale des Usines Renault, 103 F.R.D. 453, 455 (W.D. Tenn. 1984).

18. *Volkswagenwerk Aktiengesellschaft*, 486 U.S. 694, 699 (1988).

19. *See* David Sloss, *Schizophrenic Treaty Law*, 43 Tex. Int'l L.J. 15 (2007).

20. *See* David Sloss, *United States*, in THE ROLE OF DOMESTIC COURTS IN TREATY ENFORCEMENT: A COMPARATIVE STUDY (Sloss ed., 2009).

21. Estate of Herzog v. Herzog, 33 Cal.App.5th 894 (2019), is one such outlier, insofar as the court apparently thought that self-execution doctrine was at least relevant to analysis of a treaty supremacy argument in a private law case. *See id.*, at 907-10.

22. Oona Hathaway et. al., *International Law at Home: Enforcing Treaties in U.S. Courts*, 37 Yale J. Int'l L. 51, 64-68 (2012).

23. *See id.*, at 73-76.

24. 539 F.3d 485 (D.C. Cir. 2008).

25. 549 F.3d 605 (3d Cir. 2008).

INTRODUCTION

1. The Federalist, No. 22 (Alexander Hamilton).

2. 552 U.S. 491 (2008).

3. *See* Balkin (2011); Kramer (2004); Ackerman (2000); Tushnet (1999).

4. *See* Siegel (2006).

5. United Nations Charter, art. 55 (emphasis added).

6. Fujii v. California, 217 P.2d 481 (Cal. App. 2d 1950).

7. *See* Chapters 10 and 11.

8. Restatement (Second).

9. The Federalist, No. 44 (James Madison).

10. 552 U.S. 491 (2008). Article 94 requires the United States to comply with decisions of the International Court of Justice (ICJ) in cases where the United States is a party. The death row prisoner in *Medellín* sought a court order to compel compliance with a decision in which the ICJ ruled against the United States.

11. The rationale can be explained as follows: under the traditional rule, the Supremacy Clause meant that courts must resolve all conflicts between treaties and state law in favor of treaties. Hence, if a litigant claimed that a state law conflicted with a treaty, the court was generally required to address the merits of that claim. Under the NSE exception, though, courts are permitted to apply state law, regardless of whether the state law conflicts with a treaty. Therefore, when presented with an alleged conflict between a treaty and state law, courts do not have to decide whether state law actually conflicts with the treaty, because they are permitted to apply state law even if there is a conflict.
12. *See* Chapter 14, pp. 295–96 (summarizing current controversies).
13. *See* Henkin (1995); Sloss (1999).
14. *See, e.g.,* U.N. Doc. A/HRC/30/12 (July 20, 2015) (documenting gaps between international standards and domestic human rights protection in the United States).
15. U.S. CONST. art. II, § 2.
16. U.S. CONST. art. VI, cl. 2 (emphasis added).
17. Maiorano v. Baltimore & Ohio R.R. Co., 213 U.S. 268, 272–73 (1909).
18. Ware v. Hylton, 3 U.S. 199, 237 (1796) (Chase, J.).
19. Restatement (Second), Preliminary Draft 5, § 3.04, cmt. c (emphasis added).
20. Wright (1951).
21. *See* Balkin & Siegel (2006), at 930–33.
22. Cook v. United States, 288 U.S. 102, 119 (1933).
23. 112 U.S. 580 (1884).
24. *Id.* at 598–99.
25. Fujii v. State, 242 P.2d 617, 620 (Cal. 1952).
26. Foster v. Neilson, 27 U.S. 253, 314 (1829). Marshall did not actually use the term "non-self-executing" in *Foster*, but the quoted passage is frequently cited as the basis for modern NSE doctrine.
27. *See* Chapter 4.
28. Medellin v. Texas, 552 U.S. 491, 504–05, 508, 514–15 (2008).
29. U.N. Charter, arts. 55, 56 (emphasis added).
30. Universal Declaration of Human Rights (1948).
31. *See, e.g.,* Fujii v. State, 242 P.2d 617 (Cal. 1952) (invalidating California's Alien Land Law); Namba v. McCourt, 204 P.2d 569 (Or. 1949) (invalidating Oregon's Alien Land Law).
32. *See, e.g.,* Hurd v. Hodge, 334 U.S. 24 (1948) (holding that courts may not enforce racially restrictive covenants in the District of Columbia); Shelley v. Kraemer, 334 U.S. 1 (1948) (holding that state courts may not enforce racially restrictive covenants in Missouri and Michigan).
33. *See* Dudziak (2000).
34. *See* Lockwood (1984).
35. *See* Goodman & Jinks (2013), at 4, 26, 153.
36. Bolling v. Sharpe, Brief for Petitioners (1954).
37. Brown v. Bd. of Education (1954) & Bolling v. Sharpe (1954), Brief for United States as Amicus Curiae.
38. Fairman (1952).
39. Brown v. Bd. of Education, 347 U.S. 483 (1954); Bolling v. Sharpe, 347 U.S. 497 (1954).

40. Goodman & Jinks (2013), at 153.
41. Chapter 11 presents this argument in more detail. I have previously advanced a version of this argument in Sloss, *Human Rights* (2016). Professor Resnik has also made a similar argument. *See* Resnik (2006), at 1598–1606.
42. *See, e.g.,* Klarman (2004).
43. Fujii v. State, 242 P.2d 617, 620 (Cal. 1952).
44. Fujii v. California, 217 P.2d 481 (Cal. App. 2d 1950).
45. Reasonable people may disagree about whether there was actually a conflict between the U.N. Charter and the Alien Land Law. The answer to that question hinges on treaty interpretation. However, assuming that there was a conflict, the court's conclusion that the treaty trumped California law under the Supremacy Clause was firmly grounded in constitutional text, judicial precedent, and original understanding.
46. *See* Chapters 9 to 11. *See also* Tananbaum (1988); Kaufman (1990).
47. *See* Chapters 10 and 11.
48. Fujii Case File, Petition for Hearing in the Supreme Court of the State of California, at 14–15.
49. Fujii v. State, 242 P.2d 617, 620 (Cal. 1952).
50. *See id.*, at 619–22.
51. The California Supreme Court did not decide whether there was a conflict between the Charter and the Alien Land Law. Instead, the Court said that Fujii could not prevail on his Charter argument, even if the Alien Land Law did conflict with the Charter, because the Charter was not self-executing. Ultimately, the Court ruled in favor of Fujii on the basis of the Equal Protection Clause.
52. The leading originalist defense of NSE doctrine tacitly concedes the treaty supremacy point and defends NSE doctrine purely on federal separation of powers grounds. *See* Yoo, Globalism (1999).

Part 1

1. *See* Golove & Hulsebosch (2010).
2. Emmerich de Vattel, an influential figure in the United States during the Founding era, considered treaties to be one branch of the law of nations. He divided the law of nations into four parts: necessary, voluntary, conventional, and customary. Under his framework, the "conventional" law of nations equated to treaties. *See* Vattel (1758).
3. *See generally* Morris (1984), at 194–219 (discussing the U.S. failure to fulfill its international legal obligations).
4. Golove & Hulsebosch (2010), at 947.

Chapter 1

1. Treaty of Amity and Commerce, U.S.-Fr., Feb. 6, 1778, 8 Stat. 12; Treaty of Alliance, U.S.-Fr., Feb. 6, 1778, 8 Stat. 6.
2. Articles of Confederation, art. II.
3. Articles of Confederation, art. IX.
4. *See* 2 Miller, at 59–227 (reproducing text of treaties).
5. 1783 treaty with Britain, art. 7.
6. The text of Adams's Memorial is reproduced in 31 J. Cont. Cong., at 781–82.
7. *Id.*, at 784.

8. *Id.*, at 862.
9. *Id.*, at 784.
10. Morris (1984), at 201.
11. *See id.*, at 130–61.
12. *Id.*, at 152 (quoting Thomas Paine).
13. *Id.*, at 134–35.
14. *Id.*, at 159.
15. *Id.*, at 201.
16. 32 J. Cont. Cong., at 180.
17. The Federalist, No. 15, at 156 (Alexander Hamilton).
18. *See* 1 Hamilton Practice, at 282–419.
19. *See id.*, at 289–90.
20. *Id.*, at 329 (Replication and Demurrer by John Lawrence, attorney for plaintiff).
21. *Id.*, at 373 (Brief No. 6).
22. *Id.*, at 377 (Brief No. 6).
23. *See id.*, at 392, 397–99 (opinion of court).
24. *Id.*, at 411.
25. *Id.*
26. *Id.*, at 412.
27. *Id.*, at 414.
28. *See* Golove & Hulsebosch (2010), at 962 ("When beneficiaries of the new state laws used them against loyalists or Britons, most state courts enforced the statutes and refused to hold the peace treaty as a trump against contrary state laws.").
29. 1 Hamilton Practice, at 380 (Brief No. 6).
30. *Id.*, at 415 (opinion of court).
31. *Id.*, at 377 (Brief No. 6).
32. *Id.*, at 413 (opinion of court).
33. *Id.*, at 378–80 (Brief No. 6).
34. *Id.*, at 405–06 (opinion of court).
35. *Id.*, at 417.
36. *Id.*, at 418.
37. *See* 1783 treaty with Britain, arts. 4–6.
38. 31 J. Cont. Cong., at 797.
39. *Id.*, at 862.
40. *Id.*, at 868.
41. *Id.*, at 869–70.
42. *Id.*, at 870.
43. *Id.*
44. *See* 32 J. Cont. Cong., at 124–25.
45. *See id.*, at 176–84.
46. *Id.*, at 177.
47. *Id.*, at 178–79.
48. Ramsey (2007), at 39.
49. 9 Madison Papers, at 348–49.
50. 1 Records, at 19.
51. The Federalist, No. 15, at 158 (Alexander Hamilton).
52. 1 Records, at 229 (June 13). *See also* 2 Records, at 27 (reproducing slightly different version considered on July 17).

53. *See* Rakove (1996), at 81–83, 171–74.
54. *See* 2 Records, at 27–28.
55. 1 Records, at 245.
56. William Paterson first proposed the New Jersey Plan on June 15. *See* 1 Records, at 243–45. The delegates approved a modified version of what became the Supremacy Clause on July 17. *See* 2 Records, at 27–29; Rakove (1996), at 81–82. The Committee of Detail met from July 27 to August 5. They replaced the phrase "any thing in the respective laws of the individual States to the contrary notwithstanding" with the phrase "any Thing in the *Constitutions* ·or Laws of the several States to the Contrary notwithstanding," thereby clarifying that federal law supersedes state constitutions, as well as state statutes. *See* 2 Records, at 169; Rakove (1996), at 173. John Rutledge proposed an additional amendment on August 23. Earlier drafts made clear that federal statutes and treaties supersede conflicting state laws, but they did not mention the U.S. Constitution. Rutledge's modified language stated: "*This Constitution* & the laws of the U.S. . . .," thereby clarifying that the U.S. Constitution also supersedes conflicting state laws. *See* 2 Records, at 389; Rakove (1996), at 173–74.
57. 2 Records, at 27.
58. *Id.*, at 28–29.
59. Rakove (1996), at 82.
60. Vázquez (1992), at 1106.
61. *See* U.S. CONST. art. III, sec. 2 (granting Supreme Court appellate jurisdiction over cases arising under treaties).
62. *See id.*, art. III, sec. 1 (vesting federal judicial power "in such inferior Courts as the Congress may from time to time ordain and establish"); *id.*, art. III, sec. 2 (extending federal judicial power to cases arising under treaties).
63. *Id.*, art. I, sec. 10.
64. *Id.*, art. II, sec. 2, cl. 2.
65. *Id.*, art. I, sec. 3, cl. 1. The Seventeenth Amendment, which took effect in 1913, provides for direct, popular election of U.S. senators.
66. *Id.*, art. II, sec. 3.
67. *See* Ramsey (2007), at 163–65; Swaine (2008), at 342–48.
68. U.S. CONST. art. I, sec. 8, cl. 18.
69. *See* Missouri v. Holland, 252 U.S. 416 (1920).
70. *See* Rosenkranz (2005) (contending that the Necessary and Proper Clause does not grant Congress power to enact legislation to implement treaties). In *Bond v. United States*, 134 S. Ct. 2077 (2014), Justices Scalia and Thomas endorsed Professor Rosenkranz's theory. *See id.*, at 2098–99 (Scalia, J., concurring).
71. U.S. CONST. art. III, sec. 2, cl. 1.
72. *See* Vázquez (1992), at 1101–10; *see also* 32 J. Cont. Cong., at 178–79 (quoting letter from Congress to the states, which affirmed the crucial role of state courts in enforcing treaties).
73. U.S. CONST. art. VI, cl. 2.
74. Nelson (2000), at 246.
75. *Id.*, at 250.
76. *Id.*, at 254–57. In his opinion for the court in *Rutgers v. Waddington*, Mayor Duane applied the presumption against implied repeals to justify his conclusion that the New York trespass statute was not intended to repeal applicable principles of the

law of nations. Moreover, he noted explicitly that "the statute under our consideration, doth not contain even the common *non obstante clause*, tho' it is so frequent in our statute book." 1 Hamilton Practice, at 417 (opinion of court). Thus, in Duane's view, the absence of a non obstante clause in the statute supported his decision to apply the presumption against implied repeals. Similarly, the affirmative decision to include a non obstante clause in the Supremacy Clause manifests the Framers' determination that state courts should *not* apply the presumption against implied repeals to resolve conflicts between federal law and state law.

CHAPTER 2

1. 5 Ann. Cong. (April 4, 1796), at 776.
2. *See, e.g.,* Rosenkranz (2005); Golove (2000); Bradley (1998).
3. *See, e.g.,* Kesavan (2006); Flaherty (1999); Yoo, Globalism (1999); Vazquez (1992).
4. Kesavan (2006).
5. Yoo, Globalism (1999); Yoo, Public Lawmaking (1999).
6. Rakove (1984), at 264.
7. *Accord* Parry (2009), at 1263–64 ("By the end of ratification, participants on both sides appear to have concluded that treaties would trump state law under the Supremacy Clause ... On other issues, such as the role of the House of Representatives and the interaction between treaties and federal law, no consensus emerges.")
8. Warren (1934), at 297.
9. *Id.,* at 280.
10. *Id.,* at 283.
11. *See id.,* at 283–86.
12. 9 DHRC, at 1039.
13. 10 DHRC, at 1192 (William Grayson).
14. *See id.,* at 1380 (George Mason) (contending that the Treaty Clause is dangerous because "five states might make a treaty; ten Senators, the Representatives of five States, being two-thirds of a quorum").
15. James Madison to George Nicholas, May 17, 1788, 9 DHRC, at 804–09.
16. *Id.,* at 808.
17. *See, e.g.,* 9 DHRC, at 1129–31 (George Nicholas); 10 DHRC, at 1241–42 (James Madison).
18. *Id.,* at 1556.
19. *Id.,* at 1554.
20. *See* 4 Elliott's Debates, at 223–51.
21. Federal Farmer IV, 14 DHRC, at 42, 43.
22. Brutus II, 13 DHRC, at 524, 529.
23. Cato VI, 14 DHRC, at 428, 431–32.
24. 4 Elliott's Debates, at 215 (William Lancaster).
25. 10 DHRC, at 1384 (Patrick Henry).
26. *Id.*
27. *See* Yoo, Globalism (1999), at 2040–74.
28. James Iredell, Essay III, the Norfolk and Portsmouth Journal, Mar. 5, 1788, *reprinted in* 1 Bailyn, at 383.
29. The Federalist, No. 22 (Alexander Hamilton).
30. *Id.*

31. The Federalist, No. 42 (James Madison).
32. *Id.*
33. 2 DHRC, at 517–18 (James Wilson).
34. *Id.*, at 520 (James Wilson).
35. 10 DHRC, at 1392 (Francis Corbin).
36. *Id.*, at 1396 (James Madison). *See also id.*, at 1388–89 (George Nicholas).
37. 2 DHRC, at 561 (James Wilson).
38. James Madison to George Nicholas, May 17, 1788, 9 DHRC, at 806–08.
39. The Federalist, No. 75 (Alexander Hamilton).
40. 9 DHRC, at 1130–31 (George Nicholas).
41. 2 Bailyn, at 882 (James Iredell).
42. 10 DHRC, at 1395–96 (James Madison). For a modern defense of this position, see Hollis (2015).
43. 10 DHRC, at 1389 (George Nicholas).
44. *Id.*, at 1396 (James Madison).
45. *Id.*, at 1389 (George Nicholas).
46. *Id.*, at 1395 (James Madison).
47. The New York Convention adopted a resolution with a long list of declarations that they claimed "are consistent with said Constitution." One such declaration stated that "no treaty is to be construed, so to operate, as to alter the Constitution of any State." 2 Bailyn, at 539. Hence, one could argue that the New York delegates challenged the view that treaties would trump state constitutions under the Supremacy Clause.

    However, other evidence suggests that the claim that the various declarations were "consistent with said Constitution" was really a statement about the Constitution they hoped to achieve by means of amendments, not a statement about the correct interpretation of the Constitution as written. After the list of declarations, the New York Convention proposed a long list of amendments, including a proposed amendment stating that "all executive and judicial officers of the United States, shall be bound by oath or affirmation not to infringe or violate the constitutions or rights of the respective states." *Id.*, at 545. In general, the proposed amendments in the second half of the New York resolution were designed to accomplish by constitutional amendment many of the objectives expressed as declarations in the first half of the resolution. Thus, if we construe the New York resolution as a whole, the proposed amendments suggest that the New York delegates were not really convinced that the declarations in the first half of the resolution were consistent with the Constitution as written, despite the stated claim of consistency.
48. Rhode Island held a referendum in March 1788 in which the voters overwhelmingly rejected ratification of the Constitution. Two years later, in May 1790, the Rhode Island Convention voted in favor of ratification. *See* Ratification Chronology: 1786–1790, 2 DHRC, at 19–25.
49. Texts of state resolutions and proposed amendments are reprinted in 2 Bailyn, at 536–74; and 1 Elliott's Debates, at 319–32. The amendments proposed by the Pennsylvania dissent are reprinted in 2 DHRC, at 623–25.
50. *See* 2 Bailyn, at 536–74 (resolutions adopted by New York, Massachusetts, New Hampshire, Maryland (including amendments proposed by anti-Federalists), South Carolina, Virginia, and North Carolina; and 2 DHRC, at 623–25 (amendments proposed by Pennsylvania dissenters).

51. 2 Bailyn, at 563.
52. *See id.*, at 571.
53. *See* Chapter 1, pp. 21–22.
54. 2 DHRC, at 623–25 (The Address and Reasons of Dissent of the Minority of the Convention of the State of Pennsylvania to Their Constituents).
55. *Id.*, at 624–25.
56. 2 Bailyn, at 555 (amendment proposed by anti-Federalists in Maryland).
57. *Id.*, at 545.
58. *Id.*, at 539.
59. U.S. Const. art. VI, cl. 2.
60. *See* 2 DHRC, at 624–25.
61. 2 Bailyn, at 555.
62. *Id.*, at 571–72.
63. *See* 2 Elliott's Debates, at 542–46 (Proceedings of the Meeting at Harrisburg, in Pennsylvania).
64. *Id.*, at 542.
65. *Id.*, at 546.
66. *See, e.g.*, 13 DHRC, at 348–50 (George Mason's objections to the Constitution).
67. *See* Kesavan (2006), at 1544–45 (citing numerous sources); An Old Whig III, 13 DHRC, at 425, 426.
68. *See* Yoo, Globalism (1999), at 1961–62; 10 DHRC, at 1393–95 (Patrick Henry).
69. 2 DHRC, at 562–63 (James Wilson).
70. Yoo, Globalism (1999), at 2048.
71. The Federalist, No. 53 (James Madison).
72. James Madison to George Nicholas, May 17, 1788, 9 DHRC, at 808.
73. The Federalist, No. 69 (Alexander Hamilton).
74. *Id.*
75. *See* Chapter 7.
76. U.S. Const. art. I, sec. 9, cl. 7.
77. *See, e.g.*, Statement of James Iredell to the North Carolina Convention, *reprinted in* 2 Bailyn, at 886 (stating that the House of Representatives possesses the right "of exclusively originating money bills. The authority over money will do everything. A government cannot be supported without money."); Letter from James Madison to George Nicholas, 9 DHRC, at 808 (stating that the cooperation of the House of Representatives "may often be necessary in carrying treaties into full effect . . . [because] support of the Government . . . must be drawn from the purse which they hold.").
78. *See* Chapter 3.
79. 9 DHRC, at 1131 (George Nicholas).
80. 10 DHRC, at 1251 (George Nicholas).
81. 2 Bailyn, at 886 (James Iredell) (the British House of "Commons have generally been able to carry everything before them. The circumstance of their representing the great body of the people, alone gives them great weight. . . . Our Representatives may at any time compel the Senate to agree to a reasonable measure, by with-holding supplies till the measure is consented to.").
82. Yoo, Public Lawmaking (1999), at 2220.
83. *See* Parry (2009); Kesavan (2006); Flaherty (1999).
84. Yoo, Globalism (1999).

85. 10 DHRC, at 1256 (Francis Corbin).
86. *Id.*, at 1392–93 (Francis Corbin).
87. *See* Federal Farmer XI, 17 DHRC, at 308–10; *see also* Kesavan (2006), at 1546–47 (analyzing the views of the Federal Farmer).
88. Yoo, Public Lawmaking (1999), at 2220.
89. 2 Bailyn, at 562.
90. *Id.*, at 569.
91. U.S. Const. art. II, sec. 2, cl. 2.
92. 2 Bailyn, at 562 (Virginia proposal); *id.*, at 569 (North Carolina proposal).
93. Kesavan (2006), at 1486.
94. *See id.*, at 1484–86.
95. *See id.*, at 1529–92.
96. The Federalist, No. 64 (John Jay).
97. 2 DHRC, at 618, 624.
98. 2 Bailyn, at 571–72.
99. *See* Kesavan (2006), at 1567–69 (discussing the amendment proposed by the Pennsylvania dissenters).
100. 2 DHRC, at 623.
101. *Id.*, at 625.
102. 2 Bailyn, at 565.

Chapter 3

1. *See* Parry (2009), at 1276–94 (analyzing Jay Treaty debates about conflicts between treaties and statutes).
2. *See, e.g.,* Bradley (2008).
3. *See* pp. 6–7 for discussion of the distinction between the congressional-executive concept and the political-judicial concept.
4. 3 U.S. 199 (1796). *Georgia v. Brailsford*, 2 U.S. 402 (1792) also involved a conflict between a treaty and state law. However, the Court's decision did not address treaty supremacy issues. Instead, the Court issued a temporary injunction to allow more time for the parties to develop their arguments in a way that would facilitate judicial resolution of the issues.
5. *Ware*, 3 U.S. at 200.
6. 1783 treaty with Britain.
7. *Id.*, art. 4.
8. *Ware*, 3 U.S. at 209 (Tilghman, for Plaintiff in Error).
9. *Id.*, at 210–13 (Marshall, for Defendant in Error).
10. *Id.*, at 213 (Marshall, for Defendant in Error).
11. *Id.*, at 213–14 (Marshall, for Defendant in Error).
12. *Id.*, at 284 (Cushing, J.).
13. *Id.*, at 256 (Paterson, J.).
14. *Id.*, at 281 (Wilson, J.).
15. *Id.*, at 236 (Chase, J.).
16. *Id.*, at 237 (Chase, J.).
17. Justice Iredell expressed his views, but he did not technically cast a vote, because he participated in the decision at the circuit court level. *See* Parry (2009), at 1268.
18. *Ware*, 3 U.S. at 277 (Iredell, J.).
19. *See id.*, at 278–80 (Iredell, J.).

20. Seven of the ten lawyers and judges in *Ware* attended either the Constitutional Convention or a state ratifying convention or both. Justices James Wilson and William Patterson both attended the Constitutional Convention, as did future chief justice John Marshall (who represented the defendants). Justices Samuel Chase, William Cushing, and James Iredell, respectively, attended the Maryland, Massachusetts, and North Carolina Conventions. Justice Wilson attended the Pennsylvania Convention. Alexander Campbell, who represented the plaintiff, attended the Virginia Convention. *See generally* Elliott's Debates.

21. Conventional wisdom holds that Marshall created the doctrine of non-self-execution in his opinion in *Foster v. Neilson*, 27 U.S. 253 (1929). However, the conventional wisdom is wrong on two counts. First, as discussed later in this chapter, the doctrine can be traced back at least as far as the House debates over the Jay Treaty in 1796. Second, Marshall's treaty interpretation analysis in *Foster* focused on the distinction between executory and executed treaty provisions, not the distinction between self-executing and non-self-executing treaty provisions. *See* Chapter 4.

22. *Ware*, 3 U.S. at 271–73 (Iredell, J.).

23. 2 Blackstone, Commentaries *443.

24. *Ware*, 3 U.S. at 272 (Iredell, J.).

25. *Id.*

26. *Id.*

27. Although the terms "self-executing" and "non-self-executing" are ambiguous, there is general agreement that the distinction hinges on whether the treaty requires legislative implementation. The ambiguity involves what it means to say that legislation is "necessary." Is legislation necessary to incorporate the treaty into domestic law? Or are non-self-executing treaties part of domestic law, but legislation is necessary to authorize implementation by executive and/or judicial officers?

28. *See* Golove (2000), at 1154–88.

29. 1783 treaty with Britain, art. 7. *See* Chapter 1.

30. *See generally* Bemis (1962).

31. 1794 treaty with Britain [hereinafter Jay Treaty].

32. The Jay Treaty was the first treaty signed by the United States after adoption of the Constitution. The Jay Treaty was signed in November 1794 and entered into force in October 1795. However, the first treaty to enter into force after adoption of the Constitution was a consular convention with France. *See* 1788 treaty with France. The U.S. and France signed the consular convention in November 1788, before the Constitution took practical effect. The Senate consented in July 1789, after the Constitution took effect, and the treaty entered into force in 1790.

33. *See* Elkins & McKitrick (1993), at 415–49.

34. For detailed analysis of the political context of the Jay Treaty debates, see Combs (1970).

35. *See* 4 Ann. Cong., at 853–63 (1795).

36. *See* Golove (2000), at 1154–58, and sources cited therein.

37. The House debate can be divided into two phases. The first phase lasted from March 7 to April 7. *See* 5 Ann. Cong, at 426–783 (1796). The second phase lasted from April 13 to May 3. *See* 5 Ann. Cong., at 940–1292 (1796).

38. 4 Ann. Cong., at 861–62 (1795). The official Senate records do not name Senator Tazewell as the author of the motion. However, Professor Golove cites other materials that clearly identify Tazewell as the author. *See* Golove (2000), at 1159, n.249.

39. Jay Treaty, art. 9.
40. U.S. CONST. amend. X.
41. For a detailed defense of this constitutional argument, see Tucker (1915). For a more recent version of a similar argument, see Bradley (1998).
42. 4 Ann. Cong., at 862–63 (1795).
43. Supreme Court decisions also tend to support the constitutional validity of Article 9. Between 1812 and 1830, the Supreme Court decided six cases in which it awarded judgment to individual litigants whose rights were protected under Article 9 of the Jay Treaty. *See* Shanks v. DuPont, 28 U.S. 242 (1830); Hughes v. Edwards, 22 U.S. 489 (1824); Orr v. Hodgson, 17 U.S. 453 (1819); Craig v. Radford, 16 U.S. 594 (1818); Jackson v. Clarke, 16 U.S. 1 (1818); and Fairfax's Devisee v. Hunter's Lessee, 11 U.S. 603 (1812). All six cases assume, without deciding explicitly, that Article 9 was a constitutionally valid exercise of the Treaty Power. Based on available records, it appears that no opposing party in any of these cases challenged the constitutional validity of Article 9.
44. Robert Livingston, Cato No. XVI (quoted in Golove (2000), at 1166–67).
45. *See* Golove (2000), at 1163–68.
46. Atticus, No. IX (quoted in Golove (2000), at 1168). Atticus's statement includes a partial quotation of the Tenth Amendment. *See* U.S. CONST. amend X.
47. In theory, one could conceivably argue that Article 9 was internationally valid, but states had to enact implementing legislation to make it domestically effective. However, it does not appear that anyone advocated that position in the debates over the Jay Treaty.
48. Among the Federalists, Alexander Hamilton provided the most comprehensive defense of the constitutional validity of Article 9. *See The Defence No. XXXVI* (Jan. 2, 1796), *reprinted in* 20 Hamilton Papers, at 3; *The Defence No. XXXVII* (Jan. 6, 1796), *reprinted in* 20 Hamilton Papers, at 13; *The Defence No. XXXVIII* (Jan. 9, 1796), *reprinted in* 20 Hamilton Papers, at 22. Hamilton did not state explicitly that Article 9 superseded conflicting state law by virtue of the Supremacy Clause, but that proposition was implicit in his argument.
49. Disagreement about this issue was one of the main points of contention between Republicans and Federalists during the first month of House debates on the treaty. *See* 5 Ann. Cong., at 426–783 (1796). For detailed analysis of the House debate, see Parry (2009), at 1276–94.
50. 5 Ann. Cong., at 427–28 (1796).
51. *Id.*, at 481 (statement of Roger Griswold).
52. *Id.*, at 771 (text of resolution); *id.* at 782–83 (vote on resolution).
53. *See* 1 Stat. 459 (May 6, 1796) (final text of law enacted by Congress); 5 Ann. Cong., at 1292–98 (1796) (House debate over appropriations bill).
54. Currie (1997), at 215; *see also* Henkin (1996), at 204–05 ("Like some other constitutional debates, this one, too, has not been authoritatively resolved in principle.").
55. *See* Restatement (Third) § 111 cmt. i.
56. 5 Ann. Cong. 771 (1796).
57. It is helpful in this context to distinguish between prohibitions and mandates. If treaties "contain prohibitory provisions on both parties, the agreement in those respects is concluded, for such things cannot be done by either party." Tucker

(1915), at 203. Prohibitory treaty provisions do not require affirmative steps to be executed; House Republicans were presumably not thinking about prohibitions when they drafted their resolution. In contrast, "if such treaty requires the doing of certain things by the parties to the convention," then the treaty is "executory as to such subjects," and affirmative steps are needed to execute the treaty. *Id.* The House resolution seems to contemplate legislation for such executory treaty provisions within the scope of Congress's legislative powers.

58. *The Defence No. XXXVII*, 20 Hamilton Papers, at 16.

59. 5 Ann. Cong., at 548 (1796).

60. *Id.* Congressman Bradbury defended this position at some length. *See id.*, at 548–54.

61. *See, e.g.*, Yoo, Globalism (1999), at 2080–86. Yoo claims that "Congress declared that treaties that conflicted with its power to legislate were non-self-executing." *Id.*, at 2081. This claim is manifestly false. The House of Representatives adopted a resolution along these lines, but Congress as a whole never endorsed this proposition.

62. *See* 5 Ann. Cong., at 940–76 (1796).

63. *Id.*, at 940.

64. *Id.*, at 966–67.

65. Jay Treaty, art. 15.

66. *See* 1 Stat. 459-60 (May 6, 1796) for the final text of both appropriations bills. The House passed a resolution for the Spanish treaty stating "[t]hat, in the opinion of this Committee, it is expedient to pass the laws necessary for carrying the Treaty with Spain into effect." 5 Ann. Cong., at 943 (1796). *See also id.*, at 969. ("The motion was put and carried.") However, the House resolution is not a "law." The only law that Congress passed to carry the treaty into effect was the one appropriating money. The House followed a similar course with the Jay Treaty. It passed a resolution stating that "it is expedient to pass the laws necessary for carrying into effect" the Jay Treaty. *See id.*, at 954, 1290–91. But the only law enacted was the appropriations measure.

67. A consensus developed in the nineteenth century that treaties affecting import duties were constitutionally non-self-executing. *See* Chapter 6, pp. 109–13. However, the Supreme Court rejected that view, at least implicitly, in *De Lima v. Bidwell*, 182 U.S. 1 (1901). *See* Chapter 7, pp. 135–37.

68. Parry (2009), at 1292.

PART 2

1. Oxford English Dictionary, at http://www.oed.com.

2. Wright (1951), at 64.

3. *See* pp. 6–8.

4. Dickinson, Am. J. Int'l L. (1926). *See* Chapter 8.

5. *See* Sloss, *Executing Foster* (2012), at 136–39 (explaining the distinction between the one-step and two-step approaches).

6. There may be a small number of treaties that create an international legal obligation to enact legislation. Professor Ramsey cites Article 5 of the 1783 peace treaty with Britain as an example of such a treaty provision. *See* Ramsey (2016), at 1650. For such treaties, there is no practical distinction between the

international obligation question and the domestic implementation question. Regardless, it is exceedingly rare for a treaty to create an international legal obligation to enact legislation. Typically, a treaty creates an obligation to accomplish some objective and gives states discretion to determine how best to accomplish that objective—whether by legislation, executive action, or some other means.

7. I contend that there are constitutional limits on the treaty makers' Article II power to prevent courts from applying treaty provisions that are otherwise within the scope of judicial authority. *See* Chapter 14.

8. 27 U.S. 253 (1829).

9. *See* Balkin & Siegel (2006), at 930–33.

10. Two other variants of NSE doctrine developed in the nineteenth century. I refer to these variants as the "contract doctrine" and the "condition precedent doctrine." Both apply a two-step approach. Both involve the congressional-executive concept of self-execution. Hence, both can be seen as variants of the constitutional doctrine. *See* Table Three, p. 127.

11. 112 U.S. 580 (1884). I believe that Professor Vázquez coined the term "justiciability doctrine," as applied to NSE treaties. *See* Vázquez (1995), at 710–15. He also uses the term "constitutionality doctrine" to describe what I am calling the "constitutional doctrine." *See id.,* at 718–19.

CHAPTER 4

1. Foster v. Neilson, 27 U.S. 253, 314 (1829).

2. This section borrows liberally from Sloss (2006), at 79–85.

3. 3 Papers of Daniel Webster, pt. 2, at 960–80 (Andrew J. King ed., 1989) [hereinafter Webster Papers].

4. The Perdido River currently forms the western boundary of Florida that separates the Florida panhandle from Alabama. The 31st parallel now forms the border between the Florida panhandle and that portion of southern Alabama that lies east of the Perdido River. The 31st parallel also forms part of the border between Mississippi and Louisiana.

5. The facts in this paragraph are taken from *Foster,* 27 U.S. at 300–01, and from *Harcourt v. Gaillard,* 25 U.S. 523, 524 (1827).

6. *See* 1783 treaty with Britain, art. 2.

7. The facts in this paragraph are taken from *Foster,* 27 U.S. at 300–01, and from *Henderson v. Poindexter's Lessee,* 25 U.S. 530, 534 (1827).

8. *Foster,* 27 U.S. at 301 (quoting Treaty of St. Ildefonso).

9. *See id.,* at 302–03.

10. *See* 1803 treaty with France, art. 1.

11. *See Foster,* 27 U.S. at 303–09.

12. *See* 1819 treaty with Spain, arts. 2 and 3.

13. *See Foster,* 27 U.S. at 253–55.

14. *Id.,* at 255.

15. *Id.,* at 306–07.

16. *Id.,* at 307.

17. Garcia v. Lee, 37 U.S. 511, 516 (1838) (restating the holding of *Foster*). *See also* Delacroix v. Chamberlain, 25 U.S. 599, 600 (1827) (foreshadowing *Foster's*

political question holding in the following terms: "A question of disputed boundary between two sovereign independent nations is, indeed, much more properly a
subject for diplomatic discussion . . . than of judicial investigation.").

18. *See Foster*, 27 U.S. at 303–09.
19. Webster Papers, at 994.
20. Keene v. Heirs of Clark, 35 U.S. 291 (1836), involved land in Floriana, but the
     Court dismissed the case for lack of subject matter jurisdiction.
21. Garcia v. Lee, 37 U.S. 511, 520 (1838).
22. *Id.*, at 520.
23. *Foster*, 27 U.S. at 307.
24. 1819 treaty with Spain, art. 8.
25. *See Foster*, 27 U.S. at 310–14.
26. *See id.*, at 313–14.
27. *Id.*, at 313.
28. *See id.*, at 312–13.
29. *Garcia*, 37 U.S. at 520–21 (emphasis added).
30. *See* White (1988), at 184 ("Throughout most of Marshall's tenure, the Court had
     a remarkable percentage of unanimous or near unanimous decisions . . . . For ex-
     ample, between 1816 and 1823, a period in which the Court's composition was
     unchanged, the Justices produced a total of 302 majority opinions. In all these
     cases, only twenty-four dissents and eight concurrences were recorded.")
31. *See Foster*, 27 U.S. at 310–13.
32. *See* pp. 76–84 for discussion of Marshall's non-self-execution rationale.
33. *See Foster*, 27 U.S. at 256.
34. Webster Papers, at 961.
35. *Foster*, 27 U.S. at 293 (emphasis added) (argument of counsel).
36. *See, e.g.*, Medellín v. Texas, 552 U.S. 491 (2008) (citing *Foster* repeatedly as author-
     ity for NSE doctrine); *id.*, at 522–23 (stating that an NSE treaty "does not of its
     own force constitute binding federal law that pre-empts [contrary] state" law);
     Restatement (Second) § 141 (discussed in Chapter 13); Fujii v. State, 242 P.2d 617
     (Cal. 1952) (discussed in Chapter 11).
37. This section borrows liberally from Sloss, *Executing Foster* (2012), at 146–53.
38. Ware v. Hylton, 3 U.S. 199, 272 (Iredell, J.) (1796).
39. *See* 10 Ann. Cong. (1800), at 532–33 (resolution introduced by Representative
     Livingston); 10 Ann. Cong. (1800), at 605–15 (statement by Congressman John
     Marshall); Van Alstine (2008) (discussing Marshall's role in the Robbins affair).
40. *See* 1794 treaty with Britain, art. 27.
41. Letter from Timothy Pickering to Thomas Bee (June 3, 1799), *in* 4 State
     Papers and Publick Documents of the United States 304 (2d ed., T.B. Wait &
     Sons 1817).
42. *See* United States v. Robbins, 27 F. Cas. 825, 833 (D.S.C. 1799).
43. 10 Ann. Cong. (1800), at 614.
44. *Id.*, at 613.
45. U.S. CONST. art. II, sec. 3.
46. 10 Ann. Cong. (1800), at 614.
47. *Id.*, at 606. It is noteworthy that Marshall's Republican opponents thought the
     judiciary could execute the treaty without waiting for legislative authorization,
     but the executive had to await legislative authorization before implementing the

treaty. This is precisely the opposite of the view espoused by many modern scholars, who think that the president can execute treaties on his or her own authority, but the courts must await legislative implementation. *See, e.g.*, Stephan (2009).

48. 10 Ann. Cong. (1800), at 615.

49. *See id.*, at 608 (comparing the 1788 treaty with France, which specified a particular mode of treaty implementation, with Article 27 of the 1794 treaty with Britain, which contained no such provision).

50. *See* 1803 treaty with France, art. 3; 1819 treaty with Spain, art. 8.

51. One source indicates that the Supreme Court decided "some fifty cases" involving the Louisiana Treaty and "about fifty Florida cases." Cummings & McFarland (1937), at 124–25. Their figures may include some cases decided after 1860. The author identified seventy-five cases decided between 1829 and 1859. *See* Sloss, *Executing Foster* (2012), at 149–50 (listing cases).

52. *See, e.g.*, Bradley (2008); Flaherty (1999); Parry (2009); Vázquez (2008); Yoo, Globalism (1999). *But see* Sloss, Ramsey & Dodge (2011), at 18–23.

53. The Court never used the term "self-executing" or "non-self-executing" to modify the term "treaty" in any of the Louisiana/Florida property cases. *Bartram v. Robertson*, 122 U.S. 116, 120 (1887) was the first case in which the Court used the term "self-executing" to refer to treaties.

54. *See, e.g.*, United States v. Roselius, 56 U.S. 31, 34 (1853) ("If the grant of the French government to Duport was a complete title, then no act on the part of the American government was required to give it additional validity, as the treaty of 1803, by which Louisiana was acquired, sanctioned perfect titles[.]"); McDonogh v. Millaudon, 44 U.S. 693, 706 (1845) ("The perfect title of McDonogh being clothed with the highest sanction, and in full property, on the change of governments . . . the general law of nations and the treaty of 1803 . . . secured in full property such titles.")

55. United States v. Wiggins, 39 U.S. 334, 350 (1840).

56. It is helpful here to distinguish between two types of "future action." In some cases, affirmative judicial action is necessary to resolve a treaty-related dispute between two private parties. Such disputes might arise with respect to either executed or executory treaty provisions. For example, if a private party trespassed on land for which another person held a perfect title, the judiciary might need to take future action to protect the owner's title, even though the title is protected by an executed treaty provision. In contrast, some treaties obligate the United States to take future action, even in the absence of any dispute between private parties. Such treaties are "executory" in the sense in which Justice Iredell used that term. *See* Chapter 3, pp. 50–51.

57. United States v. Kingsley, 37 U.S. 476, 477 (1838).

58. *McDonogh*, 44 U.S. at 706. *See also* Strother v. Lucas, 37 U.S. 410, 436 (1838) (explaining that an "inchoate" or "equitable" title was a property right, "which before the treaty with France in 1803, or with Spain in 1819, had so attached to any piece or tract of land, great or small, as to affect the conscience of the former sovereign, 'with a trust,' and make him a trustee for an individual").

59. *See Wiggins*, 39 U.S. at 350 (stating that "the United States were bound, after the cession of the country, to the same extent that Spain had been bound before the ratification of the treaty, to perfect" these inchoate titles); *see also* Chouteau v. Eckhart, 43 U.S. 344, 374 (1844); Florida Treaty (1819), art. 8 ("All the grants

of land made before the 24th of January 1818 . . . shall be ratified and confirmed to the persons in possession of the lands, *to the same extent, that the same grants would be valid if the territories had remained under the dominion of his Catholic Majesty.*") (emphasis added).

60. *See, e.g.*, United States v. Reynes, 50 U.S. 127, 153 (1850) ("And it has been invariably held, and indeed must follow as of necessity, that imperfect titles derived from a foreign government can only be perfected by the legislation of the United States."); Menard's Heirs v. Massey, 49 U.S. 293, 307 (1850) ("It was therefore manifest, that . . . [inchoate titles] must depend for their sanction and completion upon the sovereign power . . . No standing, therefore, in an ordinary judicial tribunal has ever been allowed to these claims, until Congress has confirmed them and vested the legal title in the claimant.").

61. *See* Chouteau v. Eckhart, 43 U.S. 344, 374–75 (1844).

62. *See, e.g.*, Keene v. Whitaker, 39 U.S. 170 (1840); Garcia v. Lee, 37 U.S. 511 (1838).

63. *See, e.g.*, Lessee of Pollard v. Files, 43 U.S. 591, 603 (1844) ("Very many permits to settle on the public domain and cultivate, were also granted about the same time; which were in form incipient concessions of the land, and intended by the governor to give title, and to receive confirmation afterwards from the king's deputy, so as to perfect them into a complete title . . . . Although the United States disavowed that any right to the soil, passed by such concessions; still they were not disregarded as giving no equity to the claimant: on the contrary . . ." [explaining how Congress passed legislation to recognize equitable claims]).

64. *See* Lessee of Pollard v. Files, 43 U.S. 591 (1844); Lessee of Pollard's Heirs v. Kibbe, 39 U.S. 353 (1840).

65. *Foster*, 27 U.S. at 315.

66. United States v. Percheman, 32 U.S. 51, 89 (1833).

67. *See* Vázquez (2008), at 631 ("the need for implementing legislation has its source in the treaty itself").

68. *Medellín*, 552 U.S. 491, 514 (2008). *See also* Restatement (Third), § 111 n.5 (endorsing the modern interpretation of *Foster* and *Percheman*).

69. The statement that self-execution is a treaty interpretation issue does not mean that courts or other "interpreters" are precluded from looking beyond the text of the treaty to determine whether a treaty is self-executing. However, under the one-step approach, courts look beyond the text of the treaty to ascertain the intent of the treaty makers. In contrast, under the two-step approach, courts are trying to determine how the Constitution and federal statutes allocate power over treaty implementation.

70. An 1850 decision by the Supreme Judicial Court of Maine may have construed *Foster* in accordance with the one-step approach, although the decision is open to conflicting interpretations. *See* Little v. Watson 32 Me. 214 (1850) (discussed in Chapter 5, pp. 93–94.). Regardless, that decision had no significant influence on the subsequent evolution of self-execution doctrine.

71. *See Percheman*, 32 U.S. at 54–56.

72. *See* pp. 69–70.

73. *See* p. 76.

74. *Foster*, 27 U.S. at 313–14.

75. *Id.*, at 313.

76. Lessee of Pollard v. Files, 43 U.S. 591, 603 (1844).

77. Strother v. Lucas, 37 U.S. 410, 436 (1838).

78. *Percheman*, 32 U.S. at 86–87.
79. *Id.*, at 88.
80. *Id.*, at 88–89.
81. Ware v. Hylton, 3 U.S. 199, 272 (1796) (Iredell, J.). *See* Chapter 3, pp. 48–51 for additional discussion of *Ware*.
82. *Percheman*, 32 U.S. at 87.
83. *Id.*
84. *See* Strother v. Lucas, 37 U.S. 410, 436 (1838).
85. McDonogh v. Millaudon, 44 U.S. 693, 706 (1845).
86. 31 U.S. 691 (1832).
87. Although modern lawyers have fixated on *Foster* and *Percheman*, leading commentators in the 1930s correctly noted that *Arredondo* "served as the most important legal precedent for the entire body of Louisiana, Florida, and later California land cases." Cummings & McFarland (1937), at 127.
88. *Arredondo*, 31 U.S. at 742.
89. *Id.*, at 712.
90. The Court also distinguished *Arredondo* from *Foster* on the grounds that Congress enacted legislation granting federal courts jurisdiction to decide questions involving the validity of land titles in East Florida derived from Spanish grants. *See id.*, at 710–12. In contrast, the Court's political question holding in *Foster* said that courts were required to accept Congress's view that Spanish grants in Floriana were invalid. So, legislation was "necessary" in *Arredondo* (and *Percheman*) to grant federal courts jurisdiction to decide which claimants already held legal titles. However, legislation was not necessary to convey legal title to individuals who held perfect titles before the treaty because they already had valid, legal titles.
91. *Arredondo*, 31 U.S. at 718.
92. *Arredondo* was the first Supreme Court decision involving a claimant who held a perfect title protected by the Florida Treaty. Beginning with *Arredondo*, and continuing for almost sixty years, the Court consistently held that no legislative or administrative action was necessary to validate the titles of individuals who held perfect titles protected by the Louisiana and Florida treaties. *See, e.g.*, McDonogh v. Millaudon, 44 U.S. 693, 706 (1845); United States v. Wiggins, 39 U.S. 334, 350 (1840). However, in *Botiller v. Dominguez*, 130 U.S. 238 (1889), the Court ruled against an individual who claimed to hold a perfect title protected by an 1848 treaty with Mexico, because he failed to present his claim to an administrative tribunal created by Congress. The Court's decision in *Botiller* is inconsistent with prior cases from Louisiana and Florida. Later decisions involving land in California that the United States acquired under the 1848 treaty with Mexico followed the precedent set by *Botiller. See, e.g.*, Barker v. Harvey, 181 U.S. 481 (1901).
93. *See, e.g.*, Medellín v. Texas, 552 U.S. 491, 514 (2008); Restatement (Third), § 111 n.5 (endorsing the modern interpretation of *Foster* and *Percheman*); Vázquez (2008), at 632–45.
94. 1819 treaty with Spain, art. 8.
95. *Foster*, 27 U.S. at 314.
96. *Id.*
97. *Id.*

98. Webster Papers, at 994 (emphasis added).

99. *Arredondo*, 31 U.S. at 741.

100. *See id.*, at 741–42.

101. *Percheman*, 32 U.S. at 69 (emphasis added).

102. *Compare Percheman*, 32 U.S. at 88–89 (Marshall's opinion), *with id.*, at 68–70 (White's argument).

103. *Id.*, at 88–89.

104. *Id.*, at 86–89.

105. *See, e.g.*, Rhode Island v. Massachusetts, 37 U.S. 657, 746 (1838) (stating that *Foster* "recognised the distinction between an executory treaty . . . and an executed treaty"); *see also* Sloss (2002), at 19–23.

106. Vázquez (2008), at 631.

107. 1819 treaty with Spain, art. 8.

108. *Foster*, 27 U.S. at 315.

109. *See* 1 Jennings & Watts (1992) § 21; 2 Hyde (1922) § 523 (stating that the process by which states effect performance of treaty obligations "is primarily a matter of domestic concern"); *id.* § 524 n.4 (citing eighteenth and nineteenth century authorities).

110. 10 Ann. Cong. (1800), at 615.

111. *See* pp. 74–76.

112. *Foster*, 27 U.S. at 314.

113. *See Ware*, 3 U.S. at 271–73.

114. *See* pp. 73–74.

115. *Foster*, 27 U.S. at 313.

116. 1819 treaty with Spain, art. 8.

117. *See* pp. 73–74; *see also* Sloss, *Executing Foster* (2012), at 146–49.

118. *See, e.g.*, United States v. Reynes, 50 U.S. 127, 153 (1850); Menard's Heirs v. Massey, 49 U.S. 293, 307 (1850); Chouteau v. Eckhart, 43 U.S. 344, 374–75 (1844).

119. U.S. Const. art. IV, § 3, cl. 2.

120. McDonogh v. Millaudon, 44 U.S. 693, 706 (1845).

121. U.S. Const. art. IV, § 3, cl. 2.

122. *See* Sloss, *Executing Foster* (2012), at 149–50 (listing seventy-five property cases, forty-five of which involved the United States as a party).

123. U.S. Const. art. IV, § 3, cl. 2.

Chapter 5

1. Missouri v. Holland, 252 U.S. 416 (1920) (rejecting argument that the subject treaty violated federalism limits on the Treaty Power).

2. This point has been generally accepted by almost all relevant authorities since the Founding. Scholars have debated the proper rules to apply in determining whether a treaty provision is constitutionally valid. *Compare* Tucker (1915) (defending fairly strict constitutional restrictions on the Treaty Power) *with* Butler (1902) (defending an expansive view of the Treaty Power). However, no important scholar or government officer has defended the claim that the Treaty Power is free from all constitutional restraints.

3. Professor Duncan Hollis coined the term "executive federalism." *See* Hollis (2006).

4. All sixty cases are cited in notes 6–13.
5. An amicus brief in *Missouri v. Holland*, 252 U.S. 416 (1920), uses the term "self-executing." *See* Brief of Richard J. Hopkins, Attorney General, and Samuel W. Moore, Amici Curiae, and in Behalf of the State of Kansas, *available in The Making of Modern Law: U.S. Supreme Court Records and Briefs, 1832–1978* (electronic database). The brief states: "This is nothing more than an executory agreement of the two governments . . . . It does not create a right or impose an obligation upon any individual. It is not, therefore, the law of the land. It is not operative, as a rule of conduct, *ex proprio vigore*. It is not self-executing or self-enforcing." *Id.*, at 78. The brief for appellee in *Holland* also makes reference to the concept of self-execution without using that term. Brief for Appellee, at 12 ("Whenever a treaty operates of itself, it is to be regarded in the courts as equivalent to an act of Congress. But if it is only promissory and does not operate of itself, it is then clearly within the province of Congress to enact legislation necessary to put it into effect.")

    One could cite these briefs as evidence that some Supreme Court litigators before 1945 believed that the concept of self-execution was relevant to treaty supremacy cases. However, the classification of the subject treaty as non-self-executing relied on the constitutional version of NSE doctrine. The treaty obligated the United States to impose criminal penalties on individuals for prohibited conduct. Congress enacted implementing legislation because the treaty, by itself, did not purport to create criminal penalties, and because the prevailing understanding at the time was that a treaty, by itself, could not create federal criminal penalties. Therefore, assuming that the relevant treaty was constitutionally non-self-executing, the quoted language from the briefs does not support the claim that Supreme Court litigators, circa 1920, believed there was an NSE exception to the treaty supremacy rule.
6. *See* United States v. Pink, 315 U.S. 203 (1942) (conflict between executive agreement and state law); Bacardi Corp. v. Domenech, 311 U.S. 150 (1940) (conflict between treaty and Puerto Rican law); United States v. O'Donnell, 303 U.S. 501 (1938); United States v. Belmont, 301 U.S. 324 (1937) (conflict between executive agreement and state law); Jordan v. Tashiro, 278 U.S. 123 (1928); Nielson v. Johnson, 279 U.S. 47 (1928); Asakura v. City of Seattle, 265 U.S. 332 (1924); Geofroy v. Riggs, 133 U.S. 258 (1890); Coffee v. Groover, 123 U.S. 1 (1887); Hauenstein v. Lynham, 100 U.S. 483 (1880); The Kansas Indians, 72 U.S. 737 (1866); The Passenger Cases, 48 U.S. 283 (1849); Worcester v. Georgia, 31 U.S. 515 (1832); Shanks v. Dupont, 28 U.S. 242 (1830); Carver v. Jackson, 29 U.S. 1 (1830); Carneal v. Banks, 23 U.S. 181 (1825); Hughes v. Edwards, 22 U.S. 489 (1824); Soc'y for the Propagation of the Gospel in Foreign Parts v. Town of New Haven, 21 U.S. 464 (1823); Orr v. Hodgson, 17 U.S. 453 (1819); Jackson v. Clarke, 16 U.S. 1 (1818); Craig v. Radford, 16 U.S. 594 (1818); Chirac v. Chirac's Lessee, 15 U.S. 259 (1817); Fairfax's Devisee v. Hunter's Lessee, 11 U.S. 603 (1813); Higginson v. Mein, 8 U.S. 415 (1808); Hopkirk v. Bell, 8 U.S. 164 (1807); Hopkirk v. Bell, 7 U.S. 454 (1806). All cases cited in this footnote involved Article II treaties, except for *Belmont* and *Pink*, which both involved executive agreements. All cases cited in this footnote involved legislative or executive action by a U.S. state or a constituent local government, except for *Bacardi*, which involved a Puerto Rican law.
7. Guaranty Trust v. United States, 304 U.S. 126 (1938) (alleged conflict between executive agreement and state law); Pigeon River Co. v. Charles W. Cox, Ltd.,

291 U.S. 138 (1934); Todok v. Union State Bank, 281 U.S. 449 (1930); Ohio *ex rel.* Clarke v. Deckebach, 274 U.S. 392 (1927); Cockrill v. California, 268 U.S. 258 (1925); Terrace v. Thompson, 263 U.S. 197 (1923); Frick v. Webb, 263 U.S. 326 (1923); Webb v. O'Brien, 263 U.S. 313 (1923); Heim v. McCall, 239 U.S. 175 (1915); Patsone v. Pennsylvania, 232 U.S. 138 (1914); Rocca v. Thompson, 223 U.S. 317 (1912); Maiorano v. Baltimore & Ohio R.R. Co., 213 U.S. 268 (1909); Mali v. Keeper of the Common Jail (Wildenhus's Case), 120 U.S. 1 (1887); Ker v. Illinois, 119 U.S. 436 (1886); Pennock v. Commissioners, 103 U.S. 44 (1881); Haver v. Yaker, 76 U.S. 32 (1870); Frederickson v. Louisiana, 64 U.S. 445 (1859); Prevost v. Greneaux, 60 U.S. 1 (1856); Davis v. Police Jury of Parish of Concordia, 50 U.S. 280 (1850); The License Cases, 46 U.S. 504 (1847); Lattimer v. Poteet, 39 U.S. 4 (1840); City of New York v. Miln, 36 U.S. 102 (1837); New Orleans v. United States, 35 U.S. 662 (1836); Soc'y for the Propagation of the Gospel in Foreign Parts v. Town of Pawlet, 29 U.S. 480 (1830); Blight's Lessee v. Rochester, 20 U.S. 535 (1822); Smith v. Maryland, 10 U.S. 286 (1810). All cases cited in this footnote involved Article II treaties, except for *Guaranty Trust*, which involved an executive agreement.

8. *See* Harden v. Fisher, 14 U.S. 300 (1816) (where British plaintiff raised claim based on Article 9 of Jay Treaty, Court remanded to circuit court for additional fact-finding); Owings v. Norwood's Lessee, 9 U.S. 344 (1809) (where defendant raised treaty-based defense, Court dismissed for lack of jurisdiction, holding that case did not "arise under" a treaty).

9. *See* Hines v. Davidowitz, 312 U.S. 52 (1941) (Court refrained from deciding whether Pennsylvania law conflicted with treaties, because it held that federal statutes preempted state law); Ogden v. Blackledge, 6 U.S. 272 (1804) (where defendant raised state statute of limitations defense to a claim based partly on a treaty, Court held that statute of limitations defense failed as a matter of state law).

10. 163 U.S. 504 (1896).

11. 143 U.S. 621 (1892).

12. 246 US 297 (1918).

13. 123 U.S. 131, 182 (1887).

14. *Id.* Professor Hollis comments that *Spies* anticipates modern cases applying procedural default rules to treaty claims. *See* Hollis (2011), at 70–71. He is not incorrect, but there are important differences between *Spies* and modern procedural default cases. *Spies* did not involve a treaty that specifically obligated the United States to provide a judicial hearing for individual petitioners. In contrast, *Sanchez-Llamas v. Oregon*, 548 U.S. 331 (2006), involved a treaty that, according to the International Court of Justice (ICJ), created an international legal obligation for the United States to provide additional judicial hearings for certain individual petitioners. The Supreme Court held that states could apply their procedural default rules to bar such judicial hearings. The Court justified that result by asserting that the ICJ's interpretation of the treaty was incorrect, because the treaty did not actually obligate the United States to provide additional judicial hearings for the named individuals.

15. Hines v. Davidowitz, 312 U.S. 52, 62–63 (1941).

16. *See, e.g.,* Geofroy v. Riggs, 133 U.S. 258, 267 (1890) ("the treaty, being part of the supreme law of the land, controlled the statute and common law of Maryland whenever it differed from them"); Soc'y for the Propagation of the Gospel in

Foreign Parts v. Town of New Haven, 21 U.S. 464, 493 (1823) ("But if the Court has been correct in its opinion upon the two first points, it will follow, that the above act was utterly void, being passed in contravention of the treaty of peace, which, in this respect, is to be considered as the supreme law.").

17. Owings v. Norwood's Lessee, 9 U.S. 344, 348 (1809).

18. *See, e.g.,* Mali v. Keeper of the Common Jail (Wildenhus's Case), 120 U.S. 1, 17 (1887) ("The treaty is part of the supreme law of the United States, and has the same force and effect in New Jersey that it is entitled to elsewhere. . . . [W]e see no reason why he may not enforce his rights under the treaty by writ of *habeas corpus* in any proper court of the United States.").

19. Maiorano v. Baltimore & Ohio R.R. Co., 213 U.S. 268, 272–73 (1909).

20. All ten cases are cited in notes 21–32.

21. 265 U.S. 332, 341 (1924).

22. 213 U.S. 268, 272–73 (1909) (emphasis added).

23. 311 U.S. 150, 161–62 (1940) (internal citations omitted).

24. 100 U.S. 483, 490 (1880) (emphasis added).

25. The statement in *Asakura* that the treaty "operates of itself" is clearly a reference to *Foster.* In *Foster,* Chief Justice Marshall said that a treaty is "the law of the land . . . whenever it operates of itself without the aid of any legislative provision." *Foster,* 27 U.S. 253, 314 (1829). Marshall added that some treaties do not "operate of themselves," and therefore require legislation to make them operative. (Later, courts and commentators applied the NSE label to the class of treaties that require legislation to make them operative, but Marshall did not use the term "non-self-executing.") Thus, one could read *Asakura* to imply, however obliquely, that the treaty supremacy principle does not apply to NSE treaties. But the Court in *Asakura* did not say that some treaties do not "operate of themselves." Moreover, the only "rationale" the Court offered in support of its conclusion that the specific treaty at issue "operates of itself"—if one can call it a "rationale"—was a citation to the Supremacy Clause, coupled with a citation to other Supreme Court decisions affirming the treaty supremacy rule. Thus, *Asakura* seems to suggest that the Constitution's treaty supremacy rule applies to all treaties, not just self-executing ones. In any case, one is hard-pressed to find support in *Asakura* for an NSE exception to the treaty supremacy rule.

26. 123 U.S. 1, 25–26 (1887).

27. 50 U.S. 280, 285 (1850).

28. In fact, much of Marshall's analysis in *Foster* concerns Spain's power to issue land grants in Louisiana. *See* Chapter 4.

29. 39 U.S. 4, 15–16 (1840) (Taney, C.J., concurring).

30. 143 U.S. 621, 639 (1892).

31. 246 U.S. 297, 302 (1918).

32. 291 U.S. 138, 160 (1934).

33. One other Supreme Court decision from the period has some intersection with state law, cites *Foster,* and suggests that not every treaty "operates of itself." *See* United States v. Forty-Three Gallons of Whiskey, 93 U.S. 188, 196 (1876). *Forty-Three Gallons* is not included in the group of sixty cases cited above because no party alleged a conflict between a treaty and state law. I discuss the case more fully in Chapter 7.

34. Chapter 7 addresses cases involving the intersection among treaties, federal stat-
    utes, and Congress's regulatory authority. In many of those cases, the Supreme
    Court and lower courts cited *Foster* and/or *Head Money* to support some variant
    of NSE doctrine.

35. *See* Bradley (1998), at 419–20. For a contrary view, see Golove (2000), at 1193–1205,
    1243–54.

36. *See* Holden v. Joy, 84 U.S. 211 (1872) (affirming validity of land title that derived, in
    part, from a treaty with the Cherokee nation); Holmes v. Jennison, 39 U.S. 540 (1840)
    (holding that the governor of Vermont lacked power to extradite fugitive to Canada
    because extradition power belonged to federal government) (plurality opinion).

37. *See* 133 U.S. 258, 267 (1890) ("the treaty, being part of the supreme law of the land,
    controlled the statute and common law of Maryland whenever it differed from
    them").

38. Prevost v. Greneaux, 60 U.S. 1 (1857); *see infra* pp. 103–05.

39. *See* The Passenger Cases, 48 U.S. 283, 466 (1849) (Taney, C.J., dissenting); The
    License Cases, 46 U.S. 504, 613 (1847) (Daniel, J., concurring); New Orleans
    v. United States, 35 U.S. 662, 736–37 (1836).

40. 35 U.S. 662 (1836).

41. *Id.,* at 711.

42. *Id.,* at 736.

43. *Id.,* at 731.

44. Professor Bradley's analysis of *New Orleans v. United States* suggests that the city
    prevailed because of constitutional limits on the Treaty Power. *See* Bradley (1998),
    at 419. His analysis ignores the Court's discussion of French and Spanish law,
    which precluded the king of France from conveying the land to the United States
    in the first place. Thus, under the Court's analysis, any ostensible limits on the
    Treaty Power were irrelevant. The United States lost because the king of France
    lacked power to convey the disputed property to the United States.

45. 46 U.S. 504 (1847).

46. *Id.,* at 555 (argument of counsel).

47. *See id.,* at 598 (Catron, J., concurring); *id.,* at 617 (Daniel, J., concurring) ("These
    laws are, therefore, in violation neither of the constitution of the United States,
    nor of any law nor treaty made in pursuance or under the authority of the consti-
    tution."); *id.,* at 630 (Woodbury, J., concurring) (state law "does not appear to be
    repugnant to any part of the constitution, or a treaty, or an act of Congress").

48. *Id.,* at 598 (Catron, J., concurring).

49. 48 U.S. 283 (1849).

50. *Id.,* at 408 (McLean, J.).

51. *Id.,* at 412–13 (Wayne, J.).

52. *Id.,* at 444 (Catron, J.).

53. *Id.,* at 466 (Taney, C.J., dissenting).

54. *Id.*

55. *See* notes 58–60 for a complete list of cases.

56. To select cases, I relied primarily on a list of cases published in *American Law
    Reports,* first published in 1919, and then updated in 1941. *See* "Relation of Treaty
    to State and Federal Law," 134 ALR 882 (1941); "Relation of Treaty to State and
    Federal Law," 4 ALR 1377 (1919). I supplemented these lists by consulting 5

Hackworth, §§ 487–488. I included all state court decisions cited in these sources that involved an alleged conflict between a treaty and state law.

57.　Butschkowski v. Brecks, 143 N.W. 923, 924 (Neb. 1913) ("a self-executing treaty requires no legislation to put it into operation").

58.　*See In re* Blasi's Estate, 15 N.Y. Supp. 2d 682 (1939); *In re* Ostrowski's Estate, 290 N.Y. Supp. 174 (1936); Urbus v. State Compensation Com'r, 169 S.E. 164 (W.Va. 1933); Goos v. Brocks, 223 N.W. 13 (Neb. 1929); *In re* Romaris, 218 P. 421 (Cal. 1923); *In re* Terui, 200 P. 954 (Cal. 1921); Vietti v. Mackie Fuel Co., 197 P. 881 (Kan. 1921); Poon v. Miller, 234 S.W. 573 (Tex. 1921); Techt v. Hughes, 128 N.E. 185 (N.Y. 1920); Brown v. Peterson, 170 N.W. 444 (Iowa 1919); Trott v. State, 171 N.W. 827 (N.D. 1919); Brown v. Daly, 154 N.W. 602 (Iowa 1915); *In re* Moynihan, 151 N.W. 504 (Iowa 1915); McKeown v. Brown, 149 N.W. 593 (Iowa 1914); Erickson v. Carlson, 145 N.W. 352 (Neb. 1914); *In re* Madaloni, 141 N.Y. Supp. 323 (1913); *In re* Riccardo, 140 N.Y. Supp. 606 (1913); *In re* Vukelic, 143 N.Y. Supp. 679 (1912); *In re* Szabo, 143 N.Y. Supp. 678 (1912); *In re* Scutella, 129 N.Y. Supp. 20 (1911); *In re* Stixrud, 109 P. 343 (Wash. 1910); *In re* Wyman, 77 N.E. 379 (Mass. 1906); Ehrlich v. Weber, 88 S.W. 188 (Tenn. 1905); Doe *ex dem.* Dockstader v. Roe, 55 A. 341 (Del. 1903); *In re* Lobrasciano, 77 N.Y. Supp. 1040 (1902); *In re* Fattosini, 67 N.Y. Supp. 1119 (1900); Scharpf v. Schmidt, 50 N.E. 182 (Ill. 1898); *In re* Sala's Succession, 24 So. 674 (La. 1898); Adams v. Akerlund, 48 N.E. 454 (Ill. 1897); Doehrel v. Hillmer, 71 N.W. 204 (Iowa 1897); Wilcke v. Wilcke, 71 N.W. 201 (Iowa 1897); Opel v. Shoup, 69 N.W. 560 (Iowa 1897); *In re* Rixner's Succession, 19 So. 597 (La. 1896); *In re* Rabasse's Succession, 17 So. 867 (La. 1895); People v. Warren, 34 N.Y. Supp. 942 (1895); *In re* Tartaglio's Estate, 33 N.Y.S. 1121 (1895); Schultze v. Schultze, 33 N.E. 201 (Ill. 1893); *In re* Beck, 11 N.Y.S. 199 (1890); Blandford v. State, 10 Tex. App. 627 (1881); Commonwealth v. Hawes, 76 Ky. 697 (1878); *In re* Crusius's Succession, 19 La. Ann. 369 (1867); *In re* Amat's Succession, 18 La. Ann. 403 (1866); Watson v. Donnelly, 28 Barb. 653 (N.Y. 1859); People *ex rel.* Atty. Gen. v. Gerke, 5 Cal. 381 (1855); *In re* Dufour's Succession, 10 La. Ann. 391 (1855); Little v. Watson, 32 Me. 214 (1850); Blair v. Pathkiller, 10 Tenn. 407 (1830); Jackson *ex dem.* Folliard v. Wright, 4 Johns. 75 (N.Y. 1809).

59.　*See* Wyers v. Arnold, 147 S.W.2d 644 (Mo. 1941); Universal Adjustment Corp. v. Midland Bank, Ltd., 184 N.E. 152 (Mass. 1933); San Lorenzo Title & Improvement Co. v. Caples, 48 S.W.2d 329 (Tex. 1932); Frasca v. City Coal Co., 116 A. 189 (Conn. 1922); State *ex rel.* Tanner v. Staeheli, 192 P. 991 (Wash. 1920); Riddell v. Fuhrman, 123 N.E. 237 (Mass. 1919); Chryssikos v. DeMarco, 107 A. 358 (Md. 1919); Hamilton v. Erie R.R. Co., 114 N.E. 399 (N.Y. 1916); Pagano v. Cerri, 112 N.E. 1037 (Ohio 1916); *In re* Servas' Estate, 146 P. 651 (Cal. 1915); *In re* Bagnola, 154 N.W. 461 (Iowa 1915); *In re* D'Adamo's Estate, 106 N.E. 81 (N.Y. 1914); *In re* Anderson, 147 N.W. 1098 (Iowa 1914); Bondi v. MacKay, 89 A. 228 (Vt. 1913); *In re* Lis' Estate, 139 N.W. 300 (Minn. 1912); Commonwealth v. Patsone, 79 A. 928 (Penn. 1911); *In re* Ghio's Estate, 108 P. 516 (Cal. 1910); Ahrens v. Ahrens, 123 N.W. 164 (Iowa 1909); Lehman v. State *ex rel.* Miller, 88 N.E. 365 (Ind. 1909); Logiorato's Estate, 69 N.Y.S. 507 (1901); Compagnie Francaise de Navigation v. State Bd. of Health, 25 So. 591 (La. 1899); Wunderle v. Wunderle, 33 N.E. 195 (Ill. 1893); Baker v. Shy, 56 Tenn. 85 (1871); Yeaker v. Yeaker, 81 Am Dec. 530 (Ky. 1862); *In re* Schaffer's Succession,

13 La. Ann. 113 (1858); Siemssen v. Bofer, 6 Cal. 250 (1856); *In re* Succession of Thompson, 9 La. Ann. 96 (1854); People v. Naglee, 1 Cal. 232 (1850).

60. Butschkowski v. Brecks, 143 N.W. 923 (Neb. 1913); Minnesota Canal & Power Co. v. Pratt, 112 N.W. 395 (Minn. 1907).

61. *Butschkowski*, 143 N.W. at 924–25.

62. *Minnesota Canal & Power Co.*, 112 N.W. at 405–06.

63. In *Butschkowski*, the lower court denied plaintiff's motion to amend her pleading because she did not cite the treaty in her original pleading. The Supreme Court reversed, saying that "it was no more necessary to plead the terms of the treaty than it would be to plead the terms of a domestic statute or a provision of the Constitution of this state or of the United States." 143 N.W. at 924. In *Minnesota Canal & Power Co.*, the court said that resolution of the treaty issue was not strictly necessary to decide the case, but "elaborate briefs have been filed in which the effect of the treaty is discussed, and a few words with reference to it seem therefore appropriate." 112 N.W. at 405.

64. Urbus v. State Compensation Com'r, 169 S.E. 164 (W.Va. 1933).

65. Poon v. Miller, 234 S.W. 573, 575 (Tex. 1921).

66. Ehrlich v. Weber, 88 S.W. 188, 191 (Tenn. 1905).

67. People *ex rel.* Atty. Gen. v. Gerke, 5 Cal. 381, 385 (1855).

68. Wyers v. Arnold, 147 S.W.2d 644, 646 (Mo. 1941); *In re* Blasi's Estate, 15 N.Y. Supp. 2d 682, 684 (1939); *In re* Ostrowski's Estate, 290 N.Y. Supp. 174 (1936); Universal Adjustment Corp. v. Midland Bank, Ltd., 184 N.E. 152, 162 (Mass. 1933); San Lorenzo Title & Improvement Co. v. Caples, 48 S.W.2d 329, 331 (Tex. 1932); Goos v. Brocks, 223 N.W. 13, 14 (Neb. 1929); Frasca v. City Coal Co., 116 A. 189, 191 (Conn. 1922); *In re* Terui, 200 P. 954, 955 (Cal. 1921); Vietti v. Mackie Fuel Co., 197 P. 881, 882 (Kan. 1921); State *ex rel.* Tanner v. Staeheli, 192 P. 991, 994 (Wash. 1920); Brown v. Peterson, 170 N.W. 444 (Iowa 1919); Trott v. State, 171 N.W. 827 (N.D. 1919); Riddell v. Fuhrman, 123 N.E. 237, 238 (Mass. 1919); Chyrissikos v. DeMarco, 107 A. 358 (Md. 1919); Hamilton v. Erie R.R. Co., 114 N.E. 399, 402 (N.Y. 1916); Pagano v. Cerri, 112 N.E. 1037 (Ohio 1916); Brown v Daly, 154 N.W. 602 (Iowa 1915); McKeown v. Brown, 149 N.W. 593, 595 (Iowa 1914); *In re* Riccardo, 140 N.Y. Supp. 606, 607 (1913); Butschkowski v. Brecks, 143 N.W. 923, 924 (Neb. 1913); Bondi v. MacKay, 89 A. 228, 230 (Vt. 1913); *In re* Scutella, 129 N.Y. Supp. 20, 21 (1911); *In re* Stixrud, 109 P. 343, 345 (Wash. 1910); *In re* Ghio's Estate, 108 P. 516, 518 (Cal. 1910); Lehman v. State *ex rel.* Miller, 88 N.E. 365, 367 (Ind. 1909); Lehman v. State *ex rel.* Miller, 88 N.E. 365, 367 (Ind. 1909); Minnesota Canal & Power Co. v. Pratt, 112 N.W. 395, 405 (Minn. 1907); *In re* Wyman, 77 N.E. 379, 380 (Mass. 1906); *In re* Lobrasciano, 77 N.Y. Supp. 1040, 1044 (1902); *In re* Fattosini, 67 N.Y. Supp. 1119, 1120 (1900); Scharpf v. Schmidt, 50 N.E. 182, 183 (Ill. 1898); Opel v. Shoup, 69 N.W. 560, 562 (Iowa 1897); *In re* Rixner's Succession, 19 So. 597, 598 (La. 1896); *In re* Rabasse's Succession, 17 So. 867 (La. 1895); Wunderle v. Wunderle, 33 N.E. 195, 197 (Ill. 1893); Blandford v. State, 10 Tex. App. 627, 638 (1881); Commonwealth v. Hawes, 76 Ky. 697, 702 (1878); Yeaker v. Yeaker, 81 Am Dec. 530 (Ky. 1862); Watson v. Donnelly, 28 Barb. 653, 657 (N.Y. 1859); Siemssen v. Bofer, 6 Cal. 250, 252 (1856); *In re* Dufour's Succession, 10 La. Ann. 391, 393 (1855); Little v. Watson, 32 Me. 214, 223 (1850); People v. Naglee, 1 Cal. 232, 235 (1850).

69. *In re* Blasi's Estate, 15 N.Y. Supp. 2d 682, 684–85 (1939).

70. Frasca v. City Coal Co., 116 A. 189, 191 (Conn. 1922).

71. Trott v. State, 171 N.W. 827, 830 (N.D. 1919).

72. San Lorenzo Title & Improvement Co. v. Caples, 48 S.W.2d 329, 331 (Tex. 1932); *In re* Terui, 200 P. 954, 956 (Cal. 1921); Techt v. Hughes, 128 N.E. 185, 192 (N.Y. 1920); State *ex rel.* Tanner v. Staeheli, 192 P. 991, 994 (Wash. 1920); Chyrissikos v. DeMarco, 107 A. 358 (Md. 1919); Riddell v. Fuhrman, 123 N.E. 237, 238 (Mass. 1919); Brown v. Peterson, 170 N.W. 444 (Iowa 1919); Hamilton v. Erie R.R. Co., 114 N.E. 399, 402 (N.Y. 1916); Pagano v. Cerri, 112 N.E. 1037 (Ohio 1916); McKoewn v. Brown, 149 N.W. 593, 595 (Iowa 1914); Erickson v. Carlson, 145 N.W. 352, 353 (Neb. 1914); Butschkowski v. Brecks, 143 N.W. 923, 924 (Neb. 1913); Bondi v. MacKay, 89 A. 228, 230 (Vt. 1913); Commonwealth v. Patsone, 79 A. 928, 930 (1911); *In re* Ghio's Estate, 108 P. 516, 518 (Cal. 1910); Minnesota Canal & Power Co. v. Pratt, 112 N.W. 395, 405 (Minn. 1907); *In re* Wyman, 77 N.E. 379, 380 (Mass. 1906); Adams v. Akerlund, 48 N.E. 454, 456 (Ill. 1897); Opel v. Shoup, 69 N.W. 560, 562 (Iowa 1897); *In re* Rixner's Succession, 19 So. 597, 598 (La. 1896); *In re* Rabasse's Succession, 17 So. 867 (La. 1895); Blandford v. State, 10 Tex. App. 627, 636 (Tex. 1881); Commonwealth v. Hawes, 76 Ky. 697, 702 (1878); Siemssen v. Bofer, 6 Cal. 250, 252 (1856); People v. Naglee, 1 Cal. 232, 235 (1850).

73. The cases that cite *Foster* are: *In re* Stixrud, 109 P. 343, 345 (Wash. 1910); *In re* Ghio's Estate, 108 P. 516, 518 (Cal. 1910); *In re* Lobrasciano, 77 N.Y. Supp. 1040, 1042 (1902); Blandford v. State, 10 Tex. App. 627, 640 (1881); Commonwealth v. Hawes, 76 Ky. 697, 702 (1878); Little v. Watson, 32 Me. 214, 223–24 (1850).

74. The cases that cite *Head Money* are: Techt v. Hughes, 128 N.E. 185, 192 (N.Y. 1920) (Cardozo, J.); Hamilton v. Erie R.R. Co., 114 N.E. 399, 402 (N.Y. 1916); Butschkowski v. Brecks, 143 N.W. 923, 924 (Neb. 1913); Bondi v. MacKay, 89 A. 228, 231 (Vt. 1913); *In re* Wyman, 77 N.E. 379, 380 (Mass. 1906); Adams v. Akerlund, 48 N.E. 454, 456–57 (Ill. 1897).

75. Minnesota Canal & Power Co. v. Pratt, 112 N.W. 395, 405 (Minn. 1907) cites both *Foster* and *Head Money*.

76. *See, e.g.*, Bondi v. MacKay, 89 A. 228, 231 (Vt. 1913) (stating that courts apply treaties "when the right conferred is one that can be enforced in a court of justice, and the treaty prescribes a rule by which the right is to be determined"); Commonwealth v. Hawes, 76 Ky. 697, 702 (1878) (stating that a treaty should "be regarded in the courts of justice as equivalent to an act of the legislature whenever it operates of itself, without the aid of any legislative provision").

77. Techt v. Hughes, 128 N.E. 185 (N.Y. 1920) (Cardozo, J.) (holding that alien enemy can inherit land, despite contrary state law); *In re* Stixrud, 109 P. 343 (Wash. 1910) (holding that treaty supersedes state law requiring inheritance tax payment); *In re* Wyman, 77 N.E. 379 (Mass. 1906) (holding that treaty grants Russian Vice Consul the right to be appointed as administrator of deceased person's estate); *In re* Lobrasciano, 77 N.Y. Supp. 1040 (1902) (holding that treaty requires state court to deliver proceeds of deceased person's estate to consul general of Italy); Adams v. Akerlund, 48 N.E. 454 (Ill. 1897) (holding that nonresident aliens have right to inherit real estate in Illinois, despite contrary state law); Blandford v. State, 10 Tex. App. 627 (1881); (reversing state court criminal conviction because state violated extradition treaty with Mexico); Commonwealth v. Hawes, 76 Ky. 697 (1878)

(dismissing criminal indictment because State of Kentucky did not comply with extradition treaty); Little v. Watson, 32 Me. 214 (1850) (confirming real estate title of party who claimed under treaty, even though other party had valid title under state law before treaty).

78. Hamilton v. Erie R.R. Co., 114 N.E. 399, 402–03 (N.Y. 1916) (right of consul general under treaty did not include right to reach out-of-court settlement that deprived widow and children of statutory cause of action under state law); Bondi v. MacKay, 89 A. 228 (Vt. 1913) (treaty did not grant alien right to obtain hunting license for same fee charged to citizen of state); In re Ghio's Estate, 108 P. 516, 518 (Cal. 1910) (treaty did not grant Consul General of Italy right to appointment as estate administrator for deceased person that was superior to right of public administrator under state law).

79. See Techt v. Hughes, 128 N.E. 185, 191 (N.Y. 1920) (Cardozo, J.) (treaty at issue "is the supreme law of the land . . . and supersedes all local laws inconsistent with its terms"); Hamilton v. Erie R.R. Co., 114 N.E. 399, 402 (N.Y. 1916) (treaty "is paramount to the Constitution and statutes of the state . . . [and] [i]ts application to any case and its construction . . . are, as with any other law, questions for the court"); Bondi v. MacKay, 89 A. 228, 231 (Vt. 1913) (treaties "are the law of the land, superior to the Constitution and statutes of any state, and binding upon all courts"); In re Ghio's Estate, 108 P. 516, 518 (Cal. 1910) ("It is an established and incontrovertible principle that a treaty . . . with a foreign power becomes, upon the adoption of such treaty, a part of the law of every state of the American Union, and that where the provisions and stipulations of the treaty are at cross-purposes with the statute of any state the latter must succumb to the former."); In re Stixrud, 109 P. 343, 345 (Wash. 1910) ("It has become the settled law of this country that, when a law of a state comes in conflict with the provisions of a treaty entered into by the United States with a foreign country relating to a subject-matter within the treaty-making power, such law must give way and its application to the subject-matter covered by the treaty held in abeyance during the existence of the treaty."); In re Wyman, 77 N.E. 379, 380 (Mass. 1906) ("When, then, anything in the Constitution or laws of a state are in conflict with a treaty, the latter must prevail, and this court has not hesitated to follow this rule."); In re Lobrasciano, 77 N.Y. Supp. 1040, 1044 (1902) ("This plain language [of the Supremacy Clause] compels the elimination of all consideration of state laws while in the business of construing a treaty. State law must yield, and adjust itself to the spirit and intent of a treaty."); Blandford v. State, 10 Tex. App. 627, 640 (1881) (see text); Commonwealth v. Hawes, 76 Ky. 697, 702–03 (1878) ("It will thus be seen that with us a public treaty is not merely a compact or bargain to be carried out by the executive and legislative departments of the general government, but a living law, operating upon and binding the judicial tribunals, state and federal, and these tribunals are under the same obligations to notice and give it effect as they are to notice and enforce the constitution and the laws of congress made in pursuance thereof."); Little v. Watson, 32 Me. 214, 224 (1850) ("It is the duty of this court to consider, that treaty to be a law operating upon the grant . . . and declaring, that it shall be held valid, ratified and confirmed."). The only case in the group that does not include an explicit endorsement of treaty supremacy is Adams v. Akerlund, 48 N.E. 454 (Ill. 1897). In that case, the Supreme Court of Illinois held that Swedish citizens who lived in Sweden had a treaty-based right to inherit land in Illinois, despite contrary state law.

80. *Blandford*, 10 Tex. App. at 640.
81. *In re Stixrud*, 109 P., at 345; *In re Ghio's Estate*, 108 P. 516, 518 (Cal. 1910).
82. *Blandford*, 10 Tex. App. at 640.
83. *In re Lobrasciano*, 77 N.Y. Supp. at 1042.
84. Minnesota Canal & Power Co. v. Pratt, 112 N.W. 395, 405 (Minn. 1907) (citing *Foster* for proposition that treaty "which does not require legislation to carry its provisions into effect, is a municipal law, as well as an international contract"); Commonwealth v. Hawes, 76 Ky. 697, 702 (1878) (citing *Foster* to support claim that a treaty should "be regarded in the courts of justice as equivalent to an act of the legislature whenever it operates of itself, without the aid of any legislative provision"); Little v. Watson, 32 Me. 214, 223–24 (Me. 1850) (citing *Foster* to support claim that "[i]n the United States a treaty is to be regarded as the supreme law and operative as such, when the stipulations do not import a contract to be performed").
85. Hamilton v. Erie R.R. Co., 114 N.E. 399, 402 (N.Y. 1916).
86. *In re* Wyman, 77 N.E. 379, 380 (Mass. 1906).
87. Minnesota Canal & Power Co. v. Pratt, 112 N.W. 395, 405 (Minn. 1907).
88. Butschkowski v. Brecks, 143 N.W. 923, 924 (Neb. 1913).
89. *See* Bondi v. MacKay, 89 A. 228, 231 (Vt. 1913) (citing *Head Money* to support claim that "[t]reaty provisions which confer rights upon the subjects of another nation residing in this country partake of the nature of municipal law, and, when the right conferred is one that can be enforced in a court of justice, and the treaty prescribes a rule by which the right is to be determined, the court resorts to the treaty for the rule of decision as it would to a statute"); Adams v. Akerlund, 48 N.E. 454, 456–57 (Ill. 1897) (citing *Head Money* to support claim that "[w]here treaties concern the rights of individuals, it is frequently necessary for the courts to ascertain, by construction, the meaning intended to be conveyed by the terms used").
90. Techt v. Hughes, 128 N.E. 185, 192 (N.Y. 1920).
91. 32 Me. 214 (1850).
92. 1842 treaty with Britain.
93. *Id.*, art. IV.
94. *See Little*, 32 Me. at 221–23.
95. *Id.*, at 223.
96. *Id.*, at 223–24 (citing Foster v. Neilson, 27 U.S. 253 (1829), and United States v. Percheman, 32 U.S. 51 (1833)).
97. *Id.*, at 224.
98. *Id.*, at 224–25.
99. 9 La. Ann. 96 (1854).
100. 6 Cal. 250 (1856).
101. 1 Cal. 232 (1850).
102. *Thompson*, 9 La. Ann. at 96.
103. 5 Cal. 381 (1855).
104. *Id.*, at 387.
105. *Siemssen*, 6 Cal. at 252.
106. At two key points, Chief Justice Murray used the phrase "in my opinion," apparently to make clear that other justices did not share his opinion. *See id.* The opinion says at the beginning that "Mr. Justice Terry concurred," perhaps signaling Justice Terry's agreement with the entire opinion.

107. *See id.*, at 253–54.

108. *Naglee*, 1 Cal. at 232–33.

109. *Id.*, at 246.

110. *Id.*

111. *Id.*, at 247 (quoting The Passenger Cases, 48 U.S. 283, 466–67 (1849) (Taney, C.J., dissenting)).

112. *See supra* pp. 89–90.

113. *See, e.g.*, 1880 treaty with China, art. III; 1859 treaty with Paraguay, art. IX ("The citizens of either of the two contracting parties in the territories of the other, shall enjoy full and perfect protection for their persons and property . . . .").

114. 1871 treaty with Italy, art. III.

115. *See* 23 Cong. Rec. (1892), at 4559 (statement of Sen. Morgan); Violations of Treaty Rights of Aliens, S. Rep. No. 392, 56th Cong., 1st Sess., at 2 (1900). The riot was apparently a response to "the failure of a jury to convict some Italians, or Sicilians, who belonged to a secret oath-bound order called the Mafia." *Id.*

116. 23 Cong. Rec. (1892), at 4549.

117. *Id.*

118. *See id.*, at 4549–62; *id.*, at 4599–608.

119. *Id.*, at 4554.

120. *Id.*

121. *Id.*

122. *See id.*, at 4552–53 (statement of Sen. Palmer); *id.*, at 4554 (statement of Sen. Vilas); *id.*, at 4603–04 (statement of Sen. Vest).

123. *See id.*, at 4555–56 (statement of Sen. Davis); *id.*, at 4599 (statement of Sen. Morgan).

124. *See id.*, at 4549–50 (statement of Sen. Dolph); *id.*, at 4555–57 (statement of Sen. Davis); *id.*, at 4557–59 (statement of Sen. Morgan).

125. *See id.*, at 4549–51 (statement of Sen. Dolph); *id.*, at 4555–57 (statement of Sen. Davis); *id.*, at 4557–59 (statement of Sen. Morgan); *id.*, at 4599–601 (statement of Sen. Morgan).

126. *Id.*, at 4559 (statement of Sen. Morgan).

127. *Id.*, at 4599 (Sen. Morgan).

128. *Id.*, at 4559 (statement of Sen. Gray).

129. *See id.*, at 4552–53 (statement of Sen. Palmer); *id.*, at 4553–54 (statement of Sen. Vilas); *id.*, at 4604–06 (statement of Sen. Turpie).

130. *See* United States v. Hudson & Goodwin, 11 U.S. 32, 34 (1812) (holding that there is no federal common law of crimes).

131. 1869 treaty with Russia. This treaty was soon modified by a subsequent declaration. *See* 1874 treaty with Russia.

132. *See* 1868 treaty with Belgium (subsequently modified by 1875 treaty with Belgium, art. XV); 1869 treaty with France; 1871 treaty with Austria; 1871 treaty with Germany; 1877 treaty with Great Britain; 1878 treaty with Brazil.

133. *See* Act of Aug. 14, 1876, 19 Stat. 141; Act of July 8, 1870, 16 Stat. 198, 210.

134. *In re* Trademark Cases, 100 U.S. 82 (1879).

135. U.S. CONST. art. I, sec. 8, cl. 8.

136. *Trademark Cases*, 100 U.S. at 93–94.

137. *See id.*, at 95–99.

138. *Id.*, at 99.

139.   10 Cong. Rec. (1880), at 2702 (statement of Rep. Hammond).

140.   1874 treaty with Russia, art. 1. *See also* 1871 treaty with Germany, art. 17 (promising German citizens "the same protection as native citizens"); 1877 treaty with Great Britain (promising British citizens "the same rights as belong to native subjects or citizens"); 1878 treaty with Brazil (promising Brazilian citizens "the same rights as belong to native citizens or subjects").

141.   Taylor v. Carpenter, 23 F.Cas. 742 (C.C. Mass. 1844) (Story, J.). *See also* Coffeen v. Brunton, 5 F. Cas. 1184, 1185–86 (C.C. Ind. 1849) (McLean, J.) ("In this respect there is no difference between a citizen and an alien."); Taylor v. Carpenter, 23 F. Cas. 744 (C.C. Mass. 1846).

142.   10 Cong. Rec. (1880), at 2704 (statement of Rep. Hammond).

143.   *See, e.g.,* 1875 treaty with Belgium, art. XV; 1869 treaty with France, art. II; 1871 treaty with Austria, art. II.

144.   *See* An Act to Authorize the Registration of Trade-Marks and Protect the Same, Mar. 3, 1881, 21 Stat. 502.

145.   *See* Registration of Trademarks, H.R. Rep. No. 46-561, at 5–6 (1880). For a defense of Congress's constitutional power to implement treaties under the Necessary and Proper Clause, see Galbraith (2014).

146.   *See, e.g.,* 1869 treaty with Russia; 1868 treaty with Belgium; 1869 treaty with France, art. I; 1871 treaty with Austria, art. I.

147.   Act of July 8, 1870, 16 Stat. 198, 211 (section 79).

148.   *See* Act of Aug. 14, 1876, 19 Stat. 141.

149.   *See* Rosen (2009), at 878–81.

150.   *See id.,* at 880 n.320.

151.   *See* Registration of Trademarks, H.R. Rep. No. 46-561, at 5–6 (1880); *see also* 10 Cong. Rec. (1880), at 2702–04 (statement of Rep. Hammond).

152.   *See* An Act to Authorize the Registration of Trade-Marks and Protect the Same, Mar. 3, 1881, 21 Stat. 502.

153.   *See* 10 Cong. Rec. (1880), at 2701–02.

154.   *Id.,* at 2704.

155.   *See* An Act to Authorize the Registration of Trade-Marks and Protect the Same, § 7, Mar. 3, 1881, 21 Stat. 502, 503–04.

156.   *See* 22 U.S. Op. Atty. Gen. 214 (1898); 8 U.S. Op. Atty. Gen. 411 (1857); 8 U.S. Op. Atty. Gen. 98, 99 (1856); 2 U.S. Op. Atty. Gen. 426, 436–37 (1831); 1 U.S. Op. Atty. Gen. 659, 661 (1824); 1 U.S. Op. Atty. Gen. 275 (1819).

       When he served as attorney general, Roger Taney wrote two opinions that supported strict federalism limits on the Treaty Power. *See* Golove (2000), at 1226–29. I do not count those opinions here because they were never published formally as part of the collection of U.S. attorney general opinions. Moreover, those opinions do not alter the analysis presented in the text; they are consistent with Taney's views as Chief Justice. *See supra* pp. 89–90.

157.   1 U.S. Op. Atty. Gen. 275 (1819).

158.   2 U.S. Op. Atty. Gen. 426, 436–37 (1831).

159.   1 U.S. Op. Atty. Gen. 659, 661 (1824).

160.   8 U.S. Op. Atty. Gen. 411 (1857).

161.   22 U.S. Op. Atty. Gen. 214, 218 (1898).

162.   8 U.S. Op. Atty. Gen. 98, 99 (1856) ("*[U]nless the contrary be stipulated by treaty,* the administration of the estate of a foreign decedent is primarily a question of

the local jurisdiction, and his consul can intervene only so far as the local law may permit.") (emphasis added) (Attorney General Cushing).

163. 1853 treaty with France.

164. *Id.*, art. 7.

165. *See* 6 Miller 169, at 181–91.

166. *See id.*, at 186.

167. *See, e.g.*, 1850 treaty with Switzerland, art. V ("But in case real estate, situated within the territories of one of the contracting parties, should fall to a citizen of the other party, who, on account of his being an alien, could not be permitted to hold such property, in the State or in the Canton in which it may be situated, there shall be accorded to the said heir or other successor *such term as the laws of the State or Canton will permit* to sell such property."); *see also* 1910 treaty with Sweden, art. XIV ("In the event of any citizens of either of the two Contracting Parties dying without will or testament, in the territory of the other Contracting Party, the consul-general, consul, vice-consul-general, or vice-consul of the nation to which the deceased may belong ... shall, *so far as the laws of each country will permit* ... take charge of the property left by the deceased for the benefit of his lawful heirs and creditors ....").

168. 6 Miller 169, at 188–89.

169. *Id.*, at 189.

170. *Id.*, at 189–90.

171. In the nineteenth century, executive branch views changed over time as to whether it was constitutionally permissible to use the Article II Treaty Power to override state laws governing ownership of real property by noncitizens. *See* Hollis (2006), at 1365–67; Ku (2004), at 491–93. The negotiation between the United States and France described in the text took place in 1852–1853. At that point in time, the federal executive branch took a fairly restrictive view of its own ability to use the Treaty Power to override state law. *See id.*, at 492; Hollis (2006), at 1366.

172. Miller did not print this exact language anywhere in his account. Regardless, one can reconstruct the language based on his account. The language of the third draft is essentially the final treaty language, without the Senate amendment, which is discussed below.

173. 6 Miller 169, at 175. (This is the final treaty language.)

174. *Id.*, at 174–75.

175. The record of Senate deliberations on the Consular Convention is quite thin. *See* 22 App. Cong. Globe 122-23 (33rd Cong., Special Session, March 29, 1853). Senator Bayard moved to strike Article 7 in its entirety. That motion was defeated. Then Senator Chase moved to amend Article 7 by adding the words quoted in the text. That motion passed by a vote of 23-11. The published record does not include any statement explaining or supporting the amendment. Regardless, the text itself supports a reasonable inference about the underlying purpose.

176. At that time, some states had abolished restrictions on alien land ownership, but other states retained those restrictions. *See* Diplomatic Note from Ambassador Sartiges to Acting Secretary of State Conrad, *reprinted in* 6 Miller 169, at 188–90.

177. 60 U.S. 1 (1857).

178. *Id.*, at 7.

179. *See* Chapter 14, pp. 306–10 (discussing modern practice).
180. The correct interpretation of NSE declarations is contested. *See* Chapter 14, pp. 307–10. Here, I assume that the NSE declaration means that the treaty does not supersede conflicting state laws. This interpretation is consistent with the idea that there is an NSE exception to the treaty supremacy rule—an idea that gained support in the early 1950s. *See* Part Three.
181. Other commentators have cited *Prevost* and/or the 1853 treaty to support federalism limits on the Treaty Power. *See* Bradley (1998), at 419, n.167; Ku (2004), at 492.
182. In contemporary practice, the proper interpretation of NSE declarations attached to treaties is contested. However, there is general agreement that a provision stipulating that a treaty is not self-executing does not alter the nature or scope of the nation's international obligations under the treaty. *See* Chapter 14, p. 307.
183. *See* Chapter 1.
184. *See* Chapter 1, pp. 26–27.

CHAPTER 6

1. *See* Sloss, Ramsey, and Dodge (2011), at 7, 18–19; Ku (2005), at 373–84.
2. The Cherokee Tobacco, 78 U.S. 616, 621 (1871).
3. *See* Chapter 3.
4. 1815 Treaty with Britain.
5. Article 3 dealt with U.S. vessels engaged in commerce in British India. Article 5 addressed ratification and entry into force. *See id.*
6. *See* 29 Ann. Cong., at 419–20 (draft legislation). *Compare* 1815 Treaty with Britain.
7. Article 1 granted British subjects a right to live and conduct business in the United States; it also granted reciprocal rights to U.S. citizens. Article 4 authorized each party to appoint consuls to reside in the territory of the other party. Article 4 also permitted punishment of consuls who engaged in illegal conduct. *See* 1815 Treaty with Britain.
8. U.S. CONST. art. I, sec. 10, cl. 2.
9. U.S. CONST. art. I, sec. 8, cl. 1.
10. For a detailed account of congressional debates about the 1815 Treaty with Britain, *see* Parry (2009), at 1303–16.
11. Senator Eligius Fromentin argued that legislation was not needed because a treaty "repeal[s] every law anterior to that treaty, which is in opposition to the provisions of that treaty." 29 Ann. Cong., at 58–59.
12. Representative John Forsyth believed that legislation was "indispensable; because the power of legislation was vested in Congress, and could be exercised by no other authority." *Id.*, at 457. Representative Rufus Easton explained: "A treaty though made has not force . . . without a law of Congress . . . to carry it into effect." *Id.*, at 595.
13. *Id.*, at 478.
14. *See* pp. 54–55.
15. *Id.*, at 477.
16. *See id.*, at 557–62.
17. *Id.*, at 558.
18. *Id.*

19. *See* Chapter 3, pp. 50–51; Chapter 4, pp. 76–83.
20. 29 Ann. Cong., at 562–63.
21. *Id.*, at 46.
22. *Id.*, at 50.
23. *Id.*, at 52 (stating that "the Legislature must act to fix the amount of such penalty, to prescribe the manner in which it should be prosecuted, and to fix the tribunal which should have cognizance of the case.").
24. *Id.*, at 53.
25. *Id.*, at 53–54. Interestingly, Senator Barbour's three categories are similar to the types of treaty provisions for which the Restatement (Third) says implementing legislation is constitutionally required. *See* Restatement (Third), § 111, cmt. i.
26. 29 Ann. Cong., at 51.
27. *Id.*, at 36–37.
28. *Id.*, at 419–20.
29. *Id.*, at 1019.
30. *Id.*, at 1020.
31. *Id.*
32. *Id.*, at 1022.
33. *See* Crandall (1904), at 135–47.
34. 1867 Treaty with Russia.
35. 1884 Treaty with Hawaii.
36. 1867 Treaty with Russia, art. VI.
37. 39 Cong. Globe 4055 (40th Cong., 2nd Sess., July 14, 1868).
38. 15 Stat. 198 (July 27, 1868).
39. 1875 Treaty with Hawaii.
40. *Id.*, art. V.
41. 19 Stat. 200 (Aug. 15, 1876).
42. *See* 1 Malloy, at 915, 918–19.
43. 1884 Treaty with Hawaii.
44. It is unclear why there was a two-year delay between signature and Senate action on the treaty.
45. Treaty with the Hawaiian Islands, H.R. Rep. 49–4177, at 1 (1887).
46. *Id.*
47. *Id.*, at 23.
48. *See* Galbraith (2014), at 89–91.
49. *See* Chapter 5, pp. 95–101.
50. 1854 Treaty with Britain; 1857 Treaty with Denmark; 1871 Treaty with Britain; 1875 Treaty with Hawaii; 1883 Treaty with Mexico; 1902 Treaty with Cuba.
51. *See* Hathaway (2008), at 1286–97.
52. 182 U.S. 1 (1901). *De Lima* was a suit to recover import duties paid under protest for items imported from Puerto Rico. A federal statute authorized collection of import duties. However, after enactment of the statute, the United States and Spain concluded a treaty in which Spain ceded Puerto Rico to the United States. The Court held that the treaty was self-executing, in the sense that the treaty itself incorporated Puerto Rico into the United States for the purpose of federal tariff laws. Therefore, the treaty superseded the statute and deprived the government of its prior statutory authority to collect import duties. *See* Chapter 7 for additional analysis of *De Lima*.

53. 1857 Treaty with Denmark, Preamble.

54. For background information on the treaty with Denmark, *see* 7 Miller, at 524–70.

55. 1857 Treaty with Denmark, arts. I, III and VI.

56. *Id.*, art. V.

57. *Id.*, art. VI.

58. 11 Stat. 261 (Mar. 4, 1858).

59. *See* 1826 Treaty with Denmark. For example, in Article 2 of the 1826 treaty, the United States and Denmark agreed "that the citizens and subjects of each may frequent all the coasts and countries of the other . . . and reside and trade there in all kinds of produce, manufactures and merchandize, and they shall enjoy all the rights, privileges and exemptions . . . which native citizens or subjects do or shall enjoy."

60. *See* Nielsen v. Johnson, 279 U.S. 47 (1929).

61. Ironically, the NSE Clause in Article VI did not have any practical effect because the treaty entered into force before Congress enacted implementing legislation, despite the fact that Article VI said that such legislation was a condition precedent for the treaty to "take effect."

62. 1875 Treaty with Hawaii.

63. *Id.*, art. V. I reconstructed the original text based on information in 8 Bevans.

64. 8 Bevans, at 874.

65. 19 Stat. 200 (Aug. 15, 1876).

66. *See* 1 Malloy, at 915, 918–19.

67. 1883 Treaty with Mexico.

68. *Id.*, art. VIII, as amended by the U.S. Senate. For the original version, *see* 9 Bevans, at 855, 857–58. For the text of Senate amendments, *see* Protocol 6, 9 Bevans, at 863.

69. *See* Protocol 2, 9 Bevans, at 859–60.

70. The Senate added certain amendments, which are not material for present purposes. *See* Protocol 6, 9 Bevans, at 863.

71. 1885 Treaty with Mexico.

72. 1886 Treaty with Mexico.

73. 1902 Treaty with Cuba.

74. *See id.*, arts. I–IV.

75. *See id.*, arts. VI and VIII.

76. *Id.*, art. XI.

77. *Id.*

78. 33 Stat. 3 (Dec. 17, 1903).

79. *Id.* The statute's drafters basically copied the substantive provisions of the treaty into the statute, with appropriate modifications to reflect the fact that the statute is unilateral, whereas the treaty is bilateral.

80. 202 U.S. 563 (1906).

81. *Id.* at 564.

82. 33 Stat. 2136, 2144.

83. 202 U.S. at 579.

84. The statute actually says that it will take effect "on the tenth day after exchange of ratifications." 33 Stat. 3. As the Court noted, though, ratifications had already

been exchanged more than eight months before the statute was enacted, so this particular statutory phrase did not make sense. Under the Court's interpretation, both the statute and the treaty took effect on December 27, ten days after the parallel proclamations of the two presidents.

85. 1902 Treaty with Cuba, art. IX.
86. *Id.*, art. XI.
87. *See* 33 Stat. 3, 4 (Sec. 2).
88. *See id.*; *see also* 1902 Treaty with Cuba, art. IX.
89. 33 Stat. 3, at 3–4 (Sec. 1).
90. 1854 Treaty with Britain.
91. 10 Stat. 587–88 (Aug. 5, 1854).
92. 6 U.S. Op. Atty. Gen. 748, 748.
93. *See* 6 Miller, at 667, 735–36.
94. 6 U.S. Op. Atty. Gen. 748.
95. *Id.*, at 749.
96. *See id.* at 749–50. *See also* 1854 Treaty with Britain, art. III.
97. 6 U.S. Op. Atty. Gen., at 750.
98. 1854 Treaty with Britain, art. II.
99. *Id.*, art. IV.
100. 6 U.S. Op. Atty. Gen., at 749. Cushing said this specifically with respect to British fishing rights under Article II. He did not refer specifically to freedom of navigation for British citizens under Article IV, but he did refer specifically to freedom of navigation for U.S. citizens under Article IV, so it is reasonable to infer that the statement applies equally to freedom of navigation for British citizens.
101. *See* U.S. CONST. art. I, sec. 10, cl. 2.
102. *See* 22 U.S. Op. Atty. Gen. 214, 215–16 (1898) ("The regulation of fisheries in navigable waters within the territorial limits of the several States, in the absence of a Federal treaty, is a subject of State rather than of Federal jurisdiction.")
103. Cushing's analysis did not specifically address the impact on conflicting state laws, but this conclusion necessarily follows from what he did say. *See also* 6 U.S. Op. Atty. Gen. 291, 292 (1854) (Cushing) (stating, with respect to a different treaty with Britain, that "the convention, if duly ratified between the two nations, will become, by the Constitution of the United States, a supreme law, obligatory everywhere within the United States, binding on all, a rule of decision for all judges, whether of the United States or of the several States.").
104. 1871 Treaty with Britain.
105. *See* Bingham (2005).
106. 1871 Treaty with Britain, art. XXXIII.
107. 1873 Treaty with Britain.
108. *See* An Act to Carry into Effect the Provisions of the Treaty between the United States and Great Britain, signed in the City of Washington the eighth Day of May, eighteen hundred and seventy-one, relating to the Fisheries, 17 Stat. 482 (Mar. 1, 1873).
109. 1871 Treaty with Britain, arts. XVIII, XIX, XX.
110. Section 1 of the legislation implemented Article 21. Section 2 implemented Article 32 (related to Newfoundland). Section 3 implemented Article 29. Section 4 implemented Articles 30 and 31. *See* 17 Stat. 482, 482–83 (Mar. 1, 1873).

111. Article 29 addressed British goods arriving at U.S. ports and destined for Canada. Article 31 permitted the United States to suspend certain rights granted to British subjects under Article 30 if Canada or New Brunswick imposed export duties in contravention of Article 31.

112. Ultimately, the arbitrators awarded Britain 5.5 million dollars in compensation. *See* 1 Malloy, at 709. Of course, Congress had to enact legislation to appropriate the necessary funds.

113. Congress's decision not to enact implementing legislation for Articles 26–28 reinforces this point. Those articles dealt with navigation on internal lakes, rivers, and canals—matters that are generally subject to state regulatory authority in the absence of treaties. The decision not to enact implementing legislation for Articles 26–28 manifests Congress's view that implementing legislation was not needed for those portions of the 1871 treaty that intersected with state law.

114. *See* Chapter 14, pp. 306–07.

115. *See, e.g.,* S. Exec. Rep. 102-23, at 19 (1992) (stating expressly that "implementing legislation is not contemplated" for the International Covenant on Civil and Political Rights).

116. *See* Chapter 14, pp. 306–10.

117. *See, e.g.,* H.R. Rep. 49-4177 (1887); Crandall (1904), at 135–47.

118. 21 U.S. Op. Atty. Gen. 347 (1896).

119. 22 U.S. Op. Atty. Gen. 201, 204 (1898).

120. 23 U.S. Op. Atty. Gen. 545 (1901).

121. 1909 Treaty with Britain.

122. 30 U.S. Op. Atty. Gen. 217, 219 (1913).

123. *Id.* at 220–21.

124. 30 U.S. Op. Atty. Gen. 351, 354 (1915).

125. *Id.* at 354.

126. *See* pp. 119–20.

127. 6 U.S. Op. Atty. Gen. 748, 749 (1854).

128. 6 U.S. Op. Atty. Gen. 291, 297 (1854).

129. *Id.* at 298.

130. *Id.* at 298–99.

131. 13 U.S. Op. Atty. Gen. 354 (1870).

132. 19 U.S. Op. Atty. Gen. 273 (1889).

133. 30 U.S. Op. Atty. Gen. 84, 88 (1913).

134. 1883 Paris Convention, art. 2.

135. U.S. CONST. art. I, sec. 8, cl. 8.

136. 19 U.S. Op. Atty. Gen. 273, 275–78 (1889).

137. 27 US 253, 314 (1829).

138. 19 U.S. Op. Atty. Gen. 273, 278–79.

139. *Id.* at 278–79.

140. *See, e.g.,* Cameron Septic Tank Co. v. City of Knoxville, 227 U.S. 39, 48–50 (1913); Rousseau v. Brown, 21 App. D.C. 73, 76–77 (D.C. Cir. 1903).

141. 30 U.S. Op. Atty. Gen. 84 (1913).

142. *Id.* at 87.

143. *Id.* at 86.

144. *Id.* at 87.

145. *See id.* at 87–88. Overall, Wickersham's opinion is open to two competing interpretations that correspond, respectively, to the *contract doctrine* and the *intent doctrine.* I discuss the intent doctrine in Chapter 8. I credit Professor Dickinson with inventing the intent doctrine in 1926, but Wickersham's 1913 opinion could be construed as a precursor to the intent doctrine. In any case, Wickersham's reasoning is sufficiently opaque that it is difficult to link it definitively to any particular version of NSE doctrine.

CHAPTER 7

1. Professor Van Alstine says that "the Court applied treaties in more than three hundred substantive treaty cases" between 1900 and 1945. Van Alstine (2011), at 193. Professor Hollis identified 136 Supreme Court cases between 1861 and 1900 that "involved some treaty question." Hollis (2011), at 55. A book chapter that I coauthored says: "Between 1789 and 1860, the U.S. Supreme Court decided more than 150 cases in which one or more parties raised a claim or defense that relied, at least in part, on a treaty." Sloss, Ramsey & Dodge (2011), at 13. The estimate in the text excludes cases decided before 1800.
2. 27 U.S. 253 (1829).
3. 112 U.S. 580 (1884).
4. *Aguilar,* 318 U.S. 724, 738 (1943) (Stone, C.J., concurring/dissenting); *Factor,* 290 U.S. 276, 300 (1933); *Cook,* 288 U.S. 102, 119 n.19 (1933); *Maul,* 274 U.S. 501, 530 n.34 (1927) (Brandeis, J., concurring); *Cameron Septic,* 227 U.S. 39, 47–50 (1913); *Fok Young Yo,* 185 U.S. 296, 303 (1902); *Lee Yen Tai,* 185 U.S. 213, 221 (1902); *De Lima,* 182 U.S. 1, 195 (1901); *Mitchell,* 180 U.S. 402, 428 (1901); *Whitney,* 124 U.S. 190, 194 (1888); *Bartram,* 122 U.S. 116, 120 (1887).
5. *Whitney,* 124 U.S. at 194. *See also Cook,* 288 U.S. at 119 (defining self-executing to mean "that no legislation was necessary to authorize executive action pursuant to its provisions").
6. *Whitney,* 124 U.S. at 194.
7. *De Lima,* 182 U.S. at 195 (quoting *Whitney,* 124 U.S. at 194).
8. 290 U.S. 276, 300 (1933).
9. 185 U.S. 213, 221 (1902).
10. 180 U.S. 402, 428 (1901).
11. 122 U.S. 116, 120 (1887).
12. 185 U.S. 296, 303 (1902).
13. *Id.*
14. Aguilar v. Standard Oil Co., 318 U.S. 724, 738 (1943) (Stone, C.J., concurring/dissenting).
15. *See* Cook v. United States, 288 U.S. 102, 119 n.19 (1933); Maul v. United States, 274 U.S. 501, 530 n.39 (1927) (Brandeis, J., concurring).
16. Cameron Septic Tank Co. v. City of Knoxville, 227 U.S. 39, 47–50 (1913).
17. *See* De Lima v. Bidwell, 182 U.S. 1, 181–96 (1901). *See also* pp. 135–37 *infra* (discussing *De Lima* in more detail).
18. Mitchell v. Furman, 180 U.S. 402, 430 (1901).
19. *Head Money,* 112 U.S. 580 (1884); *Whitney,* 124 U.S. 190 (1888); *De Lima,* 182 U.S. 1 (1901); *Downes,* 182 U.S. 244 (1901); *Cameron Septic,* 227 U.S. 39 (1913); and *Cook,* 288 U.S. 102 (1933).

20. 112 U.S. 580 (1884). The summary of *Head Money* in this paragraph closely tracks the summary in Lee & Sloss (2011), at 140.
21. *Head Money*, 112 U.S. at 597.
22. *Id.*, at 597–99.
23. *Id.*, at 598–99.
24. *Id.*, at 598.
25. *See* Sloss, *Domestic Application* (2012), at 376–79.
26. *Head Money*, 112 U.S. at 598.
27. *See* Sloss, *Domestic Application* (2012), at 376–77.
28. *Head Money*, 112 U.S. at 598–99.
29. *See* Vázquez (1995), at 713–15.
30. *See* Chapter 6, pp. 125–26.
31. This statement assumes that the NSE "holding" in *Foster* was a minority view. *See* Chapter 4, pp. 70–71.
32. *See Whitney*, 124 U.S. 190, 190–91 (1888). The account of *Whitney* presented here closely follows the account presented in Sloss (2002), at 31–35. *See also* Crandall (1904), at 146–47.
33. 1867 Treaty with Dominican Republic; 1875 Treaty with Hawaii.
34. 1867 Treaty with Dominican Republic, art. IX.
35. *See Whitney*, 124 U.S. at 191–92.
36. *See id.*, at 192–95.
37. *See* Hollis (2011), at 79.
38. Professor Hollis contends that the Court held the 1867 treaty with the Dominican Republic to be non-self-executing. *See id.*, at 78–79. Under the logic of the later-in-time rule, though, if the Court was simply resolving a conflict between the 1870 statute and the 1867 treaty, it would not matter whether the treaty was self-executing or non-self-executing, because the statute would trump the treaty either way.
39. *See* Sloss (2002), at 33–35.
40. *Whitney*, 124 U.S. at 194.
41. The best explanation is that the Court believed that treaties modifying tariff laws are constitutionally non-self-executing. *See supra* pp. 112–14; *see also* Sloss (2002), at 33–35.
42. 1898 Treaty with Spain.
43. *De Lima*, 182 U.S. 1, 180 (1901).
44. *Id.*, at 181.
45. *Id.*, at 196.
46. *See id.*, at 181–94.
47. *Id.*, at 194.
48. *See supra* p. 131.
49. Between 1900 and 1945, only one lower federal court cited *De Lima* as an authority on self-execution issues. *See* M.H. Pulaski Co. v. United States, 6 U.S. Cust. App. 291, 336 (1915).
50. Memorandum from Attorney Adviser Diven to Legal Adviser Gross (Apr. 22, 1948), *reprinted in* 14 Whiteman, at 304.
51. 182 U.S. 244 (1901).
52. An Act Temporarily to Provide Revenues and a Civil Government for Porto Rico, Apr. 12, 1900, 31 Stat. 77.

53. *Downes*, 182 U.S. at 247–48.
54. U.S. CONST. art. I, sec. 8, cl. 1.
55. *See Downes*, 182 U.S., at 249–87.
56. 1898 Treaty with Spain, art. II.
57. The Restatement of Foreign Relations Law acknowledges that a single treaty might contain some provisions that are self-executing and other provisions that are non-self-executing. *See* Restatement (Third), § 111, cmt. h. However, in *Medellín v. Texas*, 552 U.S. 491 (2008), the Supreme Court ridiculed the idea that a single treaty article could be self-executing for some purposes and non-self-executing for others. *Id.*, at 514–15. Chief Justice Roberts asserted that such a "judgment-by-judgment analysis" would be inconsistent with the Court's approach in *Foster* and *Percheman*. In fact, though, Roberts's methodology in *Medellín* was inconsistent with the context-specific approach that the Court applied in *Foster, Percheman, Downes*, and *De Lima*.
58. 1900 Treaty of Brussels.
59. *Cameron Septic*, 227 U.S. 39, 40–42 (1913).
60. *Id.*, at 44.
61. *Id.*, at 45. *See also id.*, at 44–47.
62. *See id.*, at 48. *See also* Chapter 6, pp. 125–26.
63. *Cameron Septic*, 227 U.S. at 49. *See also id.*, at 50 (stating that it "seems also to be the sense of some of the other contracting nations" that Article 4 *bis* required legislative implementation).
64. *Compare* Crandall (1904), at 106–50 (discussing treaties in the United States) *with id.*, at 151–68 (discussing treaties in the United Kingdom).
65. 32 Stat. 1225 (Mar. 3, 1903).
66. 227 U.S. at 49.
67. *Id.*, at 50.
68. *Id.*
69. 288 U.S. 102 (1933).
70. 1924 Treaty with Britain.
71. *See Cook*, 288 U.S. at 107–10.
72. 1924 Treaty with Britain, art. II.
73. *See Cook*, 288 U.S. at 111–19.
74. *Id.*, at 119. This statement is a bit puzzling. The relevant question was not whether legislation was necessary to authorize executive action pursuant to the treaty. Rather, the relevant question was whether legislation was necessary to constrain executive action in accordance with treaty limitations.
75. *See id.*, at 119 n.19.
76. *Id.*, at 119.
77. *Id.*, at 119–20.
78. *Id.*, at 120.
79. *Id.*
80. The following cases cite *Foster, Head Money*, or both, but no party asserted any treaty-based right: Coleman v. Miller, 307 U.S. 433 (1939); Cincinnati Soap Co. v. United States, 301 U.S. 308 (1937); Keller v. United States, 213 U.S. 138 (1909); Moore v. McGuire, 205 U.S. 214 (1907); Brown v. Walker, 161 U.S. 591 (1896); Pollock v. Farmers' Loan & Trust Co., 158 U.S. 601 (1895); Pollock v. Farmers' Loan & Trust Co., 157 U.S. 429 (1895); Nishimura Ekiu v. United States, 142 U.S.

651 (1892); Jones v. United States, 137 U.S. 202 (1890); Bryan v. Kennett, 113 U.S. 179 (1885); Kentucky v. Dennison, 65 U.S. 66 (1860); Luther v. Borden, 48 U.S. 1 (1849); Scott v. Jones, 46 U.S. 343 (1847); Groves v. Slaughter, 40 U.S. 449 (1841); Williams v. Suffolk Ins. Co., 38 U.S. 415 (1839); Rhode Island v. Massachusetts, 37 U.S. 657 (1838); and Poole v. Fleeger, 36 U.S. 185 (1837).

81. All forty-five cases are cited in notes 82–87.

82. *See* United States v. Texas, 143 U.S. 621, 639 (1892); Coffee v. Groover, 123 U.S. 1, 25–26 (1887); United States v. Lynde, 78 U.S. 632, 638–39, 641 (1870); Doe v. Braden, 57 U.S. 635, 650, 653 (1853) (counsel's argument); United States v. Boisdore, 52 U.S. 63, 73, 77 (1850) (counsel's argument); Goodtitle *ex dem.* Pollard v. Kibbe, 50 U.S. 471, 477 (1850) (counsel's argument); Davis v. Police Jury of Concordia, 50 U.S. 280, 285 (1850); LaRoche v. Jones' Lessee, 50 U.S. 155, 158 (1850) (counsel's argument); United States v. Reynes, 50 U.S. 127, 154 (1850); Pollard v. Hagan, 44 U.S. 212, 228 (1845); Lessee of Pollard v. Files, 43 U.S. 591, 603 (1844); City of Mobile v. Emanuel, 42 U.S. 95, 102–03 (1843) (Catron, J., dissenting); Pollard's Heirs v. Kibbe, 39 U.S. 353, 360 (1840) (counsel's argument); Keene v. Whittaker, 39 U.S. 170, 171 (1840); Lattimer v. Poteet, 39 U.S. 4, 15–16 (1840); Garcia v. Lee, 37 U.S. 511, 516–17, 520–21 (1838); United States v. Arredondo, 31 U.S. 691, 710–11 (1832).

83. *See* Oetjen v. Central Leather Co., 246 U.S. 297, 302 (1918); *Ex parte* Cooper, 143 U.S. 472, 503 (1892).

84. *See* Pigeon River Co. v. Charles W. Cox, Ltd., 291 U.S. 138, 160 (1934) (citing *Head Money*); Rainey v. United States, 232 U.S. 310, 316 (1914) (citing *Head Money*); Barker v. Harvey, 181 U.S. 481, 488 (1901) (citing *Head Money*); La Abra Silver Mining Co. v. United States, 175 U.S. 423, 460 (1899) (citing *Head Money*); Thomas v. Gay, 169 U.S. 264, 271 (1898) (citing *Foster*); Lem Moon Sing v. United States, 158 U.S. 538, 549 (1895) (citing *Head Money*); Fong Yue Ting v. United States, 149 U.S. 698, 721 (1893) (citing both *Foster* and *Head Money*); Horner v. United States, 143 U.S. 570, 578 (1892) (citing *Head Money*); Chae Chan Ping v. United States, 130 U.S. 581, 600 (1889) (citing *Head Money*); Botiller v. Dominguez, 130 U.S. 238, 247 (1889) (citing *Head Money*); Chew Heong v. United States, 112 U.S. 536, 565 (1884) (Field, J., dissenting) (citing *Head Money*); The Cherokee Tobacco, 78 U.S. 616, 620–21 (1871) (citing *Foster*).

85. *See* Bacardi Corp. v. Domenech, 311 U.S. 150, 161–62 (1940) (citing *Head Money*); Asakura v. City of Seattle, 265 U.S. 332, 341 (1924) (citing both *Foster* and *Head Money*); Maiorano v. Baltimore & Ohio R.R. Co., 213 U.S. 268, 272–73 (1909) (citing both *Foster* and *Head Money*); Hauenstein v. Lynham, 100 U.S. 483, 490 (1880) (citing *Foster*). *See* Chapter 5 for additional analysis of these cases.

86. *See* The Diamond Rings, 183 U.S. 176, 182 (1901) (Brown, J., concurring) (citing both *Head Money* and *Foster* to support the proposition that a Senate resolution, adopted after the subject treaty had already been ratified, was not part of the treaty); Kinkead v. United States, 150 U.S. 483, 511 (1893) (Shiras, J., dissenting) (citing *Head Money* to support the principle that treaties should be construed liberally).

87. *See* Valentine v. United States *ex rel.* Neidecker, 299 U.S. 5, 10 (1936); Terlinden v. Ames, 184 U.S. 270, 288 (1902); *Ex parte* Cooper, 143 U.S. 472, 501–02 (1892); Baldwin v. Franks, 120 U.S. 678, 703 (1887) (Field, J., dissenting); United States v. Rauscher, 119 U.S. 407, 418–19 (1886); Chew Heong v. United States, 112 U.S. 536, 540 (1884); United States v. Forty-Three Gallons of Whiskey, 93 U.S. 188,

196 (1876); Holden v. Joy, 84 U.S. 211, 247 (1872); United States v. Brooks, 51 U.S. 442, 444 (1850) (counsel's argument); *In re* Metzger, 46 U.S. 176, 182–83 (1847); Pollard's Heirs v. Kibbe, 39 U.S. 353, 365 (1840); United States v. Arredondo, 31 U.S. 691, 710–11, 734 (1832).

Astute readers will observe that the numbers in the text associated with notes 82–87 add up to forty-nine cases, because four cases included in this footnote are also included in one of the preceding footnotes: *Cooper, Chew Heong, Pollard's Heirs,* and *Arredondo.*

88. *Rauscher*, 119 U.S. 407, 419 (1886).
89. *Chew Heong*, 112 U.S. 536, 540 (1884).
90. *Id.,* at 543.
91. *See id.,* at 543–54.
92. *Brooks*, 51 U.S. 442, 444 (1850) (counsel's argument).
93. *Id.,* at 460.
94. On the vested property rights exception, see Jones v. Meehan, 175 U.S. 1 (1899). *See also* Lee & Sloss (2011), at 136–37; Paust (1988), at 410–14.
95. *Baldwin*, 120 U.S. 678, 680–81 (1887).
96. *See id.,* at 682–94.
97. *Id.,* at 701–02 (Field, J., dissenting).
98. *Id.,* at 703 (Field, J., dissenting).
99. *Id.,* at 705 (Field, J., dissenting).
100. For additional analysis of Justice Field's dissent in *Baldwin*, see Hollis (2011), at 76–78.
101. 1852 Treaty with Prussia.
102. *See Terlinden*, 184 U.S. 270, 280–88 (1902). In this context, the Court stated that "[t]reaties of extradition are executory in their character, and fall within the rule laid down by Chief Justice Marshall in" *Foster. Id.,* at 288 (quoting *Foster*). This statement is legal gibberish, but it did not detract from the rest of the opinion.
103. Act of August 12, 1848, 9 Stat. 302.
104. *Id.,* sec. 1. *See also id.,* sec. 3 ("[I]t shall be lawful for the Secretary of State . . . to order the person so committed to be delivered to . . . such foreign government, to be tried for the crime of which such person shall be so accused.").
105. *See, e.g.,* Factor v. Laubenheimer, 290 U.S. 276 (1933); Charlton v. Kelly, 229 U.S. 447 (1913); Benson v. McMahon, 127 U.S. 457 (1888).
106. 1863 Treaty with Chippewa Indians, art. VII.
107. *Forty-Three Gallons*, 93 U.S. 188, 196 (1876).
108. *See id.,* at 192–98.
109. *Holden*, 84 U.S. 211, 236 (1872).
110. *Id.,* at 247.
111. *Id.*
112. Additionally, the Court said: "Acts of Congress were subsequently passed recognizing the treaty . . . and the supplemental treaty as valid, and making appropriations to carry the same into effect." *Id.,* at 252.
113. *See* Chapter 4, pp. 79–81.
114. *Kibbe*, 39 U.S. 353, 360 (1840) (counsel's argument).
115. *Id.,* at 365.
116. Congress passed a statute in 1836 to confirm the title of "the heirs of William Pollard." *See id.,* at 366 (quoting Act of July 2, 1836).

117. 46 U.S. 176, 182–83 (1847) (counsel's argument) (citing *Foster*).
118. *Id.*, at 188–89.
119. For additional analysis of *Metzger, see* Parry (2002), at 126–34.
120. 299 U.S. 5, 10 (1936) (quoting *Foster* and citing *Head Money*).
121. 143 U.S. 472, 501–02 (1892) (quoting *Head Money*).
122. In many of these cases, the self-execution issue was arguably not relevant because Congress had enacted some type of legislation that could plausibly be construed as treaty-implementing legislation. If Congress has authorized courts to apply the treaty, then courts need not engage in a self-execution analysis.
123. Downes v. Bidwell, 182 U.S. 244 (1901); De Lima v. Bidwell, 182 U.S. 1 (1901); Whitney v. Robertson, 124 U.S. 190 (1888); Bartram v. Robertson, 122 U.S. 116 (1887).
124. Fok Young Yo v. United States, 185 U.S. 296 (1902); United States v. Lee Yen Tai, 185 U.S. 213 (1902); The Head Money Cases, 112 U.S. 580 (1884); Chew Heong v. United States, 112 U.S. 536 (1884).
125. Valentine v. United States *ex rel.* Neidecker, 299 U.S. 5 (1936); Factor v. Laubenheimer, 290 U.S. 276 (1933); Terlinden v. Ames, 184 U.S. 270 (1902); *In re* Metzger, 46 U.S. 176 (1847).
126. Aguilar v. Standard Oil Co., 318 U.S. 724 (1943); Cook v. United States, 288 U.S. 102 (1933); Maul v. United States, 274 U.S. 501 (1927); *Ex parte* Cooper, 143 U.S. 472 (1892).
127. Mitchell v. Furman, 180 U.S. 402 (1901); Holden v. Joy, 84 U.S. 211 (1872); United States v. Brooks, 51 U.S. 442 (1850); Pollard's Heirs v. Kibbe, 39 U.S. 353 (1840); United States v. Percheman, 32 U.S. 51 (1833); United States v. Arredondo, 31 U.S. 691 (1832); Foster v. Neilson, 27 U.S. 253 (1829).
128. Cameron Septic Tank Co. v. City of Knoxville, 227 U.S. 39 (1913); United States v. Rauscher, 119 U.S. 407 (1886).
129. Baldwin v. Franks, 120 U.S. 678 (1887); United States v. Forty-Three Gallons of Whiskey, 93 U.S. 188 (1876).
130. Before creation of the federal courts of appeals, circuit courts sometimes sat as trial courts and sometimes as appellate courts. I counted cases in which circuit courts sat as appellate courts, but not those where they sat as trial courts. I excluded cases in which the term "self-executing" appears only in the headnotes, unless the case cited *Foster* or *Head Money* and at least one party raised a treaty-based argument. I also excluded cases that were later appealed to the Supreme Court if the Supreme Court decision was discussed earlier in this chapter.
131. *See* John T. Bill Co. v. United States, 104 F.2d 67, 73 (C.C.P.A. 1939) ("The treaty was reciprocal and it was self-executing, requiring no legislation other than its own enactment, so far as any matter here involved was concerned."); Minerva Automobiles v. United States, 96 F.2d 836, 838–39 (C.C.P.A. 1938) (citing *Head Money* to support the later-in-time rule); George E. Warren Corp. v. United States, 94 F.2d 597, 599 (2d Cir. 1938) (citing *Head Money* to support the statement that the treaty "addresses itself, exclusively, to the legislative power"); United States v. Garrow, 88 F.2d 318, 320–23 (C.C.P.A. 1937) (holding that Article 3 of the Jay Treaty was "self-executing and granted to the Indians named therein the right to bring their own proper goods and effects of whatever nature into the United States," but Article 9 of the 1814 Treaty of Ghent was not self-executing); George E. Warren Corp. v. United States, 71 F.2d 434, 437 (C.C.P.A.

1934) ("Most-favored nation treaties are always reciprocal in character, whether they be executory or self-executing."); United States v. Domestic Fuel Corp., 71 F.2d 424, 433–34 (C.C.P.A. 1934) ("The treaty and the statute are laws *pari materia* and must be construed together. Such being the situation . . . we fail to perceive any necessity for considering" whether the treaty is self-executing); M.H. Pulaski Co. v. United States, 6 U.S. Cust. App. 291, 328 (C.C.A. 1915) (citing *Foster* to support the statement that "whether or not a treaty is self-executing depends upon whether it is operative *ex proprio vigore*, or whether it requires some legislation to make it effective."); American Express Co. v. United States, 4 U.S. Cust. App. 146, 150 (C.C.A. 1913) (citing *Foster* for the proposition that if "a treaty speaks in the nature of an executory promise it is the rule that it is not self-executing, and before it can be given the same force and effect as the law of the land action by Congress so legislating must be had"); Shaw v. United States, 1 U.S. Cust. App. 426, 429 (C.C.A. 1911) (same); Tartar Chem. Co. v. United States, 116 F. 726, 730 (C.C. S.D.N.Y. 1902) (citing *Foster*'s political question holding); North German Lloyd S.S. Co. v. Hedden, 43 F. 17, 22 (C.C.D. N.J. 1890) (citing *Foster* to support the later-in-time rule); Taylor v. Morton, 23 F. Cas. 784, 787 (C.C.D. Mass. 1855) (citing *Foster* to support the statement that "this clause in the treaty is merely a contract, addressing itself to the legislative power").

132. *See* Robertson v. Gen. Elec. Co., 32 F.2d 495, 499–502 (4th Cir. 1929) (discussed in Chapter 8); *In re* Stoffregen, 6 F.2d 943, 944 (D.C. Cir. 1925) (rejecting claim that peace treaty with Germany was self-executing, as applied to patents); Hennebique Const. Co. v. Myers, 172 F. 869, 880–91 (3d Cir. 1909) (Archbald, J., concurring) (concluding that Article 4 *bis* of the Brussels Convention of 1900 was self-executing); Rousseau v. Brown, 21 App. D.C. 73, 76 (D.C. Cir. 1903) (holding that the Paris Convention of 1883 is not self-executing); Appert v. Schmertz, 13 App. D.C. 117, 121 (D.C. Cir. 1898) (stating that it was not necessary to decide whether the treaty at issue was self-executing).

133. *See* Haff v. Yung Poy, 68 F.2d 203, 204 (9th Cir. 1933) (stating that "treaty between the United States and China . . . is not self-executing"); Weedin v. Wong Tat Hing, 6 F.2d 201, 202 (9th Cir. 1925) (same); Hong Wing v. United States, 142 F. 128, 129 (6th Cir. 1906) (citing *Head Money* in support of the later-in-time rule); *In re* Lee Gon Yung, 111 F. 998, 1002 (C.C. N.D. Cal. 1901) ("the treaty recognizes the binding force of these regulations, and to that extent, at least, the treaty is self-executing, and is as much the law of the land as an act of congress").

134. *See* Albany v. United States, 152 F.2d 266, 266 (6th Cir. 1945) (citing *Head Money* and holding that member of Iroquois tribe was not entitled to exemption from military service); *Ex parte* Green, 123 F.2d 862, 863 (2d Cir. 1941) (citing *Head Money* and holding that Native American was not entitled to exemption from military service); Wadsworth v. Boysen, 148 F. 771, 774 (8th Cir. 1906) (using the term "self-executing" and holding that there was no "conflict between the agreement made with the Shoshone and Arapahoe Indian tribes and the act of Congress"); Godfrey v. Beardsley, 10 F. Cas. 520, 522 (C.C.D. Ind. 1841) (citing *Foster* and *Percheman* and holding that treaty with Indian tribe conveyed perfect title to individual landowner).

135. *See* Lakos v. Saliaris, 116 F.2d 440, 444–45 (4th Cir. 1940) (citing *Head Money* in support of the later-in-time rule); Warshauer v. Lloyd Sabaudo S.A., 71 F.2d 146, 148 (2d Cir. 1934) (holding that international salvage treaty was self-executing, and therefore limited the shipowner's liability); The Sagatind, 11 F.2d 673, 675 (2d Cir. 1926) (holding that liquor treaties were not self-executing, and therefore did not extend the territorial jurisdiction of the United States into the ocean beyond the twelve-mile statutory limit).

136. Z&F Assets Realization Corp. v. Hull, 114 F.2d 464, 470–71 (D.C. Cir. 1940) (citing both *Foster* and *Head Money* and stating that "when the alleged controversies arising out of treaty relationships are political in nature they are not cases within the meaning of Article III of the Constitution and, consequently, are not subject to judicial determination"); La Ninfa, 75 F. 513, 518 (9th Cir. 1896) (applying decision of international arbitration panel, and citing *Head Money* to support the statement that "a treaty, when accepted and agreed to, becomes the supreme law of the land. It binds courts as much as an act of congress.").

137. Leitensdorfer v. Campbell, 15 F. Cas. 270, 272 (C.C.D. Colo. 1878) (citing *Foster* and holding that the validity of claims derived from Mexican grants "should be decided by the executive instead of the judicial department of the government"); United States v. Flint, 25 F. Cas. 1107, 1116–17 (C.C.D. Cal. 1876) (citing *Foster* in a case involving Mexican land grants, and stating that Congress "called to its assistance the courts, and for that purpose invested them with a jurisdiction in all respects special and extraordinary").

138. *Ex parte* Ortiz, 100 F. 955, 959 (C.C.D. Minn. 1900) (citing *Head Money* to support the later-in-time rule).

139. 91 F.2d 14 (9th Cir. 1936).

140. 24 F. Cas. 344 (C.C.D. Mich. 1852).

141. 27 F. Cas. 91 (C.C.D. Mass. 1847).

142. *See O'Donnell*, 91 F.2d at 19.

143. *See id.*, at 17–18.

144. *Id.*, at 39.

145. United States v. O'Donnell, 303 U.S. 501, 505 (1938).

146. *O'Donnell*, 91 F.2d at 20.

147. *O'Donnell*, 303 U.S. at 514.

148. 24 F. Cas. 344 (C.C.D. Mich. 1852).

149. 1836 Treaty with the Ottawa, art. 8.

150. *See Turner*, 24 F. Cas. 344.

151. *Id.*, at 345.

152. Act of June 23, 1836, 5 Stat. 59.

153. 24 F. Cas. at 346.

154. An Act to Grant Preemption Rights to Settlers on the Public Lands, June 22, 1838, 5 Stat. 251.

155. 24 F. Cas. at 345.

156. *Id.*, at 346.

157. *Id.*, at 345.

158. *Id.*, at 346.

159. 27 F. Cas. 91, 91 (C.C.D. Mass. 1847).

160. *Id.*, at 107.
161. *Id.*
162. *See id.*, at 104 (stating that an "indictment cannot be sustained in this court, unless some law of the United States has declared it to be a crime, and given to this court jurisdiction over it").
163. *Id.*, at 124.
164. *Id.*
165. *Hines*, 312 U.S. 52 (1941); *Pigeon River*, 291 U.S. 138 (1934); *Oetjen*, 246 U.S. 297 (1918); *Thomas*, 169 U.S. 264 (1898); *Baldwin*, 120 U.S. 678 (1887); *Forty-Three Gallons*, 93 U.S. 188 (1876).
166. Brief for the United States, Amicus Curiae, Hines v. Davidowitz, at 35–37 (1940).
167. *Hines*, 312 U.S. at 62–63.
168. *Id.*, at 61.
169. *See Pigeon River*, 291 U.S. at 147–52.
170. *Id.*, at 158.
171. *Id.*, at 151.
172. *Id.*, at 160–61.
173. Oetjen v. Central Leather Co., 246 U.S. 297, 299–301 (1918).
174. *Id.*, at 301.
175. *Id.*, at 302–03.
176. *Id.*, at 303.
177. Thomas v. Gay, 169 U.S. 264 (1898).
178. *Id.*, at 271.
179. *Id.*, at 272.
180. *Id.*, at 273.
181. *See supra* pp. 141–43.
182. *See supra* pp. 141–43.
183. *Pigeon River*, 291 U.S. at 156.

CHAPTER 8

1. *See* Chapter 1.
2. *See generally* Herring (2008).
3. *See generally* Janis (2004).
4. Fujii v. State, 242 P.2d 617 (Cal. 1952).
5. *See* Chapters 10 and 11.
6. Dickinson, *Liquor Treaties* (1926).
7. *See* Gardbaum (1994).
8. U.S. CONST. amend XVIII.
9. National Prohibition Act, 41 Stat. 305 (Oct. 25, 1919).
10. 1922 Attorney General Report (quoted in Dickinson, *Jurisdiction* (1926), at 16 n.61).
11. *See* 1 Moore §§ 144–45; 1 Hackworth § 92.
12. *See* Tariff Act of 1922, Sec. 581, 42 Stat. 858, 979 (1922). The United States had similar statutes in place since 1790 that authorized extraterritorial enforcement of specific federal laws beyond U.S. territorial waters. *See* Dickinson, *Jurisdiction* (1926), at 12–18.
13. *See* Cook v. United States, 288 U.S. 102, 109 n.2 (1933) (citing treaties).

14. *See* Tariff Act of 1922, Sec. 581, 42 Stat. 858, 979 (1922). The statute authorizes search and seizure "within four leagues of the coast." Four leagues is equal to twelve miles. The statute also makes vessels liable to forfeiture. The twelve-mile rule did not restrict the government's authority to seize U.S. vessels.

15. *See infra* pp. 156–57.

16. *See* Ford v. United States, 273 U.S. 593 (1927) (upholding a conspiracy conviction for a defendant seized outside U.S. territorial waters).

17. 1924 Treaty with Britain, at 1761. The sixteen liquor treaties were substantially identical, except for Article I. Treaties with "the Netherlands, Germany, Cuba, Panama, and Japan," like the treaty with Britain, affirmed the three-mile rule. *Cook*, 288 U.S. at 109 n.2. In the other treaties, the parties retained their "claims, without prejudice by reason of this agreement, with respect to the extent of their territorial jurisdiction." 1924 Treaty with Denmark, at 1809.

18. 1924 Treaty with Britain, art. II, paras. 1 and 2.

19. *Id.*, art. II, para. 3.

20. 273 U.S. 593 (1927).

21. *Id.*, at 604.

22. *Id.*, at 605–06.

23. *Id.*, at 606.

24. *Id.*

25. *See* Chapter 7.

26. *See* United States v. Ferris, 19 F.2d 925 (N.D. Cal. 1927); United States v. Schouweiler, 19 F.2d 387 (S.D. Cal. 1927).

27. *Ferris*, 19 F.2d at 926.

28. *Schouweiler*, 19 F.2d at 388.

29. The court in *Ferris*, referring to the liquor treaties generally, said: "in so far as they are self-executing and relate to private rights [they] are to be given effect by the courts to the extent that they are capable of judicial enforcement." *Ferris*, 19 F.2d at 926. However, the court did not actually analyze the question of whether the treaty with Panama was self-executing.

30. Dickinson, *Liquor Treaties* (1926).

31. *Id.*, at 449.

32. Attorney General Wickersham's 1913 opinion could be construed as a precursor to the intent doctrine. *See* Chapter 6, pp. 126–27.

33. *See, e.g.*, Restatement (Third), at § 111(4) ("An international agreement of the United States is 'non-self-executing' . . . if the agreement manifests an intention that it shall not become effective as domestic law without the enactment of implementing legislation"); Medellin v. Texas, 552 U.S. 491, 505 (2008) (stating that treaties "are not domestic law unless Congress has either enacted implementing statutes or the treaty itself conveys an intention that it be 'self-executing' ").

34. Dickinson, *Liquor Treaties* (1926).

35. Dickinson, *Jurisdiction* (1926).

36. Dickinson specifically cited *The Over the Top*, 5 F.2d 838 (D. Conn. 1925), *United States v. The Sagatind*, 8 F.2d 788 (S.D.N.Y. 1925), and *The Sagatind*, 11 F.2d 673 (2d Cir. 1926), as examples of lower court cases holding that the liquor treaties were not self-executing.

37. Dickinson, *Liquor Treaties* (1926), at 452.

38. Ford v. United States, 273 U.S. 593, 606 (1927).
39. *See* The Over the Top, 5 F.2d 838 (D. Conn. 1925).
40. Dickinson, *Liquor Treaties* (1926), at 449–50 (citing Wright (1922), at 355).
41. *Id.,* at 450.
42. One can observe a similar dynamic at play twenty-five years later in an important exchange between Quincy Wright, the constitutionalist, and Manley Hudson, the internationalist. *See* Chapter 10, pp. 214–15.
43. Dickinson, *Liquor Treaties* (1926), at 448.
44. For discussion of condition precedent clauses, see Chapter 6, pp. 114–22.
45. *See* pp. 167–68 for further discussion of this point.
46. Dickinson, *Liquor Treaties* (1926), at 448.
47. *Id.,* at 449.
48. *Id.*
49. *See* Chapter 6, pp. 125–26.
50. Dickinson used slightly different formulations at different points in the article. In one key sentence he said that an NSE treaty "requires legislation before it can become a rule for the courts." Dickinson, *Liquor Treaties* (1926), at 449. Read in isolation, this sentence could be construed to indicate that Dickinson conceived of self-execution in terms of the political-judicial concept. However, the article as a whole suggests that he conceived of self-execution in terms of the congressional-executive concept. As noted previously, he argued that if the liquor treaties are not self-executing, then individuals seized pursuant to the treaties would be "guilty of no offense." *Id.,* at 452. This statement demonstrates clearly that Dickinson's concept of self-execution was not simply about the role of courts in applying the law (as in the political-judicial concept). In his view, the SE/NSE distinction mattered because an SE treaty operated in a legislative fashion to change the substantive criminal law, but an NSE treaty did not.
51. *See* Sloss, *Madison's Monster* (2016) for additional discussion of this point.
52. *See* Chapter 4, pp. 80–82.
53. The hypothetical NLE clause here differs in significant ways from modern NSE declarations. I discuss modern NSE declarations in Chapter 14. I use the term NLE here to distinguish the two types of clauses.
54. *See* pp. 166–69.
55. *See* Chapter 3, pp. 54–57 (analysis of Jay Treaty debates) and Chapter 6, pp. 108–13 (later congressional debates).
56. Professor Vázquez contends that Chief Justice Marshall's opinions in *Foster* and *Percheman* support something very much like Dickinson's intent doctrine. *See* Vázquez (2008), at 672–85. However, as discussed previously, *Foster* is best explained as an application of the constitutional version of NSE doctrine. *See* Chapter 4, pp. 82–84.
57. The justiciability doctrine is based on the political-judicial concept and applies a two-step approach. *See* Chapter 7. In contrast, the intent doctrine is based on the congressional-executive concept and applies a one-step approach. See Table Two, p. 64.
58. *See* 5 Hackworth, § 488.
59. *See* Restatement (Second), § 141.
60. *See* White (1999).
61. 299 U.S. 304, 320 (1936). *See* White (1999), at 98–111. *See also* Purcell (2013).

62. *Belmont*, 301 U.S. 324 (1937); *Pink*, 315 U.S. 203 (1942). *See* White (1999), at 111–34. *See also* Hathaway (2009), at 169–81. A "sole executive agreement" is an international agreement concluded by the president on the basis of his own constitutional authority, without authorization by Congress or approval by the Senate.

63. *Ex parte* Peru, 318 U.S. 578 (1943); Mexico v. Hoffman, 324 U.S. 30 (1945). *The Navemar*, 303 U.S. 68 (1938), was also an important case in the transformation of foreign sovereign immunity doctrine. *See* White (1999), at 134–45.

64. Hackworth.

65. Moore.

66. *See* 5 Moore, § 778; 5 Hackworth, § 488. There is one important difference between the two texts in regard to treaty supremacy. Moore's *Digest* addressed treaty supremacy in a section devoted exclusively to conflicts between treaties and state law. *See* 5 Moore, § 778. In contrast, Hackworth's *Digest* addressed treaty supremacy in a section entitled "Treaties as Law of the Land." That section addressed not only the relationship between treaties and state law, but also the relationship between treaties and federal executive power. Thus, the comparison suggests that the conceptual firewall separating federal supremacy issues from federal separation-of-power issues had begun to erode by 1944.

  However, the erosion was fairly minor. A comparison between Hackworth's analysis of treaties as "Law of the Land" (§ 487) and his discussion of self-execution (§ 488) suggests that he retained the traditional bifurcated view that isolated treaty supremacy issues from self-execution issues. Section 487, on treaties as "Law of the Land," quotes the Supremacy Clause, followed by a lengthy citation to about two dozen cases involving conflicts between treaties and state law. In contrast, Section 488, on self-execution, addresses treaties involving the laws of war, liquor smuggling, patents, import duties, international boundaries, and other matters governed exclusively by federal law. Granted, Section 488 also cites a couple of cases implicating federal-state conflicts. Overall, though, the discussion in Hackworth's Digest is generally consistent with the view that treaty supremacy doctrine governs federal-state conflicts, and self-execution doctrine governs other issues.

67. *See* 5 Hackworth, § 488.

68. *See* 5 Moore, §§ 750, 758, 765, 776, and 777. These five sections address: exchange of ratifications, legislative aid to treaties, most-favored-nation clauses, repeal of treaties by later statutes, and repeal of statutes by later treaties.

69. *See* 5 Hackworth, § 488, pp. 177–78.

70. 5 Moore, § 750, pp. 208–09.

71. *See* Chapter 7, pp. 132–34 (discussing the justiciability doctrine).

72. 5 Moore, § 758, p. 222. *See also* Chapter 6, pp. 116–17.

73. 5 Moore, § 758, p. 223. *See also* Chapter 6, pp. 108–11.

74. 5 Moore, § 758, p. 221 (stating that *Foster* decided "that art. 8 of the Florida treaty merely imported a contract for future legislation"). The statement that Article 8 "imported a contract" is ambiguous, but it probably indicates that Moore believed that Marshall construed Article 8 to be executory, rather than executed, in accordance with the contract version of NSE doctrine. Moore's separate, and much lengthier analysis of *Foster* and *Percheman* in § 99 of his Digest also supports the view that he did not construe *Foster* in accordance with the intent doctrine. Section 99 addressed the effects of a change of sovereignty on

private property rights. In that section, Moore emphasized that Article 3 of the Louisiana treaty and Article 8 of the Florida treaty were "merely declaratory of the law of nations," and he cited *Percheman* to support that view. *See* 1 Moore, § 99, pp. 414–17. Marshall's lengthy discussion of the law of nations in *Percheman*, which Moore endorsed, tends to negate the claim that Marshall applied the intent doctrine in *Foster. See* Chapter 4.

75. *Toscano*, 208 F. 938 (S.D. Cal. 1913); *Robertson*, 32 F.2d 495 (4th Cir. 1929) (both cited in 5 Hackworth, § 488, pp. 177–78).

76. 208 F. at 939.

77. *See id.*, at 939–42.

78. *Id.*, at 943.

79. *Id.*, at 942.

80. *Robertson*, 32 F.2d at 496.

81. *Id.*, at 496.

82. *See id.*, at 498–99.

83. *Id.*, at 500.

84. *Id.*, at 501. *See* Chapter 6, pp. 125–26.

85. *See* Hackworth, at vol. 5, § 488, pp. 177–78.

86. The key limitation is that the executive branch cannot make a treaty provision self-executing by manifesting its intent to do so if the provision is constitutionally non-self-executing.

87. *See* Koh (2012), at 1749–51.

88. *See* Chapter 6, pp. 125–26.

89. *See* Chapter 6, pp. 122–23.

90. *See* Vázquez (2008), at 672–85. Professor Vázquez's concept of a "*Percheman* stipulation" is similar, but not identical, to what I am calling an NLE clause.

91. *See* Chapter 4, pp. 80–84.

92. Youngstown Sheet & Tube Co. v. Sawyer, 343 U.S. 579, 610–11 (1952) (Frankfurter, J., concurring).

93. Dickinson, *Liquor Treaties* (1926), at 448.

94. 1824 Treaty with Russia, art. V.

95. 1884 Convention for Protection of Submarine Cables, art. XII.

96. *Id.*, art. XII.

97. 1916 Treaty with Britain, art. VIII. This is the treaty at issue in *Missouri v. Holland*, 252 U.S. 416 (1920).

98. 1911 Convention for the Protection of Fur Seals, art. VI.

99. *See, e.g.*, General Elec. Co. v. Robertson, 25 F.2d 146, 146 (D. Md. 1928) (in a patent case where the government was a party, the Commissioner of Patents argued "that it was not the intention of the parties to the Treaty of Berlin that it should be effective until ratified by congressional action").

100. *See* Chapter 6, pp. 123–27 (discussing attorney general opinions).

101. Regarding the use of condition precedent clauses, see Chapter 6, pp. 114–22. Regarding the distinction between condition precedent clauses and NLE clauses, see pp. 160–61.

102. *See* Chapter 1. *See also* Nelson (2000).

103. U.S. Const. art. I, § 7, cl. 1.

104. At first blush, the argument presented in this paragraph may appear to be inconsistent with the view, elaborated in the previous section, that the intent doctrine

augmented federal executive power. However, the asserted inconsistency is more apparent than real. There is a fairly broad category of cases where it is unclear whether a particular treaty provision is SE or NSE under the constitutional doctrine. In those cases, the intent doctrine allows the president, in his treaty-making capacity, to resolve the ambiguity in favor of self-execution by adopting treaty language that manifests an intention to make the treaty self-executing. If the Senate approves the treaty on that basis, courts are very unlikely to hold that the treaty is NSE. Thus, the intent doctrine enables the president, in his treaty-making capacity, to enhance the treaty-implementing power of federal executive officers.

105. Kurns v. Railroad Friction Prods. Corp., 132 S. Ct. 1261, 1265 (2012) (quoting Brown v. Hotel Employees, 468 U.S. 491, 501 (1984)).

106. Gardbaum (1994), at 770–71.

107. Id., at 782.

108. See, e.g., Ware v. Hylton, 3 U.S. 199 (1796) (applying treaty to override conflicting state law).

109. 222 U.S. 424 (1912). See Gardbaum (1994), at 803–04. Professor Gardbaum adds the following helpful caveat: "I am not arguing that no Justice of the Supreme Court ever accepted the power of preemption before 1912, but rather, (a) that whether or not Congress had the power to preempt state law was an unresolved, and at times highly controversial, issue throughout the nineteenth century; (b) that, at least before 1876, preemption was generally understood to be quite distinct from, and a more radical intrusion upon state power than, supremacy; and (c) that no state law was actually overturned on preemption grounds until 1912." Id., at 785.

110. See Gardbaum (1994), at 804–05 (discussing Chicago, Rock Island & Pacific Ry. Co. v. Hardwick Farmers Elevator Co., 226 U.S. 426 (1913), and Charleston & Western Carolina Ry. Co. v. Varnville, 237 U.S. 597 (1915)).

111. See Gardbaum (1994), at 805–07; see also Rice v. Santa Fe Elevator Corp., 331 U.S. 218, 230 (1947) ("[W]e start with the assumption that the historic police powers of the States were not to be superseded by the Federal Act unless that was the clear and manifest purpose of Congress.").

112. Before World War II, very few judicial precedents supported the intent version of NSE doctrine. Hackworth cited Robertson in support of the intent doctrine. See 5 Hackworth, § 488, p. 178. In Robertson, the Fourth Circuit said that the relevant treaty provision "was not intended to be, and is not, such a self-executing provision." Robertson v. Gen. Electric Co., 32 F.2d 495, 500 (4th Cir. 1929). Although this sentence provides modest support for the intent doctrine, the primary rationale relies on the contract doctrine. See supra pp. 164–65 (discussing Robertson).

113. See Part Three.

114. Gardbaum (1994), at 784 (emphasis added).

115. See Sloss, Treaty Preemption Defense (2009), at 983–86.

PART 3

1. Chapters 3 through 7 provide detailed support for the claims in this paragraph.

2. See Chapter 1.

3. Fujii v. California, 217 P.2d 481 (Cal. App. 2d 1950). See Chapter 10, pp. 208–13.

4. See Chapter 3, pp. 54–57; Chapter 6, pp. 108–13.

5. *See* Chapter 6, pp. 122–23.
6. *See* Chapter 8, pp. 157–61.
7. *See* Chapter 10, pp. 208–15; Chapter 11, pp. 231–35.
8. Fujii v. State, 242 P.2d 617 (Cal. 1952). *See* Chapter 11, pp. 231–35.
9. *See* Chapter 11, pp. 253–56.
10. *See* Chapter 12.
11. *See* Chapter 13.
12. *See* Siegel (2006); Dorf (2002), at 984–85; Strauss (2001), at 1476–78.
13. 347 U.S. 483 (1954).
14. 347 U.S. 497 (1954). *See* Chapter 11, pp. 241–45.
15. I recounted portions of this story in an abbreviated form in Sloss, *Human Rights* (2016).

CHAPTER 9

1. 1948 Genocide Convention (entered into force Jan. 12, 1951).
2. Universal Declaration of Human Rights (1948).
3. Quoted in Schabas (2009), at 79.
4. For detailed accounts of the negotiation and drafting of the Universal Declaration, see Humphrey (1984); Glendon (2001); Schabas (2013).
5. *See* Schabas (2009) at 59–90.
6. Although the Universal Declaration was initially conceived and drafted as a non-binding statement of principles, it has since come to be viewed as an important source of legal obligations for States. The nature of that legal obligation is contested. Some commentators maintain that the Universal Declaration expresses generally accepted principles of customary international law. Others view it as an authoritative interpretation of the treaty obligations embodied in the U.N. Charter. Regardless, it is widely recognized that the drafters of the Universal Declaration did not believe in 1948 that they were creating new legal obligations for States.
7. Universal Declaration, Preamble.
8. *Id.*, art. 2.
9. Genocide Convention, art. II.
10. To Secure These Rights: The Report of the President's Committee on Civil Rights, at 146–47 (1947) (quoting letter from Dean Acheson, Acting Secretary of State, to Fair Employment Practice Committee).
11. Anderson (2003), at 108 (quoting statement by Attorney General Tom Clark).
12. Shelley v. Kraemer, McGhee v. Sipes, Hurd v. Hodge, Urciolo v. Hodge, Brief for the United States as Amicus Curiae, at 4–5.
13. *See generally* Dudziak (2000).
14. *See* Klarman (2004), at 8–170.
15. *See* Herring (2008), at 353–54.
16. *See* Barcelona Traction, Light and Power Co., Ltd., (Belg. v. Spain), 1970 I.C.J. 3, ¶¶ 33–34 (noting that obligations *erga omnes* derive "from the principles and rules concerning the basic rights of the human person, including protection from slavery and racial discrimination").
17. *See* Dudziak (2000), at 29–39.
18. *See, e.g.,* Fahy (1948), at 138–40 (summarizing U.N. General Assembly debates in 1946–1947 concerning resolutions introduced by India that criticized the practice of apartheid in South Africa).

19. *See* Anderson (2003), at 41–56.

20. *See id.*, at 79-81; National Negro Congress (1946).

21. *See* Anderson (2003), at 92–94.

22. On shaming as an international human rights strategy, see Keck & Sikkink (1998), at 23; Goodman & Jinks (2013), at 27–28.

23. *See* Anderson (2003), at 94–96.

24. Commission on Human Rights, Report to the Economic and Social Council, U.N. Doc. E/259, para. 22 (1947). *See also* Alston (1992), at 126–31.

25. *See* Anderson (2003), at 101–02.

26. *Id.*, at 102–03. *See* Nat'l Ass'n for the Advancement of Colored People (1947).

27. George Streator, "Negroes to Bring Cause before UN: Statement Charges that South Offers Greater U.S. Threat than Soviet Activities," New York Times, Oct. 12, 1947, at 52.

28. *See* Anderson (2003), at 103–04.

29. *Id.*, at 104–05.

30. Robert S. Abbott, "An Important Appeal," Chicago Defender, Nov. 1, 1947.

31. Anderson (2003), at 108 (quoting article by Saul Padover).

32. *Id.*, at 108 (quoting statement by Attorney General Tom Clark).

33. *Id.*, at 108–09.

34. *Id.*, at 108 (quoting article from the Morgantown Post).

35. *Id.*, at 111.

36. *Id.*, at 112.

37. *See id.*, at 128–44.

38. Shelley v. Kraemer, 334 U.S. 1 (1948), *reversing* Kraemer v. Shelley, 198 S.W.2d 679 (Mo. 1946), *and reversing* Sipes v. McGhee, 25 N.W.2d 638 (Mich. 1947).

39. Hurd v. Hodge, 334 U.S. 24 (1948), *reversing* Hurd v. Hodge, 162 F.2d 233 (D.C. Cir. 1947) (joined with Urciolo v. Hodge).

40. Oyama v. California, 332 U.S. 633 (1948); Takahashi v. Fish & Game Comm'n, 334 U.S. 410 (1948).

41. 333 U.S. 28 (1948).

42. *See* Bob-Lo Excursion Co. v. Michigan, Motion and Brief for the National Association for the Advancement of Colored People, American Civil Liberties Union, and National Lawyers Guild as Amici Curiae; Hurd v. Hodge, Urciolo v. Hodge, Consolidated Brief for Petitioners; McGhee v. Sipes, Brief for Petitioners; Oyama v. California, Brief of American Civil Liberties Union, as Amicus Curiae; Shelley v. Kraemer, McGhee v. Sipes, Hurd v. Hodge, Urciolo v. Hodge, Motion for Leave to File Brief and Brief for the American Association for the United Nations as Amicus Curiae; Takahashi v. Fish & Game Comm'n, Brief for Petitioner; Takahashi v. Fish & Game Comm'n, Motion and Brief for the National Association for the Advancement of Colored People as Amicus Curiae.

43. Oyama v. California, Brief of American Civil Liberties Union, as Amicus Curiae.

44. Bob-Lo Excursion Co. v. Michigan, Motion and Brief for the National Association for the Advancement of Colored People, American Civil Liberties Union, and National Lawyers Guild as Amici Curiae.

45. Takahashi v. Fish & Game Comm'n, Motion and Brief for the National Association for the Advancement of Colored People as Amicus Curiae; Takahashi v. Fish & Game Comm'n, Brief of American Civil Liberties Union, Amicus Curiae;

Takahashi v. Fish & Game Comm'n, Brief for the American Jewish Congress as Amicus Curiae; Takahashi v. Fish & Game Comm'n, Brief of American Veterans Committee, Amicus Curiae; Takahashi v. Fish & Game Comm'n, Motion and Brief for the National Association for the Advancement of Colored People and the National Lawyers Guild as Amicus Curiae.

46. Shelley v. Kraemer, McGhee v. Sipes, Hurd v. Hodge, Urciolo v. Hodge, Brief of American Civil Liberties Union, Amicus Curiae; Shelley v. Kraemer, McGhee v. Sipes, Hurd v. Hodge, Urciolo v. Hodge, Motion for Leave to File Brief and Brief for the American Association for the United Nations as Amicus Curiae; Shelley v. Kraemer, McGhee v. Sipes, Hurd v. Hodge, Urciolo v. Hodge, Brief of the American Indian Citizens League of California, Inc., as Amicus Curiae; Shelley v. Kraemer, McGhee v. Sipes, Hurd v. Hodge, Urciolo v. Hodge, Application for Leave to File Brief Amicus and Brief Amicus Curiae on Behalf of Congress of Industrial Organizations and Certain Affiliated Organizations; Hurd v. Hodge, Brief of the Japanese-American Citizens League, Amicus Curiae; McGhee v. Sipes, Brief for Non-Sectarian Anti-Nazi League to Champion Human Rights, Inc., as Amicus Curiae; and Shelley v. Kraemer, Brief of the St. Louis Civil Liberties Committee, Amicus Curiae.

47. *See* Anderson (2003), at 18, 30.

48. Hurd v. Hodge, Brief of the Japanese-American Citizens League, Amicus Curiae, at 2–3.

49. Takahashi v. Fish & Game Comm'n, Brief for Petitioner, at 32–38.

50. McGhee v. Sipes, Brief for Petitioners, at 9.

51. Hurd v. Hodge, Urciolo v. Hodge, Consolidated Brief for Petitioners, at 108–10.

52. Oyama v. California, Brief of American Civil Liberties Union, as Amicus Curiae, at 13.

53. Takahashi v. Fish & Game Comm'n, Motion and Brief for the National Association for the Advancement of Colored People as Amicus Curiae, at 10.

54. *See also* Bob-Lo Excursion Co. v. Michigan, Motion and Brief for the National Association for the Advancement of Colored People, American Civil Liberties Union, and National Lawyers Guild as Amici Curiae, at 13–14; Oyama v. California, Brief for Petitioners, at 52–53; Shelley v. Kraemer, Brief of the St. Louis Civil Liberties Committee, Amicus Curiae, at 16; Shelley v. Kraemer, McGhee v. Sipes, Hurd v. Hodge, and Urciolo v. Hodge, Application for Leave to File Brief Amicus and Brief Amicus Curiae on Behalf of Congress of Industrial Organizations and Certain Affiliated Organizations, at 4; Shelley v. Kraemer, McGhee v. Sipes, Hurd v. Hodge, and Urciolo v. Hodge, Brief of American Civil Liberties Union, Amicus Curiae, at 27; Shelley v. Kraemer, McGhee v. Sipes, Hurd v. Hodge, and Urciolo v. Hodge, Brief of the American Indian Citizens League of California, Inc., as Amicus Curiae, at 6; Shelley v. Kraemer, McGhee v. Sipes, Hurd v. Hodge, and Urciolo v. Hodge, Motion for Leave to File Brief and Brief for the American Association for the United Nations as Amicus Curiae, at 6–9; Takahashi v. Fish & Game Comm'n, Brief for Petitioner, at 32–33; Takahashi v. Fish & Game Comm'n, Brief of American Civil Liberties Union, Amicus Curiae, at 8–9; Takahashi v. Fish & Game Comm'n, Brief of American Veterans Committee Amicus Curiae, at 14–15; Takahashi v. Fish & Game Comm'n, Motion and Brief for the National Association for the Advancement of Colored People and the National Lawyers Guild as Amicus Curiae, at 14.

55. *See* Bob-Lo Excursion Co. v. Michigan, Brief for the State of Michigan, Appellee. The appellant's brief in Bob-Lo also did not mention the U.N. Charter. *See* Bob-Lo Excursion Co. v. Michigan, Brief for Appellant. In *Bob-Lo*, only one amicus brief raised a Charter-based argument. *See* Bob-Lo Excursion Co. v. Michigan, Motion and Brief for the National Association for the Advancement of Colored People, American Civil Liberties Union, and National Lawyers Guild as Amici Curiae.

56. *See* Oyama v. State, Brief for Respondent, at 66.

57. *See* Takahashi v. Fish & Game Comm'n, Brief for Respondents, at 34–35.

58. The decision by respondents' counsel in *Oyama* and *Takahashi* not to address the self-execution issue may be attributable to the fact that neither petitioner made a treaty supremacy argument. Petitioner in *Takahashi* cited the Charter in support of a broad foreign affairs preemption argument. Petitioners in *Oyama* cited the Charter in support of an argument to overrule a prior Supreme Court decision holding that California's Alien Land Law did not violate the Equal Protection Clause. *See* Oyama v. State, Brief for Petitioners, at 52–53; Takahashi v. Fish & Game Comm'n, Brief for Petitioner, at 32–38.

59. *See* McGhee v. Sipes, Brief for Petitioners, at 84–90; Hurd v. Hodge, Urciolo v. Hodge, Consolidated Brief for Petitioners, at 108–11.

60. McGhee v. Sipes, Brief for Respondents, at 8. The brief also notes in passing that "Congress has not enacted any legislation on the subject affecting such private rights," *id.*, but it does not explain why the presence or absence of congressional legislation is significant.

61. *Id.*, at 23 (emphasis in original).

62. *See* Hurd v. Hodge, Urciolo v. Hodge, Consolidated Brief for Respondents, at 22–23.

63. Takahashi v. Fish & Game Comm'n, Motion and Brief for the National Association for the Advancement of Colored People and the National Lawyers Guild as Amicus Curiae, at 14–17.

64. Shelley v. Kraemer, McGhee v. Sipes, Hurd v. Hodge, Urciolo v. Hodge, Motion for Leave to File Brief and Brief for the American Association for the United Nations as Amicus Curiae, at 5–20.

65. *Id.*, at 21.

66. To Secure These Rights: The Report of the President's Committee on Civil Rights, at vii (1947).

67. *Id.*, at 139–41.

68. *Id.*, at 146.

69. *Id.*, at 147.

70. *Id.*, at 100–01.

71. Dudziak (2000), at 82.

72. Harry S. Truman, "Special Message to the Congress on Civil Rights" (Feb. 2, 1948).

73. *Compare* Anderson (2003), at 2–3, 115–19 (suggesting that Truman's effort to obtain equality for African Americans was a political strategy to gain black votes) *with* McCullough (1992), at 587–88 (suggesting that Truman's proposed civil rights legislation was not purely a political strategy because it cost him many Southern votes).

74. E.O. 9981, 13 Fed. Reg. 4313 (July 26, 1948).

75. *See* Dudziak (2000), at 83–88.

76. *See generally id.*, at 90–102.
77. Shelley v. Kraemer, McGhee v. Sipes, Hurd v. Hodge, Urciolo v. Hodge, Brief for the United States as Amicus Curiae.
78. Takahashi v. Fish & Game Comm'n, Brief for the United States as Amicus Curiae.
79. *See* Dudziak (2000), at 275–76.
80. Shelley v. Kraemer, McGhee v. Sipes, Hurd v. Hodge, Urciolo v. Hodge, Brief for the United States as Amicus Curiae, at 92.
81. *Id.*, at 97–102.
82. *See* Takahashi v. Fish & Game Comm'n, 334 U.S. 410 (1948).
83. Takahashi v. Fish & Game Comm'n, Brief for the United States as Amicus Curiae, at 16–17.
84. McCullough (1992), at 586 (quoting President Truman).
85. 333 U.S. 28 (1948).
86. Bob-Lo Excursion Co. v. Michigan, Motion and Brief for the National Association for the Advancement of Colored People, American Civil Liberties Union, and National Lawyers Guild as Amici Curiae, at 13.
87. *Bob-Lo*, 333 U.S. at 34.
88. 334 U.S. 410 (1948).
89. *See* Takahashi v. Fish & Game Comm'n, Brief for Petitioner; Takahashi v. Fish & Game Comm'n, Motion and Brief for the National Association for the Advancement of Colored People as Amicus Curiae; Takahashi v. Fish & Game Comm'n, Brief of American Civil Liberties Union, Amicus Curiae; Takahashi v. Fish & Game Comm'n, Brief for the American Jewish Congress as Amicus Curiae; Takahashi v. Fish & Game Comm'n, Brief of American Veterans Committee, Amicus Curiae; Takahashi v. Fish & Game Comm'n, Motion and Brief for the National Association for the Advancement of Colored People and the National Lawyers Guild as Amicus Curiae.
90. *See Takahashi*, 334 U.S. at 415–21.
91. 332 U.S. 633, 642 (1948).
92. *Id.*, at 644.
93. *Id.*, at 640.
94. *See id.*, at 647–49 (Black, J., concurring).
95. *Id.*, at 649–50 (Black, J., concurring).
96. *Id.*, at 662 (Murphy, J., concurring).
97. *Id.*, at 672–73 (Murphy, J., concurring).
98. *Id.*, at 673 (Murphy, J., concurring).
99. *See* McGhee v. Sipes, Brief for Petitioners, at 84–90; Hurd v. Hodge, Urciolo v. Hodge, Consolidated Brief for Petitioners, at 108–11; Shelley v. Kraemer, McGhee v. Sipes, Hurd v. Hodge, Urciolo v. Hodge, Brief of American Civil Liberties Union, Amicus Curiae; Shelley v. Kraemer, McGhee v. Sipes, Hurd v. Hodge, Urciolo v. Hodge, Motion for Leave to File Brief and Brief for the American Association for the United Nations as Amicus Curiae; Shelley v. Kraemer, McGhee v. Sipes, Hurd v. Hodge, Urciolo v. Hodge, Brief of the American Indian Citizens League of California, Inc., as Amicus Curiae; Shelley v. Kraemer, McGhee v. Sipes, Hurd v. Hodge, Urciolo v. Hodge, Application for Leave to File Brief Amicus and Brief Amicus Curiae on Behalf of Congress of Industrial Organizations and Certain Affiliated Organizations; Hurd v. Hodge, Brief of the Japanese-American

Citizens League, Amicus Curiae; McGhee v. Sipes, Brief for Non-Sectarian Anti-Nazi League to Champion Human Rights, Inc., as Amicus Curiae; and Shelley v. Kraemer, Brief of the St. Louis Civil Liberties Committee, Amicus Curiae.

100. Shelley v. Kraemer, 334 U.S. 1, 20 (1948).

101. Hurd v. Hodge, 334 U.S. 24, 34 (1948).

102. See Oyama v. California, 332 U.S. 633, 674–84 (1948) (Reed, J., dissenting, joined by Justice Burton); id., at 684–89 (Jackson, J., dissenting); Takahashi v. Fish & Game Comm'n, 334 U.S. 410, 427–31 (1948) (Reed, J., dissenting, joined by Jackson, J.).

103. See Kluger (1975), at 254; Ellmann (2004), at 751–52.

104. The Senate confirmed Justice Reed in 1938, Justice Jackson in 1941, and Justice Rutledge in 1943. In that era, it is difficult to imagine that a senator would have argued that ownership of a home subject to a racial covenant was a significant factor in evaluating a nominee's qualifications for the Supreme Court.

105. Curran v. City of New York, 77 N.Y.S.2d 206 (Sup. Ct., Queens Cty. 1947).

106. Id., at 211.

107. Id., at 212 (emphasis added).

108. Charter of the United Nations, Report to the President on the Results of the San Francisco Conference by the Chairman of the United States Delegation, at 160 (June 26, 1945).

109. See id., at 109–19 (addressing the Charter's human rights provisions).

110. See Chapter 11, pp. 231–35 (discussing California Supreme Court decision in Fujii).

111. In Medellín v. Texas, 552 U.S. 491 (2008), the U.S. Supreme Court held that Article 94 of the U.N. Charter is not self-executing. The Court relied heavily on the ostensible "intent of the treaty makers" to buttress that holding. However, there is not a shred of evidence to support the Court's assertion that the treaty makers intended Article 94 to be non-self-executing. See Sloss, Madison's Monster (2016).

112. See Kaufman (1990), at 16–30 (discussing Frank Holman and his leading role in the ABA).

113. See 73 Ann. Rep. ABA 94, 101–02 (1948).

114. See Glendon (2001), at 111–21; see also Lake Success Draft, reproduced in Glendon (2001), at 294–99.

115. See Report of the Third Session of the Commission on Human Rights, U.N. Doc. E/800, paras. 12–17 (28 June 1948).

116. 73 Ann Rep. ABA 283, 284 (1948).

117. Id.

118. See Glendon (2001), at 107–21.

119. 73 Ann. Rep. ABA 283, 284 (1948).

120. See generally Kaufman (1990).

121. See 73 Ann. Rep. ABA 94, 100–01 (1948).

122. See id., at 101–02.

123. Holman (1948).

124. See id., at 985–86.

125. Id., at 985.

126. 73 Ann Rep. ABA 283, 287–88 (1948).

CHAPTER 10

1. There was apparently a similar unpublished decision from Idaho. *See* Treaties and Executive Agreements: Hearings Before a Subcommittee of the Committee on the Judiciary (1953) (hereinafter, "1953 Hearings"), at 818, 869 (statement of Senator Everett Dirksen).

2. *See* U.N. Doc. E/CN.4/350 (June 23, 1949); U.N. Doc. E/CN.4/507 (May 29, 1950); and U.N. Doc. E/CN.4/640 (May 24, 1951).

3. E/CN.4/224 (May 23, 1949).

4. E/CN.4/SR.125, at 5 (summary of meeting held on June 13, 1949).

5. *Id.* at 6–7.

6. *Id.* at 8.

7. *Id.* at 17.

8. *Id.* at 19.

9. *See* Chapter 5.

10. Eleanor Roosevelt was not trained as a lawyer, so it is unlikely that she would have drafted the quoted language herself. Moreover, during her tenure as U.S. representative on the U.N. Human Rights Commission, she received frequent, detailed instructions from the State Department. *See* Glendon (2001), at 80–82.

11. Pechota (1981), at 41.

12. A/RES/421(V)E (Dec. 4, 1950).

13. A/RES/543(VI) (Feb. 5, 1952).

14. Holman (1950), at 788.

15. Dudziak (2000), at 66.

16. Civil Rights Congress (1951). *See also* Dudziak (2000), at 63–66; Anderson (2003), at 179–83.

17. Civil Rights Congress (1951), at 48.

18. Anderson (2003), at 179.

19. *Id.*, at 182.

20. *Id.*, at 199–200.

21. Kaufman (1990), at 16 (describing Frank Holman's views).

22. *See* Message from the President of the United States transmitting the Genocide Convention (1949).

23. *Id.*, at 5.

24. Rix (1949), at 554. Rix's essay in the *ABA Journal* was a printed copy of a speech he delivered earlier that year at the annual meeting of the American Society of International Law.

25. *Id.*, at 618.

26. *See* The International Convention on the Prevention and Punishment of the Crime of Genocide, Hearings Before a Subcommittee of the Committee on Foreign Relations (1950) (hereinafter, "1950 Genocide Hearings"), at 31–32 (statement of Philip B. Perlman, Solicitor General of the United States).

27. See U.N. Doc. E/1371, E/CN.4/350, Annex I, p. 39 (June 1949) (text of then-current draft of Covenant).

28. 252 U.S. 416 (1920).

29. *See* 1950 Genocide Hearings, at 30–31 (statement of Philip B. Perlman,); *id.* at 265 (statement of Adrian Fisher, Legal Adviser, Department of State). For a modern defense of a similar position, see Cleveland & Dodge (2015).

30. 74 Ann. Rep. ABA 101, 145 (Sept. 1949).
31. 74 Ann. Rep. ABA 316 (Sept. 1949).
32. *Id.*, at 330.
33. 74 Ann. Rep. ABA 101, 146–47 (Sept. 1949).
34. *Id.*, at 147.
35. *See* 1950 Genocide Hearings, at 31–32 (statement of Philip B. Perlman).
36. 74 Ann. Rep. ABA 101, 149–50 (Sept. 1949).
37. *Id.*, at 146.
38. *Id.*, at 150.
39. *See* 1950 Genocide Hearings.
40. *See id.*
41. *See id.*, at 154–205 (testimony of Alfred Schweppe, with appendices); *id.*, at 206–13 (testimony of Carl Rix); *id.*, at 213–21 (testimony of George Finch).
42. *See supra* pp. 204–06. For more detailed analysis of arguments raised by treaty opponents, see Kaufman (1990), at 42–59 (analyzing seven distinct arguments advanced by treaty opponents).
43. Staff Memorandum on the Convention on the Prevention and Punishment of the Crime of Genocide, Committee on Foreign Affairs (Aug. 15, 1950).
44. *Id.*, at 2.
45. *Id.*, at 13.
46. *Id.*, at 8.
47. *Id.*, at 9.
48. Walter George was a Democratic senator from Georgia who would later play a key role in the Bricker Amendment debates. *See* Chapter 11, pp. 249–53.
49. Committee on Foreign Relations, U.S. Senate, Executive Session, International Convention on the Prevention and Punishment of the Crime of Genocide (Sept. 6, 1950).
50. *See* Genocide Convention, S. Exec. Rep. 99-2, at 3–4 (1985).
51. *See, e.g.*, Sipes v. McGhee, 316 Mich. 614, 25 N.W.2d 638 (1947), *rev'd sub nom* Shelley v. Kraemer, 334 U.S. 1 (1948); Namba v. McCourt, 185 Ore. 579, 204 P.2d 569 (1949); Kemp v. Rubin, 188 Misc. 310, 69 N.Y.S.2d 680 (Sup. Ct. 1947).
52. *See* Fujii Case File. The case is often called "Sei Fujii v. California," but that name is based on a misunderstanding. The petitioner's first name was Sei. His last name was Fujii. It is customary to use only the individual's last name as part of the case name.
53. Factual material in this paragraph and the following one draws on the Fujii Case File. In addition, I consulted the following sources: LaMoree (1990); Christine Fukushima, *Keeping JA History Newsworthy, in* Lil Tokyo Reporter, Sept. 2, 2011, *available at*; http://www.pacificcitizen.org/wp-content/uploads/bsk-pdf-manager/19_SEPT._2_ISSUEWEB.PDF

    A History of Japanese Americans in California, available at the National Park Service website at https://www.nps.gov/parkhistory/online_books/5views/5views4.htm
54. Jordan v. Tashiro, 278 U.S. 123 (1928).
55. The Alien Land Law permitted noncitizens to own land if the right to own land was specifically protected by a bilateral treaty. As noted above, Fujii could not claim the protection of a bilateral treaty because the United States had terminated the

relevant treaty with Japan in 1940. Moreover, even when the treaty was in force, it did not protect the right of Japanese citizens to own real property in the United States.

56. Fujii v. California, 217 P.2d 481, 484 (Cal. App. 2d 1950).
57. *Id.*, at 485.
58. Fujii Case File, Respondent's Brief, pp. 24–43 (Feb. 20, 1950).
59. Fujii Case File, Appellant's Opening Brief, p. 100 (Nov. 15, 1949).
60. United Nations Charter, arts. 55, 56.
61. Fujii v. California, 217 P.2d 481 (Cal. App. 2d 1950).
62. *Id.*, at 484.
63. *Id.*, at 484–88.
64. "Ruling Holds Alien Land Law Invalid," L.A. Times, Apr. 25, 1950, at A1; "Charter of United Nations Held to Invalidate California Alien Land Act," L.A. Daily J., Apr. 25, 1950 (*reprinted in* 96 Cong. Rec. 5993, 6000).
65. *See* Gladwin Hill, "U.N. Charter Voids a California Law," N.Y. Times, Apr. 26, 1950.
66. *See* 96 Cong. Rec. 5993-6000 (April 28, 1950). The Congressional Record does not record the time spent on a subject. The one-hour estimate is based on the length of printed material.
67. *Id.*, at 5996–98.
68. Missouri v. Holland, 252 U.S. 416 (1920).
69. 96 Cong. Rec. at 5997-99.
70. U.N. Charter, art. 55.
71. Fujii Case File, Petition for Rehearing (May 9, 1950).
72. See Evelyn M. Cherpak, Register of the Papers of Manley O. Hudson, Naval Historical Collection, Naval War College, *available at* http://www.usnwc.edu/Academics/Library/Naval-Historical-Collection-%281%29/Register-of-Papers.aspx.
73. American Society of International Law, "ASIL Presidents: Manley Ottmer Hudson," *available at* http://www.asil.org/presidents/hudsonmo.html.
74. "Dr. Manley O. Hudson Gets U.N. Law Post," N.Y. Times, Nov. 3, 1948. The Commission is a body of distinguished international law experts created by the U.N. General Assembly in 1947; its mandate is to promote "the progressive development of international law and its codification." Statute of the International Law Commission, U.N. Doc. A/RES/174(II) (Nov. 21, 1947).
75. The telegram is quoted in full on page 5 of the Petition for Rehearing. *See* Fujii Case File, Petition for Rehearing. Around this time, Hudson was working for the State of California on an unrelated legal matter. *See* United States v. California, 332 U.S. 19 (1947) (dispute between United States and California related to submerged lands along California's coastline). Hudson probably knew the California attorney general from working together on that case.
76. *See* Hudson (1950).
77. *See* Fujii Case File, Petition for Rehearing, Appendix A.
78. 74 Ann. Rep. ABA 316, 317–18 (Sept. 1949).
79. *Id.*, at 318.
80. Holman, Rix, and Phillips had all expressed their opposition to the International Covenant and/or the Genocide Convention in essays published in the *ABA Journal*. *See* Holman (1948); Rix (1949); Phillips (1949). Additionally, Schweppe, Rix, and Finch all testified against the Genocide Convention in Senate hearings.

See 1950 Genocide Hearings, at 154–205 (testimony of Alfred Schweppe, with appendices); *id.*, at 206–13 (testimony of Carl Rix); *id.*, at 213–21 (testimony of George Finch).

81. *See* Hudson (1950); Hudson (1948).
82. *See* Fujii v. State, 242 P.2d 617 (Cal. 1952).
83. Fujii Case File, Brief of American Civil Liberties Union, Southern California Branch, and American Jewish Congress, Amici Curiae in Support of Appellant in Opposition to Petition for Rehearing (May 12, 1950).
84. Fujii Case File, Application for Leave to Join with Brief Amici Curiae (May 16, 1950).
85. Fujii v. State, 218 P.2d 595 (Cal. App. 2d 1950).
86. *See, e.g.,* Monzingo (1950); Comment, *UN Charter Invalidates Alien Land Law*, 2 STAN. L. REV. 797 (1950).
87. *See* Hudson (1950); Wright (1951); Schachter (1951).
88. Wright's academic training was in political science, not law. Nevertheless, much of his published writing addressed the constitutional law of U.S. foreign affairs.
89. When Schachter published the law review article at issue here, he was working as the Deputy Director of the United Nation's Legal Department.
90. Hudson (1950), at 545.
91. *See* Wright (1951), at 62–63.
92. *Id.*, at 64. Wright's reference to "instances where the treaty itself makes execution contingent upon State action" merits comment. In a separate footnote, Wright cited two examples of such treaty provisions: Article 7 of an 1853 treaty with France and Article 4 of an 1854 treaty with Great Britain. *Id.*, at 69 n.23. However, neither provision is properly described as a treaty provision that makes execution contingent upon action by state governments. As discussed in Chapter 6, the 1854 treaty with Britain made execution contingent upon action by Congress and the provincial legislatures of certain British colonies in Canada, but it did not make execution contingent upon action by state legislatures in the United States. *See* Chapter 6, pp. 119–20. As discussed in Chapter 5, Article 7 of the 1853 treaty with France did not make execution contingent upon future legislative action. Rather, it incorporated state law as a substantive limitation on the scope of the international obligation. *See* Chapter 5, pp. 102–05. Thus, Wright failed to identify any actual treaty provision to support his claim that there are "rare instances where the treaty itself makes execution contingent upon State action." Apart from this minor error, though, Wright's constitutional analysis was flawless.
93. Wright (1951), at 68.
94. *See* Chapter 4, pp. 72–73.
95. Wright (1951), at 68.
96. *Id.*, at 70.
97. Schachter (1951), at 646.
98. *See id.*, at 646–49; Wright (1951), at 69–72.
99. U.N. Charter, arts. 55, 56 (emphasis added).
100. Hudson (1950), at 544.
101. *See* U.N. International Law Commission, Doc. A/CN.4/SR.23, p. 10 (May 19, 1949).

102. Wright (1951), at 70.
103. *Id.*, at 71–72.
104. *Id.*, at 72.
105. *See* Schachter (1951), at 649–52.
106. *Id.*, at 649–50.
107. Hudson (1950), at 548.
108. *Id.*, at 545.
109. Wright (1951), at 68 (quoting 1833 letter from Secretary of State Edward Livingston, *reprinted in* 2 Wharton § 138).
110. Wright (1951), at 69.
111. Hudson (1950), at 546.
112. Schachter (1951), at 655.
113. *Id.*, at 651.
114. *Id.*, at 655.
115. *Id.*, at 656.
116. One could argue that the real issue in *Fujii* was not racial discrimination, but discrimination on the basis of nationality. The Universal Declaration of Human Rights specifically prohibits discrimination on the basis of "national or social origin," but the U.N. Charter refers only to "race, sex, language, or religion." Regardless, for understandable reasons, California did not rely on the distinction between race and nationality to defend the validity of the Alien Land Law.
117. Hudson (1950), at 545.
118. Holman (1950).
119. *Id.*, at 787–90.
120. 75 Ann. Rep. ABA 286 (1950).
121. *Id.*, at 296. Article 55 of the U.N. Charter addresses discrimination on the basis of "race, sex, language, or religion." The Universal Declaration of Human Rights expands this list to include "race, colour, sex, language, religion, political or other opinion, national or social origin, property, birth or other status." In *Fujii*, the California Court of Appeal invoked the Declaration as an aid to interpreting the scope of the nation's human rights obligations under the Charter. *See Fujii*, 217 P.2d 481, 487–88. Hence, the Committee worried that affirmance of *Fujii* would provide a basis for invalidating laws that discriminate on the basis of any of the criteria listed in the Universal Declaration.
122. 75 Ann. Rep. ABA 286, 296 (1950).
123. 388 U.S. 1 (1967).
124. 383 U.S. 663 (1966).
125. *See* 75 Ann. Rep. ABA 102, 117–18 (1950).
126. *Id.*, at 118. The Committee also suggested an amendment stipulating "that the basic structure of the United States Government . . . shall not be abolished nor altered by any treaty or executive agreement." Such an amendment, if adopted, would probably not have had any practical effect, because it has long been established that a treaty purporting to alter the structure of our government would be invalid. *See* Geofroy v. Riggs, 133 U.S. 258, 267 (1890).
127. *See* Kaufman (1990), at 64–65.
128. *See* 75 Ann. Rep. ABA 403, 414–15 (1950).
129. *See* 75 Ann. Rep. ABA 102, 118–19 (1950).

130. *Id.*, at 119. The resolution also provided an alternative formulation as follows: "[T]his treaty is not intended to be self-executing nor to become a part of the domestic law of any of the contracting parties unless implemented by domestic legislation."

131. *Id.*, at 119.

132. 1950 Genocide Hearings, at 31 (statement of Philip B. Perlman) (quoting The Over the Top, 5 F.2d 838 (D. Conn. 1925)).

133. *See supra* pp. 215–18.

134. Draft Covenant, art. 1, para. 1 (included in U.N. Doc. E/CN.4/507 (May 1950), Annex I).

135. *See id.*

136. *See* Chapter 6, pp. 114–22.

137. 75 Ann. Rep. ABA 102, 119 (1950).

138. *See* 6 U.S. Op. Atty. Gen. 748 (Oct. 3, 1854) (discussed in Chapter 6, pp. 119–20).

139. 75 Ann. Rep. ABA 102, 119 (1950).

140. *See* Chapter 8, pp. 157–66.

141. U.N. Doc. E/CN.4/224 (23 May 1949). *See* pp. 202–03.

142. *See* pp. 202–03.

143. *See* pp. 174–76.

144. The Stassen proposal did include draft language for insertion into particular treaties that was designed as an "opt out" from the constitutional rule announced by the Supreme Court in *Holland*—that is, the rule that Congress has power under the Necessary and Proper Clause to enact legislation to implement treaties. *See id.* Stassen and other Section members may have thought that the treaty makers could use language in specific treaties to opt out of the *Holland* rule, but that view is difficult to justify.

145. I discuss those purposes more fully in Chapter 11, pp. 237–40, 245–48, and Chapter 13, pp. 283–84.

146. *See* Tananbaum (1988), at 20–24; Caro (2002), at 522–28.

147. The text of the resolution is at 97 Cong. Rec. 8254. Bricker delivered two long speeches explaining his opposition to the Covenant. *See* 97 Cong. Rec. 8254–63 (July 17, 1951); 97 Cong. Rec. 11509–14 (Sept. 18, 1951).

148. For analysis of Bricker's concerns about the Covenant, see Tananbaum (1988), at 24–31; Kaufman (1990), at 64–93.

149. Tananbaum (1988), at 34–35 (summarizing correspondence between Bricker and Holman, and Bricker and Schweppe, July 18–24, 1951).

150. For the text of S.J. Res. 102, see Tananbaum (1988), at 221–22.

151. S.J. Res. 102 would have modified the Supremacy Clause so that treaties could be the "law of the land" only if made "in pursuance" of the Constitution. The actual text of the Supremacy Clause states that treaties are the "law of the land" if they are "made under the Authority of the United States." In light of dicta in *Missouri v. Holland*, Bricker was concerned that the Court might construe the phrase "under the Authority of the United States" to allow treaties to evade or override constitutional limitations. *See* 97 Cong. Rec 8261. His amendment was crafted to address that problem.

152. *See* Tananbaum (1988), at 221–22.

153. 97 Cong. Rec. 8263 (July 17, 1951). Bricker made this statement with respect to S. Res. 177, but it applied equally to the proposed amendment in S.J. Res. 102.

154. United States v. Pink, 315 U.S. 203 (1942); United States v. Belmont, 301 U.S. 324 (1937).
155. *See* Tananbaum (1988), at 221–22.
156. *See* pp. 219–20.
157. *See* 97 Cong. Rec 8261.
158. Henderson v. United States, 339 U.S. 816 (1950); Sweatt v. Painter, 339 U.S. 629 (1950); McLaurin v. Oklahoma State Regents, 339 U.S. 637 (1950).
159. *See Henderson*, 339 U.S. at 818–22.
160. Henderson v. United States, Brief for Elmer W. Henderson, at 75.
161. Henderson v. United States, Brief for the United States, at 56-66.
162. *Id.*, at 62–63.
163. Henderson v. United States, Motion for Leave to File Brief and Brief of American Veterans Committee, at 7.
164. *Henderson*, 339 U.S. at 818 (quoting statute).
165. Henderson v. United States, Brief for Southern Railway Company.
166. *Henderson*, 339 U.S. at 824.
167. *See* Dudziak (2000), at 92–94.
168. Sweatt v. Painter, 339 U.S. 629, 631–32 (1950).
169. McLaurin v. Oklahoma State Regents, 339 U.S. 637, 640 (1950). The university modified its practices after the lower court issued its decision and before the Supreme Court issued its decision so that some of the stated facts were no longer true by the time the Supreme Court decided the case. *See id.*, at 640–41.
170. McLaurin v. Oklahoma State Regents, Brief for Appellant, at 33 (quoting *Oyama v. California*). *See* Chapter 9, pp. 195–96 for discussion of *Oyama*.
171. Sweatt v. Painter, Brief for Petitioner, at 66.
172. McLaurin v. Oklahoma State Regents, Memorandum for the United States as Amicus Curiae.
173. *Id.*, at 1–2.
174. *Id.*, at 12–13.
175. *See* Dudziak (2000), at 82–83; Anderson (2003), at 30–32, 156–57.
176. *See, e.g.*, Brief of Amici Curiae in Support of Petitioner, Sweatt v. Painter; Brief for Appellant, McLaurin v. Oklahoma State Regents.
177. *See Sweatt*, 339 U.S. at 849–51; *McLaurin*, 339 U.S. at 853–54.
178. Balkin and Siegel (2006), at 928.
179. *Id.*, at 929.

CHAPTER 11

1. Fujii v. State, 242 P.2d 617 (Cal. 1952).
2. Fujii Case File, Petition for Hearing.
3. *See* Chapter 10, p. 212.
4. Fujii Case File, Petition for Hearing, at 12–13.
5. *See* Whitney v. Robertson, 124 U.S. 190, 194 (1888) (discussed in Chapter 7, pp. 134–35).
6. Fujii Case File, Answer to Petition for Hearing.
7. Wright (1951), at 64.
8. Fujii v. State, 242 P.2d 617, 620 (Cal. 1952).
9. *See* Chapter 10, pp. 202–03.
10. Hudson (1950).
11. *See* Chapter 10, pp. 220–23.

12. Fujii Case File, Petition for Hearing, at 22–24.
13. *Fujii*, 242 P.2d at 621–22.
14. *See* Schachter (1951), at 655–56.
15. *Id.*, at 655.
16. *See* pp. 6–8 (summarizing three distinct concepts of self-execution).
17. *See* pp. 61–63 (explaining the difference between the one-step and two-step approaches).
18. Fujii Case File, Petition for Hearing, at 15–22.
19. As discussed in Chapter 8, Dickinson's intent doctrine makes the "intent of the treaty makers" the controlling factor in precisely those cases where the treaty makers have not expressed their intentions. Moreover, his intent doctrine had gained widespread support before 1950. *See* pp. 157–62.
20. Fujii Case File, Answer to Petition for Hearing, p. 16.
21. *Fujii*, 242 P.2d at 620.
22. *Id.*, at 622.
23. *See* Sloss, *Madison's Monster* (2016), at 1721–33 (demonstrating that the Senate record associated with ratification of the U.N. Charter does not support the claim that the United States intended the human rights provisions to be non-self-executing).
24. *Fujii*, 242 P.2d at 630.
25. 263 U.S. 225 (1923).
26. Oyama v. California, 332 U.S. 633, 647 (1948) ("Since the view we take of petitioners' first contention requires reversal of the decision below, we do not reach their other contentions: that the Alien Land Law denies ineligible aliens the equal protection of the laws ....").
27. *Fujii*, 242 P.2d at 640 (Schauer, J., dissenting).
28. *Id.*, at 639 (Schauer, J., dissenting).
29. *Id.*, at 630–31 (Carter, J., concurring).
30. *See* Chapters 9 and 10 (discussing criticism of the United States and the U.S. response).
31. In *Oyama v. California*, 332 U.S. 633 (1948), a case in which the U.S. Supreme Court reversed the California Supreme Court, both Justice Murphy and Justice Black emphasized the negative foreign policy consequences of California's Alien Land Law in their concurring opinions. *See Oyama*, 332 U.S. at 649–50 (Black, J., concurring); *id.*, at 672–73 (Murphy, J., concurring). The California Supreme Court justices must have been familiar with those opinions. Moreover, the statement in Justice Schauer's dissent—that the majority invalidated the Alien Land Law because it was "obnoxious to their ... concepts of desirable international relations," *Fujii*, 242 P.2d at 639—reinforces the point that foreign affairs considerations influenced the majority decision.
32. *Fujii*, 242 P.2d at 627.
33. *See, e.g.*, Terrace v. Thompson, 263 U.S. 197, 217–21 (1923); Porterfield v. Webb, 263 U.S. 225, 233 (1923); People v. Oyama, 173 P.2d 794, 29 Cal. 2d 164, 174–76 (Cal. 1946).
34. *Fujii*, 242 P.2d at 628.
35. *Id.*, at 627.
36. Fujii Case File, Appellant's Opening Brief, at 85.

37. Los Angeles Cty. v. S. Cal. Tel. Co., 196 P.2d 773, 781 (CA 1948). *See also* Fujii Case File, Appellant's Opening Brief, at 85-87.
38. *See* Franck (1990), at 26.
39. *Fujii*, 242 P.2d at 622.
40. 77 Ann. Rep. ABA 425, 447–48 (1952).
41. *See* Fujii Case File, Letter from W. Jefferson Davis to California Supreme Court, Nov. 30, 1950 (advising Supreme Court about resolutions pending before the ABA that were relevant to the *Fujii* case).
42. *See* Chapter 9. The justices may not have been aware of the Bricker amendment before they issued their decision in *Fujii*. Senator Bricker first introduced his proposed amendment in September 1951. However, the first Senate hearings on the Bricker Amendment were in May 1952, one month after the *Fujii* decision.
43. Fairman (1952), at 689.
44. Professors Goodman and Jinks argue persuasively that a nation's internalization of international human rights norms often results from efforts by individuals "to avoid the unpleasant state of cognitive dissonance between what they profess in public and what they believe in private." Goodman & Jinks (2013), at 153. That appears to be a powerful explanation of the California Supreme Court's behavior in *Fujii*.
45. Treaties and Executive Agreements: Hearings Before a Subcommittee of the Committee on the Judiciary, at 138 (1953) (Testimony of Mr. Frank Holman) [hereinafter, "1953 Bricker Hearings"].
46. 263 U.S. 225 (1923).
47. 332 U.S. 633 (1948).
48. 334 U.S. 410 (1948).
49. *See* People v. Oyama, 29 Cal. 2d 164, 173 P.2d 794 (1946); Takahashi v. Fish & Game Comm'n, 30 Cal. 2d 719, 185 P.2d 805 (1947).
50. Fujii v. State, 242 P.2d 617, 623 (Cal. 1952).
51. *Takahashi*, 334 U.S. 410 (1948).
52. *Id.*, at 415–16 (quoting Truax v. Raich, 239 U.S. 33 (1915)) (internal quotations omitted).
53. *Id.*, at 422.
54. Oyama v. California, 332 U.S. 633, 637 (1948).
55. *Id.*, at 639.
56. *Id.*, at 641.
57. *Id.*, at 642.
58. *Id.*, at 644.
59. *Id.*, at 640.
60. *See id.*, at 647.
61. *Brown*, 347 U.S. 483 (1954); *Bolling*, 347 U.S. 497 (1954).
62. *See* Brief for Petitioners, Bolling v. Sharpe.
63. *See* Klarman (2004); Tushnet (1994); Kluger (1976).
64. Brief for Petitioners, Bolling v. Sharpe, at 54.
65. *Id.*, at 55.
66. *Id.*, at 57.
67. *See* Wright (1951), at 64 (discussed in Chapter 10, pp. 214–15).
68. Brief for Petitioners, Bolling v. Sharpe, at 55.

69. *Id.*, at 61.

70. Brief for Respondents, Bolling v. Sharpe, at 40.

71. *See id.*, at 41–49.

72. *Id.*, at 40 (emphasis added).

73. Interestingly, one of the Court's central concerns in *Brown* was whether a judicial ruling based on the Fourteenth Amendment was "capable of judicial enforcement." Some of the justices feared widespread political resistance in the South. Petitioners' brief in *Bolling* did not address that issue, in part because the problem was much less salient in the District of Columbia than it was in South Carolina.

74. Dickson (2001), at 652.

75. U.S. CONST. amend XIV.

76. *See* Brief for Appellants, Brown v. Bd. of Educ., at 7 (contending "that the state may not validly impose distinctions and restrictions among its citizens based upon race or color alone").

77. *See* Tushnet (1994), at 150–67.

78. Brief for Respondents, Bolling v. Sharpe, at 17.

79. 163 U.S. 537 (1896).

80. *See* Klarman (2004), at 294; Kluger (1976), at 590.

81. Klarman (2004), at 296. *See also* Dickson (2001), at 652.

82. U.S. CONST. amend V.

83. *See* Brief for Respondents, Bolling v. Sharpe, at 16–21.

84. *See* Dickson (2001), at 646–53; *see also* Klarman (2004), at 292–301; Kluger (1976), at 589–614; Tushnet (1994), at 187–95.

85. *See* Dickson (2001), at 649–51. Justice Frankfurter was especially troubled by the prospect that the Court might issue a remedial order and one or more states would refuse to comply. Klarman (2004), at 295; Kluger (1976), at 600–02. The prospect of noncompliance in the District of Columbia was not a serious risk, but that risk was far more serious in South Carolina.

86. I rely here on secondary sources. The authors of those sources do not agree fully among themselves how best to construe the conference notes. *See* Klarman (2004), at 292–301; Kluger (1976), at 589–614; Tushnet (1994), at 187–95.

87. Dickson's edited conference notes provide the most detailed record of the Court's private discussions. *See* Dickson (2001), at 646–53. Those notes do not mention the U.N. Charter. The accounts of the justices' deliberations in Klarman, Kluger, and Tushnet—all of which rely on unpublished conference notes—do not mention the U.N. Charter. One of Justice Reed's former law clerks recalled many years later that Justice Reed asked him during the Court's next term to do some research to find out "what has been the position of the United Nations and its Declaration of Rights with respect to segregation?" Barrett (2004), at 546 (panel discussion moderated by John Q. Barrett) (statement by John David Fassett).

88. U.N. Charter, arts. 55, 56.

89. *See* 2 Simma (2012), at 1569–70; Anderson, at 40–46.

90. *See* Anderson, at 48–50.

91. U.N. Charter, art. 2(7).

92. *See* Brief for Petitioners, Bolling v. Sharpe, at 59 ("Articles 55 and 56 . . . prohibit government enforced racial segregation in the public schools."). The brief did

not defend this point in great detail because the attorneys devoted most of their Charter argument to the self-execution issue.

93. Brief for Respondents, Bolling v. Sharpe, at 52–54.

94. Article 26(1) of the Universal Declaration affirms that "[e]veryone has the right to education." During the 1950s, many governmental and international sources began to consult the Universal Declaration of Human Rights as a guide to construing the human rights provisions of the U.N. Charter. *See* Schwelb (1959). Hence, as a matter of treaty interpretation, the Court could reasonably have construed the phrase "human rights and fundamental freedoms" in the Charter to include a right to education.

95. Oyama v. California, 332 U.S. 633 (1948). *See* Chapter 9, pp. 195–96 (discussing concurring opinions in *Oyama*).

96. Brief on Behalf of American Civil Liberties Union, American Ethical Union, American Jewish Committee, Anti-Defamation League of B'nai B'rith, Japanese American Citizens League, and Unitarian Fellowship for Social Justice as Amici Curiae, Brown v. Bd. of Education.

97. *Id.*, at 28.

98. *Id.*, at 31.

99. *See* Brief for the United States as Amicus Curiae, Brown v. Bd. of Education.

100. *Id.*, at 45.

101. *Id.*, at 6–8.

102. Klarman, at 299. Justice Reed, who was probably the last justice to agree to support Chief Justice Warren's opinion in *Brown*, was also probably swayed by foreign policy considerations. *See* Barrett (2004), at 547.

103. *See infra* pp. 248–49.

104. *See* Caro (2002), at 530 ("All that Fall and Winter (1953-54), the Bricker Amendment stayed on the front pages of the nation's newspapers.")

105. *See* Kluger (1976), at 593 (stating that Justice Black "agreed with Vinson that South Carolina might well abolish its public schools [in response to a judicial order requiring desegregation] as Governor Byrnes had threatened").

106. *See id.*, at 599–601.

107. *See* Klarman (2004), at 348–63.

108. Goodman & Jinks (2013), at 153.

109. Fairman (1952), at 689.

110. Goodman & Jinks (2013), at 153.

111. *See generally* Dudziak (2000); Tushnet (1994), at 188.

112. Brief for the United States as Amicus Curiae, Brown v. Bd. of Education, at 8.

113. S.J. Res. 130, 82nd Cong., 2nd sess., Feb. 7, 1952; 98 Cong. Rec. 907-14 (1952); Tananbaum (1988), at 41–44.

114. 77 Ann. Rep. ABA 425, 447–48 (1952).

115. 1953 Bricker Hearings; Treaties and Executive Agreements, Hearings Before a Subcommittee of the Committee on the Judiciary (1952) [hereinafter "1952 Bricker Hearings"].

116. Constitutional Amendment Relative to Treaties and Executive Agreements, S. Rep. 412 (1953).

117. *See* Tananbaum (1988), at 175–90. For a fascinating account of Lyndon Johnson's behind-the-scenes role as Senate minority leader, see Caro (2002), at 519–41.

118. Executive branch materials related to the Bricker Amendment are collected in 1 FRUS, pp. 1768–856.
119. *Id.*, at 1825.
120. *See* Tananbaum (1988), at 146, 224–25.
121. *See, e.g.,* S. Rep. 412 (1953), at 3–8 (contending that the proposed amendment "removes any possible doubt whether a treaty must be consistent with the Constitution. It gives unequivocal constitutional effect to early judicial dicta not yet incorporated in binding decisions."); Testimony of Mr. Alfred J. Schweppe, Chairman of the ABA Committee on Peace and Law Through the United Nations, 1953 Bricker Hearings, at 50–54.
122. *See* 1 FRUS, pp. 1822–24; Tananbaum (1988), at 97–103, 107–12.
123. Reid v. Covert, 354 U.S. 1 (1957).
124. 99 Cong. Rec. 1078–79 (Feb. 16, 1953); S. Rep. 412 (1953), at 2; Tananbaum (1988), at 81, 223–24.
125. Missouri v. Holland, 252 U.S. 416 (1920).
126. *See, e.g.,* President's News Conference, Jan. 13, 1954, *in* Public Papers of the Presidents (1954), at 51–53; 1953 Bricker Hearings, at 901–05, 924–28 (testimony of Attorney General Herbert Brownell); *id.*, at 839–40 (memorandum submitted by Secretary of State John Foster Dulles); 1952 Bricker Hearings, at 420 (memorandum submitted by Solicitor General Philip Perlman).
127. *See* Tananbaum (1988), at 80–82 (discussing Bricker's initial opposition to the ABA proposal); *id.*, at 91–92 (discussing Bricker's capitulation to the ABA in the spring of 1953).
128. S. Rep. 412 (1953), p. 1 (full text of amendment); pp. 13–24 (explaining majority's support for the "which clause"); pp. 41–47 (explaining minority's opposition to the "which clause"). For more detailed analysis of the relationship between *Missouri v. Holland* and the Bricker Amendment, see Sloss (2015), at 1595–1602.
129. *See generally* 1 FRUS, at 1826–52; Tananbaum (1988), at 133–56.
130. United States v. Pink, 315 U.S. 203 (1942); United States v. Belmont, 301 U.S. 324 (1937). After *Belmont* and *Pink*, the scope of the president's power to supersede conflicting state law by means of sole executive agreements remained unclear. However, *Belmont* and *Pink* established that the president had some power to supersede state laws by adopting sole executive agreements.
131. S.J. Res. 130, 82nd Cong., 2nd sess., Feb. 7, 1952; 98 Cong. Rec. 907–14 (1952).
132. 77 Ann. Rep. ABA 425, 447–48 (1952).
133. *See* 1 FRUS, at 1781–82; Tananbaum (1988), at 71–72.
134. 100 Cong. Rec. 853 (Jan. 27, 1954); 100 Cong. Rec. 1103 (Feb. 2, 1954).
135. *See* 1 FRUS, at 1851–52; Tananbaum (1988), at 175–90.
136. *See generally* Caro (2002), at 519–41.
137. S. Rep. 412 (1953), at 1.
138. *Id.*, at 8.
139. *See generally id.*, at 8–13 (majority views); *id.*, at 41–47 (minority views).
140. *Id.*, at 10.
141. 1953 Bricker Hearings, at 54 (testimony of Mr. Alfred J. Schweppe).
142. 1953 Bricker Hearings, at 7 (testimony of Senator Bricker). *See also id.*, at 138 (testimony of Frank Holman, former ABA president) ("The final judicial result

in the *Fujii* case makes it clearer than ever that the only way to protect the rights of the American people in their domestic affairs is to adopt a constitutional amendment which will indicate in language too clear to be misunderstood that no provision of a treaty is to be given any judicial consideration or effect unless it has been implemented by act of Congress.").

143. S. Rep. 412 (1953), at 10.
144. *Id.*, at 11.
145. *See* Tananbaum (1988), at 107–12.
146. 1 FRUS, at 1825; Public Papers of the Presidents (1953), at 509–11.
147. 1 FRUS, at 1825.
148. *See* Chapter 10, pp. 220–23 (discussing proposal by ABA section on international law).
149. 1953 Bricker Hearings, at 54 (testimony of Mr. Alfred J. Schweppe).
150. 1 FRUS, at 1825.
151. *See* Tananbaum (1988), at 150–56, 225–26.
152. 100 Cong. Rec. 1239–40 (Feb. 3, 1954); Tananbaum (1988), at 225.
153. 100 Cong. Rec. 2358 (Feb. 26, 1954); Tananbaum (1988), at 175–77.
154. *See* Caro (2002), at 531–40.
155. The George substitute would have made executive agreements non-self-executing, but it did not address the self-executing character of treaties.
156. 1 FRUS, at 1848; Tananbaum (1988), at 152–53.
157. 100 Cong. Rec. 2262 (Feb. 25, 1954); Tananbaum (1988), at 166–69; Caro (2002), at 536.
158. The quoted language is taken from the text proposed by Senator Bricker in February 1954. *See* 1 FRUS, at 1848.
159. The texts of all the referenced versions of the amendment are reproduced in Tananbaum (1988), at 222–26.
160. The phrase "effective as internal law" also implied that treaties were judicially enforceable, in accordance with the political-judicial concept of self-execution.
161. *See* Chapter 10, pp. 219–20, 223–25; *see also* Kaufman (1990).
162. *See* testimony of Secretary of State John Foster Dulles, 1953 Bricker Hearings, at 824–26 (opposing constitutional amendment, but expressing policy objections to human rights treaties); testimony of Harold E. Stassen, Director for Mutual Security, *id.*, at 1054–59 (opposing constitutional amendment, but expressing "serious reservations" about the proposed Covenant on Human Rights). President Eisenhower appointed Stassen as director of the Mutual Security Administration in 1953. The Mutual Security Administration was an independent agency that oversaw foreign aid programs. Stassen is remembered primarily as a failed presidential candidate, but he played a key role in the Bricker Amendment debates, both as a member of the ABA (see Chapter 10, pp. 220–23) and as a senior official in the Eisenhower administration.
163. 1953 Bricker Hearings, at 921–22 (testimony of Attorney General Herbert Brownell); *id.*, at 835 (memorandum submitted by Secretary of State John Foster Dulles); *id.*, at 1059 (testimony of Harold Stassen).
164. *Id.*, at 244–46 (report submitted by New York City Bar Association).
165. S. Rep. 412 (1953), at 41–42 (minority views).
166. 100 Cong. Rec. 2200, 2204 (Feb. 24, 1954) (statements by Senator George).

167.   1 FRUS, at 1833–34 (letter from the president to John J. McCloy, Jan. 13, 1954).
168.   *See* Chapter 6, pp. 114–23.
169.   *See* Chapter 8, pp. 157–62.
170.   *See* Chapter 8, pp. 163–66.
171.   *See, e.g.,* testimony of Harold Stassen, 1953 Bricker Hearings, at 1059 (contending that a constitutional amendment was unnecessary because, under existing law, "any treaty which is thought undesirably to affect local rights can be limited by a clause in the treaty or by a reservation by the Senate, so that it would not be self-executing and would require State legislative action before becoming effective"); testimony of Attorney General Brownell, *id.,* at 922; Memorandum submitted by Secretary of State John Foster Dulles, *id.,* at 835; S. Rep. 412 (1953), at 42 (minority views) ("[A]ny treaty can be limited by a clause in the treaty or by a reservation of the Senate, so that it could not be self-executing. If the words of the [proposed constitutional amendment] . . . are adequate to effect a change in the requirements for conclusion of treaties under the Constitution, then these same words would be just as effective when inserted in a treaty or in a reservation thereto.").
172.   *See* Part One.
173.   *See* Chapters 4 to 7.
174.   United States representatives in the U.N. Human Rights Commission had expressed the view that the Covenant on Human Rights would be non-self-executing, but the Covenant was still in draft form at that time. *See* Chapter 9, pp. 202–03. In his official Senate testimony, Attorney General Brownell implied that the United States ratified the U.N. Charter with the understanding that Articles 55 and 56 would be non-self-executing. Testimony of Attorney General Brownell, 1953 Bricker Hearings, at 922. In fact, though, the question of whether the Charter's human rights provisions would be self-executing in the United States was never raised during Senate deliberations over ratification of the U.N. Charter. *See* Sloss, *Madison's Monster* (2016). Moreover, the widely shared background assumption in 1945, when the Senate consented to ratification of the U.N. Charter, was that the self-execution issue was not relevant to the relationship between treaties and state law.

CHAPTER 12

1.   Fujii v. State, 242 P.2d 617 (Cal. 1952); Camacho v. Rogers, 199 F. Supp. 155 (S.D.N.Y. 1961).
2.   United States v. California, 381 U.S. 139 (1965) (relying partly on the Convention on the Territorial Sea and the Contiguous Zone to help resolve a dispute about the extent of submerged lands granted to the State of California by the Submerged Lands Act of 1953); McCulloch v. Sociedad Nacional de Marineros de Honduras, 372 U.S. 10 (1963) (citing bilateral treaty with Honduras and holding that the National Labor Relations Act does not extend to maritime operations of foreign-flagged vessels employing alien seamen); Maximov v. United States, 373 U.S. 49 (1963) (holding that bilateral tax treaty with United Kingdom did not grant federal income tax exemption to American trust whose beneficiaries were British subjects and residents); Kolovrat v. Oregon, 366 U.S. 187 (1961) (discussed in text); United States v. Louisiana, 363 U.S. 1 (1960) (citing numerous treaties in a lengthy opinion addressing U.S. suit against Louisiana, Texas, Mississippi,

Alabama, and Florida involving dispute about sovereign power over the lands and natural resources underlying the waters of the Gulf of Mexico more than three geographical miles seaward from the coast); Reid v. Covert, 354 U.S. 1 (1957) (holding that the Constitution prohibits exercise of court martial jurisdiction over wives of military personnel for capital offenses committed on overseas military bases, and that treaty purporting to authorize court martial is invalid insofar as it conflicts with Fifth and Sixth Amendments); Wilson v. Girard, 354 U.S. 524 (1957) (discussing bilateral treaties with Japan and affirming power of executive branch to deliver U.S. army specialist to Japanese authorities to be prosecuted for a crime committed in Japan); Harisiades v. Shaughnessy, 342 U.S. 580 (1952) (citing the 1907 Hague Convention in the course of an opinion upholding deportation of foreign nationals who were former members of the Communist Party); Moser v. United States, 341 U.S. 41 (1951) (relying partly on a bilateral treaty with Switzerland to support its holding that petitioner did not waive his right to apply for citizenship by claiming exemption from military service); Warren v. United States, 340 U.S. 523 (1951) (discussed in text); Johnson v. Eisentrager, 339 U.S. 763 (1950) (rejecting habeas petition by German nationals who invoked the Geneva Conventions in support of their challenge to the jurisdiction of a military commission); Farrell v. United States, 336 U.S. 511 (1949) (discussing the Shipowners' Liability Convention in the context of an admiralty action by a member of the merchant marine against the United States); Oyama v. California, 332 U.S. 633 (1948) (Murphy, J., concurring) (discussed in Chapter 9, pp. 195–96); Clark v. Allen, 331 U.S. 503 (1947) (discussed in text); Federal Trade Commission v. A.P.W. Paper Co., 328 U.S. 193 (1946) (ruling against the Federal Trade Commission in a case where the Commission invoked the Geneva Conventions in support of its order prohibiting a private company from using the words "Red Cross" to describe its products); In re Yamashita, 327 U.S. 1 (1946) (upholding the authority of a military commission to try a Japanese General for violation of the laws of war).

3. 331 U.S. 503 (1947).
4. 366 U.S. 187 (1961).
5. In *Oyama v. California*, 332 U.S. 633 (1948), two different concurring opinions cited the U.N. Charter in support of the view that California's Alien Land Law was invalid. However, the majority opinion did not reference the U.N. Charter. See Chapter 9, pp. 195–96. In *Rice v. Sioux City Memorial Park Cemetery*, 349 U.S. 70 (1955), plaintiff invoked the Charter's human rights provisions in support of her claim, but the Court dismissed the writ as improvidently granted without addressing the merits of that claim.
6. *Clark*, 331 U.S. at 505–06.
7. *Id.*, at 508.
8. *See id.*, at 508–10.
9. *Id.*, at 517.
10. *Id.* (holding "that disposition of the realty is governed by Article IV of the treaty").
11. 366 U.S. 187 (1961).
12. *Id.*, at 188.
13. *Id.*, at 191.
14. *Id.*, at 190.
15. 340 U.S. 523 (1951).

16. "Maintenance and cure" is a traditional remedy in admiralty law that compensates seamen for injuries sustained while in service of the ship. *See* Anonymous author, *The Tangled Seine* (1947), at 247–51.
17. *Warren*, 340 U.S. at 525.
18. *Id.*
19. Chief Justice Stone had endorsed this position in *Aguilar v. Standard Oil Co.* 318 U.S. 724, 738 (1943) (Stone, C.J., concurring/dissenting). *See* Chapter 7, p. 131.
20. *Warren*, 340 U.S. at 526.
21. *Id.*, at 529.
22. Professor Stephan suggests that a single footnote in *Johnson v. Eisentrager*, 339 U.S. 763 (1950), provides a "template" that the Court applied in later cases to analyze self-execution issues. *See* Stephan (2011), at 317, 324. The Court did not use the term "self-executing" in *Eisentrager*, but the footnote Stephan quotes can be construed as an application of the justiciability version of NSE doctrine. Construed in this way, *Eisentrager* reinforces the point that self-execution doctrine in the Supreme Court during this period had no bearing on the relationship between treaties and state law, because there was no state law at issue in *Eisentrager*.
23. Felsenfeld v. Societe Anonyme Belge, 234 N.Y.S.2d 351 (Cty. Civ. Ct. 1962); Baldwin-Lima-Hamilton Corp. v. Superior Court, 208 Cal. App. 2d 803 (1962); People v. Coumatos, 32 Misc. 2d 1085 (Gen. Sess. N.Y. Co. 1962); Galli v. Brazilian Int'l Airlines, 29 Misc. 2d 499 (N.Y. Sup. Ct. 1961); In re Carrizzo's Estate, 28 Misc. 2d 943 (N.Y. Misc. 1961); Milliken v. State, 131 So. 2d 889 (Fla. 1961); Scandinavian Airlines, Inc. v. Los Angeles County, 56 Cal. 2d 11 (Cal. 1961); Guiseppe v. Cozzani, 118 So. 2d 189 (Miss. 1960); Testa v. Sorrento Restaurant, 10 A.D.2d 133 (N.Y. App. Div. 1960); In re Ronkendorf's Estate, 324 P.2d 941 (Cal. App. 1958); Parke, Davis & Co. v. BOAC, 11 Misc. 2d 811 (N.Y. City Ct. 1958); Sinclair Crude Oil Co. v. Oklahoma Tax Comm'n, 326 P.2d 1051 (Okla. 1958); In re Wieboldt's Estate, 92 N.W.2d 849 (Wis. 1958); Heaton v. Delco Appliance Div., 7 A.D.2d 10 (N.Y. App. Div. 1958); Lazarou v. Moraros, 143 A.2d 669 (N.H. 1958); State v. Satiacum, 314 P.2d 400 (Wash. 1957); State *ex rel.* Port Sewall Realty Co. v. Green, 91 So. 2d 306 (Fla. 1956); Iannone v. Radory Constr. Corp., 141 N.Y.S 2d 311 (N.Y. App. Div. 1955); Brownell v. San Francisco, 271 P.2d 974 (Cal. App. 1954); In re Siegler's Will, 132 N.Y.S.2d 392 (N.Y. Sup. Ct. 1954); Rice v. Sioux City Memorial Park Cemetery, 60 N.W.2d 110 (Iowa 1953); Fujii v. State, 242 P.2d 617 (Cal. 1952); Goepp v. Am. Airlines, 281 A.D. 105 (N.Y. Sup. Ct. 1952); Salamon v. Royal Dutch Airlines, 107 N.Y.S.2d 768 (N.Y. Sup. Ct. 1951); L&C Mayers Co. v. Royal Dutch Airline, 108 N.Y.S.2d 251 (N.Y. Sup. Ct. 1951); Ex parte Backstron, 220 P.2d 742 (Cal. App. 1950); Fujii v. California, 217 P.2d 481 (Cal. App. 1950); Ross v. Pan Am. Airways, 299 N.Y. 88 (N.Y. Ct. App. 1949); Kraus v. Royal Dutch Airlines, 92 N.Y.S.2d 315 (Sup. Ct. N.Y. Cty. 1949).
24. *See* Chapter 10, pp. 202–03.
25. Restatement (Second), Proposed Official Draft (1962).
26. *See, e.g.,* Ioannou v. New York, 371 U.S. 30, 31 (1962) (citing the Proposed Official Draft as authority for the proposition that international law does not mandate a rule of foreign sovereign immunity for states acting in a commercial capacity).
27. *In re* Siegler's Will, 132 N.Y.S.2d 392, 394 (N.Y. Sup. Ct. 1954).
28. State v. Satiacum, 314 P.2d 400, 402 (Wash. 1957).
29. Guiseppe v. Cozzani, 118 So. 2d 189, 191 (Miss. 1960).

30. Scandinavian Airlines, Inc. v. Los Angeles Cty., 56 Cal. 2d 11, 37 (Cal. 1961).

31. See also Baldwin-Lima-Hamilton Corp. v. Superior Court, 208 Cal. App. 2d 803, 819–20 (Cal. App. 1962) ("The United States Constitution provides in Article VI therefor that 'Treaties made . . . under the Authority of the United States, shall be the supreme Law of the Land.' When a state statute conflicts with any such treaty, the latter will control."); In re Ronkendorf's Estate, 324 P.2d 941, 947 (Cal. App. 1958) ("It is elementary, of course, that in the event of a conflict between domestic law and a treaty the latter prevails.").

32. In a few cases, courts reached the merits of the treaty supremacy issue without reaching the merits of the underlying claim. See, e.g., Galli v. Brazilian Int'l Airlines, 29 Misc. 2d 499 (N.Y. Sup. Ct. 1961) (declining to address merits of plaintiff's state tort law claim because the Warsaw Convention, a multilateral treaty regulating international aviation, precluded the court from exercising jurisdiction otherwise provided under state law). For present purposes, I classify Galli as a case in which the court addressed the merits of the treaty supremacy issue because it applied the treaty to decide the specific (jurisdictional) issue to which the treaty related.

33. Fujii v. State, 242 P.2d 617 (Cal. 1952).

34. Ex parte Backstron, 220 P.2d 742 (Cal. App. 1950).

35. Baldwin-Lima-Hamilton Corp. v. Superior Court, 208 Cal. App. 2d 803 (Cal. App. 1962) (holding that "buy American" provision in contract between city and contractor was illegal because it conflicted with treaties); Galli v. Brazilian Int'l Airlines, 29 Misc. 2d 499 (N.Y. Sup. Ct. 1961) (holding that Warsaw Convention deprived state courts of jurisdiction otherwise available under state law); In re Carrizzo's Estate, 28 Misc. 2d 943 (N.Y. Misc. 1961) (holding that treaty with Italy authorized Italian consul general to receive payment in estate proceeding); Scandinavian Airlines, Inc. v. Los Angeles Cty., 56 Cal. 2d 11 (Cal. 1961) (holding that treaty with Sweden granted owners of foreign aircraft exemption from local taxation); Guiseppe v. Cozzani, 118 So. 2d 189 (Miss. 1960) (holding that treaty with Italy overrides state law that precludes non-resident aliens from acquiring land); Testa v. Sorrento Restaurant, 10 A.D.2d 133 (N.Y. App. 1960) (holding that treaty with Italy overrides provision of state workmen's compensation law); In re Ronkendorf's Estate, 324 P.2d 941 (Cal. App. 1958) (holding that treaty with Germany overrides conflicting provision in California Probate Code); Parke, Davis & Co. v. BOAC, 11 Misc. 2d 811 (N.Y. City Ct. 1958) (holding that Warsaw Convention barred state law claim for economic loss resulting from failure to deliver cargo); Sinclair Crude Oil Co. v. Okla. Tax Comm'n, 326 P.2d 1051 (Okla. 1958) (holding that treaty with Cherokee Tribe granted exemption from state taxation); State v. Satiacum, 314 P.2d 400 (Wash. 1957) (holding that 1855 Treaty of Medicine Creek superseded Washington state fishing laws); Iannone v. Radory Constr. Corp., 141 N.Y.S.2d 311 (N.Y. App. Div. 1955) (holding that treaty with Italy overrides state workmen's compensation law); Brownell v. San Francisco, 271 P.2d 974 (Cal. App. 1954) (holding that treaty with Germany barred city from collecting property taxes on real property owned by German government); Goepp v. Am. Airlines, 281 A.D. 105 (N.Y. Sup. Ct. 1952) (holding that Warsaw Convention limited defendant's liability for death caused by plane crash); Salamon v. Royal Dutch Airlines, 107 N.Y.S.2d 768 (N.Y. Sup. Ct. 1951) (holding that plaintiff had valid cause of action against airline under

Warsaw Convention); L&C Mayers Co. v. Royal Dutch Airline, 108 N.Y.S.2d 251 (N.Y. Sup. Ct. 1951) (holding that Warsaw Convention limited defendant's liability for lost cargo); Fujii v. California, 217 P.2d 481 (Cal. App. 2d 1950) (holding that human rights provisions of U.N. Charter superseded California's Alien Land Law); Ross v. Pan Am. Airways, 299 N.Y. 88 (N.Y. Ct. App. 1949) (holding that Warsaw Convention limits defendant's liability for injury caused by plane crash); Kraus v. Royal Dutch Airlines, 92 N.Y.S.2d 315 (Sup. Ct. N.Y. Cty. 1949) (holding that Warsaw Convention limits defendant's liability for lost cargo).

36. People v. Coumatos, 32 Misc. 2d 1085 (Gen. Sess. N.Y. Co. 1962) (holding that U.N. Charter did not grant immunity from criminal prosecution to a U.S. citizen employed as an inventory clerk at U.N. Headquarters); Felsenfeld v. Societe Anonyme Belge, 234 N.Y.S.2d 351 (Cty. Civ. Ct. 1962) (holding that Warsaw Convention did. not deprive state court of jurisdiction over claim involving flight from Tel Aviv to Brussels); Milliken v. State, 131 So. 2d 889 (Fla. 1961) (holding that treaty with Cuba did not conflict with state law that regulated taking of shrimp); In re Wieboldt's Estate, 92 N.W.2d 849 (Wis. 1958) (holding that treaty did not prohibit taxation of bequest made to president of Germany); Heaton v. Delco Appliance Div., 7 A.D.2d 10 (N.Y. App. Div. 1958) (holding that treaties with Britain did not conflict with state workmen's compensation law); Lazarou v. Moraros, 143 A.2d 669 (N.H. 1958) (holding that treaty with Greece did not grant nonresident Greek citizens the right to inherit real estate in the United States); State ex rel. Port Sewall Realty Co. v. Green, 91 So. 2d 306 (Fla. 1956) (holding that company who sought tax exemption failed to show that treaty with Canada granted such an exemption); In re Siegler's Will, 132 N.Y.S.2d 392 (N.Y. Sup. Ct. 1954) (holding that treaty with Hungary had expired, and was therefore not binding); Rice v. Sioux City Memorial Park Cemetery, 60 N.W.2d 110 (Iowa 1953) (holding that private cemetery's refusal to permit burial of plaintiff's non-Caucasian husband did not violate human rights provisions of U.N. Charter).

37. 107 N.Y.S.2d 768 (N.Y. 1951).

38. Id., at 771.

39. Id., at 772–73.

40. 141 N.Y.S 2d 311 (N.Y. 1955)

41. Id., at 315.

42. See note 35 (listing cases).

43. One could argue that all sixteen cases were poorly reasoned, in that they failed to consider whether the treaty at issue was self-executing. However, that argument is an attempt to view 1950s cases through a "post-Restatement" lens. Before the ALI published the Restatement (Second), the dominant view in state courts was that self-execution doctrine was simply not relevant to treaty supremacy cases. As discussed in detail in Parts One and Two, that was the prevailing view from the Founding until World War II.

44. People v. Coumatos, 32 Misc. 2d 1085 (Gen. Sess. N.Y. Co. 1962); Felsenfeld v. Societe Anonyme Belge, 234 N.Y.S.2d 351 (N.Y. Civ. Ct. 1962); In re Wieboldt's Estate, 92 N.W.2d 849 (Wis. 1958); Heaton v. Delco Appliance Div., 7 A.D.2d 10 (N.Y. App. Div. 1958); Lazarou v. Moraros, 143 A.2d 669 (N.H. 1958); State ex rel. Port Sewall Realty Co. v. Green, 91 So. 2d 306 (Fla. 1956); In re Siegler's Will, 132 N.Y.S.2d 392 (N.Y. Sup. Ct. 1954); Rice v. Sioux City Memorial Park Cemetery, 60 N.W.2d 110 (Iowa 1953).

45. 131 So. 2d 889 (Fla. 1961).

46. *Id.*, at 891.
47. *Id.*
48. *Id.*, at 892.
49. *Id.*, at 891.
50. *Id.*
51. The number "nineteen" counts the Supreme Court decision and the Second Circuit decision in *Warren* as two separate cases. Warren v. United States, 340 U.S. 523 (1951); Warren v. United States, 179 F.2d 919 (2d Cir. 1950).
52. Bowater S.S. Co. v. Patterson, 303 F.2d 369 (2d Cir. 1962); Yee Si v. Boyd, 243 F.2d 903 (9th Cir. 1957); Vanity Fair Mills, Inc. v. T. Eaton Co., 234 F.2d 633 (2d Cir. 1956); Jordine v. Walling, 185 F.2d 662 (3d Cir. 1950); Warren v. United States, 179 F.2d 919 (2d Cir. 1950).
53. Camacho v. Rogers, 199 F. Supp. 155 (S.D.N.Y. 1961); Aerovias Interamericanas de Panama v. Dade County, 197 F. Supp. 230 (S.D. Fla. 1961); *In re* D'Amico, 185 F. Supp. 925 (S.D.N.Y. 1960); Pauling v. McElroy, 164 F. Supp. 390 (D.D.C. 1958); Noel v. Linea Aeropostal Venezolana, 144 F. Supp. 359 (S.D.N.Y. 1956); United States v. Gredzens, 125 F. Supp. 867 (D. Minn. 1954); United States v. Coplon, 84 F. Supp. 472 (S.D.N.Y. 1949).
54. Etlimar Societe Anonyme of Casablanca v. United States, 106 F. Supp. 191 (Ct. Cl. 1952); Hannevig v. United States, 84 F. Supp. 743 (Ct. Cl. 1949).
55. There are many possible ways to define the term "treaty cases." The difficulty in ascertaining the number of treaty cases during the relevant time period relates partly to definitional problems, and partly to the fact that electronic searches designed to identify such cases are invariably both under and overinclusive.
56. *In re* D'Amico, 185 F. Supp. 925, 928 (S.D.N.Y. 1960) (in a habeas corpus proceeding challenging the validity of relator's detention pending surrender to Italy pursuant to 1868 extradition treaty, the court noted in passing that other extradition treaties adopted before enactment of the 1848 federal extradition statute were deemed to be self-executing).
57. Pauling v. McElroy, 164 F. Supp. 390, 393 (D.D.C. 1958) (in a suit against the Commissioner of Atomic Energy and the Secretary of Defense to enjoin nuclear weapons testing in the Marshall Islands, the court said that relevant provisions of the U.N. Charter and the Trusteeship Agreement for the Trust Territory of the Pacific Islands were not self-executing).
58. Yee Si v. Boyd, 243 F.2d 203, 205 (9th Cir. 1957) (in a case challenging deportation of a Chinese national to China, the court said that an 1880 treaty with China was not self-executing).
59. United States v. Gredzens, 125 F. Supp. 867, 869 (D. Minn. 1954) (in a federal prosecution against a Latvian national who failed to report for induction into the armed services, the court said that the controlling federal statute overrode inconsistent provisions of a prior treaty with Latvia, which "may have been self-executing"); United States v. Coplon, 84 F. Supp. 472, 474 (S.D.N.Y. 1949) (in a federal espionage case, where defendant claimed immunity under Article 105 of the U.N. Charter, the court held that "[t]he Charter provision in and of itself—assuming it to be self-executing—does not shield the defendant.").
60. Etlimar Societe Anonyme of Casablanca v. United States, 106 F. Supp. 191, 195–96 (Ct. Cl. 1952) (in an action against the United States seeking compensation

related to sale of goods to U.S. Army in Morocco, the court ruled in favor of the government and rejected plaintiff's argument that treaty with France was not self-executing); Hannevig v. United States, 84 F. Supp. 743, 744–45 (Ct. Cl. 1949) (in an action against the United States seeking compensation related to contracts with U.S. naval shipyards, the court ruled in favor of the government and rejected plaintiff's argument that treaty with Norway was not self-executing).

61. Jordine v. Walling, 185 F.2d 662, 669 (3d Cir. 1950) (where appellate court held that district court lacked jurisdiction because claim should have been filed as an admiralty claim, not a civil claim, the court expressed doubt as to whether the Shipowners Liability Convention was self-executing); Warren v. United States, 179 F.2d 919, 922 (2d Cir. 1950) (in a libel against the United States as the owner of a steamship, the court noted in passing Chief Justice Stone's opinion about the self-executing character of the Shipowners Liability Convention); Noel v. Linea Aeropostal Venezolana, 144 F. Supp. 359, 360 (S.D.N.Y. 1956) (where district court dismissed civil action under the Death on the High Seas Act because it should have been filed as an admiralty claim, the court said that Article 17 of the Warsaw Convention is self-executing).

62. 303 F.2d 369 (2d Cir. 1962).

63. *Id.*, at 378.

64. *Id.*

65. 234 F.2d 633 (2d Cir. 1956).

66. *Id.*, at 640.

67. *Id.*

68. 199 F. Supp. 155 (S.D.N.Y. 1961).

69. 197 F. Supp. 230 (S.D. Fla. 1961).

70. *Camacho*, 199 F. Supp. at 158.

71. *Aerovias Interamericanas*, 197 F. Supp. at 248.

72. Bd. of Cnty. Comm'rs of Dade County v. Aerolineas Peruanasa, S.A., 307 F.2d 802 (5th Cir. 1962).

CHAPTER 13

1. In *Hitai v. Immigration and Naturalization Service*, 343 F.2d 466 (2d Cir. 1965), the Second Circuit cited *Fujii* for the proposition that Article 55 of the U.N. Charter is not self-executing. However, *Hitai* was a federal immigration case that did not implicate any state law issues.

2. 199 F. Supp. 155 (S.D.N.Y. 1961).

3. *See* Chapter 11, pp. 250–56.

4. *See* Federal Judicial Center, History of the Federal Judiciary, *available at* http://www.fjc.gov/history/home.nsf/page/index.html; Greenwald (2009); Tweed (1962).

5. Memo from Dickinson to Goodrich, Jan. 24, 1951, ALI Archives, Box 16, Folder 10.

6. *See* Goodrich (1961); Newman (1961); Editorial Comment, *Edwin D. Dickinson 1887–1961*, 55 Am. J. Int'l L. 637 (1961); "Edwin Dickinson, A Law Professor," N.Y. TIMES, Mar. 27, 1961.

7. Memo to the Directors of the Ford Foundation, Nov. 12, 1951, ALI Archives, Box 17, Folder 4.

8. Dickinson to Goodrich, Mar. 17, 1958, ALI Archives, Box 16, Folder 10.

9. Goodrich to Kenneth Thompson, Rockefeller Foundation, May 26, 1954, ALI Archives, Box 17, Folder 4.

10. *See* Obituary, "Adrian S. Fisher, 69, Arms Treaty Negotiator," N.Y. Times, Mar. 19, 1983; Paige Mulhollan, Transcript, Adrian Fisher Oral History Interview I, Oct. 31, 1968, LBJ Library, *available at* http://www.lbjlib.utexas.edu/johnson/archives.hom/oralhistory.hom/Fisher-A/Fisher.asp.

11. Memo from Paul Wolkin, ALI Assistant Director, to Herbert Goodrich, ALI Director, Dec. 27, 1960, ALI Archives, Box 18, Folder 17 (stating that "we received notification of our grant" on Oct. 25, 1955).

12. Goodrich to Dickinson, Dec. 12, 1955, ALI Archives, Box 16, Folder 10.

13. The first drafts presented to the ALI Council that addressed international agreements were Council Drafts No. 4 and No. 5, which were sent to the Council in February and March, 1959, respectively. Copies of those documents in the ALI archives include handwritten notes in the margins indicating which Reporters were responsible for which portions of the document. According to those handwritten notes: Olmstead drafted chapter 1, on the authority to conclude and scope of international agreements; Oliver drafted chapter 2, on the formation of international agreements; Olmstead drafted chapter 3, on the binding effect of international agreements and their relation to domestic law; and Oliver drafted chapter 4, on the interpretation of international agreements. ALI Archives, Box 11, Folders 9 and 10.

14. *See* Schachter (1979).

15. *See* Rogers (2007); Leech (1979); Dennis Hevesi, C.T. Oliver, 93, Envoy and Professor, N.Y. Times, Feb. 28, 2007; "Law Professor Covey T. Oliver, 93, Served as Ambassador to Colombia," Wash. Post, Feb. 25, 2007.

16. *Cecil Olmstead, Associate Reporter for Foreign Relations Restatement, Is Dead at 92*, Am. Law Institute, ALI Reporter, vol. 35, No. 1 (2013); *Cecil J. Olmstead*, American Branch of the International Law Association Newsletter, vol. 90, No. 1 (2013); "Cecil J. Olmstead, An International Lawyer and Retired Texaco Executive Dies at 92," Wash. Post, July 8, 2013.

17. Minutes of Advisory Committee Meeting, Jan. 15–17, 1959, ALI Archives, Box 10, Folder 13.

18. *See* Chapter 10, pp. 213–18 (discussing Wright's work in this area).

19. Dickinson to Goodrich, Feb. 21, 1947, ALI Archives, Box 16, Folder 9.

20. A Proposal for Work in International Law to the American Philosophical Society (undated ten-page memorandum), ALI Archives, Box 16, Folder 9; Letter from Goodrich to Charles Dollard, President of the Carnegie Corporation, Sept. 12, 1952 (with nine-page proposal attached), ALI Archives, Box 16, Folder 10; To the Directors of the Ford Foundation, A Project in International Law, Nov. 12, 1951 (ten-page proposal), ALI Archives, Box 17, Folder 4.

21. Goodrich to R. Ammi Cutter, Apr. 13, 1954, ALI Archives, Box 17, Folder 13.

22. Rockefeller Foundation to Goodrich, June 8, 1954, ALI Archives, Box 17, Folder 13.

23. Goodrich to Harrison Tweed, Apr. 20, 1954, ALI Archives, Box 17, Folder 13.

24. *See infra* note 70.

25. Goodrich to Kenneth Thompson, Rockefeller Foundation, May 3, 1954, ALI Archives, Box 17, Folder 4.

26. Agenda for Discussion (1955).

27. Dickinson to Goodrich, Mar. 2, 1955, ALI Archives, Box 18, Folder 8.
28. Transcript of Conference (1955), at 95.
29. *Id.*, at 100.
30. Agenda for Discussion (1955).
31. Transcript of Conference (1955), at 103.
32. Report on Foreign Relations Law Project (1955). *See also* Letter from Goodrich to Members of the Committee on the Foreign Relations Law of the United States, Aug. 22, 1955 (transmitting Fisher's report), ALI Archives, Box 16, Folder 19.
33. Excerpt from Letter from Joseph M. McDaniel, Jr., Secretary, the Ford Foundation, Oct. 25, 1955, ALI Archives, Box 17, Folder 4; Memorandum from Paul Wolkin, ALI Assistant Director, to Herbert Goodrich, Dec. 27, 1960, ALI Archives, Box 18, Folder 17.
34. Dickinson to Goodrich, Nov. 5, 1956 (discussing initial meeting of reporters), ALI Archives, Box 16, Folder 10.
35. *See* Preliminary Draft 4 (1958); Preliminary Draft 5 (1959).
36. Minutes of Advisory Committee Meeting, Jan. 15–17, 1959, ALI Archives, Box 10, Folder 13. Dickinson did not attend the meeting. As of January 1959, he was a member of the Advisory Committee, but he had previously relinquished his position as "Chief Adviser" to the reporters.
37. Goodrich to Dickinson, Jan. 20, 1959, ALI Archives, Box 16, Folder 17; Goodrich to the Honorable George Wharton Pepper, Jan. 20, 1959, ALI Archives, Box 17, Folder 3.
38. *See* Council Draft 4 (1959); Council Draft 5 (1959).
39. *See* Tentative Draft 3 (1959).
40. Restatement (Second) § 117(1)(a) and § 117, cmt. a.
41. Restatement (Second) § 117(1)(b) and § 117, cmt. d.
42. Restatement (Second) § 118(2) and § 118, cmt. a.
43. Restatement (Second) § 118(2) and § 118, cmt. b.
44. *See* Restatement (Second) § 118, Reporters' Note.
45. *See* Preliminary Draft 4, §§ 1.05; 1.05, cmt. c; 1.07(2); 1.07(3); and 1.07, cmts. b & c.
46. *See generally* Council Draft 4, §§ 104 and 106; Tentative Draft 3, §§ 104 and 106; Proposed Official Draft, §§ 120 and 121.
47. *See* Chapter 11, pp. 248–50.
48. Agenda for Discussion (1955), at 24.
49. Transcript of Conference (1955), at 105.
50. Report on Foreign Relations Law Project (1955), at 23. For a modern defense of the "international concern" test, supported by extensive historical research, see Hollis (2015).
51. Transcript of Conference (1955), at 106.
52. *Id.*, at 106–07.
53. Report on Foreign Relations Law Project (1955), at 24–25.
54. The ALI Council met in March 1959 to discuss Council Drafts 4 and 5. There are no records of the Council's discussions at that meeting, but one can make reasonable inferences based on drafting changes that occurred between March and May 1959.
55. Tentative Draft 3, § 106, Note.
56. *See* Restatement (Second), § 118, Reporters' Note.

57. 252 U.S. 416 (1920). The Restatement endorses both aspects of *Holland*: (1) that the Treaty Power can address matters beyond the scope of Article I, and (2) that the combination of the Treaty Power and the Necessary and Proper Clause empowers Congress to enact legislation that would otherwise be beyond the scope of Article I. The reference to *Holland* in the text should be understood as a reference to the first point.

58. Restatement (Second), § 141(1).

59. Restatement (Second), § 141(2).

60. *See* Transcript of Conference (1955), at 95–110.

61. *Id.*, at 106.

62. *See* Chapter 5.

63. Preliminary Draft 5, § 3.04, cmt. c (emphasis added).

64. Preliminary Draft 5, § 3.04.

65. Preliminary Draft 5, § 3.04, cmt. a (emphasis added).

66. *See* Chapter 3, pp. 48–50 (discussing *Ware v. Hylton*); Chapter 5, pp. 85–95 (reviewing cases decided between 1800 and 1945); Chapter 12, pp. 258–63 (reviewing cases decided between 1945 and 1965).

67. *See* Council Draft 4, § 124, cmt. c; Tentative Draft 3, § 124, cmt. c.

68. Proposed Official Draft, § 144.

69. *See supra* note 13.

70. Fisher worked at the *Washington Post* from 1955 to 1961. Throughout that period, Goodrich complained about Fisher's failure to communicate. *See, e.g.,* Goodrich to Fisher, Nov. 21, 1955, ALI Archives, Box 17, Folder 5 (referring to Fisher's "sphinx-like silence"); Dickinson to Goodrich, Oct. 2, 1956, ALI Archives, Box 16, Folder 10 ("Has your office had any word of late from Fisher?"); Goodrich to Dickinson, Oct. 8, 1956, ALI Archives, Box 16, Folder 10 ("Fisher is not a person who gives you a whole lot of letters"); Goodrich to Dickinson, Jan. 9, 1961, ALI Archives, Box 16, Folder 17 (complaining that Fisher "does not get around to using the mail very much).

71. *See* Council Draft 4, § 124; Council Draft 5, § 140; Tentative Draft 3, §§ 124, 137.

72. Cook v. United States, 288 U.S. 105 (1933) (seizure of vessel at sea, discussed in Chapter 7, pp. 138–40); Johnson v. Browne, 205 U.S. 309 (1907) (habeas petition brought by prisoner who had been extradited from Canada to the United States to be punished for a federal offense); Ribas y Hijo v. United States, 194 U.S. 315 (1904) (suit against the United States seeking compensation for use of merchant vessel seized by U.S. military); United States v. Lee Yen Tai, 185 U.S. 213 (1902) (Chinese immigration, cited in Chapter 7); Whitney v. Robertson, 124 U.S. 190 (1888) (import duties, discussed in Chapter 7, pp. 134–35); United States v. Percheman, 32 U.S. 51 (1833) (title to land in Florida, discussed in Chapter 4); Foster v. Neilson, 27 U.S. 253 (1829) (title to land in Louisiana, discussed in Chapter 4); Robertson v. General Electric Co., 32 F.2d 495 (4th Cir. 1929) (patent case, discussed in Chapter 8, pp. 164–65).

73. Fujii v. State, 242 P.2d 617 (Cal. 1952).

74. Bacardi Corp. v. Domenech, 311 U.S. 150 (1940) (discussed in Chapter 5, pp. 87–88); Santovincenzo v. Egan, 284 U.S. 30 (1931) (holding that treaty with Italy required distribution of decedent's assets to Italian consul, and reversing decision of New York state court ordering that the balance of estate be paid into the

New York City treasury); Asakura v. City of Seattle, 265 U.S. 332 (1924) (discussed in Chapter 5, pp. 87–88); Chirac v. Chirac, 15 U.S. 259 (1817) (cited in Chapter 5); Ware v. Hylton, 3 U.S. 199 (1796) (discussed in Chapter 3, pp. 48–50).

75. See pp. 269–70.
76. See Report on Foreign Relations Law Project (1955), at 29–30; Agenda for Discussion (1955), at 33–34.
77. Id., at 33; Report on Foreign Relations Law Project (1955), at 30.
78. Id.; see also Agenda for Discussion (1955), at 33–34.
79. Preliminary Draft 5, § 4.09, cmt. b.
80. See Chapter 6, pp. 114–22.
81. See Chapter 10, pp. 220–23.
82. Preliminary Draft 5, § 4.09, cmt. b.
83. See Council Draft 5, § 140, cmt. b; Tentative Draft 3, § 137, cmt. b; Proposed Official Draft, § 157, cmt. b.
84. Preliminary Draft 5, § 4.09, cmt. a.
85. See Council Draft 5, § 140, cmt. a; Tentative Draft 3, § 137, cmt. a; Proposed Official Draft, § 157, cmt. a.
86. See 1 Jennings & Watts (1992) § 21; 2 Hyde (1922) § 523; id. § 524 n.4 (citing eighteenth and nineteenth century authorities).
87. See Chapter 10, pp. 202–03.
88. The final version of the Restatement says that "an international agreement may involve a commitment by the parties that its provisions will be effective under the domestic law of the parties at the time it goes into effect." Restatement (Second), § 154, cmt. a.
89. Restatement (Second), § 154(2).
90. See Chapter 6, pp. 114–22. When the Senate consented to ratification of the Genocide Convention in 1986, it adopted a declaration specifying that "the President will not deposit the instrument of ratification until after the implementing legislation referred to in Article V [of the Convention] has been enacted." 132 Cong. Rec. S1378 (1986).
91. The term "dualist," as used here, refers to a domestic legal system in which no treaties have domestic legal force in the absence of implementing legislation. For further discussion of the distinction between monist and dualist legal systems, see Sloss, Domestic Application (2012). With respect to Canada and the United Kingdom, see Van Ert (2009) (Canada), and Aust (2009) (United Kingdom).
92. See Nollkaemper (2009).
93. See Sloss, Madison's Monster (2016) (discussing the Supreme Court's reliance on fictitious intent in Medellín v. Texas, 552 U.S. 491 (2008), and presenting a detailed critique of the fictitious intent doctrine).
94. For a summary of different versions of the one-step approach, see Tables Eight and Nine, pp. 292 and 296. For analysis of judicial opinions on self-execution after 1965, see Sloss, United States (2009).
95. See Chapter 11, pp. 253–55.
96. See Goodman & Jinks (2013), at 4, 26, 153.
97. See 5 Hackworth; 14 Whiteman.
98. 5 Hackworth § 488, at 177–85.
99. In the section on self-execution, Hackworth also discusses a U.S. Supreme Court decision holding that a multilateral trademark treaty trumped a Puerto Rican

statute regulating the use of trademarks for liquor. Inasmuch as the Puerto Rican government is a local government subordinate to the United States, the relationship between treaties and Puerto Rican law is similar to the relationship between treaties and state law. However, as a formal matter, the treaty supremacy rule does not address local Puerto Rican law because Puerto Rico is not a state.

100. 5 Hackworth § 487, at 174–75.
101. 14 Whiteman § 28, at 298.
102. *See id.*, § 28, at 299–302.
103. *Id.*, § 29, at 302.
104. *Id.*, § 29, at 303.
105. Wright (1922); Hyde (1922).
106. Henkin (1972).
107. 2 Hyde (1922), at 55.
108. *Id.*, at 58
109. *See id.*, at 51–54.
110. Wright (1922), at 154.
111. *See, e.g., id.*, at 90–91 ("in no case has a clear treaty provision been superseded by the state law. On the contrary, state statutes of this character have frequently been declared void when conflicting with clear treaty provisions."); *id.*, at 129 ("state judges are expressly enjoined to observe treaties as the supreme law of the land"); *id.*, at 161–62 ("If a state law disregards a treaty it is void. The courts both federal and state are obliged to apply treaties … "); *id.*, at 175 (noting that courts "refuse to apply state constitutions and statutes in conflict with treaty"). Wright's treatise indicates that the political question doctrine, not self-execution doctrine, is the key limitation on the judicial duty to apply treaties. *See id.*, at 172–74.
112. *See id.*, at 228–29 (noting that Congress has insisted that treaties requiring a modification of the tariff system are not self-executing); *id.*, at 353–56 (analyzing the types of treaties that have traditionally been considered to be non-self-executing).
113. *See id.*, at 74–75 (noting that "self-executing treaties have limited state power without congressional action"); *id.*, at 206–08 (discussing the distinction between self-executing and non-self-executing treaties).
114. Wright (1919), at 263–64.
115. *See* Henkin (1972), at 156–61.
116. *See id.*, at 156–58.
117. Henkin published a second edition in 1996. In the second edition, Henkin made some effort to divorce the treaty supremacy rule from self-execution doctrine. *See* Henkin (1996), at 198–204.
118. Dickinson (1929); Hudson (1936).
119. *See* Dickinson (1929), at 1053–70.
120. Foster v. Neilson, 27 U.S. 253 (1829) (discussed in Chapter 4); United States v. Schooner Peggy, 5 U.S. 103 (1801); The Pictonian, 3 F.2d 145 (E.D.N.Y. 1924); Asakura v. City of Seattle, 265 U.S. 332 (1924) (discussed in Chapter 5, pp. 87–88); The Head Money Cases, 112 U.S. 580 (1884) (discussed in Chapter 7, pp. 132–34).

121. Dickinson inserted this parenthetical comment: "Only so much of the opinion is reproduced as deals with the argument that the [federal statute] was invalid because inconsistent with prior treaties." Dickinson (1929), at 1068.

122. *Id.*, at 1068 n.30 (citing Crandall (1916) and *Ware v. Hylton*).

123. *See* Chapter 8, pp. 154–57 for discussion of bilateral liquor treaties.

124. *See Schooner Peggy*, 5 U.S. at 109–10 (quoted in Dickinson (1929), at 1059–60) ("The constitution of the United States declares a treaty to be the supreme law of the land. Of consequence its obligation on the courts of the United States must be admitted. . . . [W]here a treaty is the law of the land, and as such affects the rights of parties litigating in court, that treaty as much binds those rights and is as much to be regarded by the court as an act of congress.").

125. *See* Hudson (1936), at 843–84.

126. People v. Gerke, 5 Cal. 381 (CA 1855) (discussed in Chapter 5, p. 94); Milliken v. Stone, 16 F.2d 981 (2d Cir. 1927); Missouri v. Holland, 252 U.S. 416 (1920); Davis v. Police Jury, 50 U.S. 280 (1850) (cited in Chapter 7); Haver v. Yaker, 76 U.S. 32 (1870); Taylor v. Morton, 23 F. Cas. 784 (C.C.D. Mass. 1855) (cited in Chapter 7); Robertson v. General Electric Co., 32 F.2d 495 (4th Cir. 1929) (discussed in Chapter 8, pp. 164–65).

127. Davis v. Police Jury, 50 U.S. 280 (1850).

128. Haver v. Yaker, 76 U.S. 32, 34–35 (1870) (reproduced in Hudson (1936), at 865–67).

129. Taylor v. Morton, 23 F. Cas. 784 (C.C.D. Mass. 1855).

130. Missouri v. Holland, 252 U.S. 416 (1920).

131. In *Milliken v. Stone*, 16 F.2d 981 (2d Cir. 1927), plaintiffs sought to enjoin enforcement of the bilateral liquor treaty between the United States and Great Britain on the grounds that the treaty was unconstitutional. The court dismissed the claim because "[a] court of equity will not give injunctive relief of this character, unless it be to protect property rights against injuries otherwise irremediable. . . . The averments of this bill fail to show the existence of any proprietary right in the appellants suffering an irremediable injury." *Id.*, at 983 (reproduced in Hudson (1936), at 855–56).

132. People v. Gerke, 5 Cal. 381 (CA 1855).

133. *Taylor v. Morton* addresses self-execution obliquely. Justice Curtis said that the treaty "addresses itself, exclusively, to the legislative power. It is a rule of their action, and not of the action of courts of justice." Taylor v. Morton, 23 F. Cas. 784, 787 (C.C.D. Mass. 1855) (reproduced in Hudson (1936), at 879–84). However, the main holding of *Taylor* is that a later-enacted treaty takes precedence over a prior conflicting statute.

134. *Robertson*, 32 F.2d at 500. *See* Chapter 8, pp. 164–65 for additional analysis of *Robertson*.

135. *See, e.g.*, Bishop (1971); Chayes, Ehrlich & Lowenfeld (1969).

136. Friedmann, Lissitzyn & Pugh (1969); Leech, Oliver & Sweeney (1973).

137. *See* Letter from Leech to Goodrich, June 6, 1961, ALI Archives, Box 16, Folder 17; Letter from Goodrich to Leech, Nov. 27, 1961, ALI Archives, Box 16, Folder 20; Leech Comments on Tentative Draft 3, Feb. 5, 1962, ALI Archives, Box 12, Folder 2.

138. *See* Friedmann, Lissitzyn & Pugh (1969), at 359–64.

139. 197 F. Supp. 230 (S.D. Fla. 1961).

140. *See* Chapter 12, p. 265.
141. *See* Leech, Oliver & Sweeney (1973), at 929–1033.
142. *See id.*, at 1024–33.
143. 265 U.S. 332 (1924).
144. *See* Chapter 12.
145. 501 F. Supp. 544 (S.D. Tex. 1980).
146. *Id.*, at 589.
147. *Id.*, at 590.
148. Part of the court's opinion could be construed as an application of the justiciability doctrine. *See id.*, at 589–90.

PART 4

1. 552 U.S. 491 (2008).
2. The eight versions of NSE doctrine referenced here do not include the contract doctrine because that variant of NSE doctrine effectively disappeared after about 1930.
3. Bradley (2008).
4. *See especially* Balkin (2011); Balkin & Siegel (2006); Siegel (2006).
5. *See*, e.g., Siegel (2006); Strauss (2001), at 1476–78; Dorf (2002), at 984–85.

CHAPTER 14

1. 552 U.S. 491 (2008).
2. The constitutional doctrine is addressed in Chapter 3, pp. 54–56 and Chapter 6, pp. 108–13. The condition precedent doctrine is covered in Chapter 6, pp. 122–23, and the justiciability doctrine is addressed in Chapter 7, pp. 132–34. The intent doctrine is covered in Chapter 8, pp. 157–62. The *Fujii* doctrine is discussed in Chapters 10, 11, and 13.
3. *See* pp. 6–8 for a more detailed explanation of these three concepts.
4. I use the term "allocation-of-powers," rather than the more familiar "separation-of-powers," because modern NSE doctrine implicates the division of power between state and federal governments, as well as the division of power among the three branches of the federal government.
5. *See* pp. 61–63 for a more detailed explanation of the one-step and two-step approaches.
6. *See*, e.g., Touche Ross & Co. v. Redington, 442 U.S. 560, 578 (1979); Cort v. Ash, 422 U.S. 66, 78 (1975); *see also* Fallon et al. (2009), at 705–08.
7. Tel-Oren v. Libyan Arab Republic, 726 F.2d 774, 808 (D.C. Cir. 1984) (Bork, J., concurring); *see also* Mannington Mills, Inc. v. Congoleum Corp., 595 F.2d 1287, 1298 (3d Cir. 1979) ("Thus, unless a treaty is self-executing, it must be implemented by legislation before it gives rise to a private cause of action.").
8. *See* Vázquez (1992), at 1143–57.
9. 19 U.S.C. § 3312(c) (2015) (emphasis added).
10. 19 U.S.C. § 3312(b)(2) (2015).
11. 19 U.S.C. § 3512 (2015).
12. These include bilateral agreements with Australia, Bahrain, Chile, Jordan, Morocco, Oman, Peru, and Singapore, as well as a multilateral agreement with the Dominican Republic and Central American states. *See* 19 U.S.C. § 4012 (2015)

(implementing legislation for agreement with Dominican Republic and Central American states); 19 U.S.C. § 2112 (2015) (implementing legislation for agreement with Jordan); 19 U.S.C. § 3805 (2015) (implementing legislation for agreements with Australia, Bahrain, Chile, Morocco, Oman, Peru, and Singapore).

13. Protocol on Prohibitions or Restrictions on the Use of Incendiary Weapons, S. Treaty Doc. 105-1(B) (resolution of ratification at 154 Cong. Rec. 20171). *See also infra* pp. 308–09 (discussing other treaties with similar declarations).

14. An alternative construction of these "no private enforcement" provisions is possible. Under this view, the statutory provisions are based on Congress's power to interpret the underlying international agreements, and the declarations attached to Article II treaties are based on the treaty makers' power to interpret treaties. Hence, the declarations and statutory provisions express an opinion that, as a matter of treaty interpretation, the agreements do not create primary rights for individuals. As the treaties do not create primary rights for individuals, individual claims based on those treaties are non-justiciable. If this view is correct, then the declarations and statutory provisions do not presuppose an affirmative power to restrict judicial enforcement of otherwise justiciable treaty provisions. Instead, they presuppose that both Congress and the treaty makers have an affirmative power to interpret international agreements. Under this construction, though, the judiciary would presumably not be bound by any interpretive statement adopted by the political branches.

15. *See* Vázquez (1995), at 710–15.

16. Bradley (2008).

17. *See* Restatement (Fourth): Treaties, Discussion Draft (Apr. 2015).

18. In fact, the Supreme Court has never held that Article I grants Congress the power to opt out of the federal supremacy rule in this manner. *See* Chapter 8, pp. 171–72; *see also* Sloss, *Treaty Preemption Defense* (2009), at 983–86. However, commentators have mistakenly construed the Court's preemption doctrine to support this proposition, and have defended NSE doctrine on this basis. *See, e.g.,* Bradley & Goldsmith (2000), at 447.

19. Restatement (Second), Preliminary Draft 5, § 3.04, cmt. c.

20. Restatement (Second), § 141.

21. U.S. Const. art. VI, cl. 2.

22. *See, e.g.,* City of Boerne v. Flores, 521 U.S. 507, 516–20 (1997).

23. *See* Part One.

24. *See* Part Two.

25. Youngstown Sheet & Tube Co. v. Sawyer (Steel Seizure), 343 U.S. 579, 610–11 (1952) (Frankfurter, J., concurring).

26. U.N. Doc. E/CN.4/224 (23 May 1949).

27. *See* Chapter 11, p. 254.

28. S. Rep. 412, at 41–42 (minority views).

29. 100 Cong. Rec. 2200, 2204 (Feb. 24, 1954) (statements by Senator George).

30. FRUS, v.1, at 1833–34 (letter from the president to John J. McCloy, Jan. 13, 1954).

31. *See* Chapter 10, pp. 220–23.

32. *See* Treaties and Executive Agreements: Hearings Before a Subcommittee of the Committee on the Judiciary (1953), at 244–46 (report submitted by New York City Bar Association).

33. *See* Chapter 5 (documenting support for both elements of the traditional treaty supremacy rule).
34. *See* Chapter 11, pp. 248–50.
35. Restatement (Second), sec. 141, cmt. a.
36. 14 Whiteman § 29, at 302. *See also* Chapter 13, pp. 284–87.
37. *See* Henkin (1972), at 157.
38. Convention on the Rights of the Child, Nov. 20, 1989, art. 37(a).
39. 132 S. Ct. 2455 (2012).
40. *See* p. 307.
41. Boddie v. Connecticut, 401 U.S. 371, 379 (1971). This paragraph is copied almost verbatim from Sloss, *Treaty Preemption Defense* (2009), at 988–89.
42. *See* Bouie v. City of Columbia, 378 U.S. 347, 354 (1964).
43. *Boddie*, 401 U.S. at 377 (quoting Hovey v. Ellliott, 167 U.S. 409, 417 (1897)).
44. *Boddie*, 401 U.S. at 377.
45. 321 U.S. 414 (1944).
46. *Id.*, at 430.
47. *Id.*, at 428.
48. *See id.*, at 427–29 (describing statutory scheme).
49. *Id.*, at 446.
50. 481 U.S. 828, 838 n.15 (1987).
51. *Id.*, at 837–38.
52. 330 U.S. 386, 393–94 (1947).
53. 135 S. Ct. 1378, 1383 (2015).
54. *Id.*, at 1384.
55. The material in this section draws heavily on Sloss, *Madison's Monster* (2016).
56. *See* S. Exec. Rep. 112-6 (2012), at 121–24 (listing treaties for which the Senate resolution of advice and consent includes an NSE declaration).
57. S. Exec. Rep. 103-29 (1994), at 26. *See also* S. Exec. Rep. 112-6 (2012), at 14 (stating that implementing legislation is not necessary because "current United States law fulfills or exceeds the obligations of the Convention").
58. International Human Rights Treaties: Hearings Before the Committee on Foreign Relations (1979), at 40–41 (prepared statement of Jack M. Goldklang, attorney adviser in the Department of Justice).
59. S. Exec. Docs. C, D, E and F, 95-2 (1978).
60. *Id.*, at vi.
61. International Human Rights Treaties: Hearings Before the Committee on Foreign Relations (1979), at 29 (statement of Roberts B. Owen).
62. 132 Cong. Rec. S1378 (1986).
63. S. Exec. Rep. 99-2 (1985), at 26 (emphasis added).
64. *See* Chapter 6, pp. 122–23 (discussing the condition precedent doctrine).
65. 138 Cong. Rec. S4783–84 (1992).
66. The Senate consented to ratification of the Convention Against Torture in 1990, subject to an NSE declaration. However, the United States did not ratify that treaty until 1994.
67. S. Exec. Rep. 102-23 (1992), at 19.
68. *See* Sloss (1999) (providing a detailed defense of the "private right of action" interpretation of NSE declarations attached to human rights treaties).
69. *See* S. Exec. Rep. 112-6 (2012), at 121–24.

70. *See* 154 Cong. Rec. 20166–74; 154 Cong. Rec. 21775–78; 154 Cong Rec. 22464–65.

71. 552 U.S. 491 (2008).

72. *See* 1992 Partial Revision of the Radio Regulations, S. Treaty Doc. 107-17 (resolution of ratification at 154 Cong. Rec. 20170–71); 1995 Revision of the Radio Regulations, S. Treaty Doc. 108-28 (resolution of ratification at 154 Cong. Rec. 20171); Land-Based Sources Protocol to the Cartagena Convention, S. Treaty Doc. 110-1 (resolution of ratification at 154 Cong. Rec. 21776); 1998 Amendments to the Constitution and the Convention of the International Telecommunication Union, S. Treaty Doc. 108-5 (resolution of ratification at 154 Cong. Rec. 21778); 2002 Amendments to the Constitution and the Convention of the International Telecommunication Union, S. Treaty Doc. 109-11 (resolution of ratification at 154 Cong. Rec. 21778); 2006 Amendments to the Constitution and the Convention of the International Telecommunication Union, S. Treaty Doc. 110-16 (resolution of ratification at 154 Cong. Rec. 21778); International Convention on the Control of Harmful Anti-Fouling Systems on Ships, S. Treaty Doc. 110-13 (resolution of ratification at 154 Cong. Rec. 22465).

73. *See* 154 Cong. Rec. 20166–74; 154 Cong. Rec. 21775–78; 154 Cong Rec. 22464–65. The two treaties for which the Senate did not adopt either an SE declaration or an NSE declaration are: Protocol to the North Atlantic Treaty of 1949 on the Accession of the Republic of Albania, S. Treaty Doc. 110-20 (resolution of ratification at 154 Cong. Rec. 21777); Protocol to the North Atlantic Treaty of 1949 on the Accession of the Republic of Croatia, S. Treaty Doc. 110-20 (resolution of ratification at 154 Cong. Rec. 21777).

74. Protocol on Prohibitions or Restrictions on the Use of Incendiary Weapons, S. Treaty Doc. 105-1(B) (resolution of ratification at 154 Cong. Rec. 20171) (emphasis added). *See also* Protocol on Blinding Laser Weapons, S. Treaty Doc. 105-1(C) (resolution of ratification at 154 Cong. Rec. 20171); Amendment to Article 1 of Convention on Conventional Weapons, S. Treaty Doc. 109-10(B) (resolution of ratification at 154 Cong. Rec. 20171).

75. International Convention for the Suppression of Acts of Nuclear Terrorism, S. Treaty Doc. 110-4 (resolution of ratification at 154 Cong. Rec. 21776–77) (emphasis added). *See also* Hague Convention for the Protection of Cultural Property in the Event of Armed Conflict, S. Treaty Doc. 106-1(A) (resolution of ratification at 154 Cong. Rec. 21776); Amendment to the Convention on the Physical Protection of Nuclear Material, S. Treaty Doc. 110-6 (resolution of ratification at 154 Cong. Rec. 21776); 2005 Fixed Platforms Protocol, S. Treaty Doc. 110-8 (resolution of ratification at 154 Cong. Rec. 21777); Protocol on Explosive Remnants of War, S. Treaty Doc. 109-10(C) (resolution of ratification at 154 Cong. Rec. 22464–65).

76. *See* treaties cited in two previous notes.

77. An early draft of the ALI's Restatement (Fourth) on Treaties claims that one of the eight key declarations—the one attached to the Hague Convention on Cultural Property—shows only that the Senate rejected the "private right of action" version of SE doctrine. *See* Restatement (Fourth): Treaties, Discussion Draft (Apr. 2015) § 106, n.4. With due respect for the Reporters, that claim is not plausible. None of the eight declarations uses the term "private right of action." All eight say that the treaties are not "enforceable in United States courts." The statement that the treaties are not enforceable in courts, combined with the statement that

the treaties are partially or wholly self-executing, demonstrates clearly that the
Senate understood self-execution in terms of the congressional-executive concept, not the political-judicial concept.

78. Convention on the Rights of Persons with Disabilities, S. Treaty Doc.
    112-7, at 2.

79. S. Exec. Rep. 112-6 (2012), at 14; *see also* S. Exec. Rep. 113-12 (2014), at 23 (re-
    peating the identical language).

80. Here, I assume that the statement that a treaty "does not supersede conflict-
    ing state laws" is equivalent to a statement that it is not "the supreme Law of
    the Land."

81. 552 U.S. 491 (2008).

82. *See* Vázquez (2008) (defending the first interpretation); Bradley (2008) (defend-
    ing the third interpretation).

83. *See Ex parte* Medellín, 223 S.W.3d 315, 321 (Tex. Crim. App. 2006).

84. *Id.*, at 321–22.

85. Avena and other Mexican Nationals (Mex. v. U.S.), 2004 I.C.J. 1 (Mar. 31).

86. *See id.*, ¶¶ 128–41, 153.

87. *Medellín*, 552 U.S. at 503.

88. *Ex parte* Medellín, 223 S.W.3d 315, 323 (Tex. Ct. Crim. App. 2006).

89. Tex. Code Crim. Pro, art. 11.071, § 5(a)(1) (emphasis added).

90. *Medellín*, 223 S.W.3d at 348–52.

91. *Medellín*, 552 U.S. at 504–23.

92. *Id.*, at 523–32.

93. In his brief to the Supreme Court, the Texas solicitor general argued that Texas
    courts had already provided the judicial hearing mandated by *Avena*. *See* Brief
    for Respondent, Medellín v. Texas, at 49–50. However, Texas devoted only one
    page of a fifty-page brief to supporting this argument. *See id.* Moreover, the
    Supreme Court did not rely on this argument to support its decision in *Medellín*,
    and Medellín himself vigorously denied that he had received the required judi-
    cial hearing. *See* Brief for Petitioner, Medellín v. Texas, at 12–15.

94. U.N. Charter, art. 94.

95. *Medellín*, 552 U.S. at 508.

96. *Id.*, at 510.

97. *Id.*, at 511.

98. *See* Vázquez (2008), at 660–67.

99. *See Medellín*, 552 U.S. at 511 (describing the decision "whether and how to
    comply with an ICJ judgment" as a "sensitive foreign policy decision" that is
    best left to "the political branches").

100. *Id.*, at 504.

101. *Id.*, at 508.

102. *Id.*, at 536 (Stevens, J., concurring).

103. *See, e.g.*, International Court of Justice, Written Observations of the United
    States of America on the Application for Interpretation of the Judgment of
    31 March 2004 in the *Case Concerning Avena and Other Mexican Nationals
    (Mexico v. United States of America)* (Aug. 29, 2008), at 1–2; Bradley (2008),
    at 169–71.

104. *See* Vázquez (2008), at 666–67.

105. *Medellín*, 552 U.S. at 505 n.2.
106. *Id.*, at 505 (quoting Igartua de la Rosa v. United States, 417 F.3d 145, 150 (1st Cir. 2005)).
107. *Id.*, at 504.
108. *Id.*, at 508–09.
109. *Id.*, at 513.
110. Bradley (2008), at 173–76.
111. *Id.*, at 173.
112. *Medellín*, 552 U.S. at 527.
113. *Id.*, at 525–26.
114. *Id.*, at 526.
115. *See id.*, at 532 (stating that the president's constitutional authority under the Take Care Clause "allows the President to execute the laws, not make them").
116. *Id.*, at 527.
117. *See id.*, at 533–37 (Stevens, J., concurring).
118. *See* Sloss, *Madison's Monster* (2016), at 1721–33.
119. *See id.*, at 1722–33 (reviewing the Senate record associated with ratification of the U.N. Charter).
120. 19 U.S.C. § 3312(c) (2015) (emphasis added).
121. 19 U.S.C. § 3312(b)(2) (2015).
122. The statement in the text assumes that NAFTA is federal law. That claim is contestable; I have defended the claim in detail elsewhere. *See* Sloss, *Treaty Preemption Defense* (2009), at 979–83.
123. *See* p. 298.
124. *See* pp. 308–09.
125. *See* pp. 303–06 (analyzing a similar NJE declaration).
126. United States v. Mendoza-Lopez, 481 U.S. 828, 838 n.15 (1987).
127. The NPE declaration might be construed to bar a suit against the DOJ under the APA. The declaration says that "no private party may invoke the treaty as the basis for a claim or defense." In this APA action, the Florida defendant-turned-federal-plaintiff would presumably argue that he is not invoking the treaty as the basis for his claim. Rather, he might say, the basis for his claim is the DOJ's refusal to file suit, despite its authority to do so, and despite its duty to enforce federal law.
128. 5 U.S.C. § 702 (2015).
129. 5 U.S.C. § 706(2)(A) (2015). In addition, the individual would have to overcome several other procedural hurdles to win an APA claim against the DOJ. *See* Jinks & Sloss (2004), at 192–93 (analyzing use of the APA as a procedural mechanism to enforce the Geneva Conventions).
130. Even assuming that the NPE declaration would satisfy constitutional due process standards as applied to a state prosecution, it would probably not satisfy due process standards as applied to a federal prosecution, unless Congress creates some administrative mechanism that allows a federal defendant to challenge the validity of the federal criminal law that is being used to prosecute him. The APA is probably not an "adequate" mechanism in this context because the APA does not permit a federal criminal defendant to challenge the federal prosecutor's decision to prosecute him.
131. *See* pp. 298, 308–09.

132. *See* pp. 308–09.
133. *See* Sloss, *Madison's Monster* (2016), at 1736–40 (recommending clarification of terminology associated with NSE declarations).

CHAPTER 15

1. U.S. CONST. art V.
2. *See* Ackerman (1998) (analyzing the New Deal revolution); Ackerman (2014) (analyzing the civil rights revolution).
3. *See* Strauss (1996).
4. *See, e.g.,* Balkin & Siegel (2006), Siegel (2006).
5. *See, e.g.,* Balkin (2011); Strauss (2010); Kramer (2004).
6. *See* Chapter 5.
7. *See* Medellín v. Texas, 552 U.S. 491 (2008); *see also* Chapter 14, pp. 310–16 (analyzing *Medellín*).
8. 27 U.S. 253 (1829). *See* Chapter 4 (analyzing *Foster*).
9. *See* Kramer, *Interest of Man* (2006), at 699–701; Siegel (2006), at 1352–58.
10. Siegel (2006). For other scholarly accounts of the de facto ERA, see Strauss (2001), at 1476–78; Dorf (2002), at 984–85.
11. Siegel (2006), at 1327.
12. Balkin & Siegel (2006), at 928–29.
13. Siegel (2006), at 1367–69.
14. *See* Chapters 9 and 10.
15. Fujii v. California, 217 P.2d 481 (Cal. App. 2d 1950) (discussed in Chapter 10, pp. 208–13).
16. *See* Chapters 10 and 11.
17. *See* Balkin & Siegel (2006), at 949 ("Successful social movements almost always produce countermobilizations that arise to contest them.")
18. Siegel (2006), at 1378.
19. *See id.,* at 1389–1402.
20. *See* Chapter 11, p. 248; Tananbaum (1988), at 175–90; Caro (2002), at 519–41.
21. *See* Chapters 10 and 11.
22. Siegel (2006), at 1365.
23. *Id.,* at 1403.
24. West (2006), at 1471.
25. *See* Siegel (2006), at 1403–09.
26. Brown v. Bd. of Educ., 347 U.S. 483 (1954). *See* Chapter 11, pp. 240–48 (analyzing *Brown* as a human rights case).
27. Henkin (1995).
28. 97 Cong. Rec. 8263 (July 17, 1951) (statement of Senator Bricker).
29. *See* Henkin (1995).
30. United States v. Pink, 315 U.S. 203 (1942); United States v. Belmont, 301 U.S. 324 (1937). *See* Chapter 11, pp. 248–50; Tananbaum (1988).
31. Missouri v. Holland, 252 U.S. 416 (1920). *See* Chapter 11, pp. 248–50; Tananbaum (1988). In *Bond v. United States*, 134 S. Ct. 2077 (2014), petitioner tried to persuade the Court to overrule *Holland* by construing the Constitution in a manner consistent with the revised Constitution that would have resulted if the ABA's proposed version of the Bricker Amendment had succeeded. Justices Scalia and

Thomas were prepared to overrule *Holland*, but the majority refused to do so. *See* Sloss (2015), at 1595–1602 (analyzing the relationship between *Bond* and the Bricker Amendment).

32. *See* Siegel (2006), at 1389–98.
33. During the Bricker debates, Quincy Wright was the only important voice speaking out in defense of the traditional treaty supremacy rule, but he had very little impact on the political debate, despite his standing as the leading scholar of U.S. foreign relations law. For a discussion of Wright's defense of the traditional treaty supremacy rule, see Chapter 10, pp. 213–15.
34. 75 Ann. Rep. A.B.A. 102, 119 (1950) (statement of Harold Stassen). *See* Chapter 10, pp. 219–21. *See also* Kaufman (1990).
35. Recall that Bricker and his allies sought to accomplish three distinct goals. They wanted to overrule *Missouri v. Holland*, overrule *Belmont* and *Pink*, and abolish the treaty supremacy rule. *See* Chapter 11, pp. 248–49. Bricker's opponents argued that amendments designed to accomplish the first two goals would be dangerous. However, with respect to the third goal, they argued instead that an amendment was unnecessary.
36. Schlafly and STOP ERA also argued that the ERA was unnecessary, but they did not make that argument until after the Supreme Court had begun to incorporate elements of the women's movements claims into its equal protection jurisprudence. *See* Siegel (2006), at 1403–406.
37. *See* Chapter 10, pp. 220–23; Chapter 11, pp. 250–55.
38. On the "settlement function" of law, see Alexander and Schauer (2000), at 467–78; Alexander and Schauer (1997), at 1371–81.
39. *See* Siegel (2006), at 1403–09. Leading Supreme Court decisions include Reed v. Reed, 404 U.S. 71 (1971); Frontiero v. Richardson, 411 U.S. 677 (1973); Weinberger v. Wiesenfeld, 420 U.S. 636 (1975); Craig v. Boren, 429 U.S. 190 (1976); and Califano v. Goldfarb, 430 U.S. 199 (1977).
40. *See* Chapter 11, p. 254.
41. *See* Chapter 12.
42. *See* Chapter 13.
43. 552 U.S. 491 (2008).
44. *See* Chapter 4.
45. Kramer (2004).
46. Cooper v. Aaron, 358 U.S. 1 (1958). *See* Kramer (2004), at 220–21.
47. *See* Chapter 10, pp. 220–23; Chapter 11, pp. 250–55; Chapter 13, pp. 276–80 (explaining this process in detail).
48. *See* Table Three, p. 128; Table Six, p. 176.
49. West (2006), at 1476.
50. *See* Chapter 8, pp. 157–62.
51. *See* pp. 175–77 (explaining the evolution from nineteenth century doctrine to Dickinson's intent doctrine to the transformation of the treaty supremacy rule after World War II).
52. *See generally* Katyal (2006).
53. *See* Ingber (2013), at 397–403 (discussing speechmaking by senior executive officials as a catalyst for generating new legal positions within the executive branch).

54. *See, e.g.,* Hamdan v. Rumsfeld, 548 U.S. 557 (2006) (judicial review of executive branch action related to the war on terror); Hamdi v. Rumsfeld, 542 U.S. 507 (2004) (same).
55. *See, e.g.,* Vladeck (2015); Vázquez (2015); Bradley (2015).
56. *See, e.g.,* Fisher (2014).
57. Bradley (2014) (documenting an important change in the constitutional understanding that governs the allocation of power between Congress and the president with respect to treaty termination, and showing how the executive branch played the dominant role in the process of constitutional change).
58. *See generally* Ackerman (2014).
59. *See, e.g.,* Brown v. Bd. of Educ., 347 U.S. 483 (1954); Brown v. Allen, 344 U.S. 443 (1953).
60. Cooper (2007), at 7 (quoting, in part, Festinger (1957)).
61. Fujii v. California, 217 P.2d 481 (Cal. App. 2d 1950) (discussed in Chapter 10, pp. 208–13).
62. *See, e.g.,* Kramer, *Constitutional Meaning* (2006), at 1446 ("The near-sacred status of our Constitution . . . is by now a deep and well-established part of our political culture.").
63. *See* Ackerman (2014); Balkin (2011); Strauss (2010); Kramer (2004).
64. *See* Chapter 9, pp. 188–89; Anderson (2003).
65. *See* Chapters 9 and 10.
66. *See, e.g.,* Resnik (2010); Resnik (2006); *see also* Witt (2004).
67. *See* Ackerman (2014); Ackerman (1998); Kramer (2004).
68. *See* Chapters 10 and 11.
69. *See* Chapter 13.
70. *See* Balkin & Siegel (2006); Siegel (2006).
71. On this point, I tend to agree with Professor Ackerman's critique of Professor Siegel. *See* Ackerman (2006), at 1425, 1430–31 (distinguishing between "civic culture" and the "professional culture" of attorneys, and claiming that the "internal dynamic of the professional culture, not other aspects of the constitutional culture . . . served as the prime mover in the Court's decision to move forward on women's rights in the 1970s").
72. Livermore & Revesz (2013), at 1343.
73. *See* Chapters 9 to 11.
74. Kramer, *Interest of Man* (2006), at 697.
75. *See id.,* at 724–27 (explaining Madison's "representation-based alternative to Jefferson's direct popular constitutionalism"); *id.,* at 734–38 (explaining how "the people themselves" retain control of constitutional meaning through their elected representatives).
76. *See generally* Currie (2005); Currie (2001); Currie (1997). *See also* Chapter 3, pp. 51–57 (congressional deliberations on constitutional issues related to treaties in the 1790s); Chapter 6, pp. 108–13 (congressional deliberations on constitutional issues related to treaties in the nineteenth century).
77. *See generally* Wills (2010).
78. *See* Balkin (2011), chapters 13 and 14.
79. Balkin (2012), at 842.
80. *Id.*

Bibliography

BOOKS AND ARTICLES

Ackerman, Bruce. 1998. *We the People, Volume 2: Transformations.*

Ackerman, Bruce. 2006. Interpreting the Women's Movement, *California Law Review* 94: 1421.

Ackerman, Bruce. 2014. *We the People, Volume 3: The Civil Rights Revolution.*

Alexander, Larry and Frederick Schauer. 1997. On Extrajudicial Constitutional Interpretation. *Harvard Law Review* 110: 1359.

Alexander, Larry and Frederick Schauer. 2000. Defending Judicial Supremacy: A Reply. *Constitutional Commentary* 17: 455.

Alston, Philip. 1992. *The United Nations and Human Rights: A Critical Appraisal.*

Anderson, Carol. 2003. *Eyes off the Prize: The United Nations and the African American Struggle for Human Rights, 1944–1955.*

Anonymous author. 1919. Relation of Treaty to State and Federal Law. *American Law Reports* 4: 1377.

Anonymous author. 1941. Relation of Treaty to State and Federal Law. *American Law Reports* 134: 882.

Anonymous author. 1947. The Tangled Seine: A Survey of Maritime Personal Injury Remedies. *Yale Law Journal* 57: 243.

Anonymous author. 1950. Comment: U.N. Charter Invalidates Alien Land Law. *Stanford Law Review* 2: 797.

Anonymous author. 1961. Editorial Comment: Edwin D. Dickinson 1887–1961. *American Journal of International Law* 55: 637.

Aust, Anthony. 2009. United Kingdom, in *The Role of Domestic Courts in Treaty Enforcement: A Comparative Study* (David Sloss ed.).

Bailyn, Bernard, ed. (1993). *The Debate on the Constitution: Federalist and Antifederalist Speeches, Articles, and Letters during the Struggle over Ratification* (2 vols.).

Balkin, Jack M. 2011. *Living Originalism.*

Balkin, Jack M. 2012. Nine Perspectives on Living Originalism. 2012 *University of Illinois Law Review* 2012: 815.

Balkin, Jack M. and Reva D. Siegel. 2006. Principles, Practices, and Social Movements. *University of Pennsylvania Law Review* 154: 927.

Barrett, John Q. 2004. Supreme Court Law Clerks' Recollections of *Brown v. Board of Education*, *St. John's Law Review* 78: 515.

Bemis, Samuel Flagg. 1962. *Jay's Treaty: A Study in Commerce and Diplomacy* (2d ed.).

Bingham, Tom. 2005. The Alabama Claims Arbitration. *International and Comparative Law Quarterly* 54: 1.

Bishop, Jr., William W. 1971. *International Law: Cases and Materials* (3d ed.).

Blackstone, William. 1765–1769. *Commentaries on the Laws of England* (4 vols.).

Bourguignon, Henry J. 1977. *The First Federal Court: The Federal Appellate Prize Court of the American Revolution 1775–1787.*

Bradley, Curtis A. 1998. The Treaty Power and American Federalism. *Michigan Law Review* 97: 390.

Bradley, Curtis A. 2008. Self-Execution and Treaty Duality. *Supreme Court Review* 2008: 131.

Bradley, Curtis A. 2014. Treaty Termination and Historical Gloss. *Texas Law Review* 92: 773

Bradley, Curtis A. 2015. Foreign Relations Law and the Purported Shift away from Exceptionalism. *Harvard Law Review Forum* 128: 294.

Bradley, Curtis A. and Jack L. Goldsmith. 2000. Treaties, Human Rights, and Conditional Consent. *University of Pennsylvania Law Review* 149: 399.

Butler, Charles Henry. 1902. *The Treaty-Making Power of the United States* (2 vols.). .

Caro, Robert A. 2002. *The Years of Lyndon Johnson: Master of the Senate.*

Charnovitz, Steve. 2012. Correcting America's Continuing Failure to Comply with the *Avena* Judgment. *American Journal of International Law* 106: 572.

Chayes, Abram, Thomas Ehrlich, and Andreas F. Lowenfeld. 1969. *International Legal Process: Materials for an Introductory Course.*

Civil Rights Congress. 1951. *We Charge Genocide: The Historic Petition to the United Nations for Relief from a Crime of the United States Government against the Negro People.*

Cleveland, Sarah H. 2002. Powers Inherent in Sovereignty: Indians, Aliens, Territories, and the Nineteenth Century Origins of the Plenary Power over Foreign Affairs. *Texas Law Review* 81: 1.

Cleveland, Sarah H. and William S. Dodge. 2015. Defining and Punishing Offenses under Treaties, *Yale Law Journal* 124: 2202.

Combs, Jerald A. 1970. *The Jay Treaty: Political Battleground of the Founding Fathers.*

Cooper, Joel. 2007. *Cognitive Dissonance: Fifty Years of a Classic Theory*

Crandall, Samuel B. 1904. *Treaties: Their Making and Enforcement.*

Crandall, Samuel B. 1916. *Treaties: Their Making and Enforcement* (2d ed.).

Cummings, Homer and Carl McFarland. 1937. *Federal Justice: Chapters in the History of Justice and the Federal Executive.*

Currie, David P. 1997. *The Constitution in Congress: The Federalist Period, 1789–1801.*

Currie, David P. 2001. *The Constitution in Congress: The Jeffersonians, 1801–1829.*

Currie, David P. 2005. *The Constitution in Congress: Democrats and Whigs, 1829–1861.*

Dickinson, Edwin D. 1926. Are the Liquor Treaties Self-Executing? *American Journal of International Law* 20: 444.

Dickinson, Edwin D. 1926. Jurisdiction at the Maritime Frontier. *Harvard Law Review* 40: 1.

Dickinson, Edwin D. 1929. *A Selection of Cases and Other Readings on the Law of Nations, Chiefly as It Is Interpreted and Applied by British and American Courts* (1st ed.).

Dickson, Del. 2001. *The Supreme Court in Conference, 1940–1985: The Private Discussions behind Nearly 300 Supreme Court Decisions.*

Dorf, Michael C. 2002. Equal Protection Incorporation. *Virginia Law Review* 88: 951.

Dudziak, Mary L. 2000. *Cold War Civil Rights: Race and the Image of American Democracy.*

Elkins, Stanley and Eric McKitrick. 1993. *The Age of Federalism.*

Ellmann, Stephen. 2004. The Rule of Law and the Achievement of Unanimity in *Brown*. *New York Law School Law Review* 49: 741.

Fahy, Charles. 1948. Legal Aspects of the Work of the United Nations, *Illinois Law Review* 43: 135.

Fairman, Charles. 1952. Editorial Comment, Finis to *Fujii*. *American Journal of International Law* 46: 682.

Fallon, Richard H. et al. 2009. *Hart and Wechsler's the Federal Courts and the Federal System* (6th ed.).

Festinger, Leon. 1957. *A Theory of Cognitive Dissonance.*

Fisher, Louis. 2014. *Presidential War Power* (3d ed.).

Flaherty, Martin S. 1999. History Right?: Historical Scholarship, Original Understanding and Treaties as Supreme Law of the Land. *Columbia Law Review* 99: 2095.

Franck, Thomas M. 1990. *The Power of Legitimacy among Nations.*

Friedmann, Wolfgang, Oliver J. Lissitzyn, and Richard C. Pugh. 1969. *International Law: Cases and Materials.*

Galbraith, Jean. 2014. Congress's Treaty Implementing Power in Historical Practice. *William & Mary Law Review* 56: 59.

Gardbaum, Stephen A. 1994. The Nature of Preemption. *Cornell Law Review* 79: 767.

Glendon, Mary Ann. 2001. *A World Made New: Eleanor Roosevelt and the Universal Declaration of Human Rights.*

Golove, David M. 2000. Treaty-Making and the Nation: The Historical Foundations of the Nationalist Conception of the Treaty Power. *Michigan Law Review* 98: 1075.

Golove, David M. and Daniel J. Hulsebosch. 2010. A Civilized Nation: The Early American Constitution, the Law of Nations, and the Pursuit of International Recognition. *New York University Law Review* 85: 932.

Goodman, Ryan and Derek Jinks. 2013. *Socializing States: Promoting Human Rights through International Law.*

Goodrich, Herbert F. 1961. Edwin Dewitt Dickinson. *University of Pennsylvania Law Review* 109: 919.

Greenwald, Michael. 2009. *The Yale Biographical Dictionary of American Law.*

Hathaway, Oona A. 2008. Treaties' End: The Past, Present, and Future of International Lawmaking in the United States. *Yale Law Journal* 117: 1236.

Hathaway, Oona A. 2009. Presidential Power over International Law: Restoring the Balance. *Yale Law Journal* 119: 140.

Henkin, Louis. 1972. *Foreign Affairs and the Constitution.*

Henkin, Louis. 1995. U.S. Ratification of Human Rights Conventions: The Ghost of Senator Bricker. *American Journal of International Law* 89: 341.

Henkin, Louis. 1996. *Foreign Affairs and the United States Constitution* (2d ed.).

Herring, George C. 2008. *From Colony to Superpower: U.S. Foreign Relations since 1776.*

Hollis, Duncan B. 2006. Executive Federalism: Forging New Federalist Constraints on the Treaty Power. *Southern California Law Review* 79: 1327.

Hollis, Duncan B. 2008. Treaties—A Cinderella Story. *ASIL Proceeding* 102: 412.

Hollis, Duncan B. 2011. Treaties in the Supreme Court, 1861–1900, in *International Law in the U.S. Supreme Court: Continuity and Change* (David Sloss, Michael Ramsey, and William Dodge eds.).

Hollis, Duncan B. 2015. An Intersubjective Treaty Power. *Notre Dame Law Review* 90: 1415.

Hudson, Manley O. 1936. *Cases and Other Materials on International Law* (2d ed.).

Hudson, Manley O. 1948. Editorial Comment: Integrity of International Instruments. *American Journal of International Law* 42: 105.

Hudson, Manley O. 1950. Editorial Comment: Charter Provisions on Human Rights in American Law. *American Journal of International Law* 44: 543.

Humphrey, John P. 1984. *Human Rights and the United Nations: A Great Adventure.*

Hyde, Charles Cheney. 1922. *International Law, Chiefly as Interpreted and Applied by the United States* (2 vols.).

Ingber, Rebecca. 2013. Interpretation Catalysts and Executive Branch Legal Decisionmaking. *Yale Journal of International Law* 38: 359.

Janis, Mark Weston. 2004. *The American Tradition of International Law: Great Expectations, 1789–1914.*

Jennings, Sir Robert and Sir Arthur Watts. 1992. *Oppenheim's International Law* (9th ed.) (2 vols.).

Jinks, Derek and David Sloss. 2004. Is the President Bound by the Geneva Conventions?. *Cornell Law Review* 90: 97.

Katyal, Neal Kumar. 2006. Checking Today's Most Dangerous Branch from Within. *Yale Law Journal* 115: 2314.

Kaufman, Natalie Hevener. 1990. *Human Rights Treaties and the Senate: A History of Opposition.*

Keck, Margaret E. and Katheryn Sikkink. 1998. *Activists beyond Borders: Advocacy Networks in International Politics.*

Kesavan, Vasan. 2006. The Three Tiers of Federal Law. *Northwestern University Law Review* 100: 1479.

King, Andrew J., ed. 1989. Papers of Daniel Webster (vol. 3, pt. 2).

Klarman, Michael J. 2004. *From Jim Crow to Civil Rights: The Supreme Court and the Struggle for Racial Equality.*

Kluger, Richard. 1976. *Simple Justice: The History of* Brown v. Board of Education *and Black America's Struggle for Equality.*

Koh, Harold Hongju. 2012. The State Department Legal Advisor's Office: Eight Decades in Peace and War. *Georgetown Law Journal* 100: 1747.

Kramer, Larry D. 2004. *The People Themselves: Popular Constitutionalism and Judicial Review.*

Kramer, Larry D. 2006. "The Interest of Man": James Madison, Popular Constitutionalism, and the Theory of Deliberative Democracy, *Valparaiso University Law Review* 41: 697.

Kramer, Larry D. 2006. Generating Constitutional Meaning, *California Law Review* 94: 1439.

Ku, Julian G. 2004. The State of New York Does Exist: How the States Control Compliance with International Law. *North Carolina Law Review* 82: 457.

Ku, Julian G. 2005. Treaties as Laws: A Defense of the Last-in-Time Rule for Federal Statutes. *Indiana Law Journal* 80: 319.

Kunz, Josef L. 1949. The United Nations Declaration of Human Rights. *American Journal of International Law* 43: 316.

LaMoree, Janice Marion Wright. 1990. J. Marion Wright: Los Angeles' Patient Crusader, 1890–1970. *Southern California Quarterly* 72: 41.

Lee, Thomas H. and David L. Sloss. 2011. International Law as an Interpretive Tool in the Supreme Court, 1861–1900, in *International Law in the U.S. Supreme Court: Continuity and Change* (David Sloss, Michael Ramsey, and William Dodge eds.).

Leech, Noyes E. 1979. Covey Oliver. *University of Pennsylvania Law Review* 127: 882.

Leech, Noyes E., Covey T. Oliver, and Joseph Modeste Sweeney. 1973. *The International Legal System: Cases and Materials.*

Livermore, Michael A. and Richard L. Revesz. 2013. Regulatory Review, Capture, and Agency Inaction. *Georgetown Law Journal* 101: 1337.

Lockwood Jr., Bert B. 1984. The United Nations Charter and United States Civil Rights Litigation: 1946–1955. *Iowa Law Review* 69: 901.

McCullough, David. 1992. *Truman.*

Monzingo, Cloy D. 1950. International Law—United Nations Charter—Statutes in Conflict with the Charter—*Sei Fujii v. State. Texas Law Review* 29: 263.

Moore, David H. 2009. Law(Makers) of the Land: The Doctrine of Treaty Non-self-execution. *Harvard Law Review Forum* 122: 32.

Morris, Richard. 1984. *The Forging of the Union.*

Nat'l Ass'n for the Advancement of Colored People. 1947. *An Appeal to the World: A Statement on the Denial of Human Rights to Minorities in the Case of Citizens of Negro Descent in the United States of America and an Appeal to the United Nations for Redress.*

National Negro Congress. 1946. *A Petition to the United Nations on Behalf of 13 Million Oppressed Negro Citizens of the United States of America.*

Nelson, Caleb. 2000. Preemption. *Virginia Law Review* 86: 225.

Newman, Frank C. 1961. Edwin D. Dickinson. *California Law Review* 49: 4.

Nollkaemper, André. 2009. The Netherlands, in *The Role of Domestic Courts in Treaty Enforcement: A Comparative Study* (David Sloss ed.)

Parry, John T. 2002. The Lost History of International Extradition Litigation. *Virginia Journal of International Law* 43: 126.

Parry, John T. 2009. Congress, the Supremacy Clause, and the Implementation of Treaties. *Fordham International Law Journal* 32: 1209.

Paust, Jordan J. 1988. Rediscovering the Relationship between Congressional Power and International Law: Exceptions to the Last in Time Rule and the Primacy of Custom. *Virginia Journal of International Law* 28: 393.

Pechota, Vratislav. 1981. The Development of the Covenant on Civil and Political Rights, in *The International Bill of Rights: The Covenant on Civil and Political Rights* (Louis Henkin ed.)

Purcell, Jr., Edward A. 2000. *Brandeis and the Progressive Constitution.*

Purcell, Jr., Edward A. 2013. Understanding Curtiss-Wright. *Law and History Review* 31: 653.

Rakove, Jack N. 1984. Solving a Constitutional Puzzle: The Treatymaking Clause as a Case Study. *Perspectives in American History* 1: 233.

Rakove, Jack N. 1996. *Original Meanings: Politics and Ideas in the Making of the Constitution.*

Ramsey, Michael D. 2007. *The Constitution's Text in Foreign Affairs.*

Ramsey, Michael D. 2016. A Textual Approach to Treaty Non-self-execution. *Brigham Young University Law Review* 2015: 1639.

Resnik, Judith. 2006. Law's Migration: American Exceptionalism, Silent Dialogues, and Federalism's Multiple Ports of Entry. *Yale Law Journal* 115: 1564.

Resnik, Judith. 2010. Drafting, Lobbying, and Litigating VAWA: National, Local, and Transnational Interventions on Behalf of Women's Equality, *Georgetown Journal of Gender and the Law* 11: 557.

Rogers, William D. 2007. Covey T. Oliver (1913–2007). *American Journal of International Law* 101: 404.

Rosen, Zvi S. 2009. In Search of the Trade-Mark Cases: The Nascent Treaty Power and the Turbulent Origins of Federal Trademark Law. *Saint John's Law Review* 83: 827.

Rosenkranz, Nicholas Quinn. 2005. Executing the Treaty Power. *Harvard Law Review* 118: 1867.

Schabas, William A. 2009. *Genocide in International Law: The Crime of Crimes* (2d ed.)

Schabas, William A. 2013. *The Universal Declaration of Human Rights: The Travaux Préparatoires* (3 vols.).

Schachter, Oscar. 1951. The Charter and the Constitution: The Human Rights Provisions in American Law. *Vanderbilt Law Review* 4: 643.

Schachter, Oscar. 1979. On Covey Oliver. *University of Pennsylvania Law Review* 127: 892.

Schwelb, Egon. 1959. The Influence of the Universal Declaration of Human Rights on International and National Law, *American Soc'y of Int'l Law Proceedings* 53: 217.

Siegel, Reva B. 2001. Text in Contest: Gender and the Constitution from a Social Movement Perspective. *University of Pennsylvania Law Review* 150: 297.

Siegel, Reva B. 2006. Constitutional Culture, Social Movement Conflict and Constitutional Change: The Case of the de Facto ERA. *California Law Review* 94: 1323.

Simma, Bruno et al. eds. 2012. *The Charter of the United Nations: A Commentary* (3d edition) (2 vols.).

Sloss, David. 1999. The Domestication of International Human Rights: Non-self-executing Declarations and Human Rights Treaties. *Yale Journal of International Law* 24: 129.

Sloss, David. 2002. Non-self-executing Treaties: Exposing a Constitutional Fallacy. *U.C. Davis Law Review* 36: 1.

Sloss, David. 2006. When Do Treaties Create Individually Enforceable Rights?. *Columbia Journal of Transnational Law* 45: 20.

Sloss, David. 2009. United States, in *The Role of Domestic Courts in Treaty Enforcement: A Comparative Study* (Sloss ed.).

Sloss, David. 2009. The Constitutional Right to a Treaty Preemption Defense. *University of Toledo Law Review* 40: 971.

Sloss, David ed. 2009. *The Role of Domestic Courts in Treaty Enforcement: A Comparative Study*.

Sloss, David L., Michael D. Ramsey, and William S. Dodge eds. 2011. *International Law in the U.S. Supreme Court: Continuity and Change*.

Sloss, David L., Michael D. Ramsey, and William S. Dodge. 2011. International Law in the Supreme Court to 1860, in *International Law in the U.S. Supreme Court: Continuity and Change* (Sloss, Ramsey, and Dodge eds.).

Sloss, David. 2012. Executing *Foster v. Neilson*: The Two-Step-Approach to Analyzing Self-Executing Treaties. *Harvard International Law Journal* 53: 135.

Sloss, David. 2012. Domestic Application of Treaties, in *The Oxford Guide to Treaties* (Duncan Hollis ed.).

Sloss, David. 2015. *Bond v. United States*: Choosing the Lesser of Two Evils, *Notre Dame Law Review* 90: 1583.

Sloss, David. 2016. How International Human Rights Transformed the U.S. Constitution. *Human Rights Quarterly* 38: 426.

Sloss, David. 2016. Taming Madison's Monster: How to Fix Self-Execution Doctrine. *Brigham Young University Law Review* 2015: 1691.

Stephan, Paul B. 2009. Open Doors. *Lewis & Clark Law Review* 13: 11.

Stephan, Paul B. 2011. Treaties in the Supreme Court, 1946–2000, in *International Law in the U.S. Supreme Court: Continuity and Change* (David Sloss, Michael Ramsey, and William Dodge eds.).

Strauss, David A. 1996. Common Law Constitutional Interpretation. *University of Chicago Law Review* 63: 877.

Strauss, David A. 2001. The Irrelevance of Constitutional Amendments. *Harvard Law Review* 114: 1457.

Strauss, David A. 2010. *The Living Constitution*.

Swaine, Edward T. 2008. Taking Care of Treaties. *Columbia Law Review* 108: 331.

Tananbaum, Duane. 1988. *The Bricker Amendment Controversy: A Test of Eisenhower's Political Leadership*.

Tucker, Henry St. George. 1915. *Limitations on the Treaty-Making Power under the Constitution of the United States*.

Tushnet, Mark V. 1994. *Making Civil Rights Law: Thurgood Marshall and the Supreme Court, 1936–1961*.

Tushnet, Mark. 1999. *Taking the Constitution Away from the Courts*.

Tweed, Harrison. 1962. Herbert F. Goodrich. *University of Pennsylvania Law Review* 111: 1.

Van Alstine, Michael P. 2008. Taking Care of John Marshall's Political Ghost. *Saint Louis University Law Journal* 53: 93.

Van Alstine, Michael P. 2011. Treaties in the Supreme Court, 1901–1945, in *International Law in the U.S. Supreme Court: Continuity and Change* (David Sloss, Michael Ramsey, and William Dodge eds.).

Van Ert, Gib. 2009. Canada, in *The Role of Domestic Courts in Treaty Enforcement: A Comparative Study* (David Sloss ed.)

Vattel, Emmerich de. 1758. *The Law of Nations or the Principles of Natural Law Applied to the Conduct and to the Affairs of Nations and of Sovereigns* (Joseph Chitty trans. 1883).

Vázquez, Carlos Manuel. 1992. Treaty-Based Rights and Remedies of Individuals. *Columbia Law Review* 92: 1082.

Vázquez, Carlos Manuel. 1995. The Four Doctrines of Self-Executing Treaties. *American Journal of International Law* 89: 695.

Vázquez, Carlos Manuel. 2008. Treaties as Law of the Land: The Supremacy Clause and the Judicial Enforcement of Treaties. *Harvard Law Review* 122: 599.

Vázquez, Carlos Manuel. 2015. The Abiding Exceptionalism of Foreign Relations Doctrine, *Harvard Law Review Forum* 128: 305.

Vladeck, Stephen I. 2015. The Exceptionalism of Foreign Relations Normalization, *Harvard Law Review Forum* 128: 322.

Warren, Charles. 1934. The Mississippi River and the Treaty Clause of the Constitution. *George Washington Law Review* 2: 271.

West, Robin. 2006. Constitutional Culture or Ordinary Politics: A Reply to Reva Siegel. *California Law Review* 94: 1465.

White, G. Edward. 1999. The Transformation of the Constitutional Regime of Foreign Relations. *Virginia Law Review* 85: 1.

White, G. Edward. 1988. *The Marshall Court and Cultural Change, 1815–35.*

Wills, Garry. 2010. *Bomb Power: The Modern President and the National Security State.*

Witt, John Fabian. 2004. Crystal Eastman and the Internationalist Beginnings of American Civil Liberties, *Duke Law Journal* 54: 705.

Wright, Quincy. 1919. The Constitutionality of Treaties. *American Journal of International Law* 13: 242.

Wright, Quincy. 1922. *The Control of American Foreign Relations.*

Wright, Quincy. 1951. National Courts and Human Rights: The *Fujii* Case. *American Journal of International Law* 45: 62.

Yackle, Larry W. 2009. *Federal Courts: Habeas Corpus* (2d ed.).

Yoo, John C. 1999. Globalism and the Constitution: Treaties, Non-self-execution, and the Original Understanding. *Columbia Law Review* 99: 1955.

Yoo, John C. 1999. Treaties and Public Lawmaking: A Textual and Structural Defense of Non-self-execution. *Columbia Law Review* 99: 2218.

TREATIES AND INTERNATIONAL DOCUMENTS

Treaty of Amity and Commerce, U.S.-Fr., Feb. 6, 1778, 8 Stat. 12

Treaty of Alliance, U.S.-Fr., Feb. 6, 1778, 8 Stat. 6

Definitive Treaty of Peace, U.S.-Gr. Brit., Sept. 3, 1783, 8 Stat. 80

Convention Defining and Establishing the Functions and Privileges of Consuls and Vice Consuls, U.S.-Fr., Nov. 14, 1788, 8 Stat. 106

Treaty of Amity, Commerce and Navigation, U.S.-Gr. Brit., Nov. 19, 1794, 8 Stat. 116 ("Jay Treaty")

Treaty for the Cession of Louisiana, U.S.-Fr., Apr. 30, 1803, 8 Stat. 200

A Convention to Regulate Commerce, U.S.-Gr. Brit., July 3, 1815, 8 Stat. 228

Treaty of Amity, Settlement and Limits, U.S.-Spain, Feb. 22, 1819, 8 Stat. 252

Convention as to the Pacific Ocean and Northwest Coast of America, U.S.-Russia, Apr. 17, 1824, 8 Stat. 302

Treaty of Friendship, Commerce and Navigation, U.S.-Denmark, April 26, 1826, 8 Stat. 340

Treaty with the Ottawa, Etc., Mar. 28, 1836, 2 Indian Aff. L. & Treaties 450

Webster-Ashburton Treaty, U.S.-Gr. Brit., Aug. 9, 1842, 8 Stat. 572

Convention on Friendship, Reciprocal Establishments, Commerce, and Extradition, U.S.-Swiss, Nov. 25, 1850, 11 Stat. 587

Convention for the Mutual Delivery of Criminals, Fugitives from Justice, U.S.-Prussia, June 16, 1852, 10 Stat. 964

Consular Convention, U.S.-Fr, Feb. 23, 1853, 10 Stat. 992

Reciprocity Treaty, U.S.-Gr. Brit., June 5, 1854, 10 Stat. 1089

Discontinuance of Sound Dues, U.S.-Denmark, April 11, 1857, 11 Stat. 719

Treaty of Friendship, Commerce, and Navigation, U.S.-Paraguay, Feb. 4, 1859, 12 Stat. 1091

Treaty Between the United States and the Red Lake and Pembina Bands of Chippewa Indians, Oct. 3, 1863, 13 Stat. 667

General Convention of Amity, Commerce, and Navigation, and for the Surrender of Fugitive Criminals, U.S.-Dom. Rep., Feb. 8, 1867, 15 Stat. 473

Cession of Alaska, U.S.-Russ., Mar. 30, 1867, 15 Stat. 539

Trademarks, U.S.-Belg., Dec. 20, 1868, 16 Stat. 765

Trademarks, Additional Article to the Treaty of Commerce, U.S.-Russ., Jan. 27, 1869, 16 Stat. 725

Trademarks, U.S.-Fr., Apr. 16, 1869, 16 Stat. 771

Treaty on Commerce and Navigation, U.S.-Italy, Feb. 26, 1871, 17 Stat. 845

Treaty of Washington, U.S.-Gr. Brit., May 8, 1871, 17 Stat. 863

Convention on Trademarks, U.S.-Austria, Nov. 25, 1871, 17 Stat. 917

Convention Respecting Consuls and Trademarks, U.S.-Ger., Dec. 11, 1871, 17 Stat. 921

Protocol on Fisheries, U.S.-Gr. Brit., June 7, 1873, 18 Stat. 372

Trademarks, U.S.-Russ., Mar. 28, 1874, 18 Stat. 829

Treaty of Reciprocity, U.S.-Hawaii, Jan. 30, 1875, 19 Stat. 625

Treaty on Commerce and Navigation, U.S.-Belg., Mar. 8, 1875, 19 Stat. 628

Declaration on Trademarks, U.S.-Gr. Brit., Oct. 24, 1877, 20 Stat. 703

Agreement for the Protection of Trademarks, U.S.-Brazil, Sept. 24, 1878, 21 Stat. 659

Treaty on Immigration, U.S.-China, Nov. 17, 1880, 22 Stat. 826

Convention on Commerce, U.S.-Mexico, Jan. 20, 1883, 24 Stat. 975

Protection of Industrial Property, multilateral, Mar. 20, 1883, 25 Stat. 1372 ("Paris Convention")

Convention for Protection of Submarine Cables, multilateral, Mar. 14, 1884, 25 Stat. 1425

Reciprocity Convention, U.S.-Hawaii, Dec. 6, 1884, 25 Stat. 1399

Additional Article to the Commercial Convention, U.S.-Mex., Feb. 25, 1885, 25 Stat. 1370

Supplemental Article to the Commercial Convention, U.S.-Mex., May 14, 1886, 24 Stat. 1018.

Treaty of Peace, U.S.-Spain, Dec. 10, 1898, 30 Stat. 1754

An Additional Act for the Protection of Industrial Property, multilateral, Dec. 14, 1900, 32 Stat. 1936 ("Treaty of Brussels").

Convention on Commercial Relations, U.S.-Cuba, Dec. 11, 1902, 33 Stat. 2136

Treaty Relating to Boundary Waters Between the United States and Canada, U.S.-Gr. Brit., Jan. 11, 1909, 36 Stat. 2448

Consular Convention, U.S.-Sweden, June 1, 1910, 37 Stat. 1479

Convention Providing for the Preservation and Protection of Fur Seals, multilateral, July 7, 1911, 37 Stat. 1542

Convention for the Protection of Migratory Birds, U.S.-Gr. Brit., Aug. 16, 1916, 39 Stat. 1702

Convention for Prevention of Smuggling of Intoxicating Liquors, U.S.-Gr. Brit., Jan. 23, 1924, 43 Stat. 1761

Convention for the Prevention of Smuggling of Intoxicating Liquors, U.S.-Denmark, May 29, 1924, 43 Stat. 1809

Charter of the United Nations, multilateral, Oct. 24, 1945, 1 UNTS 16

Commission on Human Rights, Report to the Economic and Social Council, U.N. Doc. E/259 (Supp.) (Jan. 1, 1947)

Statute of the International Law Commission, G.A. Res. 174 (II), U.N. Doc. A/RES/174(II) (Nov. 21, 1947)

Report of the Third Session of the Commission on Human Rights, U.N. Doc. E/800 (June 28, 1948)

Convention on the Prevention and Punishment of the Crime of Genocide, multilateral, Dec. 9, 1948, 78 U.N.T.S. 277

Universal Declaration of Human Rights, G.A. Res. (III), U.N. Doc. A/810 (Dec. 10, 1948)

U.N. International Law Commission, Summary Record of the 23rd Meeting, U.N. Doc. A/CN.4/SR.23 (May 19, 1949)

Commission on Human Rights, Draft International Covenant on Human Rights, U.N. Doc. E/CN.4/224 (May 23, 1949)

Commission on Human Rights, Summary Record of the Hundred and Twenty-Fifth Meeting, U.N. Doc. E/CN.4/SR.125 (June 22, 1949)

Economic and Social Council, Report of the Fifth Session of the Commission on Human Rights, U.N. Doc. E/1371 (June 23, 1949)

Report of the Sixth Session of the Commission on Human Rights, U.N. Doc. E/CN.4/507 (May 29, 1950)

Draft International Covenant on Human Rights and Measures of Implementation, A/RES/ 421(V)E, (Dec. 4, 1950)

Draft International Covenant on Human Rights, included as Annex I to Commission on Human Rights, Report to the Economic and Social Council on the seventh session of the Commission, E/CN.4/640 (May 24, 1951)

Preparation of Two Draft International Covenants on Human Rights, A/RES/543(VI) (Feb. 5, 1952)

Convention on the Rights of the Child, multilateral, Nov. 20, 1989, 1577 U.N.T.S. 3

Protocol on Prohibitions or Restrictions on the Use of Incendiary Weapons, multilateral, Oct. 10, 1980, S. Treaty Doc. 105-1(B) (1997)

Protocol on Blinding Laser Weapons, multilateral, May 3, 1996, S. Treaty Doc. 105-1(C) (1997)

Hague Convention for the Protection of Cultural Property in the Event of Armed Conflict, multilateral, May 14, 1954, S. Treaty Doc. 106-1(A) (1999)

Partial Revision of the Radio Regulations, multilateral, Mar. 3, 1992, S. Treaty Doc. 107-17 (2002)

Amendments to the Constitution and the Convention of the International Telecommunication Union, multilateral, Nov. 6, 1998, S. Treaty Doc. 108-5 (2003)

Revision of the Radio Regulations, multilateral, Nov. 17, 1995, S. Treaty Doc. 108-28 (2004)

Amendment to Article 1 of Convention on Conventional Weapons, multilateral, Dec. 21, 2001, S. Treaty Doc. 109-10(B) (2006)

Protocol on Explosive Remnants of War, multilateral, Nov. 28, 2003, S. Treaty Doc. 109-10(C) (2006)

Amendments to the Constitution and the Convention of the International Telecommunication Union, multilateral, Oct. 18, 2002, S. Treaty Doc. 109-11 (2006)

Land-Based Sources Protocol to the Cartagena Convention, multilateral, Oct. 6, 1999, S. Treaty Doc. 110-1 (2007)

International Convention for the Suppression of Acts of Nuclear Terrorism, multilateral, Apr. 13, 2005, S. Treaty Doc. 110-4 (2007)

Amendment to the Convention on the Physical Protection of Nuclear Material, multilateral, July 8, 2005, S. Treaty Doc. 110-6 (2007)

Fixed Platforms Protocol, multilateral, Oct. 14, 2005, S. Treaty Doc. 110-8 (2007)

International Convention on the Control of Harmful Anti-Fouling Systems on Ships, multilateral, Dec. 12, 2002, S. Treaty Doc. 110-13 (2008)

Amendments to the Constitution and the Convention of the International Telecommunication Union, multilateral, Nov. 24, 2006, S. Treaty Doc. 110-16 (2008)

Protocols to the North Atlantic Treaty of 1949 on the Accession of the Republic of Albania and Croatia, multilateral, July 9, 2008, S. Treaty Doc. 110-20 (2008)

Convention on the Rights of Persons with Disabilities, multilateral, Dec. 13, 2006, S. Treaty Doc. 112-7 (2012)

Human Rights Council, Report of the Working Group on the Universal Periodic Review: United States of America, U.N. Doc. A/HRC/30/12 (July 20, 2015)

CONGRESSIONAL DOCUMENTS

Registration of Trademarks, H.R. Rep. 46-561, 46th Cong., 1st Sess. (1880)

Treaty with the Hawaiian Islands, H.R. Rep. 49-4177, 49th Cong., 2d Sess. (1887)

Violations of Treaty Rights of Aliens, S. Rep. 392, 56th Cong., 1st Sess. (1900)

The Charter of the United Nations for the Maintenance of International Peace and Security: Hearings Before the Senate Committee on Foreign Relations, 79th Cong., 1st Sess. (1945)

Compulsory Jurisdiction, International Court of Justice, Hearings on S. Res. 196 before the Subcommittee of the Senate Committee on Foreign Relations, 79th Cong., 2d Sess. (1946)

Message from the President of the United States Transmitting the Genocide Convention, Executive O, U.S. Senate, 81st Cong., 1st Sess. (1949)

The International Convention on the Prevention and Punishment of the Crime of Genocide, Hearings Before a Subcommittee of the Committee on Foreign Relations, U.S. Senate, 81st Cong., 2d Sess. (1950)

Staff Memorandum on The Convention on the Prevention and Punishment of the Crime of Genocide, Committee on Foreign Affairs, 81st Cong., 2d Sess., Committee Print (Aug. 15, 1950)

Committee on Foreign Relations, U.S. Senate, Executive Session, International Convention on the Prevention and Punishment of the Crime of Genocide (Sept. 6, 1950)

Treaties and Executive Agreements, Hearings Before a Subcommittee of the Committee on the Judiciary, U.S. Senate, 82nd Cong., 2d Sess. (1952)

Treaties and Executive Agreements: Hearings Before a Subcommittee of the Committee on the Judiciary, U.S. Senate, 83rd Cong., 1st Sess. (1953)

Constitutional Amendment Relative to Treaties and Executive Agreements, S. Rep. 412, 83rd Cong., 1st Sess. (1953)

Message from the President of the United States Transmitting Four Treaties Pertaining to Human Rights, S. Exec. Docs. C, D, E and F, 95-2 (1978)

International Human Rights Treaties: Hearings Before the Committee on Foreign Relations, U.S. Senate, 96th Cong., 1st Sess. (1979)

Senate Committee on Foreign Relations, Genocide Convention, S. Exec. Rep. 99-2 (1985)

Senate Committee on Foreign Relations, International Covenant on Civil and Political Rights, S. Exec. Rep. 102-23 (1992)

Senate Committee on Foreign Relations, International Convention on the Elimination of all Forms of Racial Discrimination, S. Exec. Rep. 103-29 (1994)

Senate Committee on Foreign Relations, Convention on the Rights of Persons with Disabilities, S. Exec. Rep. 112-6 (2012)

Senate Committee on Foreign Relations, Convention on the Rights of Persons with Disabilities, S. Exec. Rep. 113-12 (2014)

EXECUTIVE BRANCH MATERIALS

Right of Aliens to Hold Property, 1 U.S. Op. Atty. Gen. 275 (1819)

Validity of the South Carolina Police Bill, 1 U.S. Op. Atty. Gen. 659 (1824)

Validity of the South Carolina Police Bill, 2 U.S. Op. Atty. Gen. 426 (1831)

Reciprocity Treaty with Great Britain, 6 U.S. Op. Atty. Gen. 748 (1854)

Copyright Convention with Great Britain, 6 U.S. Op. Atty. Gen. 291 (1854)

Estates of Foreign Decedents, 8 U.S. Op. Atty. Gen. 98 (1856)

Droit D'Aubaine, 8 U.S. Op. Atty. Gen. 411 (1857)

Choctaw Indians, 13 U.S. Op. Atty. Gen. 354 (1870)

Caveats for Patents for Inventions, 19 U.S. Op. Atty. Gen. 273 (1889)

Treaties—Chinese, 21 U.S. Op. Atty. Gen. 347 (1896)

Treaties—Fisheries, 22 U.S. Op. Atty. Gen. 214 (1898)

Chinese Laborers—Return Certificates, 23 U.S. Op. Atty. Gen. 545 (1901)

Diversion of Water from Niagara River, 30 U.S. Op. Atty. Gen. 217 (1913)

Apparatus for Radio Communication of Steam Vessels, 30 U.S. Op. Atty. Gen. 84 (1913)

Canadian Boundary Waters, 30 U.S. Op. Atty. Gen. 351 (1915)

Charter of the United Nations, Report to the President on the Results of the San Francisco Conference by the Chairman of the United States Delegation (June 26, 1945)

To Secure These Rights: The Report of the President's Committee on Civil Rights (1947)

Harry S. Truman, "Special Message to the Congress on Civil Rights," 1948 Public Papers of the Presidents 121 (Feb. 2, 1948)

Establishing the President's Committee on Equality of Treatment and Opportunity in the Armed Services, Executive Order 9981, 13 Fed. Reg. 4313 (July 26, 1948)

Public Papers of the Presidents of the United States: Dwight D. Eisenhower (1953–1954).

LEGAL BRIEFS

Bob-Lo Excursion Co. v. Michigan, 333 U.S. 28 (1948) (No. 374), Brief for Appellant, *available at* 1947 WL 44419.

Bob-Lo Excursion Co. v. Michigan, 333 U.S. 28 (1948) (No. 374), Brief for the State of Michigan, Appellee, *available at* 1947 WL 44420.

Bob-Lo Excursion Co. v. Michigan, 333 U.S. 28 (1948) (No. 374), Motion and Brief for the National Association for the Advancement of Colored People, American Civil Liberties Union, and National Lawyers Guild as Amici Curiae, *available at* 1947 WL 44321.

Bolling v. Sharpe, 347 U.S. 497 (1954) (No. 8), Brief for Petitioners, *available at* 1952 WL 47257.

Bolling v. Sharpe, 347 U.S. 497 (1954) (No. 8), Brief for Respondents, *available at* 1952 WL 47280.

Brown v. Bd. of Educ., 347 U.S. 483 (1954) (No. 1), Brief for Appellants, *available at* 1952 WL 82041.

Brown v. Bd. of Educ., 347 U.S. 483 (1954) (Nos. 1, 2, 3, 4, 5), Brief for United States as Amicus Curiae, *available at* 1952 WL 82045.

Brown v. Bd. of Educ., 347 U.S. 483 (1954) (No. 1), Brief on Behalf of American Civil Liberties Union, American Ethical Union, American Jewish Committee, Anti-Defamation League of B'nai B'rith, Japanese American Citizens League, and Unitarian Fellowship for Social Justice as Amici Curiae, *available at* 1952 WL 47256.

Henderson v. United States, 339 U.S. 816 (1950) (No. 25), Brief for Elmer W. Henderson, *available at* 1949 WL 50667.

Henderson v. United States, 339 U.S. 816 (1950) (No. 25), Brief for Southern Railway Co., *available at* 1949 WL 50331.

Henderson v. United States, 339 U.S. 816 (1950) (No. 25), Brief for the United States, *available at* 1949 WL 50329.

Henderson v. United States, 339 U.S. 816 (1950) (No. 25), Motion for Leave to File Brief and Brief of American Veterans Committee, *available at* 1949 WL 50668.

Hines v. Davidowitz, 312 U.S. 52 (1941) (No. 22), Brief for the United States, Amicus Curiae, *available at* 1940 WL 71236.

Hurd v. Hodge, 334 U.S. 24 (1948) (Nos. 290, 291), Brief of the Japanese-American Citizens League, Amicus Curiae, *available at* 1947 WL 44430.

Hurd v. Hodge, Urciolo v. Hodge, 334 U.S. 24 (1948) (Nos. 290, 291), Consolidated Brief for Petitioners, *available at* 1947 WL 44429.

Hurd v. Hodge, Urciolo v. Hodge, 334 U.S. 24 (1948) (Nos. 290, 291), Consolidated Brief for Respondents, *available at* 1947 WL 44432.

McGhee v. Sipes, 331 U.S 804 (1947) (No. 87), Brief for Non-Sectarian Anti-Nazi League to Champion Human Rights, Inc., as Amicus Curiae, *available at* 1947 WL 44174.

McGhee v. Sipes, 331 U.S 804 (1947) (No. 87), Brief for Petitioners, *available at* 1947 WL 44154.

McGhee v. Sipes, 331 U.S 804 (1947) (No. 87), Brief for Respondents, *available at* 1947 WL 30429.

McLaurin v. Oklahoma State Regents, 339 U.S. 637 (1950) (No. 34), Brief for Appellant, *available at* 1950 WL 78675.

McLaurin v. Oklahoma State Regents, 339 U.S. 637 (1950) (No. 34), Memorandum for the United States as Amicus Curiae, *available at* http://galenet.galegroup.com.

Medellin v. Texas, 552 U.S. 491 (2008) (No. 06-984), Brief for Petitioner, *available at* 2007 WL 1886212.

Medellin v. Texas, 552 U.S. 491 (2008) (No. 06-984), Brief for Respondent, *available at* 2007 WL 2428387.

Oyama v. California, 332 U.S. 633 (1947) (No. 44), Brief for Petitioners, *available at* 1947 WL 44264.

Oyama v. California, 332 U.S. 633 (1947) (No. 44), Brief for Respondent, *available at* 1947 WL 44265.

Oyama v. California, 332 U.S. 633 (1947) (No. 44), Brief of American Civil Liberties Union, as Amicus Curiae, *available at* 1947 WL 44267.

Shelley v. Kraemer, 334 U.S. 1 (1948) (No. 72) & McGhee v. Sipes, 331 U.S 804 (1947) (No. 87) & Hurd v. Hodge, Urciolo v. Hodge, 334 U.S. 24 (1948) (Nos. 290, 291), Application for Leave to File Brief Amicus and Brief Amicus Curiae on Behalf of Congress of Industrial Organizations and Certain Affiliated Organizations, *available at* 1947 WL 44164.

Shelley v. Kraemer, 334 U.S. 1 (1948) (No. 72) & McGhee v. Sipes, 331 U.S 804 (1947) (No. 87) & Hurd v. Hodge, Urciolo v. Hodge, 334 U.S. 24 (1948) (Nos. 290, 291), Brief for the United States as Amicus Curiae, *available at* 1947 WL 44159.

Shelley v. Kraemer, 334 U.S. 1 (1948) (No. 72) & McGhee v. Sipes, 331 U.S 804 (1947) (No. 87) & Hurd v. Hodge, Urciolo v. Hodge, 334 U.S. 24 (1948) (Nos. 290, 291), Brief of American Civil Liberties Union, Amicus Curiae, *available at* 1947 WL 44163.

Shelley v. Kraemer, 334 U.S. 1 (1948) (No. 72) & McGhee v. Sipes, 331 U.S 804 (1947) (No. 87) & Hurd v. Hodge, Urciolo v. Hodge, 334 U.S. 24 (1948) (Nos. 290, 291), Brief of the American Indian Citizens League of California, Inc., as Amicus Curiae, *available at* 1947 WL 30437.

Shelley v. Kraemer, 334 U.S. 1 (1948) (No. 72) & McGhee v. Sipes, 331 U.S 804 (1947) (No. 87) & Hurd v. Hodge, Urciolo v. Hodge, 334 U.S. 24 (1948) (Nos. 290, 291), Motion for Leave to File Brief and Brief for the American Association for the United Nations as Amicus Curiae, *available at* 1948 WL 47412.

Shelley v. Kraemer, 334 U.S. 1 (1948) (No. 72), Brief of the St. Louis Civil Liberties Committee, Amicus Curiae, *available at* 1947 WL 44169.

Sweatt v. Painter, 339 U.S. 629 (1950) (No. 44), Brief for Petitioner, *available at* 1950 WL 78681.

Sweatt v. Painter, 339 U.S. 629 (1950) (No. 44), Brief of Amici Curiae in Support of Petitioner, *available at* 1950 WL 78683.

Takahashi v. Fish & Game Comm'n, 334 U.S. 410 (1948) (No. 533), Brief for Petitioner, *available at* 1948 WL 47429.

Takahashi v. Fish & Game Comm'n, 334 U.S. 410 (1948) (No. 533), Brief for Respondents, *available at* 1948 WL 47430.

Takahashi v. Fish & Game Comm'n, 334 U.S. 410 (1948) (No. 533), Brief for the American Jewish Congress as Amicus Curiae, *available at* 1948 WL 47438.

Takahashi v. Fish & Game Comm'n, 334 U.S. 410 (1948) (No. 533), Brief for the United States as Amicus Curiae, *available at* 1948 WL 47431.

Takahashi v. Fish & Game Comm'n, 334 U.S. 410 (1948) (No. 533), Brief of American Civil Liberties Union, Amicus Curiae, *available at* 1948 WL 47437.

Takahashi v. Fish & Game Comm'n, 334 U.S. 410 (1948) (No. 533), Brief of American Veterans Committee, Amicus Curiae, *available at* 1948 WL 47432.

Takahashi v. Fish & Game Comm'n, 334 U.S. 410 (1948) (No. 533), Motion and Brief for the National Association for the Advancement of Colored People and the National Lawyers Guild as Amicus Curiae, *available at* 1948 WL 47439.

Takahashi v. Fish & Game Comm'n, 334 U.S. 410 (1948) (No. 533), Motion and Brief for the National Association for the Advancement of Colored People as Amicus Curiae, *available at* 1948 WL 47434.

AMERICAN BAR ASSOCIATION DOCUMENTS

Proceedings of the House of Delegates, 71st Annual Meeting, 73 Ann. Rep. ABA 94 (Sept. 1948)

Report of the Special Committee on Peace and Law Through United Nations, 73 Ann. Rep. ABA 283 (1948)

Holman, Frank E. 1948. An International Bill of Rights: Proposals Have Dangerous Implications for U.S., *American Bar Association Journal* 34: 984.

Proceedings of the House of Delegates, 72nd Annual Meeting, 74 Ann. Rep. ABA 101 (Sept. 1949)

Report of the Special Committee on Peace and Law Through United Nations, 74 Ann. Rep. ABA 316 (1949)

Rix, Carl B. 1949. Human Rights and International Law: Effect of the Covenant Under Our Constitution, *American Bar Association Journal* 35: 551.

Phillips, Orie L. 1949. The Genocide Convention: Its Effect on Our Legal System. *American Bar Association Journal* 35: 623.

Proceedings of the House of Delegates, 73rd Annual Meeting, 75 Ann. Rep. ABA 102 (Sept. 1950)

Proceedings of the House of Delegates, Midyear Meeting, 75 Ann. Rep. ABA 403 (Feb. 1950)

Report of the Special Committee for Peace and Law Through United Nations, 75 Ann. Rep. ABA 286 (1950)

Holman, Frank E. 1950. Treaty Law-Making: A Blank Check for Writing a New Constitution. *American Bar Association Journal* 36: 707.

Proceedings of the House of Delegates, Midyear Meeting, 77 Ann. Rep. ABA 425 (Feb. 1952).

AMERICAN LAW INSTITUTE DOCUMENTS

Agenda for Discussion of Possible Work in the Field of Foreign Relations Law (Mar. 1955), *available on* Hein Online, American Law Institute Library.

Transcript of Conference on Possible Project in Foreign Relations Law (Mar. 31 to Apr. 2, 1955), *available on* Hein Online, American Law Institute Library.

Report on Foreign Relations Law Project (Aug. 1955), *available on* Hein Online, American Law Institute Library.

Restatement (Second), Preliminary Draft 4 (Dec. 1958), *available on* Hein Online, American Law Institute Library.

Restatement (Second), Preliminary Draft 5 (Jan. 1959), *available on* Hein Online, American Law Institute Library.

Restatement (Second), Council Draft 4 (Feb. 1959), *available on* Hein Online, American Law Institute Library.

Restatement (Second), Council Draft 5 (Mar. 1959), *available on* Hein Online, American Law Institute Library.

Restatement (Second), Tentative Draft 3 (May 1959), *available on* Hein Online, American Law Institute Library.

Restatement (Second), Proposed Official Draft (1962), *available on* Hein Online, American Law Institute Library.

Restatement (Fourth): The Foreign Relations Law of the United States—Treaties, Discussion Draft (Apr. 2015), *available on* Hein Online, American Law Institute Library.

Index

discriminatory state laws. *See* state laws.
domestic human rights litigation
  and treaty supremacy arguments 189
  based on U.N. Charter 187–90
  in lower federal courts 190
  in state courts 187
  in U.S. Supreme Court 190–91
Donnell, Forrest (Senator) 210–11
Douglas, William (Associate Justice)
  196, 243
Downes v. Bidwell 132, 135–37, 144–45
Du Bois, W.E.B. 185–87
dualist states 90, 281
Duane, James 19
Due Process Clause 10, 164, 243,
  304–06, 317–18
Dulles, John Foster (Secretary of State)
  244, 254, 301

East Florida 77, 79–80
economic and social rights 185, 203,
  220, 223
Eighteenth Amendment 154
Eisenhower, Dwight 12, 224, 245, 248–49,
  252–54, 301
Eisenhower administration
  and optional treaty supremacy rule
  249, 252–53
  Senate testimony on Bricker
  Amendment 3, 11, 176, 301, 323
  views on Bricker Amendment 12, 174,
  176, 249–54, 323, 328
Eleventh Amendment 300. *See also* state
  sovereignty.
Equal Protection Clause 4, 9–10, 12, 177–
  78, 196, 209, 228–29, 236, 238, 240,
  242, 321
Equal Rights Amendment (ERA) 2, 177,
  292, 320–23
Everett, Edward (Secretary of
  State) 102–03
Ex parte Toscano 164
executive discretion in foreign affairs
  and changes in self-execution
  doctrine 154
  and intent doctrine 154, 162–66,
  rise of executive power after World
  War I 154, 162–64

executive federalism 85, 88, 102
executive power to implement treaties 3,
  6–7, 25–26, 42, 47–48, 62, 64, 74, 82,
  107, 113, 127–28, 158, 165–69, 175,
  292–93, 303, 324–25
Executive Vesting Clause 25–26
executory and executed treaty
  provisions
  distinction between executory and
  executed treaties 50–51, 73, 79, 81
  distinction between executory
  and non-self-executing treaties
  80–81, 159–60
  in *Foster v. Neilson* 73–76, 80–81,
  125, 160
  in Louisiana/Florida property cases
  75–76, 79
  in *Ware v. Hylton* 50–51, 74
extradition 73, 130–31, 140, 142, 144–45,
  261, 264, 286

Fairman, Charles 247
federal preemption 147
  and Supremacy Clause 169
  distinction between preemption and
  supremacy 154
  preemption doctrine and treaty
  supremacy rule 169–71
  preemption doctrine and
  self-execution 170–71
federal supremacy 38, 162, 169–70, 215,
  217, 299. *See also* federal preemption,
  treaty supremacy.
federalism 29–30, 85, 88, 94–95, 98,
  101–02, 105, 114, 127, 205. *See also*
  state sovereignty.
Federalist Papers 3, 36
Federalists
  and Bill of Rights 33, 36, 46
  and limitations on Treaty Power 33, 36,
  40, 74, 108
  defense of Constitution's treaty
  provisions 34–36, 54, 73–74
  Treaty Power and procedural
  safeguards 32, 35, 55, 108
  understanding of treaty supremacy rule
  32–34, 36–39, 46, 54
Ferguson, Homer (Senator) 211, 253